Spencer

FAMILY TREE

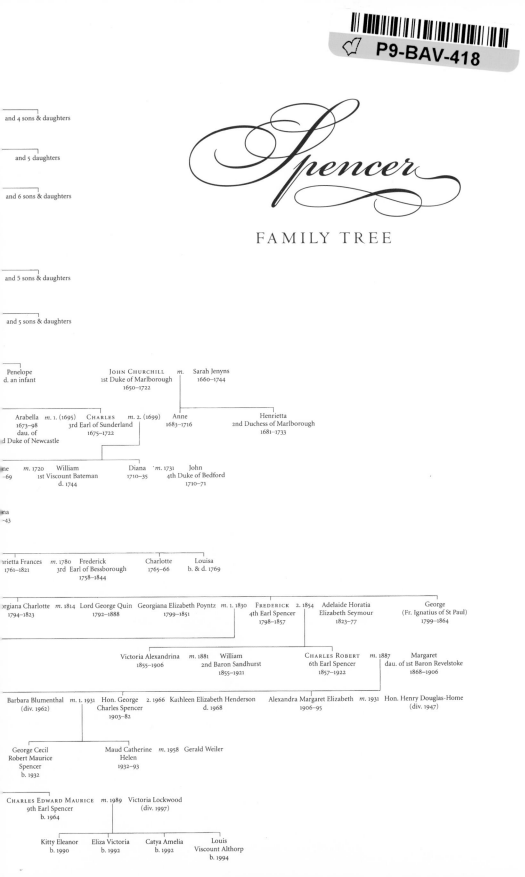

and 4 sons & daughters

and 5 daughters

and 6 sons & daughters

and 5 sons & daughters

and 5 sons & daughters

Penelope
d. an infant

JOHN CHURCHILL   *m.*   Sarah Jenyns
1st Duke of Marlborough   1660–1744
1650–1722

Arabella   *m.* 1. (1695)   CHARLES   *m.* 2. (1699)   Anne   Henrietta
1673–98   3rd Earl of Sunderland   1683–1716   2nd Duchess of Marlborough
dau. of   1675–1722   1681–1733
d Duke of Newcastle

ne   *m.* 1720   William   Diana   *m.* 1731   John
–69   1st Viscount Bateman   1710–35   4th Duke of Bedford
d. 1744   1710–71

na
–43

nrietta Frances   *m.* 1780   Frederick   Charlotte   Louisa
1761–1821   3rd Earl of Bessborough   1765–66   b. & d. 1769
1758–1844

orgiana Charlotte   *m.* 1814   Lord George Quin   Georgiana Elizabeth Poyntz   *m.* 1. 1830   FREDERICK   2. 1854   Adelaide Horatia   George
1794–1823   1792–1888   1799–1851   4th Earl Spencer   Elizabeth Seymour   (Fr. Ignatius of St Paul)
1798–1857   1823–77   1799–1864

Victoria Alexandrina   *m.* 1881   William   CHARLES ROBERT   *m.* 1887   Margaret
1855–1906   2nd Baron Sandhurst   6th Earl Spencer   dau. of 1st Baron Revelstoke
1855–1921   1857–1922   1868–1906

Barbara Blumenthal   *m.* 1. 1931   Hon. George   2. 1966   Kathleen Elizabeth Henderson   Alexandra Margaret Elizabeth   *m.* 1931   Hon. Henry Douglas-Home
(div. 1962)   Charles Spencer   d. 1968   1906–95   (div. 1947)
1903–82

George Cecil   Maud Catherine   *m.* 1958   Gerald Weiler
Robert Maurice   Helen
Spencer   1932–93
b. 1932

CHARLES EDWARD MAURICE   *m.* 1989   Victoria Lockwood
9th Earl Spencer   (div. 1997)
b. 1964

Kitty Eleanor   Eliza Victoria   Catya Amelia   Louis
b. 1990   b. 1992   b. 1992   Viscount Althorp
b. 1994

Georgiana

Duchess of Devonshire

Georgiana, Duchess of Devonshire, by Maria Cosway,
1782. Georgiana, aged twenty-five, is portrayed as the goddess
Diana, flying through the clouds.

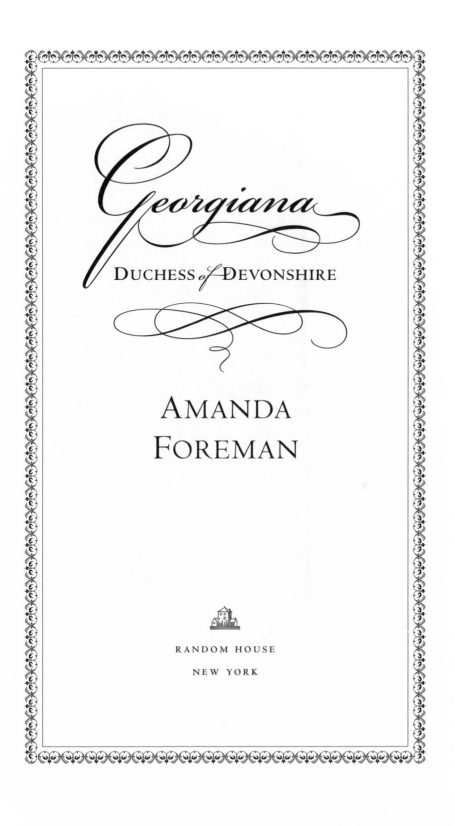

Georgiana

DUCHESS *of* DEVONSHIRE

AMANDA
FOREMAN

RANDOM HOUSE

NEW YORK

ACKNOWLEDGEMENTS

The accumulation of several years' research inevitably means that enormous debts of gratitude are owed to many institutions and individuals. I am very grateful to the following owners of manuscript collections for allowing me access to their materials: His Grace the Duke of Devonshire, Drummonds Bank, the Hon. Simon Howard, Hugh Seymour, Esq., and the Earl Spencer.

I was on the road for much of my research and I am grateful to the following people for their generous hospitality: Mr. and Mrs. Piers Paul Read, Celia and Tom Read, Bernard and Marie Scrope, and Sir Simon and Lady Towneley and Cosima Towneley.

I never met with anything but interest and helpfulness from librarians and archivists up and down the country. Hundreds of people gave of their expertise, in particular Ian McIver of the National Library of Scotland, who brought to my attention the letters of Mary Graham. I would also like to thank Peter Day, head librarian of Chatsworth, Dr. R. C. E. Hayes of the Royal Commission on Historical Manuscripts, and the staff at the British Library Manuscript Reading Room. The British Library, the Bodleian Conservation Department, New Scotland Yard, and the Oxford University Computer Centre did their utmost to help me decipher those Chatsworth letters which had been censored with black ink. The fact that we did not succeed does not lessen my profound gratitude to all four institutions for the time and effort they willingly spent on the problem.

I have received an extraordinary amount of help over the past six years. While I worked on the U.S. edition a number of people were particularly kind; I wish to express my gratitude to Jonathan Barton for his unfailing good humour and encouragement, and to Marisol Arguetta, Anthea

Craigmyle, Caroline Dalmeny, Alice Lucas-Tooth, Lizzie Pitman, Jessica Pulay, and Hugh Smith.

I am also indebted to the following readers for their comments and criticism: Elaine Chalus, Jemima Fishwick, Jonathan Foreman, Stephen Howard, Anthony Lejeune, Andrew Roberts, Justin Shaw, Fredric Smoler, Philip Watson, and particularly my supervisor, Dr. Leslie Mitchell, who inspired me with his devotion to the Whig cause.

I would not have embarked on *Georgiana* were it not for my agent, Alexandra Pringle, and I would not have finished it without my editor, Michael Fishwick. I can hardly put into words the gratitude and admiration I feel for both of them. They have been patient, supportive, inspirational, and generous. They contributed to the book in a number of profound ways and, along with the dedicated and painstaking copy-editing by Rebecca Lloyd and Sophie Nelson, helped to bring *Georgiana* to its completed form.

The U.S. edition of *Georgiana* was made possible only by the enthusiasm and hard work of Susanna Porter and Kate Niedzwecki. Their vision has helped to produce a book which stands on its own, without reference to its British cousin.

I also wish to thank my parents, Eve and Michael Williams-Jones, for their unstinting and generous support. Four years is a long time to have remained interested and willing to listen while I went on and on about Georgiana. I owe them much more than I can repay and am more grateful than my demeanour sometimes showed. Finally I would like to thank my brother Jonny, my soulmate, best friend, and fellow conspirator, who has always been my champion and ready to offer help or advice, day or night. I hope I have rewarded his patience.

I dedicate this book to my father, Carl Foreman, in the certain knowledge that, had he lived, by now we too would be friends.

CONTENTS

Introduction . . . . *xiii*

A Note on Eighteenth-Century Politics . . . . *xvii*

Chronology . . . . *xix*

PART ONE: DÉBUTANTE

1 Débutante: 1757–1774 . . . . *3*

2 Fashion's Favourite: 1774–1776 . . . . *21*

3 The Vortex of Dissipation: 1776–1778 . . . . *43*

4 A Popular Patriot: 1778–1781 . . . . *61*

5 Introduction to Politics: 1780–1782 . . . . *83*

PART TWO: POLITICS

6 The Newcomer: 1782–1783 . . . . *95*

7 An Unstable Coalition: 1783 . . . . *108*

8 A Birth and a Death: 1783–1784 . . . . *117*

9 The Westminster Election: 1784 . . . . *133*

10 Opposition: 1784–1786 . . . . *155*

11 Queen Bess: 1787 . . . . *182*

12 *Ménage à Trois:* 1788 . . . . *192*

13 The Regency Crisis: 1788–1789 . . . . *204*

PART THREE: EXILE

14 The Approaching Storm: 1789–1790 .... *223*

15 Exposure: 1790–1791 .... *240*

16 Exile: 1791–1793 .... *258*

17 Return: 1794–1796 .... *276*

18 Interlude: 1796 .... *290*

19 Isolation: 1796–1799 .... *296*

PART FOUR: GEORGIANA REDUX

20 Georgiana Redux: 1800–1801 .... *317*

21 Peace: 1801–1802 .... *330*

22 Power Struggles: 1802–1803 .... *335*

23 The Doyenne of the Whig Party: 1803–1804 .... *346*

24 "The Ministry of All the Talents": 1804–1806 .... *357*

Epilogue *372*

Notes *387*

Select Bibliography *423*

Index *433*

ILLUSTRATIONS

FRONTISPIECE: Georgiana, Duchess of Devonshire, by Maria Cosway, 1782. *(By Kind Permission of the Trustees of the Chatsworth Settlement)*

SECTION ONE

George, 1st Earl Spencer, by Thomas Gainsborough, c. 1763. *(By Kind Permission of Earl Spencer)*

Georgiana, Countess Spencer, by Pompeo Batoni, c. 1764. *(By Kind Permission of Earl Spencer)*

Photograph of Althorp House. *(By Kind Permission of Earl Spencer)*

Lady Spencer with Lady Georgiana Spencer by Reynolds, c. 1760. *(By Kind Permission of Earl Spencer)*

Viscount Althorp with his sisters Lady Georgiana and Lady Henrietta-Frances (Harriet) Spencer by Angelica Kauffmann, 1774. *(By Kind Permission of Earl Spencer)*

Chatsworth, west front. *(By Kind Permission of the Trustees of the Chatsworth Settlement)*

Interior of Chatsworth, the Painted Hall. *(By Kind Permission of the Trustees of the Chatsworth Settlement)*

Georgiana, Duchess of Devonshire, by Sir Joshua Reynolds. *(By Kind Permission of the Trustees of the Chatsworth Settlement)*

5th Duke of Devonshire by Pompeo Batoni. *(By Kind Permission of the Trustees of the Chatsworth Settlement)*

Mary Graham by Gainsborough. *(National Gallery of Scotland)*

Marie Antoinette by L. Cournerie. *(Reproduced by Permission of the Trustees of the Wallace Collection)*

Georgiana, Duchess of Devonshire, and Lady Elizabeth Foster by Jean-

Urbain Guérin. *(Reproduced by Permission of the Trustees of the Wallace Collection)*

Lady Elizabeth Foster by Reynolds, 1787. *(By Kind Permission of the Trustees of the Chatsworth Settlement)*

Lady Elizabeth Foster by Sir Thomas Lawrence, 1803. *(National Gallery of Ireland)*

A view of Green Park, English School, c. 1760. *(By Kind Permission of Earl Spencer)*

Georgiana, Duchess of Devonshire, and Lady Georgiana Cavendish by Reynolds, 1784. *(By Kind Permission of the Trustees of the Chatsworth Settlement)*

SECTION TWO

BM Cat. 5395. "A Hint to the Ladies to take Care of their Heads." *(British Museum)*

Spencer House, north-west view; watercolour drawing, c. 1780. *(London Metropolitan Archives)*

Spencer House, north front, 1942. *(London Metropolitan Archives)*

Wimbledon Park House, Surrey. *(London Metropolitan Archives)*

Front of Devonshire House, c. 1890. *(London Metropolitan Archives)*

Lady Georgiana Spencer aged three, after Reynolds. *(Castle Howard Collection: Photograph Courtauld Institute of Art)*

Georgiana, Duchess of Devonshire, by Richard Cosway. *(Castle Howard Collection: Photograph Courtauld Institute of Art)*

Georgiana, Duchess of Devonshire, by an unknown artist. *(The Viscount Hampden: Photograph Courtauld Institute of Art)*

Georgiana, Duchess of Devonshire, by John Downman. *(Castle Howard Collection: Photograph Courtauld Institute of Art)*

George, Prince of Wales, by John Hoppner. *(Reproduced by Permission of the Trustees of the Wallace Collection)*

Charles James Fox by John Powell after Reynolds. *(Castle Howard Collection: Photograph Courtauld Institute of Art)*

A Gaming Table at Devonshire House by T. Rowlandson. *(Private Collection: Courtesy of Spink and Son)*

Lady Georgiana Cavendish and Lady Harriet Cavendish as children. *(Castle Howard Collection: Photograph Courtauld Institute of Art)*

Harriet, Lady Granville, by Thomas Barber. *(Hardwick Hall, The Devonshire Collection [The National Trust]: Photograph Courtauld Institute of Art)*

William, 6th Duke of Devonshire, by Thomas Lawrence. *(Castle Howard Collection: Photograph Courtauld Institute of Art)*

Eliza Courtney. *(The Viscount Hampden: Photograph Courtauld Institute of Art)*

William Pitt by John Jackson after Hoppner. *(Castle Howard Collection: Photograph Courtauld Institute of Art)*

Charles, 3rd Duke of Richmond, by George Romney. *(Private Collection: Photograph Courtauld Institute of Art)*

Thomas Grenville by Camille Manzini. *(By Courtesy of the National Portrait Gallery, London)*

Charles, 2nd Earl Grey, by James Northcote. *(Private Collection: Photograph Courtauld Institute of Art)*

Sir Philip Francis by James Lonsdale. *(By Courtesy of the National Portrait Gallery, London)*

Lord Granville Leveson Gower after Sir Thomas Lawrence. *(The Sutherland Trust: Photograph Courtauld Institute of Art)*

3rd Duke of Dorset by Reynolds. *(Private Collection: Photograph Courtauld Institute of Art)*

Harriet, Lady Bessborough, by Reynolds. *(By Kind Permission of Earl Spencer: Photograph Courtauld Institute of Art)*

Attributed as Frederick, Lord Bessborough, after Reynolds. *(Leeds Museums & Galleries [Temple Newsam House]: Photograph Courtauld Institute of Art)*

BM Cat. 6520. Rowlandson. "The Devonshire, or the most Approved Method of Securing Votes." *(British Museum)*

R. B. Sheridan by John Hoppner. *(Private Collection: Photograph Courtauld Institute of Art)*

James Hare after Reynolds. *(By Kind Permission of the Trustees of the Chatsworth Settlement: Photograph Courtauld Institute of Art)*

Whig Statesmen and their Friends, c. 1810, by William Lane. *(By Courtesy of the National Portrait Gallery, London)*

Francis, 5th Duke of Bedford, by John Hoppner. *(The Lord Egremont: Photograph Courtauld Institute of Art)*

Elizabeth, Viscountess Melbourne, by Thomas Phillips. *(The Lord Egremont: Photograph Courtauld Institute of Art)*

"Witches Round the Cauldron" by Daniel Gardner. *(Private Collection: Photograph Courtauld Institute of Art)*

George, 2nd Earl Spencer, by John Singleton Copley. *(By Kind Permission of Earl Spencer)*

House of Commons in 1793 by K. A. Hickel. *(By Courtesy of the National Portrait Gallery, London)*

Lord Morpeth by Henry Birch. *(Castle Howard Collection: Photograph Courtauld Institute of Art)*

George Canning after Lawrence. *(Castle Howard Collection: Photograph Courtauld Institute of Art)*

South view of Castle Howard by William Marlow. *(Castle Howard Collection: Photograph Courtauld Institute of Art)*

Devonshire House, ballroom, c. 1920. *(London Metropolitan Archives)*

Demolition of Devonshire House. *(RCHME, © Crown Copyright)*

BM Cat. 6533. "A Certain Dutchess Kissing old Swelter-in-Grease for His Vote." *(British Museum)*

BM Cat. 10253. Gillray. "L'Assemblée Nationale:—or—Grand Co-operation Meeting at St. Ann's Hill." *(British Museum)*

ILLUSTRATIONS IN TEXT

p. 141 BM Cat. 6494. Rowlandson. "The Two Patriotic Duchess's on Their Canvass" *(British Museum)*

p. 142 BM Cat. 6524. "The Chairing of Fox" *(British Museum)*

p. 150 BM Cat. 6560. Aitken. "The Tipling Dutchess Returning From Canvassing" *(British Museum)*

p. 150 BM Cat. 6566. Rowlandson. "Every Man Has His Hobby Horse" *(British Museum)*

p. 151 BM Cat. 6594. Humphry. "Vox Populi, Vox Dei" *(British Museum)*

p. 170 BM Cat. 6668. Dent. "British Balloon, and D——— Aerial Yacht" *(British Museum)*

p. 200 BM Cat. 7360. Dent. "The Miscarriage or His Grace Stopping the Supplies" *(British Museum)*

INTRODUCTION

Biographers are notorious for falling in love with their subjects. It is the literary equivalent of the Stockholm Syndrome, the phenomenon which leads hostages to feel sympathetic towards their captors. The biographer is, in a sense, a willing hostage, held captive for so long that he becomes hopelessly enthralled.

There are obvious, intellectual motives which drive a writer to spend years, and sometimes decades, researching the life of a person long vanished, but they often mask a less clear although equally powerful compulsion. Most biographers identify with their subjects. It can be unconscious and no more substantial than a shadow flitting across the page. At other times identification plays so central a role that the work becomes part autobiography as, famously, in Richard Holmes's *Footsteps: Adventures of a Romantic Biographer* (1995).

In either case, once he commits himself to the task, the writer embarks on a journey that has no obvious route for a destination that is only partly known. He immerses himself in his subject's life. The recorded impressions of contemporaries are read and re-read; letters, diaries, hastily scribbled notes, even discarded fragments are scrutinised for clues; and yet the truth remains maddeningly elusive. The subject's own self-deception, mistaken recollections, and the hidden motives of witnesses conspire to make a complete picture impossible to assemble. Finally, it is intuition and a sympathy with the past which supply the last missing pieces. It is no wonder that biographers often confess to dreaming about their subjects. I remember the first time Georgiana appeared to me: I dreamt I switched on the radio and heard her reciting one of her poems. That was the closest she ever came to me; in later dreams she was always a vanishing figure, present but beyond my reach.

Such profound bonds have obvious dangers, not least in the disruption they can inflict upon a biographer's life. Sometimes the work suffers; its integrity becomes jeopardised when, without realizing it, a biographer mistakes his own feelings for the subject's, ascribing characteristics that did not exist and motives that were never there. In his life of Charles James Fox, the Victorian historian George Trevelyan insisted that Fox held to a strict code of morality regarding the sexual conquest of aristocratic women; he seduced only courtesans. Trevelyan, perhaps, had such a code, but Fox did not. There is ample evidence to suggest that the Whig politician had several affairs with married women of quality, including Mrs. Crewe and possibly Georgiana, Duchess of Devonshire. Her first biographer, Iris Palmer, was similarly wishful in her description of Georgiana as a "simple woman" without ambition except in her desire to help others. Palmer also claimed, in the face of contrary evidence, that Georgiana was unfaithful to her husband with only one man, Charles Grey. Both biographers illustrate how easy it is to fall prey to the temptation to suppress or ignore unwelcome evidence.

Fortunately, the emotional distance required to construct a narrative from an incoherent collection of facts and suppositions provides a powerful counterbalance. By deciding which pieces of the puzzle are the most significant—not always an easy task—and thereby asserting their own interpretation, the biographer achieves a measure of separation. The demands of writing, of style, pace, and clarity, also force a writer to be more objective. Numerous decisions have to be made about conflicting evidence, or where to place the correct emphasis between certain events. Having previously dominated the biographer's waking and sleeping life, the subject gradually diminishes until he or she is contained on the page.

I discovered Georgiana in 1993, while researching a doctoral dissertation on English attitudes to race and colour in the late eighteenth century. I was reading a biography of Charles Grey, later Earl Grey, by E. A. Smith, and came across one of her letters. I was already familiar with Georgiana's career as a political hostess and as the duchess who once campaigned for Charles James Fox, but I had never read any of her writing, and knew little of her character. I was struck by her voice; it was so strong, so clear, honest, and open that she made everything I subsequently read seem dull by comparison. I lost interest in my doctorate, and after six months I had read just one book on eighteenth-century racial attitudes and thirty-two novels. Whenever I did go to the library it was to look for biographies of Georgiana.

Nothing I read about her portrayed the Georgiana I felt I had heard. Eventually I realized I would never be satisfied until I had followed the trail to its source. Oxford accepted my explanation and graciously allowed me to start again and begin a new Ph.D. on Georgiana's life and times. A short while later I decided to write her biography in addition to the doctorate.

As Georgiana's letters are scattered around England, I planned to be on the road for eighteen months and set off in the summer of 1994, having finally passed my driving test on the seventh attempt. My fears about starting a new project were subsumed by the act of driving on the motorway for the first time. I began my search at Chatsworth in Derbyshire, Georgiana's home during her married life. Its archives, hidden away inside a subterranean labyrinth of corridors, contain over one thousand of her letters. They revealed so much of her daily life that it seemed as though I were watching a play from the corner of the stage. The impression of being an invisible, perhaps even an uninvited, spectator remained with me throughout my research.

The Stockholm Syndrome came upon me suddenly, and I was caught even before I noticed it happening. One day in the Public Record Office at Kew, while reading a vicious letter from one of Georgiana's rivals, I found myself becoming furious on her behalf. This was the beginning of my obsession with Georgiana, fuelled by frustration at the empty spaces in the Chatsworth archives where someone had either destroyed her letters or censored them with black ink. It only began to wane after I had filled in the missing days and months in Georgiana's life from other sources: the archives at Castle Howard, private collections, the British Library, and libraries and record offices all over Britain.

By the time I had consigned Georgiana to the page a different picture of her had emerged. Previous accounts portrayed her as a charismatic but flighty woman; I see her as courageous and vulnerable. Georgiana indeed suffered from the instability which often accompanies intelligent and sensitive characters. She was thrust into public life at the age of sixteen, unprepared for the pressures that quickly followed, and unsupported in a cold and loveless marriage. Though most of her contemporaries adored her because she seemed so natural and vibrant, only a few knew how tormented she was by self-doubt and loneliness. Georgiana was not content to lead the fashionable set nor merely to host soirées for the Whig party, but instead she became an adept political campaigner and negotiator, respected by the Whigs and feared by her adversaries. She was the first woman to conduct a modern electoral campaign, going out into the streets to persuade ordinary people to vote for the Whigs. She took advantage of the country's rapidly expanding newspaper trade to increase the popularity of the Whig party and succeeded in turning herself into a national celebrity. Georgiana was a patron of the arts, a novelist and writer, an amateur scientist and a musician. It was her tragedy that these successes were overshadowed by private and public misfortune. Ambitious for herself and her party, Georgiana was continually frustrated by restrictions imposed on eighteenth-century women. She was also a woman who needed to be loved, but the two people whom she loved most—Charles Grey and the Duke of Devonshire's mistress Lady Elizabeth Foster—proved incapable of reciprocating her feelings in full measure. Georgiana's unhappiness expressed itself destructively in her addiction to gambling, her early eating disorders, and her deliberate courting of risk. Her battle to overcome her problems was an achievement equal to the triumphs she enjoyed in her public life.

Georgiana's relationships with men and women cannot be categorized by twentieth-century divisions between what is strictly heterosexual and homosexual. Nor did she think about the rights of women or entertain the same notions of equality that characterize modern feminism. It would be foolish to separate Georgiana from her era and call her a woman before her time; she was distinctly of her time. Yet her successful entry into the male-dominated world of politics, her relationship with the press, her struggle with addiction, and her determination to forge her own identity make her equally relevant to the lives of contemporary women. In writing this book, I hope that her voice is heard once more, by a new generation.

A Note on
Eighteenth-Century
Politics

Georgiana, Duchess of Devonshire, lived during a period of rapid change. The population was sharply increasing, the national income was rising, roads were improving, and literacy was spreading. Britain was on the verge of becoming a great power, driven by its burgeoning factories at home and fertile territories abroad. But with fewer than ten million people, the country was still small enough to be governed by an aristocratic oligarchy.

There were roughly two hundred peers (as British aristocrats are called) when Georgiana married the Duke of Devonshire. There were only twenty-eight dukes, but because of their wealth and rank they exerted a disproportionate influence in politics. As a duchess, Georgiana was one tier below royalty; below her the titles descended in the order of marquess and marchioness, earl and countess, viscount and viscountess, and lord and lady. The peers sat by right of birth in the House of Lords, the upper chamber of the Houses of Parliament. The only form of retirement for a peer was death. Indeed, in 1778 the Earl of Chatham made a dramatic exit from the floor of the Lords, dying of a heart attack in mid-speech.

While the two hundred or so peers sat in isolated splendour in the Lords, their sons, cousins, brothers-in-law, friends, and hangers-on filled up the House of Commons, the lower chamber in Parliament. Britain was a democracy in the sense that every five years a general election took place and voters elected 558 members of Parliament, known as MPs, to sit in the Commons. However, property restrictions kept the number of voters small—roughly three hundred thousand, or 3 percent of the population. There were all kinds of legal anomalies and customs which enabled peers and gentlemen of sufficient wealth to actually own a seat outright, or have so much influence in the constituency, that democracy did not enter into

the equation at all. The peerage spent a great deal of money and effort trying to control as many seats in the Commons as possible. But aristocratic
patronage never extended to more than two hundred MPs, leaving the
majority open to some form of contest.

There was enough popular participation to make politics as big a national obsession as sport, if not bigger. The emergence of national newspapers turned politicians into celebrities. The talk in coffee houses and
inns up and down the country was on the quality of the speeches the day
before, on who had acquitted himself in the finest manner and whether
the government—meaning the monarchy—had won the argument. For
the aristocracy, politics was not just a sport but a business. It dominated
their lives, destroying some in the process and elevating others to even
greater wealth and glory.

Although women did not have the vote, were barred from the House of
Commons, and could not hold an official position, Georgiana was a passionate contestant in the political arena. She devoted herself to the Whig
party: campaigning, scheming, fund-raising, and recruiting for it right up
until the day she died. The story of her extraordinary life is a mirror of the
past; look into it and you will see the turbulent history of late-eighteenth-
century politics unfold.

CHRONOLOGY

1757 Birth of Lady Georgiana Spencer
      First public concert in Philadelphia

1758 Colonel George Washington and John Forbes take Fort Duquesne,
      later renamed Pittsburgh

1760 George III becomes king on the death of his grandfather, George II

1763 End of French and Indian War. Canada and Nova Scotia ceded to
      Britain

1769 Lord North becomes prime minister

1770 Boston Massacre

1774 Marriage of Lady Georgiana Spencer to 5th Duke of Devonshire
      Continental Congress of Philadelphia

1775 War of Independence starts
      British Whig party states its support for the American colonists

1782 George Washington's victory over the British forces Prime Minis-
      ter Lord North to resign
      Lady Elizabeth Foster (Bess) enters Georgiana's life

1783 Peace declared between Britain and America
      Birth of Georgiana's first child, Lady Georgiana Cavendish

1789 George III recovers from insanity. Resolution of the Regency crisis
      George Washington inaugurated as president of the United States
      Beginning of the French Revolution
      Georgiana, the Duke, and Bess go to France

1791 Georgiana sent into exile
      Thomas Paine publishes *The Rights of Man*

1793 Georgiana and Bess allowed to return to London
      France declares war on Britain

1796 Georgiana suffers catastrophic illness
      George Washington refuses to accept a third term as president

1806 The Whig party wins power
      The Burr plot in the United States
      Death of Prime Minister William Pitt, Georgiana, Duchess of
         Devonshire, and Charles James Fox

PART ONE

Débutante

CHAPTER I

DÉBUTANTE

1757—1774

I know I was handsome . . . and have always been fashionable, but I do assure you," Georgiana, Duchess of Devonshire, wrote to her daughter at the end of her life, "our negligence and ommissions have been forgiven and we have been loved, more from our being free from airs than from any other circumstance."*[1] Lacking airs was only part of her charm. She had always fascinated people. According to the retired French diplomat Louis Dutens, who wrote a memoir of English society in the 1780s and 1790s, "When she appeared, every eye was turned towards her; when absent, she was the subject of universal conversation."[2] Georgiana was not classically pretty, but she was tall, arresting, sexually attractive, and extremely stylish. Indeed, the newspapers dubbed her the Empress of Fashion.

The famous Gainsborough portrait of Georgiana succeeds in capturing something of the enigmatic charm which her contemporaries found so compelling. However, it is not an accurate depiction of her features: her eyes were heavier, her mouth larger. Georgiana's son Hart (short for Marquess of Hartington) insisted that no artist ever succeeded in painting a true representation of his mother. Her character was too full of contradictions, the spirit which animated her thoughts too quick to be caught in a single expression.

Georgiana Spencer was the eldest child of the Earl and Countess

---

* Misspellings have been corrected only where they intrude on the text.

Spencer.* She was born on June 7, 1757, at the family country seat, Althorp Park, situated some one hundred miles north of London in the sheep-farming county of Northamptonshire. She was a precocious and affectionate baby and the birth of her brother George, a year later, failed to diminish Lady Spencer's infatuation with her daughter. Georgiana would always have first place in her heart, she confessed: "I will own I feel so partial to my Dear little Gee, that I think I never shall love another so well."[3] The arrival of a second daughter, Harriet, in 1761 did not alter Lady Spencer's feelings. Writing soon after the birth, she dismissed Georgiana's sister as a "little ugly girl" with "no beauty to brag of but an abundance of fine brown hair." The special bond between Georgiana and her mother endured throughout her childhood and beyond. They loved each other with a rare intensity. "You are my best and dearest friend," Georgiana told her when she was seventeen. "You have my heart and may do what you will with it."[4]

By contrast, Georgiana—like her sister and brother—was always a little frightened of her father. He was not violent, but his explosive temper inspired awe and sometimes terror. "I believe he was a man of generous and amiable disposition," wrote his grandson, who never knew him. But his character had been spoiled, partly by almost continual ill-health and partly by his "having been placed at too early a period of his life in the possession of what then appeared to him inexhaustible wealth." Georgiana's father was only eleven when his own father died of alcoholism, leaving behind an estate worth £750,000—roughly equivalent to $74 million today.† It was one of the largest fortunes in England and included 100,000 acres in twenty-seven different counties, five substantial residences, and a sumptuous collection of plate, jewels, and old-master paintings. Lord Spencer had an income of £700 a week in an era when a gentleman could live off £300 a year.

Georgiana's earliest memories were of travelling between the five houses. She learnt to associate the change in seasons with her family's move to a different location. During the "season," when society took up residence "in town" and Parliament was in session, they lived in a draughty,

---

* Georgiana became Lady Georgiana Spencer at the age of eight when her father, John Spencer, was created the first Earl Spencer in 1765. For the purpose of continuity the Spencers will be referred to as Lord and Lady throughout.

† The usual method for estimating equivalent twentieth-century values is to multiply by sixty.

old-fashioned house in Grosvenor Street a few minutes' walk from where
the American embassy now resides. In the summer, when the stench of the
cesspool next to the house and the clouds of dust generated by passing traffic became unbearable, they took refuge at Wimbledon Park, a Palladian
villa on the outskirts of London. In the autumn they went north to their
hunting lodge in Pytchley outside Kettering, and in the winter months,
from November to March, they stayed at Althorp, the country seat of the
Spencers for over three hundred years.

When the diarist John Evelyn visited Althorp in the seventeenth century he described the H-shaped building as almost palatial, "a noble
pile . . . such as may become a great prince."[5] He particularly admired the
great saloon, which had been the courtyard of the house until one of
Georgiana's ancestors covered it over with a glass roof. To Lord and Lady
Spencer it was the ballroom; to the children it was an indoor playground.
On rainy days they would take turns to slide down the famous ten-foot-
wide staircase or run around the first-floor gallery playing tag. From the
top of the stairs, dominating the hall, a full-length portrait of Robert, first
Baron Spencer (created 1603), gazed down at his descendants, whose
lesser portraits lined the ground floor.*

Georgiana was seven when the family moved their London residence
to the newly built Spencer House in St. James's, overlooking Green Park.
The length of time and sums involved in the building—almost £50,000
over seven years—reflected Lord Spencer's determination to create a
house worthy of his growing collection of classical antiquities. The travel
writer and economist Arthur Young was among the first people to view
the house when Lord Spencer opened it to the public. "I know not in England a more beautiful piece of architecture," he wrote, "superior to any
house I have seen. . . . The hangings, carpets, glasses, sofas, chairs, tables,
slabs, everything, are not only astonishingly beautiful, but contain a vast
variety."[6] Everything, from the elaborate classical façade to the lavishly

---

* The Spencers originally came from Warwickshire, where they farmed sheep. They
were successful businessmen, and with each generation the family grew a little richer. By
1508 John Spencer had saved enough capital to purchase the 300-acre estate of Althorp. He
also acquired a coat of arms and a knighthood from Henry VIII. His descendants were no
less diligent, and a hundred years later, when Robert Spencer was having his portrait
painted for the saloon, he was at the head of one of the richest farming families in England.
King James I, who could never resist an attractive young man, gave him a peerage and a
diplomatic post to the court of Duke Frederick of Württemberg. From then on the
Spencers left farming to their agents and concentrated on court politics.

decorated interior, so much admired by Arthur Young, reflected Lord Spencer's taste. He was a noted connoisseur and passionate collector of rare books and Italian art. Each time he went abroad he returned with a cargo of paintings and statues for the house. His favourite room, the Painted Room, as it has always been called, was the first complete neo-classical interior in Europe.

The Spencers entertained constantly and were generous patrons. Spencer House was often used for plays and concerts, and Georgiana grew up in an extraordinarily sophisticated milieu of writers, politicians, and artists. After dinner the guests would sometimes be entertained by a solilo-quy delivered by the actor David Garrick or a reading by the writer Lau-rence Sterne, who dedicated a section of *Tristram Shandy* to the Spencers. The house had been built not to attract artists, however, but to consolidate the political prestige and influence of the family. The urban palaces of the nobility encircled the borough of Westminster, where the Houses of Par-liament reside, like satellite courts. They were deliberately designed to combine informal politics with a formal social life. A ball might fill the vast public rooms one night, a secret political meeting the next. Many a career began with a witty remark made in a drawing room; many a government policy emerged out of discussions over dinner. Jobs were discreetly sought, positions gained, and promises of support obtained in return. This was the age of oligarch politics, when the great landowning families enjoyed un-challenged pre-eminence in government. While the Lords sat in the cham-ber known as the Upper House, or the House of Lords, their younger brothers, sons, and nephews filled up most of the Lower House, known as the House of Commons. There were very few electoral boroughs in Britain which the aristocracy did not own or at least have a controlling in-terest in. Since the right to vote could only be exercised by a man who owned a property worth at least forty shillings, wealthy families would buy up every house in their local constituency. When that proved impossible there were the usual sort of inducements or threats that the biggest em-ployer in the area could employ to encourage compliance among local voters. Land conferred wealth, wealth conferred power, and power, in eighteenth-century terms, meant access to patronage, from lucrative gov-ernment sinecures down to the local parish office, worth £20 ($1,980 today) per annum.

Ironically, there was a condition attached to Lord Spencer's inheritance: by the terms of the will he could be a politician so long as he always re-tained his independent voice in Parliament. He was never to accept a government position or a place in the Cabinet.* He retained great influence because he could use his wealth to support the government, but his political ambitions were thwarted. As a result he had no challenges to draw him out, and little experience of applying himself. He led a life dedicated to pleasure and, in time, the surfeit of ease took its toll. Lord Spencer became diffident and withdrawn. The indefatigable diarist Lady Mary Coke, a distant relation, once heard him speak in Parliament and thought "as much as could be heard was very pretty, but he was extremely frightened and spoke very low."[7] The Duke of Newcastle awarded him an earldom in 1765 in recognition of his consistent loyalty. But Lord Spencer's elevation to the peerage failed to prevent him from becoming more self-absorbed with each passing year. His friend Viscount Palmerston reflected sadly: "He seems to be a man whose value few people know. The bright side of his character appears in private and the dark side in public. . . . it is only those who live in intimacy with him who know that he has an understanding and a heart that might do credit to any man."[8]

Lady Spencer knew her husband could be generous and sensitive. Margaret Georgiana Poyntz, known as Georgiana, met John Spencer in 1754 when she was seventeen, and immediately fell in love with him. "I will own it," she confided to a friend, "and never deny it that I do love Spencer above all men upon Earth."[9] He was a handsome man then, with deep-set eyes and thin lips which curled in a cupid's bow. His daughter inherited from him her unusual height and russet-coloured hair. When Lady Spencer first knew him he loved to parade in the flamboyant fashions of the French aristocracy. At one masquerade he made a striking figure in a blue and gold suit with white leather shoes topped with blue and gold roses.[10]

Georgiana's mother had delicate cheekbones, auburn hair, and deep

---

* His father, the Hon. John Spencer, was in fact a younger son and, given the law of primogeniture, had always expected to marry his fortune or live in debt. However, his mother was the daughter of the first Duke of Marlborough, and the Marlboroughs had no heir. To prevent the line from dying out the Marlboroughs obtained special dispensation for the title to pass through the female line. John's older brother Charles became the next Duke. John, meanwhile, became head of the Spencer family and subsequently inherited Althorp. Charles had inherited the title but, significantly, he had no right to the Marlborough fortune until his grandmother Duchess Sarah, the widowed Duchess of Marlborough, died. Except for Blenheim Palace, she could leave the entire estate to whomever she chose. Sarah had strong political beliefs and she was outraged when Charles disobeyed her instruction to oppose the government of the day. In retribution she left Marlborough's £1 million estate to John, with the sole proviso that neither he nor his son should ever accept a government post.

brown eyes which looked almost black against her pale complexion. The fashion for arranging the hair away from the face suited her perfectly. It helped to disguise the fact that her eyes bulged slightly, a feature which she passed on to Georgiana. She was intelligent, exceptionally well read, and, unusually for women of her day, she could read and write Greek as well as French and Italian. A portrait painted by Pompeo Batoni in 1764 shows her surrounded by her interests: in one hand she holds a sheaf of music— she was a keen amateur composer—near the other lies a guitar; there are books on the table and in the background the ruins of ancient Rome, referring to her love of all things classical. "She has so decided a character," remarked Lord Bristol, "that nothing can warp it."[11]

Her father, Stephen Poyntz, had died when she was thirteen, leaving the family in comfortable but not rich circumstances. He had risen from humble origins—his father was an upholsterer—by making the best of an engaging manner and a brilliant mind. He began his career as a tutor to the children of Viscount Townshend and ended it a Privy Councillor to King George II. Accordingly, he brought up his children to be little courtiers like himself: charming, discreet, and socially adept in all situations. Vice was tolerated so long as it was hidden. "I have known the Poyntzes in the nursery," Lord Lansdowne remarked contemptuously, "the Bible on the table, the cards in the drawer."

"Never was such a lover," remarked the prolific diarist and chronicler of her times Mrs. Delany, who watched young John Spencer ardently court Miss Poyntz during the spring and summer of 1754. The following year, in late spring, the two families, the Poyntzes and the Spencers, made a week-long excursion to Wimbledon Park. There was no doubt in anyone's mind about the outcome and yet Spencer was in an agony of anticipation throughout the visit. At the last moment, with the carriages waiting to leave, he drew her aside and blushingly produced a diamond and ruby ring. Inside the gold band, in tiny letters, were the words: "MON COEUR EST TOUT À TOI. GARDE LE BIEN POUR MOI."*

The first years of their married life were happy. The Duke of Queensberry, known as "Old Q," declared that the Spencers were "really the happiest people I ever saw in the marriage system." They delighted in each other's company and were affectionate in public as well as in private. In middle age, Lady Spencer proudly told David Garrick, "I verily believe that we have neither of us for one instant repented our lot from that time

---

* My heart is yours. Keep it well.

to this."[12] They had "modern" attitudes both in their taste and in their attitude to social mores. Their daughter Harriet recorded an occasion when Lord Spencer took her to see some mummified corpses in a church crypt because "it is foolish and superstitious to be afraid of seeing dead bodies."[13] Another time he "bid us observe how much persecution encreased [the] zeal for the religion [of the sect] so oppressed, which he said was a lesson against oppression, and for toleration."[14]

The Spencers were demonstrative and affectionate parents. "I think I have experienced a thousand times," Lady Spencer mused, "that commendation does much more good than reproof."[15] She preferred to obtain obedience through indirect methods of persuasion, as this letter to eleven-year-old Georgiana shows: "I would have neither of you go to the Ball on Tuesday, tho' I think I need not have mentioned this, as I flatter myself you would both chose rather to go with me, than when I am not there. . . ."[16] It was a sentiment typical of an age influenced by the ideas of John Locke and Jean-Jacques Rousseau, whose books had helped to popularize the cult of "sensibility." In some cases the new, softer attitudes ran to ridiculous excesses. The biographer and sexual careerist James Boswell, whose views on children were as tolerant as his attitude towards adultery, complained that his dinner party was ruined when the Countess of Rothes insisted on bringing her two small children, who "played and prattled and suffered nobody to be heard but themselves."[17]

Georgiana's education reflected her parents' idea of a sound upbringing. During the week a succession of experts trooped up and down the grand staircase to the bare schoolroom overlooking the courtyard. There, for most of the day, Georgiana studied a range of subjects, both feminine (deportment and harp-playing) and practical (geography and languages). The aim was to make her polished but not overly educated. The royal drawing-master and miniaturist John Gresse taught her drawing. The composer Thomas Linley, later father-in-law to the playwright Richard Sheridan, gave her singing lessons. The distinguished orientalist Sir William Jones, who was preparing her brother, George, for Harrow, taught her writing. She also learned French, Latin, Italian, dancing, and horsemanship.[18] Everything came easily to her, but what delighted Georgiana's mother in particular was her quick grasp of etiquette. Lady Spencer's own upbringing as a courtier's daughter made her keenly critical of Georgiana's comportment in public; it was almost the only basis, apart from religion, on which she judged her, praised her, and directed her training.

Lady Spencer's emphasis on acquiring social skills encouraged the performer in Georgiana. In quiet moments she would curl up in a window seat in the nursery and compose little poems and stories to be recited after dinner. She loved to put on an "evening" and entertain her family with dramatic playlets featuring heroines in need of rescue. While Georgiana bathed in the limelight, George concentrated on being the dependable, sensible child who could be relied upon to remember instructions. Harriet, despite being the youngest, enjoyed the least attention of all. Perhaps in another family, her obvious sensitivity and intelligence would have marked her out as a special child. But with a precocious and amusing sister and model brother, she had no special talent of her own to attract her parents' notice. Instead she attached herself to Georgiana, content to worship her and perform the duties of a faithful lieutenant. Even here poor Harriet often had to compete with George. He was proud of Georgiana's talent and at Harrow would show round the verse letters he had received from her. "By this time there is not an old Dowager in or about Richmond that has not a copy of them; there's honour for you!" he informed her. On one occasion he imagined the two of them achieving fame by publishing her letters under the title, "An epistle from a young lady of quality abroad to her Brother at School in England."[19]

Georgiana could think of nothing more delightful than a public exhibition of her writing. Despite being the clear favourite of the family she was anxious and attention-seeking, constantly concerned about disappointing her parents. "Although I can't write as well as my brother," she told them plaintively when she was seven, "I love you very much and him just as much."[20] Adults never failed to be charmed by Georgiana's lively and perceptive conversation and yet she valued their praise only if it made an impression on her mother and father. Her ability to attract notice pleased Lady Spencer as much as its origins puzzled her: "Without being handsome or having a single good feature in her face," she remarked to a friend, "[she is] one of the most showy girls I ever saw."[21] Lady Spencer never understood her daughter's need for attention or its effect on her development. In later years, when forced to examine her part in Georgiana's misfortunes, she blamed herself for having been too lenient a parent.

In 1763, when Georgiana was six, the stability she had enjoyed came to an abrupt end when the Spencers embarked on a grand tour. Lord Spencer had trouble with his lungs and his invalid condition made him bad-tempered. Lady Spencer, worn down by his moods, urged him to rest and heal in the warmer climate of the Continent. Most of their friends were going abroad. Britain had been at war with France for the previous seven years and, although the fighting had largely taken place in outposts—in Canada, India, and the Caribbean—visits across the Channel were severely curtailed. With the advent of peace, travel became possible again and the English aristocracy could indulge in its favourite pastime: visiting "the sights."

Georgiana accompanied her parents while George and Harriet, both considered too young to undertake such a long journey, stayed behind. The Spencers' first stop was Spa, in what is now Belgium, in the Ardennes forest. Its natural warm springs and pastoral scenery made it a fashionable watering place among the European nobility, who came to drink the waters and bathe in the artificially constructed pools. But Lady Spencer's hopes that its gentle atmosphere would soothe her husband's nerves were disappointed. A friend who stayed with them for a short while described the visit as one of the worst he had ever made: "If you ask me really whether I had a great deal of pleasure in it I must be forced to answer in the negative. Lord S's unhappy disposition to look always on the worst side of things, and if he does not find a subject for fretting to make one, rendered both himself and his company insensible to much of the satisfaction which the circumstances of our journey might have occasioned us."[22]

Undaunted, Lady Spencer decided they should try Italy. She wrote to her mother in July and asked her to come out to Spa to look after Georgiana while they were away. She admitted that she was leaving Georgiana behind "with some difficulty," but she had always placed her role as a wife before that of motherhood. For Georgiana, already missing her siblings, her mother's sudden and inexplicable abandonment was a profound shock. "Miss Spencer told me today she lov'd me very well but did not like to stay with me without her mama," her grandmother recorded in her diary.[23] For the next twelve months Georgiana lived in Antwerp with her grandmother, who supervised her education. Believing, perhaps, that her parents had left her behind as a punishment for some unnamed misdeed, Georgiana became acutely self-conscious and anxious to please. She imitated her grandmother's likes and dislikes, training herself to anticipate the expectations of adults. "We are now 38 at table," Mrs. Poyntz wrote in June 1764, ten months after Georgiana's parents had left Spa. "Miss Spencer is adored by all the company, they are astonished to see a child of her age never ask for anything of the dinner or desert but what I give her."[24]

When her daughter and son-in-law returned Mrs. Poyntz was amazed at the intensity of Georgiana's reaction: "I never saw a child so overjoy'd, she could hardly speak or eat her dinner."[25] Lady Spencer immediately noticed that there was something different about her daughter but she decided she liked the change. "I had the happiness of finding my dear Mother and Sweet girl quite well," she wrote to one of her friends; "the latter is vastly improved."[26] Although Lady Spencer did not realize it, the improvement was at the cost of Georgiana's self-confidence. Without the inner resources which normally develop in childhood, she grew up depending far too much on other people. As a child it made her obedient; as an adult it made her susceptible to manipulation.

Three years later, in 1766, a tragedy occurred which had repercussions for the whole family. Lady Spencer had become pregnant with her fourth child and, in the autumn of 1765, gave birth to a daughter named Charlotte. The child symbolized a much needed fresh start after the Spencers' eighteen-month absence from England, which was perhaps why she engrossed Lady Spencer's attention just as Georgiana had done nine years before. "She is a sweet little poppet," she wrote.[27] This time Lady Spencer breastfed the baby herself instead of hiring a wet nurse, and persevered even though it hurt and made her "low." Georgiana's notes to her mother when Lady Spencer was in London suggest that she was more than a little jealous of the new arrival.[28] But infant mortality, although improved since the seventeenth century, was still high. Charlotte died shortly after her first birthday.

Lord and Lady Spencer were shattered by the loss. "You know the perhaps uncommon tenderness I have for my children," Lady Spencer explained to her friend Thea Cowper. Three years later, in 1769, Charlotte was still very much in her heart when she had another daughter, whom they called Louise. But she too died after only a few weeks. After this the Spencers travelled obsessively, sometimes with and sometimes without the children, never spending more than a few months in England at a stretch. Seeking an answer for their "heavy affliction," they turned to religion for comfort and Lady Spencer began to show the first signs of the religious fanaticism which later overshadowed her life.

At night, however, religion was far from their thoughts as they sought distraction in more worldly pursuits. They set up gaming tables at Spencer House and Althorp and played incessantly with their friends until the small hours. Lady Spencer tried to control herself: "Played at billiards and bowls and cards all evening and a part of the night," she wrote in her diary. "Enable me O God to persevere in my endeavour to conquer this habit as far as it is a vice," she prayed on another occasion.[29] The more hours she spent at the gambling table, the more she punished herself with acts of self-denial. By the time Georgiana was old enough to be conscious of her mother's routine,

Lady Spencer had tied herself to a harsh regimen: up at 5:30 every morning, prayers for an hour, the Bible for a further hour, followed by a meagre breakfast at nine, and then household duties and good works until dinner. But in her heart she knew that her actions contained more show than feeling. "I know," she wrote, "that there is a mixture of Vanity and false humility about me that is detestable."[30] However, knowledge of her faults did not change her ways. Twenty years later a friend complained: "She is toujours Lady Spencer, Vanity and bragging will not leave her, she lugg'd in by the head and shoulders that she had been at Windsor."[31]

The children were silent witnesses to their parents' troubled life. Sometimes Georgiana and Harriet would creep downstairs to watch the noisy scenes taking place around the gaming table. "I staid till one hour past twelve, but mama remained till six next morning," Harriet wrote in her diary.[32] When the children were older they were allowed to participate. Harriet recorded on a trip to Paris: "A man came today to papa to teach him how he might always win at Pharo, and talked of it as a certainty, telling all his rules, and when papa told him he always lost himself, the man assur'd him it was for want of money and patience, for that his secret was infallible. Everybody has given him something to play for them, and papa gave him a louis d'or for my sister and me."[33]

Georgiana reacted to the loss of Charlotte and Louise by worrying excessively about her two younger siblings. She also became highly sensitive to criticism and the smallest remonstrance produced hysterical screams and protracted crying. Lady Spencer tried many different experiments to calm Georgiana, forcing her to spend hours in prayer and confining her to her room—to little effect.[34] It was in her nature to oversee every aspect of a project, and from this time forward Lady Spencer left nothing in Georgiana's development to chance. Even her thoughts were subject to scrutiny. "Pray sincerely to God," Lady Spencer ordered her, "that he would for Jesus Christ's sake give his assistance without which you must not hope to do anything."[35]

When she reached adolescence Georgiana's tendency to over-react became less marked, but not enough to allay her mother's fear for her future happiness. In November 1769 both George and Harriet were dangerously ill and Lady Spencer confided to a friend that the twelve-year-old Georgiana had shown "upon this as upon every other occasion such a charming sensibility that it is impossible not to be pleased with it, tho when I reflect upon it I assure you it gives me concern as I know by painful experience how much such a disposition will make her suffer hereafter."[36]

Georgiana was only fourteen when people began to speculate on her choice of husband. Lady Spencer thought it would be a dreadful mistake if she married too young. "I hope not to part with her till 18 at the soonest," she told a friend in 1771.[37] Her daughter's outward sophistication led many to think that she was more mature than her years. In 1772 the family embarked upon another grand tour, this time with all three children in tow. The rapturous reception which greeted Georgiana in Paris confirmed Lady Spencer's fears. According to a fellow English traveller, "Lady Georgiana Spencer has been very highly admired. She has, I believe, an exceedingly good disposition of her own, and is happy in an education which it is to be hoped will counteract any ill effect from what may too naturally turn her head."[38]

Georgiana combined a perfect mastery of etiquette with a mischievous grace and ease which met with approval in the artificial and mannered atmosphere of the French court. Wherever Georgiana accompanied Lady Spencer people marvelled at the way in which she seemed so natural and yet also conscious of being on show. Many were daunted by the complex and highly choreographed set-pieces which passed for social discourse in French salons. "It was no ordinary science," reminisced a retired courtier, "to know how to enter with grace and assurance a salon where thirty men and women were seated in a circle round the fire, to penetrate this circle while bowing slightly to everyone, to advance straight to the mistress of the house, and to retire with honour, without clumsily disarranging one's fine clothes, lace ruffles, [and] head-dress of thirty-six curls powdered like rime. . . ."[39]

The family travelled around France for a few months and then moved on to Spa, where Georgiana celebrated her sixteenth birthday, in the summer of 1773. They found many friends already there, including the twenty-four-year-old Duke of Devonshire. His family had always been regular visitors: it was at Spa that his father the fourth Duke had died in 1764, aged forty-four, worn out after his short but harrowing stint as Prime Minister in 1756.* The Devonshires ranked among the first fami-

---

* Political life had not suited the reserved and honest Duke. But for the rivalry between Henry Fox and William Pitt, neither of whom would support a government with the other as its leader, George II would not have chosen this "amiable, straightforward man," who was noted "for common sense rather than statesmanship." The Duke shared with Lord

lies of England and commanded a special place in British history. They had been involved in politics since the reign of Henry VIII, when Sir William Cavendish oversaw the dissolution of the monasteries. Sir William was the second husband of four to the redoubtable Bess of Hardwick, the richest woman in England after Elizabeth I and the most prolific builder of her age. He was the only one whom she married for love, and when she died all her accumulated wealth went to her Cavendish sons. The eldest, William, used his mother's fortune to purchase the earldom of Devonshire from James I for £10,000. His descendants followed his example and devoted their lives to increasing the family's wealth and power.

Seventy years later, on June 30, 1688, the fourth Earl of Devonshire joined with six other parliamentary notables (the Immortal Seven) and issued a secret invitation to William of Orange to come to England and take the throne from the Catholic James II. When William arrived the Earl personally toured the Midlands with his own militia and subdued the countryside around Derbyshire and Cheshire. He received a dukedom for his bravery, as did several of his Whig colleagues. It was not bigotry which had prompted the first Duke to act but political idealism; he, along with many other Whigs, had suspected King James of plotting to reduce the power of Parliament in order to establish an absolutist monarchy, similar to that enjoyed by his cousin Louis XIV in France. William's acceptance of their offer of the crown, as well as the conditions imposed by Parliament, resulted in the establishment of the Revolution Settlement. This guaranteed the sovereignty of Parliament over a constitutional monarchy, and restricted the succession to royal members of the Protestant faith. Subsequent generations of Whigs revered the 1688 revolutionaries as the guardians of English liberty. They looked to the descendants of the Immortal Seven to maintain the Whig party and to keep its ideals alive.

At first the fortunes of the party fluctuated as its leaders gained or lost favour at court, and factions fought for control. By 1714, however, the Whigs had crushed the rival Tory party and from then on they experienced

---

Spencer, with whom he enjoyed a close friendship, a total lack of aptitude for the bravado of parliamentary politics. Dr. Johnson said of him, "If he promised you an acorn, and none had grown that year in his woods, he would have sent to Denmark for it." But if asked to formulate a strategy for dealing with the French he sat there helplessly, waiting for someone to suggest an idea. He only participated in government out of a sense of duty and the effort it cost him ruined his health and destroyed his peace of mind.

little opposition except from disgruntled members within their own party. By the time the twenty-two-year-old George III ascended the throne in 1760 the same Whig families had been pulling the levers of power for over fifty years. The Duke's family, known collectively as the Cavendishes (the Duke is always referred to by his title, the family by its surname), had been in power for so many years that political office seemed theirs by right; they and their supporters were entirely unprepared for their sudden disgrace. The new King's first act was to dismiss the Whig cabinet. He had long regarded the Whig leaders as a cynical and corrupt rabble, and in their place he appointed his tutor, Lord Bute, to form a new government.

The fourth Duke of Devonshire was among the casualties. Without warning the King removed him from his post as Lord Chamberlain and had his name scratched from the honorary Royal advisory group known as the Privy Council. After a lifetime spent serving the court this graceless demotion was an insult which the Duke would never forgive nor the party forget. When he died a few years later his sixteen-year-old son William (who was never referred to as anything except "the Duke") inherited the quarrel and automatically became heir-presumptive to the leadership of the Whig party. But a contemporary politician, Nathaniel Wraxall, who knew him well, bemoaned the fact that the Whigs had to rely on a man so ill-suited to public life: "Constitutional apathy formed his distinguishing characteristic. His figure was tall and manly, though not animated or graceful, his manners, always calm and unruffled. He seemed to be incapable of any strong emotion, and destitute of all energy or activity of mind. As play became indispensable in order to arouse him from his lethargic habit, and to awaken his torpid faculties, he passed his evenings usually at Brooks's, engaged at whist or faro."[40]

The Duke had had a lonely upbringing, which was reflected in his almost pathological reserve. One of his daughters later joked that their only means of communication was through her dog: "the whole of tea and again at supper, we talked of no one subject but the puppies. . . . I quite rejoice at having one in my possession, for it is never a failing method of calling his attention and attracting his notice."[41] However, behind the Duke's wooden façade was an intelligent and well-educated mind. According to Wraxall, his friends regarded him as an expert on Shakespeare and the classics: "On all disputes that occasionally arose among the members of the club [Brooks's] relative to passages of the Roman poets or historians, I know that appeal was commonly made to the Duke, and his decision or opinion was regarded as final."[42]

The Duke had barely known his mother, Lady Charlotte Boyle, who died when he was six. The fourth Duke had married her against his own mother's wishes. There was no clear reason for the Duchess's objection— she called it "an accursed match"—particularly since Lady Charlotte brought a vast fortune to the family, her father, the Earl of Burlington, having no heir. But the Duchess would have nothing more to do with her son; when he died ten years later she made no attempt to see her grand-children. The fifth Duke, his two brothers Lords Richard and George, and sister Lady Dorothy were brought up in cold splendour in the care of their Cavendish uncles.

Georgiana's future husband was only sixteen when he came into an in-come that was twice Lord Spencer's; by one account it amounted to more than £60,000 a year. His property included not only the magnificent Chatsworth in Derbyshire and Devonshire House in London, but five other estates of comparable grandeur: Lismore Castle in Ireland, Hard-wick House and Bolton Abbey in Yorkshire, and Chiswick House and Burlington House in London. He was one of the most sought-after bach-elors in London—although Mrs. Delany was mystified as to the reason why. "The Duke's intimate friends say he has sense, and does not want merit," she wrote. But in her opinion he was boring and gauche: "To be sure the jewell *has not been well polished:* had he fallen under the tuition of the late Lord Chesterfield he might have possessed *les graces,* but at present only that of his dukedom belongs to him."[43] As one newspaper delicately put it, "His Grace is an amiable and respectable character, but *dancing* is not his forte."[44]

Superficially, the Duke's character seemed not unlike Lord Spencer's: however, behind a shy exterior Georgiana's father concealed strong feel-ings. One of his few surviving letters to Georgiana, written after her mar-riage, bears eloquent witness to his warm heart: "But indeed my Dearest Georgiana, I did not know till lately how much I loved you; I miss you every day and every hour."[45] The twenty-four-year-old Duke had no such hidden sweetness, although Georgiana thought he did. Knowing how awkward her father could be in public, she assumed that the Duke masked his true nature from all but his closest confidants. The fact that her parents treated him so respectfully also elevated the Duke in her eyes. The Spencers were extremely gratified by the interest he showed in their eldest daughter, and it did not escape Georgiana's notice that she was being watched; she knew that her parents wanted her to succeed.

By the end of summer, having danced with the Duke on several occa-

sions and sat near him at numerous dinners, Georgiana had fallen in love
with the idea of marrying him. His return home upset her greatly; she
feared that he would make his choice before she was grown up. "I have
not heard that the Duke of Devonshire is talked of for anybody," her
cousin reassured her after receiving an enquiry about a rumour linking
him with Lady Betty Hamilton. "Indeed I have heard very little of him
this Winter."[46] Lady Spencer, on the other hand, was relieved that the
Duke had not made a formal offer. Even though there could be no more
illustrious a match, she did not want her daughter to be a child-bride.
Georgiana "is indeed a lovely young woman," she confided to a friend,
"very pleasing in her figure, but infinitely more so from her character and
disposition; my dread is that she will be snatched from me before her age
and experience make her by any means fit for the serious duties of a wife,
a mother, or the mistress of a family."[47]

In fact the Duke had already made up his mind to marry Georgiana.
She was an obvious choice: socially the Spencers were almost equal to
the Cavendishes, she had a large dowry, she seemed likely to be popular,
and, most important, she was young and malleable. Despite Lady
Spencer's reservations, discussions between the two families began in
earnest while the Spencers were still abroad, and were concluded after
they returned to England in the spring of 1774. By now Georgiana was
almost seventeen and preparing to make her entrance into society. Hers
was not to be an arranged marriage in the sense of those common a generation before.[48] She was not exchanged in lieu of gambling debts, nor
thrown in as part of a political alliance.* However, it cannot be said that
Georgiana had been free to make a proper choice. Unlike her mother
she had not been out for several seasons before her marriage, and she
had not accepted the Duke because she loved him "above all men upon
Earth." She would go to any lengths to please her parents, and that included thinking herself in love with a man she hardly knew. But her
happiness at his proposal convinced the Spencers that they were facili-
tating a love-match.

As the marriage approached, Georgiana's faults became an obsession

---

* In 1719 the Duke of Richmond, finding himself unable to meet his obligations, paid
off his debts by agreeing to have his eighteen-year-old heir married to the thirteen-year-old
daughter of the Earl of Cadogan. The ceremony took place almost immediately, after
which the girl was returned to the nursery and did not see her husband again until she was
sixteen.

with her mother, who feared that her daughter did not understand the responsibilities which would come with her new role as a society wife and political hostess: "I had flatter'd myself I should have had more time to have improv'd her understanding and, with God's assistance to have strengthened her principles, and enabled her to avoid the many snares that vice and folly will throw in her way. She is amiable, innocent and benevolent, but she is giddy, idle and fond of dissipation."[49] Whenever they were apart, Lady Spencer criticized Georgiana's behaviour in long letters filled with "hints to form your own conduct . . . when you are so near entering into a world abounding with dissipation, vice and folly."[50] In one, she included a list of rules governing a married woman's behaviour on Sundays. Georgiana would have to rise early, pray, instruct the children or servants, then read an improving book, and above all "make it a rule to be among the first [to church], and to shew by my good humour and attention to everybody that I saw nothing in religion or a Sunday to make people silent, ill-bred or uncomfortable. . . ." Flirting and gossip were to be absolutely avoided on this day.[51]

Most observers shared Lady Spencer's disquiet, although not for the same reason.

> We drank tea in the Spring Gardens [recorded Mary Hamilton in her diary]: Lady Spencer and daughter, Lady Georgiana, and the Duke of Devonshire joined us: he walked between Lady Georgiana and I, we were very Chatty, but not one word spoke the Duke to his betrothed nor did one smile grace his dull visage.—Notwithstanding his rank and fortune I wd not marry him—they say he is sensible and has good qualities—it is a pity he is not more ostensibly agreeable, dear charming Lady Georgiana will not be well matched.[52]

Mrs. Delany had come to a similar conclusion. She happened to be at a ball in May where Georgiana danced for so long that she fainted from the heat and the constriction of her dress—"Which of course made a little bustle," she informed her friend. "His (philosophical) Grace was at the other end of the room and ask'd 'what's that?' They told him and he replied with his usual demureness (alias dullness), '*I thought the noise— was—among—the—women.*' " He did not even make a pretence of going over to where Georgiana lay to see how she was.[53]

Meanwhile the Spencers assembled a trousseau more lavish than those of many princesses on the Continent. In three months they spent a total of £1,486 on hundreds of items: sixty-five pairs of shoes filled one trunk, forty-eight pairs of stockings and twenty-six "and a half" pairs of gloves filled another.[54] They bought hats, feathers, and trimmings; morning dresses, walking dresses, riding habits, and ball gowns. There was her wedding dress to be made, her court dress, her first visiting dress, as well as cloaks, shawls, and wraps. The prospect of a union between two such wealthy and powerful families naturally caught the attention of the press—there had been no Duchess of Devonshire for over two decades. People described the marriage as the wedding of the year and anticipated that the new Duchess of Devonshire would revive the former splendour of Devonshire House. The Whig grandees also looked upon the match with favour, hoping that the married state would have a beneficial effect on the Duke.

The wedding took place on June 7, 1774, two days earlier than the official date. There had been so much publicity about the marriage that the Spencers feared the church would be mobbed with curious onlookers. They persuaded the Duke to leave the comfort of his home temporarily and stay with them at Wimbledon Park, so that the marriage could take place in the peace and quiet of the local parish church. According to Mrs. Delany, Georgiana knew nothing of their plans until the morning of the ceremony. She did not mind at all; a secret marriage appealed to her. "She is so peculiarly happy as to think his Grace *very agreeable*" and, to Mrs. Delany's surprise, "had not the least regret" about anything. She wore a white and gold dress, with silver slippers on her feet and pearl drops in her hair. Eighteenth-century weddings were small, private occasions. There were only five people present at Georgiana's: the Duke's brother Lord Richard Cavendish and his sister Dorothy, who had married the Duke of Portland, and on Georgiana's side only her parents and paternal grandmother, Lady Cowper.[55] George and Harriet remained at Wimbledon, waiting for the wedding party to return. Georgiana's feelings clearly showed on her face, while the Duke appeared inscrutable. His new wife may have occupied his thoughts, although they may well have turned to another Spencer. Not very far away in a rented villa, on a discreet road where a carriage could come and go unseen, Charlotte Spencer, formerly a milliner and no relation to the Spencers, was nursing a newborn baby: his—their—daughter Charlotte.[56]

CHAPTER 2

FASHION'S FAVOURITE

1774—1776

The heads of Society at present are the Duchess of Devonshire, Duchess of Marlborough, Duchess of Bedford, Lady Harrington, and Co. etc.

Morning Post, *Saturday, July 29, 1775*

The excess to which pleasure and dissipation are now carried amongst the ton exceeds all bounds, particularly among women of quality. The duchess of D——e has almost ruined her constitution by the hurrying life which she has led for some time; her mother, Lady S——r has mentioned it with concern to the Duke, who only answers, "Let her alone—she is but a girl."

Morning Post, *Monday, March 11, 1776*

Three days after the wedding the Duke was spotted with his drinking companions trawling the pleasure gardens of Ranelagh at Chelsea. He provoked more gossip when he turned up four hours late for his presentation at court with Georgiana. All newly married couples were required to present themselves to the Queen at one of her twice-weekly public audiences at St. James's Palace, known as Drawing Rooms. "The Drawing-room was fuller than ever I saw it," a witness recorded, "excepting that of a Birthday [of the King or Queen], owing, as I suppose, to the curiosity to see the Duchess of Devonshire." Georgiana was wearing her wedding dress and "look'd very pretty. . . . happiness was never more marked in a countenance than hers. She was properly fine for the time of year, and her diamonds are very magnificent."[1] The formidable Lady

Mary Coke wondered why the Duke ambled in on his own several hours after Georgiana. He "had very near been too late; it was nearly four o'clock when he came into the Drawing-Room." She watched him for some time and noticed that he showed no emotion. "His Grace is as happy as his Duchess," she decided charitably, "but his countenance does not mark it so strongly."[2] Lady Mary's opinion might have been different had she known about Lady Spencer's frantic messages to the Duke, imploring him not to be late.

Protocol demanded that Georgiana should pay a call on every notable person in society. For the next three weeks she went from house to house, making polite conversation for fifteen minutes while her hosts scrutinised the new Duchess of Devonshire. In an era when social prestige was itself a form of currency, Georgiana's visits were highly prized. Lady Mary Coke was not among the five hundred whom Georgiana managed to see, which soured her feelings towards her cousin for ever after.

In early July Georgiana set off with the Duke on the three-day journey northwards from London to Derbyshire, to stay at Chatsworth for the summer. The long hours on the road, with no amusement save the view from the window, were the first she had spent alone with her husband. He had hardly addressed a word to her since the day of their marriage. His taciturnity made her nervous and she overcompensated by being excessively lively. There were plenty of scenes for her to point out: a picturesque church here, a field of poppies there—rural villages in England were much more prosperous and better kept than in Europe. A Frenchman on a tour of Britain in 1765 was amazed to see that labourers had shoes on their feet, and instead of grey rags wore "good cloth" on their backs. In contrast to the mud cottages of the peasantry in France, all the dwellings he saw were "built of brick and covered with tiles, [and] have glass windows."[3]

The road had dwindled to little more than a bumpy track by the time the cavalcade of wagons and baggage carts reached Derbyshire. Here rocky moorland and fast-flowing waterfalls replaced the green hedgerows and rich hay fields of the south. Daniel Defoe toured England at the beginning of the century and described the countryside around Chatsworth as a "waste and howling wilderness with neither hedge nor tree." But Horace Walpole, visiting the area half a century later, when tastes inclined towards the romantic, was spellbound by its ruggedness. "Vast woods hand down the hills," he wrote, "and the immense rocks only serve to dignify the prospect." He admired the terrain; but Chatsworth itself—the

Palace of the Peak—with its gloomy grandeur and isolated situation, low-ered his spirits.

Successive generations of Cavendishes had transformed the original Elizabethan design until it was unrecognizable. In 1686 the first Duke of Devonshire, who was of "nice honour in everything, but the paying of his tradesmen," ordered the architect William Talman to tear down Chatsworth's pointed turrets and design something more modern in their place. He continued adding to the house until the result was a novel evocation of the English baroque style. Georgiana's first glimpse was of a rectangular stone box, some 172 feet long and three storeys high, topped by a cornice and balustrade which bore elaborately deco-rated urns at regular intervals. The façade was a bold design of double-height windows alternating with fluted pilasters, with the Cavendish symbol of interlocking serpents carved along the length of the cornice. As a whole the house and parkland was far more imposing than Althorp, except for one note of light relief in the garden—a tree made of lead. Unsuspecting visitors who stood beneath it were drenched by water spurting from its leaves. Not everyone appreciated the joke: the traveller and diarist Joseph Torrington thought it "worthy only of a tea garden in London."

Torrington also criticized the grounds as lacking in taste, even though they were the work of Capability Brown, and the house as "vile and un-comfortable."[4] He disliked the heavy use of gilt on every available surface; the combination of unpainted wainscoting and inlaid wood floors made the rooms appear dark even in the middle of the day. By the 1770s Chatsworth had an old-fashioned feel; its layout, which followed the seventeenth-century practice of linking public and private rooms along a single axis, was inconvenient and impractical; newer houses had their family apartments entirely separate from their entertaining rooms.[5] But Chatsworth was meant to be more than a family home. Its sumptuous rooms, with their classical wall paintings and triumphant gods staring down from the ceilings, performed a public function. Their purpose was to inspire awe among the lower orders who trooped round on Public Days, and respect—as well as envy—among the aristocracy. Comfort was a secondary consideration. The dining room could easily accommodate over a hundred but—as Georgiana discovered—there were only three water closets in the entire house.

She was not alone with the Duke for long. The Spencers came to stay for an extended visit, bringing with them her sister Harriet and an assort-ment of pets, favourite horses, and servants. They came in part to provide

Georgiana with the support and guidance she desperately needed. The Duke's brothers and uncles were already there to check on her behaviour as the new Duchess and chatelaine of Chatsworth. Georgiana was on show from the moment she stepped out of her carriage. Aristocratic life in the eighteenth century had little in the way of privacy: almost every activity took place before an audience of servants. Rank determined behaviour, and the social pressure on Georgiana to remain "within character" was intense. She was now the wife of one of the most powerful men in the country. Everyone—from the staff assembled outside Chatsworth to welcome her on her arrival, to the neighbours who came to pay their respects, to the people who met her at public functions, saw her from afar, or read about her in the papers—expected her to know precisely what to say and how to perform.

What help the Cavendishes were prepared to give Georgiana lay waiting in her bed chamber. The Duke's agent, Heaton, had prepared a list of the household expenses, which included the names of the parishioners and tenants who received charity from the estate and whose welfare was now in her trust. Some received food, others alms; when the Duke was in residence the poorer tenants were given bread on Mondays and Thursdays. His arrival, and likewise his departure, was always marked by a gift of ox meat to the local parishioners. Georgiana's first task was to fulfil her social obligations and, with the importance of the Cavendish name in mind, to establish goodwill between herself and the Duke's many dependants.

These duties gave a rhythm to Georgiana's first days and weeks at Chatsworth. In the morning the men went out riding or shooting, while she made exploratory visits to the neighbourhood accompanied by Lady Spencer, who was pregnant again. She quickly made friends with all the Duke's tenants, displaying the charm and sympathy for which she would become renowned. On one of their walks they found a disused building which Georgiana decided should be used for her first charity school. This was the sort of thing she enjoyed; as a little girl she had given her pocket money to street children and, according to her grandmother, "seemed as glad to give [the coins] as they were to have them."[6]

They would return at mid-day, rest, and prepare for dinner at three. It was the most important meal of the day and could last up to four hours. Instead of one course following another, there were two "covers," or servings, of fifteen or so sweet and savoury dishes, artfully arranged in geometric patterns and decorated with flowers. Georgiana self-consciously practised being the hostess in front of her parents and the Duke, giving orders to footmen and displaying a command which she did not necessarily feel. Eighteenth-century dinners were less formal than those in the century to follow, but their rules, though subtle, were strictly observed.* Although diners could sit where they chose, the host and hostess always sat at the head and foot of the table with the principal guests on either side. It was considered ill-bred to ask for a dish or to reach too far across for one—the servants standing along the walls were supposed to ensure that the guests' plates were never empty. Not only did Georgiana have to keep up a lively flow of conversation, she also had to watch the servants for neglect, the guests for boredom, and the Cavendishes for signs of displeasure.

In the evening she played cards with some of the guests or listened to music performed by Felix Giardini, the violinist and director of the London Opera and a friend of the Spencers. At her request he composed pieces for small orchestra which Georgiana and some of her musical guests would perform under his direction. The house was filling up as more of the Duke's friends and relatives came to inspect his bride. Georgiana did her best to appear composed and friendly towards the sophisticated strangers who often arrived at short notice and expected to be entertained. That she succeeded in fulfilling her role was thanks to the presence of Lady Spencer by her side as much as to her careful upbringing. Georgiana had little acquaintance with her husband or with his world; training was all that she could rely upon to take her through the first few months.

By late September autumn colours were returning to the park and the sun was casting longer shadows. It was easy to stay outside for too long after dinner and catch a chill, as Lady Spencer did one afternoon. She seemed to have only a slight fever; but a few days later she suffered a miscarriage. When she recovered, her only desire was to return to Althorp; she had lost three children in ten years, and Georgiana's steps towards independence may have caused her to feel she was losing another. Geor-

---

* When French visitors attended aristocratic dinners they had difficulty with the table forks, and the English predilection for toasts bored them witless. Regarding the former, the usual complaint, as expressed by Faujas de Saint-Fond, was that they "prick my mouth or my tongue with their little sharp steel tridents." Regarding the latter, it was their inordinate number. The practice of proposing and replying continued throughout the dinner and with even more vigour after the women had left. Toasting the ladies, the food, each other, and whatever else came to mind went on for so long there were chamber pots in each corner, and "the person who has occasion to use it does not even interrupt his talk during the operation." André Parreaux, *Daily Life,* p. 36.

giana came downstairs one morning to discover that her parents had left without saying goodbye. In a hastily scribbled note Lady Spencer apologized for running away, and blamed it on "my Spirits having been lower'd by my late illness. . . . Do not think I shall ever be so nonsensical about quitting you again," she promised, "but the number of people that are here are so formidable and I felt so afraid of disgracing myself and distressing you, that I think it better to get out of the way."[7] Georgiana was distraught and full of guilt: "Oh my dearest Mama," she wrote immediately, "how can I tell [you], how can I express how much I love you and how much I felt at your going."[8]

Lady Spencer was relieved to receive Georgiana's letter; its tone reassured her that independence was still some way off. She replied with a description of the trust and obedience she expected of Georgiana in their future relationship:

> Here commences our correspondence, my dear Georgiana, from which I propose myself more real pleasure than I can express, but the greatest part of it will quite vanish if I do not find you treat me with that entire Confidence that my heart expects. Seventeen years of painful anxiety and unwearied attention on my part, and the most affectionate and grateful return on yours is surely a sufficient [reason] to give me the very first place. I will not say your heart because that the D of D will have, but in your friendship.[9]

Georgiana was happy to comply, as her days were lonely now. "As soon as I am up and have breakfasted I ride," she wrote. "I then come in and write and or do anything of employment, I then walk, dress for Dinner and after Dinner I take a short walk if it is fine and I have time 'till the Gentlemen come out, and then spend the remainder of the evening in Playing at Whist, or writing if I have an opportunity and reading."[10] Not caring for his wife's after-dinner concerts, the Duke usually took his friends off to drink and play billiards. Georgiana would not see him until much later, when, already in bed and fast asleep, she would be woken up by a noise at the door—he was impatient for her to become pregnant.

❧❧

She often rose full of dread at what lay ahead in the day. Sometimes she stayed in bed as long as possible, but this evasive measure brought its own problems.

Lord Charles and Lady D. Thompson and Miss Hatham arrived and
I was obliged (for they were let in before I knew anything about it)
to pretend that I was gone walking and at last went down Drest the
greatest figure you can Imagine [she wrote sadly to her mother]. To
compleat my Distress another Coachful arrived—of People I had
never seen before. As I could not have much to say for myself, and
some of the Company were talking about things I knew nothing of,
I made the silliest figure you can conceive, and J [Lord John
Cavendish] says I broke all the rules of Hospitality in forgetting to
offer them some breakfast.[11]

She also had to preside over the Public Days, which had resumed after
Lady Spencer's departure. Chatsworth still maintained the tradition of
holding a Public Day every week. On these occasions the house was
open to all the Duke's tenants, as well as to any respectable stranger who
wished to see the house and have dinner with its owners. Georgiana and
the Duke stood in the hall wearing their finest clothes, as if attending a
state occasion, and personally greeted each visitor. They had to remain
gracious and sober while their guests helped themselves to the free food
and drink. "Some of the men got extremely drunk," Georgiana recorded
after one dinner, and her friends, "if they had not made a sudden retreat,
would have been the victims of a drunken clergyman, who very nearly
fell on them."[12] Her first appearance naturally caused great excitement
in Derbyshire, but after a few weeks the Public Days became less
crowded. She learned how to orchestrate a room full of strangers, how
to pick out those whom she ought particularly to distinguish, and how
to detach herself from those who would otherwise cling to her arm all
day.*

Public Days were a feudal relic from the era of vassals and private
armies. Because of the expense only the grandest of families continued the

---

* On one occasion she met the celebrated Dr. Johnson, who was visiting a friend in the
neighbourhood. The Devonshires were as gratified to be in his presence as he was in theirs.
Georgiana was awed by his conversation but, she noted, "he din'd here and does not shine
quite so much in eating as in conversing, for he ate much and nastily." Chatsworth MSS
644: GD to LS, September 4–10, 1784. Nevertheless, she sat next to him throughout the
day and, according to Nathaniel Wraxall, was "hanging on the sentences that fell from
Johnson's lips. . . . All the cynic moroseness of the philosopher and moralist seemed to dis-
solve under so flattering [an] approach." Nathaniel Wraxall, *Posthumous and Historical Memoirs of My Own Time* (London 1904), I, pp. 113–14.

tradition. Such lavish entertainment was now a means of cultivating good relations with the tenantry and of safeguarding local political influence. In the eighteenth century the maintenance of an electoral borough was a family matter; it was part of the estate, as tangible and valuable as land. The Cavendish influence in Parliament depended on the number of MPs who sat in the family's "interest." At its height, thirteen MPs owed their seats to the Duke's financial and political might, the second largest grouping within the Whig party after the Marquess of Rockingham, who had eighteen.[13] Since the Duke's brother-in-law the Duke of Portland controlled ten, when the Cavendishes collaborated they presented a formidable faction.

That year the Public Days had a particular purpose; a general election was scheduled in October and the Cavendishes were defending their electoral interests in Derbyshire. Since peers were barred from personally campaigning in parliamentary elections, their wives and relatives had to look after their interests for them. On October 8 Georgiana went to her first election ball in Derby, dressed in fashionable London clothes for the benefit of the locals. The Duke's brothers were already drunk by the time she arrived and Lord Frederick Cavendish, the Duke's uncle, almost fell on her as she climbed the stairs to the assembly room. An open-door policy operated, and the heat and sweat of so many bodies crammed together made the room suffocating. The musicians—the usual country players— made an appalling noise, each following a different measure.[14] Nevertheless Georgiana kept her poise and danced to the tunes from memory, smiling graciously at her partners and at any townspeople who caught her eye. The next ball she attended revealed the Derbyshire voters' opinion of the new Duchess: "we were received there by a great huzza," she recorded. "The room was very much crowded but they were so good as to split in 2 to make room for us."[15] Although the Whigs did not do well as a party in the election, the Duke's candidates were voted in without any trouble. His bill came to £554, which was low compared to the average £5,000 spent on a contested election.[16]

The Spencers had to pay considerably more. Lady Spencer went to the borough of Northampton Town because Lord Spencer's nominee Mr. Tollemache was facing a challenge from a newcomer, Sir James Langham. "I have dined each day during the Poll at the George with all the gentlemen and am extremely popular among them," she wrote contentedly to Georgiana.[17] She not only courted the gentlemen voters but bravely went out to rally the whole town:

I set out on Thursday morning with Mrs Tollemache in my Cabrio-
let and four, in hopes of putting a little spirit into our people who
were sadly discompos'd at having neither money or drink offer'd
them [she informed her daughter on October 9, 1774]. I succeeded
beyond my expectations, for I no sooner got to the George than a little mob surrounded us and insisted on taking off our horses and
drawing us around the town. . . . in a very few minutes we had a mob
of several hundred people screaming Spencer for ever—Tollemache
and Robinson—No Langham. In this manner did they drag us about
thro' every street in the town, and were so delighted with my talking
to them and shewing no signs of fear at going wherever they chose,
that it was with the utmost difficulty I could in the evening . . . prevent their drawing me quite home to Althorp. I went thro' the same
ceremony again on Friday, when very luckily my chaise was
broke. . . . it has ensur'd Mr Tollemache a great majority, by putting
such numbers of people in spirits and good humour who before
were cross and sulky and would not vote because there was nothing
to enliven them.[18]

Despite the fact that people responded favourably to her youth and enthusiasm, Georgiana was constantly terrified of forgetting herself and commit-
ting some *faux pas*. This worry was exacerbated by the Cavendishes, who
sternly demanded that she conform to their ways. A century of political
leadership and proud public service had made them self-conscious and introverted in their dealings with the outside world. The Cavendish way of
doing things stamped itself on all members of the family, from the relent-
less self-control they exerted on their emotions to the peculiar drawl which
marred their speech. They pronounced her name "George-aina" (as in
rain-a), as opposed to George-i-ahna. In her eagerness to be accepted Georgiana adopted all their mannerisms, vigorously applying the Cavendish
drawl and insisting that everyone should call her "George-ayna." This was
how she became known for the rest of her life.

෧෧

By now, three months into her marriage, Georgiana could not help but
suspect the true nature of the Duke's feelings towards her. He was kind in
a distant sort of way, but he was naturally reticent and she soon realized
that they had little in common. Her innocence bored him and Georgiana
was too acute not to notice his lack of interest in her. She told her mother

that she was secretly making an effort to be more attractive to him. Since
he was so much more worldly than she, she read Lord Chesterfield's *Letters to His Son;* and knowing of his interest in history and the classics, she
began several books on ancient Greece and on the reign of Louis XIV, "for
as those two periods are so distant there will be no danger of their interfering so as to puzzle me."[19]

At first Lady Spencer tried to reassure her that the Duke "was no less
happy than herself."[20] She also supplied her daughter with advice on how
to please him, suggesting that she should curb any thoughts of independence and show her submission by anticipating his desires:

> But where a husband's delicacy and indulgence is so great that he
> will not say what he likes, the task becomes more difficult, and a wife
> must use all possible delicacy and ingenuity in trying to find out his
> inclinations, and the utmost readiness in conforming to them. You
> have this difficult task to perform, my dearest Georgiana, for the
> Duke of D., from a mistaken tenderness, persists in not dictating to
> you the things he wishes you to do, and not contradicting you in
> anything however disagreeable to him. This should engage you by a
> thousand additional motives of duty and gratitude to try to know his
> sentiments upon even the most trifling subjects, and especially not
> to enter into any engagements or form any plans without consulting
> him. . . .[21]

Unwilling to disappoint her mother, Georgiana made sincere efforts to
appear cheerful, sending her carefully composed accounts of her life. Lady
Spencer was particularly delighted when Georgiana wrote her letters in
French and interspersed her news with little poems or religious reflections. Since she had been told that she ought to be content, Georgiana asserted that she was: "I have been so happy in marrying a Man I so sincerely
lov'd, and experience Dayly so much of his goodness to me, that it is impossible I should not feel to the greatest degree that mutual happyness you
speak of." But she could not help adding anxiously, "My only wish is to
deserve it and my greatest pleasure the thought of being in any manner
able to add to His Happyness."[22] She was quite sure that she did not add
to his happiness in the slightest degree.

Georgiana had entered into marriage thinking that, like her mother, she
would be a wife and companion. She soon discovered that her chief role
was to produce children and carry out her social obligations. The Duke

was used to his bachelor life: love he received from his mistress, companionship from his friends; from his wife he expected loyalty, support, and commitment to the family's interests. His was an old-fashioned view, greatly out of step with an age which celebrated romantic sentiment and openly shed tears over Samuel Richardson's novel *Clarissa*. The Duke did not know how to be romantic; never having experienced tenderness himself he was incapable of showing it to Georgiana. He did not mean to hurt her, but there was a nine-year age difference between them and a gulf of misunderstanding and misplaced expectations.

They left Chatsworth in January, much to Georgiana's relief. In London she would be surrounded by her own family and friends and no longer reliant on the monosyllabic Duke or his critical relations. The caravan of carriages and coaches, piled high with boxes of plate and linens, set off once more. Most of the servants joined the back of the train to take up their duties at Devonshire House, leaving behind a skeleton staff until the family's return in the summer.

⌘

Devonshire House lay in London's western end, known as the "polite" end, encompassing Piccadilly, St. James's, and Hyde Park. Before the eighteenth century the grand nobility lived in private palaces along the Strand, overlooking the river Thames, but after the Glorious Revolution in 1688, when William and Mary, the Protestant rulers of Holland, sailed to England at the Whig party's request and helped to depose the Catholic King James II, the nature of political life changed. Parliament no longer met at the King's command but according to a set calendar, while the court resided permanently at St. James's Palace when Parliament was in session. The aristocracy had to be in London for much longer periods of time, and in a location convenient for both the Houses of Parliament at Westminster and the Palace of St. James's nearby. The concentration of so much wealth and power transformed the city. By the mid-eighteenth century one in ten Englishmen had lived in London at some point in his life. There was a frenzy of building as the capital spread out westwards. Speculators widened country lanes into streets, turned fields into smart squares, and built shops, arcades, and churches on previously empty spaces. By the 1770s modern London was envied throughout Europe for its glass-fronted shops and spacious roads that easily accommodated two lanes of traffic.

The aristocratic "season" came into existence not only to further the marriage market but to entertain the upper classes while they carried out their political duties. The season followed the rhythm of Parliament: it began in late October with the opening of the new session, and ended in June with the summer recess. The two most popular nights of the week were Wednesday and Saturday, when Parliament was not in session and the men's attendance could be assured. A completely new form of public architecture appeared, the sole purpose of which was to facilitate social intercourse. Coffee houses—where men of all classes gathered during the day to read newspapers and discuss politics—sprang up. White's, the first of the London clubs, opened in St. James's in 1697; Almack's, Boodles, and Brooks's followed half a century later. For evening entertainment people went to Covent Garden or to the Italian Opera House in the Haymarket to hear Handel, or to Drury Lane to watch David Garrick. Afterwards they could amuse themselves at the commercial gardens of Ranelagh, or visit its riverside competitor, Vauxhall, to dance at a masquerade, attend a concert, or watch the fireworks.

Baron Archenholtz came to London at this time and was amazed by the difference between the east and the west, the old and the new. East was the City, home of the country's banking, insurance, and commercial institutions. It retained a medieval feel with its tiny slipways and hidden courtyards. Further east were the manufacturing districts, where artisans laboured in run-down workshops without heat or ventilation to produce luxury goods to be sold in the West End—jewellery, clocks, saddles, furniture, and cutlery. Further east still were the Spitalfields silk-weavers, the soap-making factories, tanneries, and the slum-dwellings of the marginal poor. "The East end," Archenholtz wrote, "especially along the shores of the Thames, consists of old houses, the streets there are narrow, dark and ill-paved; inhabited by sailors and other workmen who are employed in the construction of ships and by a great part of the Jews.

"The contrast between this and the West end," Archenholtz continued, "is astonishing: the houses here are mostly new and elegant; the squares superb, the streets straight and open. . . . If all London were as well built, there would be nothing to compare it with."[23] Another visitor commented on how "pure air circulates in the new streets [compared to the fetid stench in the alleyways behind Westminster]; and the squares are carefully planned, and pleasing to the eye; the upper-class society who live there find these squares salubrious since within each of them is a magnificent garden; the surrounding houses are tall with plenty of big windows. . . . admirable pavements very wide protect the passers-by from carriages and carts."[24] New lighting systems were being introduced and stucco was being applied to the front of buildings: they "lifted" the city from under the thick fog of coal dust "which envelops London like a mantle; a cloud which the sun pervades rarely."

Situated opposite what is now the Ritz Hotel, Devonshire House commanded magnificent views over Green Park. The original house had burnt down in 1733 and the third Duke of Devonshire commissioned William Kent to rebuild it. Aesthetically it was a failure. The house was stark and devoid of architectural detail; the bottom windows were too large, the top windows too small. The whole building was enclosed behind a brick wall which hid the ground floor from view and made the street unattractive to passers-by. The London topographer James Ralph wrote, "It is spacious, and so are the East India Company's warehouses; and both are equally deserving of praise."[25] As well as attracting every graffiti writer within two miles, the brick wall ruined the architectural line of Piccadilly. One contemporary complained: "The Duke of Devonshire's is one of those which present a horrid blank of wall, cheerless and unsociable by day, and terrible by night. Would it be credible that any man of taste, fashion, and figure would prefer the solitary grandeur of enclosing himself in a jail, to the enjoyment of the first view in Britain, which he might possess by throwing down this execrable brick screen?"[26]

The chief attraction of Devonshire House was the public rooms, which were larger and more ornate than almost anything to be seen in London. A crowd of 1,200 could easily sweep through the house during a ball, a remarkable contrast to some great houses where the crush could lift a person off his feet and carry him from room to room. Guests entered the house by an outer staircase which took them directly to the first floor. Inside was a hall two storeys high—flanked on either side by two drawing rooms of identical size. Beyond the hall was another, even larger drawing room, several anterooms, and the dining room. Some of the finest paintings in England adorned the walls, including Rembrandt's *Old Man in Turkish Dress* and Poussin's *Et in Arcadia Ego.*

Georgiana and the Duke were naturally placed to become the leaders of society's most select group, known as the *ton* or the World—the ultra-fashionable people who decided whether a play was a success, an artist a genius, or what colour would be "in" that season. Henry Fielding was only half-joking when he said that "Nobody" was "all the people in Great Britain, except about 1200."[27] The *ton* certainly believed this to be the case. The writer and reluctant courtier Fanny Burney made fun of its self-absorption in *Cecilia:* "Why, he's the very head of the ton," Miss Larolles

says of Mr. Matthews. "There's nothing in the world so fashionable as taking no notice of things, and never seeing people, and saying nothing at all,
and never hearing a word, and not knowing one's own acquaintance, and
always finding fault; all the ton do so."

The social tyrants who made up the *ton* also considered it deeply unfashionable for a wife and husband to be seen too much in each other's
company. The Duke escorted Georgiana to the opera once and then resumed his habit of visiting Brooks's, where he always ordered the same
supper—a broiled blade-bone of mutton—and played cards until five or six
in the morning.[28] Occasionally they went to a party together but Georgiana
was expected to make her own social arrangements. There was no shortage
of invitations and she accepted everything—promenades in the park, card
parties in the afternoon, routs in the evening where she exchanged fashionable gossip with her friends, assemblies and balls at night—anything—
in an effort to avoid sitting alone in Devonshire House.

With her instinctive ability to make an impression, Georgiana immediately caused a sensation. She always appeared natural, even when she was
called upon to open a ball in front of 800 people. She could engage in
friendly chatter with several people simultaneously, leaving each with the
impression that it had been a memorable event. She was "so handsome, so
agreeable, so obliging in her manner, that I am *quite* in love with her," Mrs.
Delany burbled to a friend. "I can't tell you all the civil things she said, and
really they deserve a better name, which is *kindness* embellished by *politeness.* I hope she will *illumine* and *reform* her contemporaries!"[29] Even cynics
like Horace Walpole found their resistance worn down by Georgiana's
unforced charm and directness. Observing her transformation into a society figure, Walpole marvelled that this "lovely girl, natural, and full of
grace" could retain these qualities and yet be so much on show. "The
Duchess of Devonshire effaces all," he wrote a few weeks after her arrival
in London. She achieved it "without being a beauty; but her youth, figure,
flowing good nature, sense and lively modesty, and modest familiarity,
make her a phenomenon."[30]

The few voices raised in criticism of Georgiana were not heeded, except by Lady Spencer. "I think there is too much of her," was one woman's
opinion. "She gives me the idea of being *larger* than life."[31] Lady Mary
Coke thought Georgiana was making herself ridiculous and that her behaviour occasionally verged on hysteria. The Duchess went to visit Lady
Harriet Foley, she wrote, just as her house and contents were being seized
by the bailiffs, and "as her Grace's misfortune is a very unnatural one, that

of being too happy and of being delighted with everything she hears and sees, so the situation in which she found Lady Harriet was, in her Grace's opinion, Charming; Lady Harriet told her she had no clothes, this was charming above measure."[32]

Occasionally Georgiana drank too much, especially when she was nervous, and showed off as a result: "nothing is talked of but the Duchess of Devonshire: and I am sorry to say not much in her favour," wrote a society lady after Georgiana upset a dignified matron by pulling out her hair feathers.[33] Lady Mary Coke went to Ranelagh and was disgusted to see Georgiana and her new friends amusing themselves by puffing out their cheeks and popping them.[34] She could be persuaded to do anything: once she even appeared on stage at Hampton Court and danced in an opera organized by the fashionable wit and playwright Anthony Storer. Lady Spencer was worried when she saw how easily her daughter could be influenced: "when others draw you out of your own character, and make you assume one that is quite a stranger to you, it is difficult to distinguish you under the disguise," she warned.[35] Mrs. Delany feared that rather than reforming her contemporaries Georgiana was more likely to be corrupted by them: "This bitter reflection arises from what I hear *every* body says of a *great* and *handsome* relation of ours just *beginning* her part; but I do hope she will be like the young actors and actresses, who begin with *over* acting when they first come upon the stage . . . but I tremble for her."[36]

Lady Spencer could see that her daughter was adopting the ways of the fast set. Gossip that some of them were encouraging Georgiana to gamble at high stakes worried her: "let me entreat you to beware of it, and if [gambling] is mention'd to you any more, to decline the taking any part in it," she begged.[37] Gaming was to the aristocracy what gin was to the working classes: it caused the ruin of families and corrupted people's lives. "A thousand meadows and cornfields are staked at every throw, and as many villages lost as in the earthquake that overwhelmed Herculaneum and Pompeii," wrote Horace Walpole, who had seen men lose an entire estate in a single night. "Play at whist, commerce, backgammon, trictrac or chess," Lady Spencer urged, "but never at quinze, lou, brag, faro, hazard or any games of chance, and if you are pressed to play always make the fashionable excuse of being tied up not to play at such and such a game. In short I must beg you, my dearest girl, if you value my happiness to send me in writing a serious answer to this."[38]

Lady Clermont, who had known the Spencer family for many years, counselled Lady Spencer against being too critical: "I hope you don't talk to her too often about trifles, when she does any little thing that is not right. . . . If we can but keep her out of the fire for a year or two, or rather from being burn'd, for in the fire she is, it will all be well."[39] But Lady Spencer was too worried to listen; instead she tried to frighten Georgiana into adopting a more mature exterior. "You must learn to respect yourself," she wrote in April 1775, "and the world will soon follow your example; but while you herd only with the vicious and the profligate you will be like them, pert, familiar, noisy and indelicate, not to say indecent in their contempt for the censures of the grave, and their total disregard of the opinion of the world in general, you will be lost indeed past recovery."[40]

Georgiana—as dependent on parental approval as ever—felt guilty and went to even greater lengths to distract herself with frivolity. Her recklessness entranced society even as it caused disapproval. Whatever she wore became instantly fashionable. Women's hair was already arranged high above the head, but Georgiana took the fashion a step further by creating the three-foot hair tower. She stuck pads of horse hair to her own hair using scented pomade and decorated the top with miniature ornaments. Sometimes she carried a ship in full sail, or an exotic arrangement of stuffed birds and waxed fruit, or even a pastoral tableau with little wooden trees and sheep. Even though the towers required the help of at least two hairdressers and took several hours to arrange, Georgiana's designs inspired others to imitate her. "The Duchess of Devonshire is the most envied woman of the day in the *Ton*," the newspapers reported.[41] It was true; women competed with each other to construct the tallest head, ignoring the fact that it made quick movements impossible and the only way to ride in a carriage was to sit on the floor.

Another of Georgiana's innovations was the drooping ostrich feather, which she attached in a wide arch across the front of her hair. In April Lord Stormont, the British ambassador in Paris, presented her with one that was four feet long.[42] Overnight it became the most important accessory in a lady's wardrobe, even though the tall nodding plumes were difficult to find and extremely expensive.[43] The *ton* wore them with a smug arrogance which infuriated the less fortunate. The fashion generated resentment: it was too excessive and too exclusive. The Queen banned ostrich feathers from court, and according to Lady Louisa Stuart, "the unfortunate feathers were insulted, mobbed, hissed, almost pelted wherever they appeared, abused in the newspapers, nay even preached at in the pulpits and pointed out as marks of reprobation."[44]

In less than a year Georgiana had become a celebrity. Newspaper editors noticed that any report on the Duchess of Devonshire increased their sales. She brought glamour and style to a paper. A three-ring circus soon developed between newspapers who saw commercial value in her fame, ordinary readers who were fascinated by her, and Georgiana herself, who enjoyed the attention. The more editors printed stories about her, the more she obliged by playing up to them. Her arrival coincided with the flowering of the English press. A growing population, increased wealth, better roads, and an end to official censorship had resulted in a wider readership and more news to report. By the end of the 1770s there were nine daily newspapers, all based in London, and hundreds of bi- and tri-weekly provincial papers which reprinted the London news. For the first time national figures emerged, Georgiana among them, which the whole country read about and discussed, and with whom they could feel some sort of connection.

The *Morning Post* reported Georgiana's progress to a nation whose appetite for news about her was constantly growing:

> The Duchess of D——e has a fashionable coat of mail; impregnable to the arrows of wit or ridicule; many other females of distinction have been made to moult, and rather than be laughed at any longer, left themselves featherless; while her Grace, with all the dignity of a young Duchess is determined to keep the field, for her feathers increase in enormity in proportion to the public intimations she receives of the absurdity. Her head was a wonderful exhibition on Saturday night at the Opera. The Duke is quoted as saying she is welcome to do as she likes as long as she doesn't think it "necessary that I should wear any *ornaments on my head* in compliment to her notions of taste and dress."

The *London Chronicle* reported with outrage that a crowd had almost attacked Georgiana when she visited the pleasure gardens at Ranelagh

> dressed in a stile so whimsically singular as quickly collected the company round her, they behaved with great rudeness, in so much that she was necessitated to take shelter in one of the boxes, and there remained prisoner for some time, until the motley crew had retired, and left only those behind who scorned to offer insult to a

fine woman for indulging her fancy in the most innocent and inof-
fensive manner, and who were capable of discovering, amidst her
levity, an understanding that would distinguish her in any court in
Europe.[45]

On the whole, society took Georgiana's fashion excesses in good part, and
even when people teased her it was done with gentle humour. One night
at the opera she entered her box just as the celebrated Signor Lovattini
came on stage to sing. He was wearing an enormous headdress of red and
white flowers in imitation of the one Georgiana had worn on her last visit.
The audience burst out laughing and Georgiana, rather than taking offence, turned to Lovattini and made him a low bow which earned her
cheers of approval.[46] People were enraptured by a duchess who was happy
to exchange banter with the crowd. On another occasion the *Morning Post*
reported that the audience in the Haymarket Theatre had lapsed into gig-
gles when a couple appeared in the stalls dressed up in a parody of the
Devonshires. The woman wore ostrich feathers in her hair and enormous
breeches which extended up to her armpits while her male companion
was wearing an oversized petticoat with a ducal coronet and jewels on his
head.[47] It was not an attack on Georgiana so much as a comment on the
Duke's inadequacies. In less than a year she had eclipsed her husband and
become a popular figure in her own right.

❧❦

During that year Georgiana had also brought herself to a state of nervous
and physical exhaustion. She had suffered at least one miscarriage, which
convinced Lady Spencer that her daughter should leave England, if only to
remain quiet for a while. In July the Spencers and the Devonshires set off
for a holiday in Spa. After a few weeks in the open air Georgiana's health
returned and her unnatural pallor disappeared. On their return they
stopped at Versailles to pay their respects to Louis XVI. Georgiana already
had more than a passing acquaintance with Marie Antoinette, having met
her during previous trips to France. On this visit a close friendship developed which lasted until the Queen's execution in 1793. They discovered
they had much in common, not only in having married a position rather
than a lover, but also in their relations with their mothers. Empress Marie
Thérèse combined an intense, almost suffocating love for her children
with a manipulative and dominating manner. While Georgiana was in

Paris Marie Antoinette received the following scolding from her mother, which sounded uncannily like many of Lady Spencer's letters:

> What frivolity! Where is the kind and generous heart of the Archduchess Antoinette? All I see is intrigue, low hatred, a persecuting spirit, and cheap wit. . . . Your too early success and your entourage of flatterers have always made me fear for you, ever since that winter when you wallowed in pleasures and ridiculous fashions. Those excursions from pleasure to pleasure without the King and in the knowledge that he doesn't enjoy them and that he either accompanies you or leaves you free out of sheer good nature. . . . Where is the respect and gratitude you owe him for all his kindness?[48]

Three weeks later Georgiana received a similar inquiry from Lady Spencer, who complained, among other things, about her inattentiveness towards the Duke. "You do not say anything of [him]—how does he employ and amuse himself?" she asked.[49]

Similar words have often been used to describe both Georgiana and Marie Antoinette. Horace Walpole thought Marie Antoinette grace itself, and called her a "statue of beauty." She had immense charm, which at first endeared her to the court and the people, but she shared Georgiana's tendency to take everything to excess. On a typical evening she would go to the opera, leave early for an intimate supper, rush to several balls, and finish off the night gambling with Mme. de Guémène, whom everyone suspected of cheating. Her addiction to trivial amusements has been attributed to her frustration with her marriage. A naturally romantic woman, she had little in common with her reserved and awkward husband. "The great obstacle to this perfect union is the incompatibility of the tastes and characters of the two spouses," wrote an observer. "The King is calm, rather passive, loving the solitude of his library. . . . His wife is . . . extremely vivacious, loving a quick succession of pleasures and their diversity."[50] Marie Antoinette loved extravagant coiffures and clothes and, like Georgiana, enjoyed being at the forefront of fashion. But she chose her friends unwisely, from among the most dissipated in French society. They led the tractable Queen into one scrape after another.

It was on this visit, too, that Georgiana formed life-long friendships with members of Marie Antoinette's set, particularly with the ambitious Polignacs. The Austrian ambassador to France complained to the Empress

Marie Thérèse that Marie Antoinette was infatuated with the Duchesse de Polignac. The "Little Po," as she was nicknamed, was a sweet-natured, elegant brunette, very much under her husband's thumb, who nevertheless exerted a powerful attraction on both Marie Antoinette and Georgiana. Throughout Georgiana's stay the three women went everywhere together, wore each other's favours on their bosoms, and exchanged locks of hair as keepsakes. They met in a highly charged feminine atmosphere where feelings ruled and kisses and embraces were part of the ordinary language of communication. Georgiana's passionate nature, thwarted in her marriage to the Duke, found fulfilment in such an atmosphere.

On her return to England Georgiana made a renewed effort to please her husband. Initially he responded with unaccustomed sensitivity. "The Duke is in very good spirits," she wrote in September 1775. "I sincerely hope he is contented with me, tho' if he is not he hides it very well, for it is impossible to say how good and attentive he is to me, and how much he seems to make it his business to see me happy and pleas'd—with so much reason as he has had to be discontented at such a number of things, I have very little right to expect [it]."[51] Lady Spencer's friend Miss Lloyd thought that Georgiana was telling the truth and that they appeared to be getting on well together: "I think they are grown quite in love with each other," she wrote.[52]

But they had so little in common that their efforts to establish a deeper intimacy had petered out by Christmas. It was not a question of dislike; neither understood the other. The Duke was used to being flattered and cosseted by his mistress, Charlotte Spencer, and resented the emotional demands that Georgiana made upon him. Georgiana, on the other hand, treated him as if he were part of her audience and then wondered why her reserved and shy husband failed to respond. A family tale reveals the misunderstanding between them. The Duke was drinking a dish of tea with Lady Spencer and Harriet when Georgiana walked into the room and sat on his lap with her arms around his neck. Without saying a word he pushed her off and left the company.[53]

Rejected by the Duke, Georgiana once more sought consolation in the fashionable world as soon as the season began. Newspapers speculated on how long she could keep up the frantic pace of her life before her health collapsed.[54] They only had to wait a couple of months. In April 1776 Georgiana went into premature labour. No one was surprised by her miscarriage. "The Duchess of Devonshire lies dangerously ill," reported the *Morning Post,* "and we hear the physicians have ascribed her indisposition to the reigning fashionable irregularities of the age."[55] The next day it claimed with gloomy pleasure that the physicians had given up and her death was imminent.

Georgiana denied the prophets of doom their satisfaction, but her recovery was much slower than it should have been. She was harbouring a secret: she was deeply in debt. She had placed all hope of repaying her gambling dues in the birth of the lost child, positive that the Duke would forgive her in the general glow of happiness. Now that her plans had gone awry she had no idea what to do and the worry affected her health. She was not the first woman to find herself in such a predicament; it was a popular theme in the press. The *Guardian* was blunt: "The Man who plays beyond his income, pawns his Estate; the Woman must find something else to Mortgage when her Pin Money is gone. The Husband has his Lands to dispose of; the Wife, her Person."[56] Georgiana could not even bring herself to think how she might tell the Duke or her mother that her gambling debts amounted to at least £3,000 ($297,000 in today's money) when her pin money, the allowance granted to her by the Duke, came to £4,000 a year. Like everyone else, the Duke blamed the miscarriage on her reckless living.

In July Georgiana's creditors threatened to apply directly to the Duke, which frightened her into confessing the truth to her parents. They were so angry that Lady Clermont felt obliged to intercede on her behalf:

> The conversation you had with the Duchess made so great an impression on her that it made her quite ill. She has not seen anybody since she came to town, except myself, not one of the *set*. I am convinced she will be very different in everything. She goes to you this evening to stay till the Duke returns from Newmarket. I do beg you will not say any more to her. Look in good spirits whether you are or not, try this for once. For God's Sake don't let Lord Spencer say anything to her. I would give the World to go to Wimbledon and not to Newmarket but that is impossible. I told her today that if I could ever be of the least use to her, let me be in France or whatever part of the world I was in, I should go to her. I am sorry. I love her so much.[57]

The Spencers listened to Lady Clermont's plea for calm. They paid Georgiana's debts but insisted that she reveal everything to the Duke. When she told him, falteringly and with many tears, he hardly said a word. He promptly repaid her parents and then never referred to the matter again. This unnerved Georgiana more than a display of anger. After a measured period of silence Lady Spencer began writing to her daughter again. She had suffered a profound shock on discovering that Georgiana hid things from her, and she no longer felt so confident about their relationship. "Pray take care if you play to carry money in your pocket as much as you care to lose and never go beyond it," she repeated. "If you stick to commerce and play carefully I think you will not lose more than you can afford, but I beg you will never play quinze or lou, and I shall be very glad if you will tell me *honestly* in each letter what you have won or lost and at what games every day."[58]

For the first time since Georgiana's marriage two years earlier Lady Spencer sensed that she was losing her hold over her daughter and she feared for the future.

CHAPTER 3

THE VORTEX OF DISSIPATION

1776—1778

Gaming among the females at Chatsworth has been carried to such a pitch that the phlegmatic Duke has been provoked to express at it and he has spoken to the Duchess in the severest terms against a conduct which has driven many from the house who could not afford to partake of amusements carried on at the expense of £500 or £1000 a night.

Morning Post and Daily Advertiser, *Wednesday, September 4, 1776*

As you are the loveliest and best tempered woman in his Majesty's dominions, learn to be the most prudent and wise. If you do, your dominion will be universal, and you will have nothing to lament, but that you have no more worlds to conquer.

Editorial addressed to Georgiana, Morning Post and Daily Advertiser, *July 4, 1777*

Coming here has made a strong impression on me," Georgiana wrote during a visit to the Devonshires' Londesborough estate in October 1776. "Alas," she continued, "I can't help but make an unhappy comparison between the emotions I experienced two years ago during my first visit, and what I feel now."[1] She was suffering from a profound sense of disillusionment, not only with her marriage but also with fashionable life.

For those who could moderate their pursuit of pleasure, Whig society was sophisticated, tolerant, and cosmopolitan. Whigs prided themselves on their patronage of the arts as much as they venerated their contribution to statecraft. They were the oligarchs of taste, proselytizers of their superior cultivation. But the *ton,* by definition, inhabited the realm of the extreme. Moderation was not a part of its world: elegance bowed to artifice, pleasure gave way to excess. "You must expect to be class'd with the company you keep," was Lady Spencer's constant warning to Georgiana.[2] Embarrassed by her own previous association with the *ton,* Lady Spencer nursed a visceral dislike towards its members. She regarded it as a magnet for the least respectable elements of her class, and Georgiana's friends as the worst among the bad.

The people who gathered around Georgiana and the Duke shared an attachment to the Whig party, a worldly attitude, a passion for the theatre, and a love of scandal. Fashion was the only "career" open to aristocratic women; politics the only "trade" that a man of rank might pursue. Georgiana's friends engaged in both regardless of their sex. Women aspired to be political hostesses of note, men to be arbiters of taste. Their collective ambition and competitiveness made them distinct even within the exclusive circle of the *ton,* and it was not long before society labelled the *habitués* of Devonshire House the "Devonshire House Circle." All Whigs were welcome, of course, but the older, staider members felt ill at ease among the more rakish elements. Among the older group was the philosopher and statesman Edmund Burke, whose legacy to conservative political ideology remains strong in America and Britain. He was the first conservative thinker to recognize that the State has a duty to safeguard the political and religious freedoms of its citizens, which was one of the reasons why he supported the American colonists against the British government. Burke rarely went to Georgiana's parties except to accompany his patron, the Marquess of Rockingham. Devonshire House was too frivolous and louche for him, and its casual attitude towards sexual misconduct made the middle-class Irishman uncomfortable. Some of the men took a delight in being overtly crude, as the following wager illustrates: "Ld Cholmondeley has given two guineas to Ld Derby, to receive 500 Gs. whenever his lordship fucks a woman in a Balloon one thousand yards from Earth."[3]

Those who embraced the Circle maintained a lofty disdain for the world outside.* Serious Devonshire House acolytes identified themselves by their imitation of the Cavendish drawl. By now Georgiana never spoke in any other way, and the more it became one of her personal mannerisms,

---

* Georgiana was not herself a snob. When Monsieur Tessier, the celebrated French actor, visited England the Duchess of Manchester refused to speak to him because he earned his living. Her behaviour disgusted Georgiana, and to make the point she danced with him at Almack's.

the more compelling it was to her admirers. What began as playful mimicry evolved with popular usage into a kind of dialect, called the Devonshire House Drawl. It has been characterized as part baby-talk, part refined affectation: hope was written and pronounced as "whop"; you became "oo." Vowels were compressed and extended so that cucumber became "cowcumber," yellow "yaller," gold "goold," and spoil rhymed with mile. Stresses fell on unexpected syllables, such as bal-*cony* instead of *bal*cony and con-*tem*plate.[4] By the middle of the next century all Whigs would speak in the Drawl, transforming a family tradition into a symbol of political allegiance, but in Georgiana's time it remained the Circle's own *patois*. Lord Pelham was moved to warn a friend: "I hope you will love the Dss and forgive some of her peculiarities—but above all do not adopt their manners. . . . I have never known anybody that has lived much with them without catching something of their manner."[5]

At its broadest the Circle numbered more than a hundred people; at its most intimate, thirty. In modern terms they were London's "café society": the racier members of the aristocracy mixed with professional artists and actors, scroungers, libertines, and wits. The playwright and arch-scrounger Richard Brinsley Sheridan was one of its stars. An incorrigible drinker, womanizer, and plotter, he embodied the best and worst of the Circle. He was brilliant yet lazy, kind-hearted and yet remiss over honouring his debts to the point of dishonesty. Sheridan disliked paying his creditors on the grounds that "paying only encourages them." He once shook his head at the sight of a friend settling his account, saying, "What a waste. . . ."[6] He was introduced to Georgiana through his wife, the beautiful and talented singer Elizabeth Linley. Then at the pinnacle of her career, Elizabeth consented to perform at Devonshire House so long as she could be accompanied by her husband. Sheridan's sole success at the time, *The Rivals,* did not gain him an invitation on his own account. Notwithstanding his inauspicious introduction as Elizabeth's escort, Sheridan worked feverishly to ingratiate himself into the Circle. He made it his business to be entertaining, to be useful, to know every secret, and to have a hand in every intrigue. Having secured his place, he encouraged his wife to relinquish her career and only the very fortunate heard her sing again.*

David Garrick was another celebrated theatrical member of the Circle.

---

* Sheridan's friend and biographer Thomas Moore remembered his hatred of perceived rivals: "It was Burke chiefly that S. hated and envied (they indeed hated each other)—Being both Irishmen—both adventurers—they had every possible incentive to envy." Wilfrid S. Dowden, ed., *The Journal of Thomas Moore* (London 1983), I, p. 161.

After watching him give a pre-supper performance, Georgiana wrote: "I have no terms to express the horror of Mr Garrick's reading *Macbeth*. I have not recovered yet, it is the finest and most dreadful thing I ever saw or heard, for his action and countenance is as expressive and terrible as his voice. It froze my blood as I heard him. . . ."[7] Second to Garrick in celebrity was the sculptress Mrs. Damer, whose heads of Father Thames and the goddess Isis still adorn Henley Bridge. Rumour hinted that she had lesbian tendencies although there was a more obvious explanation for the failure of her marriage: the Hon. John Damer was a pathetic drunk and gamester. In August 1775 he shot himself through the head in a room above the Bedford Arms at Covent Garden after having ruined them both in a single night.

The Craufurd brothers—the Francophile James, known as Fish because he could be extraordinarily selfish, and Quentin, known as Flesh—were renowned connoisseurs of art whose presence lent an intellectual quality to Devonshire House suppers. Their conversational skill was matched by the famous wit James Hare, Georgiana's particular favourite. "He has a manner of placing every object in so new a light," she explained to her mother, "that his kind of wit always surprises as much as it pleases."[*8] Hare was also discreet and trustworthy—rare attributes, Georgiana discovered, in the Devonshire House world. Even the "mere" politicians of the Circle were celebrated for their other achievements, like the playwright and satirist General Richard Fitzpatrick, who wrote the enormously successful *Rolliad*. Georgiana also felt a special affection for the Whig politician and bibliophile Thomas Grenville, who reputedly never married because of his hopeless love for her. These conquerors of the drawing room were joined by such sportsmen as the Duke of Dorset, who, when he was not making a reputation for himself as the debaucher of other men's wives, transformed cricket into the national game. The Earl of Derby, whose wife was one of Dorset's conquests, and Lord Clermont promoted British horse racing with the establishment of the Oaks and the Derby.

The women, who were no less extraordinary, divided into those who were received by polite society and those who were not. The socially pro-

---

* Hare's seat in Parliament—courtesy of the Duke—was the only barrier between him and debtors' prison. He was fortunate enough to be the grandson of a bishop, but also unfortunate in being the son of an apothecary. He had gambled away his small inheritance and thereafter survived as a permanent house guest in Whig society. He was stick-thin, with a face so white he appeared more dead than alive.

scribed women included Georgiana's cousin Lady Diana Spencer, who had committed adultery with Topham Beauclerk in order to provoke her violent husband Lord Bolingbroke into divorcing her. Although an outcast in society, Lady Diana enjoyed equal status at Devonshire House with the "beauties" and celebrated hostesses. Among these were Lady Clermont, a great favourite at Versailles; Lady Derby, who had once hoped to marry the Duke of Devonshire; and Lady Jersey, who used her "irresistible seduction and fascination" to wreck the marriages of her friends. According to a contemporary, she was "clever, unprincipled, but beautiful and fascinating."[9] Mrs. Bouverie, whom Reynolds painted to much acclaim, and the conversationalist Mrs. Crewe completed the inner group of respectable women. They were highly competitive and spent much of their time putting one another down. Although greatly respected by her politician friends, and a confidante of Edmund Burke, Mrs. Crewe was dismissed by Lady Douglas as "very fat with a considerable quantity of visible down about her mouth. . . . her ideas came so quick that [Lady Douglas] could not follow them, nor she believed Mrs Crewe herself."

Lady Spencer had mixed feelings about the female members of the Circle, but she loathed one woman in particular: Lady Melbourne. Beautiful, clever, and ruthless, Lady Melbourne epitomized the decadence of Georgiana's friends. The incurable gossip Lord Glenbervie recorded in his diary, "it was a very general report and belief that . . . Lord Coleraine sold Lady Melbourne to Lord Egremont for £13,000, that both Lady and Lord Melbourne were parties to this contract and had each a share of the money."[10] The story might even have been true. Lord Melbourne was an enigma, a silent figure in the drawing room whom visitors to Melbourne House barely noticed. Once Lady Melbourne had presented him with an heir he allowed her the freedom to do and see whom she pleased. He also profited by it. She was not a woman to give her affections indiscriminately. Through her efforts Lord Melbourne was made a viscount in 1781, and later a Gentleman of the Bedchamber in the Prince of Wales's household. Two of her five children were the offspring of Lord Egremont; another, George, the result of her affair with the Prince of Wales. Only the eldest and possibly the youngest were Lord Melbourne's.

Before Georgiana's entry into the *ton* Lady Melbourne had reigned as its leading hostess. People naturally assumed that they would become rivals, but Lady Melbourne had no intention of setting herself up in opposition to Georgiana. She befriended her and adopted the role of benign older counsel instead. "My dearest Thémire" (the French term for

Themis, the Goddess of Justice) was how Georgiana usually addressed her. Lady Melbourne was a natural manager of people. She had a firm grasp of the recondite laws which governed life within the *ton,* and an unsentimental, even cynical view of humanity. "Never trust a man with another's secret," she is reputed to have said, "never trust a woman with her own." Ferociously practical and discreet, she could also be sarcastic and cutting when irritated. Georgiana was in awe of her temper; "I believe I have been a little afraid of you," she once admitted.[11] "Pray write to me, tell me that you love me and are not angry with me," she pleaded on another occasion.[12]

Lady Melbourne provided the comradeship that was missing in Georgiana's relationship with her mother. Lady Spencer was always commenting and offering advice, but it was hardly ever of the practical kind that could help her daughter out of scrapes. She was too far removed from the Circle to understand the sort of pressures that it exerted. Jealous of Lady Melbourne's influence, she tried to make Georgiana drop her. Uncharacteristically, Georgiana refused to obey:

> I conjure you my Dst. Mama to forgive my warmth about Lady Melbourne today [she wrote after a painful argument]. But I do assure you that everything I have known of her has been so right and her conduct to me so truly friendly and for my good, [that] I was miserable to see her so low in your opinion—I hope you will not object to my continuing a friendship which it would be so terrible for me to break off, and I am sure that next year from a thousand things you will not have to be uneasy about my goings on.[13]

Georgiana's "goings on" had become an obsession with the press. Her clothes, her movements, her friends—in short anything new or unusual about her—was considered newsworthy. Rarely did a week go by without a snippet of gossip appearing somewhere. On December 30, 1776, the *Morning Post* reported that Georgiana and Lady Jersey had all their friends playing "newly invented aenigmas" which, the *Post* learned, they called "charades."[14] Throughout 1777 a series of anonymous publications appeared addressed to Georgiana, some of them attacking her slavish devotion to fashion, others defending her.[15] More often, though, the scandal sheets embroiled her in fictitious escapades with numerous lovers. There were enough stories of licentious behaviour attached to members of the Circle to give any allegation the veneer of plausibility.

Audiences flocked to Drury Lane in May 1777 to see Sheridan's new play *The School for Scandal,* partly because it was known to be a satire on the Devonshire House Circle. "I can assure you that the Farce is charming," enthused Mrs. Crewe to Lady Clermont; "the Duchess of Devonshire, Lady Worseley, and I cut very good figures in it."[16] Sheridan pandered to the audience's expectations by portraying Georgiana's friends as a set of louche aristocrats whose moral sensibilities had been blunted by a life of wealth without responsibility. Georgiana is Lady Teazle: young, easily influenced, possessed of a good heart but needing a firm husband to manage her properly. As the play opens Sir Peter Teazle is quarrelling with Lady Teazle over her spendthrift ways and her preoccupation with fashion. "I'm sure I'm not more extravagant than a woman of fashion ought to be," she retorts. The evil Lady Sneerwell (a mixture of Lady Jersey and Lady Melbourne) connives with the journalist Snake (Sheridan) and Joseph Surface to bring about Lady Teazle's ruin. But the play ends with Lady Teazle resisting Surface's attempt to seduce her and renouncing her scandal-loving friends as worthless and silly. Members of the Circle thought it was a tremendous joke to see themselves caricatured on stage, and helped to publicize the play by ostentatiously arriving *en masse* to watch the first night.

Georgiana's thoughts on being portrayed as Lady Teazle have not survived, but the play almost certainly made her uneasy. Behind the broad humour was a semi-serious message which did not escape her notice. "I am alarm'd at my own dispositions because I think I know them now," she told Lady Spencer in August. "I am afraid that the minute I think seriously of my conduct I shall be so shocked, especially with regard to all that has happened this year. . . ."[17] Lacking the maturity and confidence to stand up to her friends, Georgiana was being drawn into a life of heavy drinking and compulsive gambling. She often found herself acting against her own judgement but she felt unable to resist the pressures on her to conform.

In November 1777 Lady Sarah Lennox observed that Georgiana seemed to have no ballast. "The Pretty Duchess of Devonshire who by all accounts has no faults but delicate health in my mind, dines at seven, summer as well as winter, goes to bed at three, and lies in bed till four: she has hysteric fits in the morning and dances in the evening; she bathes, rides, dances for ten days and lies in bed the next ten." Georgiana made periodic attempts to reform. As often as she could she presented Lady Spencer with a positive picture of her life, emphasizing the time she spent with the Duke, her involvement in charity work, the frequent prayers she said, and the sermons she heard. "You see my dearest Mama, how happy I am to tell you of anything I think you will approve of," she had written in September 1776; "it gives me such real pleasure to feel that I am doing anything that makes me more pleasing to the best of mothers."[18] Inspired by such sentiments, Georgiana would adopt a starvation diet, lock herself away in her room, and see no one for a week, but as soon as she emerged she compensated with all-night drinking and eating binges until she was too exhausted to get out of bed. Her weight fluctuated wildly as a consequence. "You are very apt to be too much so, and run into extremes which your constitution will not bear," Lady Spencer complained.[19] The effect on Georgiana's general health was catastrophic: she had one miscarriage after another, leading the Duke and the Cavendishes to accuse her of deliberately sabotaging their hopes for an heir. Only Lady Sarah Lennox questioned whether the Duke might not be to blame for neglecting Georgiana when she was young and so vulnerable to suggestion. "Indeed," she concluded, "I can't forgive her or rather her husband, the fault of ruining her health."[20]

❦❧

Just as Lady Sarah Lennox made her astute observation, towards the end of 1777, Georgiana met two quite different people, Charles James Fox and Mary Graham, whose impact on her would have far-reaching consequences. She was introduced to Mary in October while taking the sea air in Brighton. Mary was there with her husband, Thomas, and was recuperating from a bout of pneumonia. Georgiana was there in the hope of improving her fertility. Medical opinion cited a weak placenta as the cause of serial miscarriages like Georgiana's; the only remedy was to take water cures, either bathing in sea water or drinking warm spa water. (There was no concept of male infertility in the eighteenth century, except in cases of impotence.)

Georgiana was immediately captivated by her. "Mr and Mrs Graham came the same day as the Duke and Dss," reported Lady Clermont to Lady Spencer; "she is a very pretty sort of woman, the Dss likes her of all things; they are inseparable, which is no bad thing. I wish she had half a dozen more such favourites."[21] Mary's father, Lord Cathcart, was formerly the British envoy to Russia, and she had lived abroad for much of her life. Lady Cathcart had died when Mary was fourteen and she had since been obliged to act as a surrogate mother to her baby sister, Charlotte. Georgiana and Mary were the same age and had married in the same year, but Mary lived a very different, sheltered life. She was quiet, serious, and gentle—Georgiana might not have noticed her were it not for her breathtaking beauty: she was known as "the beautiful Mrs Graham." Gainsborough painted her portrait at least four times in an attempt to capture the serenity of her features.

The obvious mutual attachment between the two women was remarked upon at Brighton, although Georgiana made light of it to Lady Spencer. "I live very much with Mrs Graham," she wrote *en passant*. "I think her extremely amiable and we like him too very much—but Lady Sefton does not approve of it as I suppose she expected I should live entirely with her."[22] However, the letters Georgiana wrote to Mary after she had returned home to London show that their feelings for each other had grown into infatuation. The first surviving letter of Georgiana's is a response to a reproach from Mary for not writing more often. Georgiana was staying at Althorp with Lady Spencer, who regarded the interlude as her chance to initiate some remedial training. She kept a tight rein on her daughter, insisting that she imitate her own daily regimen of early morning walks, hours of improving literature, and endless fussing about the servants. The unaccustomed harshness of the regime so exhausted Georgiana that she was too tired to keep up the promised letter-journal to Mary.

> I cannot bear the thought of your thinking me negligent [she replied in anguish after receiving a furious letter from Mary]. I have had scarce any opportunity lately—and besides I have been very busy—in the first place with writing the verses to my Father on his birthday and with the picture—(As soon as I have time to write them out I will send them to you) and then, I have been working very hard for Mama to compose her some reflections to read to the servants on their taking the Sacrament. Would you believe me capable of so serious a work? My dear friend, despite my giddiness I am capable of thought sometimes. You would not think from appearances that I am able to have deep friendships, but, nevertheless you must know how tenderly I love you. It is the same with other things. I am full of madness but I also have a little sense. I perceive I am eulogising myself, but that is characteristic of a bad heart and I have often told you mine is bad. . . . I am falling asleep and must leave you now, but I want to say to you above all that I love you, my dear friend, and kiss you tenderly.[23]

By the spring of 1778 it was Lady Spencer's turn to complain that Georgiana's letters had slowed to a trickle.[24] Not only did Georgiana spend all her free time writing to Mary; no other subject interested her: "I made Mr James set by me at supper last night to have the pleasure of talking about you—it is so deliciously sweet for me, my adorable friend, to speak constantly of you—as I am continuously thinking of you it is a subject that I am very well prepared for. . . . I went to see Lady Anne and Lady Margaret, they both talk a great deal about you and my heart applauds their good taste—I have seen your picture too at Gainsborough's."[25]

Both of them were frightened that the intensity of their friendship would become the subject of gossip. Georgiana's passionate imprecations went far beyond the ordinary endearments written between women friends. "*Je t'aime mon coeur bien tendrement,* indeed, indeed, indeed, I love you dearly" is one of her typical messages to Lady Melbourne.[26] However, even taking hyperbole into account, Georgiana's letters to Mary were more personal, more intense, clearly separating them from her other correspondence. It was almost impossible to keep such things hidden. Maids and footmen were not above reading their employers' mail, and there was always the danger of letters going astray or falling into the wrong hands. In one fragment Georgiana wrote: "I have been reading over this curious letter and I am almost sorry I put so much about what vex'd me when I began writing, I must tell you I am quite easy about it now and if I was sure you would get this letter safe, I would tell you all about it—but I don't dare."[27] Despite the risk of exposure, she urged Mary to accept a small drawing of herself: "You desire me to give you my opinion about the picture, I can not see why you should not have it, I understand what you mean, but I don't think it would appear odd—consider that in a little time we shall be *old friends*—however I think I can send you a drawing when I go to town which will not have any of the inconveniences you thought of as you need not shew it—for I shall like you to have something like me."[28]

Whether or not Mary actually received the picture is not known. Almost nothing else survives from their lengthy correspondence except a couple of later fragments. Discouraged by the Duke's freezing civility, Georgiana longed for the tenderness, companionship, and affection she experienced with Mary—and also something else, equally if not more important: relief from having to perform for her relatives or the *ton.* Lady Spencer, her friends, the Duke and his family all placed expectations on her, often forcing her to play roles which made her feel uncomfortable or inadequate. Only with Mary could Georgiana unburden herself and talk about her confusion and dismay.

> The hurry I live here distracts me [she wrote in 1778], when I first came into the world the novelty of the scene made me like everything but my heart now feels only an emptiness in the beau monde which cannot be filled—I don't have the liberty to think or occupy myself with the things I like as much as I would wish and all my desires are turned upside down—you are the only person to whom I would say this, anybody else would only laugh at me and call it an affectation—I seem to enjoy every thing so much at the minute that nobody can think how much I am tired sometimes with the dissipation I live in.[29]

Georgiana's sense of unease about her life of dissipation was turning to disgust but, as she remarked sadly, her friends would only laugh if she tried to explain herself. Her intimacy with Mary helped her to gain a perspective on her situation, particularly on the limitations of her marriage. It was unthinkable, however, for a woman to take a lover before she had supplied her husband with a son. Convention allowed aristocratic women a *cicisbeo*—a term borrowed from the Italian to mean a platonic lover who provided escort duties and other practical services in place of the husband. In *The School for Scandal* Lady Teazle says she will admit the wicked Joseph Surface "as a lover no farther than fashion sanctions." "True," he replies, "a mere Platonic cicisbeo—what every wife is entitled to."[30] Despite the large crowd of suitors eager to comply, Georgiana was the exception in lacking even this.[31] In 1779 her cousin Lady Pembroke remarked to Lord Herbert: "You wrote some time ago terrible things you had heard about the poor Dss of Devonshire, which made me laugh, they were so totally without foundation, and I forgot to answer it. She has never been even talked for any body in the flirting way yet. . . ."[32]

Whether and to what extent physical intimacy played a part in Georgiana's relationship with Mary is impossible to determine. Several of her friendships contained an element of flirtatiousness: it was a French habit she had acquired from Madame de Polignac and Marie Antoinette. Since the publication of Jean-Jacques Rousseau's enormously successful *Julie ou La nouvelle Héloïse* French women had self-consciously imitated the loving friendship between Julie and Claire. However, there were rumours that Marie Antoinette and the Little Po were more than simply friends, which their displays of physical affection encouraged.[33]*

Rousseau made a deep impression on Georgiana, and her own copy of *La nouvelle Héloïse* at Chatsworth is scored with her markings.[34] She lived on a plane of heightened feeling which her English friends found alluring but also disturbing. "Some part of your letter frightened me," Lady Jersey once wrote, not altogether sure how to interpret Georgiana's declarations of love.[35] In Mary, Georgiana was seeking her Claire, who would know her every thought, be at her side during the day, share her bed at night, and hold her in her arms when she died. But it was not to be. In 1781 the doctors ordered Mr. Graham to take Mary to a warmer climate: it was the only hope for her weak lungs. They had diagnosed her as consumptive. Georgiana was bereft and searched without success for a replacement.

Charles James Fox, her second new acquaintance, made a great impression on Georgiana, not in a romantic way—that would emerge later—but intellectually. It was Fox, more than anyone else, who led Georgiana to her life's vocation—politics. Fox was a brilliant though flawed politician. Short and corpulent, with shaggy eyebrows and a permanent five o'clock shadow, he was already at twenty-eight marked down as a future leader of the Whig party when the Marquess of Rockingham retired. Georgiana became friends with him when he came to stay at Chatsworth in 1777. His career until then had veered between political success and failure, between unimaginable wealth and bankruptcy. He confounded his critics with his irrepressible confidence, and exasperated his friends by his incontinent lifestyle. Eighteenth-century England was full of wits, connoisseurs, orators, historians, drinkers, gamblers, rakes, and pranksters, but only Fox embodied all these things.

He was born in 1749, the second of the three surviving sons of the Whig politician Henry Fox, first Lord Holland, and Lady Caroline Lennox, daughter of the second Duke of Richmond. Although an unscrupulous and—even for the age—corrupt politician, Lord Holland was

---

* Apparently the Queen's brother-in-law surprised them one day while they were making up after an argument, hugging each other tightly and kissing each other's tear-stained cheeks. He burst out laughing and left, saying, "Pray don't let me disturb you!" and told everybody how he had interrupted the two friends.

a tender husband and an indulgent father who shamelessly spoilt his children. No eighteenth-century upbringing has received more attention or encountered such criticism as Fox's. By contemporary social standards the Holland household was a kind of freak show. There were stories of Fox casually burning his father's carefully prepared speeches, smashing his gold watch to see how it would look broken, disrupting his dinners—and never being punished.

Having enjoyed such an unrestricted existence, both materially and emotionally, Fox was similarly open and generous with his friends. He was incapable of small-mindedness or petty ambition. It was this, coupled with his natural talent for leadership, which won him instant popularity at Eton and enduring friendships throughout his life. Before he joined the Whig party Fox seemed to have no ambition except pleasure and no political loyalties except to his father's reputation. This he vigorously defended in Parliament against charges that, as Paymaster-General during the Seven Years' War, Lord Holland had embezzled the country out of millions. No one could deny that the family had become unaccountably rich during this period. However, after his father's death in 1774 Fox did his best to return the fortune to the nation by gambling it away at Newmarket and Brooks's.

Lord Holland's last act before he died had been to pay off his son's £140,000 debt,[36] but this generous gift had no effect on Fox's behaviour. He stayed up night after night, fighting his body's urge to sleep with coffee and platefuls of food. According to one anecdote, he played hazard continuously from Tuesday to Wednesday night, winning, losing, recovering, and finally losing all his money. He stopped on Thursday to rush to the House of Commons to participate in a debate on the Thirty-nine Articles of the Church of England, and went straight back to White's afterwards. There he drank until Friday morning, when he walked to Almack's and gambled until 4 p.m. Having won £6,000 he rode to Newmarket, where he lost £10,000.[37] Though he very quickly frittered everything away, Fox could always count on friends, including the Duke, to support him financially and politically.* Occasionally he won money, but he

* Fox even brought a few of his friends to near bankruptcy by persuading them to provide security for him in the form of annuities to money-lenders. At one point the Earl of Carlisle was paying one sixth of his income towards the interest on Fox's debts. Leslie Mitchell, *Charles James Fox* (Oxford 1991), p. 102.

avoided games of skill, which he was very good at, for the excitement of games of chance. He spent so many hours at Brooks's that he was rarely out of his gambling clothes.*

Fox displayed a sense of fun and theatre that equalled Georgiana's. The term "macaroni" was coined to describe the fashionable young fops of the 1770s who wore exaggerated clothes about town. The term probably originated in the 1760s, when members of the short-lived Macaroni Club brought attention to themselves by their predilection for all things foreign, especially food. Macaronis were much criticized in the press. The *Oxford Magazine* complained: "There is indeed a kind of animal, neither male nor female, a thing of the neuter gender, lately started up amongst us. It is called a Macaroni. It talks without meaning, it smiles without pleasantry, it eats without appetite, it rides without exercise, it wenches without passion."[38] Until his gambling debts made him poor, Fox was one of its most visible exemplars. Like Georgiana, he had an eye for colour and a talent for whimsy. The macaroni uniform strove for a super-slim elegance with narrow breeches and short, tight-fitting waistcoats. The flourish was in the finishes: large buttons and extravagant nosegays were essential; high-heeled shoes and a small hat perched on the side of the head added a certain flair. Fox's particular contribution was to experiment with hair colour, powdering his hair blue one day, red the next. He wore multicoloured shoes and velvet frills, a daring combination which challenged the fainthearted to follow him.

He went to stay at Chatsworth in August 1777, joining a large house party that included the Jerseys, the Clermonts, the Duke of Dorset, all the Cavendishes as well as their cousins the Ponsonbys, and the violinist Giardini. The week before his arrival Georgiana had written of her alarm and distress "at my own dispositions." But she hid her feelings from her guests and no one noticed that her liveliness was as much a performance as the after-dinner entertainments.

Fox's presence wrought an immediate change in Georgiana; he in-

---

* Contemporary descriptions show how peculiar this uniform was: "The gamesters began by pulling off their embroidered clothes, and putting on frieze greatcoats, or turned their coats inside outwards for good luck. They put on pieces of leather (such as are worn by footmen when they clean knives) to save their laced ruffles; to shield their eyes from the light and hold up curls, etc., they wore high-crowned straw hats with broad brims, adorned with flowers and ribbons: [and] masks to conceal their emotions when they played at quinze." J. Timbs, *Clubs and Club Life in London* (London 1872), p. 72.

trigued and stimulated her. For the first time since her initial attempts to educate herself two years before, she had found someone to emulate.

> The great merit of C. Fox is his amazing quickness in seazing any subject [she wrote to her mother in August]. He seems to have the particular talent of knowing more about what he is saying and with less pains than anyone else. His conversation is like a brilliant player at billiards, the strokes follow one another piff puff—and what makes him more entertaining now is his being here with Mr Townsend and the D. of Devonshire, for their living so much together makes them show off to one another. Their chief topic is Politics and Shakespear. As for the latter they all three seem to have the most astonishing memorys for it, and I suppose I shall be able in time to go thro' a play as they do. . . .[39]

In her next letter Georgiana informed her mother that she was reading Vertot's *Revolutions of Sweden.* "I think it is the most interesting book in the world, I really was quite agitated with my anxiety for Gustavas Vasa," she wrote. "Especially at seeing a generous and open hearted Hero fighting for the liberty of his country and to revenge the memory of an injur'd friend against lawless cruelty and oppressive tyranny."[40] This was the Whig political creed in a single line: the hero fighting for liberty against lawless cruelty and oppressive tyranny. In practical terms, for the Whig party of the 1770s it meant opposition to George III, a mistrust of the powers of the crown, and a vigilance over civil liberties. Fox had probably suggested Vertot to Georgiana. He had only lately converted to the Whig cause, having previously served as a junior minister in the current government under Lord North. Like his father, Fox had planned his political career in the service of the King. But his sybaritic behavior and erratic loyalty to the government line drove George III and Lord North to remove him. "Indeed," the King wrote in disgust, "that young man has so thoroughly cast off every principle of common honour and honesty that he must become as contemptible as he is odious."[41] After his dismissal Fox became the protégé of Edmund Burke, and under his tutelage he began to absorb the Whig preoccupation with constitutional rights and political autonomy. The politician who declared his contempt for the people: "[I] will not be a rebel to my King, my country or my own heart, for the loudest huzza of the inconsiderate multitude" now claimed that the King "held nothing but what he held in trust for the people, for their use and benefit."[42]

Fox's ardour moved Georgiana. He talked to her as no one else did, treating her as his equal, discussing his ideas, and encouraging her participation. She had once visited the House of Commons out of curiosity with Lady Jersey (women were banned from the gallery in 1778), but had not repeated the experiment. Fox awakened in her a sense of loyalty and commitment to the Whig party. By the time he left Chatsworth she was his devoted follower. Twenty years later she was still his most loyal supporter. "Charles always had faults," was all she would concede, "that may injure him and have as a Statesman—but never as the greatest of men."[43] Like his contemporaries at Eton and later at Brooks's she had fallen under Fox's spell. His following in Parliament depended as much on his personality as on his views. To be a Foxite meant that one belonged to a gang whose single bond was an uncritical admiration of Fox.

Fox and Mary's belief in Georgiana persuaded her that she could make something more of herself. In April 1778 she wrote of her desire to begin afresh. "I have the strongest sense of having many things to repent of and my heart is fully determined to mend," she told Lady Spencer; she planned to take Holy Communion (a rite less commonly performed in the eighteenth century) after her trip to Derby. But the same letter also hints at entanglements—gambling debts—which she regretted and feared. "By going there I break off many unpleasant embarrassments I am in with regard to others and the quiet life I shall lead there will give me time to think. . . ."[44]

The result was a thinly disguised autobiographical novel called *The Sylph*. Notwithstanding its exaggerations, the book can be read as a *roman à clef*. Written as a series of letters, the story follows the misadventures of Julia Stanley, a naive country girl married to the dissipated Sir William Stanley, a rake whose only interests are fashion and gambling. When Julia first comes to London she does not understand the ways of the *ton*, but slowly it seduces her and she becomes trapped. She learns how to live *à la mode*, how to spend hours dressing for a ball, how to talk, sing, dance, and think like a fashionable person. She realizes that her soul is being corrupted by the cynicism and heartlessness which pervades the *ton*, but sees no hope of escape. Sir William is cruel, even brutal towards her. His only concern is that she should be a credit to him in public. He flaunts his mistress in front of her, punishes her when she suffers a miscarriage, and is not above assaulting her when angered. As his creditors close in, Sir William forces Julia to sign over all her personal property. (Nor is she the only woman in the book to suffer from male abuse. An aristocratic lady who loses a fortune at the gaming table is blackmailed by a friend into sleeping with him in return for his silence.)* Julia's friend Lady Besford, who is obviously modelled on Lady Melbourne, urges her to accept her life and find happiness where she can. Julia is facing moral ruin when an anonymous protector, calling himself "the Sylph," begins sending her letters of advice. Finally Sir William becomes so desperate for money that he sells the rights to Julia's body to his chief creditor. She runs away, and he shoots himself in a shabby room above an inn.† The Sylph then reveals himself to be Julia's childhood sweetheart. They marry and live happily ever after.

Georgiana wrote *The Sylph* in secret and published it anonymously as "a young lady."[45] The novel was a creditable success, quickly going through four editions; it was not long before people guessed the identity of the author. When challenged in public Georgiana refused to comment, but it became common knowledge that she had admitted the truth in private. There were plenty of clues pointing in her direction, not only in her choice of names, which are all variations on those of her friends, but in the sly references to herself: Julia's hairdresser protests that "he had run the risk of disobliging the Duchess of D——, by giving me the preference of the finest bunch of radishes that had yet come over from Paris." Like Georgiana, Julia has a younger sister whom she adores and a worldly, older female companion to whom she turns for advice. The similarities in style and phrasing between the novel and Georgiana's letters allayed any lingering doubts. Georgiana often wrote of her longing for a moral guide: "Few can boast like me of having such a friend and finding her in a mother," she once wrote to Lady Spencer, adding how much she depended on her for moral and spiritual advice. "I should be very happy if I could borrow some friendly Sylph (if any are so kind as to hover about Hardwick) and a pair of wings that I might Pay you now and then a visit."[46]

Part of *The Sylph*'s success was due to its notoriety. Readers were shocked by the sexual licence and violence it depicted. The *Gentleman's Magazine* was appalled: the anonymous female author, it thought, showed "too great a knowledge of the *ton*, and of the worst, though perhaps highest part of the world." Mrs. Thrale, doyenne of the Blue Stocking Circle,

---

* When he wrote his memoirs in 1801 Colonel George Hanger, a former lover of Lady Melbourne's, claimed that several ladies in the Devonshire House Circle had fallen into the same trap.

† In circumstances very similar to the suicide of Mrs. Damer's husband in 1775.

denounced the book as "an obscene Novel."[47] She objected to passages such as the following, where Lady Besford expresses a breath-takingly cynical view of marriage:

> you do not suppose my happiness proceeds from my being married, any further than that I enjoy title, rank and liberty, by bearing Lord Besford's name. We do not disagree because we seldom meet. He pursues his pleasure one way, I seek mine another, and our dispositions being opposite, they are sure never to interfere with each other. . . . My Lord kept a mistress from the moment of his marriage. What law excludes a woman from doing the same? Marriage now is a necessary kind of barter, and an alliance of families;—the heart is not consulted. . . .

The Sylph touches on many subjects, not least the loneliness of a bad marriage and the vulnerability of women in a society where they are deprived of equal rights. Georgiana obviously wrote the novel in a hurry, and it does not compare well with Fanny Burney's *Evelina,* for example. The significance of *The Sylph* lies in the rare insider's glimpse it provides of the *ton*. Georgiana describes a competitive, unfriendly world peopled predominantly by opportunists, liars, and bullies, a world which encourages hypocrisy and values pretence. The irony did not escape her that even as she hated it she was also its creature. However, in publishing *The Sylph* she was also claiming her independence.

CHAPTER 4

A POPULAR PATRIOT

1778—1781

Saturday Morning the Derbyshire Militia passed through the city on their road to Cox Heath. The Duke of Devonshire marched at their head. The whole regiment made a very noble appearance, equal to any regulars whatever. If the militia of the other counties prove but as good, there is no doubt but that they are a match for any force that can be brought against them. The Duchess of Devonshire followed the regiment, dressed en militaire, and was escorted by several attendants.

London Chronicle, *June 20–23, 1778*

One day last week, her Grace the Duchess of Devonshire appeared on the hustings at Covent Garden. She immediately saluted her favourite Candidate, the Hon. Charles Fox.

Morning Post, *September 25, 1780*

Georgiana's political awakening coincided with a disastrous year for the Whigs. The Declaration of Independence of July 4, 1776, proclaimed the American colonies "Free and Independent States . . . absolved from all allegiance to the British crown." The Whigs supported the colonists against the government but their rousing talk of safeguarding the liberty of the people had signally failed to impress the country. The public rejected their contention that the government was at fault for having tried to force an unjust system of taxation on the colonists, and the press accused the party of conniving with Britain's enemies to break up the empire. It was an unfair accusation, although it touched on a dilemma for the Whigs: they viewed

the American conflict through the prism of Westminster politics and regarded it as part of the struggle between the people and the crown. For this
reason they privately hoped that the Americans would win.

In February 1778 France entered the war on the side of the Americans,
transforming what had hitherto been a set of military skirmishes in New
England into a trans-continental war. Britain now had to fight on several
fronts. Shaken by this new threat, the Prime Minister Lord North hoped
to strengthen the cabinet by poaching Charles Fox and one or two others,
but his overtures were rejected. The debates in Parliament became bitter
as Whig and government MPs accused each other of betraying the country's interests. The sense of crisis was heightened in April by the dramatic
death of William Pitt the Elder during a debate in the House of Lords. The
former Prime Minister, now the Earl of Chatham, had risen from his sick
bed to make his final speech. He arrived draped in black velvet, and
dragged himself to his old seat with the help of crutches. Speaking in the
government's defence, he argued that a surrender to the Americans would
signal the end of the empire—the empire he had won for Britain almost
thirty years earlier. Only the Duke of Richmond, Fox's uncle and a committed Whig, dared to answer the respected statesman. He argued that it
was impossible to fight a war on two fronts against the Americans and the
French. Chatham slowly pulled himself to his feet to reply, but no words
came out. He shuddered, clutched his heart, and collapsed to the floor. To
many MPs Chatham's death in the throes of a patriotic speech seemed to
symbolize Britain's approaching demise.

Having enjoyed two years of a distant war, the country now began to
mobilize its defences against the threat of a French invasion. As Lord
Lieutenant of Derbyshire the Duke of Devonshire returned to the country to organize a voluntary militia. Most able-bodied men were either already in the army or in stable employment; those available to join the
home defence force made unpromising material. This did not deter the
aristocracy, who threw themselves into the task of training their corps with
almost childish enthusiasm. Many of them proudly wore their regimental
uniforms to the King's birthday celebrations at St. James's.[1]

Since the French were likely to target London first, the government set
up two campsites for its protection: Coxheath in Kent and Warley in
Essex. So many sightseers flocked to the camps that a London–Coxheath
coach service started. The *London Chronicle* reported that Coxheath camp
would be three miles long, holding 15,000 men and representing the
"flower of the nobility." Workers were building a stone pavilion in antici-

pation of a royal visit. Meanwhile "the Tradespeople of the neighbouring places are deserting their town residents, and are likewise encamping round us in the various temporary streets. The whole will form one of the most striking military spectacles ever exhibited in the country."[2]

Georgiana accompanied the Duke to Coxheath, where they were joined by many of their friends. She was enthralled by the spectacle of thousands of men mobilizing for war. She walked behind the Duke as he inspected his regiment, imagining herself bravely leading a battalion of men in a bloody engagement against the invaders. Although women were not usually tolerated on the field, the officers indulged her desire to take part in the preparations. "There is a vacant company which the soldiers call mine," she confided to her brother. "I intend to make it a very good one."[3] The Duke rented a large house for her nearby, but she persuaded him to allow her to live in the camp with him. Their "tent" was made up of several marquees, arranged into a compound of sleeping quarters, entertaining rooms, kitchens, and a servants' hall. Refusing to equate a state of readiness with austerity, Georgiana decorated it with travelling tables, oriental rugs, and silver candlesticks from Chatsworth. Nevertheless conditions in the camp were primitive and sanitary arrangements nonexistent.

Her letters during these weeks are full of military matters—manoeuvres and parades. In May she wrote to Lady Spencer:

> I got up very early and went to the field. The soldiers fir'd very well and I stood by the Duke and Cl Gladwin, who were near enough to have their faces smart with gun-powder, but I was not fortunate enough to have this honour. After the firing was over, Major Revel, whose gout prevents him from walking, sat a horseback to be saluted as General. The Duke of Devonshire took his post at the head of his company, and after marching about they came by Major Revel and saluted him. The D. really does it vastly well. . . .[4]

By mid-June, however, Georgiana was feeling less welcome on the field: the Duke had grown tired of her presence and the soldiers no longer regarded her as a novelty. She stopped loitering around the guns and reluctantly joined her friends in their card parties, carriage rides, and jolly picnics on the hills overlooking the camp. Over veal cake and tea with Lady Melbourne and Mrs. Crewe she discovered that they too were bored and wished to do more than simply observe the soldiers. Their complaints gave her courage. It occurred to her that even though women were barred

from taking part in military action, there was nothing to stop her from organizing a female auxiliary corps. She had soon designed a smart uniform
that combined elegance with masculinity, using a tailored version of a
man's riding coat over a close-fitting dress. In July the *Morning Post* informed its readers: "Her Grace the Duchess of Devonshire appears every
day at the head of the beauteous Amazons on Coxheath, who are all
dressed *en militaire;* in the regimentals that distinguish the several regi-
ments in which their Lords, etc., serve, and charms every beholder with
their beauty and affability."[5] She continued to parade throughout the summer, inspiring women in other camps to follow suit. The Marchioness of
Granby bought a half share in a sixteen-gun ship and had it renamed after
her.[6]

   Although Georgiana and her friends did little more than dress up in uniforms and provide good cheer for the men, she had broken with tradition.
For the first time aristocratic women organized themselves as a voluntary
group, taking up duties to help their men in time of war. Following the
publicity they generated Georgiana was particularly gratified by the con-
gratulations she received from the Whig grandees. Her idea of dressing up
in patriotic uniforms was a propaganda coup for the Whigs, who had suffered for their opposition to the war. They had been labelled by the press as
"Patriots" in reference to Dr. Johnson's apothegm about patriotism being
the last refuge of the scoundrel. Georgiana's display of military fervour
helped to mitigate the Whigs' pro-American stance by showing that when
the country was in danger, they were as ready to defend it as anyone.

   Georgiana's pleasure at her success was short-lived: one day she discovered that the Duke and Lady Jersey had been taking advantage of her
parades through the camp to visit each other's tents. Possibly jealous of
the attention Georgiana was receiving and feeling neglected, the Duke
made no effort to keep the affair a secret. Lady Jersey went further and
flaunted her conquest in front of Georgiana, who was too frightened and
inexperienced to assert herself.[7] Lady Jersey regarded all married men—
except her husband, who was twice her age—as an irresistible challenge.
(When a ribald article appeared about her in the *Morning Post* in 1777 it
shocked only Lord Jersey. They happened to be staying at Chatsworth at
the time and he embarrassed everyone by announcing that he loved his
wife and would "shew the world he did not believe them.")[8] Lady Jersey
always tormented the wives of her conquests, and fond though she was of
Georgiana she couldn't resist the urge to humiliate her friend. According
to Lady Clermont, she "asked the Duchess if she could give her a bed [at

Coxheath]. She said she was afraid not, the other said, 'then I will have a bed in your room.' So that in the house she is to be. Pray, write to the Duchess," she asked Lady Spencer, "that you hope, in short, I don't know what . . ."[9]

Georgiana's timidity puzzled her mother—although hurt and mortified it seems that she said nothing to either party. For once Lady Spencer showed a certain sensitivity and, instead of remonstrating with her daughter, made an unaccustomed effort to praise her and boost her confidence. "Your behaviour is in every respect just what it ought to be," she wrote in July, referring to Georgiana's visit to nearby Tunbridge Wells. A local newspaper had reported that the townspeople felt snubbed by the grandees at Coxheath, so Georgiana attended the Assembly Rooms with Lady Clermont and Mrs. Crewe, where the master of ceremonies welcomed them to much applause. "I believe it with great reason," Lady Spencer continued, "that if you continue as you have begun you will gain the love and admiration of all who see you."*[10]

It was not long, however, before the chiding resumed: "I suspect," she complained in August, "you put on . . . a great deal more familiarity and ease than is necessary or proper to the men about you."[11] As usual, Lady Spencer's criticisms were not without cause. "I believe the Dss of D one of the most amiable beings in the world," Mrs. Montagu wrote after meeting her at Tunbridge Wells. "She has a form and face extremely angelick, her temper is perfectly sweet, she has fine parts, the greatest purity of heart and innocence possible." But, Mrs. Montagu added, "as goodness thinks no ill where no ill seems, she does not keep so far aloof from the giddy and imprudent part of the World as one could wish."[12]

The liaison between Lady Jersey and the Duke was short-lived. Fortunately for Georgiana, Lady Spencer ordered an end to the affair. Angered by Georgiana's unwillingness to interfere, she had called on Lady Jersey and outlined the consequences she would face if it continued.[13] The Spencers also gave the Duke to understand that they were disgusted with him.

By the time the King and Queen made their long-awaited official visit

---

* Georgiana had learned the importance of "mixing" from her first days of married life when the Duke had sent her off to Derby to foster good relations with the local voters. She also knew, without the Cavendishes having to tell her, that her behaviour had political implications. The year before at Brighton she wrote, "we are very popular here from mixing so much with the people, for Lady Sefton and Mrs Meynel never mixed with the people till we came."

to Coxheath on November 4, 1778, Lady Jersey had acquired a new lover. The rain poured down on the day—"cats and dogs," Georgiana complained—and while the Duke marched his soldiers past the King, Georgiana led the delegation of ladies standing in slippery mud up to their ankles waiting on the Queen. Georgiana's discomfort was greatly increased by the onset of what she termed "the Prince," a common euphemism for menstruation. Although the rain prevented many of the planned manoeuvres from taking place, the newspapers considered the visit a success. According to Georgiana, the Duke of Devonshire was "reckon'd to have saluted the best of anybody."[14] However, the Devonshires' patriotism did not extend to spending the winter in a mud pit; immediately after the royal visit they returned to Devonshire House.

Georgiana's sense of isolation had increased as a result of the Duke's adultery. Her ebullience became a screen which she employed to distance herself from people. She did not mind public occasions, but quiet *tête-à-têtes* made her uncomfortable and she tried to avoid them, though not always with success. Her reluctance to give offence made her incapable of declining an invitation. "I am to dine with Lady Jersey," Georgiana wrote to Lady Spencer a few months later. "To tell you the truth tho' I love her tenderly, I have learnt to feel a kind of uneasiness in being with her, that makes our society very general—I am discontented in being with her and can't tell her so, et ma bonhomie en souffre."[15]* Despite her unease, she continued to behave towards Lady Jersey as if nothing had happened.

Other inhabitants of the camp were less fortunate than Lady Jersey—not all escaped the consequences of their actions so lightly. Lady Melbourne became pregnant with Lord Egremont's child, while Lady Clermont's affair with the local apothecary resulted in a secret abortion. But it was Lady Derby and the Duke of Dorset who, in social terms, paid the highest price.[16] Lady Mary Coke saw them together in June and rued Lady Derby's recklessness. She wrote in her diary: "Lady Derby, like the Duchess of Devonshire, has bad connexions which lead her into many things that she had better not do, and for which I am sorry. . . ."[17] Her intuition proved correct. In December 1778 Lady Derby fled from her husband's house, leaving behind her children and all her belongings. It was a widely broadcast secret that she was hiding with the Duke of Dorset. Her desertion broke one of eighteenth-century society's strongest taboos re-

---

* I cannot feel at ease.

garding the sanctity of the family and a wife's obedience to her husband. According to Lady Mary Coke, she had "offended against the laws of man and God."[18] She heard that Lady Derby's brother the Duke of Hamilton was trying to force the Duke of Dorset to sign a legal document agreeing to marry her as soon as the divorce came through. There were other rumours: Lady Derby was pregnant; the Duke of Dorset had made another mistress pregnant; he was now in love with someone else. In February, two months after the initial excitement, Lady Sarah Lennox had this to say to her sister:

> It is imagined the Duke of Dorset will marry Lady Derby, who is now in the country keeping quiet and out of the way. There is a sort of party in town of who is to visit her and who is not, which makes great squabbles, as if the curse or blessing of the poor woman depended on a few tickets more or less. . . . I am told she has been and still is more thoroughly attached to the Duke of Dorset, and if so I suppose she will be very happy if the lessening of her visiting list is the only misfortune, and what with giving up her children, sorrow for a fault, and dread of not preserving his affections, I think she is much to be pitied.[19]

The "party" who went to visit her consisted mostly of the younger generation of Whigs—Lady Carlisle and Lady Jersey in particular. Georgiana was caught between her friends, who sought the additional weight of her celebrity, and her parents, who forbade her to have anything more to do with the unfortunate woman. Everyone was waiting to see what Georgiana would do, said Lady Mary Coke, "lest such bad company should influence her."[20] Georgiana argued that it would be hypocritical of her to turn against Lady Derby. Fearing her father's temper, she begged Lady Spencer not to tell him of her request to accompany her friends:

> I have the greatest horror of her crime, I can not nor do not try to excuse her. But her conduct has been long imprudent, and yet, I have sup'd at her house, and I have enter'd with her into any scheme of amusement, etc., and now it does seem shocking to me, that at the time this poor creature is in distress, that at the time all her grandeur is crush'd around her, I should entirely abandon her, as if I said, I know you was imprudent formerly, but then you had a gay house

and great suppers and so I came to you but now that you have nothing of all this, I will avoid you.[21]

The Spencers disagreed. They gave Georgiana a choice: either she dropped Lady Derby or they would never allow her sister Harriet to visit Devonshire House or Chatsworth. "If you sacrifice so much for a person who was never on a footing of friendship," wrote Lady Spencer, "what are you to do if Lady J or Lady M should proceed (and they are already far on their way) to the same lengths?"[22] Georgiana surrendered, a little relieved to be excused from the unpleasant bickering which surrounded the affair. Lady Carlisle had issued an invitation to a party which included Lady Derby as a test of her friends' loyalty. For four months society thought about nothing else. Then, in April, Lord Derby announced that he would not be divorcing her. It was a terrible revenge; by his refusal—it was almost impossible for a wife to divorce her husband except on the grounds of non-consummation—he consigned his wife to social limbo, disgraced, separated, and unprotected. Only marriage to the Duke of Dorset would have brought about her social rehabilitation. Their relationship did not survive the strain of her ostracism, confirming Lady Sarah Lennox's prediction. Two years later Lady Mary Coke recorded a rumour that Lady Derby had left for Italy with a certain Lord Jocelyn, which, she wrote spitefully, merely confirmed her opinion of her.[23]

The reputation of the Duke of Dorset did not suffer. He had seduced another man's wife, but while many people looked askance at his behaviour there was no question of excluding him from society. He even remained friends with Lord Derby and continued to be invited to his house. The Derby affair illustrates the point made by Georgiana in *The Sylph*: eighteenth-century society tolerated anything so long as there was no scandal. Publicly immoral behaviour earned public censure; private transgressions remained whispered gossip. In Lady Spencer's words, Lady Derby "insulted the World with her Vice."[24]

In July 1779, once the season was over, Georgiana went with her parents to Spa. The Duke did not accompany them, pleading military duty, and spent the summer marching his soldiers at the camp. The English and French aristocrats on holiday at Spa behaved as if the two countries were still at peace. Good breeding and fine manners counted for more than martial spirits. Madame de Polignac had been waiting for Georgiana to arrive and they passed the vacation together, walking arm in arm through the wooded fields surrounding the village. They were such conspicuous companions that their friendship reached the notice of the English press. The *Morning Herald and Daily Advertiser* reported: "The reigning female favourite of the Queen of France is Madame Polignac, a great encomiast of the English, and a particular admirer of her Grace the Duchess of Devonshire. . . ."[25]

On her return in September Georgiana experienced her first battle. They were travelling in a convoy of two packet boats, escorted by a naval sloop, *The Fly,* for protection. At dawn on September 14 French privateers attacked her boat. *The Fly* moved in to engage the French ships, enabling the packet boats to escape. Although he possessed only fourteen guns, Captain Garner fought for over two hours until both sides were too exhausted to continue. The half-sinking ship then managed to rejoin its frightened escorts and sail for England. Captain Garner immediately became a hero and the adventure was seized upon by the press as welcome propaganda.[26] Spain had also declared war against Britain. The country was now fighting against a triple alliance.

When Georgiana rejoined the Duke at the camp in October 1779 she was appalled by the soldiers' low morale as well as the lethargy of their leaders. The combined French and Spanish fleets had been sighted in the Channel; the government expected an invasion force to arrive at any day.

> Lord Cholmondeley and Cl Dalrymple arriv'd here from Plymouth at 7—they give a terrible account of the defenceless state of the place and the danger of the troops encamp'd on the Mount Edgcumb side [she wrote]. In case of the enemy's landing they must all either perish by the invaders or be drown'd in making their escape. They say the troops are all out of spirits and looking on themselves as a forlorn hope, and the Duke of Rutland says he should think himself lucky to escape with the loss of an arm or a leg.[27]

She was determined to stay and watch the fight, telling her mother: "I rather think there will be an invasion and that I shall see something of it to complete the extraordinary sights I have been present at this year."[28] But the camp waited in readiness for an invasion which never came. The strain of anticipation was reflected in the drinking and debauchery that went on after dark; during one all-night party the stables burned down and six horses were killed.

Georgiana was soon fed up with camp life. She was more sensitive now to the sycophancy she perceived in some of her friends. Mrs. Crewe, she complained, was caressing her without ceasing. Lady Frances Masham, she noticed, "always talks to me as if she thought I had not my five senses like other people."[29] She returned to Devonshire House without the Duke. Her departure annoyed the Cavendishes, who thought she had no right to go anywhere on her own when she had not yet given them an heir. "I found the Dss in town," wrote Lord Frederick Cavendish to Lady Spencer on November 11, 1779. "I never saw her Grace look better, [but] she laments that she has grown fat. To say the truth she does look bigger, I would fain have dropt the last syllable."[30]

Fearing that she would never have a child, Georgiana noted every variation in her menstrual cycle with obsessive diligence. "The Prince is not yet come," she wrote to her mother in October, "but my pains are frequent and I continue the Spa water."[31] After five and a half years of marriage she was so desperate to conceive that she went to the notorious quack Dr. James Graham. Lady Spencer was dismayed. "Let me entreat you not to listen to Dr Graham with regard to internal medicines," she urged, "but consult Warren."[32] Graham's use of electricity, milk baths, and friction techniques to encourage fertility in women and cure impotency in men left her unimpressed. Society, however, had taken him up and Graham was earning sufficient money to practise out of the Adelphi, where his Temple of Health and Hymen attracted long queues of desperate women. "Lady Carlisle went to see Dr Graham's Electrical Machinery in the Adelphi," wrote Miss Lloyd to Lady Stafford, "[it is] a most curious sight, and he is a most wonderful man. She and I agree that he might be of use to you."*[33] Georgiana saw him for a couple of months, and then abruptly stopped. Her wish for a child had been answered, only the child was not hers: the Duke had asked her to accept his daughter Charlotte by his late mistress.[34]

Charlotte Spencer had remained his mistress until at least 1778, but what had happened to her then remains a mystery; it is known only that

---

* Educated opinion excoriated the doctor as a charlatan and his patients as pathetic gullibles, but this did not prevent the credulous from seeking his help. Infertile couples paid an exorbitant £50 a night to make love on the "electro-magnetic bed" in his "celestial chamber" to the strains of an orchestra playing outside, while a pressure-cylinder pumped "magnetic fire" into the room. It was also recommended that they drink from Graham's patented elixir, costing a guinea a bottle. The *Morning Herald and Daily Advertiser* ran a successful campaign against Graham, pillorying both him and his clients and eventually he went bankrupt in 1782.

she died shortly afterwards. Georgiana's thoughts on the situation have not survived—she almost certainly knew of the relationship: articles about it had appeared in the *Bon Ton Magazine* and the *Town and Country Magazine*. The latter had declared, "it was the greatest paradox" that the Duke must be the only man in England not in love with the Duchess of Devonshire. After Charlotte's death the Duke sent for their daughter and her nurse, Mrs. Gardner. It was not uncommon among aristocratic families for a husband's illegitimate children to be brought up by his wife. Georgiana was in raptures at the prospect of adopting the girl. She met her for the first time on May 8, 1780, and told her mother:

> she is a very healthy good humour'd looking child, I think, not very tall; she is amazingly like the Duke, I am sure you would have known her anywhere. She is the best humour'd little thing you ever saw, vastly active and vastly lively, she seems very affectionate and seems to like Mrs Gardner very much. She has not good teeth and has often the toothache, but I suppose that does not signify as she has not changed them yet, and she is the most nervous little thing in the world, the agitation of coming made her hands shake so, that they are scarcely recover'd today.[35]

The Duke, Georgiana wrote, was also "vastly pleased" with the little girl. Lady Spencer was baffled by her daughter's excitement. "I hope you have not talk'd of her to people," she warned, "as that is taking it out of the Duke's and your power to act as you shall hereafter choose about her." Georgiana was sending the wrong message to the Duke, she thought; she would do better to appear neutral about the child.[36] Georgiana ignored her advice; little Charlotte was all she had of her own to love, and she didn't care where the girl came from. However, her gambling sharply increased just before Charlotte's arrival and continued afterwards at the same level. "You say you play'd on Sunday night till two," wrote Lady Spencer in distress. "What did you do? I hope you are not meant by the beautiful Duchess who has taken to the gaming table and lost £2000. Pray, my dearest G. take care about play . . . and deserve to be what I doubt you are, whether you deserve it or not, the idol of my heart."[37]

Charlotte had no surname but Georgiana resisted any move which might alert the child to her irregular background. "We have not been able to fix on a name," she wrote to Lady Spencer, "but I think it will be

William without the S if it will not look too peculiar."[38] The usual practice was to use the father's Christian name or, if he had several titles, one of his lesser ones, in the place of a surname. After much discussion they agreed on Williams instead and decided to present Charlotte as a distant, orphaned relation of the Spencers.

Meanwhile both George and Harriet became engaged. The twenty-two-year-old George confessed that he was "out of his senses" over a certain Lady Lavinia Bingham.[39] Although Lavinia had no money of her own, and did not come from a particularly distinguished family—her father, Lord Lucan, was a mere Irish peer—the Spencers made no objection to the match. At first glance she seemed to be a good choice. She was pretty in a conventional way with blue eyes and fair hair, talkative, intelligent, and possessed of a strong sense of propriety, which Lady Spencer applauded. Less obvious until later were her more unattractive traits: she was moody, vindictive, hypocritical, and a calm liar who maintained a veneer of politeness to her in-laws while freely abusing them in conversation elsewhere. She was also neurotically jealous of anything which diverted George's attention from herself and loathed Georgiana and Harriet. Georgiana tried not to show her misgivings even though she could sense Lavinia's dislike. "My Dearest Dearest Dearest Brother," she wrote on May 9, 1780, after the announcement of their engagement. "Happiness, 'tho' not to be had directly, is in store for you—That every hour, every minute of your life may be full of happiness is the sincere and fervent wish of my heart for it loves you dearly in the double character of friend and brother."[40]

Harriet's engagement took place two months later, in July. She was now an attractive nineteen-year-old, tall like Georgiana, slim, and the image of Lord Spencer with his dark eyebrows and pale skin. She was quieter than her sister, more analytical, and less prone to flights of fancy, and she still worshipped Georgiana with a devotion which bordered on fixation. Most people compared her unfavorably to Georgiana—a judgment Harriet had made little effort to correct since childhood. Yet on her own she revealed herself to be every bit as individual in her character: passionate, vulnerable, witty, and intuitive. Far from being "unremarkable," Harriet was an extraordinarily gifted linguist and letter writer. Georgiana had never shared her parents' dismissal of her sister and now, ironically, it was her appreciation of Harriet which was helping to show her neglected sister in a more glamorous light. The *Morning Herald and Daily Advertiser* put it neatly in saying that Harriet "never appeared to greater advantage than on Thursday at the Opera; without detracting from her ladyship's good graces, part of this effect may be imputed to comparison—her sister, the Duchess *not* 'being by.' "[41]

Her choice was the Duke of Devonshire's cousin Frederick, Lord Duncannon, the eldest son of the Earl of Bessborough. She explained to her friends that "he was very sensible and good tempered and by marrying him she made no new connections, for now her sister's and hers would be the same."[42] Georgiana was slightly surprised by her sister's choice. Even though the Cavendishes had been pushing for the match she had not thought him the type of man to attract Harriet. He was quiet, not particularly good looking, and not even financially secure—his father was known to have mortgaged all his estates. Harriet admitted to her cousin that his proposal had come as a surprise; she had "not the least guess of [his regard] till the day papa told me, for from your letters I thought his coming to St James's Place was merely on Miss Thynn's account."[43] She added sadly:

> I wish I could have known him a little better first, but my dear Papa and Mama say that it will make them the happiest of creatures, and what would I not do to see them happy, to be sure the connections are the pleasantest that can be . . . when one is to choose a companion for life (what a dreadful sound that has) the inside and not the out is what one ought to look at, and I think from what I have heard of him, and the great attachment he professes to have for me, I have a better chance of being reasonably happy with him than with most people I know. But there are some things which frighten me sadly, he is so grave and I am so very giddy. . . . I will not plague you any more with my jeremiads for I am very low, pray write to me.[44]

Lord and Lady Spencer approved of the marriage because of the Cavendish connection, and probably influenced Harriet more than they realized, but they were also concerned about the couple's financial situation. Harriet's marriage portion of £20,000 went to pay off part of Lord Bessborough's £30,000 debt. She would be left with a mere £400-a-year pin money and £2,000-a-year joint income with her husband.[45] Lady Spencer begged Georgiana not to lead her impressionable sister into bad habits, and above all, to keep her away from the Devonshire set. "I am sure

I need not assure you of my doing everything in the world (should this take place) to prevent her falling into either extravagance or dissipation," she promised.[46]

Georgiana was confident that if she could reform her own life, protecting Harriet would be simple. Since her return from Coxheath she had sought to impress Fox and the other Whig leaders with her political understanding. She followed the debates in Parliament, never missing an opportunity to discuss their implications at party dinners. Only a short time before, people had described her as a novice: "I have also some hopes that she will turn Politician too," remarked a family friend in 1775, "for she gave me an account of some of the speeches in the House of Lords, Ld Grove made an odd one, and the Bishop of Peterborough a prodigious good one, only she said it was rather too much like Preaching." As an afterthought the friend added, "She must have heard all this from the Duke."[47] No doubt it was true then, but Georgiana soon became sufficiently well informed to have her own strong opinions about political debates. She had also perfected the skills required of a political hostess: her dinners at Devonshire House served a useful purpose: waverers could be kept in line and supporters rewarded. She had also learned how to extract information without betraying any secrets in return. She knew when to appear knowledgeable and when to appear ignorant.

Georgiana absorbed the minutiae of party politics. To an outsider the House of Commons was an inchoate system of temporary factions and alliances. In reality the 558 MPs could be divided into three broad categories: the largest being MPs who supported the Prime Minister Lord North, followed by MPs who supported Charles James Fox and the other Whig leaders, and finally those who liked to portray themselves as independently minded gentlemen who were above party politics. The House of Lords, which is where titled aristocrats, known as peers, sat was much smaller and simpler. There were only 150 peers, made up of lords, viscounts, marquesses, and dukes. The majority of them were utterly loyal to the King and they were known as the "King's Friends." The Whigs were numerically inferior in both the House of Commons and the House of Lords but, unlike in the Commons where elections can help to shift the balance, each peer sits in the Lords for life and the Whig party had little hope of making an impact.

Despite being outnumbered and frequently outmanoeuvred, the Whigs never ceased to put on a display in Parliament of brave opposition. Their chief line of attack was that George III and his Prime Minister Lord North were trying to increase the influence of the crown at the expense of civil liberties. They used the American war of independence as evidence of the King's despotism. While they, the Whigs said, believed in a bicameral government in which each chamber would balance the other—like the American House of Representatives and the Senate today—and also keep the power of the King in check, George III, so went their argument, was only interested in ruling through his cronies and had no respect for the House of Commons as an institution. The Whigs liked to portray themselves as political martyrs, popular in the country (which they were not), but barred from government because of the King's dislike.

Georgiana fervently believed this to be the case even if some members of the opposition were rather more cynical.

When she wore the adopted Whig colours of blue and buff (taken from the colours of the American army) she did so out of conviction and expected her friends to do the same. It was precisely because she was a fervent believer that she was able to carry off her military uniforms and women's auxiliary corps at Coxheath without being ridiculed. She had become one of the party's best-known representatives. Fox was the first to recognize her talent for propaganda—they shared a flair for the public aspect of politics. They understood, for example, the potency of symbols in raising or lowering morale, in attracting or repelling support.

Fox encouraged Georgiana to play a greater role in increasing the party's public presence. As a result, in January 1780 she failed to appear at court for the annual celebration of the Queen's birthday. Society and the press remarked upon her absence. It was the first time she had shunned the court and people read it as a sign of the Whigs' confidence that they would soon drive Lord North from office. When Parliament reconvened on February 8 the government was beset by a number of crises. Not only was the war going badly; there was unrest in Ireland and a widespread fear that it might follow the example of America and declare independence. There was also popular discontent at home, fuelled by the Whigs, and hundreds of petitions poured in from around the country demanding democratic reform of the parliamentary system.

The session began promisingly enough. Prodded by the Whigs, the Duke of Devonshire at last gave his maiden speech in the Lords on March 17. Edmund Burke congratulated Georgiana, saying with more hope than conviction, "it will become, by habit, more disagreeable to him to continue silent on an interesting occasion than hitherto it has been to him, to speak upon it."[48]

On April 6, 1780, the Whigs ambushed North with a surprise resolution. John Dunning, a lawyer MP who had honed his rhetorical technique
at the Inns of Court, rose to give a speech. With clear and precise logic, he
pointed out that over 100,000 people had petitioned Parliament for
change, and that the government's response was merely to crush it. He
paused theatrically, holding the House in rapt attention, before, his voice
rising to a crescendo, he urged the following resolution: "The influence of
the Crown has increased, is increasing, and ought to be diminished." The
House was electrified; MPs jumped from their seats and waved their papers at him. The vote was 233 to 215 in favour. Westminster was in pandemonium and the government thrown into confusion.

North's immediate response was to tender his resignation, but George
III insisted that he remain in office. The Speaker fell ill, preventing the
Commons from meeting for a week, and Georgiana feared that the delay
would cost them votes. "Lord Westmoreland [*sic*] as much as told me he
should vote with North on Tuesday," she recorded.[49] When the Commons
met again her presentiment proved correct. The independent MPs voted
with the ministry against the resolution. "We were sadly beat last night in
the House of Commons," Georgiana informed Lady Spencer; "the ministry people are all in great spirits."[50]

A few weeks later she reported, "We go on vilely indeed in the House
of Commons."[51] Her friend Lord Camden concurred: "Our popular exertions are dying away, and the country returning to its old state of luke-
warm indifference, the Minority in the House of Commons dwindle
every day, and the Opposition is at variance with itself."[52] But there was
one piece of good news. The eighteen-year-old Prince of Wales, the future
George IV, had allied himself with the Whigs. His support, as the heir apparent to the throne, absolved them of the charge of disloyalty to the
crown, which made it easier for them to attack the King.

In supporting the Whigs against his father the Prince was following an
established tradition among the Hanoverians. From George I onwards,
father and son had hated each other. Each successive Prince of Wales had
thrown in his lot with the opposition, and the future George IV was no
different from his predecessors. He feared and resented his parents while
they despised him as weak, duplicitous, and lazy. Georgiana recorded her
first impressions of him in a scrapbook, which she entitled "Annecdotes
Concerning HRH the Prince of Wales." Knowing that the memoir would
be seen only by future generations she was absolutely candid in her opinion of him:

Above: George, first Earl Spencer, by Thomas Gainsborough, c. 1763. Lord Spencer "seems to be the man whose value few people know," wrote Viscount Palmerston. "The bright side of his character appears in private and the dark side in public."

Above right: Georgiana, Countess Spencer, by Pompeo Batoni, c. 1764. Georgiana was waiting disconsolately in Amsterdam for her parents to return when this portrait was painted. It shows Lady Spencer surrounded by her interests: books, a musical instrument, and classical ruins.

Photograph of Althorp House. The historian John Evelyn visited Althorp in the seventeenth century and described it as a "noble pile . . . such as may become a great prince." Lord and Lady Spencer were married at Althorp in 1755, during a ball held to commemorate Spencer's coming of age.

Lady Spencer with Lady Georgiana Spencer, by Reynolds, c. 1760. Lady Spencer confessed, "I will own I feel so partial to my Dear Little Gee, that I think I shall never love another so well."

Viscount Althorp with his sisters Lady Georgiana and Lady Henrietta-Frances (Harriet) Spencer, by Angelica Kauffmann, 1774. The portrait was painted just before Georgiana married the Duke of Devonshire.

Chatsworth, west front. Georgiana felt that Chatsworth never really belonged to her. Horace Walpole thought it had an air of gloomy grandeur. When the diarist Lord Torrington visited the house, he dismissed it as "vile and uncomfortable."

The Painted Hall, Chatsworth. Georgiana's son, the sixth Duke, extensively remodeled this hall to suit his taste for gilt and grandeur. His "improvements" were ripped out in 1912 and the room restored to seventeenth-century designs.

Georgiana, by Reynolds. "The Duchess of Devonshire is the most envied woman of the day," wrote the *Morning Post* shortly after her marriage in 1774. Horace Walpole described Georgiana as a "phenomenon." Yet, as the unfinished portrait shows, Georgiana was not a conventional beauty.

Fifth Duke of Devonshire, by Pompeo Batoni. The Duke was on the Grand Tour when Batoni painted this portrait. The trip abroad failed to improve his manners: "To be sure the jewell has not been well polished," wrote Mrs. Delany. "Had he fallen under the tuition of the late Lord Chesterfield he might have possessed *les graces*, but at present only that of his dukedom belongs to him."

Marie Antoinette (1755–93), by L. Courniere. The queen was a great friend to Georgiana, whose code name for her was Mrs. Brown. After Marie Antoinette's imprisonment, Georgiana urged Lafayette to protect her from harm.

Above: Mary Graham, known in society as the "beautiful Mrs. Graham," by Gainsborough. She and Georgiana wrote passionate letters to each other and secretly exchanged portraits. Georgiana was besotted with Mary until she met Lady Elizabeth Foster while visiting Bath with the Duke of Devonshire.

Right: Georgiana, Duchess of Devonshire, and Lady Elizabeth Foster, by Jean-Urbain Guérin. Georgiana is in the foreground, resting her hand on Bess's shoulder.

Lady Elizabeth "Bess" Foster, by Reynolds, 1788, painted after she had been with the Devonshires for six years.

Lady Elizabeth Foster, by Thomas Lawrence, 1802. Georgiana's love for her friend was undiminished even while the woman was her husband's mistress. "My dear Bess," she wrote in 1803. "Do you hear the voice of my heart crying to you? Do you feel what it is for me to be separated from you . . . ?"

A view of Green Park, English School, c. 1760, from Devonshire House looking across the park. Buckingham House is on the right; Spencer House is on the left.

Georgiana, Duchess of Devonshire, and Lady Georgiana Cavendish, by Joshua Reynolds. Georgiana gave birth to Lady Georgiana, "Little G," at Devonshire House in the summer of 1783. Instead of giving the child to a wet nurse, Georgiana insisted on breast-feeding the baby herself. In 1804, Little G, by then a mother of two children, told Georgiana, "One cannot know till one has separated from you how different you are from everyone else, how superior to all mothers, even good ones."

The Prince of Wales is rather tall, and has a figure which, though striking is not perfect. He is inclined to be too fat and looks too much like a woman in men's clothes, but the gracefulness of his manner and his height certainly make him a pleasing figure. His face is very handsome, and he is fond of dress even to a tawdry degree, which young as he is will soon wear off. His person, his dress and the admiration he has met with . . . take up his thoughts chiefly. He is good-natured and rather extravagant . . . but he certainly does not want for understanding, and his jokes sometimes have the appearance of wit. He appears to have an inclination to meddle with politics—he loves being of consequence, and whether it is in intrigues of state or of gallantry he often thinks more is intended than really is.[53]

He was clever, well read, and possessed of exquisite taste in art and decoration, but he was wholly deficient in self-knowledge. Following the King's orders the Prince had been isolated from companions of his own age and tutored by dry old men who saw to it that his life was one long regime of worthy activities. But instead of creating a paragon of virtue, the Prince's strict and joyless upbringing had made him vain, petulant, and attention-seeking. As soon as he could he rebelled against everything he had been taught. The King relaxed the *cordon sanitaire* around the Prince when he turned eighteen only to the extent of holding a few private balls for him, "from which I and many others were banished," wrote Georgiana, "as no opposition person was asked"—which only increased his desire to mix with people who did not meet with his parents' approval.

"As he only went out in secret, or with the King and Queen," she also recorded, "he formed very few connections with any other woman other than women of the town." On his first trip to the theater in 1779 he saw *The Winter's Tale* at Drury Lane, and immediately fell in love with the twenty-one-year-old actress Mary Robinson, a protégée of Georgiana's. She was delighted to conduct a very public affair with him, and even went so far as to emblazon a simulacrum of his crest—three feathers—on her carriage. The Prince foolishly wrote her explicit letters, in which he called her "Perdita"—her role in the play—and signed himself "Florizel." Like any astute woman on the make, she kept his adolescent declarations—he promised her a fortune as soon as he came of age—and blackmailed him when he grew tired of her.

It was during the Prince's visits to Drury Lane that he first came into contact with the Devonshire House Circle, and in particular with Geor-

giana and Fox. George III blamed Fox for deliberately and calculatingly
debauching his son, but he had no malicious intent. The Prince had already started to drink and gamble before he met Fox, who simply showed
him how to do it in a more refined way. The Prince worshipped Fox who,
for his part, genuinely liked the boy, despite the thirteen-year age gap, seeing in him, perhaps, something of his younger, reckless self. The two
made an unlikely pair, one of them dressed in exquisite finery, the other
unwashed, unshaven, his clothes askew and his linen soiled. On most
nights they could be found either at Brooks's or Devonshire House, playing faro until they fell asleep at the table.

The Prince's marked attentions to Georgiana, the fact that he constantly sought her advice on every matter—from his clothes to his relations with his father—fanned rumours that they were having an affair.
Nathaniel Wraxall was loath to characterize it definitely, and ventured no
further than saying, "of what nature was that attachment, and what limits
were affixed to it by the Duchess, must remain a matter of conjecture."[54]
The Prince was almost certainly in love with Georgiana, but she never
reciprocated his feelings. Throughout their lives they always addressed
each other as "my dearest brother" and "sister," although the Prince was
often madly jealous of rivals.[55] It was his lack of success with Georgiana,
when every other woman in Whig society (including, it was rumoured,
Harriet) was his for the asking, that made her so irresistible to him.

The Prince shared with Fox, Lord Cholmondeley, and Lord George
Cavendish a round robin of the three most famous courtesans of the era:
Perdita, Grace Dalrymple, and Mrs. Armistead. Georgiana heard that Lord
George had paid a drunken visit to Mrs. Armistead one night only to find
the Prince hiding behind a door. Luckily, rather than take offence he burst
out laughing, made him a low bow, and left. The Prince also pursued Lady
Melbourne and Lady Jersey, or perhaps it was the other way round. Less
well-informed people speculated that Georgiana was in competition with
her friends for the Prince's affection, but a letter from Lady Melbourne
suggests collusion rather than rivalry:

> The Duke of Richmond has been here, and told me you and I were
> two rival queens, and I believe, if there had not been some people in
> the room, who might have thought it odd, that I should have slapped
> his face for having such an idea; and he wished me joy of having the
> Prince to myself. How odious people are, upon my life, I have no pa-
> tience with them. I believe you and I are very different from all the

rest of the world—as from their ideas they do such strange things in certain situations or they never could suspect us in the way they do.[56]

The Whigs continued their onslaught against the government. On June 3, 1780, the Duke of Richmond, then a radical on the extreme left of the party, moved a resolution that the constitution should be rewritten to allow annual parliaments and universal suffrage. His plan was based on the proposals drawn up by the Westminster Association, an offshoot of Christopher Wyvill's Association Movement which had led the petitions for parliamentary reform. By an unlucky chance, while the Lords were debating the Duke of Richmond's proposals, Lord George Gordon, a mentally unbalanced Protestant fanatic, chose to march on Parliament at the head of a large mob. He carried with him a petition from the Protestant Association, a sectarian body which opposed giving legal rights to Catholics.

Eighteenth-century society was rarely bothered by the occasional eruptions of the lower orders; the establishment ignored them and the fracas would die down of its own accord. But this mob, intoxicated by drink and whipped up by a crazed demagogue, was more dangerous than the usual over-excited rabble. The crowd blocked all the entrances to Parliament while Lord George Gordon stormed into the Commons. The MPs fell silent at his entrance and sat spellbound as he harangued them on the evils of popery. He then rushed out to do the same in the Lords. In between speeches he ran to a window to shout at the crowd outside. Fearing for their lives, MPs made a dash for the stairs, and as they tried to leave the House they were punched and kicked by the marchers. The Lords followed suit, ignominiously leaving older peers such as the eighty-year-old Lord Mansfield to fend for themselves. The Duke of Devonshire's carriage was stopped by the mob until he agreed to shout "No Popery." By nightfall the protest had turned into a riot. Thieves and looters joined in as bands of club-wielding rioters burned down foreign chapels and attacked the shops and houses of known Catholics.

At first Georgiana did not realize the danger facing the capital. Her friend Miss Lloyd, she joked, was dreaming about enraged Protestants hammering on her door.

Lord George Gordon's people continued to make a great fracas, there is a violent mob in Moorfields, and I have learnt that five hundred guards are gone down there. I could not go to the Birthday—

my gown was beautiful, a pale blue, with the drapery etc., of an em-
broider'd gauze in *paillons*. I am a little comforted for not going by
the two messages I have received from Lady Melbourne and the
Duke from the Prince of Wales to express his disappointment at having missed dancing with me for the 3rd time.[57]

But by the next day, June 6, the mob was on the point of taking over the
city. Ministers and opposition alike hurriedly sent their wives and children
out of town and prepared to mount a defence of the streets. But the mag-
istrates were nowhere to be seen and, following a misunderstanding over
which authority had the power to mandate the use of firearms against
civilians, there were no troops in place. The rioting continued unchecked.
The mob sacked Newgate Prison and burned down the King's Bench.
They exploded the distilleries at Holborn so that the streets were flooded
with spirits and the water supply to Lincoln's Inn Fields became alcoholic.
Lord John Cavendish condemned the Lord Mayor's cowardice in standing by while London burned to the ground. He had good reason; the mob
targeted the houses of prominent Whigs because of the party's support for
religious toleration. Edmund Burke's house was surrounded, but he managed to fend them off. Sir George Savile was less fortunate and narrowly
escaped being burnt to death. Poor Lord Mansfield watched as rioters
looted his house and destroyed his celebrated library. The Whig grandees
mounted a round-the-clock defence of their houses. Georgiana wrote on
June 7, forgetting her birthday in the midst of the chaos:

> I shall go to Chiswick tomorrow, for tho' there could be no kind of
> danger for me, yet a woman is only troublesome. I hope and think
> that it will be over tonight as the Council has issued orders that the
> soldiers may fire. . . . the mob is a strange set, and some of it com-
> posed of mere boys. I was very much frightened yesterday, but I keep
> quiet and preach quiet to everybody. The night before last the Duke
> was in garrison at Ld Rockingham's till five, which alarmed me not a
> little, but now Ld R's is the safest place, as he has plenty of guards, a
> justice of peace, a hundred tradesmen arm'd, besides servants and
> friends.[58]

Burke persuaded those MPs who had braved the streets to reach Parliament not to revoke religious tolerance legislation, even though some
sought only to placate the mob. At last, on June 8, the army arrived and,

aided by volunteers that included MPs, barristers, coalheavers, and Irish chairmen, organized a well-armed defence. The mob attempted to seize the Bank of England, but its defenders, ably led by Captain Holroyd, beat them off. Devonshire House was well guarded and the expected attack never came. By the ninth only pockets of resistance remained. Lord George Gordon gave himself up and was imprisoned in the Tower. Georgiana was badly shaken. "I feel mad with spirits at [it] all being over," she wrote; "it seems now like a dream."[59] She had stayed on the balcony for four nights, staring at the orange sky as Piccadilly reverberated to the sound of gunfire and explosions. The number of people killed or seriously wounded stood at 458; whole blocks of the city lay in ruins.

The immediate aftermath saw the total discrediting of the reformers and all the Association movements. The Whigs were blamed for irresponsibly fomenting discontent "Without Doors"—the term for the world outside Parliament. Lord North seized the political advantage and called a snap general election on September 1. Georgiana's assistance was demanded from many quarters: in addition to the canvassing she had to do for the Cavendishes in Derby, the Duke's family pressured her to persuade Lord Spencer to align his interests with theirs. "Lord Richard is very anxious for my father to give his interest in Cambridgeshire to Lord Robert Manners, the Duke of Rutland's brother," she told Lady Spencer. "I told him I dare say my father would, and they are very anxious as it is of great consequence to have Mr Parker wrote to directly, that he may speak to the tenants as otherwise they might be got by other people."[60] Her brother's former tutor Sir William Jones, who was contesting the seat for Oxford University, also asked her to write letters on his behalf.

Sheridan wanted to become a politician, but his lack of wealth and family connections made it impossible for him to contest a seat on his own cognizance. His vanity prevented him from making a direct application to the grandees. It suited him far better to approach his target by a more circuitous route, and for this reason he pressed Georgiana to help him. Although she thought it was a shame for him to throw away his literary career, she arranged for him to stand in the Spencer-dominated borough of Stafford. He was duly elected and wrote her a grovelling letter of thanks: "I profited by the Permission allow'd to me to make use of your Grace's letter as my first and best introduction to Lord Spencer's Interest in the Town. . . . It is no flattery to say that the Duchess of Devonshire's name commands an implicit admiration wherever it is mentioned."[61] A week later, on September 25, Charles Fox invited Georgiana to accompany him on the hustings when he contested the borough of Westminster. The press was shocked by her boldness, even though she stood on the platform for only a few minutes. Fox was magnificent on the hustings, whipping up his supporters with speeches about parliamentary reform, the rights of the British people, and the consequences of royal tyranny. It was on this campaign that he earned his title "Man of the People."

Fox won with a comfortable majority, and his success was unexpectedly duplicated around the country. Despite its recent setbacks, the party had managed to run a well-organized election, clawing back the ground it had lost following the Gordon Riots. North's majority was much reduced; on paper it was only 28, and he would have to rely on the independent MPs to give their support. The Whigs' success was all the more remarkable because they had funded their campaign out of their own pockets while North had almost unlimited funds from the treasury. The near-parity of numbers convinced them that it would be only a matter of time before the government collapsed.

CHAPTER 5

INTRODUCTION TO POLITICS

1780—1782

The concourse of Nobility, etc., at the Duchess of Devonshire's on Thursday night were so great, that it was eight o'clock yesterday morning before they all took leave. Upwards of 500 sat down to supper, and near 1000 came agreeable to invitation; and so numerous were the servants, that no less than 3500 tickets were delivered out, which entitled each of them to a pot of porter. The company consisted of the most fashionable "characters." With respect to the ladies, the dresses were for the prevailing part, white. . . . The best dressed ladies were her Royal Highness the Duchess of Cumberland, her Grace the Duchess of Devonshire, Lady Duncannon, Lady Althorpe, Lady Waldegrave, and Lady Harrington. . . . The gentlemen best dressed were his Royal Highness the Prince of Wales, the Marquis of Graham, and the Hon. Charles Fox.

London Chronicle, *March 21–23, 1782*

We hear the amiable Duchess of Devonshire is about to propose and promote a subscription among her female friends for building a fifty gun ship, in imitation of the Ladies in France who set the laudable example at the beginning of the war.

Morning Post, *September 21, 1782*

Lord North clung to office despite the government's poor showing in the election. Exasperated, the Whigs consoled themselves by fêting the Prince of Wales, who amused them by being rude about his father. He took great delight in annoying his parents; at the ball to mark his official presentation to society on January 18, 1781, he snubbed the ladies of the court by dancing all night with Georgiana. The *Morning Herald* could not help remarking, "The Court beauties looked with an eye of envy on her Grace of Devonshire, as the only woman honoured with the hand of the heir apparent, during Thursday night's ball at St James's."[1]

Much against her inclination, Georgiana left London just as the new Parliament was getting under way. In February she accompanied the Duke to Hardwick, in the words of a friend, "pour faire un enfant."*[2] Lady Clermont had paid the Devonshires a visit while little Charlotte was still new to the household and was pleasantly surprised. "I never saw anything so charming as [Georgiana] has been," she wrote to Lady Spencer, "her fondness for the Duke, and his not being ashamed of expressing his for her."[3] But relations between them had deteriorated rapidly after Harriet's marriage to Lord Duncannon in November. To Georgiana's embarrassment, her sister delighted the Cavendishes by becoming pregnant at once. Despite Harriet's initial reservations her marriage appeared to be free of the tensions which plagued Georgiana's. In February 1781 Lady Spencer wrote to inform Georgiana that Harriet's "closet is becoming a *vrai bijou,* and she and her husband pass many comfortable hours in it. I trust indeed that all will go very well in that quarter."[4]

Harriet's good fortune contributed to Georgiana's fear that her own failure to produce a baby was a punishment from God.[5] "I will not hear you give way to disappointment so much," chided Lady Spencer. "If you were of my age there would be some reason why you should suppose you would never have children, but as it is there is no reason why you should give it up."[6] Sitting alone in cheerless Hardwick every day while the Duke went out hunting, Georgiana saw every reason why she should. The empty, silent afternoons were too much for her to bear and she blotted out her days with large doses of opiates. "I took something today," she wrote, "but I shall ride tomorrow."[7]

The Duke was disgusted when Georgiana still showed no sign of pregnancy after a month at Hardwick. Deciding that their stay was a waste of time, he gave orders for Devonshire House to be prepared for their imminent arrival. After their return Georgiana rarely appeared in public. The papers remarked that she had "become the gravest creature in the world" and complained about her absence from society.[8] On March 24 she appeared briefly at the King's Theatre to support the dancer Vestris, an Italian immigrant and one of the most famous dancers of the time. He was

---

* To make a baby.

performing a new dance which he and Georgiana had invented together during a private lesson at Devonshire House. Nine hundred people filled the theatre. "We were in the greatest impatience for the Duchess of Devonshire's arrival," reported the *Morning Herald and Daily Advertiser,* "and our eager eyes were roaming about in search of her. We spied her Grace at last sitting in her box . . . alas! We soon found out, that her Grace was only there to pay a kind of public visit to the Vestris, for the Devonshire minuet, which was received with very warm applause, and was no sooner over than the Duchess disappeared."[9]

The reason for Georgiana's sudden retirement was not only the disappointment of Hardwick but a crisis concerning Harriet. Less than two months after Lady Spencer had written of the Duncannons' "comfortable hours" together Lord Duncannon shocked them all by shouting at Harriet in public. Questioned afterwards, Harriet confessed that she was frightened to be alone with him, since the slightest provocation made him lose his self-control. The Cavendishes regarded Duncannon's abusiveness towards his wife as a disgrace to the entire family. Another incident at a ball in April moved his cousin, the Duke's sister the Duchess of Portland, to write him a warning:

You say I did you great injury by exposing you publicly to all the room—You exposed yourself, and I am concerned to say I have too often seen you do the same before. . . . when you left the room, there was not any of the company present (your father in particular) who did not applaud my conduct, and censure yours in the strongest terms possible. . . . Indeed, the very first evening that you came to me after that conversation, the *night of the Ridotto,* I never felt more ashamed or hurt than I did for you, and I must tell you that your Behaviour did not escape the notice of the Company who heard it as well as myself with astonishment. The cards were going to your mind, nothing had happened to put you out of humour, but upon Lady Duncannon's coming into the Room, as I thought very properly dressed, your temper was immediately ruffled because she had put on her diamonds (a consideration I should not have thought worthy of the mind of a man). Indeed such sort of behaviour in a man is so perfectly new that I do not know how to account for it or reason upon it. You are very young and have had very little experience. . . . The World in general was inclined to think well of you. Your friends and relations thought you were all their hearts could have wished, but do not flatter yourself that your conduct has escaped observation. It is becoming the subject of ridicule, and your best Friends begin to fear your want of understanding.[10]

Lord Duncannon apologized; his behaviour, he explained, was caused by worry over Harriet's pregnancy: he feared that she would miscarry like Georgiana. The Duchess of Portland's reply showed her contempt: "the frequent agitations that I have perceived your conduct to occasion her may have been the cause of this unhappy event. I trust in God she will recover [from] this, and that it will hereafter be uppermost in your mind to reward her affection for you with that confidence which she so well deserves."[11] Threats and warnings were the only weapons available to the Spencers or the Cavendishes. Eighteenth-century law granted a husband the freedom to treat his wife as he pleased, except in the case of imprisonment and physical torture. Even then, the shame of public scandal deterred upper-class women from seeking legal redress in all but the most extreme circumstances.*

Georgiana had ceased to entertain at Devonshire House immediately after the discovery and spent her time caring for Harriet. The Spencers were frightened to leave their daughter alone with Duncannon when she was so vulnerable. They kept her away from him as much as they could until she gave birth to a son, the Hon. John William Ponsonby, on August 31, 1781. Not long afterwards Lord Spencer became deaf and suffered a partial paralysis on one side of his body. The double anxiety over Harriet and Lord Spencer drove Georgiana to the gaming tables, and Lady Spencer with her. "I can never make myself easy about the bad example I have set you and which you have but too faithfully imitated," Lady Spencer had written bitterly in November 1779.[12] Now she found herself writing again: she had committed "twenty enormities which oblige me to conclude my letter with the usual charge that you must attend more to what I say than what I do."[13] Harriet followed her mother and sister, but with less than a tenth of their income, and without the resources to pay her creditors.

George Selwyn described incredible scenes at Devonshire House to

---

* The patriarchal right to "discipline and punnish" a wife was not in question. If there was any doubt, a judge's verdict on a case in 1782 resolved the issue. He declared that, if there was a good cause, a husband could legally beat his wife so long as the stick was no thicker than his thumb. Lawrence Stone, *Road to Divorce* (Oxford 1990), p. 201.

Lord Carlisle. "The trade or amusement which engrosses everybody who lives in what is called the pleasurable world is [faro]," he wrote. Georgiana had arranged the drawing room to resemble a professional gaming house, complete with hired croupiers and a commercial faro bank. Lady Spencer was there most nights, throwing her rings on to the table when she had run out of money:

> poor Mr Grady is worn out in being kept up at one Lady's house or another till six in the morning. Among these, Lady Spencer and her daughter, the Duchess of D. and Lady Harcourt are the chief punters. Hare, Charles [Fox], and Richard [Fitzpatrick] held a bank the whole night and a good part of the next day . . . by turns, each of the triumvirate punting when he is himself a dealer. There is generally two or three thousands lying on the table in rouleaus till about noon, but who they belong to, or will belong to, the Lord knows.[14]

Faro was a complicated game, involving one banker and an unlimited number of players who staked their bets upon the dealer turning over particular combinations of cards. Although it was a game of chance, the odds in favour of the banker were second only to those in roulette. It was first played in resort towns such as Tunbridge Wells, but in fifty years it had become the most popular game in high society. Women were said to be particularly addicted to it, but it was also the favourite of Charles Fox. Georgiana set a new trend by illegally charging faro-dealers fifty guineas a night for the right to set up tables in her house.*[15] But she relied on professionals of questionable honesty to run the faro table and bank, and Selwyn complained of underhand dealings "at Devonshire House. . . . Charles [Fox] says, he is not allowed to take money from the bank; he means for the payment of debts, but yet I hear some are paid, such as O'Kelly and other blacklegs." The carelessness with which people threw their money about attracted shady characters to the house. One in particular, a man called Martindale, lured Georgiana into a ruinous agreement. According to Sheridan, "the Duchess and Martindale had agreed that whatever the two won from each other should be sometimes double, sometimes treble the sum which it was called. . . . the Duchess . . . was lit-

---

* In 1797 Lady Buckinghamshire and Lady Elizabeth Luttrell were actually arrested and fined £50 each for running a gambling concern with a faro-banker in Lady Buckinghamshire's house.

erally sobbing at her losses—she perhaps having lost £1500, when it was supposed to be £500."[16]

Lady Mary Coke told her relations in Scotland that the Duchess of Devonshire was living a twenty-four-hour day of gambling and amusement. Last week, she wrote, Georgiana had attended a breakfast at Wimbledon (which continued all day), then an assembly at Lady Hertford's, where she had proposed a visit to Vauxhall Gardens. She took all the Duchesses, sniffed Lady Mary, as well as the most popular men, including Lord Egremont and Thomas Grenville, "a professed admirer of the Duchess of Devonshire for two years past." There they stayed until the small hours, keeping the musicians at their posts long after the gardens were officially closed. She did the same thing the next day and the day after that until, returning from another late party at Vauxhall with the Duchess of Rutland, Lady Melbourne, Lord Egremont, and Thomas Grenville, she fell asleep in the boat.[17]

The newspapers also reported on Georgiana's activities to the wider world, but she was still their darling. The *Morning Herald and Daily Advertiser* increased its coverage of her to almost an item a week. On June 11 it proudly reported having seen "the Duchess of Devonshire, with a smart cocked hat, scarlet riding habit and a man's domino, [who] looked divinely."[18] In July it informed readers that Georgiana was sitting for Gainsborough for a full-length portrait intended as a present to the Queen of France. It continued to follow her progress after the end of the season, when she and the Duke accompanied the Derbyshire militia to the military camp on the Roxborough Downs, near Plymouth.

On September 6, 1781, the French fleet once again appeared in the Channel, but for the press the event paled in comparison to Georgiana's launch of HMS *Anson:* she christened the ship in front of a delirious crowd of several thousand who had streamed into the port for the day.[19] When the Duke and Duchess of Rutland, contemporaries of the Devonshires, came for a visit the press invented a rift between the two women, calling them "the rival and beautiful Duchesses." Georgiana had become so famous that her name was enough to make anything fashionable. The entrepreneur Josiah Wedgwood understood the principles of selling better than any manufacturer in the country: "Few ladies, you know, dare venture at anything out of the common stile [*sic*] 'till authoris'd by their betters—by the Ladies of superior spirit who set the ton."[20] To entice the middle classes to buy his china sets he named them after royalty and famous aristocratic families. "They want a name—a name has a wonderful effect I assure you," he told his partner. "Suppose you present the Duchess of Devonshire with a Set and beg leave to call them Devonshire flowerpots."[21]

The *Morning Herald*'s love affair with Georgiana showed no signs of tiring. In December it stated that "her heart, notwithstanding her exalted situation, appears to be directed by the most liberal principles; and from the benevolence and gentleness which marks her conduct, the voice of compliment becomes the offering of gratitude."[22] These fawning notices revealed more than just a weakness for society hostesses. A recent upturn in the Whig party's fortunes made the paper eager to be associated with the future regime. The war looked certain to end: General Cornwallis had surrendered at Yorktown to the combined forces of the French and the Americans, under the leadership of the Marquis de Lafayette and George Washington. When Lord North heard the news he threw back his arms and cried, "Oh God. It is all over."[23] He offered his resignation to the King without delay, but after five years of war George III could not accept the defeat. He ordered the Prime Minister to remain in office and to prepare a counter attack.

Driven by his implacable master, North limped on until March 20, when at last the King accepted that the ministry had lost the confidence of the House and could not continue. George Selwyn told Lord Carlisle that the report of North's resignation had spread to all the coffee houses within hours.[24]

The Whigs felt certain that they would soon be in power. But George III refused to accept the Whigs *en masse* and insisted on their sharing power with his preferred minister the Marquess of Shelburne. The party accepted this bitter pill, hoping it might eventually be able to push Shelburne out. Having agreed to the terms, the Whigs went to Devonshire House to celebrate. "I was at Devonshire House till about 4," wrote Selwyn to Lord Carlisle, "and then left most of the company there."[25] Georgiana threw a series of celebratory balls, each one lasting the whole night and part of the following day. The furniture downstairs was cleared out to make room for the crowds and the ceilings decorated with thick festoons of roses. Keeping the ten Van Dycks in the hall, Georgiana transformed all the other rooms into a fantasy with painted scenery and strategically hung mirrors. Public excitement about the balls grew, and on one night the managers of the Opera House shortened the last act to enable the Prince of Wales to leave on time. The next day the *Morning Herald and Daily Ad-*

vertiser, which had devoted several columns to the Devonshire "galas," reported, "none was ever more admired than the minuets at the Devonshire Gala, the Prince of Wales and the Duchess of Devonshire in particular."[26]

Having so long avoided St. James's Palace, the Whigs now trooped into court to pay their respects. The King was too disgusted to hold a proper Drawing Room and sat glumly next to Queen Charlotte, while Georgiana and her friends made polite conversation with the Prince of Wales and the Duke of Cumberland.[27] Tradition demanded that the King recognize the new ministers with the awards of office, and he grudgingly offered the garter to senior Whigs. They accepted with a shameless delight which disgusted Nathaniel Wraxall. He watched with embarrassment as "The Duke of Devonshire . . . advanced up to the Sovereign, with his phlegmatic, cold, awkward air, like a clown. Lord Shelburne came forward, bowing on every side, smiling and fawning like a courtier." Only the Duke of Richmond, in his opinion, "presented himself, easy, unembarrassed and with dignity as a gentleman."[28]

Fox approached Georgiana during the celebrations and made her a proposal. He was now Foreign Secretary, and under parliamentary rules MPs selected for office had to re-offer themselves to their constituents. Having been impressed by the crowd's reaction to Georgiana's appearance on the hustings at Covent Garden in 1780, Fox asked her to repeat her performance, only this time with more fanfare. She accepted without hesitation. The Duke and other grandees agreed to the proposal and allowed her to participate in discussions on how to plan the event. They decided that Georgiana should lead a women's delegation. Since the crowds had responded so enthusiastically to one woman on the platform, they reasoned that five or six would be even more popular.

On April 3 Georgiana performed her first official duty for the party by helping Fox in his re-election campaign. The diarist Silas Neville was enjoying a stroll when he stumbled on the proceedings: "[I] was present in the Garden at the re-election of the Arch-Patriot Secretary. The Crowd was immense of carriages and people of all ranks. The Duchess of Devonshire and another lady were on the hustings and waved their hats with the rest in compliment to Charles, who was soon after chaired under a canopy of oak leaves and mirtle amidst the acclamations of thousands."[29] The *London Chronicle* reported the event in some amazement. In an age of free beer and bloody noses at election time the Whigs' polished handling of public events was disconcerting. Fox stood on a platform beneath three large banners that read, THE MAN OF THE PEOPLE, FREEDOM AND INDEPEN-

DENCE, and INDEPENDENCE. Shouting above the roaring crowd, Fox thanked them for their confidence and promised he would unite the country in defence of liberty. "His friends wore orange and blue ribbons, with the word Fox on them," reported the paper.[30] Georgiana was there with several other women, all wearing the Whig colours of blue and buff, and they raised their hats each time the crowd huzzahed. Nothing like it had ever been witnessed before. Milliners' shops began making fans bearing Georgiana's portrait, which sold in their hundreds; Charles Fox and the Prince of Wales also became fashionable subjects: "The fans are quite new, and beautiful, designed and executed by the first masters of that art, and are striking likenesses of the exalted characters they represent; the prices are very moderate," claimed Hartshorn and Dyde's of Wigmore Street.[31]

A week later, on April 8, the Whigs made their first appearance in the Commons. At first MPs were disoriented: Lord North and his followers were no longer sitting on the treasury benches; in their place were the Whigs. Their uniform of blue and buff was gone and they wore the formal dress of government, all of them—even Fox—with hair powder, ruffles, lace around their necks, and swords by their sides.

Lady Spencer, trapped at home with the ailing Lord Spencer, felt excluded from her children's lives. The drum beat which accompanied Georgiana's activities barely sounded in Wimbledon. On May 22 she recalled a recent conversation with the Duchess of Annenberg, who had congratulated her on the family's reputation for being one of the "happiest and closest" in Britain.[32] But Georgiana paid no attention to her mother's hints; for the first time since her wedding in 1774 she looked forward to the future. According to James Hare, she appeared "very handsome and seems easier and happier than she used to do."[33]

Georgiana's optimism was born out of a new-found sense of purpose. In September 1782 she recorded her thoughts about the year.

> The secret springs of events are seldom known [she wrote]. But when they are, they become particularly instructive and entertaining. . . . the greatest actions have often proceeded from the intrigues of a handsome woman or a fashionable man, and of course whilst the memoires of those events are instructive by opening the secret workings of the human mind, they likewise attract by the interest and events of a novel. . . . If some people would write down the events they had been witness to . . . the meaning of an age would be

transmitted to the next with clearness and dependence—to the idle reader it would present an interesting picture of the manners of his country. . . . I wish I had done this—I came into the world at 17 and I am now five and twenty—in these eight years I have been in the midst of action. . . . I have seen partys rise and fall—friends be united and disunited—the ties of love give way to caprice, to interest, and to vanity. . . ."

She hoped one day to be "a faithful historian of the secret history of the times."[34]

PART TWO

Politics

CHAPTER 6

THE NEWCOMER

1782—1783

The Duchess of Devonshire, it is said, means to introduce a head piece which is to be neither hat, cap, nor bonnet, and yet all three, a sort of trinity in unity, under the appellation the "Devonshire Whim." Whenever the Duchess of Devonshire visits the capital, a Standard may be expected to be given to the Fashion. At present scarce any innovation is attempted even in the head-dress. This does not arise from the Town being destitute of Women of elegance; many ladies of the first rank being on the spot; but rather proceeds from the dread each feels that the Taste she may endeavour to take the lead in may be rejected.

Morning Herald and Daily Advertiser, *October 21, 1782*

As soon as Parliament adjourned for the summer Georgiana and the Duke retreated west to the popular spa town of Bath, where the fashionable young hoped to meet eligible partners and the fashionable old sought relief from their ailments. They did not return to Devonshire House until the autumn, when the new session was well under way. Accompanying them to London was Lady Elizabeth Foster, described by the papers as the "Duchess of Devonshire's intimate friend."

Georgiana met Elizabeth, or Bess, as she affectionately called her, during their first week at Bath. The Duke had rented the Duke of Marlborough's house, one of the finest in town, for the whole summer. The Devonshires were both there to "take the cure": the Duke for his gout, Georgiana for her "infertility"—she had suffered two early miscarriages the previous year.[1] The tone of her letters betrays her misery at having to abandon London just when the Whigs had come to power. She rarely went out and attended few of the fee-paying balls and nightly concerts. Twice a day she drank the thermal waters in the King's Bath, the most fashionable of the three pump rooms. The company there was hardly uplifting, comprising the unfortunate casualties of eighteenth-century living: the incurables, the rheumatics, the gout sufferers, and those afflicted with rampant eczema and other unsightly skin diseases. Georgiana sat each morning in a semicircle near the bar with the other childless wives, cup and saucer in either hand, listening to a band of provincial musicians. Bath was, in her opinion, "amazingly disagreeable, I am only surprised at the Duke bearing it all as well as he does, but he is so good natur'd he bears anything well."[2]

Two things made life tolerable: watching the new Shakespearean actress Sarah Siddons at the Theatre Royal, and the acquaintance of two sisters living in straitened circumstances in an unfashionable part of town. On June 1 Georgiana informed Lady Spencer, "Lady Erne and Lady E. Foster are our chief support or else it would be shockingly dull for the D. indeed."[3] These were the eldest daughters of the Earl of Bristol; Lady Mary Erne was a great friend of Mary Graham, who was probably responsible for the sisters' introduction to Georgiana. Both were separated from their husbands, and lived with their aunt, a Methodist convert, on the tiny income allocated to them by their father.

Georgiana's letters to her mother were full of praise for her new friends: "You cannot conceive how agreeable and amiable they are, and I never knew people who have more wit and good nature."[4] But after a short time there was no more mention of Lady Mary Erne, and Lady Elizabeth Foster—Bess—became the sole topic of her correspondence. She was the same age as Georgiana and already the mother of two sons, yet there was something surprisingly girlish about her. Physically, she was the opposite of Georgiana: slimmer, shorter, more delicate, with thin dark hair framing her tiny face. Her appearance of frailty, coupled with a feminine helplessness and coquettish charm, made most men want to protect and possess her. The historian Edward Gibbon, who had known Bess since she was a little girl, described her manners as the most seductive of any woman he knew. "No man could withstand her," was his opinion. "If she chose to beckon the Lord Chancellor from his Woolsack in full sight of the world, he could not resist obedience."[5]

Bess's family, the Herveys, were not the sort that recommended themselves to Lady Spencer. Lady Mary Wortley Montagu is alleged to have said: "When God created the human race, he created men, women, and Herveys."* The quip could apply to each generation: eccentric, libertine, and untrustworthy, the Herveys were an extraordinary family who had made their fortune in the early eighteenth century as professional courtiers. Bess's father, the fourth Earl of Bristol, had succeeded unexpectedly to the title on the death of his two elder brothers without legitimate heirs.† He took the well-worn path to a career in the Church, eventually becoming the Bishop of Derry, which brought him a modest salary. But the Earl-Bishop's spendthrift habits meant that Bess, her brother, and two sisters were brought up in relative poverty. He had two great passions: one was for art, and the other a morbid fascination with human misery. He was constantly rushing to the scene of wars, riots, and natural disasters. The family spent years roaming the Continent from one terrible situation to another while he searched for antiquities and *objets d'art* along the way.

On succeeding to the title in 1779 Bess's father inherited Ickworth Park in Suffolk, and with it an income of £20,000 a year.[6] Immediately he embarked on a grandiose building scheme to house his planned art collection.

---

* She was referring to Bess's grandfather Lord Hervey, who died before he could become the second Earl of Bristol. Despite suffering from severe epilepsy and general ill-health, Lord Hervey was, for a time, a brilliantly successful courtier. He recorded his career in the witty and scabrous *Memoirs of George II,* which was published after his death. Although he married the clever and beautiful Molly Lepel, his real love was for Stephen Fox, Charles Fox's uncle. The poet Alexander Pope wrote a vicious poem about him: "Amphibious thing! that acting either part,/The Trifling head, or the corrupted heart/Fop at the toilet, flatterer at the board,/Now trips a lady, now struts a lord . . ."

† George, the eldest son of Lord Hervey, died unmarried. The second son, Augustus, who became the third Earl of Bristol, did so in a blaze of scandal. Many years before, he had secretly married Elizabeth Chudleigh, a rambunctious lady-in-waiting at court with ambition and a reputation to match. The alliance was short-lived and both of them agreed to maintain the pretence of there never having been a marriage. Elizabeth then married the Duke of Kingston, who knew nothing of her previous life, but after the Duke died her past was exposed in a court case over the will. The Countess-Duchess—as Horace Walpole called her—was tried for bigamy in the House of Lords in 1776 in front of 6,000 spectators. One of the many peeresses who crammed into the gallery during the lengthy trial was Georgiana. Because of her age and status, the Duchess of Kingston escaped branding on the hand, the usual punishment, and was allowed to retire abroad. Augustus was condemned for conniving in the deception and his punishment was severe: the Lords insisted the original marriage was indissoluble, thus depriving him of legitimate heirs.

But the Earl-Bishop's good fortune had come too late for his daughters, especially for Bess. She had married in 1776 while still Miss Elizabeth Hervey, a mere bishop's daughter with no dowry and few acquaintances. Her husband, John Thomas Foster, was a family friend and a member of the Irish parliament. At the time general opinion congratulated Bess on her advantageous match. Foster was careful with money, serious (if a little humourless), and uninterested in city life. Later Bess claimed she had married him under duress: "I really did on my knees ask not to marry Mr F. and said his character terrified me, and they both have since said it was their doing my being married to him," she told Georgiana.[7] However, her parents' letters suggest a different story—a love match between a respectable squire and a young bride impatient for her own establishment. "I like the young man better than ever," the Earl-Bishop told his daughter Mary, "and think him peculiarly suited to her."[8]

Whatever the truth, by 1780 the marriage was in jeopardy. Bess's father, who was busy supervising his building works, ordered his wife to bring the couple to heel. Bess was pregnant with her second child and the two were at Ickworth, bickering constantly. Lady Bristol obeyed reluctantly, complaining to Lady Mary, "With regard to the reconciliation, I do not think there is a ray of comfort or hope in it. It was totally against my opinion as to *happiness,* but your Father's orders and her *situation* call'd for it. . . . dejection and despair are wrote on her countenance, and tho' I have no doubt that time might wear out her *attachment,* I believe nothing *can remove* her disgust. . . . I have no hope of getting rid of him. . . ." She was also furious with her husband, whose sole motive in seeking a reconciliation was to avoid paying for his daughter's upkeep: "For his part I am convinced that he is perfectly well pleased—affection, vanity and avarice being all gratified."[9] Lady Bristol does not name the object of Bess's "attachment" but he was clearly not Mr. Foster, for whom Bess felt "disgust."

In public the Herveys blamed the breakdown of the marriage on Mr. Foster, who had seduced Bess's maid. This was obviously a factor in Bess's dislike. Nevertheless, she was willing to attempt a reconciliation, if only for the sake of her own two children, and was shocked when Foster demanded a complete separation. He ordered her to surrender their child and the infant as soon as it was weaned, refusing to pay a penny towards her support. The first act was legal in the eighteenth century as the father always had custody of his children, but the second was not under normal circumstances. Unless legally separated or divorced, a husband was liable for his wife's debts and most families ensured that marriage contracts contained provisions for their daughters if there was a separation. Either Bess's family had failed to do so, or Mr. Foster had evidence of his wife's adultery and threatened to divorce her if provoked.

In November 1781 Mrs. Dillon, a distant relation of the Herveys, visited Ickworth and was appalled by Lord Bristol's callousness: "Lady Elizabeth Foster has the most pleasing manner in the world. She is just at this moment in the most terrible situation. Her odious husband will settle so little on her that she must be dependent on her father, which is always an unpleasant thing. Her children, who are now here, are to be taken from her. All this makes her miserable. . . . [Lord Bristol] has not taken his seat, nor will he let Lady Bristol go to Court or to town."[10] The Earl was shortly to abandon his family in England and resume his jaunts across Europe. In 1782 he rented out their London house and locked his wife out of her rooms at Ickworth.

> Never was a story more proper for a novel than poor Lady Elizabeth Foster's [wrote Mrs. Dillon]. She is parted from her husband, but would you conceive any father with the income he has should talk of her living alone on such a scanty pittance as £300 a year! And this is the man who is ever talking of his love of hospitality and his desire to have his children about him! Might one not imagine that he would be oppos'd to a pretty young woman of her age living alone? It is incredible the cruelties that monster Foster made her undergo with him; her father knows it, owned him a villain, and yet, for fear she should fall on his hands again, tried first to persuade her to return to him.[11]

To compound matters, the Earl managed to "forget" Bess's allowance whenever it came due.

Mrs. Dillon's horror at Bess's situation—respectable but alone and without financial support—was understandable. Fanny Burney wrote *The Wanderer* to highlight the dreadful vulnerability of such women to pimps and exploitation. Their status demanded that appearances they could not afford should be maintained while the means to make an independent living were denied them. Bess's newly inherited title made it impossible for her to find work either as a governess or a paid companion.[12] She could easily fall for a man who offered her a better life as his mistress, hence

Mrs. Dillon's amazement at Lord Bristol's lack of concern. Many years later Bess tried to defend her subsequent conduct to her son:

> Pray remember, when you say that my enthusiasm has had a fair and well-shaped channel, that I was younger than you when I was without a guide; a wife and no husband, a mother and no children . . . by myself alone to steer through every peril that surrounds a young woman so situated; books, the arts, and a wish to be loved and approved . . . a proud determination to be my own letter of recommendation . . . with perhaps a manner that pleased, realised my projects, and gained me friends wherever I have been.[13]

A wish to be loved and approved, and a manner that pleased: it was an irresistible combination to Georgiana. Bess's desire to serve her new friend was greater than anything Georgiana had ever encountered before. Both the Devonshires were also deeply moved by her misfortunes. "If you see Lady Bristol," wrote Georgiana to her mother, "I wish you would say as from yourself that the D and I are very happy in seeing a great deal of Lady Erne and Lady Eliz., for that strange man Lord Bristol is, I have a notion, acting the strangest of parts by Lady Eliz and we thought perhaps if it was known we saw something of them it might make him ashamed of not doing something for her."[14]

It never occurred to Georgiana that Bess's untiring enthusiasm for her company might be inspired by her own poverty. The idea that her generosity made Bess a *de facto* paid companion never entered her mind. Bess was good with the Duke, too; indeed he appeared to like her almost as much, and Georgiana congratulated herself on discovering such a perfect friend. Bess realized that both Georgiana and the Duke were lonely—Georgiana obviously so, but the Duke suffered no less in his own way. Since Charlotte Spencer's death he had been without steady female companionship. Georgiana was too involved in her own life, and too much in awe of him to take the place of Charlotte. Bess could see that they both needed a confidante, a role that she was very happy to play, although it required her to act two quite different parts: with the Duke she was submissive and flirtatious; with Georgiana she was passionate and sensitive. Almost everyone except the Devonshires saw through Bess immediately. Much later James Hare gently tried to explain to Georgiana what all their friends had thought for many years. "I agree with you in every word you say of Ly Elizabeth, there cannot be a warmer, steadier, more disinterested friend: [but] she shews, perhaps, too great a distrust in her natural graces, for I never will be brought to say that she is not affected, tho' I allow it is the most pardonable sort of affectation I ever met with, and is become quite natural."[15]

The seventh of June was Georgiana's twenty-fifth birthday and Lady Spencer used the occasion to denounce her daughter's mode of living. "In your dangerous path of life you have almost unavoidably amassed a great deal of useless trash—gathered weeds instead of flowers," she wrote sternly. "You live so constantly in public you cannot live for your own soul."[16] The harshness of the letter stunned Georgiana, who replied that on her "nervous days" she cried whenever she thought about it: "When the 7th of June gave you a Daughter, wild, unworthy, careless as she is, and of course, a cause of many fears, many troubles to you, yet it gave her to you, with a heart that longs and dares too, to think it shall make it up to you."[17] The following week she repeated her promise, pleading, "I could write it in my blood Dearest M."[18]

Feeling hurt and rejected, Georgiana turned to the sympathetic and understanding Bess for comfort. She could confide in her new friend as she had done with Mary Graham, and without any of the inconvenience—Bess had no husband or home to call her away; there was no question of their being parted. The news that Bess had accompanied Georgiana and the Duke to Plympton camp for the annual military review alarmed Lady Spencer. She had no illusions about Bess, but she was astonished that both Georgiana and the Duke had fallen under her spell. She gathered from her daughter's letters that the three were inseparable, sharing Plympton House together, passing their evenings reading Shakespeare aloud. Bess never seemed to leave Georgiana alone, nor was there any facet of Georgiana's life closed off to her. Little realizing its bad effect, Bess wrote on Georgiana's letters to Lady Spencer, addressing her as if she were an old friend and adding postscripts about her daughter's health and good behaviour. Sometimes she wrote almost the whole body of the letter on the excuse that her friend was too tired to write. She was always deferential, but her familiarity with Georgiana grated on Lady Spencer. Her tone revealed a person desperate to make a permanent home for herself.

The harmonious threesome remained at Plympton until the end of September, when Bess developed a bad cough. Georgiana complained she was being very annoying, loudly insisting one minute that she was perfectly all right, and the next admitting to a troublesome cough for the past two years, "tho' she considers all this very ridiculous, and says she is only a little nervous."[19] Georgiana became anxious and full of self-doubt. On September 30 she wrote, "I did not go out as I was sulky and uneasy and locked myself up all morning."[20] She admitted she was taking sedatives again which made her groggy and prevented her from receiving friends.[21]

Georgiana blamed her unhappiness on her infertility.

> You accepted *Zyllia* [she wrote to Lady Spencer, referring to a play she had written about a girl who discovers that her best friend is her mother], and therefore I am going to open the foolish nonsense of my heart, to my *friend*—I am discontented with myself—I feel a sentiment something like uneasiness and envy at the accounts I receive of Lady George [Cavendish] and her grossesse. I did not mind it at all at first, but now that it draws near its event I feel a sensation at it that I hate myself for, and yet nobody can form more sincere and heartfelt vows than I do for her well-being—I should not feel this if it did not appear to me that there was a possibility of my being so, I am convinc'd could I master the lying in bed, could I lead a strengthening kind of life, and have a calm heart and mind for some time together that it would succeed—and strong as my wishes and persuasions are, so weak am I that I yield to things that hurt me, with my eyes open— you must direct and save me Dst M, for you only can.[22]

There were other worries: her debts for one. On October 19 Lady Spencer told her that she had paid some money on her behalf to a Mr. Hicks who had seemed quite shifty.

> In short [she wrote, somewhat alarmed by the meeting], I suspect some mischief or other—that you have bespoke more things than you can possibly pay for and have given him things of value in exchange. If this is the case I wish you would let me enquire into the particulars, for I am afraid you are often much impos'd upon—at all events I beg you will never part with Jewells. I have often told you they are not your own and should be look'd upon as things only entrusted to your care—do not pass over this article without answering.[23]

Georgiana was, as usual, mired in debt, but it was not the only reason for her distress. The envy she felt towards Lady George had a much closer object.

The ease with which Bess had made herself the centre of attention during her illness had been a revelation to Georgiana. She deeply resented the Duke's behaviour over her and had suffered pangs of jealousy when he earnestly discussed Bess's health with the doctors. Conveniently, Georgiana then fell ill herself. It had the desired effect of turning Bess's attention back to her and she wrote contentedly, "I was bad with my head but as I have already told you, I was so well nursed by the Duke and Ly Eliz that there was quite a comfort in being ill."[24] The crisis was over, and Bess was once more her special friend. Yet she was unable to rid herself of the suspicion that Bess was not quite all that she seemed. She tried to explain her feelings to Lady Spencer in a long letter on October 29:

> You will not suspect me of overdeep penetration, but I very often have, more than you would imagine, amus'd myself with observing the characters of those around me. I do not know if this is a good occupation, it is not least a negative one for it does neither good nor harm to myself or anybody else. It has happened to me with people who have influence over me, to have perfectly seized the reason of their wishing me to do some one thing or other which I did not like to do, and that tho' they did not disclose their real motive, I have been saying to myself all the time they have been persuading me, "I know what you are at and why you wish me to do so and so," and yet with this full conviction, instead of owning it and inspite of disliking the thing, I have done it because I was desired and have pretended to believe every word that was said to me, so that I actually have taken more pains to appear a Dupe than most people do, to show they cannot be outwitted. In things of consequence I hope I should be stronger, but in common events I have so great an antipathy to the word *no* that I expose myself to many inconveniences not to pronounce it. It seems almost as if the activity of my nature spent itself in my mind, and gave me force to feel and reason, but that tir'd with the effort it yielded to indolence the moment I was to perform.[25]

Lady Spencer gave no sign that she understood Georgiana's cry, and in her reply merely agreed, "your stopping short of acting so, must be an effect of Indolence and will I hope with a little time be got the better of."[26] It was only many years later, when suffering forced her to acknowledge things she would ordinarily have buried, that Lady Spencer accepted she might have been responsible for fostering a certain weakness in Georgiana's character. "I cannot deceive myself," she wrote sadly, "that to that easiness of temper and fear of giving pain which they both (the Duchess especially) inherit from me they owe the want of that persevering resolution which would have led them into much good and away from much evil."[27] All Lady Spencer could see in 1782, however, was an interloper who was stealing her own rightful place in Georgiana's heart. She complained about Bess's influence:

> Those were happy days, my dearest child, when every thought of your innocent heart came rushing out without a wish to disguise it, when my eternal rummages were born with perfect composure without any previous precautions and no little drawers or porte-feuille were reserved. . . . I see you on the edge of a thousand precipices, in danger of losing the confidence of those who are dearest to you. . . . I see you running with eagerness to those—must I miscall them friends?—Who tho' their intentions may not be wrong, are by constantly talking to you on subjects which are always better avoided becoming imperceptibly your most hurtful enemies, all these and more keep me on the rack.[28]

Lady Spencer spent much of her time thinking up ways to get rid of her rival. She asked Georgiana and the Duke to visit them at Hotwells in Bristol, politely adding that Bess would not be welcome since Lord Spencer was "too ill to see a stranger with any comfort."[29] Bess was bitterly disappointed to be called a stranger after all her carefully composed postscripts. "Poor little Bess," as she styled herself, went into hysterics at the thought of being left alone and whipped up the Devonshires into an equally distraught state. Georgiana hurriedly wrote to her mother, "Lady Eliz. comes with us, Dst Mama, and poor little soul, it is impossible it should be otherwise." She tried to soften the blow by pointing to Bess's obedient nature: "My father need not mind her in the least, she is the quietest little thing and will sit and draw in a corner of the room, or be sent out of the room, or do whatever you please."[30] She ended the letter with the only sentence that brought comfort to Lady Spencer: "I hope to see her set out for Nice within the month."

The two weeks in Bristol were strained and awkward for everyone except Bess. If she was aware of the tensions around her, she gave no sign of it: her smile never dropped and her eagerness to oblige never flagged. Lady Spencer, however, noticed that she ate very little; it almost appeared as if she were deliberately starving herself. Nearly every morning the Duke and

Bess left Georgiana with her to go riding together; they returned before supper and joined the group, playing cards or reading, without looking or glancing at each other again. Their behaviour was suspicious enough for anyone to question their relationship, but Georgiana chose to remain ignorant. In only a short space of time she had become so dependent on Bess that the possibility of losing her devotion was too painful to contemplate.

The Duke left for London after ten days and Bess remained in Bristol with Georgiana and Lady Spencer. His departure enabled Lady Spencer to examine Bess's relationship with her daughter. When the Duke was not present she appeared to think of nothing but Georgiana's comfort. She displayed a combination of servility and bossiness, taking a great delight in fussing round her. She hardly ever used "I," Lady Spencer noticed; it was always "we." Her voice, hair, and clothes were all arranged in a faithful, if not disconcerting, imitation of Georgiana's—Lady Spencer was sure that most of her clothes had once belonged to her daughter. Yet Georgiana not only didn't seem to mind Bess's behaviour; she encouraged it. They used code words and nicknames for each other which made Lady Spencer feel excluded. The Duke was called Canis, which was obviously a reference to his fondness for dogs. But for reasons which have never been clear Georgiana was Mrs. Rat, and Bess, Racky. Lady Spencer feared that Harriet would also become infected by Bess's charm. "I do beg you will comply with my earnest request of letting me know at the very first moment of anything that distresses, vexes, or ails you," she wrote anxiously, "unless you think any body else has a sincerer affection for you and is from that more worthy of your confidence."[31]

Shortly after their return to London Georgiana announced that she was pregnant again. She was healthier than she had been for many years, drinking less and eating properly without the destructive cycle of bingeing and starving. But her mental state seemed precarious: she was beset by "feels" which made her cry constantly and prevented her from sleeping. "I wrote you a letter in very bad spirits this morning," Georgiana confessed to her mother on December 1. "It is but justice to tell you how much I am mended now and not all uncomfortable, the feels [are] abated and am not near so nervous." But the spectre of Bess loomed: "Lady Eliz. desires me to express to you," she added, "how much she is touch'd and flatter'd by your goodness to her . . . and how sensible she is of any interest you take in her."[32] Lady Spencer's response to Bess's overtures was curt: "I hope Lady Eliz does not lose sight of going abroad."[33]

Georgiana's emotional state disturbed Lady Spencer, who feared it

might induce a miscarriage. She told Harriet she was sure the ones she
herself had suffered as a young woman had been caused by an "agitation
of spirits."[34] But she had neither the sensitivity nor the imagination to understand that Bess might be the cause of her daughter's torment, and her
advice to Georgiana was limited to the practical. Firstly she suggested that
Georgiana should stay at home; otherwise she would be accused of loving
parties "better than a child."[35] Secondly she recommended laudanum;
"take a few drops (5 or 6) . . . if you feel any violent [attacks] or agitation. . . . be assured whatever may happen *this time,* your health is much
improved in the main, that if you can but contrive by any means this winter, to keep your mind and body in a calm and quiet state, I have no doubt
of your soon obtaining all you wish. . . . do not make yourself unhappy."[36]
Finally, as usual, disturbed by Georgiana's fear that she was too sinful to
take the Sacrament, she urged her to put her trust in God. She enlisted
Harriet's help in persuading Georgiana that it was "not necessary to be too
scrupulous about what is past—the merits of the Saviour are more than
sufficient to atone for the blackest of crimes, of which she certainly has
none to reproach herself with."[37]

Bess was due to pack her bags and leave for France on December 25.
The Devonshires had officially engaged her to be Charlotte Williams's
governess at £300 a year and she was to take her pupil abroad for the winter. The plan had a neatness to it which pleased everyone. It solved the
problem of Charlotte, who had not thrived with her nurse Mrs. Gardner,
offered hope for Bess's health, and provided her with an income. The
Duke was firmly convinced that only the warm conditions of the south of
France would cure Bess's terrible cough. There may have been other reasons for Bess going away.* She begged Georgiana and the Duke to keep
her informed of "the stories you hear of me, pray communicate to me that
at least I may be justified to you, and that you may know truth from false-

---

* There is also a vague hint in surviving letters that Bess had become, or contemplated
becoming, the mistress of that great seducer the Duke of Dorset. The clues come from
gossip repeated by Lady George Cavendish, who baldly stated that Bess had an affair with
Dorset, but also from some little admissions in Bess's own letters. In one fragment she
refers to her separation from Mr. Foster and that she told him, "I never would quit him in
any misfortune—it was after all that, that he went down to Ickworth and my mother would
not see him. Yet I think I should not have answered at all, but to deny the thing." She does
not say what she should have denied to Mr. Foster, except that they were "imprudencies,
which though no cause of my separation were subjects of blame." Chatsworth 532.4: Bess
to GD, circa Sept. 1783.

hood." The threat of some scandal would explain why she was sent abroad for so long when the friendship was in its early stages.

Georgiana was distraught at her departure. "I am to lose my dear little Bess and my dear Little Charlotte tomorrow," she wrote. "It will do them so much good that I don't allow myself to be much vex'd. But I shall miss them both very much."[38] Lady Spencer hoped, as much as Bess feared, that the separation would mean the end of her reign over the Devonshires. But neither reckoned on the strength of Georgiana's attachment. "My dearest, dearest, dearest Bess, my lovely friend," she wrote in a letter accompanying a box stuffed with gifts. "If I am mistaken and that you are grown "*Ah te voilà ma petite*" to your G. throw this into the sea. *Mais non c'est impossible, pardonnez moi, mon ange, Je crois que je vous dis quelquefois des brutalités pour avoir le bonheur de m'entendre contredire.*"*[39] Bess's mother, Lady Bristol, informed her daughter that Georgiana had written and visited several times just to talk to her. "You have done well, most certainly," she congratulated, "to leave your interest in her hands."[40]

---

* But that is not possible. Forgive me, my angel. I believe I say these terrible things merely in order to hear them contradicted.

CHAPTER 7

AN UNSTABLE COALITION

1783

Her Grace the Duchess of Devonshire has determined not to appear in public till after her lying-in; as she had long been leader of the fashion, we hope the ladies will follow her example, and get into the straw as fast as possible.

Morning Herald and Daily Advertiser, *February 8, 1783*

Once Bess had set sail on the packet to France, enriched with money, new clothes, and a letter of introduction to the Polignacs, Georgiana was free to resume her former activities. Her long absence from London during 1782 had reduced her to the role of spectator of most of the developments affecting the Whigs. Defying reports by the *Morning Herald* and other newspapers that she would withdraw from public life until the end of her pregnancy, Georgiana now re-established herself as Fox's ally and political confidante. He frequently stopped by Devonshire House to discuss his worries. The strain he was under showed in his bloodshot eyes and in the weight he had put on since the previous summer. "He says ev'ry body is grown fat even Mr Hare," Georgiana replied to her mother's enquiry; "and that the people who are said to be thin are only call'd so because they have not increas'd with the rest of the world."[1]

The Rockingham-Shelburne Coalition had been in trouble from the beginning. George III would only talk to Lord Shelburne and pointedly ignored Lord Rockingham and all the Whigs' requests for patronage. As early as June 1782 some Whigs were already condemning the coalition as unworkable. Then Lord Rockingham came down with the flu; within two weeks he was dead. He had been in office for just three months, after almost two decades in opposition. Shortly after Rockingham's death, Fox became disillusioned with the coalition government and surrendered his seal of office. Several other Whigs followed suit.

The man who benefited most from Fox's resignation was the twenty-three-year-old William Pitt. Fox's mother, Lady Caroline Holland, had met Pitt when he was a child and immediately saw that he possessed such vital qualities as patience and attention to detail which her own son lacked. "*Not eight years old,*" she wrote, "and really the cleverest child I ever saw *and brought up so proper in his behaviour that, mark my words,* that little boy will be a thorn in Charles's side as long as he lives." Pitt's maiden speech in Parliament, in 1781, had indicated that his political sympathies on economical and parliamentary reform lay with the Whigs. Notwithstanding the fact that their fathers had been bitter enemies all their working lives, Fox hailed him as a rising new star.* He was generous enough to perceive the young man's potential and within a month of Pitt taking his seat Fox had put him up for Brooks's. Despite their contrasting physiques—Pitt was tall and slender with pointed features and an almost hairless face—they were both heavy drinkers and, for the first few months at least, seemed to have much in common. But Pitt was too proud and too sure of his own destiny to play the part of the eager young acolyte for long.

By 1782 Pitt had disentangled himself from Fox's embrace and made it clear to all parties that, as the son of the former Prime Minister the Earl of Chatham, he expected to be treated seriously. When Fox's resignation created three spaces in the cabinet, Shelburne, thinking the young man would be easy to manage, invited Pitt to take Lord John Cavendish's place as Chancellor of the Exchequer. To Fox's indignation his former protégé stepped into office over the heads of the departing Whigs. From that moment Fox and Pitt were implacable rivals.

The unpopular Shelburne found himself rapidly losing support as MPs gravitated to either Lord North or Fox. He had to form a coalition with

* William Pitt the Elder had so loathed his rival that in 1756, while advising the Duke of Devonshire on the new ministry, he blocked Henry Fox's appointment as Chancellor of the Exchequer in favour of a less qualified colleague. The Fox family's resentment knew no bounds after Pitt received an earldom from George III in 1763, when two years previously Henry Fox had been fobbed off with a mere barony.

one of them or he would find himself outvoted in the House of Commons. His difficulties were increased by William Pitt's hatred of Lord North, whom he despised more than Fox. That left Shelburne with the only option of joining with Fox, which was not likely given the mutual antipathy between the two men.

Georgiana saw Fox during these negotiations when it was by no means clear whether any of the three parties would be able to stifle its dislike of the other two for long enough to make a pact.[2] On February 11, 1783, Shelburne ordered Pitt to meet with Fox in private to see if they could reconcile their differences. In the course of the negotiations Pitt made contemptuous remarks about the Whig party, which Fox took personally and never forgave him.

Shelburne's failure to woo Fox pushed the Whigs into an unlikely pairing with Lord North. The ex–Prime Minister had several cautious discussions with Fox and, despite their previously bitter encounters, they agreed to put their past enmity behind them. As soon as the Whigs and North's supporters began voting together Shelburne was lost. "The political bustle still continues," Georgiana wrote to Bess shortly before Shelburne accepted defeat. "Lord Shelburne is not yet out, but today's question will probably do it—Ld Camden, the Duke of Grafton and Gl Conway have resigned. . . . Canis sends his love to you but he must go to the House of Commons and therefore has not time to write today."[3]

On February 24 Shelburne resigned in the face of overwhelming numbers against him. Once again George III resisted the idea of allowing the Whigs back into office. He begged Pitt to form his own government, but the young politician declined, knowing he would have no support. Lord North refused to renege on his deal with Fox and come in on his own. The King approached every senior parliamentary figure, and a few minor ones, including a cousin of Pitt's. "Get me Mr Thomas Pitt or Mr Thomas Anybody," he cried. Seeing that no one was prepared to challenge Fox, the King contemplated leaving England. He even drafted his abdication speech. Finally, though, on April 1 North, Fox, and the Duke of Portland tripped up the stairs of St. James's to receive the Great Seals of State, loudly congratulating themselves on their success. North became Prime Minister, Fox was once more Foreign Secretary, and Lord John Cavendish the Chancellor of the Exchequer.

Georgiana kept Bess informed of political developments as they unfolded, although Bess was more concerned with her own affairs—chiefly with the behaviour of Mr. Foster. He had made some enquiries about Bess since learning of her friendship with the Devonshires, wanting to know who was giving her money, among other things. Georgiana and the Duke replied coldly to his letters but they gave Georgiana an idea. "Do you know the kind appearance in Mr Foster's letter has set me wild about a scheme," she told Bess. "As to your ever living with him again that your own Dr feelings must decide—But I think it plain that Mr Foster's seeing that his bad or good conduct to you *now* will be known to more than your family, as he is a vain man, seems to actuate him to behave better. Therefore I would wish you to keep the good terms you are upon now on the same footing."[4] Georgiana advised her to hint that if he would allow his younger son to be educated at school in England, the Devonshires would act as godparents throughout his career. They would pay for his upkeep so there would be no pecuniary disadvantage to either her or Foster.

Georgiana's favourite subject, after politics, was their relationship and how it would be when Bess returned. She managed to be explicit and yet circumspect at the same time:

I promised you my Dearest Dearest Love, a plan, of my ideas for your future life—here it is, but remember, that one word of yours as to any other intentions will be adopted by me, unless indeed they were such as would hurt your health or deprive me of the happiness of seeing you.

The summit of my wishes would be that whilst you remain abroad you would not only attend strictly to your dear health, but likewise to every amusement for your mind that would not be hurtful to it or imprudent, for it is certain that the line of conduct you have used in your present situation, young and beautiful as you are, is absolutely necessary. . . . Tho' for fear of the agitation it would cause us both and of the hurt it would do your dear health, you must not come before I am brought to bed. . . . When you do return it will be to Devonshire House, for a month at least, and as your little pride, and perhaps circumstances, may make it as well that you should not absolutely live in the house always with your brother and sister, I will look out immediately for a house for you near us, on condition that you are less in it than here. The summers you shall pass at Chatsworth. . . . the autumns hunting with Canis and the winters in London. You shall have your children with you, or at least Augustus. You shall be on the best and most friendly terms with all your family and *all your cousins,* but independent of them, and your Brother and

Sister—Canis and G—shall be the only ones whom you shall allow to share with you.[5]

Bess must never leave her, she insisted. One paragraph of hers was blacked out by a later hand: "Am I too presuming in making myself and Canis the principal movers in the scheme of your future life? But remember . . ." are the tantalizing opening words of the inked-over passage. Hidden here, perhaps, are references to Bess's previous liaison with Dorset. The passage may also have revealed something of the inner workings of Bess's relationship with the Devonshires, and explained the sexual dynamics between them. It is clear, however, despite the erasures and the imprecise language, that Georgiana could not tolerate an affair between Bess and her husband. She did not say it outright, but her repeated references to the Duke as "your dear Brother" must have left Bess in no doubt about the kind of relationship she envisaged between them.

Georgiana's feelings for Bess threatened to overcome her devotion to the party. She was horrified when the Duke of Portland suggested that her husband should become Lord Lieutenant of Ireland. The third Duke of Devonshire had governed Ireland for eight years between 1737 and 1745, and, since the huge Cavendish estates over there generated a large part of the family wealth, the choice seemed extremely apposite. But Bess would not be able to accompany them because of Mr. Foster's injunction that she stay out of Ireland. "Ah, Bess, I am half dead," Georgiana wrote when she relayed the news on April 5. "I can only tell you I am afraid we are to go to Ireland. . . . I declare to God I am half mad."[6] On the one hand, she at last had an opportunity to play an official role in politics: she would have her own court at Dublin, her own duties, and the Duke would have to shake off his lethargy and behave like a statesman. On the other hand, she would be separated from Bess for months at a stretch. The dilemma tore her apart; she made up her mind to go but then instantly regretted doing so. "I found it so much the wish of the Duke of Portland and the whole country, that Canis should go, that I took a resolution and went and told him yesterday that I not only advised him but wished it. I am sure I did right—but I am half mad. Only, if I do go, I will make Mr Foster give me Augustus—Bess, Dearest Bess," she wailed. A few hours later she scratched another note: "My fate is deciding. I find Canis gone out and the Duchess [of Portland] is gone in to the Duke of Portland to know what has passed. Oh Bess, every sensation I feel but heightens my adoration of you."[7]

The matter was decided by the Duke, who for similar reasons disliked

the idea of moving to Ireland. They were to stay. Georgiana tried to persuade her brother to go in their place. It was partly family pride which mo-
tivated her and partly a wish to remain vicariously connected to the office.
She told him that everyone was "anxious to see you in a situation that
would do justice to your abilities and to the rectitude of your heart and
mind, and that besides it would be essential service to your country and
strengthen the administration you support."[8] George, however, de-
murred. He felt too inexperienced to cope with the volatile situation in
Ireland. The country was on the verge of revolution, and the Irish parliament in almost open revolt against Dublin Castle. Why, he asked, if the
service was essential, was the Duke not prepared to do his patriotic duty?
Georgiana replied truthfully that she had tried to change the Duke's mind,

> tho' I was averse to it, especially in my present situation. When I
> did everything to persuade him I was certain as they were that his
> name, his family, and his extraordinary good judgement and ability
> would enable him to succeed. But I own I trembled at the thought
> of what his hitherto great inaptitude to business would cost him
> when obliged to force himself to it. For he has that kind of turn
> that being forced to anything gives him a disgust to it—this is not
> the case with you.

She argued against each of her brother's objections and even engaged the
Duke of Portland to try to persuade him: "I think in all events you should
speak again to the Duke of Portland and I write this to tell you he will expect you tomorrow any time before or after twelve."[9] But George remained firm and, in the end, the Whigs allowed Lord Temple, Shelburne's
man, to remain in his post.

Although she was five months pregnant, Georgiana continued to host
political dinners several times a week. When the Duc de Chartres—a
cousin of Louis XVI—and several other members of the French court
came to London they treated Georgiana as if she were their official hostess. Lady Mary Coke recorded jealously that they "did not go anywhere
but by [her] direction."[10] The new French ambassador, the Comte d'Adhémar, was already a regular visitor at Devonshire House, having arrived
in London two months earlier with a letter of introduction from the
Duchesse de Polignac. He was not a professional diplomat and owed his
position to his friendship with the Polignac clan. The Little Po, sweet and
pliant as she was, allowed herself to be ruled by her violent lover, the

Comte de Vaudreuil, and her greedy sister-in-law Comtesse Diane. Un-
blemished by ambition or greed, she was an easy cipher, enabling Vaudreuil to obtain gifts and favours for his friends. The Baron de Bésenval
and d'Adhémar were his two great cronies. According to the Comte de la
Marck, d'Adhémar "was, of all the Polignac set, the one with most wit, but
not less ability than the Baron de Bésenval to attain his ends. . . . he sang
well, was an excellent comedian, wrote delightful verses. That was more
than was needed for success in society."[11] Such was the man who represented France's interests in the continuing peace negotiations between the
two countries. Georgiana did not particularly like his silky manner, but
she accepted his company because of his connections. For d'Adhémar's
part, the weekly invitation to the elegant dinners at Devonshire House
gave him access to all the social and political gossip he needed for his secret reports to Paris.

On May 8, 1783, Georgiana told her mother that the Duc de Chartres
was sporting oversized buttons with pornographic pictures on his waist-
coat, "which my sister very nearly died of."[12] The entertainments she was
providing for the French visitors were so original and lavish that even the
London Chronicle, which normally eschewed reporting such frivolities,
printed full descriptions:

> On Sunday morning, the Duke and Duchess of Devonshire gave a
> most elegant breakfast to a select number of the nobility at Burling-
> ton House, Chiswick. The natural beauties of this delightful spot
> were enlivened on this occasion by the most pleasing decorations
> that an elegant fancy, controlled by a just judgement, could possibly
> supply. The trees and shrubberies were hung with festoons of flow-
> ers, desposed in easy and unaffected variations. All the figures were
> ornamented with sashes of roses, intermingled with oranges and
> myrtles. The company began to assemble about 1 o'clock, among
> which the most distinguishable were the Prince of Wales, the Duc de
> Chartres, attended by the Duc de Fitzjames, and most of the foreign
> nobility, besides whom were Lords Carlisle, Althorp, Jersey, Mel-
> bourne, Duncannon, Herbert, Colonels Fitzpatrick, St. Leger,
> Ladies Melbourne, Duncannon, with many more select friends of
> the Duchess's. The company were entertained with tea, coffee,
> chocolate, fruits of all sorts, ices, etc., til four o'clock when they re-
> turned to town.[13]

Georgiana's popularity with the foreigners inspired envy among the *ton:* not only did she enjoy first place in society; her party was also now in power—it was all too much. Lady Mary Coke raged,

> As her Grace seems to fancy by the Duke of Portland being First Minister and the Prince of Wales always at her house, she is to carry any point she has a mind to, for these reasons, I am not sorry she has met with a repulse. Her Grace asked the Prince of Wales to desire the Queen to let the French ladies see Her Majesty's house . . . [which the King refused] So the French ladies will return to Paris with the certainty that the Duchess of Devonshire and the bon ton does not absolutely govern the nation.[14]

It hurt Bess to hear about Georgiana's success while she was plodding through France with the ungainly Charlotte. Reading of the gulf between their lives was cruel, but the days when no letters arrived were worse. "Dearest ever ever dearest Love," she wrote in June, "why have I no letters from you? I cannot express nor describe the anxiety I feel from it, nor how my peace depends on everything that concerns you . . . how necessary you are to my heart."[15] She wanted to know all Georgiana's movements even though what she learned only made her more unhappy. Georgiana obliged, little imagining how the news affected her friend.

However, the government was not running as smoothly as outsiders imagined. The King was determined to remove the Whigs as soon as he found the appropriate means and the Prince of Wales seemed to provide the opportunity. "The whole world is in an uproar," wrote Georgiana on June 17, referring to a row over the Prince's desire to have a proper allowance and his own household. Now that he was twenty-one he wanted a separate establishment of his own, but he had already run up so many debts that he needed an extra one-off payment of £100,000 to clear himself. The King refused even to consider handing over such a large amount to his delinquent son, and the Prince found that few MPs sympathized with his position. The Whigs tried to make him see the damage he would cause his political friends if he insisted on trying to force the measure through Parliament: half the cabinet had threatened to resign if Fox gave in to the Prince's demand, and yet he could not, having promised the Prince that he would obtain the money for him, go back on his word.

Fox was in despair over his promise to the Prince. He asked the Duke to have a private talk with the Prince. "He [the Prince] is now in the next room with C. Fox, and has been with Canis before," Georgiana scribbled in a hasty letter to Bess on June 20. "You would have lov'd him for the manner he [Fox] talked of Canis when he went out. He said 'there is the man whose generous and feeling heart and right head and understanding may be reposed in without fear, and that's the man, who, if his indolence did not get the better of him, ought to govern the country.' "[16] Notwithstanding Fox's confidence in him, the Duke failed to move the Prince.

That night Fox predicted the end of the coalition government in a matter of days. He informed Lord Northington that the tensions between himself and his colleagues meant "it will not outlive tomorrow."[17] But while Fox sat at Brooks's, cursing his promise to the Prince, Georgiana took it upon herself to persuade the Prince to drop his demand. Knowing her voice carried its own authority, she wrote the Prince a frank letter, explaining why he would be making a terrible mistake if he caused the Whigs to resign:

> . . . attempting to carry this thro by force would be impossible—as neither Lord North or Lord John [Cavendish] would support it or go out on it—& in the case that it was attempted to be carryd thro' in these circumstances it must put an end to the Administration in 3 days. The thing therefore to be considered is whether it is not in the power of the present Administration to serve you more by staying in than going out. . . . Mr Fox looks upon himself as bound in honour to carry it thro for you & will go out rather than give up, unless you release him; but great delicacy must be used in releasing him—& and you must do it, if you think it right, as if it was of your own accord.[18]

Georgiana's letter made the Prince realize that the situation was hopeless. He capitulated and accepted the lower sum of £30,000. Thanks to her intervention the coalition was safe for the moment. Georgiana's action proved her own thesis—that great consequences often develop from "causes little imagined." No one in England knew that the fate of the government rested on a woman's influence with a spoilt youth. In five years Georgiana had matured from a girl parading in military uniform into an astute political negotiator.

CHAPTER 8

A BIRTH AND A DEATH

1783—1784

The decorative appendage of female dress and the newest taste, and highest ton, is the golden collar, epigrammatically bemottoed. Her Grace of Devonshire is said to be the fair inventress of this fashion, whose enviable collar bears this sportive inscription: "Strayed from Devonshire House!"

Morning Herald and Daily Advertiser, *August 12, 1783*

The conduct of the young, beauteous and virtuous Duchess of Devonshire is a pattern worthy of imitation; finding lately that deep play and hazard was become frequent at all fashionable routs in the beginning of this winter, at her first grand rout for the season, had written in large characters in every chamber "no higher play than crown whist permitted here, other games in proportion and no dice."

Morning Post, *February 11, 1784*

The peace negotiations with the French and American delegates, overseen by Charles Fox, had not yet been concluded when Georgiana retreated from public life for the last weeks of her pregnancy. Her confinement was a great inconvenience for the negotiators, who had relied on her suppers at Devonshire House for informal meetings. The Comte d'Adhémar had grown accustomed to dropping by every day; Georgiana's absence made him realize the extent to which he had needed her help. "Mr Fox is careful to avoid every possible opportunity to talk politics with me," he reported to his superiors in France. "The house of the Duchess of Devonshire, where I usually meet him informally, has been closed to us all for three weeks, owing to the lady's confinement. The painful consequences of this event will doubtless make her invisible for even longer, until she is obliged to leave for the country and I shall be deprived entirely of this daily means of seeing Mr Fox."[1]

Georgiana whiled away the time with Harriet, who was also eight months pregnant. Duncannon had taken to spending most nights away, and Harriet generally spent her days at Devonshire House. She knew little of his activities except that he was gambling heavily at Brooks's; this much he let her know because his losses made him irritable. In the sanctuary of Devonshire House the two women amused themselves by experimenting with new hats and drawing patterns for dresses. The fashion for false hips and bottoms made of cork to round out the figure, and padded breasts to fill out the bodice had been in vogue since the 1770s. Georgiana added a new element: the false front to disguise pregnancy. She showed her designs to her friends; they were so well received that the false fronts were soon worn even by women who were not pregnant. Georgiana was also responsible for the unprecedented sales of the "picture hat": wide-brimmed hats, worn with a large sash and adorned with drooping feathers. She had posed in one of her own design, perching it stylishly on the side of her head, for her portrait by Gainsborough. After he exhibited the painting, women up and down the country ordered their milliners to make them a copy of the "Duchess of Devonshire's picture hat."[2]

Although Georgiana was no longer receiving visitors, enquiries about her health arrived every day and the newspapers monitored her condition with keen interest. The only person who was not excited by Georgiana's pregnancy was the Duke. He was convinced that the baby would be a girl. Lady Mary Coke bumped into him and said she would congratulate him properly when his son was born. He looked at her and "laughed on one side of his mouth and told me not to bother."[3]

On July 6 Harriet gave birth to Frederick, her second boy. A week later, on the twelfth, Georgiana went into labour herself. She described the event to Bess:

> I was laid on a couch in the middle of the room. My Mother and Dennis supported me. Canis was at the door, and the Duchess of Portland sometimes bending over me and screaming with me, and sometimes running to the end of the room and to him. I thought the pain I suffered was so great from being unusual to me, but I find since I had a very hard time. Towards the end, some symptoms made

me think the child was dead. I said so, and Dr Denman only said there was no reason to think so but we must submit to providence. I had then no doubt and watching my mother's fine eyes . . . I saw she thought it dead, which they all did except Denman who dared not say too much. When it came into the world I said, "only let it be alive." The little child seemed to move as it lay by me but I was not sure when all at once it cried. Oh, God, I cried and was quite hysterical. The Duchess and my mother were overcome and cried and all kissed me.[4]

The baby was a girl as the Duke had feared. However, Georgiana insisted to Bess that he was as pleased with the child as she was. At least it proved that she was capable of bearing a son.* They decided to call the baby Georgiana Dorothy—Dorothy after her aunt and godmother, the Duchess of Portland. The Prince of Wales and Lord John Cavendish also agreed to be godparents. In accordance with custom, Georgiana lay with Little G, as she called her, for a month. But she refused to adhere to the rules which demanded her seclusion in a tightly sealed room. Visitors found the windows wide open to let in the summer breeze, and Georgiana nursing her baby, propped up by thick, white lace pillows. "[Little G] is very much admired," she wrote to Bess. "Her cradle, robes, baskets, etc., are, I am afraid, foolishly magnificent. . . . She has a present coming from the Queen of France, but I don't know what it is yet."[5]

Georgiana decided to breastfeed Little G herself, still an unusual step among the aristocracy. The *Morning Post* applauded her, remarking how sad it was "that females in high life should generally be such strangers to the duty of a mother, as to render one instance to the contrary so singular."[6] Her refusal to employ a wet nurse was a brave act of defiance.[7] The Cavendishes were annoyed and tried to bully her into changing her mind. As far as they were concerned, there was no good reason why she should not employ a healthy country girl while she got on with the business of producing an heir. On August 6 a harassed Georgiana wrote to her mother,

---

* Newspapers were unsure whether to congratulate Georgiana or commiserate with the Duke. The *Morning Herald* was typical: "We are extremely happy to inform our readers that her Grace the Duchess of Devonshire was brought to bed on Saturday morning at 5 o'clock. . . . the satisfaction on this happy occasion is perhaps a little impaired by the sex of the infant. . . . The complimentary enquiries yesterday at Devonshire House were more numerous and from persons of higher distinction than were, perhaps, ever known under similar circumstances." *Morning Herald and Daily Advertiser,* July 14, 1783.

"what makes [them] abuse suckling is their impatience for my having a boy, and they fancying I shan't soon if I suckled. I should not have minded this but the Dss of Portland said she wanted me to drink porter to fatten the little girl, and Lady Sefton and the Dss of Rutland said that Ly Lincoln's child was fatter."[8]

It was difficult to find trustworthy, sober maternity nurses in the eighteenth century and Georgiana's brief experience with one was disastrous. "She was only rather dirty till last night," she wrote to Lady Spencer, "when she was quite drunk." This was too much:

> My Dr little girl sleeps in bed with me after her first suckling as it is cold to move her, and the Rocker was to turn her dry and lay her down to sleep. I perceiv'd she had made the bed stink of wine and strong drink whenever she came near it, and that Mrs Smith was always wakeful and telling her to leave the child. This rather alarmed me, but this morning I learnt that she had been so drunk as to fall down and vomit. . . . I have therefore sent her 10 guineas and told her I would pay her journey up to town, and that I parted with her because I wanted her no longer.[9]

After the incident Georgiana let no one but the nurse, Mrs. Smith, help her with Little G. On August 12, a month after her birth, Little G was christened. Georgiana put on proper clothes for the first time in six weeks and travelled at the head of a cavalcade of Cavendishes and Spencers to Wimbledon church, where she had married the Duke nine years before. Harriet and Duncannon came with Frederick, and the two cousins were christened together.

Only one person felt unease over the event, and that was Bess, several hundred miles away and thinking constantly of home. Her letters had hitherto been eloquently pathetic: she was broken by her misfortunes, her health was ruined and her heart crushed like a "bruised plant [which] cannot regain its vigour, but droops even in the blest sunshine of your affection." Now, however, she tried to convince Georgiana that her poor Bess was in perfect health and spirits and should be allowed to come home. She repeatedly begged to be allowed to look after Georgiana and her baby. "I shall wait your directions, my angel," she wrote earnestly.[10] "You will know how anxiously my heart watched over you in the first moments of your being with child," she reminded her friend; since then, she insisted, she had spent every waking minute thinking about her.[11] "Kiss *our* child for me," she wrote enviously. "How happy are those who have a right to be its godmother, but I am to be its little Mama—Canis said so."[12] She repeated the claim in her next letter.

One of the few surviving letters from the Duke to Bess, written on July 29, shows that even he was aware of her jealousy:

> I have not had a letter from you this great while, which makes me afraid you are in a *dudgeon* with me, but I hope you will make it up with me now, as I have written to you often lately. My letters would have been more frequent and longer, but for two reasons, the one is that I am (as you must have long perceived) the worst letter writer in the world and the other that I have no news to write about that could be entertaining to you. I shall write to you again to let you know how the Duchess does, and I dare say she will be able to write to you herself in two or three days. I forgot to tell you that the Duchess thinks the child is much such a little thing as you, and I think so too, only she is not so naughty and so apt to be *vexed*.[13]

The Duke's clumsy attempt at gentle raillery did not reassure her. Convinced that they would soon forget her in their joy over Little G, Bess began saving the money she received from the Devonshires' bankers. She had previously accepted Georgiana's gifts with a great show of reluctance— "let it my love, be a debt," she would insist; now she constantly found excuses to ask for more.[14] It was easy to extract money from the credulous Georgiana.

> I find you are kept in Turin for want of money [she wrote in alarm after receiving an urgent message]. Good God—Good God—and all my fault . . . Oh God, what will you do? . . . I send £50 tonight, that's a hundred. Canis will give me the day after tomorrow 200 which I shall send, and then I will send 200 or 300 more in three weeks where you will direct me. . . . I am so miserable at the idea of your wanting money that, if I can find him, I shall send the messenger to Turin. . . . Do not talk of expense, you would break my heart and neither use Canis nor I like Brother and Sister, if you did not spend. You owe, Dumouriez says, 170. You will receive 300, and I will desire Sir Robert's people to send an order for you for 100 more. . . .

God bless you my angel love, I adore and love you beyond description, but I am miserable till I know you have received this. Canis
sends a thousand loves.[15]

The temptation of being on her own, and in receipt of large funds, was too
much for Bess. "I do think it necessary that you should have a person of
character and conduct about you," Lady Bristol had written in February,
"and not a pert, gallant, corrupt femme de chambre who may overturn
your best plans of prudence."[16] "Do not play the coquette," she begged a
month or so later. Bess paid no heed. She went about as she pleased, drag-
ging the uncommunicative Charlotte with her. In August reports reached
Devonshire House that she had taken Charlotte to Naples and was sharing
a house with two lovers. Georgiana could not bring herself to believe it:

Pray, pray, my dearest love, forgive what I am going to say [she wrote
in a state of bewilderment]. I think that the innocence of your conduct and intentions does not make you aware enough of the danger
of your situation. You see after all the resolutions you made about not
receiving men, you have been living alone with 2. . . . This is in itself
nothing, but suppose you had, at any place, seen a beautiful young
woman arrive, travelling by herself, who, tho' there was nothing
against her, had had imprudences laid to her charge, and that you saw
this young woman giving parties and living with two men, both supposed to be in love with her—with all your candour you would think
her imprudent . . . and so many of our women lately have gone into
Switzerland and Italy when in scrapes, that you should be doubly
cautious to shew that you are not that kind of person.[17]

They had also heard that Bess had fallen in love with a certain *chevalier* and
was planning to meet him in Turin. "I must entreat you not to go so soon
to Turin," Georgiana pleaded, "at least let the Chevalier be there some
days, for tho' I fear him not, do not go there purposely to meet him." Why,
she asked despairingly, could not Bess behave herself and live with a female companion like any other respectable woman? "Live with women as
much as you can," she implored, "let them be ever so disagreeable; the
amusements of the country will occupy you, and if you met with any
bearable woman who would stay some time . . . do try. My angel love, the
world is so alive [with stories] about you. . . ."[18]

Bess was horrified when she read Georgiana's letter. It had never occurred to her that she might figure in people's letters to their friends and relatives in England. She wrote a long, pleading letter to her dearest beloved Georgiana. In nine cramped pages she attempted to justify herself from every angle—knowing that her future hung in the balance. It was a masterpiece of flattery and denial. "The idea of having made you uneasy counterbalances all. I am wretched till I know you are again tranquil on my account, and assured that I cannot err against your will again," she wrote humbly, "let my ruling sentiment be to please you." She blamed her "imprudences" on her broken heart; the loss of her dear children may have possibly overturned her judgement. In a startling revelation—which discredited the self-pitying lamentations of her previous letters—she claimed she was one of the favourites at the Neapolitan court. The British ambassador Sir William Hamilton, a family friend of the Herveys, had introduced her to the King and Queen. No one in Naples objected to her living arrangements; indeed, the royal family made a point of including her in all their intimate social engagements.[19] However, she accepted Georgiana's suggestion and regretfully moved away from Naples.

Bess was prepared to embark on a lengthy correspondence to regain her friends' confidence, but the need never arose. To her surprise, one letter was enough to reassure them and the subject was never referred to again. She had imagined them reading her letter and discussing it for days. Fortunately for her, far more pressing matters claimed Georgiana's attention.

⚬⚬⚬

Georgiana was in serious trouble over her gambling debts. She had frittered away thousands during the past few years, and secretly borrowed more to hide her losses.*[20] Nor could she stop herself playing when she had no money to spare. Lady Mary Coke recorded in her diary an embarrassing incident at a party given by Lady Ailesbury. The guests were playing faro according to strict rules—no borrowing from the bank. Georgiana arrived, flushed with excitement from a previous engagement, and in-

---

* Georgiana also lent money without bothering to reclaim it. Lady Charlotte Bury recorded: "I have often heard it told of her that if she had money set apart for pleasure, or for repayment of debts, and that when some individual came to her in pecuniary distress, she would always relieve him or her, and leave her own difficulties unprovided for. Oftentimes she was wrong in doing so. . . . One must be just before one is generous. But it is impossible not to be charmed by the kindly impulse which made her, without a moment's hesitating, shield another from distress." A. Francis Steuart, ed., *The Diary of a Lady-in-Waiting* (London 1908), II, p. 35.

sisted on joining the players. But her purse was empty. She cried and made a fuss until Mr. Conway lent her ten guineas, which made her all smiles until she had lost the lot. By now nothing would stop her and she insisted on borrowing sixty guineas from the bank. This time luck was with her and she won. She scooped up her winnings amidst general acclaim and prepared to leave. As she headed towards the door there was a cough and someone gently mentioned Mr. Conway's name to her. Georgiana was aghast, and with many apologies and exclamations repaid the loan. Her departure restored the party's equilibrium, and it was half an hour before the players realized that she had left without repaying the bank.[21]

On September 30, 1783, three weeks after Bess's long letter of self-exculpation, the *Morning Herald* announced: "The town will be deprived of the amiable Duchess of Devonshire for two months longer, her Grace having determined to remain at her country seat in Derbyshire till the first week in December. . . . The amiable Duchess happily has softer and far sweeter cares."[22] However, it was not "sweeter cares" which kept Georgiana away from London. "At times," she wrote to her mother, "except when my Dear little girl calls on me, I have neither the will nor the courage to do anything."[23] She swore she would go mad or die if anything happened to Little G. (One person who remained sceptical about this was Horace Walpole, who wrote dismissively: "[she] will probably stuff her poor babe into her knotting bag, when she wants to play Macao, and forget it.")[24]

The Duke's agent John Heaton had accused Georgiana of swindling tradesmen, and worse. Since the beginning of the year Chatsworth had been undergoing a programme of improvements. Georgiana was refurbishing her private apartments and persuaded the Duke to employ the French craftsman François Hervé to design a complete set of furniture. She had also instructed builders to give Devonshire House a much-needed face-lift. But on Heaton's command the work came to a halt. He had heard a rumour that Georgiana was using the services of some craftsmen free of charge in return for passing on a recommendation to the Prince of Wales. Whether or not this was true, Heaton believed the claim and advised the Duke not to pay any of Georgiana's bills until he had investigated the matter. He also informed the Duke, without any proof, that Georgiana was having an affair with the Prince. The world, he said, knew that the Devonshires "liv'd ill together."[25]

The Duke politely listened to Heaton's accusation, and told him to keep his suspicions to himself. Unfortunately, the following week a caricature appeared in the print shops entitled "The Ladies Church Yard," which linked Georgiana with the Prince.*[26] "I set these kind of reports at defiance," Georgiana wrote to her mother, "whilst I know that the Duke's confidence in me is such that nobody but myself could hurt me with him. This he gave me every assurance of. . . ." But other parts of her conversation with the Duke were less reassuring. Why did he not sack his agent, she asked, since he was so angry at his presumption? His reply chilled her, and was to affect her actions for the rest of her life, making her fearful of being honest about her financial affairs:

> he said, *"not so easily, for I do not look enough into my own affairs."* I said I thought it was a pity he did not, and he answered me in the following remarkable words, which I shall never forget—*"If I found out that Heaton was ever so great a rascal* [to be embezzling our estate] *I should be mad to quarrel with him for it would quite ruin us."* In short, whatever he is, Mr Heaton has so puzzled our affairs that I expect he alone can have the clue. This, however, has determined me to be silent whatever I think. . . .[27]

Shocked to learn that Heaton had so much control over their affairs, Georgiana wondered what would happen if he ever learnt the true nature of her debts. In fact, the Duke was exaggerating Heaton's power because he himself knew so little about the running of his estate, but Georgiana was not to know that. On receiving her daughter's worried letters, Lady Spencer advised: "Try to show your extravagance was due to ignorance."[28] She was appalled, like the Duke, that a servant should pass comment on his employer's wife. Taking Georgiana's side against Heaton, she called him the "Corkscrew," and suggested that in the future they should all be on their guard against him. Georgiana was grateful for her understanding. However, the Duke's brother and uncles did not share Lady Spencer's sense of outrage; they accused Georgiana of deliberately wasting his money. Lord and Lady George Cavendish, who remained hopeful that Georgiana would never produce an heir, resented her depletion of what they regarded as their future estate.[29]

* The caricature was a drawing of a graveyard containing the tombstones of many of the "fallen" women of London. In the centre was the Prince of Wales's tomb, flanked on either side with the graves of Lady Melbourne and Georgiana. There was no mistaking the implication.

Georgiana was saved from further unpleasant conversations by the arrival of many stalwarts of the Devonshire House Circle, including James Hare and Thomas Grenville. The gaiety at Chatsworth temporarily lifted her spirits. On October 21 she wrote in a happier mood: "we had a bouncing public day yesterday, and many staid. We have a grand coursing this morning. . . . We never had such public days, and we have had 4 sets of people this summer who were staunch enemies before. Indeed, our being *in* may be something. Georgiana is very very fretful, and has for a fortnight past slobbered amazingly."[30] But more rumours about her reached Chatsworth and infected the atmosphere. Lady George Cavendish told Harriet that everyone knew about her sister and Charles Fox. "Lady George teazed her cruelly," Georgiana complained to Bess, "about the Eyebrow [Fox] and me, and Canis and the Infernal [Lady Jersey], and so blended with some truth that my sister was quite hurt. The odd thing is that she said many true things about my mother having found letters of the Eyebrow, but what Canis thinks most ill-natured is that she said his intrigue with the Infernal was upon his being angry with me about the Eyebrow."[31] The letter reveals the extraordinary, albeit one-sided, openness between Georgiana and the Duke. Though he obviously accepted that there was no "intrigue" between her and Fox, Lady George's comments suggest otherwise.

When Georgiana had a secret she would often "confess" it by issuing a denial to a question no one had asked. Four months earlier, in June, she had written to Bess:

But, Dear Bess, what I wanted to tell you is that the Eyebrow was to go out of town yesterday, and as I had not seen him for a long time, for am very lazy now I grow so big, and he had called several mornings, I let him call Wednesday after court. After talking of many things and expressing very affectionate tho' not improper anxiety for the situation he left me in—in the midst of all this the P. of W. arrived in the court, and as I was standing up and the other taking leave of me, without my scarcely knowing it he kissed my cheek, and went away. Je vous assure, mon adorable petite, sans la moindre emotion de ma part, but you cannot think how uneasy it made me. And what do you think I did—I told Canis, who Dear Dog, instead of being angry said it was not my fault and there was nothing in it as he was taking leave of me in such a situation. You cannot think what a load this took off my mind and heart.[32]

There is little evidence to prove or disprove the notion that Georgiana and Fox had become lovers. Their correspondence for these years does not survive. Georgiana's demeanour had certainly altered since 1779, when Lady Pembroke assured her son that Georgiana never flirted. According to Nathaniel Wraxall, she was at the time "not exempt perhaps, from vanity and coquetry," and quite obviously aware of her effect on men.[33] Perhaps Bess's skill at playing the flirt had stirred something within her, or perhaps she no longer saw any reason to remain faithful to her adulterous husband. Nothing is certain except that Georgiana shared her contemporaries' horror of breaking the patriarchal bloodline. It was an unwritten rule in eighteenth-century society that a wife should present her husband with a legitimate first son, whatever she chose to do afterwards.

If Georgiana was having an affair with Fox, it was brief and insignificant compared to their profound friendship. Towards the end of her life she claimed that he had never been her lover, only her friend. She may have been lying, of course, which would mean that she had shared him with the courtesan Mrs. Armistead, who became his mistress in 1783. Elizabeth Armistead was a handsome, good-natured cockney with no interest in politics or literature. It was not an obvious match. Nevertheless, they were happy together and Mrs. Armistead retired from her profession.

In the midst of Georgiana's troubles over rumours and debts, news came from Bath that Lord Spencer was dead. He was only forty-nine, although his continual ill health had made him prematurely old. Lady Spencer had tried to prepare herself for his death, but when it came she was devastated. The following day, November 1, she wrote in her diary, "I have passed another day half-stunned with affliction and stupefied with laudanum." The next day Lord Spencer's body was carried out to the hearse to be transported to Althorp. "I felt as if every nerve about my head and heart would break," she wrote in her next entry. "I never can describe or forget what I felt when they came to fetch me—my reason almost forsook me, I was half frantick and wanted to go into his room—I had not power to pass by his door, & my Brother and George were forced to drag me down the stairs & lift me into the coach."[34]

She had deliberately concealed Lord Spencer's final illness from Georgiana, fearing to add to her worries. The sudden news of his death made Georgiana ill. "The Duke is so good to me that it is a great comfort," she told her brother, but "I am very quiet as I stay in my room and see nobody, for seeing people is what I dread most."[35] She developed a fever and lay sick for almost two weeks. Little Georgiana and the Duke caught her fever, and a month passed before they were able to visit Lady Spencer. When the news reached Italy the English community in Rome was surprised to see Lady Elizabeth Foster go into deep mourning.

"I really feel more capable of talking to you about my sorrow, and receiving consolation from such discourse than from anything else," Georgiana wrote to Bess on January 3, 1784; "pray heaven I do not infect you with my grief."[36] She wanted her friend to return now, but she also took care to remind her that there had to be an equal partnership between the three of them. "What could be more interesting than our journey last year," she wrote, "a man and a woman endowed with every amiable quality and loving one another as Brother and Sister, nursing and taking care of a woman, who was doatingly fond of them, and who bore within her the child that was to fulfil the vows and wishes of all three."[37]

The Devonshires retreated to Bath so that the Duke, who was suffering from gout, could bathe in the springs. Every day reminded Georgiana that she had not been present as her father lay dying. She consoled herself by writing each morning to Bess:

I am gulchy, gulchy when I reflect at the length of time that is elapsed since we first knew one another here, at the length of time since I have lost you, and at the distance to our meeting, but I comfort myself by thinking what a sacredness all this gives our friendship. Thank God we have been long enough united not to blush at the short period of our friendship. Dr dr dr Bess, you grow every day more and more Canis's sister and your Georgine's friend.[38]

Bath was no less painful for the Duke. He missed his Bess, he wrote:

I have been ill for some time of a complaint in my stomach, but am better for having drank the waters for about a fortnight. This place has been very unpleasant for me compared to what it was a year and a half ago, for then I had the Rat and Bess and good health and fine weather. . . . There are many places in Bath that put me so much in mind of you that when I walk about the town I cannot help expecting upon turning the corner of a street, to see you walking along it, holding your cane at each end, and bending it over your knee. But I have never met you yet, and what surprises me likewise very much is, that somebody or other has the impudence to live in your house in Bennet Street.[39]

Bess, however, had found other attractions and was no longer in a hurry to return to England. "I have received your blessed letter about my return," she wrote in February; "what can I have force to say, my angelic friend, but that if I am well enough that I will return to you."[40] Since making her promise to Georgiana and the Duke to avoid any more flirtations, she had visited Rome with Charlotte and made a conquest of the *bon viveur* Cardinal Bernis. They appeared constantly in each other's company until the Cardinal's public affection for her became a dangerous liability. Bess hurriedly returned to Naples, where she promptly fell in love with a handsome Swedish diplomat, Count Fersen. The Count had recently come from Versailles, where his departure had caused Marie Antoinette to cry in front of her attendants. The Duc de Lévis described him in his memoirs as having a "face and manner . . . perfectly suited to the hero of a novel."[41]

Fersen was thought to reciprocate Marie Antoinette's feelings, but it did not prevent him from falling for the "tragic" and beautiful young Englishwoman in exile. According to Bess, he cried when she told him the story of her two sons, hidden away from her in Ireland. One evening, she claimed, he kissed her before she knew what was happening—by chance they were alone—but she reluctantly halted his advances. "Pray forgive me," she hurriedly wrote to Georgiana in case she had heard about Fersen from someone else. "I think better of him than anybody I have seen, but your claims and Canis's on me can never lessen. . . . I do not pretend that I shall not regret him, he is in every respect amiable and estimable, but you live in my heart and to it I confess my weakness. . . . Oh G., are you angry with me?"[42]

Georgiana begged her to return immediately. Two years later, when she finally met Count Fersen, her resentment towards her rival was just as strong. She did not think him as good looking as Bess's description, and told her: "He is reckoned ugly here, because from the idea of Mrs B's [Marie Antoinette] liking him, a great beauty was expected. He has delightful eyes, the finest countenance that can be, and the most gentleman-like air. Thank God, I an't in love with him. I was quite agitated when I first saw him, but now we are well acquainted and have talked of you. Canis has peeped at him and he peeped through the jalousie to see Canis riding."[43]

Georgiana had detailed plans for Bess and Charlotte. Bess would no longer be in charge of the girl: her life would be with them at Devonshire House. She conceded that Bess would have to live in her own little house from time to time to avoid gossip, but the three of them would never again be parted. However, the prize no longer seemed so attractive to Bess. Her replies were evasive: she wondered whether Charlotte might not benefit from another year abroad. "She does not in any respect improve as I hope she would have done—she has a quickness but no application."[44] In a moment of candour Bess let slip that she dreaded her return because it "will renew all remarks, and observations and conjectures" about her past behaviour. She reminded Georgiana that their "tender friendship makes me an object of envy, and of course of the malice of others." But it was neither malice nor envy which prompted Lady Clermont to write to Lady Spencer on February 26, 1783: "I hope you have talked to Lady Duncannon about the lady in Italy. I hear there never was anything so much admired, and that she sees a great deal of company. I wish to God she would run off with somebody. I am afraid it is a wicked wish; but it is to prevent worse."[45]

By early 1784, the prospect of Bess remaining abroad horrified Georgiana. She was pregnant again, but this time the pregnancy was proving to be difficult and painful. The physical signs were not good, and added to her many anxieties was the fear that she might miscarry. For the past few months she had been nerving herself to make a confession to the Duke, but Heaton's allegations and Lady George's troublemaking had made her keep quiet. By February, however, her debts could no longer remain hidden. "I have somehow or other lately begun an opening to the Duke about the state of my affairs," she wrote to her mother, "as I find from Heaton's letters it is necessary. He has been very kind about it, but as I wish to keep my mind free from agitation at this crucial period, I own I have been more idle than I ought to be."[46] Georgiana agonized for three more weeks until finally, at the beginning of March, she went to see the Duke.

"Before I say a word more, you must promise, my dearest dearest, dearest angelic love, never to let Canis know I have told this secret to you," she wrote to Bess after the meeting: she had incurred

> a very, very large debt. I never had courage to own it, and try'd to win it at play, by which means it became immense and was grown (I have not the courage to write the sum, but will tell you when I see you) many, many, many thousands. I would not tell Canis, (tho' I have kept absolute ruin to myself scarcely off) whilst I was with child and suckling, because I thought it ungenerous to be protected by my situation. . . . It must distress him, for besides the alterations at Chatsworth, and the buildings at Buxton, he has with a generosity unparalleled engag'd to buy the Duke of Portland's great Cumber-

land estate, which saves the D of P from raising the money. . . . I should feel myself a monster if I did not propose the strictest care and economy. Would to God that Canis would consent to come abroad next summer and to stay a year with you, Charlotte, and Georgiana—in which time everything would come right, but he minds so much the idea of the World, and what would be said that I fear he will not retrench.

What had I to offer for the kind of ruin I brought on him (for every year of my life I have cost him immense sums)—a mind he could not trust in, a person faded, and 26 years of folly and indiscretion. And how do you think he has received the avowal—with the utmost generosity, goodness and kindness. His whole care has been that I may not vex myself, and you would think he was the offender not me. . . . My angel Bess, write to me, tell me you don't hate me for this confession, Oh, love, love me ever.[47]

Georgiana lost the baby shortly after her confession. She wanted Lady Spencer to come to her, but her mother could not leave London while the executors were unravelling Lord Spencer's estate. Not only was it less than a quarter of what they had expected; his affairs were in a terrible muddle. The money had simply vanished: some of the fortune had gone on Spencer House and the art collection, but it appeared that the Spencers had lost most of it at the gaming table. Lady Spencer was no longer rich; her income would be a mere £3,000 a year, with the promise of an extra £1,000 from George, once he had paid off the outstanding creditors. Her change of status to widowhood was all the more difficult for the loss of the Spencer wealth. She blamed herself for having wasted her son's inheritance—and worse, for having corrupted her children by her example. Georgiana tried unsuccessfully to excuse her: "You talk of the bad example you have set me, you can mean but one thing—gaming, and there, I do assure you it is innate, for I remember playing from seven in the morning till 8 at night at Lansquenet with old Mrs Newton when I was nine years old and was sent to King's Road for the measles."[48] Lady Spencer would never face the world with the same self-confidence again. Georgiana was distressed at the blow to her mother's pride; and she felt ashamed to hear her situation discussed in public. "Have you any guile or anger in your dear heart," she wrote to her mother. "If you have, call it forth. . . . against the Duchess of Beaufort, who was brutal enough to dispute with Miss Fielding, insisting upon it you would play again."[49]

Although she was lonely and miserable, Georgiana preferred to remain at Chatsworth rather than go to Devonshire House, where she would be surrounded by her friends. "When as now I feel nervous and shy," she wrote, "I had much rather converse with people I know but little of, than with those I know very much better. I feel a dread of going to London, tho' Ly Melbourne, whom I love, and Ly Jersey, whose society is so remarkably amusing, would certainly do their best to entertain and dissipate me." For the moment, if she had to see anyone, she preferred the company of strangers because "their conversation [is] certain of not touching any string, that has any connection with those various irritable nerves" that plagued her.[50] She confessed to George that her health, purse, and inclination all contributed to her strong desire to avoid London. Often she fantasized about escaping to a different life. "The kind of castles I build," she explained to her mother, "and which I chiefly build when I have an uneasy thought I want to get rid of—is fancying myself in a thousand different situations but almost always different from what I really could be in."[51] The papers announced that she would be residing in Bath until the summer, but events taking place in Westminster meant that she would have no respite from her worries.

CHAPTER 9

THE WESTMINSTER ELECTION

1784

If Mr Fox is no longer the Man of the People, he must be allowed from the number of females who attend to give him their support, to be at least, the Man for the Ladies. The Duchess of Devonshire's attendance at Covent Garden, perhaps, will not secure Mr Fox's election; but it will at least establish her pre-eminence above all other beauties of that place, and make her a standing toast in all the ale-houses and gin-shops of Westminster. . . . Ladies who interest themselves so much in the case of elections, are perhaps too ignorant to know that they meddle with what does not concern them, but they ought at least to know, that it is usual, even in these days of degeneracy, to expect common decency in a married woman.

Morning Post, *April 8, 1784*

Every liberal mind revolts at the wretched abuse now levelled at the most amiable of our country women! The base and burring hand of calumny, however, is raised in vain against the lovely Devon and her sister patriots, who at this juncture, so much resemble those fair celestials of the Grecian bard, whose attributes of divinity never appeared so brilliant as when forming a shield for the heroic leader of an oppressed people!

Morning Herald and Daily Advertiser, *April 24, 1784*

The coalition had struggled to remain in power since driving out Lord Shelburne in April 1783. George III's hostility to Fox and his former Prime Minister, Lord North, was so marked that no one thought the coalition could survive for long. Self-doubt and internal divisions continually undermined the new ministry. The danger of the government appearing weak formed the chief topic of Georgiana's conversations with Fox before her confinement. They both knew that without the King's support the coalition was vulnerable to challengers.

When Parliament resumed after the summer recess, the cabinet was cautiously optimistic. The ministry announced its programme of reform for the session while Georgiana was at Chatsworth. The most controversial plan was Fox's Bill to overhaul the East India Company's rights and charters. There was cross-party agreement that something had to be done. Company employees went to India with nothing and returned with vast wealth, giving rise not only to resentment but also to suspicions that fortunes were being obtained in a less than gentleman-like manner. There were stories of unbridled corruption, exploitation—even violence against the native population. But successive governments had always been wary of meddling with private business, and many MPs regarded the East India Bill as outrageous political interference. The coalition's enemies claimed that the Whigs were planning to take control of the East India Company.

Fox was jubilant when he defeated his critics: the East India Bill passed through the House of Commons in November with a comfortable majority. However, this easy victory was a smokescreen: there were secret moves afoot to break the coalition. William Pitt held meetings with the King in early December and together they formed a plot to oust Fox. When the Bill reached the House of Lords for ratification by the peers, Pitt's cousin, Lord Temple, quietly circulated an open letter from the King. It stated clearly that anyone who voted for the Bill would henceforth be the King's enemy. Lord Frederick Cavendish told Georgiana that the Duke of Portland had confronted the King in his closet about rumours of a conspiracy; the King had fixed his glassy stare on him and ignored the question.[1] Fox refused to believe the rumours until the sight of the Lords voting down the Bill made him realize, in a dreadful moment of clarity, that he had been outwitted. George III so loathed the Whigs that when he heard the results at 10 p.m. he immediately sent his officers to Piccadilly to collect the Seals of State from Fox and North. The next morning, December 19, William Pitt kissed the King's hand and, at twenty-four, became the youngest Prime Minister in parliamentary history.

Paradoxically, the mood among the Whigs was one of exultation. Now that the King had declared open war on his ex-ministers they had proof of his despotic intentions. For the past two decades their allegations about the increasing influence of the crown had cited its "secret" patronage through the awarding of pensions and places. By issuing an order to the Lords to override the House of Commons the King had at last provided evidence of his anti-constitutional activities. Fox saw the political crisis in personal terms—as a duel between himself, George III, and William Pitt.

Georgiana had no doubt that Fox would win. As long as the House of Commons supported the coalition there was nothing either the King or Pitt could do. No bills could be passed, taxes raised, nor foreign policy enacted. "We have the majority still in the H. of C.," she wrote, "which, it is supposed, must rout them."[2] The coalition spent the Christmas break preparing for battle. No one thought Pitt could last to the New Year: "Depend on it," joked Mrs. Crewe, "it will be a mincepie administration." But they misjudged public opinion. Between Hyde Park and Piccadilly the Whigs strutted in righteous indignation with the approval of their friends, but everywhere else they were reviled for having forced their way into power in spite of the King's objections—"storming the closet" as it was known. Fox, in particular, was cast in the role of the villain for his supposed attempt to turn the East India Company into a cash cow for the Whigs. His perorations on English liberty looked spurious next to his notorious lifestyle. Of all the political cartoons which emerged during these weeks the most effective were those directed against him. James Gillray depicted him as "Carlo Khan" striding down Leadenhall Street on an elephant to take possession of the East India Company. This, and another cartoon depicting him as a latter-day Oliver Cromwell, did him more damage than all the other cartoons put together. His motives had become suspect.

The coalition held regular meetings at Devonshire House; its palatial drawing room was the only place that could comfortably accommodate all its supporters. They were depressing affairs: complaints and criticism drowned out constructive suggestions and fewer and fewer people turned out for each meeting. Their Commons majority remained substantial for the first week, but by the end of the second it had begun to slip. Pitt pressed on, showing no emotion at the cat-calls and hooting from the opposition benches as his measures were voted down. The combination of the King's support and Pitt's cool determination won over increasing numbers of MPs every week. It was a slow, humiliating torture for Fox, but he refused to accept defeat. Pitt relentlessly eroded the coalition's majority until by the first week of March it was down to nine votes. On

March 8 Fox moved that the House of Commons delay discussing the Mutiny Bill until Pitt resigned: it was carried by only one vote. This was the end. Pitt had won.

By mid-March the Devonshires were re-established in London and Georgiana was trying to make sense of her debts to Heaton. She regarded the coalition's defeat as a disaster not only for the party but for the whole country: "If Mr Pitt succeeds, he will have brought about an event that he himself, as well as every Englishman will repent ever after," she wrote.[3] She was in complete agreement with Fox that the King's interference with the will of the Commons had to be stopped. She drew on her contacts at the French court to urge their government not to recognize Pitt.[4] She also forced the reluctant d'Adhémar to hold a grand dinner in honour of the coalition at his official residence. He was humble to her face, but she knew he was disparaging them all over London. "He says nothing can equal *le despotisme de M. Fox que la bassesse de ses amis.*"*

On March 17 Georgiana went to the opera to hear *La Reine de Golconde,* which included a little piece she had composed herself. That night, however, the theatre was taking place not on the stage but in the stalls. Political rivalry divided the audience and there was much booing and hissing at the arrival of prominent politicians. Georgiana loved this kind of public participation. She went again on the twentieth: "It was very full and I had several good political fights."[5] The Duchess of Rutland jumped to her feet and shouted, "Damn Fox!" at the boisterous crowd below. Lady Maria Waldegrave retaliated from the opposite box, "Damn Pitt!" "We had quite an opposition dinner [afterwards]," recorded Georgiana at d'Adhémar's, "much against the grain with him. There was Mr Fox Grenville, Ld Malden, Cl St. Leger, all our men in short. . . ."[6] Her unconscious use of the word "our" reveals how closely she identified with the Whigs. She was not following the struggle, she was one of the contestants. Indeed, one cartoon depicted the coalition leaders—Sheridan, Burke, North, and Fox—drumming up support by invoking not just the Cavendish wealth but Georgiana herself. "Join the Coalition and you shall be cloathed," cries Burke. "All Gentlemen Voluntiers who will serve his Majesty Carlo Khan repair to the Portland Block," shouts North. "Present Pay, good Quarters, and a handsome Landlady," adds Fox.[7]

Rivalry between the parties spread to the streets, aided in many instances by *agents provocateurs.* Pitt rode down the Strand accompanied by a

---

* He says nothing can equal the despotism of Mr. Fox except the baseness of his friends.

great mob which stopped outside Carlton House and shouted abuse at the Prince. It moved on to St. James's, where with difficulty he prevented them from smashing Fox's windows. Later Lord Chatham, Pitt's elder brother, spotted James Hare exhorting a crowd of chairmen armed with broken carriage poles to attack Pitt's carriage.

> They succeeded in making their way to the carriage and forced open the door. Several desperate blows were aimed at Mr Pitt, and I recollect endeavouring to cover him as well as I could, in his getting out of the Carriage. Fortunately however . . . by ye timely assistance of a [rival] Party of Chairmen, and many Gentlemen from Whites, who saw his danger, we were extricated from a most unpleasant situation, and with considerable difficulty, got into some adjacent houses.[8]

A public debate at Westminster Hall degenerated into a riot and Fox was pelted with "filth" while his supporters hustled him out into a waiting carriage.

The threat of insults or worse did not deter Georgiana from venturing into this turbulent world to aid Fox. She spent a few days canvassing for her brother's constituency and then returned to London for the Westminster election.* There were three candidates standing for two places: Fox for the Whigs, and Sir Cecil Wray (a Whig deserter) and Lord Admiral Hood for Pitt. Since Admiral Hood was a popular hero from the American war, it was really a contest between Fox and Wray. Because of its large franchise of 18,000 voters and its proximity to Parliament, Westminster was one of the few constituencies where public opinion really mattered. Pitt would gladly have exchanged a dozen ordinary boroughs to oust Fox from this, the "people's constituency." The King cared less about public opinion and simply wanted Fox out. Do whatever is necessary, he ordered Pitt, "rather than let him be Returned for Westminster."[9]

Criticisms of political corruption and coercion levelled by later Whig historians against eighteenth-century elections would have puzzled Georgiana. As Frank O'Gorman has shown, although the total number

---

* Lady Spencer wrote to her son that Lady Salisbury had canvassed the town on the government's behalf: "we were told, with amazing success, and she threw a sort of Spirit upon their party that depressed ours. So last night I sent for your two sisters who set out an hour ago with Mrs Sloper and a very large body of friends to make a regular canvass. It is amazing what this has already done." BL Althorp G276; LS to second Earl Spencer, circa March 25, 1784.

of voters may have been small—roughly 300,000 in a population of 10 million—the public was not necessarily excluded from electoral politics; nor were elections simply a case of ratification. "While committees met to plot and plan," he writes, "while agents swarmed all over the constituency, and while the formal canvass proceeded, a veritable torrent of rival publicity—squibs, poems, songs, cartoons, handbills, letters, and advertisements—deluged the constituency. . . . Daily speeches, celebrations, parades, displays, treats, and dinners fostered and maintained the excitement, enthusiasm of the public."[10] Local issues predominated, but national ones were also important and could be used to discredit rivals. Westminster's large franchise spanned a broad range of occupations. They could be wooed, flattered, and flooded with inducements, but not controlled.

As at previous elections, the speaker platforms were erected in Covent Garden beside the polling booths, through which the voters had to shuffle, one at a time, to record their vote in front of the clerk. On the first day of the polls, which remained open for six weeks, the Whigs assembled for a mass canvass. Their helpers had strung up banners and coloured bunting along the main thoroughfares in an uneven zigzag from one supporter's house to another. Fox and a few friends stayed on the platform to harangue the crowd, while the men and women divided into three teams led by Georgiana, Mrs. Crewe, and Mrs. Damer. Most of the party members were busy fighting their own seats and the women were needed to make up the shortfall in numbers. Georgiana and Harriet, accompanied by several male escorts, walked through the cobbled streets, handing out specially struck medals to Foxites. The Whigs enjoyed themselves in spite of the pushing and shoving of the crowd. However, many observers were shocked to see women so cavalierly exposed to the dangers of a metropolitan election. A German tourist at the hustings watched the previously tranquil mob turn violent after the poll closed:

> In a very few minutes, the whole scaffolding, benches, and chairs, and everything were completely destroyed, and the mat with which it had been covered torn into ten thousand long strips or pieces, with which they encircled multitudes of peoples of all ranks. These they hurried along with them, and everything else that came in their way, as trophies of joy: and thus in the midst of exaltation and triumph, they paraded through many of the most populous streets of London.[11]

The *London Chronicle* reported that at the end of the first day Fox had polled 302, Lord Hood 264, and Wray 238.[12] But on the second and third, Hood and Wray surged ahead. The Whigs frantically urged everyone to join the canvass. By April 5 the Duchess of Portland, Lady Jersey, Lady Carlisle, Mrs. Bouverie, and the three Ladies Waldegrave were among those parading through Westminster, dressed in blue and buff with fox-tails in their hats, soliciting votes from bemused shopkeepers. According to Nathaniel Wraxall, their activities soon got out of hand: "These ladies, being previously furnished with lists of outlying voters, drove to their respective dwellings. Neither entreaties nor promises were spared. In some instances even personal caresses were said to have been permitted, in order to prevail upon the surly or inflexible, and there can be no doubt of common mechanics having been conveyed to the hustings on more than one occasion by the Duchess in her own coach."[13]

Horace Walpole was ashamed by the way in which some of the voters took advantage of Georgiana: "During her canvass, the Duchess made no scruple of visiting some of the humblest of electors, dazzling and enchanting them by the fascination of her manner, the power of her beauty and the influence of her high rank." But others shouted abuse at her and on more than one occasion she was physically threatened. One account claimed that Georgiana thoughtlessly entered a house alone to confront seven drunken Hood supporters. They would not let her leave until they had all kissed her, by which time there was a noisy mob outside, fighting to get in.[14] Whether or not this particular story is true, there were other, similar incidents. "She is in the street, they tell me almost every day," wrote Mrs. Boscawen to Lady Chatham. "And this is her sole employment from morning till night. She gets out of her carriage and walks into alleys—many feathers and fox tails in her hat—many blackguards in her suit."[15]

By the end of the first week Georgiana was exhausted and demoralized. Her voice was hoarse and her feet were sore and blistered from walking on the broken cobbles of Henrietta Street—incidentally home to some famous brothels and therefore a source of much coarse humour in the press. Despite all their efforts Fox was still trailing in the polls. "I give the Election quite up," Georgiana wrote to her mother, "and must lament all that has happened—however, the circumstances I was in will justify me to those it is most essential for me to please and I must pocket the opinions of the rest."[16] The government was jubilant. "Westminster is indeed a cruel blow upon the party," Pitt's cousin told the Duke of Rutland. "Their exertions have been incredible, particularly upon the part of her Grace of Devon, who in the course of her canvass has heard more plain English of the grossest sort than ever fell to the share of any lady of her rank. . . . Fox is now clearly defeated."[17]

Pittite newspapers concentrated their attacks on Georgiana and ignored the other women. Lady Salisbury and Mrs. Hobart, who were canvassing for Pitt, received far less attention. "It is very hard," she complained, "they should single me out when all the women of my side do as much."[18] She denied exchanging kisses for votes: it had been Harriet's idea, not hers. The men did that sort of thing at every election—candidates had to do a great deal of kissing and handshaking. Lord Palmerston heard that one butcher had made Fox kiss his wife and all his daughters in turn before shoving him out of the shop, telling him, "he might kiss his arse if he liked into the bargain; but he'd see him damned before he voted for him."[19] Georgiana was easy to attack because she was already a celebrity. The *Morning Post* was the first to run the story about her kissing voters on March 31: "We hear the D——s of D—— grants *favours* to those who promise their votes and interest to Mr Fox." Thereafter it ran vicious stories almost every day. It concentrated on three themes: she was selling her body for votes, she was Fox's mistress, and she was betraying her rank and sex by her undignified behaviour. On April 8 it sneered, "She wore as usual the insignia of the order in her hat, and by her extraordinary beauty attracted the eyes of the gaping multitude. A band of greasy musicians struck up with marrow-bones and cleavers in honour of her *Grace,* and she was followed down the whole of Southampton Street, with the acclamations of her *new* admirers." By the twelfth Georgiana could no longer endure it and informed the Duke that she was leaving London to stay with her mother in St. Albans.

Lady Spencer was relieved when her daughter finally listened to her plea to stop canvassing. In October 1774 she herself had come in for some teasing from the press for her successful canvass in Northampton, provoking great amusement among the family: Lord Spencer thought it was a great joke. "Have you seen all the compliments, abuse and satire in the London newspapers upon her and Mrs Tollemache canvassing?" he asked Georgiana.[20] But he had belonged to a generation which still regarded the daily reporting of events as something of a novelty. When he was a young man editors faced the risk of arrest if they reported parliamentary debates. This had not been the case since 1774. Now, the mass circulation of newspapers and political cartoons which together reached several hundred

Pd by W Humphrey 227 Strand.

THE TWO PATRIOTIC DUCHESS'S ON THEIR CANVASS. 3 ap. 1784

Requesting the favour of an early Poll.

Dß: Portland   Dß: Devonshire

Rowlandson

Westm Elect P 99. 193. 216

"The Two Patriotic Duchess's on Their Canvass," April 3, 1784. Georgiana is shown kissing a butcher while slipping him money. Another butcher rejects the Duchess of Portland's advances. Rowlandson. BM Cat 6494.

"The Chairing of Fox," April 12, 1784. A Whig cartoon depicting Georgiana, Harriet, and either the Duchess of Portland or Lady Archer chairing Fox through Westminster. BM Cat. 6524.

thousand readers each week ensured that the views, appearance, and debating style of all the major political figures were familiar around the country. When Baron Archenholtz visited England he was surprised by the silence which reigned in clubs, inns, and coffee houses while men read the papers. Like other foreign visitors, he was also deeply impressed by the political knowledge shown by ordinary people; such free and informal debates were not common on the Continent.

The surge in newspaper reporting since the 1770s had been accompanied by a greater boldness when it came to ridiculing public figures. This was partly because both the government and opposition were prepared to pay newspaper editors handsomely for attacking their opponents. (Lord Shelburne's ministry lasted less than a year, but still managed to spend almost £2,000 on bribes to pamphleteers and editors.)[21] The government poured money into anti-Fox and anti-Georgiana propaganda. Its tame editors on newspapers such as the *Morning Herald* printed as many nasty stories about her as possible, and print sellers who were close to the government sold thousands of cartoons attacking her campaign. On April 3 print shops were displaying a new and particularly offensive set of cartoons depicting Georgiana in a lewd embrace with a Westminster tradesman. Those who balked at paying a shilling could see the drawings in coffee houses, gentlemen's clubs, barber shops, taverns, and ale houses. Some print sellers had crossed the line between satire and pornography and were simply using Georgiana as an excuse for titillation.

In a world which prized female modesty Georgiana's drubbing by the press shamed her family. It was not the fact of her canvassing but her method, which was too free and easy, too masculine. Lady Spencer had not objected when her daughters trooped off to Northampton to campaign for George: there they had conducted themselves in a seemly manner.[22] "There is a dignity and delicacy which a woman should never depart from," Lady Spencer told Harriet. "I know it has been from the best intention you have both been led to take the part you have done, but let this be a lesson to you . . . never to go in any matter beyond the strictest rules of propriety."[23] Even Mrs. Montagu, a champion of women's education as well as a member of the Blue Stocking Circle, thought Georgiana had gone too far: "The Duchess of Devonshire has been canvassing in a most masculine manner, and has met with much abuse." But her disapproval of Georgiana did not affect her own activities on behalf of Pitt: "I hope we shall succeed at York and in the country. I have done my endeavours where I had the smallest interest and my men will all be Pittite."[24] Mary Hamilton recorded in her diary that she had "met the Dss of Devonshire in her Coach with a mob round her, canvassing in the Strand for Mr Fox. What a pity that any of our sex should ever forget what is due to female delicacy. The Scenes the Dss has been in lately, were they noted down, would not gain credit by those not in London at the time of the Election."[25]

St. Albans was a safe haven where Georgiana could forget the recent scenes at Covent Garden. The scent of pot pourri and wood fires replaced the odour of urine and rotting food which pervaded the backstreets of Westminster. However, shortly after her arrival she received a summons from the party. They wanted her to return immediately. As it turned out, she had left just as votes were shifting away from Wray and in favour of Fox. The Duchess of Portland wrote, "I am happy to tell you of our success today for Westminster—we beat them by forty-five, which has put us into great spirits, you may believe. Everybody is so anxious for your return that I do hope you will come to town at the latest tomorrow evening; for if we should lose this at last, they will think it is owing to your absence."[26]

Lady Spencer could scarcely believe the effrontery of the Cavendishes, or their willingness to sacrifice Georgiana's health and reputation for political ends. She wrote a sharp reply, her bitterness heightened by the knowledge that if her husband were alive they would not treat the Spencer name in so cavalier a fashion. Georgiana did not wish to return; she was not convinced that her efforts had been the cause of Fox's change in fortune. Her refusal horrified the Whig grandees; as far as they were concerned, the success of the election depended upon her presence. The Duke of Portland humbled himself to make a personal plea:

> The state of the Polls for these last two days is a better argument than any other I can give you for refusing to concur in your opinion of yourself. Every one is convinced that your Exertions have produced the very material alteration which has happened in Fox's favour, and will continue to preserve and improve it into a decisive victory, but be assured that if . . . a suspicion should arise of your having withdrawn yourself from the Election, a general languor would prevail, Despondency would succeed, and the Triumph of the Court would be the inevitable consequence. However it may seem, depend upon it, that this Representation is not exaggerated.[27]

Lord John Cavendish wrote directly to Lady Spencer on behalf of the Cavendishes to apologize for the treatment of her daughters. "It was entirely to be imputed to some injudicious advisers who conducted them in an absurd and improper manner." But he was also blunt in claiming that "the censure and abuse has already been incurred; and that if any votes are lost for want of similar application" Georgiana would be blamed. He promised her that they had changed their methods: "the Ladies go early in the mornings to such persons as they are told are likely to be influenced by them, and talk to them at their coach doors, after which they go to a shop that over looks the polling place and look out of the window and encourage their friends."[28] He also promised that the party would mount a better defence of Georgiana; henceforth no libel would go unchallenged.

Reluctantly, Lady Spencer allowed her daughter to set off in her coach back to London. Lord John Cavendish's assurances had not convinced either of them. "You cannot conceive how vexed I am at the newspaper abuse," Georgiana told her brother. She begged him not to read the lurid stories they printed about her or, if he did, not to believe them. She blamed the Portlands for forcing her to canvass in the first place, and cited their letters as justification for her return.[29] But even though she hated to be a figure of ridicule, she longed for the theatre and excitement of mass canvassing. St. Albans had been a welcome rest for a few days but the election made ordinary life seem insipid.

In Westminster Georgiana ignored orders to remain in her carriage. She not only chatted with voters and argued cheerfully with them, she also took an interest in their businesses and families. She met their wives and children, became godmother to tens of infants, and impressed the women with her knowledge of such homely matters as nursing and discipline. Her success lay in her ability to empathize with strangers. "I delight myself with the Idea that your unaffected good humour, civility and attention to everyone will draw all hearts towards you," Lady Spencer acknowledged. She recognized her daughter's talent and pitied those who "have not that Vivyfying spark of benevolence about them, nor know what it is to love their fellow creatures abstracted."[30] Georgiana also understood the power of money and she went with her friends from shop to shop making enormous purchases, deliberately overpaying while hinting at the promise of more if the proprietors voted for Fox. A visit to the milliners' shops in Tavistock Street with Harriet and the Ladies Waldegrave turned into a street party, with the shopkeepers hoisting foxskin muffs over their doors as a sign of their support.

The *Morning Post* complained that Georgiana and Harriet were guilty of more than paying over the odds. It accused them of threatening anti-Fox tradesmen with a Whig blacklist. Just as Lord John Cavendish had promised, the *Morning Herald and Daily Advertiser* riposted on Georgiana's behalf. "The interference of the Duchess of Devonshire in behalf of Mr Fox is but a counterpart of those Roman Ladies who sued to Coriolanus for the welfare of the City of Rome," it intoned.[31] The more scurrilous the abuse and sexual innuendo levelled at them, the loftier the rebuttals of the Foxite papers. For the Whigs, the contest was about the larger issues: Liberty, Patriotism, and Duty. In contrast, the pro-government papers concentrated on Georgiana, showing her kissing or bribing electors with favours. The Whig printers tried to raise her above the fray. In the cartoon "The Apotheosis of the Dutchess" she is lifted up to the clouds by the goddesses "Truth" and "Virtue" while "Scandal" lies grovelling on the ground clutching a copy of the *Morning Post*.[32] The anti-Fox propagandists linked Georgiana's genius for the "common touch" with being common, hence her nickname of "Doll Common." In its daily report on the election the *Morning Post* persistently associated Georgiana with free sex: she was either "granting favours," caressing her "favourite member," looking for the "right handle in politics," or grasping the "fox's tail." It also implied that her unfeminine behaviour was causing her to grow a beard. On occasion, the *Post* was even a little ironic: "A certain Duke is quite charmed with the public and political conduct of his amiable Duchess, and calls for the *Morning Post* at breakfast to read the history of her Grace's canvass."[33]

The one effective argument in the Whigs' counter-attack was the charge of misogyny and cowardice against the other side. On April 21 the *Morning Herald* scored a blow with this article:

> The following curious paper was found in Catherine Street yesterday evening, supposed to have dropped from the pocket of a ministerial editor in the environs of that place:

> My Dear Friend,
> You go on swimmingly. The women are the best subjects in the world—work them for God's Sake. HER in Piccadilly particularly. Suppose you were to say in your next . . . we hear that a certain Duchess (in great letters) has eloped with Sam House . . . having first had half a dozen amours; . . . She does a great deal of mischief to the cause—can't you throw a hint against Lady D——n or Mrs F . . . it would have an effect . . . Say a word or two about the Miss

Keppels, and just throw out that they were seen in a certain place, with a certain fishmonger, and so on, you know how to manage it.[34]

The Whigs pursued the theme with considerable success, although it meant that they had to temper their attacks on Mrs. Hobart and Lady Salisbury. But their defence of Georgiana was anaemic compared to the robust insults made by the government press. The pious images depicting her making sacrifices to the Temple of Liberty failed to neutralize those of her making love to the electors of Westminster. There seemed to be twice the number of broadsheets and handbills attacking Georgiana, who was forced to send deputies to buy up the most offensive prints as soon as they appeared in shop windows.

In the streets, earthy ballads were sold by balladmongers, who strategically placed themselves near Georgiana's canvass. Gangs of rowdy sailors followed her coach, singing at the top of their voices:

> *I had rather kiss my Moll than she;*
> *With all her paint and finery;*
> *What's a Duchess more than woman?*
> *We've sounder flesh on Portsmouth Common:*
> *So drink about to HOOD and WRAY—*
> *Their health!—and may they gain the day!*
> *Then fill our Nectar in a glass,*
> *As for kissing—Kiss my a——.[35]*

Remarkably, the government's efforts failed to turn the voters against Georgiana and her energetic canvass brought in the votes Fox needed. By April 22 he was almost level with Wray. Yet he remained despondent about his chances of winning, and one of the newspapers poked fun at him for his lack of enthusiasm: "all advertisements relative to the Westminster Election should be in the Duchess of Devonshire's name. She is the candidate to all intents and purposes. Mr Fox has not of himself polled a man this fortnight."[36] He recovered somewhat when his lead over Wray increased to three figures. By the end of April the party's spirits were sufficiently high for them to host a dinner for over 800 electors at the Freemason's Tavern. Fox sat at the top table facing his constituents so that everyone could see that the gruelling election had in no way dented his confidence. The party coffers had been raided to ensure the evening's suc-

cess; the *Morning Herald* described it as "an uninterrupted scene of con-
vivial mirth." Captain Morris led the revellers through a number of table-
thumping songs, and finally the whole company scrambled to its feet to
toast "The Duchess of Devonshire and Portland, and other fair supporters
of the Whig cause."[37]

The improved morale had a noticeable effect on the tone of Whig propaganda. For the first time since the beginning of the election a note of
humour crept into the party's advertisements. On May 1 the *Morning Herald* informed its female readers that the "Ladies of Fashion, in the interest
of Mr Fox's election, are distinguished by wearing a feather in exact imitation of a fox's brush." The only purveyor of this commodity was Mr.
Carbery, plume-master to His Royal Highness the Prince of Wales, whose
shop could be found at 34 Conduit Street, near Bond Street, while stocks
lasted.[38] With only three more weeks to go, supporters in Pitt's camp were
understandably sulky. Some suggested that Georgiana should be arraigned
before Parliament on charges of bribery. Pro-government newspapers increased their output, but the Whig counter-offensive was now working at
maximum efficiency and anti-Georgiana posters scarcely survived an hour
before being spotted and pasted over. The *Post* and the *Herald* were locked
in battle, devoting almost their entire news section to rebuttals and
counter-attacks.

Through it all, Georgiana and the other women continued to canvass.
Only Lavinia Spencer, who could not hide her jealousy of Georgiana, still
thought that the election might swing the other way. "I found Lady
Spencer very unhappy indeed about the Duchess and the Westminster
Election," she told George. "She is so abused for meddling and so hooted
at for her avowed interference that Lady Spencer is miserable about it."
Lavinia had to admit that Fox was leading in the polls, but "he knows, and
so do all the Party that he cannot carry it and this provokes the Dss and
Lady Spencer that the Portlands and Cavendishes oblige her to interfere
when they know it is for nothing."[39]

However, by the close of polling Hood was first and Fox second, the
clear winner over Wray by more than 200 votes. The final figures were:
Lord Hood—6,694; Mr. Fox—6,234; Sir Cecil Wray—5,998. Lady Spencer
no longer cared about the outcome and simply wanted Georgiana out of
the limelight. "Why should you not shirk the winding up and say that you
are unable to hold out any longer?" she asked. "There is no law against im-
possibilities. I am really afraid of your hurting yourselves, and shall be

heartily glad if you have both the courage to withstand all the flimsy arguments . . . by coming down here immediately."[40] This was not what Georgiana wanted to hear just when all her efforts were proving to be justified.
The Duke of Portland also insisted that she must stay: the party could
show no hint of regret or embarrassment, whatever its private feelings
about the Westminster campaign. It had to be a clear-cut moral victory—
especially since they had done so badly in the rest of the country. Eighty-
nine Whigs, nicknamed "Fox's Martyrs," had lost their seats.[41] Even the
leadership was not immune: in a humiliating defeat for the Cavendishes,
Lord John had lost his seat at York. Fox, someone had heard, "can't bear to
think of politics."[42] The future looked bleak for the Whigs, which was all
the more reason for squeezing every last bit of advantage out of their victory at Westminster.

As soon as the poll closed a triumphant procession of the entire party
marched from St. Paul's down the Strand, past Carlton House, the Prince
of Wales's residence, which they circled three times, and along Piccadilly
to Devonshire House. Twenty-four horsemen led the way, all dressed in
blue and buff with foxtails hanging from their hats. Behind them followed
a brass band, playing the Whig songs of the election, and then Fox in a decorated chair, garlanded with laurels and other senatorial insignia. Witnesses were shocked to see that his friends had dressed themselves in
servants' liveries and were driving his carriage. Hundreds of supporters
marched behind, many of them carrying banners proclaiming FOX AND
LIBERTY, and SACRED TO FEMALE PATRIOTISM, in reference to the women's
contribution. The aristocracy followed, dressed in full regalia, having ordered out their state carriages for the occasion. The Prince's carriage
brought up the rear of the parade accompanied by every member of his
household, all in uniform. Everyone was shouting and waving their hats at
the thousands of spectators who watched them from windows lining the
route. The Prince of Wales and Georgiana, meanwhile, had slipped
through the streets in order to greet the marchers when they reached
Devonshire House. According to one witness, the two perched themselves on ladders set against the walls of the house, holding on with one
hand and waving laurels with the other. It was a novel sight, not least because there was none of the unruly behaviour usually associated with large
crowds. The marchers applauded the speeches and then departed relatively peacably, leaving property unscathed, with the exception of Lord
Temple's windows. The conservative *London Chronicle* could not help

"The Tipling Duchess Returning from Canvassing," April 29, 1784. Georgiana is shown returning home in an inebriated state. Aitken. BM Cat. 6560.

"Every Man Has His Hobby Horse," May 1, 1784. Charles Fox is attacked for relying on Georgiana to increase his votes. Rowlandson. BM Cat. 6566.

"Vox Populi, Vox Dei," May 23, 1784. Georgiana defends herself against "woman-hating" newspapers with the "shield of virtue." Humphry. BM Cat. 6594.

praising the Whigs for this feat of organization: "The Festival concluded as it was conducted throughout, with peace and harmony. There was neither riot nor disorder. At night almost the whole of the windows of the principal streets were illuminated, and there really seemed to be a general testimony of joy on the occasion."[43]

The Prince of Wales, who had been too drunk for most of the election to be of any help, opened up Carlton House for several nights of dinners and balls. All the celebrants appeared in buff and blue, which for once solved the problem of casual gatecrashers. One of the highlights was a sumptuous banquet for 600 guests. Mrs. Crewe lived up to her reputation for wit when she replied to the Prince's toast of "True blue and Mrs Crew" with "Buff and blue and all of you." If anyone remained ignorant of the purpose behind such a determined display of spirit, it was clear by the following week on the day of the state opening of Parliament. The King had to go through St. James's Park, past Carlton House, to reach Parliament. To embarrass him, the Prince held a *fête-champêtre* in his gardens with music and dancing. The solemnity of the state occasion was disrupted by the sound of revelry coming from the other side of the brick wall.

Nevertheless, on the first day of Parliament the Whig ranks were so depleted they could only muster a miserable 114 votes against the government's majority of almost 300. Pitt's first speech to the House was relaxed and self-assured. He moved his listeners to frequent laughter with descriptions of the Westminster election and Georgiana's canvass. She would not be arraigned for bribery, but he refused to allow the election results to stand. Fox was barred from taking his seat until after an official scrutiny. It was a delaying tactic by Pitt, a piece of petty vindictiveness against the conquered. After several months the House grew tired of the game and voted to allow Fox his seat. (Fox achieved some consolation in suing the bailiff of Westminster and winning £2,000.)

Georgiana scarcely registered the fact that she had escaped prosecution; the end of the election had not stopped her hounding in the press or removed her responsibilities. Although the core membership of the party was stable, there were at least a hundred more supporters who had to be prevented from defecting. Georgiana used lavish entertainments and her own popularity to entice waverers back to meetings at Devonshire House, but turtle dinners and gambling nights could not disguise the fact that the Whigs would never be in power while the King reigned. Lord North remained loyal but many of his followers felt there was no point in supporting the defunct coalition.

The Fox-North alliance had been a disaster for the Whigs, but it was also the defining moment for their ideology. Henceforth the Foxites would always hark back to 1784: their defeat became enshrined as a near-mythological battle against a despotic King and his lackey William Pitt. For Georgiana 1784 was also a defining year—the personal cost of the Westminster election had been far greater for her than anyone else, but it also established her position. Before the election her participation in party politics had been haphazard and dependent upon circumstance. Her duties as a wife, her friendships with Fox and the Prince of Wales, and her celebrity as the leader of the *ton* had placed opportunities in her way. But it was only after the government had recognized her potency as a campaigner that Georgiana achieved political status in her own right. Her unofficial ties to the Whigs were now official, as the Duke of Portland had made clear when he recalled her to London. Fanny Burney explained Georgiana's position in just a few words: she was the "head of opposition public."[44]

At least eleven women had canvassed daily, including Harriet, the Duchess of Portland, and the Waldegrave sisters. Lady Salisbury and Mrs. Hobart had run a less successful but still a high-profile campaign for Pitt. Their participation discounts the argument put forward by some historians that it was the fact that Georgiana had campaigned for a non-relative

which enraged eighteenth-century society.[45] There was no taboo on female participation in politics, only a great deal of hypocrisy.

> So [Harriet teased Lord Granville Leveson Gower many years later,
> when she heard about his method of campaigning], your Ladies as-
> sist you in canvassing? I thought, my dear Granville, you were one of
> the people who thought my Sister and my canvassing even for our
> Brother, certainly for Mr Fox, so scandalous a thing that it could
> never be forgot or forgiven. How I have heard you . . . exclaim at the
> impropriety and indelicacy of both our conduct and the people who
> *could suffer us* to do so horrible a thing! Yet, you see, in Election fer-
> vour you can take up the same means you were so shocked at in
> others.[46]

The other women canvassers neither endured the same abuse as Georgiana, nor won the same plaudits; certainly no one libelled Lady Salisbury,
who was briefly the Prince of Wales's mistress, with the accusation of
nymphomania. Georgiana was marked out for several reasons. First, she
brought her own personality to the campaign in an era when the only
women who had public personas were actresses and courtesans. Since her
marriage she had deliberately courted attention through her patronage of
the arts and her flair for fashion. She had appeared as herself and not as a
sacrifice to female duty, and this had affronted traditionalists and made her
vulnerable to attack. Furthermore, it was one thing for Fox to recast his
public image to become the "Man of the People"—the sobriquet neatly
encapsulated his populist rhetoric and reforming ideas—but the term
could not cross over. A "Woman of the People" meant a prostitute, hence
the plethora of prints which portrayed Georgiana as sexually available.

Georgiana had also challenged eighteenth-century attitudes to class distinction. Treating the voters as her equals was a serious transgression
against propriety. The accusations of bribery were mere stock in trade for
every election. The Duchess of Northumberland used to drop trinkets
from her window to the waiting crowd below, and those who returned
them received a double bounty, but unlike Georgiana she never shared
any intimate moments with the voters, chatting over a pint of ale or a tip-
ple of gin. Indeed, the *Morning Post* calculated Georgiana's daily alcoholic
intake and wondered how she could remain standing. No one as yet had
any idea that France would soon be convulsed by revolution, but Georgiana's encouragement of her inferiors still seemed very dangerous.

It was these innovations—her own cult of celebrity and her democratic approach—which differentiated Georgiana then and later as a female pioneer in electoral politics. Her methods were too modern for eighteenth-century society. She was never allowed to canvass openly in London again, nor did other aristocratic women imitate her example. It would be another hundred years before women once more ventured boldly into street politics as Georgiana had not been afraid to do in 1784.

CHAPTER 10

OPPOSITION

1784—1786

Two presidencies have been of late given up, Lady Bridget Tollemache and the Duchess of Devonshire. The former over wit, and the latter of fashion and bon ton. Lady Bridget is succeeded by the Duchess of Gordon, and her Grace of Devon by the Countess of Salisbury, who is now supreme not only in article of dress, but in everything that depends on guste.

The Duchess of Devonshire appeared on Saturday at Drury-Lane Theatre in a mob cap; her Grace, ever since her initiation into the business of electioneering, has been much attached to mobs.

Morning Post, *May 3, 1785*

"Emblematic Designs": The Duchess of Devonshire—The Whig Heroine— reviewing the grand procession [and] the triumphant cavalcade of the Man of the People. In the background, Envy is beheld in the character of a belamiste barking at the moon with all her brazen tongues; and in a retrospect prospect, Charity is beheld in a divine attitude, showering her heavenly influence on indigent mortals. With the motto, "My Humour is my leading star."

Advertisement in the Morning Herald and Daily Advertiser, *November 18, 1785*

I am cross, miserable and unhappy. I hate myself," Georgiana wrote in June 1784, two months after the election victory.[1] She was in debt again. According to estimates in the *Morning Post*, the Westminster election personally cost the Devonshires over £30,000. Georgiana knew that she had spent more than that, although she could only guess at the true figure. Her little French writing desk was almost hidden beneath the pile of credit notes waiting to be paid, but she was terrified of asking the Duke for help. He had hardly spoken to her since her previous confession and their relationship had deteriorated further during the election. He had been mortified by the caricatures portraying him as a cuckold, but, more than that, he resented Georgiana's independence and was angry she wasn't more like Bess, who made him feel important. He showed his displeasure by allowing her bills to go unpaid. "I find my debts are much talked of, and I know not how to hurry the Duke," Georgiana complained. She tried to be philosophical about her own treatment by the press but "I think it has lowered me," she wrote, "and thrown me out of the quiet and domestic life I long for."[2]

The Duke's silence frightened her. "As much as I long to see you it is not for me I write," she wrote to Bess. "I am certain poor Canis's health and spirits depend upon your soothing friendship."[3] They were expecting her return and Georgiana had begged her friend to be in England by June at the latest. She promised Bess she could return to Italy in the winter if she wished, but at least they would have the summer together. Perhaps the four of them, little Georgiana included, would go together to the Continent. Bess had not seen England for almost a year and a half and she was beginning to tire of her nomadic life. Since she knew her place at Devonshire House was absolutely assured, there were no more obstacles to her return.

Bess informed the Devonshires that they should expect her in August, news which dismayed Lady Spencer and Lady Clermont. "I have no reason for these fears but knowing her powers, makes me wish her gone," Lady Clermont admitted.[4] Disappointed that Bess was not coming sooner, Georgiana found solace in holding suppers for the party and, as usual, in gambling. "The Duchess of Devonshire has parties almost every night for gambling purposes and factious ends," wrote Lady Mary Coke disapprovingly. Nor was she the only person to comment: emboldened by the election, pro-government newspapers printed sarcastic asides about Georgiana's inability to pay her debts. "It is a heavy punishment upon myself," cried Lady Spencer when she read about another of Georgiana's scrapes. "Could I recall past times and begin your education again my first care should be to teach you and your sister . . . to shun the abuse of money, for in not doing that I cannot but see myself [as] the cause of all the distress and anxiety you undergo." She no longer believed Georgiana's contrite promises to reform.

In July the Prince of Wales involved her in a far worse scandal than mere trouble with creditors. During a ball in May, Prinny, as he became known, had affronted his female guests by his habit of dancing only with Georgiana. "The whole company assembled at 10," complained Mrs. Boscawen to Lady Chatham. "The Duchess of Devonshire did not come till 12 and he waited for her to begin, tho' the Dss of Marlboro' and her daughters, as well as Lady Charlotte Berthe were there."[5] But it was not love, or at least not towards Georgiana, which prompted his actions. The Prince's latest passion was for Maria Fitzherbert, a respectable and wealthy Catholic widow.[6] Although gratified by his affections she refused to become his mistress, which made the Prince, who was unaccustomed to such rebuffs, love her all the more. He increased his offer from *carte blanche* to marriage, and alarmed his friends by throwing himself on the floor and pulling at his hair, sobbing and screaming that she had to be his wife or he would die. It was an impossible wish. Not only would it be unthinkable for him to marry a commoner, twice married, and several years older than himself; two parliamentary acts forbade it. The Act of Settlement stipulated that the monarch had to marry within the Protestant faith, and the 1774 Royal Marriages Act awarded the King sole discretion in choosing the spouses of the royal family. Such a marriage could only end in the Prince's exile. He swore he would go mad if Maria could not be his wife, and he begged Georgiana, as his best friend, to help him.

Despite her distaste for the whole affair Georgiana could not resist his pathetic entreaties. There was an unspoken but nevertheless keenly felt antipathy between the two women which made her reluctant to accept the role of go-between, even without the complication of the constitutional issue. Each sensed a rival in the other. Mrs. Fitzherbert had thick, gold-coloured hair and pleasant features, but she was no match for Georgiana in terms of beauty or wit. Everything about her was heavy: her figure, her walk, even her conversation. She could bring a flagging discussion down with a bump, an attribute which did her no harm at court but made her unwelcome in the Devonshire House Circle. She also had an acute sense of self-regard and, as Georgiana would later learn, a boundless memory for slights. Few females are predisposed to like the woman whom their lover employs as his emissary: Georgiana compounded her crime in the eyes of Mrs. Fitzherbert, who suspected her motives anyway, by taking every opportunity to warn her against such a marriage. Nevertheless, she agreed during one of Georgiana's difficult visits to her house that a trip abroad would be necessary if the Prince persisted in his plan to marry her.

On July 8 Georgiana was drinking on the balcony of Devonshire House with some friends when she was called inside. A footman whispered that two men were waiting to see her. She made her excuses to her guests, who had pretended not to see the urgent conversation in the corner, and went down the steps to the courtyard. There she found two of the Prince's cronies, Mr. Bouverie and Mr. Onslow, who gabbled some story about Prinny having run himself through with a sword. His dying wish, they said, was to see Mrs. Fitzherbert, but she would not go unless Georgiana accompanied her, and even now was waiting in her carriage just outside the gates. The Duke was away, and Georgiana was too frightened to consult anyone upstairs and so she agreed, leaving Harriet in charge of the party.

It was dark when they reached Carlton House. Onslow and Bouverie took them into an overheated room, where they found the Prince dramatically sprawled across a crimson sofa with bloody bandages wrapped around his hairless chest. The sight of Prinny wheezing and crying in what seemed to be his final moments moved Mrs. Fitzherbert to agree to become his wife. Prinny wanted a ring to seal the pact and so, reluctantly, Georgiana pulled off one of hers, which he falteringly slipped on Mrs. Fitzherbert's fourth finger. With that accomplished he fell back against the pillows and seemed to rest easy. There was nothing for the women to do except return home. Not all the Prince's attendants shared his satisfaction; Lord Southampton was in a panic and ready to go to the King at once, but they managed to calm him down with the assurance that the ceremony was meaningless. Before the two women parted that night they both signed a deposition stating that promises obtained in such a manner are entirely void.[7] The following morning Mrs. Fitzherbert hurriedly packed her bags and departed for France, leaving to Georgiana the task of explaining her absence to the disappointed Prince.*

---

* Georgiana immediately related the episode to her mother and the Duke. Neither was surprised at the Prince's behaviour, and she began to wonder whether it had been a hoax. She suggested to Mr. Onslow that the Prince should see an independent surgeon to establish whether or not the suicide attempt had been genuine. When Prinny heard of this he sent her a long and indignant letter about "false friends." Georgiana was too fed up to reply and left London a week later without seeing him. His letters, aggressive and pleading by turn, wore her down and she reluctantly agreed he could use her courier to write to Mrs. Fitzherbert in France. She later found out that in order to escape detection the Prince frequently wrote to Mrs. Fitzherbert using her name.

❦❧

Two weeks later Bess returned from Italy. "The greatest lady in Ireland [the Duchess of Rutland] came to pay me a visit the day before yesterday," wrote Lady Clermont to Lady Spencer in August. "There were a great many people in the room, one of the company said, 'I saw Lady E. in London, she is come from Italy to pay a visit to the Duchess.' The great lady, (who is a great fool by the by) said, 'the Duke you mean, he is very much in love with her.' Many other disagreeable things [were] said which I try'd to laugh off."[8] When Georgiana reported that they were disappointed to find Bess looking thin and pale, her mother could not refrain from replying: "Indeed she should not stay in such a climate as this, every hour may be of consequence to her."[9]

Lady Spencer noticed a change in Georgiana's letters soon after Bess joined the Devonshires at Chatsworth. They were far shorter than normal and mostly about generalities—local politics and the races—but there was anxiety beneath their flippant tone.[10] She joked that Bess was like Susannah tempted by the Elders; she had succeeded in making all the men of the house party fall in love with her. "Cl Crawfurd [*sic*] is, you know, very gallant and had been saying all manner of fine things to Ly Eliz," wrote Georgiana in September, "so the Duke threw her whip down the steepest part of the hill that he might fetch it, but his gallantry did not reach so far for he would not go."[11] Lady Spencer was worried by what she read, but she alienated Georgiana by sending her unsolicited advice and demanding that she keep up a daily letter journal. Her daughter replied evasively: "I shall quarrel with you for your letter being too much taken up with me and not enough with accounts of yourself. Do you continue to ride—do you eat pretty well—how do you sleep—remember that you cannot do more good than by telling me what you do car le meilleur sermon est prêchant d'exemple."*[12]

Lavinia and George came to stay in the middle of September, and this at last provided Lady Spencer with reliable witnesses. But despite his cautious spying, George could discover nothing concrete about Bess or her relationship with either the Duke or Georgiana: "The circumstances that you wished me to take notice of when I was here, I have not yet had an opportunity of observing. I do not think it is so much to be observed as is

---

* The best way to teach is by example.

thought in general, and I really believe much more is made of it than need be. I never saw Lady E. before, at least never for any time. She is certainly very pretty and sometimes very engaging in her manners."[13] However, George was not a man to be beguiled with pretty comments and judicious flattery. He found Bess's affectations ludicrous and "quite sufficient, I think, for anyone to be disgusted" if they weren't already in love with her. Another guest, the obliging Miss Lloyd, also supplied Lady Spencer with information, but her powers of observation were far less acute than George's. "I hope you are quite at ease about the fondness of the Husband and wife for her," she wrote. "You certainly may, for though to be sure nothing can be greater than it is, of all sides, yet I will pawn my life on it, it is perfectly innocent." While she was sanguine about the threesome, she had a word or two to say about Charlotte: "I don't like this Charlotte much, I fear there is something bad in her, I am glad she is going abroad again."[14]

Georgiana also watched Bess closely, although she felt wretched for even suspecting her friend of duplicity. No one noticed that she was anxious, although she told Lady Spencer at the end of September that her spirits were low. They had had another "brilliant" party which she could not enjoy because "I was not well and felt more nervous and unhappy and uncomfortable than I ever did almost in all my life." Yet she was unable or unwilling to explain the reason and described her depression as a "causeless woe."[15] The Duke increasingly found fault with Georgiana, and when he had nothing particular to point to he criticized her for failing to provide him with a son. Bess, on the other hand, never felt happier or more secure. "I wish I had a Plympton piece of news [where Georgiana first became pregnant] to communicate to you my dear Madam," she wrote to Lady Spencer, who was unpleasantly surprised to receive a postscript from her at the end of Georgiana's letter. "But tho' I never saw my beloved friend look better than she does now, I fear another season at Bath will be necessary for our wishes to succeed: I wish I could attend her there, for far beyond any circumstances in this world much as I have to wish for, do I most anxiously wish she had a son . . . I own I am irresistibly attached to you with all a daughter's respect and affection."[16]

Bess's flattery only prompted Lady Spencer to urge her once again to go abroad as soon as possible. Coincidentally, there was now a good reason for her departure: even by eighteenth-century standards, which encouraged women to look slight and delicate, Bess was painfully thin.[17] As soon as they returned to London the worried Devonshires called in their doctors who examined her and once again prescribed a warmer climate. She reluctantly agreed to return to France, this time without Charlotte, but with all her expenses met by the Devonshires. Georgiana forgot her doubts about Bess's loyalty and only thought of her imminent loss. Lavinia was contemptuous of her sister-in-law. "The Duchess left town the same instant that Lady Eliz did," she told George. "I did not see her for she was too much overcome with the separation to see anyone."[18]

The Devonshires supplied Bess with money and letters of introduction to all their friends in Paris to ensure that there would be no repeat of the previous year's reception. Then, the Duchesse de Polignac, jealous of Bess's relationship with Georgiana, had used her influence with Marie Antoinette to exclude her from Versailles society. Since Bess had officially been travelling as a governess to little Charlotte, Georgiana had been unable to do more than hint to her French friends that they should welcome her. "Let spite and jealousy and envy take its fill," Bess had written defiantly to Georgiana. Nevertheless, she had agreed—for Georgiana's sake, naturally—to follow her advice: "I will do all that is for your ease and comfort, let Madame P. be suffer'd, soothed, as you please. I shall give Madame P no cause for jealousy, I will try to gain her friendship."[19] Bess implied that the other reason for her ostracism was a rumour: *le tout Paris* talked of a lesbian affair between her and Georgiana. What angered her, Bess claimed, was not so much the accusation as the impertinence of having their relationship defined in so mundane a fashion. She was eloquent in her indignation, although she implied that only Georgiana was under suspicion:

> Who has any right to know how long or how tenderly we love one another! Why are excuses to be made for its sharpness and its fervency? Why am I to pay court to anybody but your mother? Why is our union to be profaned by having a lie told about it? Can I ever forget the note that contained—"the first instant I saw you, my heart flew to your service." . . . Does the warm impulse of two hearts want an excuse to be accounted for, and must your partiality to me be ushered in by another connection?[20]

The question of "another connection"—Georgiana's suspected lesbian feelings for Bess—can never be properly answered while the censored letters at Chatsworth remain indecipherable. The claim that women in the eighteenth century only experienced loving same-sex friendships but never love affairs does not stand up to scrutiny. There were both kinds, and eighteenth-century men and women were perfectly capable of telling them apart. It is entirely possible that Bess and Georgiana's relationship encompassed erotic love, at least for a while, given the louche, sexually-charged, and self-consciously rebellious nature of the Devonshire House Circle. But since both women remained ferociously heterosexual, it is also clear that their emotional attachment to each other was far more important, more complicated, and longer lasting than whatever initial bonds of physical attraction.

Georgiana's effusive letters guaranteed Bess a rapturous welcome on this occasion. The Duke of Dorset, who had been Ambassador-Extraordinary since 1783, was also in residence; his greeting left no doubt of his interest in renewing their former acquaintance. Bess's letters home contained little else except detailed descriptions of her evenings with the Polignacs, the brilliant parties at Versailles, and suppers at the embassy. No doubt she sought to make her friends just a little jealous of the wonderful time she was having without them; and she succeeded. Georgiana sent her a bitter letter in February 1785, sarcastically congratulating her on "your new acquaintances in Paris." Its vehemence frightened Bess and she wrote a humble, and honest, apology. The last half of the letter has been cut away but it reads in part: "I wished for you—Oh G may I hope you will believe this. . . . can you do yourself and me the injustice to doubt that knowing you and loving you as I have done my heart can ever alter towards you! no, never, never, never. . . . I cannot read your letter without a trembling heart that Paris or anything, or anybody . . ."[21] This was one of the few occasions when Bess allowed her mask of affectation to slip—and even then the truth was implicit rather than explicit. She was silently pleading for Georgiana's forgiveness for a far greater betrayal than the co-opting of her friends: she was three months pregnant with the Duke of Devonshire's child.

Her letter crossed with one of Georgiana's, bringing the news that she too was three months pregnant. When Bess counted the weeks she realized angrily that their babies could have been conceived within days or even hours of each other. To console herself she took up with the Duke of Dorset and remained in Paris as his mistress until her pregnancy began to show. Faced by the danger of discovery she fled to Italy to be with her brother, Lord Hervey, and from there confessed to Georgiana about her short-lived affair with Dorset, hastily adding that it in no way affected her love for her. "I must thank you over and over and over again for the Dr Secret letter,"

Georgiana replied tenderly in June, "I have not a fear about the Pride [the Duke of Dorset]." In return she assured Bess there was no need to worry about the "Eyebrow" [Fox], who had failed in his attempts to persuade her to leave the Duke: "I am not parted and Canis is triumphant, tho' the Eyebrow makes me, by his reproaches etc., feel very much sometimes."[22] This is one of few surviving references to Georgiana's suspected affair with Fox. Whatever happened between them, his "reproaches" did not impair their working relationship. There were other men courting Georgiana, including a new, unnamed suitor "whom I admire but am not in love with," though they did not mean anything to her: "Oh my Dearest Bess, how I do love you—I cannot live without you—you and Canis and G are the only comforts I have."[23]

Georgiana agreed to give up dancing while she was pregnant but she could not stop gambling. She herself could not explain the compulsion, nor did she know why it had grown worse since Bess's departure. In April the Duke at last began to take an interest in her financial plight and wrote out a note of credit for £1,300 to settle her debts. But instead of paying it in to her bankers, she took the note with her to Mrs. Sturt's and gambled it away on top of a further £500. At the end of May, when Georgiana was six months pregnant, Lady Mary Coke heard that she had lost over £1,000 at Mrs. Hobart's and stayed until 6 a.m. trying to win it back.[24] In July, with only a few weeks left before she came to term, Georgiana was still in the grip of her mania: "She sits up almost every night at faro," wrote a friend. "The Duke has paid five thousand pound for her and She owes three more."*[25]

Lady Spencer could find no peace while Georgiana continued upon her self-destructive course. It was not only the gambling which frightened her so much as the drugs and all-night binges.

For God's sake try to compose yourself [she begged]. I am terrified lest the perpetual hurry of your spirits, and the medicines you take, to obtain a false tranquillity, should injure you. I hoped the Duke

---

* The Duke was also losing a great deal of money at Brooks's, and between them the two made inroads into their capital. "I hear the Devonshire Estate is put to nurse," Mrs. Scott wrote sarcastically to Mrs. Montagu. "And that family reduced to the small pittance of £8000 a year—it will really be poverty to them who could not keep within their original immense income, and some of the hungry opposition must feel it very sensibly." Reginald Blunt, *Mrs Montagu* (London 1923), II, p. 192; Mrs. Scott to Mrs. Montagu, July 23, 1785.

knew the whole of what you had lost and that it was all settled. . . .
Why will you not say fairly: I have led a wild and scrambling life that
disagrees with me. I have lost more money than I can afford. I will
turn over a new leaf and lead a quiet sober life from this moment, as
I am sure if I do not I shall hurt myself or my child.[26]

Her letters had no effect. They still had the power to hurt, but since meeting Bess Georgiana had ceased to be so emotionally dependent on her
mother. The replies she sent to Lady Spencer no longer had a ring of sin-
cerity: "Your letter quite overcame me, my Dst Dst M.," she wrote on
June 7. "Indeed one cannot feel more forcibly than I do the errors of every
year of my life and of this year above all others, but indeed I hope that they
will be so far beneficial errors as to secure beyond doubt, years such as you
wish them."[27] As long as she remained on good terms with the Duke,
Georgiana felt reasonably sure of her position, and he had convinced himself that the baby would be a boy. After eleven years of marriage the Duke
was frantic for a son. Georgiana, on the other hand, regarded it as her only
salvation: under the terms of the Cavendish estate, the birth of an heir
would enable the Duke to borrow against a mortgage, making it possible
for her to confess her debts without ruining him.

On September 1 the papers announced that the Devonshires had had a
son, prompting a rush of congratulatory messages. But on September 2
they announced a correction: the baby was a girl. Georgiana had given
birth to a second daughter—Harriet. Well-wishers dropped by at Devonshire House to find Georgiana happily nursing her new baby, cosseted in
almost Eastern opulence. Her lying-in room had been entirely redeco-
rated with white satin. In the centre was a vast bed decked with enormous
paper flowers and silver ribbons, and crowned at the top by a gold canopy,
embellished by ducal ornaments inside and out. Lady Spencer gently
padded around so as not to disturb the patient, having left off wearing silk
to avoid making a rustle. Lady Mary Coke heard from visitors that Georgiana had composed a hymn during the labour; it would have been better,
she suggested, if she had made a vow never to gamble again.[28] Two months
later Harriet also gave birth to a girl: Caroline.* Lady Spencer decamped to

---

* Lady Caroline Ponsonby became the infamous Lady Caroline Lamb. She married
Lady Melbourne's second son, William Lamb, who became the second Viscount Mel-
bourne. Her talent as a novelist has been largely eclipsed today by her love affair with Lord
Byron and subsequent madness.

the Duncannon household, throwing Lord Duncannon out of his wife's bedroom and setting up a truckle bed in the corner. She spent a month there with her servants and prayer books while Harriet nursed her baby. People wondered why her sons-in-law put up with such interference.[29]

The birth of the Duke's other child took place in secret and in squalor; its mother was alone and frightened. The pregnancy had made her head and back ache, but mercifully her stomach still barely showed when she left Paris. In Italy her brother and sister-in-law were quarrelling bitterly and hardly noticed her. It was only in July, when the party reached the little island of Ischia, near Naples, that Bess had the courage to confess the truth to her brother. He was upset but not angry—he was a Hervey himself—and accepted his sister's indiscretion with magnanimity, but he insisted that she should go as far away from people as possible. "I must go near 100 miles at sea and in an open boat—I must go amongst strangers, perhaps leave my Infant with them. Patience, patience; my punishment is just," she cried.[30]

The need for secrecy forced Bess to choose the meanest inns along the route. A vivid account of her appalling journey survives in her diary.* It was a bitter irony for her to reflect that she had written long, indulgent letters of despair to the Devonshires when she had no reason. Now she was in great need of comfort and forced to write false letters describing non-existent events 150 miles away from her real location. She wrote to Georgiana from Ischia of "my heart full of sorrows and head of anxiety" but without stating the cause.[31] She wrote separately to the Duke when possible, with more specific complaints which he could only indirectly allude to by way of reply; he dared not write in tones greater than friendship. On the rare occasions that he could trust the courier he wrote awkwardly, unsure how to comfort her:

> I am terribly in want of you here, Mrs Bess, and am every minute reminded of the misfortune of your not being here by things that I see, such as the couch you us'd to sit on in the drawing room, amidst all your sighing lovers. . . . I have some thoughts, if I have time, of

---

* It is one of the few passages which seems to have escaped the censor's pen. In middle age Bess rewrote her entire collection of journals with a view to publication. Her son Augustus also edited extracts from his mother's diaries. What survives is not necessarily what she originally wrote or thought. In the main, the opus is a self-justification for stealing her friend's husband, and to that end her other lovers are either excised completely or their existence glossed over. Nevertheless, the terror and heartbreak she describes during her arduous experience were probably real.

going to Bolton to shoot upon the moors, and to prepare the place for you against next summer, for I intend to take you there whether you like it nor, let the consequences be what it will; I have not time to write any more but will write again very soon. So goodnight.[32]

On August 29, 1785, the Duke wrote with news of Georgiana's baby girl and added, "I am very much surpriz'd and impatient at not having heard from you upon a subject I expected to have heard something about by this time."[33] Bess was in a little town called Vietri on the Gulf of Salerno, having given birth on August 16 in a hostel which also doubled as a brothel—a place well known to her feckless brother. She had arrived two weeks before with Louis, a trusted family servant. He had agreed to pretend that Bess was his pregnant wife, and the mistress of his master Lord Hervey.

> Imagine [she wrote in her diary] a little staircase, dark and dirty, leading to the apartments of these people. The family consisted of the *Archi-Pretre des Amoureux;* his woman-servant, a coarse, ugly, and filthy creature; the doctor (his brother) and his wife—the doctor an honest man, the wife everything that one can imagine of wicked, vulgar and horrible . . . I heard everything but pretended to understand nothing . . . My faithful servant wept for me. . . . How many things increased my unhappiness! I had to dine with him, and to endure the odious company of these people; I had to live in a house which was little better than a house of ill fame.[34]

When the labour pains came Bess claims she thought only of the baby, the Duke, and Georgiana. It was a girl, whom she named Caroline Rosalie. She hurriedly rejoined her brother in Naples, and was relieved to see by her sister-in-law's manner that her secret was still safe. The baby was lodged with a poor family not far away, but Bess could do little more than visit it once a day, and she cried at having to leave Caroline with strangers. The separation affected her in other ways: she was in agony over her unused milk, which stained her bodice; she had to cover her breasts with fresh flannels, risking discovery by the servants in doing so. When Caroline was a few weeks old Louis offered to take her to his own family. There she could be cared for properly and Bess would be able to see her more easily. With Caroline safe, Bess consoled herself with a flirtation with the

Russian ambassador: "Misfortune," she wrote regretfully in her diary, "cannot cure me of my vanity."[35]

Bess remained in Italy for nearly a year, even though the Duke and Georgiana repeatedly urged her to come home. It was not only reluctance to leave Caroline which delayed her return—she knew in her heart that there would have to be changes to the *ménage à trois,* but she did not know how to present Georgiana with the truth. In his usual way, the Duke tried to make light of her fears: "The Rat does not know the chief cause of your uneasiness, and I, of course, shall never mention it to her, unless you desire me, but I am certain that if she did, she would not think you had been to blame about it, particularly after I had explain'd to her how the thing happen'd."[36] This was the question Bess often asked herself: how had this all happened?

Georgiana summed up her life during 1786 in a short poem:

> My mind can no comfort or happyness fix
> On seventeen hundred and eighty six
> For Sorry and Folly delighted to mix
> With seventeen hundred and eighty six
> Abounding alone in unpromising tricks
> Was seventeen hundred and eighty six
> And none was e'er worse I can swear by the Styx
> Than seventeen hundred and eighty six.[37]

People outside her family would have been astonished by its sadness. In the two years since the Westminster election she had silenced her critics by becoming more popular than ever. Her place within the Whig hierarchy was established and during parliamentary sessions she was usually busy behind the scenes: watching the numbers, relaying messages, and nipping signs of discontent in the bud. Fox's position as leader of the Whigs was not in doubt, but since the loss of the eighty-nine members he preferred to remain at his house in St. Anne's Hill, leaving administrative matters to the Duke of Portland, who unfortunately was incapable of organizing a systematic opposition to Pitt. In consequence, nothing much happened in the first year after the election. Edmund Burke was disgusted with the party's quiescence and complained in October 1784: "As to any plan of Conduct in our Leaders, there are not the faintest Traces of it—nor does it seem to occur to them that any such thing is necessary. Accordingly everything is left to accidents."[38] The Whigs did not begin to recover their sense of purpose until the middle of 1785.

Georgiana had grasped the essentials of a successful publicity campaign during her experiments with military uniforms in 1778. This was now the only kind of public political activity open to her, but she used what she had learned to remarkable effect. For her first venture, in December 1784, she sponsored a balloon send-off on behalf of the party.

The invention of the hot-air balloon was the most talked about wonder of the 1780s. In 1783 the Montgolfier brothers astounded the court at Versailles by floating a sixty-foot sky-blue balloon 6,000 feet into the air. Their ingenious experiment immediately inspired a number of imitators, two of whom—the Neapolitan Vincenzo Lunardi and the Frenchman Jean-Pierre Blanchard—arrived in England in 1784 to compete for the affections of the British public. On September 15 Lunardi launched his balloon from the Artillery Ground in London in front of thousands of spectators. Despite the cold, which almost killed his cat, and the loss of one of his wooden oars, he managed to stay up for twenty-four miles. The following month Blanchard succeeded in travelling further into the countryside.

Georgiana gave separate dinners at Devonshire House in honour of the two men. Lunardi repaid the compliment by wearing a silk coat to court in a colour of Georgiana's own invention, called "Devonshire brown." But the Frenchman Blanchard was particularly gratified when Georgiana asked him to carry letters to the royal family in his balloon. In return he allowed her to transform his last British aerial ascent into a Whig political occasion. On December 1 the London newspapers reported an extraordinary exhibition in Grosvenor Square. The Prince of Wales and a hundred Whigs and their ladies braved the chill air to join the crowd who had bought tickets to watch Georgiana release the ropes of Blanchard's balloon. They all wore blue and buff uniforms, and Georgiana had seen to it that even the stay-ropes were decorated with dual-coloured ribbons. "Blanchard's balloon is to be called the 'Devonshire Aerial Yacht' in the future," trumpeted the *Morning Herald and Daily Advertiser.*[39] All the surrounding streets were blocked with spectators, some standing on their carriages, while the fifty-foot advertisement floated over London.

After her triumph with Blanchard's balloon Georgiana regularly organized popular events, such as benefit nights for retiring performers and show-cases for young talent, to reinforce political and social solidarity among party members. Since arranging Perdita's first appearance on the stage as Juliet in 1776 Georgiana had helped to establish a number of the theatre's most celebrated stars, including Mrs. Siddons, who later wrote "My good reception in London I cannot but partly attribute to the enthusiastic accounts of me which the amiable Duchess of Devonshire had brought thither, and spread before my arrival. I had the honour of her acquaintance during her visit to Bath, and her unqualified approbation at my performances."*⁴⁰ Georgiana genuinely wanted to help performing artists but she was also conscious of the value of positive publicity for the Whigs. Her patronage of the arts increasingly associated Whiggery with taste, fashion, and wit.⁴¹ Glittering first nights in support of her latest discovery, and grand balls with inventive themes where the entire company arrived in prescribed dress, made life in opposition bearable and even enjoyable. "She really is a very good Politician," a Pittite complained. "As soon as ever any young man comes from abroad he is immediately invited to Devonshire House and to Chatsworth—and by that means he is to be of the Opposition."⁴²

"Why does she reign supreme?" Lady Mary Coke wondered after a tedious visit from her friends Mrs. Pitt and Miss Hope, who, although strangers to Devonshire House, talked of nothing but Georgiana's health.⁴³ One answer lay in her vitality: Lady Louisa Stuart went to a ball and was amused to observe the birth of a new fashion as Georgiana and Harriet paraded about the room in a variant of the Turkish look. "I don't think I ever saw new fashions set in with such vengeance, except in the year when feathers and high heads first began," she wrote. "Some of us are glorious figures, such wings and tails to our caps. Such shelves of plaited gauze under our chin. . . . the Duchess of Devonshire and Lady Duncannon . . . were dressed in redingotes, robes turkes, that is to say with three caps and capells. . . ."⁴⁴

Georgiana also introduced the muslin gown to English fashion. Known as *la chemise à la reine,* it was exceedingly simple, almost like a shift with a drawstring neck and a plain ribbon to tie round the middle. Although it was originally worn in France by Creole women from the West Indies, Marie Antoinette liked the style so much that she posed for a portrait

---

* Mrs. Nunns was another of Georgiana's protégées: the *Morning Herald and Daily Advertiser* reported: "The Duchess of Devonshire, in her patronage of Mrs Nunns, had behaved with her accustomed liberality. Her Grace not only introduced her to London, and supported her very powerfully on the first two nights of her appearance, but corrected her dress in the Confederacy as directed and gave the dress in the Jealous Wife." *Morning Herald and Daily Advertiser,* July 4, 1785.

"British Balloon, and D—— Aerial Yacht," December 13, 1784. A double entendre: the Prince is saying, "It rises majestically," while Georgiana replies, "Yes, I can feel it." Watching below from left to right are: Lord John Cavendish, the Duke of Devonshire, a Frenchman, Elizabeth Farren, and Lord Derby. Dent. BM Cat. 6668.

wearing her own version of the dress for Madame Vigée-Lebrun in 1783. The portrait shocked society; many thought it an indecent depiction of the Queen in a state of semi-nudity, and it was removed from the Salon. However, the gown caught on in England after Marie Antoinette sent Georgiana a present of one of "the muslin chemises with fine lace."[45] Taking advantage of the warm weather, Georgiana made one of her most successful entrances when she arrived at the Prince of Wales's ball wearing white muslin decorated with silver sprigs. Soon the *Lady's Magazine* was claiming that "all the Sex now, from 15 to 50 and upwards . . . appear in their white muslin frocks with broad sashes."[46]

The *Morning Post* had tried to topple Georgiana from "the chair of fashion," but its snide remarks on her "vulgar inventions" carried little weight with the public. Sharp of Fleet Street, purveyor of perfumes and toiletries to the gentry, made considerable profits having cornered the market in Georgiana's favourite make of French hair powder. In 1785 he advertised to the world the arrival of his latest consignment, "just imported, a quantity of curious, beautiful and sweet Powder à la Duchesse, or Devonshire Powder."[47] Likewise, Mr. Austin, Drawing Master at the Print Rooms, St. James's Street, enjoyed a brisk trade in life-size busts and "curious casts in wax of His Royal Highness the Prince of Wales, her Grace the Duchess of Devonshire . . . the Right Honourable Charles James Fox . . . intended as ornaments to mansions, public libraries, etc." His special offer for April was "proof prints and pictures ready to be engraved of the Prince of Wales and the Duchess of Devonshire."[48] In 1786 there was a minor scandal when one of Georgiana's seamstresses was bribed to reveal her latest design. Several ladies paid for the drawings, each thinking she was the only one. They were all exposed several weeks later when they arrived at a ball wearing the same dress.[49]

Georgiana's popularity meant that she was subjected to scrutiny and with it the propagation of half-truths and second-guesses which caused her untold trouble. The persistent rumour linking her with the Prince exasperated her; the obnoxious cartoons which depicted them as lovers were unhappy reminders of the Westminster election. Nor was the gossip Georgiana's fault: it was the Prince's eccentric behaviour which invited conjecture. During her confinement with baby Harriet he visited her so often—sometimes several times a day—that people wondered if the child was his. However, it was not the baby he came to discuss but Mrs. Fitzherbert. Georgiana did not dare refuse him entry although his visits were an ordeal. She was trapped on her couch while, seized by emotion, he threw himself about the room, flinging himself on his knees, clasping her hands, and banging his head against a chair. Georgiana repeated, until her head ached, that he ought to talk to Fox.

Mrs. Fitzherbert returned home in November 1785, tired of waiting for the Prince to fall out of love with her. She had been bored and lonely during her eighteen-month exile and was ready to be persuaded to become his wife. As soon as Fox heard of her return he wrote to the Prince, imploring him not to take the "desperate step" of marriage. An alliance with Mrs. Fitzherbert, a Catholic widow—especially without his father's permission—would make it impossible for him to inherit the throne. His brother the Duke of York would become heir presumptive. The consequences for the Whigs would be disastrous: the party's reputation would be fatally damaged by its connection with the Prince. However, he ignored Fox's pleas and secretly attempted to find a clergyman willing to go through with an illegal ceremony. But he could not resist revealing his plans to Georgiana and even invited her to be one of the witnesses. She was too frightened to say anything then or for a few days afterwards, but later sent him the following note:

> I write to you, my Dr Br, terrified out of my sences. I have [been] in a dreadful state of agitation ever since I saw you, and now I must tell you and Mrs F. too that I never thought this wd take place, and therefore acquiesced, but it is indeed madness in both. I have not wrote to her to tell her so and will not if you will delay it and consult Charles Fox—For God's sake do. . . . I cannot be present for it is not a marriage, and I cannot be by what I do not think one. It is not shabbyness of fear for myself, but what I fear for her and you. I always shall certainly shew her every mark of regard, but I cannot be by what I do not think a marriage. Indeed it is not. You observed something was the matter with me and indeed I have been quite wild with horror of it ever since. I never thought it could come to this—Pray see Charles Fox tomorrow or let me write to him. Let me beg you over and over to consult C.F., see him tomorrow.[50]

The letter had no effect except to make Mrs. Fitzherbert her lifelong enemy and to cool her relations with the Prince for a while. He did write to Fox but only to lie to him: "Make yourself easy, my dear friend; believe me the world will now soon be convinced that there not only is, but never was, any ground for these reports which of late have so malevolently been circulated."[51] A few days later the couple were married at Mrs. Fitzherbert's house with her uncle and brother as witnesses, leaving immediately for a short honeymoon at a house near Richmond. When they returned, the whole of London was buzzing with rumours about their marriage. Fox's naive trust in his friend led him to stand up in Parliament and categorically refute the allegations about the Prince. Mrs. Fitzherbert took the speech as a personal insult and never forgave him; for as long as she had influence over the Prince she tried to prevent the two men from seeing each other. Fox's feelings were equally vehement when he learned of Prinny's deception, and the friendship never returned to its old footing.

The dilemma was particularly acute for Georgiana who, like most people, was fairly certain the marriage had taken place. The Prince stayed away from Devonshire House, but he wrote to the Devonshires, inviting them to visit Mrs. Fitzherbert, adding that he was not asking them to visit "an improper person." Georgiana understood the Prince's anxiety, for where she led the rest of society would follow. The Spencer and Cavendish clans opposed any action which would bestow legitimacy on the union, so she had little choice but to snub them or leave London for the foreseeable future (her mother's preferred option). She steered a middle course between keeping Mrs. Fitzherbert at bay and not excluding her from Devonshire House society. "I never will go to the Opera with her," Georgiana declared, "I never did and never will, and she knows it. . . . I search into nothing and only wish to keep entirely out of it."*[52]

Georgiana was saved from further embarrassment by the Prince's debts. They had doubled since 1783 and even his cronies had lost patience with him. The King was not prepared to help without receiving certain concessions in return, including, not unreasonably under the circumstances, the Prince's renunciation of the Whigs. Instead, Prinny decided

---

* This was the one thing she was not allowed to do: Mrs. Fitzherbert was careful not to appear pushy in public, but privately she schemed to have her new status recognized. In March Lavinia wrote to George about an embarrassing incident: "The Duchess and 16 other ladies are to be in some frightful dress of Lady Beauchamp's invention, and the Dss is very angry at the scrape she has got into because when their dresses were ordered and everything was fixed on Mrs Fitzherbert sent to desire to be of it, and she could not refuse. I am sure (so is she) that it is a plan of his R.H. and she is excessively angry at it and I think with some reason." BL Althorp G290, Lavinia, Lady Spencer to George, Lord Spencer, March 1786.

on one of his dramatic gestures: he shut up Carlton House, sold his horses and carriages, dismissed the servants, and rented a little villa in Brighton. On July 15 he left London in a public coach, travelling as an outside passenger on the Brighton Dilly, much to the amazement of the other passengers. Mrs. Fitzherbert followed a short time later, and the two of them lived quietly like an ordinary couple for almost a year.[53] His departure was a great relief to the Devonshires, who decided that Southampton offered a more attractive summer retreat than Brighton that year.

⟨∞⟩

Two weeks later the press wrongly reported there had been a second elopement in the Spencer family. The first, which had taken place just a few months before, had involved Georgiana's cousin Mrs. Georgiana Fawkener, known as "Jockey," who had run off with Lord John Townshend.* Although no names were mentioned everyone knew that the latest gossip referred to Harriet and Charles Wyndham, one of the Prince's drinking companions. They had taken so few pains to hide the affair that even Lady Mary Coke noticed something between them. In January 1785 she had written to her sister, "I am sorry to say Lady Duncannon and Charles Wyndham seem to be too good friends."[54] When the erroneous reports of an elopement appeared the faithful Lady Melbourne did her best to contradict them even before she received confirmation from Geor-

---

* The two lovers took advantage of the lax attitudes at Devonshire House to begin a clandestine affair, but by 1786 neither of them could bear the pretence any longer and they deliberately revealed their secret. Remembering how Georgiana had aided Lord George Cavendish and Lady Betty when his wife's family had objected to the match, Mr. Fawkener accused Georgiana of having encouraged the adulterous couple. On this rare occasion the Duke angrily defended his wife: "I write this at the request of the Duchess and partly likewise for my own satisfaction," he responded coldly to Fawkener. "I am thoroughly convinced from conversations I have had with her that she has done nothing intentionally to promote anything that could be disagreeable to you." Chatsworth 747, Duke of Devonshire to William Fawkener, circa July 1786. But Lady Spencer was not so supportive. She accused Georgiana of bringing dishonour to the family and ordered both her daughters to regard their cousin as deceased. The Poyntzes imprisoned Jockey in a bedroom at their London house and alternately entreated and bullied her to give up Townshend. Lady Spencer joined her sister-in-law during these sessions and tried to break her niece's will. But Jockey refused to return to Fawkener. He divorced her and she immediately married her lover. Georgiana was godmother to their first child. The marriage was not a success.

giana: "I was assured yesterday that Lady Duncannon was gone off, surely
it cannot be true, do write me word that I may contradict it. . . . I am sure
that nobody can have been in Town for these past Ten days without meeting him at every place and in every street which makes me so vastly surprised at people believing it."[55]

No one felt sorry for Lord Duncannon. In 1782 the Duchess of Portland had commented sympathetically that Harriet "leads a melancholy
life, at home always, and literally alone."[56] "Lady Duncannon has a good
heart but a sad head," opined Mrs. Damer, "quite unfit for all the dangers
the circumstances of her life have exposed her to, wanting a protector, instead of which she has fallen to the share of a peevish little mortal who
teazes without correcting her."[57] Duncannon subjected her to long periods
of neglect punctuated by episodes of anger and abuse. Lady Spencer suspected him of drinking and of gambling at a faster rate than they could afford, but her preoccupation with her two daughters' faults meant that she
rarely criticized either son-in-law.

George had found out that Harriet was contemplating something rash
and immediately alerted Lady Spencer. The two of them surprised Harriet
and carried her off to St. Albans before Duncannon discovered anything.
Less in love and less robust than her cousin, Harriet crumpled very
quickly and agreed to give Wyndham up. Lady Spencer was not in a forgiving mood: Harriet was never to speak to him again. The Devonshires,
who until then had stood by helplessly, intervened at this point. "Harriet
has agreed a change must take place . . . and is anxious to do everything
you wish," Georgiana wrote to George, but she and the Duke both
thought it would look odd for her to cut him "and would certainly make
it be supposed that something had pass'd which had required our exertions. . . . as Lord Duncannon don't know, it might be informing him of it
in a very unpleasant way."[58]

The Spencers allowed Harriet to return to London, having extracted a
promise from the Devonshires to keep her under supervision. George was
not entirely unsympathetic, but he was more concerned about the family's
reputation:

> Last night I went to Devonshire House and supped en trio with
> them very comfortably; Harriet has scarcely been out since she left
> you and I understand from the Duchess is determined to act per-
> fectly as you with her. Her sweet husband never comes home till 8,

9, 10, or 11 o'clock in the morning, and that is really poor encouragement for living at home. They were at the play last night as I understand with your leave, and their box was filled with other people.
C.W. was not there I believe. I think the matter will be right, but
when it is ended, her situation still continues a most dangerous one
and requires the strictest attention on her own part as well as ours.[59]

Fortunately for Harriet the return of Bess distracted the Spencer family's
attention. "I really look upon her in every light as the most dangerous
devil," Lavinia told George.[60] The Spencers had come across her while on
holiday in Naples, during Christmas 1785. They found a different situation from the brilliant social life Bess described in her letters. "She is not
very well liked by the Italians on account of her want of facility in speaking their language, and her wearing perfume which is here an unpardon-
able offence," wrote George to Lady Spencer. "She lives almost entirely
with the French Ambassadress, and does not seem to be much attached to
her sister-in-law. . . . a great many things I have heard, many of which are
certainly not true but some must be, I don't know what to make of her."[61]
In her letters home Bess made a joke of Lavinia's rudeness: "Lady S
seemed to raise herself three feet in order to look down with contempt on
me. . . . The Ambassadress happen'd to be with me; Lady S., tho' she had
never seen her before, address'd all her conversation to her, [and] almost
turned her back to poor me."[62] The Spencers' aggressive dislike made
Bess, who was already frightened about her future, seriously consider
whether or not to remain abroad.

The Duke naturally understood her reluctance to return much better
than Georgiana and tried to reassure her by insisting there were few, if any,
rumours about the two of them. The longer she stayed away the more
Bess resented Georgiana for her good fortune: her children, her rank, her
popularity and, above all, her possession of the Duke. Bess's greatest desire was to be a society hostess—like Georgiana. She knew that a respectable woman would not sleep with her best friend's husband or with
any man who happened to pay her court. She blamed her promiscuity on
the fact that Georgiana had the things she most wanted, or, as she delicately described it, "had I been his, or could I live near him," she would
not need "to give way to the pernicious desire of attaching people to me."[63]

In June, just before she set out for England, Bess tried to explain herself
to Georgiana without admitting to the betrayal: "All my possible hopes of
friendship are connected in you. Without you the World is nothing to me.

If you could forsake me, I would not bear to live, or living should never think of any other creature."[64] The Duke had not written to her since March, and she was terrified that he was losing interest in her and his daughter. Instead of going straight to Calais, she made a detour to Aix-en-Provence, where she stayed with the elderly Comte St. Jules. There is no record of how they knew each other or of what passed between them, but when she left he agreed to accept paternity of little Caroline, who became Caroline Rosalie St. Jules, illegitimate daughter of a French count and an unknown mother. Bess found a surrogate family for her daughter, and set sail for Southampton at the end of July. According to her diary, the Duke travelled to meet her: "I fear I was glad. I arrive—he had dined out but left a note; he came; Oh, heavens, such moments do indeed efface past sorrows!" There is no mention of Georgiana except possibly in the bleak aside "it was happiness mixed with fear and agitation."[65]

As is so often the case in Bess's diary, her version of events—in which she is always the centre of attention—was more fantasy than truth. The Duke was not alone at Southampton. The Duncannons, Spencers, and Devonshires, accompanied by all their children, were holidaying there when Bess landed. Furthermore the Duke was extremely ill with gout and could only move with difficulty on crutches. Half of London society had joined them, causing the *Morning Post* to comment: "Fashion and taste have fixed their headquarters at this place, for the Season."[66] Bess was happy for the first few days; everyone was kind to her—even Lady Melbourne, who, like all Georgiana's friends, had previously resented the way Bess tried to exclude them.[67]

After spending a decent interval with her mother, Bess set off to join the Devonshires at Chatsworth. As the Duke's health returned the guests felt easier about enjoying the entertainments Georgiana had arranged for their amusement. That summer Count Joseph Mazzinghi, the director of music at the Italian Opera, was the star attraction. He arrived to great excitement, and lived up to expectations by performing with his troupe almost every night. Georgiana frequently accompanied the entourage on her harp and made such an impression that the news reached London. The *Morning Post,* which had declared a temporary ceasefire, reported: "The Duchess of Devonshire's improvement on the harp, leaves very few, out of the profession, who are able to dispute the palm of excellence on that instrument. Mazzinghi has done much, but her Grace's genius more, towards completing this superior accomplishment."[68]

Bess had not expected to find Lady Spencer at Chatsworth and she had

difficulty in hiding her disappointment. There was no repeat of the flirtatious behaviour she had shown with the other guests in 1784. She did
not attempt anything in front of Lady Spencer and, when Georgiana's
mother was not around, James Hare and Sheridan would tease her if she
seemed too attentive to the Duke. Georgiana had other things on her
mind: she had received a blackmail letter from Martindale just before
Bess's arrival. She had resumed gambling with him during the spring because she owed money to all the other faro dealers and in a short time he
had cheated her into a debt of almost £100,000.* Georgiana desperately
wanted to confide in Bess and could not understand why she avoided
being alone with her.

The Duke of Dorset arrived on September 14, 1786, and took in the situation immediately. He had never been in love with Bess and it didn't
bother him to see her flirting with the Duke of Devonshire. On the other
hand, he had always admired Georgiana. He wooed and flattered her, and
before long everyone knew there was an understanding between them.
Lady Spencer was so distressed by what she saw that she took the unusual
step—given her mistrust of servants—of informing George in a letter.
"The Duke of Dorset and Lord Thanet came yesterday, the latter is a modest well-behaved young man—the former, I think, makes a little *diversion*—
I hope you understand me."

"I am far from happy here," Lady Spencer told George, but she felt she
had to stay.[69] After Dorset returned to London Georgiana began to suffer
mysterious spasms which twisted her entire body. Lady Spencer suspected
that some hidden mental anguish was behind them, but she could not
make her daughter confide in her. Each attack left Georgiana exhausted,
and she would remain in her room for the rest of the day. With the appearance of great sorrow, Bess assumed her friend's role in her absence,
giving orders to the servants and making it clear to everyone that she was
in charge. Lady Spencer could not bear to watch her preening and joined
Georgiana in isolation. "I dine every day with your sister in her room," she
told George on October 12. "She comes out in the evening—she has had
no return of her spasms lately but her nerves and spirits are very weak."[70]
When she revealed Bess's behaviour downstairs Georgiana refused to believe her.

Lady Spencer left as soon as she could be sure there would be no more

---

* The equivalent of £6,000,000 today.

spasms. "I am wretched to feel that time here has been embittered by unpleasant events and anxieties," Georgiana wrote to her afterwards. She
promised "to get some resolution to take place about our affairs. . . . you
do not know how I do love you—I have often feared trusting to open all
my thoughts to you."[71] A week later, when the house was empty, Georgiana made a partial confession to the Duke about Martindale. Without
hesitation, the Duke demanded a separation. Georgiana was devastated;
she turned to Bess for support and found her friend unwilling to talk to
her. In her diary Bess hardly mentions the incident except to praise the
Duke's reaction when Georgiana confessed the debt: "how nobly, kindly,
touchingly did he behave."[72] She was far more concerned about her jealousy and quarrelsomeness, which the Duke nevertheless forgave. "Every
day," she wrote, while the Duke and Heaton discussed how to effect the
separation, "my tenderness for him increased, and so, I think, did his confidence and affection for me. We wish for Caroline but know not what to
do."[73] Heaton argued that there would have to be drastic cuts in the
Cavendish expenditure to pay off the debts: houses would have to be sold,
servants dismissed, and on no account was Georgiana to be allowed near
London.

George rushed to his sister's defence as soon as he heard of the Duke's
plans. The idea that the Duke and Bess might shut Georgiana away in a
hunting lodge revolted him. Bravely withstanding Lavinia's annoyance, he
invited Georgiana to take the children and live with him at Althorp. The
Duke, he added, would be welcome to visit whenever he liked; there was
no mention of Bess. When she first heard of the proposed separation Lady
Spencer complained at length about her misfortune: "It is a real consolation to me," she told Harriet, "in all the misery I have lately gone through
that your Dear Father has not shared my sufferings."[74] However, George's
offer to Georgiana revived her, and she insisted that if her daughter was to
stay with anyone it should be with her. The normally placid George lost
his temper:

> The proposal I made to my sister was made entirely under the idea
> that there were none of the Duke's houses that would be so conve-
> nient for her to be at as this . . . and not under any idea of being in
> competition with you for having her with me, as I should hope in
> case she were to accept it that you would very frequently come too
> and we might live en famille very comfortably and much in the style

of the French country houses where the different parts of the family all live together.[75]

In any case, he suspected that "there is a reason which will be equally an obstacle to her living with you or with us." The Duke did not have any grounds for a divorce, and if he wanted an heir it would still have to come from Georgiana. For this reason he wanted to have her within easy reach. Georgiana knew that the relationship between the Duke and Bess was such that, if he could not bring her with him when he came to visit, he would never come at all, and there would be no chance of a reconciliation: "which is what of all things your sister dreads," Lady Spencer told George.[76] (On the other hand, if Georgiana was publicly separated from the Duke Bess would not be able to stay at Devonshire House without scandal, nor would the Devonshire House Circle tolerate her usurpation of Georgiana's role at Chatsworth.) Lady Spencer thought that Georgiana ought to live at Londesborough, the third of the Duke's houses, which was at least fitting for her rank. There was "no time to be lost in recommending it," she wrote, "lest the *Chief Councellor* [Bess] should have settled any other plan."[77] At Chatsworth she could possibly help husband and wife to come to a sensible resolution but "alas, what can I do as the fourth in such a party, where two out of the three at least should think me de trop. If *she* was removed, I should really think all that has passed was not only retrievable but fortunate for all parties."[78]

Discussions dragged on through November and into December. "I feel an uncertainty that kills me," confessed Georgiana.[79] George complained of the "enormous obstacles" that stood in the way: either Georgiana objected to some aspect of the arrangement, or the Duke did or, as was more often the case, Bess. But as time went by the Duke seemed to lose interest and he mentioned the separation less and less. Throughout the ordeal Georgiana felt so ashamed of herself that she hardly noticed her friend's sudden quietness. Bess, who had claimed in June that their hearts were formed for each other, made no offer to follow her wherever she went: if Georgiana were to go in adversity, she would have to go alone. But to Bess's astonishment, Georgiana never reproached her.

On December 29 Georgiana wrote: "my business goes slow." Nothing was yet decided, but there seemed to be less pressure on her to leave. Lady Bristol had written several times to Bess asking her to visit, and she could put it off no longer. The Devonshires left Chatsworth at the same time. "I suspect the reason of their going by Milton is that she may join them on the road and go to Town with them, but this is only my own ill-natured conjecture," wrote Lady Spencer.[80] On the last day of the year Georgiana's future still looked uncertain but less precarious than before. George allowed himself to feel a little hope: "A calm has ensued in a certain quarter as I supposed it would when the first violence of the storm had spent itself. How long either will last it is impossible ever to conjecture, but that there will be frequent transmitting from the one to the other is all that one can be certain about."[81]

CHAPTER 11

QUEEN BESS

1787

On Monday last, the Constitutional Whig Grand Lodge of England held their anniversary at the Intrepid Fox, Wardour St, Soho, in commemoration of the Landing of the Great Deliverer, William the Third. . . . among the toasts were "The Noble House of Cavendish, root and branches—May the blossoms of Liberty never be blighted, nor the Duchess of Devonshire ever be slighted. . . ."

Morning Herald, *November 8, 1787*

The Duke regarded himself as an injured man. He required two things of Georgiana: not to gamble away the family estate, and to produce an heir, and she seemed to be incapable of performing either one. He was also furious that she had been deceiving him about her debts for the past two years. But his habit of shutting out unpleasant thoughts spared Georgiana a repetition of the scenes at Chatsworth. "He is calm," she wrote, until "an occasional event, letter, etc., that requires discussion and thought renews the sensation."[1] By Christmas, three months after her confession, the Duke was beginning to have mixed feelings about the proposed separation. He was not so blinded by his love for Bess nor so bitter towards Georgiana that he wanted to see her publicly humiliated. Although he preferred Bess's company, he liked having both women around, competing for his attention. When they were together they kept each other's quirks in check.

Bess was torn: should she complete her triumph over Georgiana or intercede on her behalf? If she pushed hard enough she could probably force the Duke to separate from Georgiana. But much as she fantasized about taking Georgiana's place, Bess knew that without her she would not be able to live at Devonshire House or at Chatsworth. Life as the Duke's acknowledged mistress would be dull and constricting. She would become a non-person—ostracized by polite society and despised by Georgiana's friends and family. That was not the sort of life Bess wanted for herself. She hesitated until Georgiana unwittingly made up her mind for her. Instead of accusing Bess of disloyalty for her wavering, Georgiana apologized to her for lying about her debts. All she hoped, Georgiana told her, was that her folly in wasting "dear Canis's" fortune would not make Bess despise her. This was the last thing Bess had expected. It had been much easier for her to resent Georgiana when she could question the strength of her friend's attachment. The realization that in Georgiana she had a friend who truly loved her was a revelation to a woman who had always believed herself to be alone. As a consequence, her behaviour towards Georgiana subtly changed. The naivety of Georgiana's love brought out a protectiveness in Bess: she became motherly, even strict, and, though the jealousy remained, there was no further attempt to usurp her place and no more talk of separation.

The Duke took Georgiana to London, where they engaged Sheridan's help to resolve the Martindale problem. No stranger to the art of putting off creditors, Sheridan coached her on what to say. "The bargain with Martindale entirely depends upon his thinking it my doing unadvis'd," she told her mother, "and therefore I must close it by seeing him."[2] She had persuaded him to consider only £25,000, but was hoping that he would accept £6,000. They met alone, as arranged, and Georgiana acted her part just as she had been told. To her surprise he believed her display of innocence and confusion and he agreed to settle at the lower sum.* With the resolution of this degrading episode life at Devonshire House returned to a semblance of normality. Yet it was a fragile truce: Georgiana was terrified of upsetting the Duke, and he was so suspicious of her now that she admitted, "I dare not press the Duke nor give him reason to imagine I have a wish or design of my own."[3]

The Duke insisted on certain conditions before he dropped his plans for separation. Georgiana was not to stay in London any longer than necessary, and her income was to be sharply reduced, not only because it

---

* Georgiana never succeeded in being completely rid of him. From time to time he would demand, and receive, "hush money" from her.

might hinder her free-spending habits but also because he agreed with Heaton that the money saved should go towards retaining a few more servants. Several had to be sacked in any case, some of the horses and carriages sold, and all capital projects halted. "We are distressed, but prudence will set us right," wrote Georgiana cheerfully.[4] "I have made a good beginning, having forbid all milliners etc., Dst. M., I shall be with you in the Lottery time and will only have 2 tickets and no insurance of any kind."[5] She was not concerned by the reduction of her income, thinking that it would be offset by her residing in Bath or in the country, where commodities were cheaper and fashion more sedate. The Duke was also determined to live quietly for a few months while Heaton straightened out their financial affairs.

Georgiana ought to have felt relief: she had owned up to her mistakes and the Duke had forgiven her. But when she confessed about Martindale she had told a stupid and terrible lie. The Duke had asked if there were any other debts, and she had admitted to only about a fifth of the total. She lost her only chance of living her life free from secret worries. The difficult steps she had taken to clear her debts should have brought about her deliverance; instead they were the beginning of a new misery. Henceforth all her ingenuity would be focused on concealing the truth from the Duke and, to a lesser extent, from Bess, all her energy spent in keeping creditors at bay.

Georgiana's encounter with Martindale had taught her how to appear plausible. The ease with which she charmed him made her realize that the same technique might be used on others. Her friends and acquaintances became a potential source of wealth that she shamelessly mined for loans and gifts. Mary Graham was one of the first to receive her begging letters and gave as much as she could until her husband found out. But there were many others, some of them near strangers, whose snobbery might be exploited by a Duchess in need. The inventor Sir Richard Arkwright soon regretted his impulse to lend her several thousand pounds when she not only defaulted on her repayments but pleaded for a further loan. In January 1788 he wrote, "I flattered myself with the hope that everything had turned out as you wished. I am sincerely sorry to find I was mistaken. . . . I must also request your Grace will say whether I *may rely* upon the other notes being all regularly paid. . . . Nothing has dropt from me to any person living that could lead to suspect what your Grace wishes to remain a secret."[6] The story was always the same: she was desperate, she needed the money to save her from immediate exposure and ruin, and it had to be a secret.

Fortunately Georgiana was not alone. Most of her close friends were like her, gamesters and always broke. Fitzpatrick, Hare, Sheridan, Fox, and the Prince of Wales were all constantly harried by creditors. None of them would have condemned her if they had known what lengths she was forced to go to in order to obtain ready money—she was not the first person in the Devonshire House Circle to beg her jewellers to buy back some of her purchases. Most of the Circle relied on the willingness of one banker, Thomas Coutts, to keep them afloat. A cautious Scot with a weakness for titles, Coutts disliked living among banking society and was determined to drag himself and his wife, a former servant, into the refined society of the *ton*. He courted the Prince of Wales and his Whig friends, seeing in the relationship future lucrative government contracts for the bank and social advancement for his daughters. He expected to be rewarded for his generosity when the King, now in his fifties and in poor health, died and Prinny inherited the throne. Coutts and Georgiana were perfect partners since they both believed that money could solve their problems.

In March 1787 Georgiana asked Coutts to become her private banker. "With very little acquaintance, and that acquaintance having only given you a knowledge of my extravagance, I feel myself perfectly unauthoriz'd to the address I am making to you, and yet I cannot help applying to you and feeling . . . a kind of confidence that you will befriend me."[7] She hinted that without his help "my distress would . . . I am afraid drive me to every ruinous expedient." He was only too glad to be of assistance to a charming woman who pleaded, "I am so ignorant of business."[8] He agreed to oversee her accounts, to provide her with unsecured loans without the Duke's knowledge (a risky and illegal undertaking), and to take on the edifying role, he thought, of her financial adviser.* He made a similar offer to the Duke of Devonshire, without revealing his arrangements with Georgiana, and loaned him £7,000 without security and with no time limit.[9]

---

* He was also in the process of securing another bankrupt for his books, Charles James Fox, who could hardly believe his good fortune when he read the following letter: "Perhaps you will laugh at my letter, but I feel an impulse to write it, & and to make you an offer, in case you have Annuities or Debts, to lend you money to pay Them provided you would like to be indebted *to me*—and that such a Sum as I can spare, would extricate you from hands that are less liberal than, I *Hope,* mine are. . . ." BL Add. MSS 51466, f. 17: Thomas Coutts to Charles Fox, July 30, 1787. Fox gladly accepted a £5,000 loan which Coutts noted in his book was "not to be press'd or any Interest ask'd for." Leslie Mitchell, *Charles James Fox* (Oxford 1992), p. 103.

Coutts assumed that he would be Georgiana's sole banker, and hoped that the personal relationship between them would be as important to her as the financial one. "I will confess a selfish view," he wrote on May 23, 1787, "tho' I disclaim any interested one, in desiring this vizt that it will give me the opportunity perhaps of more frequently having occasion to see or correspond with your Grace."[10] The truth was far more complicated than he realized: Georgiana had inveigled the Parisian banker, Comte Pérregeaux, into a similar relationship to help her manage some £40,000 or £50,000 worth of debts in France. She did not know how much she owed in total, nor did she want to. She gave everyone different figures which represented different debts: gambling debts, purchases, loans from private money lenders, as well as burdens she had assumed on behalf of others. Lady Spencer thought Georgiana's income would now be £1,000 a year; Coutts thought it £2,000 but with £500 a year marked out for annuities she had allocated to needy friends and relations, "which keep me very poor, as you may imagine, yet I cannot bear to stop them."[11] She told Coutts that the Duke knew about all her debts except for £4,500, but the figure was closer to £60,000, and perhaps even more. The first step had to be a complete cessation of all forms of gambling—Coutts urged her to reflect on what "you risk to gratify this destructive passion. . . . a gamester goes on in the vain hope of recovering lost sums, till he loses probably all that remains, and along with it everything which is precious."[12]

Even if her sincere desire to change had been matched by her will power there were almost insuperable obstacles in her way. Temptation was everywhere: the Duke was not prepared to curb his card playing and Lady Spencer saw no harm in inviting Georgiana to join her little gambling parties at home. "Tho' she has lost considerably for the moderate play we have had," she reported to the Duke on one occasion, "it has been from a most obstinate and unalterable run of ill luck and not from gambling. As a proof of this, I who have been her partner can answer for having won in the whole time but one single rubber at whist of two guineas."[13] Georgiana brazenly asserted to Coutts and others that she had indeed given up: "I have the pleasure to assure you that I have not *play'd* once the whole season. . . . I am under a sacred promise with regard to playing at faro and insurance at the lottery, which no temptation could break."[14] Yet she was secretly doing both not merely for the thrills but also, as Coutts so eloquently warned against in his homily, in the vain hope of winning back some of her losses.

Nor did Georgiana act alone. Harriet joined her in every scheme and was often the more enthusiastic of the two. She had her own reasons for seeking relief at the gaming table. Duncannon was not only unfaithful and unpredictable, he was also deeply suspicious of his wife. He opened all her correspondence and rationed the visits she might receive. Her family were afraid to interfere lest they made her situation worse. Georgiana was careful to keep her letters to Harriet light and impersonal—they communicated with each other through secret messages—so she was ignorant of Harriet's latest problem with Duncannon. It was George who discovered it by chance. He paid one of his discreet visits on a February morning in 1787, while Duncannon was out, and found Harriet crying with fear. Duncannon had just left the house, having roughly informed her that he had lost a large sum of money at faro. It had to be paid immediately and he wanted Harriet to get it for him. Rather like the evil Sir William in *The Sylph*, Duncannon promised her she would regret it if she failed.

"Harriet was quite at a loss," George wrote afterwards to Lady Spencer, "as well she might, and was very apprehensive of the consequences of his disappointment." Duncannon had ordered her not to tell anyone, which naturally made it impossible for her to raise the money from friends or family. Ominously, he also brought up the subject of her dowry—Georgiana's heroine Julia had been beaten into relinquishing hers—and he tried to make her sign it over. Harriet was too frightened to refuse, but thinking quickly had added that her brother, as her guardian, would have to give his consent. "I don't know whether it is or no, but if it is I certainly shall never grant it," George wrote.[15] He did not know how to help his sister: he could not deny her the money and yet he hated to see it go to her bullying husband. "I cannot advise giving assistance or even being security," counselled Lady Spencer hardheartedly. "Future help (when ruin which I fear is inevitable sooner or later makes it necessary) may be of essential use, but nothing else. I hope for the sake of the children nothing will be given up."[16] She wanted George to hold out until Duncannon had promised to stop gambling, but for Harriet's sake he and Georgiana insisted on going ahead. They paid the debt themselves and kept it a secret from the Cavendishes.

In May 1787 Georgiana and Harriet joined a consortium behind a new faro bank which included the Prince of Wales and the Duke of Rutland. Georgiana had to fight for her place because her creditworthiness was so poor. "The Duchess of Devonshire is in debt to all the banks she has ever been connected with; so that must keep her from a claim to be in debt to us," decided one of the organizers, Daniel Pultney, before her persistence made him relent.[17] Neither Georgiana nor Harriet could wait for the operation to begin, and they irritated him by their incessant enquiries about the scheme's progress. In the meantime they spent the money they had set aside for the bank.

> The faro project, though so essentially advanced by your Grace's means, is, from the absence of some of the gang from town, in no condition to commence this summer [Pultney wrote to Rutland], though some of our allies at Bath (the Duchess of Devonshire and Lady Duncannon) are in a rage at our having suffered Sir Watts Horton to set up a mushroom bank of £500 in their absence. Little as I can pretend to any great knowledge of the ladies, I cannot foresee what obstacles the very proposers may suggest in future. All I know is that it is as much as their interest as mine, and . . . as much as their inclination. Lady Duncannon sold £200 a year for £1600 to a Jew, about six weeks ago, and showed me overnight a £1000 note, which she was determined to keep for this subscription, and in three days it was all gone; though, as to her share for this subscription, that can easily be borrowed for her.[18]

A poignant letter of Georgiana's to Bess, written some time in 1787, reveals the extent to which she had become a victim of her addiction. It also shows the complete reversal of power between them since the happy summer of Plympton in 1782. Now it was Georgiana who desperately clung to Bess, resorting to emotional blackmail when necessary.

> This is the last time perhaps you will ever speak to or love me—I really am unworthy of you and Canis and you must be shocked at my levity all today but there was no medium. When I first told all my debts to Ca at C[hatsworth] I had reserved £500 which I had agreed to insure in this Lottery as a hope of regaining him some money— My good genius often prompted me to stop this but as I had agreed to do it and paid the money into Baker's hands for the purpose I resolved unwillingly to do it. I went to Newmarket and left an insurance meaning to stop—but I had some money distress about Mr Cater which I will explain to you. Oh God Bess, I have gone on and lost an immense sum—I dare not tell you that it is 6000—It is madness and I ought not to live on with Canis—but what am I to do? You must not tell him this—and you shall advise me when I return what I am to do—whether to tell him or not—it could be settled without

and so that it should never come to him—you know he *could* not forgive me. My Bess, I am desperate. If the Eyebrow [Fox] had been here I should have thrown myself into his arms, to have completed myself—you see that doating on Ca how I have used him. I scarcely have pleasure in looking at my Babes. Say nothing to him until I return—Oh Bess![19]

Bess could not resist such an appeal. No one had ever needed or trusted her as much as Georgiana. But that didn't prevent her from extracting her own reward. Inexorably, she eradicated the boundaries between them, the friends, the interests—even the better aspects of Georgiana's character such as her passion for the arts—she adopted or co-opted as her own. There is no mention of little Caroline in any of the correspondence but it was probably at this point that Bess disclosed her existence to Georgiana—now that her ascendancy over both Devonshires was complete there was no longer any reason to keep the child or its paternity a secret. Georgiana's reaction has not been recorded; however, she had long since renounced her claims to the Duke. But, irritatingly for Bess, the Duke did not renounce his claims to his wife. He refused to live in a monogamous relationship with Bess, or to grant her the precedence she sought over Georgiana. His sometimes brutal reminders of her position prevented her from being complacent: "I go for a week to Tunbridge," she wrote in her "diary" in August, "return and am foolish and capricious because they dined out—but suffered severely by the D taking it ill of me. We made it up at Chiswick and have never quarrelled since—passed a happy week there."[20] She also missed her sons, Augustus and Frederick, who were still in Ireland with their father, and from time to time she made attempts to see them.

Georgiana's friends accepted Bess's permanent presence, particularly Harriet, who, unlike the rest of the family, knew how much Georgiana relied on her. Bess was too clever to try to alienate Georgiana from her sister. Very early on she had made it clear to Harriet that her relationship with Georgiana was safe and, in return, Harriet had given Bess her tacit approval. Bess's connection with Devonshire House elevated her status in London society; her name even began to appear in the social columns, although sporadically and almost always behind Georgiana's. When Georgiana returned to London for the season (that part of the Duke's conditions having been forgotten) Bess never left her side. In her letters Georgiana always prefixed her descriptions with "we": "Monday we supp'd at Lady

Beauchamp's—Tuesday the opera and my party, and yesterday we breakfasted at Carlton House and in the evening Ly Lucan's, Ranelagh and a
supper at D'Adhémar's—tonight [another] ball, and tomorrow Ly
Hopetoun's . . ."[21] Such was the gaiety of Whig society that there was considerable mirth when on June 1, 1787, George III issued a royal proclamation on the suppression of vice and the encouragement of virtue.[22]

Seeing Bess so contented with the Duke, however, made Georgiana
long for something similar for herself. The Duke of Dorset could not fulfil her wish. He was in Paris most of the time and they had to be content
with writing to each other several times a week. Nor was she deeply in love
with him, although the relationship served a purpose. Since the Whigs engaged in only intermittent action during this time, with Dorset's encouragement Georgiana became more involved in French court politics. In one
letter he asked her to contact "Argus" (Sheridan): he wanted him to place
some favourable articles about the Little Po, who was the victim of a whis-
pering campaign by the Princesse de Lamballe, in the *Courier de l'Europe*.
Her efforts did not go unnoticed: Daniel Pultney reported to the Duke of
Rutland, "Amongst the news of last week was Madame Polignac's disgrace
with the Queen of France and expected arrival in England to form a female
treaty of opposition, I suppose, with the Duchess of Devonshire."[23] When
the Polignacs arrived in the late spring Georgiana arranged an uninterrupted programme of public events, attended by cabinet ministers as well
as Whigs, to enhance their reputation in France. She almost certainly wrote
to the Queen on the Little Po's behalf as well, but the letters did not survive the revolution.

Dorset flattered Georgiana by his frankness in confiding to her his real
views on the French situation. When the Finance Minister, Charles
Alexandre de Calonne, and the Director-General of Finance, Jacques
Necker, were dismissed in April 1787, Dorset described it as a disaster for
France's stability. He blamed their dismissal on Marie Antoinette's pride.
"You will have heard of Necker and Calonne's banishment," he wrote:
"what a horrid government (between friends) this is . . . jugés quel empire
a Mrs B [Marie Antoinette] sur l'ésprit de son mari:* she felt her power and
influence in danger and got rid of her rival dans un clin d'oeil [in no time
at all]."[24] This sort of intimate friendship combined with behind-the-
scenes politics was irresistible to Georgiana. She couldn't help succumbing
to Dorset's charm even though she knew he was manipulative and vain. He

* Judging by the influence Mrs. B. has over her husband.

is "the most dangerous of men," she had written before the affair. "For with that beauty of his he is so unaffected and has a simplicity and persuasion in his manner that makes one account very easily for the number of women he has had in love with him."* Horace Walpole despised him: "amorous and pleasing in his figure. . . . the French could not desire a man more qualified to be a dupe."[25]

Lady Spencer was so frightened that she would lose one or both her daughters to a scandalous elopement that she detected clandestine meetings in the most innocent situations. "I suppose you mean Wyndham and the D of Dorset," Georgiana replied impatiently to her accusing letters. "The first is hunting and would not see her if here, the other is at Paris."[26] But it was not only Lady Spencer who feared Georgiana's involvement with such a dangerous flirt. Lady Melbourne added her voice, reminding Georgiana that Dorset's indiscreet comments about his affair with Lady Derby had made her situation so impossible that elopement had been her only choice. Lady Melbourne's warning was strong enough to make Georgiana consider breaking off their affair. "The Pride [the Duke of Dorset] does come," she admitted to Lady Melbourne. "I could not help it, but my mother, who knows of it now is prepared to care he should *have nothing to tell;* however, independent of her case and she is quite right, I will and would have been upon my guard."[27] Yet, as with her gambling, Georgiana's words did not match her actions.

---

* All Dorset's correspondence with Georgiana was censored in the last century; an unknown hand has scratched over his endearments to her. Most of the letters were destroyed, and the majority of those that survive are edited copies. "My ever dearest Duchess" is one of the few lines which can be faintly detected beneath the black markings of the censor's pen. Chatsworth 833: Duke of Dorset to GD, Oct. 19, 1787.

CHAPTER 12

MÉNAGE À TROIS

1788

The Gallery of the Graces has no small acquisition in the beautiful portraits of the Duchess of Devonshire, Lady Duncannon, and Lady Elizabeth Foster.
Morning Post, *March 29, 1788*

B ess chose to remain in London for the summer while the Devonshires went ahead to Chatsworth. Lady Spencer took advantage of her absence to remain with them until mid-October. The Duke of Dorset was in Paris, and for once Lady Spencer found little to criticize during her stay. She reported to George that Georgiana was "much calmer and better" than last year, and there was no repeat of her "nervous symptoms." But it galled her to think that Bess was in London, waiting for her to leave: "I think she will measure her time by mine," she wrote.[1] In this she was mistaken; there was another reason for Bess's delay:

> The Duke of Richmond is so in love with Ly Elizabeth Foster [wrote Lady Augusta Murray spitefully], that they say he has made a ridiculous figure of himself, and it is due to his infatuation that Lord Hervey owes his new employment. The Duke of Devonshire is now less smitten. Lady Spencer est trés en colère, and Lady Jersey says she does not see why such a trifle can put her Dowagership in such a passion when she herself had Lord Harcourt and Lord Jersey at one time.[2]

The remorse Bess had once expressed in her journal over the Duke of Dorset ("How could I bear to let the D. of Dorset be attach'd to me, to think me virtuous! I shall write to tell him I don't deserve his love")[3] had not prevented her from making the Duke of Richmond fall in love with her. He was an ideal choice—a sort of insurance policy. He was middle-aged, childless, and lived a separate life from the Duchess, whose health was poor. He also had contacts in the government, and Bess's brother, Lord Hervey, needed some form of employment before his creditors had him arrested. The Duke of Richmond lobbied Pitt on his behalf for the vacant ambassadorship to Florence, and as soon as he heard of his success wrote immediately to Devonshire House to give Bess the news. There was nothing he wouldn't do for her, and she certainly knew how to make use of him.

Since Bess's recent triumph was known to everyone, guests at Chatsworth were surprised by her subdued demeanour when she arrived at the end of October. Normally she took Sheridan's arch comments about her charming attachment to the Duke of Devonshire in good part, but she showed her irritation on this occasion. When they were alone she confronted the Duke, who "hardly knew the ill I had hinted to him, and asked me if it was really so. I confirmed it." She was pregnant again. "We regret this new anxiety," Bess wrote in her diary: "But I felt a kind of pleasure that supported me. How kind he was to me, how soothing and endearing!"[4] Once again she glossed over several important details. The Duke was aware of her friendship with the Duke of Richmond, although she swore to him it was innocent. Naturally, she insisted the baby could not possibly be Richmond's, but the Duke's indifferent attitude towards the child suggests that he never wholly believed her. This time the lovers told Georgiana immediately. Her reaction was typical of what Bess had come to expect: she insisted on accompanying Bess to France in order to assist her when she went into labour. No doubt her desire to be with Bess was compounded by the prospect of seeing Dorset in Paris, but Georgiana's devotion was none the less real. There was no question that she loved her friend and infinitely preferred her company to the Duke's.

When Lady Spencer heard that Georgiana was taking Bess abroad for her health, she assumed correctly that Bess was pregnant but also that the Duke had ordered his wife to take care of his mistress during her confinement. Georgiana's assurance that she had no motive for going other than seeing her friends made her more suspicious. She accused her daughter of going to Paris with the intention of taking up with the Duke of Dorset and would not listen to her protestations. "Nothing can exceed [Georgiana and Harriet's] affectionate care and attention to me," she wrote to George. "But art has greatly lessened if not entirely deprived me of that unreserved confidence which could alone make my advice be of use to them—I cannot love them less, and loving them as I do I cannot be happy about them."[5] Georgiana reluctantly acquiesced to her order to remain in England: "Since it is disagreeable to you, however anxious I was, and desirable as it seemed to be in many circumstances, I will not go," she wrote. "I give you my word that I shall not go unless by any alteration the Duke has it in his power to come too, for all the time; which I am afraid is not likely. . . . I see your reason Dst M; but I was in hopes my not going near Paris would have prevented your apprehension."[6]

Lady Spencer held Bess responsible for her estrangement with Georgiana, but her continual criticizing and interfering were as much the cause. She had become less confident since her widowhood. Just before her visit to Chatsworth she had tried to attend a small party of Harriet's and was forced to abandon the attempt: "I got to the house but was seized with such a foolish panic and tremor that I could not go in," she told George. "I really begin to fear I shall never go into company again."[7] She compensated for her reclusiveness by becoming ever more inquisitive and censorious with her daughters. Her hectoring letters made communication a duty rather than a pleasure. "I hope you will be comfortable at Chatsworth because I hope you will see me conduct myself with *prudence*," Georgiana had written in anticipation of her mother's visit. "Tho' there will I dare say in the course of your stay be many men, and some you may not like, yet I had rather you shd see me behave well with opportunity of doing otherwise than only from having nobody to flirt with."[8]

"I don't know how I shall be able to bear my parting with Bess," Georgiana wrote on February 10, 1788. The Devonshires accompanied Bess to Dover and stood on the quayside while her luggage was loaded on to the packet. "Oh it was bitterness to lose her," admitted Bess in her diary, "but him—his last embrace—his last look drew my soul after him. . . . I see him—he is fixed in my heart—this guilty heart—Oh, why could I not love him without crime? Why cannot I be his without sin?"[9] After eighteen months of a fantasy life she was abruptly reduced to her ordinary state: Lady Elizabeth Foster, grafter, courtesan, and destitute wife of an Irish MP. This time, however, she could rely on Georgiana to make up for the Duke's previous indolence over arrangements for the birth. She travelled through France with the faithful Louis and her maidservant Lucille until she reached Rouen on May 15, supposedly having already come to term.

Instead of the filthy bordello in Vietri there was an apartment "tolerable, but in a close confined street on one part and a stinking court at the other."[10] Nothing happened for almost two weeks. "What will the Duke think?" moaned Bess; "that is the last day I was with him, and did not return till I was above two months gone."[11] Fortunately, she went into labour on the twenty-sixth, just in time for the balance of paternity to remain undecided between the Dukes of Devonshire and Richmond. After three hours she gave birth to a boy whom she called Augustus (despite already having a son with the same name) William James Clifford. She had chosen the names with care: William was his father's name and Clifford was one of the Cavendish titles. Her affair with Richmond may have made her more anxious to establish the boy's parentage than with Caroline Rosalie. Clifford, as he was always known, was deposited with another family while Bess collected Caroline from her foster parents. She and the Duke had already decided to send her to Paris to be educated with Charlotte Williams. In her diary Bess confessed to having formed a secret plan to bring Caroline over to England and have her brought up in the nursery with Little Georgiana and Harriet. She did not yet know how she would accomplish this, but she had no doubt she would succeed.

While Bess was in France Georgiana and the Duke remained in London and entertained on a lavish scale at Devonshire House nearly every night. They were getting on surprisingly well—better, in fact, than for several years. Although Georgiana could not control her gambling, she ensured that they had little to quarrel over by keeping her debts hidden. She tried to compensate the Duke for his loss by giving him the sort of attention he enjoyed from Bess. He, in turn, took Georgiana's side when Lady Spencer decided that London offered too much temptation and tried to force her to stay at St. Alban's. "If she was to stay at St Albans for six weeks or two months without any ostensible reason," finally responded the Duke to Lady Spencer's insistent letters, "it might make her feel dissatisfied and discontented, as well as give rise to conversations and surmises in the world which would be better avoided."[12] Lady Spencer was so overcome by his concern for his wife that she did not bring up the subject again.

The day after Clifford's birth across the Channel Lady Spencer was writing to George about her joy at seeing husband and wife on such good terms with each other: "the entire confidence, the easy good humours and the unaffected regard and tenderness which has been apparent in their whole conduct to each other ever since I have been here, make me but grieve the more that they ever live any other life than they now do."[13] She was disappointed to hear that they were planning to go to France in the summer to meet Bess. But she was mistaken if she hoped for any rekindling of love between them—neither would ever be in love with the other. "Dr Bess, I know you are safe and therefore not *hurt*," Georgiana wrote; "always write to him if you have not time for both."[14]

Bess pressed them to come to France, but there were obstacles to their leaving. Friends assumed that they were delaying their trip because of a serious theft in Devonshire House committed by the son of one of their most trusted servants. The truth was that they suspected Duncannon of attempting to poison Harriet. It was almost certainly fear rather than malice which guided his actions; he was trying to subjugate his wife rather than kill her. This was the verdict of Mrs. Damer, who wrote much later: "She once, I know, did suffer, and took those terrible medicines but it was some years passed. Her husband, doubting not that it was owing to his conduct, and the vile company he kept, used to carry her the medicines, and being ashamed and wishing to screen himself, endangered her life by preventing her from having proper advice."[15] It was not until he put Harriet's life in danger and the doctors had to be called out in an emergency that Duncannon's actions were exposed. He stopped feeding her drugs but the Devonshires took the precaution of putting off their visit to France until the spring.

The Duke of Dorset was extremely irritated, having gone to considerable lengths to rent a summer house for them and to arrange his leave to coincide with their visit. "The state of affairs here will not admit of my absence," he replied when Georgiana suggested he come to England. "Things now grow serious, and I hope they now feel the effects of promoting and abetting rebellion in other countries* they have learnt the people to fight for their liberties. . . . I am exceedingly concerned for Mr and Mrs B. [the King and Queen]. The latter is *amazingly* out of spirits."[16] It was late summer when he managed to visit England and by this time Georgiana's feelings had already altered. The shock turned the urbane diplomat into a sad, pleading figure. Concerned that his obvious distress

---

* i.e., in America.

would create a scandal, Lady Melbourne advised Georgiana to allow him hope. But she refused.

> however good and wise your arguments are, they are not stronger than my own heart suggests to me—and I wish fairly and honestly to make you read it as I do myself. When the Duke of Dorset returned, he express'd great misery at the idea of my having, without any cause of his side, spoken to him in an angry and harsh manner, especially as he was ready to give up every wish to mine, to be contented with seeing me and being on a friendly footing with me—he was particularly shocked at the idea of my forbidding him Chatsworth, at the time when he gave up to me what he said was the greatest sacrifice a man could make me—he has kept within the rules I laid down *nearly* tho' not quite, he has come to be sure twice a day, but that is already broke thru since he stays at Windsor to night because I told him *not* to come here—I was in spirits last night because I was in hopes it wd go on so, without any further bustle till the time of his return. . . . So far I had wrote on Wednesday. Today is Saturday—tho' I was silent I have done wonders—I have told him I do not prefer him—I have convinced him of it and he really seems desirous of keeping on some terms with me—I am sure of myself—he goes tomorrow and will not come this fortnight. . . . I think just the same of my own folly.[17]

Dorset reluctantly accepted the affair was over even though Georgiana refused to give a satisfactory explanation for her sudden change of feelings. Only Bess, and probably Harriet, knew what had prompted Georgiana to break off with him. It was the appearance at Devonshire House of a rising young politician called Charles Grey. He was only twenty-three years old, the eldest son of a general from a well-connected Northumberland family. Georgiana had met him before, when he was a schoolboy at Eton, and had visited his parents at Coxheath. In the intervening period he had grown into a tall, handsome young man with an aristocratic appearance, possessing a high forehead, thick hair, melancholy dark eyes, and a long nose. "He has the patrician thoroughbred look . . . which I dote upon," remarked Lord Byron, when he first saw him.

Grey delivered his maiden speech in the Commons on February 22, 1787; it was sufficiently eloquent for Sir Gilbert Elliot to praise it as "excessively good indeed, and such as has given everybody the highest opinion both of his abilities and character. . . . he professes not to be of a party but I think he has a warm leaning to us."[18] Following her usual practice, Georgiana quickly snatched him up into Whig society, flattering him with invitations to select dinners to meet the party grandees. For many months she tolerated his attentions with the gentle amusement she reserved for her younger admirers—she was seven years older than him and he seemed no match for the sophisticated womanizing ambassador to Paris.

Dorset had the further advantage of having been friends with Georgiana for more than thirteen years. He fitted in easily with the rest of her life; he was safe, light hearted, and not without a touch of cynicism. Grey was dangerously impulsive, vain, and moody. An acquaintance described him as "peevish and wayward . . . always desponding, always out of spirits unless he thinks he is riding the winning horse," and "always thinking of himself."[19] His violent expressions of love for Georgiana both frightened and fascinated her. She complained to Bess about the teasing she had suffered "for my liking to talk to so young a man," but she couldn't stop herself from falling in love.[20] Grey's passionate and vehement declarations appealed to the romantic in her. The thought of Georgiana juggling lovers no doubt appeased Bess's conscience and she surreptitiously encouraged Grey's suit. On the occasion of his first major speech she wrote: "I suppose you are in Town; and poor Black's [Charles Grey] day by this time is over, and he is either very happy or very sad—the others are veterans and I suppose felt little."[21] By 1788 Georgiana was more entranced by him than she was prepared to admit. Grey was in London—a great advantage over Dorset—and Georgiana was his only love while she knew for certain that Dorset kept several women about him.

While Bess was away there was a by-election in Westminster. Georgiana had no desire to expose herself to another nationally orchestrated attack on her character and she remained at home while Harriet joined the canvass. Nevertheless she attended the strategy meetings at Devonshire House which allowed her to fight the election vicariously. "We were 236 ahead today and 454 on the whole and I hope a very popular meeting tonight about the shop tax secures our success. . . . I hope our friends will not slacken their exertions," she told her mother on July 29.[22] She had secured a great coup in persuading the Duke of Bedford to donate to the subscription fund much more money than he had originally intended. "He is wonderfully eager," she wrote after her success. Lavinia informed George:

She looked well and healthy but is so coarse that I hardly knew her—she says *they* are sure of carrying the election but it will cost *us* very dear—the D of Bedford has at last . . . subscribed 3000 . . . the bribery is higher than it ever was and so are the shameful riots and excesses—such blood shedding I never heard of—your sister the Duchess does not canvass at all and I could not help saying I was very glad of it—but Lady Duncannon is most violently busy at this business—she is about all day long and has done infinite good to the party, Lady G Cavendish and Mrs Stanhope are also wonderfully active.[23]

Another correspondent, Miss Lloyd, described Georgiana's efforts behind the scenes:

all the intelligence I have had has been from the Dutchess of Devonshire, who has come once a week to dine here, and who I suppose does not tell us the whole truth, but what she does is bad enough. She has not gone about canvassing as she did the last time; she only writes about fifty notes, and sees about fifty people every day. At night the Heads of the Party meet and sup at Devonshire House, and are so jolly and so eager that she says it is quite delightful. . . .[24]

Fox and Lord John Townshend beat the opposition by a convincing margin, and once again the Whigs organized a march of their supporters from Covent Garden to Pall Mall. A procession of 120 carriages, including the state carriages of the Duchesses of Devonshire and Portland, rumbled down the Strand to Charing Cross. Two hundred Whigs on horseback, all dressed in blue and buff, followed, led by Lord Galway. The electors marched behind carrying the usual banners: SACRED TO FEMALE PATRIOTISM and NO NAVAL JUDAS in reference to the defeated Pittite candidate Admiral Lord Hood. But there were no women present; when Fox and Sheridan addressed the crowd from the balcony of Devonshire House Georgiana remained inside, ignoring calls for her appearance. Lavinia sat with her in the drawing room to make sure she did.

Bess arrived from France shortly afterwards. Despite having written in her diary, "I will cease to live in error with him," she resumed her place as the Duke's second wife as soon as she returned.[25] Her permanent residence at Devonshire House kept Georgiana and her mother apart. Lady

"The Miscarriage or His Grace Stopping the Supplies," July 30, 1788. A cartoon accusing Georgiana of depleting the Cavendish fortune to help the Whigs during the election. The Duke protests and insists that he will wear the breeches. Dent. BM Cat. 7360.

Spencer had revealed to George the year before, in 1787, that "G., makes a point of my going to D. House, but I have an insurmountable objection to being in the house with *the obstacle,* which is I think giving my sanction in some degree to that incomprehensible connexion. . . . I can have your uncle's house in Bentinck Street which is more conveniently situated for Harriet and may consequently have that pretence made for giving it preference."[26] She continued to make public her opposition to Bess.

Lady Spencer's hostility upset Georgiana, who felt she owed her security at Devonshire House to Bess, certain that were it not for Bess the Duke would have separated from her long ago. It was remarkable how much the balance of power within their relationship had moved in Bess's favour. From being "a poor little thing," she had become the mainstay of the *ménage à trois*. What had not changed was her obsessive jealousy of Georgiana. Moreover, it was Bess's single-minded pursuit of her which had proved to be the enduring attraction for Georgiana. Her need for attention was so boundless that only someone like Bess would be willing, or able, to satiate it. Georgiana would continue to love Bess for as long as her friend remained preoccupied with her. It was a love which made her blind to Bess's other faults. She simply could not understand why Lady Spencer loathed her.

> You know how anxious I am to make you happy, and to shew my regard and gratitude to the Duke for the constant tenour of his behaviour to me [Lady Spencer wrote in August 1788 after receiving another complaint from Georgiana], I always avoid naming Lady E.F., and if anybody is injudicious enough to mention her to me, I endeavour to give such answer as will shew them I am determined not to enter into the subject. My behaviour was not premeditated, it arose at Chatsworth from my own feelings at scenes I was unfortunate enough to be witness to, and finding I have so little power to command myself when I am deeply affected, I thought it better to avoid all opportunities of acting in a manner that might distress us all. I certainly mean to behave civilly to Ly E.F. whenever I meet her, and hope of late especially I have done so.[27]

But it took several months of pleading before Lady Spencer wrote, somewhat stiffly, that Bess "might come down some day" to St. Albans. Georgiana's gratitude at this small concession was pathetic: "I love you, Dearest M. as an ador'd mother, as a darling friend, nor can I express to you the delight it would be to me if some day next week we might come down for one night. . . . I do not deceive you in assuring you that [the Duke] loves you with all the affection of a son," she lied. "I should not be thus anxious if I did not know all [Bess's] merits, and if I was not certain of her virtue as of my own."[28]

Visitors to Chatsworth found the atmosphere harmonious although somewhat eccentric. Bess's confession about her pregnancy the year before had fixed the *ménage à trois* into certain patterns. It was as if, in order to accommodate the more bizarre aspects of their relationship, the two women had colluded in creating an unreal life based on fantasy and melodrama. When Harriet was there she joined in with them, tipping the balance so that everyone was obliged to play along. James Hare wrote a gentle satire on life at Chatsworth called "A Rational Day in the Country":

> The Ladies rise from one o'clock to two—breakfast in their own rooms for the convenience of having their hair combed while they drink their tea. Cold meat is brought for the Dogs at the same time. Send messages, or (if Time permits) write notes to each other, just to say, "Dearest one, how do oo do?" The usual answer is "As oo do, so does poor little I, by *itself* . . . I." This delicate complaint of solitude sets the whole house in motion. All the Ladies run from one room to another till they have mustered a sufficient force to venture among the men. . . . they write with the greatest ease and tolerable accuracy long letters on all subjects and to every sort of correspondent, standing, walking and even running, and without the least interruption of conversation, which at Chatsworth *never* goes beyond a whisper. . . . they take the precaution of beginning them all alike with the general terms of general civility that may apply to anybody, such as "My Dearest most dear ever adored Lord without whom I cannot live— *Bess oo*."
>
> . . . If by this time it is grown nearly dark and snows and freezes pretty hard, walking is usually proposed. I forgot to observe that when the Ladies first come down to a small Room with a large fire they are wrapped up with furs and waddings of various sorts, but as this heavy "furniture" might impede their agility in walking, they throw it off, and chuse lighter drapery before they venture out— such as gauze or muslin shawls, thin silk sandals, which with the help of a long Pole with a spike in the end of it (to throw over their shoulders or stick into any gentleman's foot who has the honour of accompanying them) form the walking apparatus. The reflection of the snow in the glimmering of the Moon through the trees, if it is a clear night, enables them to find their way round the pleasure ground very tolerably.
>
> . . . When the Dinner has been served up about half an hour they usually retire to dress, and then meet either in the Duchess' or Lady E.F.'s room for a quarter of an hour's social talk. At length the female cohort enter the Dining Room. It is difficult to ascertain their exact diet, as it varies according to their health and humours. . . . By the noise and chatting that ensues on their leaving the Dining Room it is concluded that they remain some time in the Drawing Room, but as

soon as the Gentlemen come out to Tea and Coffee, each Lady retires to her respective apartment, where to pass the time, for want of anything to do, she goes to sleep. . . . On waking they assemble in one of their rooms, and between eleven and twelve retire to the Music Room and crowd round the Pianoforte that each in her turn may have the pleasure of refusing to sing or play. . . . the moment that [supper] is brought in, everybody hastens to begin the day's amusements and repairs to whist, chess, backgammon, billiards, according to their fancies' direction. In the course of a few hours, the supper being sufficiently cooled, the Duke invites his friends to partake of the genial Board; every one presses eagerly for a place, especially those who do not sup. The Ladies sip by turns cowslip wine, punch, or cherry syrup, take their leave, and spend the remainder of the night in confidential discourse, dividing into small parties of two and three for this purpose, and then leaving the supper room, and separating for the night, as the Housemaids begin to twirl their mops and open the shutters to the sunshine.[29]

Among the guests during the summer was the disgraced French minister Alexandre de Calonne, whose friendship with the Polignacs ensured his *entrée* into Devonshire House society. George thought him "a great rogue," but the effervescent Frenchman had met his match in his sister. He fell in love with Georgiana, a weakness she capitalized upon to obtain loans for herself and Harriet. However, the extra income made only a tiny inroad into her worries; she still showed no sign of producing an heir. The Cavendishes referred to her failure almost every day of their visit. She had more reasons than they to want a boy, and yet they continued to blame her. Their disapproval made her feel like an outsider, tolerated but not welcomed by her husband's family. "I do think there is nothing in beauty that equals Chatsworth," she wrote sadly, "tho' I like a number of places better. I believe if I had a son I should like it best of all; but there is something in its not being my children's that makes me fancy it is not mine."[30]

CHAPTER 13

THE REGENCY CRISIS

1788—1789

Most of the Ladies of fashion appeared at the Opera on Saturday in a new head-dress in honour of the Prince of Wales. It consisted of three large white feathers connected by a band, on which was inscribed the motto of the Principality—Ich Dien, and is the most becoming ornament that has graced the female world for many years.

Morning Post, *February 9, 1789*

Dr. George Baker was called to see the King on a quiet day in October 1788 and found him drenched in sweat, unable to sit, stand, or lie down except in excruciating pain. Any movement triggered shooting cramps down his legs and up through his back. The doctor noted that his eyes were yellow; an examination of his urine showed it had turned brown, and occasionally flecks of foam appeared on the patient's lips. Even more disturbing than this precipitous decline in the King's physical health were the obvious signs of mental disorder. At times his speech was almost normal, at others rambling and agitated. He was prone to violent rages interspersed with bursts of uncontrolled jabbering, repeating the same sentence for hours. During the next two weeks the King was well enough to be aware of his worsening condition, and in moments of clarity he made pathetic appeals for help; "I wish to God I may die," he wept in front of his distraught children, "for I am going to be mad."[1] Even the Prince of Wales was so shocked by his father's state that he visited Windsor every day to console his mother and sisters.

Naturally courtiers began to whisper, first among themselves and then to family and friends. The circle of gossip widened until the King's illness became an open secret. Dr. Baker informed Pitt on October 22 that the situation was serious and yet so baffling that he could give neither a proper diagnosis nor a prognosis. Newspapers alluded to the rumours, but the lack of real news and the delicacy of the subject made their reports circumspect. The *Morning Post* claimed the King was suffering from an unusual form of dropsy.[2] To dampen speculation about his state, the King made a heroic effort to appear in public, which exacerbated his disorientating attacks. He insisted on attending a concert where, as soon as the music began, he startled the room by breaking into spasmodic movements and sudden fits of speech. The Queen and courtiers behaved as if nothing was happening, which added a surreal element to the already disconcerting display. After this, the whispers rose to a babble. Medical ignorance and royal etiquette induced a paralysis at court until, on November 5, the King jumped from his chair during dinner and attacked the Prince of Wales. He grappled with him in front of his terrified family and attendants and, with the energy of a lunatic, smashed his son's head against a wall. Several people noticed how afterwards he turned and gave the Queen, who had been screaming throughout, a strange, glaring look.

The following day her attendants were ordered to move her belongings into another bedroom. Later that night the King went in search of her. On entering her former bedroom he found Dr. Baker, the Prince of Wales and his brothers, and the entire male section of the court nervously crowding around the walls of the room. The sight of this silent chorus checked him for a moment, but no one dared approach him. Dr. Baker made a timid movement to usher the King out which enraged him, and he chased the doctor into a corner. After a few moments the Queen's Vice Chamberlain had the presence of mind to walk over to the King and pull him away from his crouching victim. George III allowed himself to be led back to his own bed. Shortly afterwards he called "Mr Pitt a rascal, & Mr Fox his friend."[3] There was no longer any doubt that the King had lost his mind.

❦❧

The Regency crisis unfolds like a morality tale in which the foolish are punished and the wise and temperate are rewarded. It is not difficult to understand its interest to historians and dramatists—the characters' foibles are so vivid: Pitt's coldness, Fox's carelessness, Sheridan's duplicity, Grey's arrogance, and the Prince of Wales's self-indulgence.[4] The reason we know so much about what went on behind the scenes is that

Georgiana kept a diary. Her eye-witness account, recorded in a daily journal for her mother—"my letters will be a regular newspaper," she had promised—remains the most quoted source material for the period.

Georgiana learned the true nature of the King's illness on November 7, two days after his assault on the Prince of Wales. Fish Craufurd dispatched a hurried note:

> I can give you no just account of the King's disorder. Nobody can get at the truth but he is certainly very ill and dangerously ill. . . . The Chancellor was sent for yesterday while he was at dinner and came back this morning. Why he was sent for, or whether he saw the King, I don't know. The truth is, I believe, that the King is quite disordered in his mind. . . . I understand that the Prince has desired Charles [Fox] to be sent for, which ought to be a secret, but is none, for I heard it at Brooks's.[5]

Georgiana arrived in London on the twentieth to find the party already riven with dissent between those who wanted to wait for Fox, who was holidaying in Italy with Mrs. Armistead, and those who were prepared to begin the political battle without him. The Duke of Portland was the nominal leader of the Whigs but his reticent nature meant that members looked to Fox for guidance. There were several men, Sheridan and Grey chief among them, who saw Fox's absence as an opportunity to assert their authority. The jostling of the young pretenders distracted the party just when it needed to be at its most disciplined and focused. By law, if the King was incapacitated, the Prince of Wales (whose marriage remained a secret) became Regent. The government would have to resign and the Regent would have the opportunity to choose a new cabinet.

The competition between the two parties was similar to that leading up to the 1784 election, but many of the faces had changed during the intervening years. Scores of Whigs, including the Duke of Richmond, had deserted the party and no longer went to Devonshire House. In their place were younger, more idealistic men. Georgiana's most frequent visitors were now Charles Grey, Sheridan, and the Duke of Bedford, Lady Melbourne's new lover. Richard Sheridan was envied and mistrusted rather than liked by many members of the party. Fox's friends resented the way he fawned on the Prince of Wales and seemed so willing to act as his errand-boy. Nor could they fathom why women found him so attractive, "having a red face and an ill look as I ever saw," mused Sir Gilbert Elliot to his wife. "He employs a great deal of art, with a great deal of pain, to gratify, not the proper passion in such affairs, but vanity; and he deals in the most intricate plotting and under plotting, like a Spanish play."[6] Although he had been a loyal friend to Georgiana she could see through him: "I do not mean to accuse him of any duplicity; in fact he has stood the test of even poverty and I feel convinc'd of the honour of his political sentiments—but he cannot resist playing a sly game."[7] During the Regency crisis Sheridan came to Devonshire House every day, not to see her but Harriet: they had recently become lovers.

Harriet's affair with Charles Wyndham had been followed by others, as a teasing letter of Sheridan's shows: "Do not listen to Jack's elegies or smile at F's epigrams or tremble at C.W.'s [Lord John Townshend, Richard Fitzpatrick, and Charles Wyndham] frowns."*[8] Their affair began shortly after he had broken off with another Whig hostess, Mrs. Crewe. Duncannon was ignorant of it but everyone else knew, including Sheridan's wife and his sister Betsy, who never missed an opportunity to malign Harriet. Devonshire House, which provided the setting for so many intrigues, was the easiest place for them to meet, although it was not without its irritations for Sheridan. Recognizing a fellow adventurer, he could not resist teasing Bess, who responded to his arch sallies with ill grace. He also derived little enjoyment from seeing Charles Grey so frequently since they were venomous political rivals. Sheridan could almost always outwit Grey in an argument, which the latter attempted to laugh off, implying that it was beneath him to engage in discussion with a playwright.

While Fox was on his way back from Italy Sheridan appointed himself master-negotiator on behalf of the Prince, a move which greatly increased his political stock and gave him the added satisfaction of watching Grey sulk over dinner at Devonshire House. His desire to hold all the cards meant that his meetings with the Prince were shrouded in secrecy, and the outcome of interviews known only to himself. It made him an unpopular leader and damaged the party's morale by encouraging suspicion and rival machinations. Georgiana complained that "he cannot resist the pleasure of acting alone, and this, added to his natural want of judgement and dislike of consultation," made him appear to be double-dealing. Yet at the same

---

* Sheridan adopted the Devonshire House Circle's patois whenever he wrote to Harriet: "I must bid 'oo good Night," etc.

time the Whigs were terrified of alienating the Prince, and if the price of office was to pander to Sheridan's egotistical posturing, most considered it one worth paying.

Fox reached England on November 24, after a breakneck journey covering 1,000 miles in nine days. He had contracted dysentery along the way and was unable to attend any meetings. His supporters wanted him to quash Sheridan's pretensions, but Fox's conversations with the Prince were disappointing: it was clear to him that Sheridan had usurped his place. Charles Grey was one of those who found their ambitions thwarted by the playwright's mischievous meddling. Primed by Sheridan that Grey expected to be given high office, the Prince made a loud speech about his talents and then offered him the "honour" of an extremely junior post.

The Duke of Devonshire, on the other hand, was offered *carte blanche* but swiftly declined any post. Georgiana and Bess tried in vain to persuade him to take something. Lord John Cavendish also displayed a mulish aversion to office and refused the Chancellorship. It dismayed Georgiana to think there would be no Cavendish presence in the new government. She, too, thought Grey was over-reaching himself in wanting the post and surreptitiously supported Sheridan's efforts to lower his expectations. It was awkward for her to have to choose between her lover and her husband's family, but the politician in her won over the romantic.

Georgiana was coy about her transactions with the Prince of Wales: "I saw the Prince this Eveg," she told Lady Spencer on December 4. "He told me he should absolutely refuse any *limited* Regency so they might do as they will." She said nothing more, and it was from other sources that Lady Spencer learned the truth; that as well as pushing her own choices for certain posts, Georgiana jockeyed with Sheridan to advise the Prince. Her mother had heard that in contrast to Sheridan's plan—for the Prince to accept whatever conditions the Pitt ministry imposed and then, once in power, to dismantle them—Georgiana thought the Prince ought to insist on being granted the full powers of Regent but to show magnanimity afterwards. She asked Georgiana whether it was true

> that you have advised the Pr. not to accept on anything but the sole Regency without any limitation, but that when he has got it he should declare that, tho' his opinion of his former friends was as high as ever, nevertheless he would act as well as he could with those now in office for a *certain given time,* out of delicacy to the K. and in hope of his recovery. It is added that this advice was as politic as it

was good, for it would conciliate the affections of the nation and greatly weaken the power of the present Ministry, who would dis-unite before the given period approached, and if, in truth, the K. did recover shortly, it would be saving the greatest confusion possible to the nation.[9]

Such a plan would certainly have been the most politic, but the party and the Prince were too distracted by the imminent prospect of power to think sensibly any more. Three weeks of exemplary behaviour towards his family had strained the Prince's nerves past breaking point. A disgusted public read about his nightly parties; he had even been seen lurching up St. James's shouting obscenities and jokes about his father. At Brooks's when he played cards he said, "I play the lunatic," meaning the King. Nothing in the Prince's attitude indicated that he was fit for the responsi-bilities of Regent, and public opinion began to side with Pitt. Yet the op-position did not care, and in their complacency lay the party's undoing. While the Whigs argued over the division of spoils, Pitt was carefully studying the options available to his government. Contrary to the Whigs' expectations, there were several complicated issues to be faced before the Prince took over as head of state. The most important of these was the prospect of the King's recovery. Since medical opinion was divided, it was not clear what form the Regency should take. It would be awkward if the King recovered and found that his greatest enemies were enjoying them-selves at his expense.

When Parliament met on December 10 to discuss the matter, Pitt had prepared himself with a list of arguments and precedents dating back to the insanity of Henry VI in 1454. His cabinet was resolved to be dismissed but nevertheless remained united in his support. By contrast, the chief spokesmen for the Whigs were barely on speaking terms with each other. There had not been a single meeting at which all the party members had been present, and no coherent strategy had been devised. Pitt opened the debate by suggesting that Parliament should set up a committee to exam-ine the precedents, which would report on its findings within a week. His cool eloquence and the sound reasons he gave for delaying any decision on the Regency made a good impression on the House. Fox leapt to his feet to oppose. It was almost the first time he had left his room since his return from Italy; he was obviously still unwell and his mind, already clouded by his anxiety to show the House he was still the leader of his party, was muddled. He opened his mouth and inflicted on his own party one of the most damaging assaults it had ever sustained. Pitt, he said, had no right to delay the Regency by one day. Parliament had no right to debate anything regarding the Prince of Wales, and the government was merely playing for time. In those few minutes Fox had destroyed the party's credibility as the defender of parliamentary rights. By so forcefully championing the Prince of Wales he made the party's battle to limit the powers of the crown appear at best a sham and at worst a sinister plot. There was nothing any of the subsequent Whig speakers could do to lessen the effect of Fox's speech.*

"The party wish'd they are rid of Charles Fox who was rash and imprudent," recorded Bess in her journal. "Different opinions, uneasiness etc., at what has past," wrote Georgiana. "When Sheridan attack[ed] Charles for bring[ing] on debate on *Right,* Charles said it's better always to take the bull by the horns. Sheridan said yes but you need not have drove him into the room that you might take him by the horns." Sheridan was particularly bitter at what he viewed as Fox's sabotage of his own plans. Two days later, however, he committed an equally disastrous blunder. He began a speech which started out as a conciliatory attempt to smooth over Fox's mistake, but his bullying tendencies got the better of him and he made a veiled threat about what the Prince might do to those who opposed him. MPs jumped to their feet when they heard this. "I never remember such an uproar as was raised by his threatening us with the danger of provoking the Prince to assert his right," wrote a witness to the pandemonium.[10]

The Whigs had destroyed any chance of a smooth passage into office, but rather than follow Pitt's example and concentrate on tactics they continued to squabble about places. "Great disturbances in the arrangements," wrote Georgiana on December 12. "The Prince has promised Ld Sandwich to the 1st Ld of the Admiralty and both the Duke of Portland and Charles refuse to have anything to do with it in that case." Four days later, in this mood of rancour and distrust, the Whigs went down to the

---

* Comparing Fox's and Pitt's style, the diarist Joseph Farington recalled: "Mr Pitt always spoke with a regular flow of expression, never requiring to go backward to correct himself but proceeding with an uninterrupted stream of delivery. On the contrary, Mr Fox went *forward* and *backward,* not satisfied with his first expression. He would put it another way. The *undertone* of Mr Fox's voice was agreeable, almost musical, but when to give force & energy to his delivery He raised his voice it became squeaking and disagreeable. . . . Mr Fox occasionally had flashes of genius beyond Mr Pitt . . . [but] Mr Pitt had the ascendancy." J. Greig, *The Farington Diary* (London 1922), June 25, 1806.

House to argue for an unrestricted and immediate Regency. Georgiana was filled with trepidation. The Duke of Richmond had boasted to Bess "that they will beat us. . . . Pitt had caught us on the hook and would keep us to it." The Prince stayed with her during the debate, "much agitated," and finally left to get drunk elsewhere. Grey sent her notes on the debate's progress, but the result, when it came through at four in the morning, was nevertheless a shock: Pitt had won by 268 to 204. Georgiana had suffered from a fierce headache all day, and the news, she said, "did not make me better." "Fox's declaration of the Prince of Wales's right has been of no small service to us," wrote Pitt's cousin, William Grenville.[11]

Pitt sent a curt letter to the Prince a few days later outlining the restrictions he would impose on him: the Prince would have no power to create peerages, and he was debarred from conferring any pensions, honours, or royal posts. As a final insult, the Queen would be in charge of the Royal Household. Georgiana and her friends were indignant at the harsh conditions. Belatedly, Sheridan stayed at home to study the precedents. But it was more than a matter of catching up; Pitt had the measure of his opponents: he knew their weaknesses and their strengths, and the former he took care to play upon while the latter he was not too proud to imitate. Chief among these was the Whigs' skill in psychological warfare—Georgiana's field. From the beginning of the crisis she had been energetic in employing the tactics which had so successfully demoralized the government in 1784. "The ladies are as usual at the head of all animosity," Lord Sydney told Lord Cornwallis, "and are distinguished by caps, ribands, and other such ensigns of party." Georgiana had designed a fetching headpiece, a "Regency cap," based on the Prince of Wales's crest, made up of three jaunty feathers with his motto "*Ich Dien*" sewn at the base. It caught on to some extent, but Pitt was ready for her this time. The Whigs were dismayed to find the government benches uniformly dressed in "constitutional coats" of blue and red, and they were further discomforted to encounter the majority of people wearing the uniform at public assemblies. The inhabitants of Devonshire House were horrified to discover one morning that its walls were plastered with handbills denouncing Fox and the Prince of Wales.

Pitt realized that Georgiana fulfilled a vital function for the Whig party and he was keen to find an equivalent. He was fortunate in having a candidate who had already put herself forward for the post. "It will not be the first time that a man of great understanding has been the dupe of a designing woman," wrote Lady Mary Coke disgustedly in 1787, having seen Jane, Duchess of Gordon, at work on Pitt: "The Duchess of Gordon resembles my Lady Bristol [Bess's mother], is like her in person, manner, contrivances, and like her, scruples nothing to gain her end, such a person must always be dangerous."[12] During the general election of 1780 she had allegedly kidnapped a supporter of Lord Frederick Campbell, who was the candidate in her constituency on the Argyll interest, and kept him locked in the cellar during the canvassing in order to secure the seat for her friend, Captain Elphinstone. Since separating from her husband, the Duchess of Gordon had entered into a semi-public affair with Henry Dundas, Pitt's best friend and chief political adviser. She was rich, handsome, and a withering opponent in argument. "The Duchess triumphs in a manly mien; Loud is her accent, and her phrase obscene," was how she was described by a Scottish wit. Her critics regarded her as a political harpy, "a horrid violent woman," incapable of acting beyond her two chief ambitions—to be the most powerful political hostess in London, and to secure rich husbands for her five daughters.

For the previous two years she had shamelessly imitated Georgiana, holding regular political dinners for Pitt and Dundas, and organizing specifically Tory assemblies to build up a sense of party as a counterbalance to Devonshire House. One observer noted that she was of "Infinite service among the Young Men, holding nightly gatherings of them in Pall Mall."[13] She tried, less successfully, to introduce her own inventions to the fashion world. However, her brashness brought her the rewards she sought: in July 1787 the pro-government *Morning Herald* reported, "The Duchess of Gordon is now amongst the Ladies most in vogue."[14] Nathaniel Wraxall thought that she was "far inferior to her rival," lacking Georgiana's charm or generosity, but that she more than compensated for her deficiencies in personality by her utter ruthlessness. Even Dundas found himself capitulating to her demands for her own candidates to be given preference in Scotland. Once the Regency debates were in progress she did not hesitate to use her influence on the government's behalf. Wraxall records: "She even acted as a *Whipper-in* of Ministers. Confiding in her rank, her sex, and personal attractions, she ventured to send for members of Parliament, to question, to remonstrate, and to use every means for confirming their adherence to the government."[15]

There is no doubt that the Duchess of Gordon was of considerable help to Pitt. In employing her, he was paying tribute to Georgiana's success as the doyenne of the Whig party and acknowledging that certain women, at least, possessed the calibre to be leaders of men. It was another example of

Pitt combining his opponents' flair with his genius for method. In contrast, the Whigs squandered their advantages by their internal bickering; there could be no whipping-in to the party line if the leadership could not agree on its content. The Lord Chancellor bluntly told Sheridan that his party were fools to waste Georgiana's talents; "he said she would have been a powerful indeed almost irresistible advocate."[16] Sheridan replied, according to Georgiana, that they "had had thoughts of employing me," but it was one more thing on which the leaders could not agree.

"Really London is now the most odious place I ever was in," complained Lavinia to George. "Party rage is so high and people all so outrageous and absurd that there is even less comfort in society now than there ever was."[17] The Duchess of Gordon trounced Georgiana's parties with showy balls which made the Whigs' thin gatherings seem insipid by comparison. The Prince of Wales asked the Duchess of Gordon to wear a Regency cap, at which she laughed rudely and said "she would sooner be hang'd."[18] In the meantime public opinion supported Pitt. By the middle of January 1789 over forty-five towns had sent public addresses to Parliament praising his leadership. The Whigs fought every restriction imposed on the Regency and lost each debate. "Nothing but treachery going forward—Sheridan heres [sic] Grey has abus'd him, Grey is abus'd by the others," Georgiana wrote despairingly on January 11; the enmity between Fox and Sheridan was being acted out by their supporters and destroying any hope of a last-ditch rally against Pitt. The Duchess of Gordon invited Georgiana and Bess to accompany her to the House of Commons to listen to the debates, making no attempt to hide her satisfaction at their disappointment. They curtly refused.

By the end of January the only barrier between the Whigs and ignominy was the King's illness. Fox had given up fighting with Sheridan and the Prince of Wales, and retired to Bath with Mrs. Armistead. In a feeble response to the loyal addresses piling up on Pitt's desk, the Whigs attempted to organize a public address from the borough of Westminster, but with Portland refusing to talk to Sheridan, and Sheridan ignoring Grey, and Grey still furious with the Prince of Wales, and Fitzpatrick, Loughborough, Craufurd, and Burke nursing their own grievances, the best the party could manage was to send a petition round various public houses. Fewer Whigs bothered to turn up for meetings at Devonshire House despite strenuous efforts by Georgiana to ensure attendance. Lord Malmesbury was among the waverers who received a summons: "Pray come here tomorrow evening any time after 9," she wrote. "You wd have been more loyal, had you come of yr own accord without being sent to; yr, ever, *however,* G. Devonshire."[19]

The Regency Bill passed through the House of Commons on February 12; by this time Pitt could afford to be magnanimous, and he accepted Daniel Pultney's suggestion that the restrictions on the Regent's power should end after three years. A week later, on the nineteenth, official bulletins announced that the King was convalescing. The Lords moved to adjourn the Regency Bill amidst noisy jubilation on the government benches. The Pittite Lady Stafford described the opposition's reaction:

> Dismay, Disappointment, and Mortification were strongly painted in their Countenances, and in the Evening at Assemblies they could not disguise their unexpected Distress. I do think it must be a sad hearing to them, after quarrelling among themselves about the Places, exulting in their approaching Power, and so late as Thursday protesting that they would come in, if it was only for a Week, to humble this proud Administration, and to torment his Majesty the more when he should resume his Government.[20]

The King's recovery released the two sides from any remaining constraints of civility. Sheridan's sister recorded that the Whigs were the object of public derision. Georgiana and her friends braved an assembly given by Lady Buckinghamshire, where they were "groan'd and hooted" at by the "Ladies on the Opposite Side."[21] Georgiana went ahead with a ball she had planned; it fell flat. The Prince made matters worse by provoking several drunken brawls in London clubs; one night the stewards actually threw him out of Ranelagh Gardens. At first the Whigs coped with the news of the King's recovery by refusing to believe the medical reports. Grey still insisted a month later that the King was "foolish" and a Regency imminent. Gradually, however, the cold truth banished their dreams. The Whigs were silenced by their defeat, their stupefaction highlighted by the joyful clamour around them.

After a short pause national celebrations began with the formal opening of Parliament on March 10. Carriages blocked every street and thoroughfare as people jostled for a clear view of the fireworks and illuminations marking the event. The Whigs who dared to venture out did so anonymously, squeezing past thousands of flag-waving citizens who cheered and hugged each other in unaffected joy. A group of artisans spotted the

Prince's carriage crawling towards Westminster and began singing "God Save the King" in sarcastic tones. William Elliot, who witnessed the incident, told his wife that at first the Prince joined in, shouting "Long live the King!" but when they also cried "Pitt for ever!" he shouted "Fox for ever," which started a mini riot: "a man pulled the coach-door open, and the Prince endeavoured to jump out amongst them in order to defend himself; but his younger brother the Duke of York kept him back with one arm, and with the other struck the man on the head and called to the coachman to drive on, which he did at great pace, the coach door flapping about as they went."[22] The carnival-like atmosphere was galling for all the losers, but the exclusion from public rejoicing was especially painful for someone like Georgiana; in other circumstances she would have been the organizer. The last time mile-long traffic jams had been seen in Piccadilly was four years ago at her famous balloon launch. This time she was trapped inside Devonshire House, forced to listen to the bickering nonsense of Grey and Sheridan.

Georgiana's next public appearance was on March 26 at the Queen's Drawing Room to mark the King's recovery. All the women had received prior notice to wear GOD SAVE THE KING in their caps in a direct riposte to Georgiana's Regency caps. "I found it was much a subject of discussion and observation whether the Duchess would have it or no," wrote George to Lady Spencer. After several heated arguments the Whigs agreed that their side would keep their heads bare.[23] The order of presentation was published in advance, and it was clear that the Queen was particularly relishing the thought of having the Whigs under her scrutiny. The day was one of the longest Harriet could remember:

> people did not get away till after eight o'clock though some were there by eleven. The Q. stood near the middle window with a small space round her, through which everybody pass'd one by one. She did not speak to any of the principal Opposition people. Fox, Sheridan, Tierney, Grey, and very cold to the Princes. . . . She was dress'd in blue and orange and had "God save the King" in her cap, as almost everybody else had except us; she look'd up at our heads as we past her.[24]

Their discomfort at this humiliating procedure was increased by the stifling heat. People pushed and shoved in an effort to get out of the slow-moving crush. "Nothing ever equalled the crowd," wrote Harriet; "one heard nothing but screams and women carrying out in fits. The whole ground was strewed with different coloured foil, and pearls and diamonds crumbled to pieces."[25]

The exhausted women returned to Devonshire House aching and dishevelled, furious at the Duke of Portland for having insisted that they expose themselves to further embarrassment. The Prince arrived a short time later for a quiet supper which he ruined by sobbing and ranting throughout. Sheridan attempted to calm him down by discussing strategies for a reconciliation between the brothers and their parents, but it was hollow talk. The Prince's agitation increased over the next few days following the announcement that a concert and supper would be held at Windsor on April 2. Neither he nor the Duke of York was invited, and when he finally summoned the courage to question his mother she replied, "she supposed they would not come, as it was meant as a compliment to those who supported her and the King."[26] On March 30 the members of White's held a ball in honour of the King at the Pantheon. Over 2,000 people danced beneath illuminated devices depicting "GR" and other symbols until the early hours of the morning. The Duchesses of Gordon and Richmond, who were the patrons for the event, had deliberately appointed only three milliners in London to make the white and gold uniforms in the expectation that the Whig ladies would humble themselves to accept their lead. To their chagrin the Prince and all the Whigs boycotted the ball. Few people noticed the absence of the opposition; patriotic fervour combined with the champagne to intoxicate the hall, and "God Save the King" was sung many times until throats were hoarse.

The uniform for the concert at Windsor three days later was deep blue trimmed with scarlet and gold. "Loyalty is a most expensive virtue at present," complained Lady Louisa Stuart to Lady Portarlington. "A good subject cannot be dressed for these three days for under a hundred pounds."[27] The Prince did attend this celebration, and it was a lesson in mortification. Many of the guests ignored him, his mother glared at him whenever their eyes met, and his sisters were forbidden to speak to him. The Prince and the Duke of York did their best to appear unconcerned even though the whole tone of the event was directed against them. Pitt's famous winning vote after the Regency debate on December 16—268—was emblazoned above the banqueting table along with his coat of arms entwined with the Lord Chancellor's. "All this," complained William Elliot, "is quite new at Court, and most excessively indecent, as the King is always expected to be of *no party*."[28]

The Whigs retaliated three weeks later on April 22, when they staged a rival ball at the Opera House. Initially the Queen forbade any friend to the court to go, which provoked such an outcry that she partly relented, forbidding only the members of the Royal Household. With such advance publicity the Whigs hoped to recapture some of their fighting spirit, but their demoralized state was apparent in the decree that there would be no uniform for the occasion. Thanks largely to Georgiana's efforts the event was sold out. But the party's usual expertise on these occasions had deserted them and the ball failed to match their former successes. There were not enough chairs, and by 4 a.m. women were sitting on the floor, too fatigued to care about their dresses. Mrs. Siddons declaimed an ode to the King which half the house couldn't hear and the other half talked through. No one had remembered to arrange for runners to fetch the carriages, which resulted in confusion and delays.

The Whigs' torture continued for one more day. The service of thanksgiving for the King took place at St. Paul's on April 23, St. George's day. The King and Queen, followed by the royal family and the entire household, rode past a clamour of cheers and ringing bells until they reached the cathedral. They were all dressed in the Windsor uniform and, though the King looked thin and frail, there was no mistaking his calm demeanour. Ministers and members of both Houses followed in a slow march behind, which allowed the crowd to give clear indications of preference. *The Times* reported that Fox's carriage was received with "an universal hiss which continued with very little intermission until he alighted at St Paul's."[29] He threw back the door to a greeting of boos and catcalls which he ignored, keeping his head up above the sightline of the crowds. The view afforded no comfort; every building was covered in banners and ribbons. "God Save the King" was strung across hundreds of streets. As a precautionary measure against the mob, even Devonshire House was decorated with flags and royal insignia.

Pro-government witnesses accused the Prince of Wales and his brother of giggling throughout the service. In contrast, Whig observers thought they had behaved surprisingly well. The Whigs themselves acted with strict decorum, as if attending a funeral rather than a celebration. At the end of the service they departed in their carriages to endure a repeat reception from the crowds. The Devonshire carriage was mostly ignored and escaped the missiles being thrown at the losers. Pitt's carriage, on the other hand, was stopped by the cheering mob and unhinged from the horses. Hundreds of people helped to pull it back to Downing Street, where another crowd was waiting to greet them. It was Pitt's day. "He is admired and adored by all who wish well to Great Britain," wrote one supporter. He was still only twenty-nine.[30]

The Duchess of Gordon was also triumphant. The night of White's ball she hosted a select party which included Pitt, Dundas, and Dr. Willis; people stopped to applaud them as they walked arm in arm. She had become a significant rival to Georgiana, whose reign over the *ton* for the past fifteen years now looked seriously in doubt. The thought that the Duchess of Gordon might topple her from her place caused widespread excitement and immense satisfaction in government circles. By common agreement Georgiana, and not the Duchess of Gordon, was blamed for having divided society down party lines. "We have seen no times when it had been so necessary to separate parties in private company," wrote a Tory peer to a friend. "The acrimony is beyond anything you can conceive."[31] The uniforms, the tribal politics, the use of private female influence to affect the voting outcome—Georgiana had perfected the technique and the Duchess of Gordon had copied her with successful results.

The Regency crisis established the future path of the two parties: the diminution of the Whigs as a credible opposition and Pitt's unassailable pre-eminence. "I have often thought," wrote the Whig peer Lord Palmerston, that "we have more Wit and Ingenuity on our side than sound judgement in managing Parliamentary matters."[32] Pitt had learned from the 1784 Westminster election how to combine both. Many Whigs expressed regret at their party's lack of professionalism. "We despise parliamentary craft too much, and are sadly deficient in it," complained Lord George Cavendish.[33] This was also Georgiana's criticism—lack of discipline among the leadership.[34] Re-reading her journal some years later, she wrote:

> I think the following journal offers two epochas. The first when there seem'd no doubt of the Prince's being Regent, and that the formation of a new administration occupied the minds and produced the circumstances of rivalship and anxiety which attend a new Ministry. The second when the King's recovery revived the hopes of Mr Pitt's friends, and when the opposition seemed only to differ on the part the Prince and themselves were to take. . . . From hence is to be trac'd the facility with which the Prince yields to the pleasure of making himself agreeable to those whom he happens to associate. . . . We can

trace . . . the Virtues and foibles of Mr Fox, the comprehensive mind, undaunted genius, . . . [but] a contempt for even necessary expedients, [and] a great imprudence in conversation. . . . I have so long lamented, and often been provoked with his negligence, sometimes even to decent attention. . . . These fragments, I think, prepare to the disunion and want of method which so soon brought the destruction of opposition about during the years '92 and '93.[35]

PART THREE

Exile

CHAPTER 14

THE APPROACHING
STORM
1789—1790

The Duchess of Devonshire has thought it proper to quit Paris during the present convulsions in that capital. The amiable Duchess was advised to this measure by Madame de Polignac, who told her Grace that she could not depend upon her own safety. The Duchess of Devonshire, it is supposed, has proceeded to Spa.

Morning Post, *July 10, 1789*

The Whigs retreated to Brooks's after the King's recovery; only small numbers bothered to turn up for debates and there was no attempt to organize a coherent strategy for the next session. Almost everyone held a grievance about the way the leadership had dealt with the crisis. Sheridan's supporters blamed Fox for having discredited the party with his claim that Parliament had no right to discuss the Regency. Fox's friends, in turn, felt Sheridan had played an underhanded game and were quick to point out that his own comments in the House had not been particularly helpful. The Cavendishes and the Duke of Portland did not have a good word to say about either of them. Georgiana adopted a conciliatory role and tried to bring the various factions together by holding quiet dinners at Devonshire House. But she, too, retreated from public life and avoided all large gatherings.

It was not only the animosity she encountered from "Tory ladies," as she started to refer to them, which made Georgiana reluctant to go out: by April she was personally bankrupt and in terror of the Duke discovering her debts.[1] Neither Coutts nor Calonne would answer her appeals for further loans. "I really think the best thing is to lay before the Duke the very worst of your situation at once," Coutts wrote after she implored him for another £6,000. "At the same time take an absolute determination to reform your system. If *his* excusing the past, together with *your viewing* the precipice you are standing on the verge of, does not cure you I can only say you have gone beyond the point of recovery."[2] Fortunately for her, she had means of persuasion: Coutt's daughters were learning French at a convent in Paris and it was within her power to introduce them to the French court. It was an unspoken *quid pro quo,* but Georgiana had no illusions about what was expected of her. She enlisted the help of the Duke of Dorset and the Little Po to welcome Coutts's daughters into society. Her efforts brought her a brief respite, especially after she had explained to Coutts that money would be forthcoming as soon as she gave birth to a son. Once she had produced the future sixth Duke of Devonshire her husband would no longer be barred from borrowing money against the estate.

At the end of May the Duke announced that he had made up his mind to take Georgiana and Bess to Spa. Both women were delighted: Georgiana hoped the waters would help her to conceive, while Bess regarded the trip as an opportunity to see her two children, Caroline and Clifford. She was still fighting to gain access to her sons by John Foster, which made her all the more determined to rescue the two she had abandoned in France. Charlotte Williams was to accompany them, and Little G and Harriet, whom they nicknamed Harryo, would stay with Lady Spencer. On June 20, 1789, Georgiana set sail for Calais with Bess and the Duke. She had managed to secure a £500 loan from her brother before setting off from London. It was all the cash she had to last her while she was abroad.[3]

The enthusiastic reception Georgiana received from the French temporarily enabled her to forget her worries.* The Devonshires' visit during such uncertain times was a reassuring sign of normality for the Parisians. French farmers were still suffering the effects of a prolonged drought which had turned grain fields into dust and caused livestock to die of

---

* Martindale had reappeared. Theoretically, Georgiana still owed him tens of thousands. Despite his agreement not to press for repayment he knew he could secure some "quiet" money from her. Writing from Paris, Georgiana could not explain to Coutts why her account was so overdrawn, and resorted to flattery instead. "You are my second father," she told him. She managed to persuade him not to charge her interest. "I hope it will be no loss to you," she wrote, playing up the part of the helpless, unworldly woman. Chatsworth 969; GD to Coutts, July 9, 1789.

thirst. Those crops that survived the scorching sun had drowned in the violent storms that followed. In some areas people were facing starvation: there were riots in the marketplace, grain stores were being attacked, and there were frequent reports of bakers being forced by the mob to sell bread at a "fair price." Rumours that the nobles and the *parlement* had conspired in a *"pacte de famine"* to use as leverage against the King, though unfounded, acted as a powerful incitement to political unrest. In April Paris had been brought to a standstill after an off-the-cuff remark at an electoral meeting by a wallpaper manufacturer called Reveillon sparked two days of rioting. Pitched battles between workers and the army left fifty dead and hundreds wounded. The bloodshed terrified the authorities at the same time as it convinced them that the King had to do something.

Having decided to delay their trip to Spa for a few weeks, the Devonshires arrived in France just after the Third Estate had voted to give itself the new title of National Assembly. Since it represented 96 percent of the country its members felt they should have the majority share of power. The Assembly lost no time in declaring that taxes could only be collected while it remained in session. This challenge to the *ancien régime* affected the various participants in different ways. Some of the clergy and a hard core of liberal nobles, including the Marquis de Lafayette and the Marquis de Condorcet, supported the Third Estate, but most were angered by its presumption. The King now had to assert his authority over the renegades or else, the Duke of Dorset wrote in his dispatches, "it will be little short of laying his crown at their feet."[4] During the five days it took Georgiana to reach Paris the King was judged to have surrendered his crown, his dignity, and any last remnants of the government's credibility. On June 19 the Royal Council met and agreed that the King should call a special session of all the Estates: it was the only hope of regaining the initiative. After much heated argument, and a tearful entrance by the Queen, who burst in on the proceedings and begged the King to take a strong line, they decided that he should annul the proceedings of June 17 and impose his own compromise plan—although quite what that would be no one could say. Unfortunately no one told the deputies that, in the meantime, all meetings were suspended. The Third Estate arrived at the great hall on June 20 to find the doors padlocked. Fearing they were the victims of some royal plot, the deputies tumbled into an indoor tennis court near by and, while a delirious crowd outside shouted *"Vive l'Assemblée,"* took an oath not to disperse until they had achieved constitutional reform.

The King's special session began in an atmosphere of belligerence on all sides, the mood of the Third Estate having been determined by the guards, who forced them to stand in the rain for an hour while the nobles (the First Estate) and clergy (the Second Estate) seated themselves first. Louis XVI did offer a compromise which entailed limiting some of the monarchy's powers, but he remained firm against the Third Estate's other demands: in particular, there would be no union of the three Estates. The nobles were to retain their privileges unless they themselves removed them by separate vote. He declared all the proceedings conducted by the Third Estate since May null and void, and then ordered the deputies to disperse until the next day. Georgiana summed up the futility of the meeting in a letter to her mother: "the King . . . made a speech to the *tiers* telling them they must desist from their proceedings. After he went, there they staid and voted to annul everything he had done and said."[5]

On June 25, three days after the Devonshires had settled at their hotel, there was a revolt among the upper Estates, and the majority of the clergy and about fifty nobles, led by the Duc d'Orléans, formerly the Duc de Chartres, joined the Third Estate. "The ferment at Paris is beyond conception," wrote Arthur Young. "10,000 people have been all this day in the Palais-Royal. . . . every hour that passes seems to give the people fresh spirit: the meetings at the Palais-Royal are more numerous, more violent, and more assured. . . . the language that was talked, by all ranks of people, was nothing less than a revolution in the government, and the establishment of a free constitution."[6]

Georgiana's experience of the London mob meant that at first she regarded the sporadic rioting around her as more of a nuisance than a danger. She told Lady Spencer that they had planned to go to Versailles on June 24 but "the tumults encrease so much at Versailles that our going would be troublesome." Her insouciance was a peculiarly English trait which the French, never having witnessed a county election, found baffling. "I could not resist making the D of Devonshire take Bess, Cha. and I to see the Palais Royal," she wrote; "there were great rejoicings."[7] Lady Sutherland, writing from the British embassy, admitted that she would like to go to Spa but that her husband, Lord Gower, "likes a riot in his heart" and he insisted they stay so he could join in with the crowds.[8] Thomas Jefferson, the American ambassador, expressed his alarm quite openly: "Yesterday at Versailles the mob was violent; they insulted, and even attacked all the clergy and nobility that are known to be strenuous for preserving the separation of Orders. . . . The confusion is so great, that the court have only the troops to depend on."[9]

Within a few days Georgiana and Bess had received visits from most members of the Paris *ton* and all the city's tradesmen. "I am overwhelm'd with stay makers," Georgiana laughed.[10] Ironically, considering the social apartheid she had helped to create at home, she received her French friends on a non-political basis, merely making sure that members of the court party arrived at different times to the "patriots," so that the Princesse de Lamballes could drink tea without fear of running into the Duc d'Orléans. At times this impartiality took on a comic aspect. When Georgiana and Bess went to the Opéra they had to alternate between sharing a box with the Comte d'Artois one night and with his arch rival, the Duc d'Orléans, the next. "You have no need to fear the Duke of Dorset," Georgiana promised her mother, who had written of her concern. "The complexion of the times is such that we can scarcely see him at all."[11] In any case, Dorset had already told her he planned to marry the first woman who would accept him.

When the Devonshires were eventually able to drive to Versailles they found the Polignacs and the King and Queen excessively glad to see them. On their first visit they arrived in the morning and were made to stay for dinner. They went each day and listened sympathetically to their friends' complaints. Georgiana found the King looking better than she expected and the Queen looking worse. "She received us very graciously indeed, tho' very much out of spirit at the times. She asked much after you and took the children's picture and admir'd it very much. She is sadly altered, her belly quite big, and no hair at all, but she has still great éclat."[12] They spent many hours with the Comte d'Artois, who raged against the complicity of his cousin d'Orléans. On June 27 Louis capitulated and ordered the other two Estates to join the Third. "The King has wrote to his nobles to join the *tiers*," Georgiana reported, "which in fact is giving up his authority entirely. The Cte D'Artois wrote to tell them if they did not join the King's life was in danger. The people are wild with joy, and all our friends miserable."[13] Three days later the Estates merged, nobles and clergy marching into the hall in total silence as a way of marking their disapproval. That night a riotous crowd surrounded Versailles shouting slogans and dancing to music until daybreak. The King and Queen briefly appeared on the balcony with their family, although the effect was spoiled when Marie Antoinette broke down in tears.

Georgiana continued to hold sumptuous dinners for her friends in spite of the deteriorating situation. "We were frightened tonight," she admitted, "as the mob at the Palais Royal were screaming and huzzaing because the guards, who had been imprison'd, were let out."[14] It was becoming difficult for her to travel about; "all is license and confusion." She was more explicit about the situation to her brother, George, to whom she wrote on July 5: "The troubles of this place are not to be described—the guards refusing to act, the people half mad and the greatest part of the nobles divided in the most surprising manner, so that families are at daggers drawn."[15] Ignoring the dangers on the streets, where roving bands of youths were prone to commit random acts of violence against the rich, Georgiana went out to meet the leaders of the "patriot" side. No stranger to political debate, she enjoyed arguing with them: "I confess I amuse myself at Paris. . . . I saw La Fayette at the Vicomte de Noailles late. They disputed amazingly on Politicks with me. I am *for* the Court on Mme Polignac's account. They are violently against it."[16] She knew her position was indefensible considering her staunch opposition to the court at home, but she didn't care. Parisian society admired her independent spirit: "they make a great fuss of me, and pay me outrageous compliments," she told Harriet.[17] This was an understatement in Lady Sutherland's opinion:

> I don't think the French bon ton a very beautiful set of people, being dingy and little, and rather rabougris [stunted]. The Dss of Devonshire looks like a creature of different species from any of them; all the men are wonderfully épris with her, and the women who have pretensions get out of her way; as I have none, but am quite a harmless stupid being, I think her the most charming creature I ever saw in my life, and it is quite impossible to see much of her without liking her extremely.[18]

The Duke, however, had had enough of Paris, and on July 8 Georgiana and Bess, dressed in mourning, made one last visit to Versailles to say goodbye to their friends. The roads were lined with foreign troops, which encouraged rumours that the King, or the Queen and her party, were planning a coup against the Assembly. Georgiana saw Marie Antoinette alone for a little while, and then the Little Po, who had been a faithful friend to her. Their correspondence had never slackened; for Georgiana's sake she had accepted Bess, helped to bring Caroline St. Jules to Paris, and provided countenance to Coutts's daughters. They knew most of each other's secrets, and had swapped advice on matters political and romantic for more than fifteen years. Georgiana said farewell not knowing when she would see her again, or in what circumstances.

The Devonshires were in Brussels, en route to Spa, when a messenger reached them with news of the storming of the Bastille. The report of the governor's lynching and the bloody outrages which accompanied his murder made them fear for their friends. To their relief they heard almost immediately that the Comte d'Artois, the Prince de Condé, and the Polignacs had escaped, fleeing Versailles in the middle of the night. They had left without servants so as not to attract notice, and even then, Georgiana told her mother, the Polignacs' sons were almost caught and murdered. Marie Antoinette had urged them to go, but their departure left her almost completely alone except for her family and a few attendants.

James Hare wrote to Georgiana at Spa on July 18 to give her an eye-witness account of the rioting and to reassure her that Charlotte was safe. They had left her with a French family, never imagining the bedlam which would overtake the city. Georgiana told Lady Spencer that the Duke of Devonshire "really cry'd from anxiety" at the thought of poor Charlotte surrounded by a "mad populace arm'd with pistols, swords and bayonets" and, even as an "Englishwoman," she admitted to being frightened by the "extraordinary events."[19] But the Duke's tears were not only (if at all) for Charlotte, but for little Caroline, to whom Georgiana referred very casually in her letters as the "other pensioner, Mlle de St Jules, a young lady from the provinces."[20] Very few people knew of her existence apart from the Little Po and James Hare. With several illegitimate children of his own he sincerely sympathized with the Duke and Bess: "The constant anxiety which I feel for my own children would of itself sufficiently dispose me to assist almost anybody when children are concerned," he had written in reply to their request for help.[21] He not only visited Charlotte and Caroline but also the infant Clifford—he even made sure Coutts's daughters were safe in their convent. Hare found the boy well cared for but shy ("how happens this?" he wrote), although he was pleased to learn from the nurse that both Bess and the Duke had seen the boy before they left Paris.

Georgiana understood Bess's desire to have Caroline with her permanently, but she dreaded the scandalous rumours which her presence at Devonshire House would generate. She had the reputation of her own two daughters to protect. Bess hesitated to force the issue until encouraged to do so by Hare. She had a duty to her daughter, he told her:

It would be dealing insincerely with you if I were to say that I think her introduction at D. House will occasion no surmises or scandal, but this consideration is in my mind infinitely over ballanced by your having her under your own care, whether one thinks of her advantage or your amusement. As to the difficulties which seem to terrify the Dss so much, I guess [what] they must be, and I wish they did not exist, but they cannot last long, and when once the little woman has gained a footing, I am not afraid of her being disturbed. As to any scruples that you may entertain about imposing on people whom you ought to love, and do, I confess it would be pleasanter if no deceit were necessary, but when things have gone so far as they have, there is no choice left, and it becomes a duty to consult the interest of the poor little helpless wretches, even at the expence of feelings . . .[22]

He was equally blunt with Georgiana; they had a chance while there was such confusion in Paris to absorb Caroline into their orbit with the minimum of fuss and she should take it. "It is a pity," he wrote, "that there should be any obstacle to you taking little Caroline more immediately under your own care, for she is the prettiest child I ever saw."[23] By mid-September Charlotte and "the other pensioner" had joined them at Spa.

Georgiana continued to receive almost daily reports of the situation in Paris from the Duke of Dorset. The mob had become distinctly Anglophobic, in reaction to Marie Antoinette's love of all things English, and briefly besieged the British embassy. Dorset, arriving by chance at just the wrong moment, had to fight his way through with his sword. The Duke of Devonshire began to talk of their going home, which dismayed Georgiana, who feared her creditors more than the revolutionaries. Coutts had discovered she had been lying to him. "You *are* not, you *cannot* be more interested in your own honour and character than I am," he wrote angrily, "which is the reason I have always wished you to tell me frankly every thing."[24] He refused her plea for another loan. James Hare guessed something was wrong when Georgiana told him how she dreaded returning to London.

If you are in any scrape about money it will be impossible for you to conceal it from the Duke [he counselled], and therefore the sooner he knows it the better, but, for God's sake, if you tell him anything tell him all, or let Ly Elizabeth or let me tell him. There is no situation so desperate where there is not something to be done, and if you were in debt more than his whole estate would sell for, it would be equally advisable to acquaint him with it, as if you owed but

£5000. . . . What I dread most is that you should be sanguine enough to trust to some future good fortune to extricate you out of your difficulties, and so get more deeply involved.[25]

He read her character well; Georgiana had placed all her hopes on conceiving a son.

To everyone's surprise the peaceful atmosphere and therapeutic waters of Spa worked their magic and at the end of September she discovered she was pregnant. "The symptoms are all the same," she wrote excitedly to Lady Spencer; "I have no *Wednesday feels,* but some that show that great care must be taken—I have been entirely free from headache this last three weeks which seems to be a sign of being with child, as I should imagine liable as I am to headache, the stoppage of the Prince would give them me sadly."[26] The pregnancy was a last-minute reprieve. Georgiana was so relieved that the first person she informed was Coutts, two days before she wrote to her mother. "The aim of my journey, I hope, is answer'd. . . . I am in hopes I am with child. . . . I shall consecrate all my time to quiet of body and mind, that I may not lose the advantage of giving the Duke a son; and before I lie in (if I really am with child), I shall lay everything before him. In the meantime . . . I send an order to Beard to pay you 300. This will, I hope answer all demands . . ."[27]

The Duke was so excited at the prospect of an heir that he immediately cancelled their plans to return to England, fearing that the Channel crossing might cause his wife to miscarry. Bess confided to Lady Melbourne that she dreaded another girl; for her own sake as much as Georgiana's she was praying for a boy. Georgiana acquiesced to his decision because "in sacrificing *all* to my situation I am pleasing the Duke—who is extremely anxious—I believe he had given up hope of my breeding—for I could not have expected him to be as anxious as he is."[28] But the situation in Belgium was hardly safe: revolutionary fever had spread to Brussels and there was rioting in the streets against Joseph II. "You know that I am a good Royalist in France," Georgiana told Calonne; "well, in Brussels I am a good Patriot."[29] Unencumbered by ties of friendship, her Whig principles reasserted themselves. This was a great help with regard to receiving mail, since letters addressed via their royal connections mysteriously disappeared while those which came via the patriots did not. Yet, in spite of Georgiana's well-known sympathy for the patriot cause, which was fighting for Belgium's independence from the Austrians, her carriage was peppered with bullets.

Whenever the fighting on the streets grew too dangerous the Devonshires retreated to Lille, just west of the French border, returning when it abated. The Spencers and Cavendishes were bewildered by the Duke's decision to remain abroad; Lady Spencer wondered if Bess was pregnant. Their concern increased when the Duke departed for England at the end of December, leaving Bess and Georgiana behind. Neither woman was happy at the prospect—Georgiana had not seen her children for six months and she missed them terribly, "but from circumstances too long for a letter, it is impossible for me to urge him," she told Lady Melbourne.[30] Bess dreaded the Duke's absence in such lawless times, but "I shall stay with her to the last," she wrote melodramatically.

The Duke had left them not to attend to business matters in England, as they claimed, but because Duncannon had initiated divorce proceedings against Harriet. He had discovered her affair with Sheridan nine months earlier, in March: "The accusations against me quite bad, told Ca. . . ." Harriet scribbled in her diary.[31] Although she had promised not to see Sheridan again they continued to meet in secret until Duncannon found out that she had lied. Georgiana may have had misgivings about Harriet's trust in Sheridan, knowing his vanity and penchant for conquests, but she had not interfered. But others, notably Betsy Sheridan, his sister, were determined to stop the affair, and it was probably she who informed Duncannon. Writing in June to her sister in Ireland, she had expressed the hope that Sheridan might be tiring of Harriet. Seeing them together at a private supper of the Prince's with Lady Jersey, Mrs. Fitzherbert, and the Duchess of Rutland, she thought that Harriet "was casting many tender looks across the table [at Sheridan] which to my great joy did not seem much attended to."[32] But she was mistaken about Sheridan's feelings. He loved Harriet and the coldness he displayed towards her in public was probably a late and clumsy attempt to protect her from calumny.

The Duke of Devonshire reached England just as the bill for the divorce was about to enter the first stage of proceedings. He found Harriet in a state of nervous collapse, and Duncannon more determined than he had ever seen him before. Sheridan had already sworn an oath never to see Harriet again, which had not changed Duncannon's mind. Eliza Sheridan was so distraught by her husband's behaviour that she, too, was demanding an immediate separation:

I don't know in my Life that ever I pass'd so many Miserable Hours [she wrote to a friend on February 5], S[heridan] had so completely involved himself with Ly D. in that a suit was actually commenced against them in the Doctors Commons—and if the Duke of Devon had not come over to England, and exerted his influence with Ld D., by this time S would have been an Object of Ridicule and abuse to all the World—however, thank God! the business is hush'd up—I believe principally on old Ld Bessborough's account—and She is going abroad very soon I believe to her Sister. You will imagine this affair gave me no little uneasiness. . . . S was pleading forgiveness to me, on this Account, before it was certain that it would be hush'd up . . . swearing and imprecating all sorts of Curses on himself, on Me and his Child, if ever he was led away by any Motive to be false to me again. . . .[33]

Once Duncannon realized that his father and all the Cavendishes were taking Harriet's side against him he dropped the suit. The Duke, however, was not prepared to take any chances while Georgiana was still liable to miscarry. He forced Duncannon to agree to accompany Harriet to Brussels and stay with them. As soon as they left Sheridan had a fling with the governess at Crewe Hall, Caroline Townsend, an intelligent but plain woman. It happened, Eliza Sheridan recorded indignantly, "at the very time when S was pleading forgiveness to me."*

The Duncannons arrived at Brussels a short time after the Duke, not in the least reconciled and their future together as bleak as the winter prospect around them. "I envy your chère soeur going to see you," Dorset wrote to Georgiana from England. "I am sure nobody has more sincerely lamented your absence from London than myself."[34] Harriet's presence gave Georgiana something to think about other than her own problems. For the past few months she had been desperately trying to raise money to

---

* By coincidence, Caroline Townsend was the daughter of the late Lord Spencer's trusted steward. When she became pregnant as a result of the affair Georgiana and Harriet helped Sheridan to arrange for her to go abroad, and on her return they adopted the baby. They named her Fanny Mortimer and she grew up at Devonshire House as a sort of foundling, inhabiting a nether world between the servants' quarters and the nursery. After Georgiana died Harriet sent Fanny to private school and eventually saw her marry quite well. Fanny always suspected that either Harriet or Georgiana was her mother and never quite recovered from learning that her true mother was a mere governess. Chichester RO Bessborough MSS 207: Mrs. Peterson to Lady Emily Ponsonby, November 1856. Mrs. Peterson was Harriet's maid. She began working for her in the 1780s, when Georgiana's black hairdresser, Gilbert, taught her how to dress hair.

satisfy her creditors. She asked the Duke's personal banker Cornelius Denne to advance her £5,000 in secret, which he sent over despite grave reservations.[35] She kept part of it and sent the rest to William Galley at the Lottery Office to lay bets for her on the Oaks, the Oatlands, and Derby races "as the risk is so little and the gain might be so much."[36] She also extracted money from the Prince of Wales:

> I look upon your secrecy my dearest brother, as the great test and trial of your affection and friendship. I am most afraid of Weltje, Jack Payne or Sheridan. I do entreat you for God's sake not to disclose it in any way to them. I should die were they to know it in any way* . . . If you find you cannot get £2000 without its being known, write me a letter telling me so, and enclose it to *Mr Baker.* . . . If you can get the 2,000 get it in common notes . . . I am quite mad and distracted at what I am doing. . . . I don't dare read over what I have written and if I did not think I could depend on you I should go quite mad. God bless you—what trouble I give you. I don't sign my name in case of accidents.[37]

She was sickened by herself:

> If I have no son I have no right to expect he [the Duke] should do anything for my children [she wrote distractedly to Lady Spencer], if I have a son, I shall have perhaps the misery of seeing *him* impoverished and my poor little girls very poor and of accusing myself that it is owing to my imprudence and to the ill opinion my husband's relations have of me. I have earnestly entreated the D. to permit me to establish myself at Chatsworth for 5 or 6 years after my lying in, and if I must come to London, to come occasionally to Chiswick and St Albans. Perhaps this may restore me in their opinions. . . .[38]

Georgiana's talk of retiring from London convinced Bess that the Duke could no longer be kept ignorant of the true state of affairs. So many people knew that the situation had almost become farcical. The Duke failed to understand what Bess was saying at first, and assumed that a significant sum meant a few thousand. "I think the best thing that can happen is that she should not be able to pay the interest of her debts regularly at present,"

---

* All three had presumably lent her money.

he wrote, "as that will make her creditors more willing to settle their accounts with her upon fair terms."[39] Gradually, he realized from her hints that the sum was much greater. But despite everyone—Coutts, Calonne, Hare, Harriet, and Bess—urging her to confess before it was too late, Georgiana once again lied when he confronted her. She wrote him a letter in March which was as subtle as it was sad in its contortions to avoid a disclosure. "Why do you force me, my dear Ca, to an avowal to you which agitates me beyond measure, and which is not necessary now?" she asked, not mentioning that the circumstance which made it unnecessary was the money she had borrowed from the Prince and Denne. She also played on the Duke's fear of her miscarrying: "This is a request made from the bottom of my heart, and I trust you will not refuse it me indeed after my various agitations. Your granting it is of more importance than I can express to me and my child." All she asked was that he wait a little longer. "Could I tell you, pay this for me, I owe no more, I should not hesitate to expose myself to all your reproof—But as I am still further involved I dread the opening of an explanation I should not dare encounter in my present situation."[40] She implored him not to confront Calonne and Denne: the true extent of her debts would, she knew, send him into a rage.

The Duke's suspicions should have been aroused by Georgiana's glib assurance that her income more than amply covered the interest on her debts. By the time the baby was due she had borrowed almost £20,000 and was still being persecuted by her creditors. In May she begged a further loan from the Prince, falsely claiming that it would clear all her debts:

> But my dearest brother, the state of my mind operates sadly on my body. As to the business of Calonne, I am determined to tell that to the Duke, but with this intention I am afraid of pressing him for some more money I want before I lie in, which will finish all my debts except Calonne's, yours and a trifling one to Mr Coutts. This determined me to write to you by Baker and if you once more can enclose 3,000 to him by Aberdeen my tranquility during my lying in is secured. But, my dearest brother and friend, how can I ask it of you? I have told my sister your kindness and generosity, therefore you may talk to her freely about it.[41]

Harriet, who had no more to spare, tried to help by paying some of the smaller creditors herself. Like everyone else, she dreaded Georgiana becoming agitated and losing the baby. The Duke even agreed to allow the children to be brought out from England because she missed them so much. It was a dangerous and complicated venture which involved the transport of over thirty adults in various capacities as outriders, footmen, nurses, nannies, maids, and grooms.[42] As a consequence little Georgiana and Harryo met their half-sister Caroline much earlier than planned. Georgiana had prepared the ground with her mother before they arrived. "Charlotte, as I mentioned before," she wrote, "will be out of the way except occasionally, and Mll de St Jules is, tho' very lively, a remarkably orderly little creature and will be of great assistance to their French."[43]

Caroline's presence among the Cavendish children did invite speculation, which all three were quick to put down. "She is a poor little thing," Bess claimed disingenuously to Lady Melbourne. There were other rumours; some people actually claimed Georgiana was not pregnant at all, which made her indignant: "If those who say I am not with child were to see me, they would, I believe, have an *evident* answer to that, as well as many other infamous lies."[44] It was not only their remaining abroad which caused talk; their choice of a young doctor named Croft seemed obscure. In fact he was the son-in-law of Dr. Denman, who had attended Georgiana's previous births. Denman had felt he was too old to make the arduous journey, whereas Croft was a gifted and ambitious obstetrician sensitive to his patients yet robust enough to withstand the rigours of Continental travel.[45] However, Georgiana was his first notable client, and people wondered why the Duke would allow someone so relatively inexperienced near his wife, unless the Devonshires were planning something to ensure that whatever happened they returned with a son. Lady Spencer joined the party at the beginning of May partly to help quash these rumours.

After the initial turmoil most of their eight-month stay in Brussels was quiet. Georgiana's contacts with the patriots were of great use in this respect. "The revolution has taken place here," she wrote in late December; "the most perfect quiet is established; all the troops have left the country. . . . The Patriots have been as humane as brave, and the revolution here was really astonishing."[46] But the Belgians did not understand her royalist links, and after some of her letters were intercepted the entire party was ordered to leave Brussels.

I suppose you have heard [wrote Lord Erskine to Mrs. Montagu] that it was with great difficulty her Grace was allowed to stay at Brussels till Lady Spencer arrived. The Duchess was put to bed, and it

A Hint to the Ladies to take Care of their HEADS.

"A Hint to the Ladies to Take Care of Their Heads," cartoon by Sayer. One of a number of cartoons appearing in 1776 that made fun of the outrageous headdresses sported by Georgiana and her friends. BM Cat. 5395.

Spencer House, northeast view; watercolor drawing, c. 1780.

Spencer House, north front. The photograph, taken in 1942, shows the damage caused by enemy bombing during the Second World War.

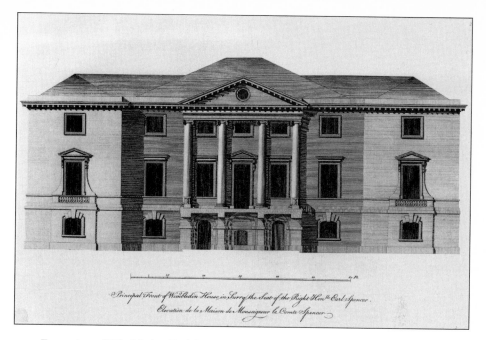

Engraving of Wimbledon Park House, Surrey. Completed in 1732, it was built by the Duchess of Marlborough to designs by Roger Morris and the Earl of Pembroke. Half a century later the house was destroyed by fire, and the second Earl Spencer decided to let it remain in ruins.

Front of Devonshire House c. 1890. The original house burnt down in 1733 and the third Duke commissioned William Kent to rebuild it. Critics condemned the house as ugly and undistinguished, and particularly hated the wall, which spoiled the view. In the nineteenth century, the sixth Duke removed the sweeping steps to the first floor and made the entrance on the ground floor.

Top left: Georgiana, aged three, after Reynolds; *top right:* Georgiana, by Richard Cosway; *bottom left:* Georgiana, by an unknown artist; *bottom right:* Georgiana, by John Downman.

The adult portraits, painted between 1776 and 1789, show Georgiana, aged nineteen to thirty-two, when she was at the height of her celebrity; yet they are all remarkably simple and unaffected.

Prince of Wales (1762–1830), by John Hoppner. In 1782 Georgiana wrote of him, "He is inclined to be too fat and looks too much like a woman in men's clothes."

Charles James Fox (1749–1806), as a young MP before becoming leader of the Whig party, by John Powell. Georgiana denied they were ever lovers.

A Gaming Table at Devonshire House, by T. Rowlandson. Georgiana throws the dice while her sister Harriet takes money from her purse. The stakes in these games were ruinously high, and they and their friends, including Charles James Fox and the Prince of Wales, lost fortunes at the tables. When not at Devonshire House, Fox and the Prince threw their money away at Brooks's Club in St. James's.

GEORGIANA'S FOUR CHILDREN

Top left: Lady Georgiana "Little G" Cavendish (1783–1858) and Lady Harriet "Harryo" Cavendish (1785–1862) as children.

Top right: Harryo after her marriage to Lord Granville Leveson Gower in 1809, by Thomas Barber.

Left: Hartington (1790–1858) after he became the sixth Duke of Devonshire in 1811, by Thomas Lawrence.

Right: Eliza Courtney (1792–1859), Georgiana's illegitimate child by Charles Grey.

Right: William Pitt the Younger (1759–1806), by John Jackson, after Hoppner. The portrait, completed after Pitt died, shows the toll of twenty-one years as Prime Minister.

Below: Charles, third Duke of Richmond (1735–1806), by George Romney. Bess was still living at Devonshire House (but no longer the Duke's mistress) when she began a four-year affair with Richmond in 1796.

Below right: Thomas Grenville (1755–1846), by Camille Manzini. Grenville reputedly never married because of his un-requited love for Georgiana. Pitt persuaded both Richmond and Grenville to desert Fox and join his government in 1784 and 1794, respectively.

Top left: Charles, second Earl Grey (1764–1845), by James Northcote. After the Duke of Devonshire discovered Georgiana's affair with Grey, he forced her to choose between her lover and her children.

Top right: Sir Philip Francis (1740–1818), by James Lonsdale, was another of Georgiana's admirers.

Above left: Lord Granville Leveson Gower (1773–1846), after Sir Thomas Lawrence. Though Harriet had two illegitimate children with him, she showed great courage and self-sacrifice in supporting his decision to marry her niece, Georgiana's daughter Harryo.

Above right: Third Duke of Dorset (1745–99), by Reynolds. Georgiana abandoned him for Grey, who became the love of her life.

was pretended that she was in labour, yet even that plea was but just able to suspend the search of the House and turning the family out of the Town; at last the favour was obtained to allow them to wait until Lady Spencer arrived, on promise they would then depart immediately, which they did. It seems some letters of her Grace's were intercepted in which there were political offences, what business she had to meddle in the affairs of the Brabantines [part of Belgium] I cannot imagine.[47]

They mobilized as quickly as was possible with four children and a hundred adults to organize. Georgiana was so large she had difficulty walking, her discomfort aggravated by chronic cystitis. Lafayette promised they would not be molested if they returned to France. Nevertheless, George wrote in consternation to Lady Spencer, "everybody here is openmouthed about the idea of their going to Paris."[48] They did not know where they would stay until by chance the unwieldy caravan bumped into the Duc d'Ahrenberg, who was fleeing in the other direction. He offered them his house at Passy, just outside Paris. They reached the city on May 19 and found it "perfectly quiet." Georgiana began to experience pains almost immediately. Lady Spencer would not allow her to give birth in a public hotel and she forced the party to hurry on. "We are thank God got safe into a magnificent house here," she wrote to George when they reached Passy, "where I trust it will not be many days before we shall be relieved from the load of anxiety."[49]

Within a few hours of their arrival Georgiana went into labour. Lady Spencer took charge of the situation. She ordered Bess to ride back to Paris and show herself at the Opéra in order to dispel the speculation about which of the women was actually pregnant. She also wrote to the secretary of the British embassy, Lord Robert Fitzgerald, and to the dowager Duchesse d'Ahrenberg, both persons of impeccable respectability, asking them to come and be independent witnesses to the birth. Bess did as she was asked and appeared in Lord St. Helen's box so that everyone might see her slim figure. She arrived back at Passy just before the birth. The message had not got through to the embassy but the Duchesse d'Ahrenberg was there. They waited outside Georgiana's door.

Just before two in the morning on May 21, 1790, the nurse lifted Georgiana's head so that she could see the tiny body in Dr. Croft's arms. It was a boy, the Marquess of Hartington. As arranged, the Duchesse d'Ahrenberg entered the room before the family and verified the newborn baby;

her cries brought the rest of the family rushing in. "There never was a more welcome child," recorded one of the servants.[50] Everyone wept and clasped each other—except Bess and Lady Spencer. Messengers were immediately dispatched to England. Church bells rang continuously in Derbyshire to relay the news across the county. The Cavendish clan could hardly believe that Georgiana had at last delivered them an heir. Lord George wrote to commend her efforts, adding ruefully, "it is not too often that I have the opportunity of doing it."[51]

For two weeks after Hartington's birth the joy at his arrival was muted by the fear that Georgiana might die. Duncannon was impatient to return to England, but Harriet refused to leave until she could be sure about her sister. It was not until mid-June that Lady Spencer was able to tell George, "since Thursday there has been a regular and gradual amendment and she is at this moment expressing with a sweet affectionate countenance her gratitude to everybody for their care and tenderness—the extraordinary instability of her nerves and the great debility of her whole frame are the difficulties we yet have to encounter but thank God, they both grow less every hour."[52] Within days Georgiana was organizing a round of parties to celebrate. Their Parisian friends descended on Passy, pleased to have any excuse to leave the city. Although it was quiet there were worrying signs of what was to come. On June 19, 1790, the Assembly issued a diktat against the display of heraldic insignia. All aristocrats hastily ordered the arms on their carriages to be painted over. However, other aspects of life remained the same, commerce went on uninterrupted, and as soon as Georgiana felt well enough she enjoyed the attentions of Paris's finest couturiers—a gift from her grateful husband. "My hair is doing by Bezier, my picture drawing by Guérin, Mlle Bertin and her diamond chimère in one room—Mlle Gaussé and her bill in another. . . ." For the first time in many months she could relax and enjoy herself.[53]

But Georgiana was not insensible to the plight of her friends. Since October the royal family had been virtual prisoners in the Tuileries, where they were subjected to the scrutiny of crowds who came daily to stare and insult them. Marie Antoinette still had some freedom of movement and was enjoying a short respite from Paris in the beautiful gardens at Saint-Cloud when Georgiana took her children and Bess to visit her. Lack of sleep and continual fear made the Queen resemble the care-worn women who taunted her at the Tuileries. She cried when they talked of the Duchesse de Polignac in Switzerland. "Tell her," she choked, "that you have seen a person who will love her to her life's end."[54]

They stayed in France until the end of August. Lady Spencer had left in July, taking the children with her. Little G had come down with a strange illness which Dr. Croft could not identify and which further convinced them that the children would be better off at home. For Bess it was a supreme irony to know that her arch enemy would be the means of transporting her daughter into Devonshire House; Lady Spencer was too anxious to leave to question Charlotte and Caroline's inclusion in the party. "I regret the Duchess's departure very much," wrote Lady Sutherland, echoing the general sentiment among the Parisians. "As for Lady Elisabeth, she is nice enough but one can do without her, but the Duchess has a thousand good qualities and an excellent heart."[55] Georgiana's experience of revolution in France and Belgium had made her wary about supporting political reform for its own sake, although she remained a steadfast Whig in her view that the monarchy must be balanced by Parliament. But some of the Whig speeches at home in support of the French Revolution struck her as rather naive. Lady Sutherland recorded that her husband "gave the Dss of Devonshire some good advice yesterday about the chance she had of being Mrs Cavendish if Sheridan has *his* way. Which did not seem to be ill taken or misunderstood."[56] The French were confused by Georgiana's attitude. "The aristocrats suspected her of being a democrate, and the Democrates thought she was an aristocrate. Whatever her opinions and inclinations may be," observed Lady Sutherland, "J'ai raison de croire that she and etc., are rather displeased with Sheridan and reverse to the *reform* of which I hope there is no danger in England."[57]

Even without the children the entourage filled four packet boats. The Devonshires sailed in the first boat, followed by their servants and luggage crammed on to the three behind. Georgiana rarely let Hartington out of her sight. The trip to the Continent had given her a long-awaited son, and returned Caroline St. Jules to Bess. Yet the purpose of the journey remained unfinished: Georgiana still had to confess her debts and Bess's son Clifford was marooned amid the chaos in Paris.

CHAPTER 15

EXPOSURE

1790—1791

The liberal, noble spirit of the Lady united to the head of [the Cavendish] family, whose charities are universal and whose benignity of heart is announced by the beaming graces of the most ingenuous, lovely, impassioned countenance ought to have operated as an example. . . . Her lively, mercurial temper was also admirably calculated to correct the phlegm of the family, with which she is connected; but fire and water cannot assimilate; and it grieves us to hear, that a separation has actually taken place.

The Jockey Club (*pamphlet*), C. Pigott, London 1792

Georgiana came home to find the Whigs split over the merits of the French Revolution. Burke and Sheridan were at the head of rival camps, with Burke claiming it as the triumph of despotic democracy, and Sheridan as a victory for citizen's rights. Georgiana's own views were closer to Sheridan's than to Burke's but her first-hand knowledge of the events also made her sympathetic to the latter. Fox wanted to remain a neutral friend to both men, but this became impossible after the publication of Burke's *Reflections on the Revolution in France* in November 1790. "Everyone is taken up with Burke's book," Bess recorded. "Sheridan means to answer it. . . . Mr. Hare admires it very much more than C. Fox does."[1]

Fox allowed Burke and Sheridan's dispute to grow until it paralysed the party. Yet he still dithered, unable to decide which man to support, until on May 6, 1791, Edmund Burke made the decision for him. He renounced their thirty-year friendship from the floor of the Commons. The debate that day was on the constitution for Quebec, a fairly innocuous issue, but Burke turned it into a platform from which to denounce the new French republican constitution and the "deplorable condition of France itself." Fox interrupted him before he provoked Sheridan into saying something cutting, but his hasty manner inflamed the sensitive Burke. He reacted as if Fox had personally slighted him and, enraged by years of collected grievances, turned to his former protégé and announced their irrevocable separation. Fox rose to his feet, too shocked to speak at first, tears streaming down his cheeks. Foxites and Pittites alike began shouting, some triumphant, others anguished. Horace Walpole recorded that when Fox recovered, his voice was broken with sobs while he "lamented on the loss of Burke's friendship, and endeavoured to make atonement; but in vain, though Burke wept too—in short, it was the most affecting scene possible."[2]

Years later, Georgiana admitted that she held Fox accountable for his failure of leadership at the critical moment.[3] If he had not been so careless about "even necessary expedients" she was sure the party could have been saved. For one thing, she knew that Burke's devastating criticism of Fox's political beliefs was based on a misunderstanding: Fox had never supported the republican movement either in England or in France. In his own brand of Whiggery the French Revolution was a tremendous event because it was meant to bring about a constitutional monarchy similar to that inspired by the Glorious Revolution of 1688. He never advocated the deposition of Louis XVI, and he made plain his support for the French monarchy three months later, when the royal family were captured while attempting to flee the country. As soon as he heard the details of the King and Queen's tragic flight to Varennes, of their return to Paris surrounded by a baying mob, and of their imprisonment in separate apartments, he wrote to Lafayette urging him to safeguard their lives.

Although Georgiana shared Fox's enthusiasm for the concept of the French Revolution, her stay in Paris the previous year had alerted her to its dangers. She would never forget the unruly hatred of the mob, nor her last visit to Marie Antoinette when the taunts of the crowd could be heard outside the gates. Since her return to England Georgiana had allied herself with a select group of Englishmen who were striving to contain the revolution within reasonable bounds. Like Fox, she maintained her contacts within the various political camps and wrote to them constantly, although she remained closest to Calonne. The flight to Varennes was a

double blow to Georgiana since she had counted on him to organize resistance on the monarchy's behalf. The abortive escape planned by
Count Fersen was a complete surprise. Georgiana did not wait for further
events before she tried to organize a letter campaign urging the Assembly
to treat the King and Queen with restraint. She also wrote to Lafayette
and warned him that his reputation was at stake. Resenting English interference, he replied indignantly that the royal family were not in any danger, and asked her to tell the same thing to the French émigrés now
residing in London.[4]

The flight to Varennes was such an unexpected blow that it briefly reunited Georgiana and the Duke of Dorset. They had not been in contact
with each other since the previous November. Georgiana had tried to re-
establish a friendly relationship on her return, but Dorset, having married
a woman whom he despised, betrayed too much anxiety to resume their
affair.

> I am happy to find there are some parts of ancient *amitié* yet remain-
> ing [he wrote in reply to her letter]. Your silence m'a fait beaucoup
> de peine, but your *oublie* me ferait un mal inexprimable,* I think
> your affections are fixed on somebody in France, at least you are oc-
> cupied with quelquechose plus qu'a ordinaire or otherwise you
> would have written to me oftener, but not more affectionately
> cependant than in your last letter, therefore I flatter myself que peu
> à peu vous retrouverei pour moi vos ancien sentiments.[†5]

He was mortified when he realized his mistake, and there was no more
communication between them until June. However, as soon as the news
of the flight to Varennes reached England he impulsively wrote to her,
apologizing first: "my silence my dear Duchess has not proceeded from
any motive of forgetfulness or méchanceté [spite], but from various reasons. . . . however I am very willing to *recommence* a letter correspondant
could I but feel that you had some degree of pleasure et intérêt in receiving my letters."[6]

---

* "Your silence was very hurtful, but your forgetting me would be painful beyond
words."

† "Therefore I flatter myself that little by little you will rediscover your former feelings
for me."

They were soon exchanging news with each other almost every day, Dorset passing on official reports from the embassy, Georgiana relaying information from Calonne. In August he sent an express to Bath; "all of Europe is anxiously waiting" to see whether the King of Prussia would go to Marie Antoinette's aid—Georgiana had to travel to London for meetings at his house.[7] She replied evasively that there were reasons why she could not leave Bath, reasons that she could not reveal to anyone.

The Duke had given Georgiana until Hartington, now nicknamed Hart, was weaned to prepare her accounts. She felt certain that he would want a separation as soon as he learned the truth and she put off the day as long as she could. It was only Bess's vehement insistence that she would take her side which made Georgiana begin the process at all. Now that Bess could have the Duke to herself the two women were closer than they had ever been before. Ironically, Lady Spencer was still scheming to have her rival removed from Devonshire House. She had befriended the children's governess, Selina Trimmer, during their stay in France, and used her to spy on and torment Bess.* Georgiana did not suspect the alliance between her mother and Selina for several months. It was small things which struck her first: Selina seemed to know about her plans in advance, and her mother's knowledge of nursery happenings was as good if not better than her own. Then she noticed that servants were taking their cue from Selina and behaving with marked insolence towards Bess. She was breastfeeding Hart in the nursery one day when the door opened and Bess walked in. The nursery staff, led by Selina, remained seated as if another member of staff had entered. The insult was pointed. Bess had originally arrived at Devonshire House in 1782 as "Charlotte's governess."

Georgiana guessed that someone with authority—it could only be her mother—was encouraging Selina. It gave rise to one of her rare acts of rebellion.

* Selina's mother, Sarah Trimmer, was a famous educationalist whose books for children consisted of worthy stories around moral themes, such as being kind to animals. Lady Spencer thought it miraculous when the religious and sober-minded Selina agreed to become her grandchildren's governess. Georgiana acquiesced to her mother's request to take Selina on, not realizing that the governess considered it her sacred duty to reform the irregularities in the Devonshire household. She fervently shared her patroness's opinion that someone had to protect the children from the immoral lifestyle of their parents. In a very short time Lady Spencer came to regard Selina as another daughter.

I shrewdly suspect that, elevated and a little spoilt, I doubt, by your kindness, [Selina] has ventur'd to talk on subjects quite out of her line. I have, Dst. M., a great opinion of Miss T's principles and talents for education, but I see her so alter'd, thinking herself so independent of me, that it is really impossible for me not to suspect her. . . . if I ever can discover that she interferes in anything but the care of their education, or that she stands between you and me in any way whatsoever, I could not submit to have a person whom I look'd upon in that light another moment in the house with me.

Georgiana explained her feelings to Lady Spencer with uncharacteristic boldness: "in the difficult part your dislike to Ly Eliz puts me to, added to my money anxieties, I cannot suffer the additional uneasiness of seeing that a young person whom you have known but 2 years has more of your confidence and knows more of your intentions than I do."[8]

Georgiana also attempted to settle the question of Bess's presence once and for all; she lived with them, she said, because both she and the Duke wanted it that way. "I am born to a most complicated misery. I had run into errors, that would have made any other man discard me," she declared, and it was owing to Bess's influence that the marriage had remained intact. "Her society was delightful to us, and her gentleness and affection sooth'd the bitterness that [my] misfortunes had brought on us. And the mother, whom I adore . . . sets herself up in the opposite scale, forgets all the affection her son-in-law has shewn her, and only says: I will deprive them of their friend or of my countenance."[9] After this simplistic description of her domestic situation Lady Spencer found it difficult to argue without going into more painful and complicated detail. She had witnessed Georgiana's unhappiness in the early days, and she would never be able to forget Bess's air of triumph that first summer at Chatsworth. Her daughter insisted that the Duke "has often told me that (if we continue to live together, which my unfortunate conduct about money renders very doubtful), if I had a moment's uneasiness about her he certainly would be far from wishing her to live with us," but Lady Spencer regarded this and other similar protestations with extreme scepticism.

While defending Bess to Lady Spencer, Georgiana also unconsciously revealed her own affair with Grey. She repeated in her next letter that the Duke was no more likely to have an affair than herself: "Was I absolutely discovered in an intrigue, you could not be more uneasy than at the possibility of your son-in-law having an attachment."[10] If Lady Spencer had not been distracted by the subject of the letter, its language might have alerted her to the fact that this was an oblique confession. As it was, her daughter's desperate tone—"for God's sake have compassion on me, I am so unwell and so miserable"—left her shaken. Lady Spencer promised she never would and never did speak about Bess to anyone, except sometimes "a little vent of impatience in talking to your sister. . . . I grieve from my soul that I hinted a word about anything that could give you pain." She swiftly returned to the question of Georgiana's debts. "Do not say that money matters are hopeless," she urged. "A firm resolution not to buy so much as a yard of ribband will soon effect wonders you are little aware of. This is a disagreeable subject but one on which I think I can sometimes be of use."[11]

Hart was weaned in November, and Georgiana had no choice but to compile a list of her creditors. Friends as well as family, Sheridan and Hare in particular, begged her not to hide anything. She finally presented a list of over thirty names, some of them surprising, such as "Scafe, £2,638: brother to a servant," and others which hinted at murky dealings in the City—"Statta: £3700: an imposition." The amount came to £61,917.* But, as some had feared, it was a sanitized version of her situation: there was no mention, for example, of the thousands borrowed from the Prince, or of the life annuity of £500 she was paying to William Galley, bookmaker to the *ton.*

In order to show her contrition Georgiana asked her trustees to sign over her settlement to the Duke, which would leave her destitute if they separated. It was a sad irony considering Harriet's bravery in refusing to relinquish hers to Duncannon. The act, impulsive as it was and driven more by guilt than sound judgement, failed to appease the Duke or the Cavendishes. Bess warned Georgiana to leave the Duke alone and to trust her to ease him slowly into accepting the sum. Georgiana listened to her advice, but the anxiety of waiting for his decision gave her headaches which left her prostrate for days at a time. "I have not a guess of my future destination," she confided to her mother.[12] Lady Mary Coke noticed that Georgiana rarely went out any more. "The Duchess of Devonshire has been less talked of this winter than I have ever known."[13]

---

* Roughly £3,720,000 today, or $6 million.

In February, while the Duke was still deliberating, the Stock Exchange suffered the major collapse of a private share syndicate. According to Lady Mary,

> tis the conversation of the town . . . [Georgiana] has it seems been gambling on the stocks, and to such an extent that her loss is now too considerable to remain any longer a secret. Tis said she is fifty thousand pounds the loser, and if the report of the day is to be believed she is posted up as a lame duck. I pity the Duke of Devonshire, and all his family, who must be secretly feeling this great folly of her Grace—for a long time all her indiscretions were pardon'd by her friends by the excuse of youth—that plea no longer to be alleged in her favour, what can they now say?[14]

Harriet was also involved. "Surely there must have been a great neglect in their education [for] two daughters to turn out so," mused a Mrs. Trevor to Lady Hestor Stanhope.[15] Others, like their sister-in-law Lavinia, attributed it to character. She had no sympathy at all and blamed Georgiana's predicament on self-indulgence. "As for your sister," she fulminated to George, "she pretends to be always ill to account for her neglect of everybody, but at the same time is able to Dine at Dinners of twenty people & to be at the opera & all assemblies & have company at home. . . . if I cared a farthing for her I should be hurt at it—but as it is now between us I heartily hope she may never trouble herself to come to me again."[16] The £500 Georgiana had borrowed and not yet repaid rankled as well. Lavinia and George had, after all, been forced to go abroad for a year to pay off the late Lord Spencer's debts against the estate.

The Cavendishes told the Duke he was a fool to support his wife any longer, and at a noisy family meeting to discuss her debts the Duchess of Portland accused her of deliberate malice. "I got into a passion," was all Georgiana would say of the confrontation, but she was aghast at the strength of the feeling against her. The Duke's formidable sister pronounced Georgiana's ostracism from the family; henceforth they would cut her in public and avoid her in private. This was worse than she had expected. "Is it not hard to have liv'd with the Dss as a sister," she wrote to Coutts. "To have shared my house with her like her own; to have ever been anxious to prove my affection to her and now that I am in distress and affliction to feel that all hope of being reconciled is over."[17]

The distress she was referring to was not only financial. Harriet had collapsed with some sort of stroke. She was paralysed down one side of her body and suffering from severe fits. What exactly had happened to her is unclear, and was a closely guarded secret at the time. "She had a most violent illness, the precise cause of which the Physicians could not account for," was all even close friends knew. Mrs. Damer thought it was "some inward disease" connected with a miscarriage. The more fanciful declared: "She was not ill at all but confined by her husband."[18] It may have been a botched abortion or, more likely, a suicide attempt. Duncannon featured so largely in the rumours that he may also have played a sinister part. There were no more stories of ill-treatment after the incident; perhaps he was shocked into changing his behaviour.

The illness occurred just before Harriet and Georgiana were exposed on the Stock Exchange. Nathaniel Wraxall hinted at dark happenings in his memoirs: "Some years later, Sheridan joined in a partnership with two ladies of the highest distinction, but whom I will not name, for the purpose of making purchases and sales, vulgarly called dabbling, in the public funds. The speculation proved most unfortunate, as they *waddled,* and became *lame ducks.* Nor was the bankruptcy of the firm the only evil that followed this experiment; but the subject is too delicate. . . ."[19] The rumours about Georgiana and Harriet reached Coutts in France; he immediately demanded an explanation from Georgiana, but she denied that her name had been posted up:

> whatever I have been foolish enough to lose has always been paid directly nor do I hear of any deficiency of any kind—What can have occasioned the report I know not. . . . The truth is my affairs are as you left, which is bad enough, but no worse than you know. There has been no discovery—my disclosure to the Duke was voluntary and lucky it was for me that I made it. I am convinced in my own mind that all will be paid; but the uncertainty of my situation is dreadful.

She also denied the reports about Harriet, saying, "her illness was a miscarriage succeeded by inflammation in the womb and bowels. For 10 days she was in the greatest danger but is thank God restored to me."[20] While she lay paralysed Harriet caught bronchial pneumonia and her coughing damaged her lungs. The family resigned itself to her imminent death.

After several months of silent pique, the Duke behaved with surprising generosity towards Georgiana and Harriet. Ignoring his family's injunction to abandon his wife and her relatives, he rented a house in Bath large enough to accommodate his and Harriet's children, and moved both families down there. No record survives explaining his precise reasons for taking charge of Harriet and protecting Georgiana. It is clear, however, that he was not only attached to his sister-in-law but had become more sympathetic to Georgiana. He was not in love with her, but after fifteen years of marriage there were indissoluble ties between them. The Duke may have felt a debt of gratitude for her acquiescence regarding Bess and Caroline St. Jules. Despite all that had passed between them, in supporting Georgiana now the Duke was trying to show he was pleased with his son and that he forgave her for lying to him. There was no reason, he thought, why they could not always live this way.

The *Morning Post* approved of the Duke's loyalty, reporting: "The Duke and Duchess of Devonshire are at Bath, giving the *best examples* of fashion, in alleviating the lingering illness of their sister, Lady Duncannon."[21] Harriet remained at Bath for several months, attended by Dr. Warren and nursed by Lady Spencer, Georgiana, and Bess. "My dear sister had a return of dreadful spasms last night," Georgiana told Coutts in July 1791, "they have left her very weak, and tho' we trace some symptoms of returning sensation these painful attacks are dreadful."[22] Dr. Warren prescribed a warmer climate as the best remedy for Harriet's health. Lisbon seemed an ideal option as the climate was warm and dry and the country was free from political turmoil. The only impediment to the plan was Harriet, who declared she would rather die than go abroad with just her husband for company.

Nothing had been decided when the novelist Fanny Burney paid her first and only call on Georgiana in August. She was staying with her friend Mrs. Ord while she became accustomed to her retirement from court as Second Keeper of the Queen's Robes. The change to a civilian routine proved to be more of a shock than she had anticipated, and she gratefully accepted her friend's invitation to stay with her at Bath while she became acclimatized to once more being sole mistress of her time. For the past five years she had lived at the beck and call of the Queen and the six princesses from seven in the morning until twelve at night. They adored and trusted her, but nevertheless Fanny was exhausted from her emotionally demanding as well as burdensome position. Naturally she shared her employers' dislike of the Whigs and readily believed the rumours which circulated about them at court. She was appalled when Mrs. Ord's friendship with

Lady Spencer brought her into contact with women of such tarnished character. Her record of her meeting with Georgiana, Harriet, and Bess is a unique description of their domestic situation by someone unconnected with the Devonshire House Circle.

Fanny had been introduced to Lady Spencer at a party once before in 1783, but had scarcely spoken to her. With the leisure of a full afternoon to study her properly she decided that for all her pious airs her chief occupation seemed to be a tedious form of self-promotion. Burney was just beginning to dismiss Lady Spencer as a prig and a bore when she began talking about Harriet: "she spoke of Lady Duncannon's situation with much sorrow, and expatiated upon her resignation to her fate, her prepared state for Death and the excellence of her principles, with an eagerness and feeling that quite overwhelmed me with surprise and embarrassment." Fanny was shocked by Lady Spencer's reference to Harriet's principles; she knew what everyone in London knew—that Harriet had never been faithful to Duncannon, that she had had an affair with Sheridan, and that Duncannon was delaying a divorce until his father died "lest the grief of such an event should shorten his days." She had even heard the rumour that Harriet had tried to poison herself. Yet Lady Spencer talked with such conviction that Fanny found herself wondering, "Can it be that she is, after all, innocent? Or is her mother deluded?"[23]

The following day she had the opportunity to decide for herself. Her visit to Lady Spencer was interrupted halfway through by Harriet's servants, who opened the door and carried in the invalid. "I felt an unconquerable repugnance to even be in a room with her," Fanny recorded, and she turned a hard and unwelcoming face to the figure lying on the sofa. Harriet invited Fanny to sit next to her in a soft voice barely stronger than a whisper which pricked her conscience a little but not enough to make her accept the invitation. Burney wanted to despise her, but as the afternoon wore on her opinion changed in spite of herself:

> I perceived her Dress was extremely becoming, though simple, and in part, that of an invalid: in part, I say, for to a *close cap* she added a *hat and feather*. . . . But in point of beauty, she never looked in my eyes, to so much advantage. Sickness has softened her features and her Expression into something so interesting and so unusually lovely, that I should by no means have known her for the same lady I had so little admired in her early Days. The tone of her voice, too,

modified by the same cause, is soft, sweet, and penetrating. She never spoke, without catching all my attention, however unwillingly, and her words and her manner enforced its power by expressing constantly something cheerful about her own wretched state, or grateful for the services offered or done her.

Duncannon then walked in and put on one of his displays of affection that could so completely fool outsiders: "Judge then, my Fresh surprise, to see him hasten up to his Wife, enquire tenderly how she did and take the seat I had declined! . . . He would let no one but himself lift her into [the wheel chair] and was so silent, quiet, and still in all he did for her, that I plainly saw his assistance was the result of affection, not ostentation."[24]

While Fanny Burney was debating whether Harriet could really be guilty of the crimes circulated against her, more family members arrived. Selina brought in the little girls, who were in high spirits because it was Harryo's birthday. Fanny disliked Selina's self-satisfied demeanour:

[she] is a pleasing, but not pretty young woman, and who, though she seems born with her excellent mother's amiableness and serenity of mind, appears to me rather too much fascinated with the charms of her altered situation. She is not absolutely affected, but she is not natural, the manner in which she deviates from simplicity is strongly imitative of those patterns in high life which are forever before her eyes. She seems, in short, not merely to enjoy being made *one* of *them,* but studiously to mark she considers herself wholly in that point of view. She was not well and Ly Spencer was extremely tender to her.[25]

The "little French lady," as she described five-year-old Caroline St. Jules, also displeased her. Caroline seemed a different creature compared to the "happy disposition" of the Cavendish girls; she was "fat and full of mincing little affectations and airs." No doubt she had learned them from her mother, Fanny thought, who had heard rumours about her too: "To the tales told about *her, scandal* is nothing—INFAMY enwraps them." The appearance of George Spencer, whose grave manner and honest face scored high marks with her, calmed Burney's inflamed feelings for a short while until Georgiana and Bess flurried in. Lady Spencer made no attempt to hide her dislike of Bess; she introduced Georgiana to Fanny with an air of pride and satisfaction and "then, slightly, as if unavoidably, said 'Lady Elizabeth Foster.' "

By this time Fanny's curiosity was stronger than her moral outrage, and she was eager to learn more about this infamous coterie. But Bess seized her, "to my great provocation," and monopolized her entirely while Georgiana went to talk to Harriet. She carried on making bright conversation, although Fanny could tell that "her general powers of shining were violently dampened by my coldness and reserve." Caroline ran up to Bess quite frequently, yet "I observed that not one other amongst the Children ever approached her, neither did she once call upon them." Georgiana, on the other hand, moved about the room leading the children in all sorts of games "like the Pied Piper." The knowledge that Bess was flaunting her illegitimate child in front of them made the respectable Fanny feel ill: "something so rose in my throat during this little scene, that I had real difficulty . . . to answer her." Their conversation convinced her that "Lady Elizabeth has the general character of inheriting all the wit, all the subtlety, all les agréments [charm], and all the wickedness of the Herveys."

This judgement of Bess coloured Fanny's view of Georgiana, whom she regarded as the victim of her friend's designs. "I did not find so much beauty in her as I expected, not withstanding the variations of accounts; but I found far more of manner, politeness and gentle quiet." When she finally managed to escape from Bess and talk to Georgiana she thought she was one of the most pleasing women she had ever met: well read, interested in others and interesting to talk to. Fanny recorded, "it is impossible to view . . . this celebrated woman without feeling the strongest disposition to admire and like her." Consequently:

> I fancied all sort of things about Lady Eliz Foster—I fancied that while—from some inevitable compact with the Duke,—she [Georgiana] consented to countenance her, and receive her as her own guest, she was secretly hurt, offended and unhappy. . . . She submitted with the best grace in her power to save her *own* character by affecting to have no doubt of Lady Elizabeth's, but that, in her inmost mind, she detested such a Companion, and felt a hopeless and helpless resentment of her own situation. . . . It is generally believed her own terrible extravagancies have extorted from her a consent to this unnatural inmating of her House, from the threats of the Duke that they should be separated! What a payement for her indiscretion. . . .

All this I thought, I imagined I read it from time to time in her own countenance,—and I found myself strongly concerned for her in the situation.

Her judgement seemed confirmed beyond doubt when she bumped into Georgiana and Lady Spencer walking in town without Bess a few days later. She seemed "more easy and lively in her spirits, and consequently more lovely in her person. . . . It struck me, also, in her favour, that her spirits had before been depressed by the presence of the odious Lady Elizabeth and were now revived by being absent from her. Certainly at all events she was quite a different woman, gay, easy and charming. Indeed that last epithet might have been coined for her."

"This has been a singular acquaintance for *me!*" wrote Burney when she left Bath, "that the first visit I should make, after leaving the Queen, should be to meet the head *of opposition public,* the Duchess of Devonshire! . . . I came away impressed with the most mixt sensations of pain and pleasure. The terrible stories circulated of the miserable conduct of a pair of this community made me shudder at their powers of pleasing."[26] Yet she resolved to like all of them except Bess, whom she thought irredeemably awful. She also detected that something was troubling Georgiana. "She seems by Nature to possess the highest animal spirits, but she appeared to me not happy. I thought she looked oppressed within—though there is a native cheerfulness about her which I fancy scarce ever deserts her."[27] She could not have known the real cause: Georgiana was carrying Charles Grey's baby.

Harriet and Bess had known ever since Georgiana discovered it herself. "There has never existed a stricter confidence and friendship than there has [been] for many years between my sister, Lady Elizabeth and myself," Harriet once said of their relationship. "But to avoid tracasseries we long ago made it a rule never to conceal anything great or small from each other that concerned ourselves, and never to impart anything that concern'd our respective friends unless by their desire or consent."[28] They had repeatedly warned Georgiana to be careful, but she was infatuated with Grey. He followed her to Bath while the Duke was away, and was often seen going in and out of the house. "She distracts me," Bess complained to Lady Melbourne, who had also admonished Georgiana, "by working herself up to think she is more attach'd to him than I know she can be."[29]

Georgiana was mesmerized by him. They made no attempt to be discreet, and the public way in which Grey would monopolize her at a party or argue with her if he felt neglected dismayed even the most tolerant members of the Circle. Nobody wanted her to become another Lady Derby. Sheridan took it upon himself to make her see sense: "There is one subject too I do most vehemently want to talk to you about—tho' I am afraid—but don't you be afraid for it relates only to *yourself* and interests me only because it is so dangerous to you."[30] But she wouldn't listen. Their lack of caution made Bess dread the arrival of the papers each day, expecting to read some item about them in the press. However, help came from an unexpected, although unpleasant source. Lady Spencer, Bess told Lady Melbourne, "had received an anonymous letter and her commands are you know absolute and her vigilance extreme. . . . [compared to Lady Spencer] your letters and my entreaties would have been a drop in the ocean." Condemning her daughter and blaming Bess and Harriet as her collaborators, Lady Spencer browbeat Georgiana until she swore to send Grey back to London. She was not even allowed to say goodbye to him. "From Friday to this morning that he has gone away we have lived in fear and misery," Bess continued in her report to Lady Melbourne. "But I have the happiness of telling you that she gave him no secret meeting, and there was no taking leave which I dreaded. . . . at least she had not entangled herself further, and his present absence must set all things right."[31]

Lady Spencer wrote to George of her satisfaction, convinced that she had been successful. George's reply was cautious: "Upon the subject of the Dss, I am glad to hear what you say, and can only add upon a subject like that it is right to hope the best, whatever we may expect or fear."[32] He was right not to share his mother's confidence—Georgiana was already pregnant when Lady Spencer arrived. After carrying three children she could detect the changes in her body immediately. As usual she had to confess to someone, and she chose to send Coutts one of her unprovoked denials. On July 17, while writing about Harriet's health, she added without warning: "I assure you I am not likely to give Hartington either a brother or a sister, which I am very glad of, as I should be very sorry to have any impediment to my attendance on my Dearest sister. I order'd half a buck for you. I hope it will be good."[33] Coutts, of course, had no idea of the letter's significance.

They managed to keep Georgiana's secret safe for as long as the pregnancy did not show. However, by October she was into her sixth month and large. Harriet's health was improving, but she still needed to convalesce in a warmer climate and this seemed Georgiana's only hope of escape. Dr. Warren had agreed to Harriet's request to recommend Cornwall rather than Lisbon; it was as far as they could go without making the Duke concerned about Georgiana's absence. But before they could put their plan into action the Duke arrived on an unannounced visit: someone in London had told him he ought to see his wife immediately. He confronted Georgiana alone; the sound of shouting and crying terrified Harriet, who lay on a couch in the adjoining room. At one point he called in Bess and berated her for covering up for Georgiana. "I never felt so frightened about her as now," wrote Harriet to Lady Melbourne. "Wherever she goes I will go with her. If it should be decided for the *parting* I will beg [Dr.] Warren to send me abroad—that will be a pretence for her going."[34]

After the Duke left, the sisters remained in their separate rooms. Harriet could hear Georgiana moving about in hers and she sent in a note of enquiry. The reply confirmed her fears. "We must go abroad—immediately." Harriet wrote to Lady Melbourne. "Nothing else will do, neither prayers nor entreaties will alter him. He says there is no choice between this, or public entire separation at home. . . . write to me, come if you can, give us some comfort but do not betray me."[35] Georgiana also wrote to Lady Melbourne but she was too frightened to admit the truth. Instead she touched on the possibility of Harriet's health sending them abroad and explained the shaky writing and blotched paper with an airy "I am out of spirits my love, so don't mind me." Her chief concern was how Charles Grey would react if she left England: "If I go you must stem the fury of the *Black Sea*."[36]

The morning after the interview Harriet talked to Bess and was relieved to find both her common sense and loyalty intact. "Bess has very generously promised to go with us. I urg'd her to it almost as much on her own account as my sister's, it must have been ruin to her to stay behind."[37] With Bess's support secured, Harriet turned her thoughts to her mother and husband: "Lord D. and my mother still both believe we are going to Penzance, and how they will ever be brought to consent I know not."[38] Lady Spencer was at Hollywell and had no idea of the scenes at Bath until Georgiana wrote to her saying that Warren had ordered Harriet abroad immediately. She hurried to her daughters, worried that Harriet had suffered a relapse. Her arrival plunged the house into crisis again. "My mother is come and our difficulties encrease," wrote Harriet. "Vexation and unhappiness surround me. I almost wish myself at the bottom of the sea."[39]

She took some comfort from Duncannon's reaction. He could be magnanimous where Georgiana was concerned and reassured Harriet that he would assist them in whatever plan they chose. In the meantime he went to London to make arrangements for the children. The women endured several more angry visits from the Duke and from Lady Spencer. Bess felt she blamed her almost as much as she did Georgiana, and Lady Melbourne's advice to ignore her insults did not help. "I shall observe all you say," she wrote, "but Lady S has begun as bad as possible about me—even to say I should not travel with them—but on your life say not a word of it to anybody—if the Dss goes I will."[40] The lapse of a few days had done nothing to diminish the Duke's rage either; Bess did not dare try to intercede, especially as she had recently managed to bring Clifford over from France: he was living with a family named Marshall in Clewer in Somerset. Every few hours the Duke announced he had changed his mind: first they were to go to Cornwall, then abroad, then not, then abroad but without Lady Spencer or Bess. "If the Duke had purposely intended to perplex and torment us, he could not have done it better," cried Harriet. "His only excuse is his being himself excessively unhappy, which indeed poor fellow I am afraid he is."[41]

When the Cavendishes heard the news they were unanimous in urging an immediate separation. This was her repayment, they said, after the Duke had stood up for her against his own relatives and accepted her debts against the advice of his agents. Only the Duke knew to what extent jealousy played a part in his anguish, but Harriet had a shrewd idea; she believed it had prompted him to insist upon secrecy, and told Lady Melbourne, "it is of the greatest consequence [to him] it should not be suspected he is in distress or that our going is at all upon *her* account."[42] Finally the Duke recovered himself sufficiently to make a firm decision: unable to trust himself with Georgiana or Bess he sought out Harriet and even then he struggled with his words for a long time. Harriet waited for what seemed several minutes and was completely taken by surprise when he burst out, "If you wish to save your sister and me from the most unpleasant disclosure, break off your going to Penzance and go abroad directly." That was it, she told Lady Melbourne: after he walked out she realized, "it is determined as far as the Duke can determine anything. . . . His soliciting an open publick separation or not depends upon my entire acquiescence in everything he wishes."[43]

"We are all in distress and confusion and shall be so till Warren comes," wrote Georgiana, still lying about the true cause. "My mother is very much agitated tho' extremely kind; and of course my Sister is nervous and I am mad. I shall make any possible use of you about Black's letters sent you when I am gone—if I *go* for all is obscure—my mother goes I believe," she continued somewhat incoherently, "and the D sees less necessity for my going but if she [Harriet] continues as anxious apart I am sure we shall— you must see my children very often."[44] By the time Dr. Warren arrived the strain on Harriet had brought about a relapse and he had no difficulty in requesting her departure. The Duke ordered Selina and Lady Spencer to take the children to London; the exiles should go immediately to Southampton. The party was to consist of Lady Spencer, the Duncannons and their youngest child, Caroline, Georgiana, Bess, and her daughter, Caroline St. Jules. However, the news that Lady Spencer was definitely going made Bess reconsider her offer to accompany Georgiana. "Bess and I had a long conversation and a half quarrel last night," Harriet told Lady Melbourne afterwards. "But I think I have [fixed] it. . . . I really believe it is nothing but the fear she has of my mother and the mistrust she feels when with her that makes her hesitate."[45]

Once again Lady Spencer's prejudices had blinded her to the exigencies of Georgiana's situation. If Bess stayed behind, her reputation might be ruined but the Duke would have little incentive to recall Georgiana from her exile. In any case, there were far more serious problems to be overcome which made her preoccupation with Bess look ridiculous. None of the party had any money. The Duncannons were massively in debt as usual and Georgiana had only the contents of her baggage. The private incomes of Bess and Lady Spencer were hardly enough to support themselves abroad, let alone seven people. Lady Melbourne gave them what money she could quickly gather without attracting notice, and George paid for Harriet's doctor to travel with them. He had little cash to spare, although he compensated for this by sending his agent, Townsend, to accompany the party and conduct all their business transactions for them. In many ways Townsend was better than a line of credit because he was practical and level-headed. However, it was impossible to imagine how they would survive if the Duke remained angry for any length of time. He had forbidden Georgiana to borrow any money, and yet, Harriet complained to Lady Melbourne, he was throwing "temptation in her face" by leaving her destitute. She could already see the day when they would be forced to sell their jewels.

The person at the centre of this drama thought about little except the choice the Duke had forced her to make. He had ordered Georgiana to renounce Grey and have the baby adopted as soon as it was born. If she refused he would divorce her and she would never see her three children again. She did not hesitate even though she had no guarantee that the

Duke would not change his mind and divorce her anyway. But Grey could not forgive her choice, and when she tried to make him understand his replies were savage. He was being "very cruel," Georgiana wrote sadly to Lady Melbourne, who was secretly forwarding their letters. She did not blame him nor did she deny that he was "deserving of pity too, and I have in leaving him for ever, left my heart and soul; but it is over now. . . . he has one consolation that I have given him up to my children only."[46]

CHAPTER 16

EXILE

1791—1793

The Duchess of Devonshire, the Dowager Lady Spencer, and Lord and Lady Dun-cannon pass the summer in Switzerland, and next winter in Nice. The Duke is going to visit them soon. This fully contradicts the vague reports that have been circulated of these noble personages.

Bon Ton Magazine, *June 1792*

Georgiana lay in an airless, shuttered room in a house near Montpel-lier, waiting to give birth. Although only thirty-four she feared that her life had run its course. A new will, dated January 27, 1792, lay hidden amongst her possessions next to a life insurance policy for £1,000. Bess and the six-year-old Caroline St. Jules were the only people with her; the others had pressed on to Nice on account of Harriet's health. The baby was due in a few days, and in the time she had left Georgiana composed letters of farewell to each of her children, in case of her death. She tried to find words that would provide them with comfort and advice long after she was gone. "As soon as you are old enough to understand this letter it will be given to you," she wrote hopefully to her two-year-old son. "It contains the only present I can make you—my blessing, written in my blood. . . . Alas, I am gone before you could know me, but I lov'd you, I nurs'd you nine months at my breast. I love you dearly."[1]

As well as giving each of them her blessing, Georgiana begged the chil-dren to learn from the mistakes which had ruined her life: "One of my greatest pains in dying," began her farewell to Little Georgiana, "is not to see you again. But I hope that this letter will influence your whole life; I die, my dearest child, with the most unfeigned repentance for many errors. Learn to be exact about expence—I beg you as the best Legacy I can leave you—never to run into debt for the most triffling sum; I have suffered enough from a contrary conduct."[2] Her final injunction was that they should always be dutiful to their father, loving to their grandmother, and "affectionate to my Dear friend Bess—love and befriend Caroline St. Jules."

The children knew that their mother had been sent away to give birth to an illegitimate child; the proof is in the blacked-out paragraphs which disfigure Georgiana's letters to them during these months. Their Victorian descendants attempted to wipe out every trace of her transgression: in the Chatsworth archives there is a gap where her letters about the birth would have been. Every letter which ever mentioned the child's name, bar one or two, has been either destroyed or mutilated. But we know from other sources that on February 20, 1791, Georgiana gave birth to a girl. She called her Eliza (a favourite name of Bess's) Courtney (a surname which belonged to the Poyntz family and therefore, unusually, gave no hint of her patrimony). Someone took Eliza from Georgiana's arms almost immediately. The baby was nursed by a foster mother and then, when she was old enough to travel, sent over to England to live with Charles Grey's parents in Falloden in Northumberland.

Somehow, a poem which Georgiana wrote just after Eliza's birth made its way into her daughter's hands and a copy lies among her descendants' papers:

> Unhappy child of indiscretion,
> poor slumberer on a breast forlorn
> pledge of reproof of past transgression
> Dear tho' unfortunate to be born
>
> For thee a suppliant wish addressing
> To Heaven thy mother fain would dare
> But conscious blushes stain the blessing
> And sighs suppress my broken prayer
>
> But spite of these my mind unshaken
> In present duty turns to thee
> Tho' long repented ne'er forgotten
> Thy days shall lov'd and guarded be

And should th'ungenerous world upbraid thee
for mine and for thy father's ill
A nameless mother oft shall assist thee
A hand unseen protect thee still

And tho' to rank and wealth a stranger
Thy life a humble course must run
Soon shalt thou learn to fly the danger
Which I too late have learnt to shun

Meanwhile in these sequestered vallies
Here may'st thou live in safe content
For innocence may smile at malice
And thou—Oh! Thou art innocent[3]

Georgiana was never allowed to acknowledge Eliza, although her existence eventually became an open secret. In 1796 Lord Glenbervie, the social magpie of the late eighteenth century, recorded in his diary: "I heard yesterday a stray anecdote of a foundling left about four years ago at Sir Charles Grey's under very mysterious circumstances. The Duchess of Devonshire was at that time abroad. Since her return about three years ago she has often visited the child, and been with it for hours at a time."[4] Mrs. Fitzherbert, whose resentment of Georgiana increased rather than diminished with each passing year, may have learned the truth from him, or from the Duchess of Leeds, another famous gossip. However she found out, she made sure that the rest of society learned of Eliza's existence. Mrs. Creevey, the wife of the Whig politician, was speechless when Mrs. Fitzherbert brought up the subject over tea and biscuits one afternoon in 1805: "She said quite naturally. . . . it is only two years since the Prince knew of that Child who lives with Lady Grey—he would not believe it at first and vowed he would ask the Duchess but I made him promise not to do so, tho' now he can have no doubts."[5]

The arrangement ultimately agreed between the Devonshires and the Greys granted Georgiana limited access to the child as her unofficial godmother, and she became the "unseen hand" which tried to protect her. She was not allowed to send her private letters or visit her at Falloden, nor does it seem that Eliza ever set foot inside Devonshire House. But Georgiana was granted permission to see her occasionally when the Greys brought her to London. These visits were painful: Georgiana could sense that Eliza lacked the sort of loving attention which her other children enjoyed, so she sent her little presents—poetry, tiny watercolour drawings, and any other scrap of nursery paraphernalia which could be tied up in a ribbon and easily conveyed. But no matter how carefully she composed her letters, she couldn't hide her thwarted maternal feelings.

One letter to Eliza when she was twelve years old begins innocently enough—"A thousand thanks for your delightful letter. I hope to hear from you again when you have received the books and that you continue well"—but ends with a poignant passage describing a children's ball, where the sight of the little girls concentrating on their steps brought tears to Georgiana's eyes.[6] In another letter, written the following year, 1804, Georgiana told a story—which sounds suspiciously like a parable—about Fortuna, an orphaned child whom she had been sponsoring for the past six years. It turned out that the girl was not an orphan; her parents had gone abroad and left her in the charge of a nurse who wickedly gave her away while keeping her allowance. Fortuna's real name was Louise Dupont and she had an English mother living in France; for the past two years Louise's family had been searching for her and, having found her, would now restore her birthright to her.[7]

In relating the miraculous end to Fortuna's troubles, Georgiana may have half wanted to awaken Eliza's suspicions about her own birthright. There were clues in all her letters, as if she hoped that one day Eliza would be able to piece the truth together for herself. For example, she made an oblique reference to her long exile and Eliza's birth in France by giving her "some memorandums I made abroad, four French lines which I send you as I thought them very pretty . . ."

> Form but few projects, cultivate few friends,
> Content with little space, do good to all
> and if alas, this happy system ends
> the recollection, with no pain recall.[8]

Sometimes Georgiana came perilously close to betraying herself: "God bless you dear Eliza," she ended one of her letters. "I will send you from time to time anything interesting I find in my papers which I am arranging. How I should like to have you here to help me."[9] But she kept her oath and also forbade Little Georgiana and Harryo, who were taken to see

Eliza occasionally, ever to reveal their knowledge of the connection: "understand she could [be] the daughter of any other person," she warned.[10]

Eliza therefore grew up in complete ignorance about her parentage, thinking that Georgiana was a kind friend and Charles Grey her much older brother. Her treatment in her grandparents' household was marked by indifference and she was made to feel inferior to the rest of the family. "We saw a great deal of old Mrs. Grey and little Eliza," Little Georgiana told Selina in 1799, "who was very much pleased with a toy we brought her."[11] Such presents were the only ones Eliza received. Harriet visited the Greys in 1808 and was miserable at what she saw: "Eliza is a fine girl, and will, I think, be handsome; but tho' they are kind to her, it goes to my heart to see her—she is so evidently thrown into the background, and has such a look of mortification about her that it is not pleasant, yet *he* [Charles Grey] seems very fond of her. Lord B. [Harriet's husband] has this moment ask'd me whether she is not the Governess."[12]

Georgiana did not live to see Eliza reach adulthood, but she would have been happy with the result. Lord Broughton met Eliza in 1814, just before she married Colonel, later General, Robert Ellice. He recorded in his diary that "the daughter of the late Duchess of Devonshire by Charles Grey" was a "fine girl, sensible and talkative, and easy mannered."[13] Eliza was the most beautiful of all Georgiana's children, which, combined with her sensitive and attractive nature, won her many friends. She married a tolerant and loving husband whose elder brother, Edward, had already married Eliza's half sister, Hannah Alethea Grey. Robert met Eliza at Edward's house, fell in love with her, and rescued her from her life of petty drudgery. In 1828 Eliza visited Southill, the home of the Whitbreads, friends of the Greys. While there she recorded the only surviving impressions of her childhood: "I have not been here since I married—all puts me too much in mind of dearest mama of my younger days," meaning that by now Eliza had learned that Mrs. Grey was not her real mother. "I feel depressed to a degree. . . . I sleep in the room poor mama used to sleep in— and when I used to study with her—I was not happy then, some oppressed me, but she was always most kind. How grateful I ought to feel for my present happy lot."[14]

❦❧

Georgiana and Bess remained apart from the group for several more weeks after Eliza's birth, giving great offence to Lady Spencer and causing

Harriet to wonder whether Georgiana reciprocated her love to the same degree. She need not have worried: Caroline St. Jules was the reason for their delay. Bess feared that her decision to accompany Georgiana had cost her the Duke's protection. She had initially delayed her departure, knowing that either way she stood to lose much.

> She was excessively [upset] [Harriet told Lady Melbourne] when she first came. Poor little soul, I felt for her from my heart, for I am certain the effort was as much as she could bear; but she is better now; she is our only security. I do not think she will go back without us now she is come, though I had very great doubts whether she would have [the] resolution to tear herself away. But that once over, I think the natural generosity of her character, and her friendship for my sister will have the leisure to act.[15]

Georgiana expressed her gratitude by accompanying Bess to Aix-en-Provence to help her to persuade the dying Comte St. Jules to adopt Caroline formally, thereby giving her some kind of legitimacy. To add to Bess's worry the Duke had, out of pique, stopped her allowance and she had no guarantee that Caroline's future would be provided for. Georgiana shared her anxiety, telling Lady Melbourne, "This poor old man continues very ill, and in the trouble of this country it really is very necessary that something should be done about securing Caroline's little income—and getting it into safe hands."[16] Nothing survives that would explain Bess's influence with the old man or why he would consider offering his protection to her child. Nevertheless, they succeeded in making him sign a paper just before he died but at considerable cost: the only way Harriet was able to prevent Lady Spencer from fetching them herself was by admitting the truth about Caroline. "My mother having been told everything was indeed unfortunate," she wrote.[17]

Lady Spencer gave the women a chilly reception when they arrived on March 9, although her anger was tempered by the horrors they had suffered on the way to Nice. The situation in France had worsened since their arrival in Paris in November. The south was particularly unsafe and minor uprisings in Provence and the Languedoc region had led to anarchy. Lawlessness and general brigandage rendered the roads almost unusable. Fearing that their carriage made them vulnerable, Georgiana and Bess opted to leave it by the roadside and rode the rest of the way. It made them less of a target but it exposed them to roving bands of looters. Lady Sutherland, cowering in comparative safety at the British embassy, heard about some of Georgiana's adventures:

I was very happy to hear of the Dss of Devonshire getting away from the Toulon Banditti, as the idea of the horrors that might have happened to her had she fallen into their hands gave me the nightmare. As to Ly Eliz [she added contemptuously], I did not care so much about it; that sort of thing for once in a way not signifying to a Hervey so much as to any other class in the animal world. If the Ds had been carried off, Ly Spencer would, like Ceres, have lighted her torch at Mount Etna and gone to seek her daughter all over the South of Europe—She is safe at Nice in the meantime where I hope the Dss now is.[18]

The party was safe but miserable and bad-tempered. Lady Spencer set everyone on edge by her hostility to Bess and the almost hysterical way in which she supervised Georgiana's every move. She insisted that Georgiana should sleep in her room like a child, show her her letters, and keep her door open at all times. Any protest was silenced by Lady Spencer's reminders "of all her sins."[19]

Georgiana had hoped that once the baby was born and safely hidden the Duke's anger would subside and he would let her return. Five months away was already enough for Bess, and she had started to hint of her longing for home. Lord Duncannon was also tired of living in hotels; furthermore his eighty-eight-year-old father was ill and wanted to make peace with his son. Even though Harriet was still weak and barely able to move on crutches Duncannon persuaded himself of her fitness to travel. The truce between husband and wife broke down over their disagreement; "nothing but absolute brute force shall make me return without [Georgiana]," Harriet declared, in spite of the pain she suffered at the separation from her sons.[20]

The Duke finally put an end to their speculation in April. His anger had not diminished, and Georgiana was to stay abroad until he fetched her himself. He gave Bess leave to do as she liked. "I lose all courage and spirit," Harriet sobbed when she heard the news. "England and everything is, it seems, remov'd twice as far." Georgiana was dismayed by his harshness. At least, she implored, let her secretly visit the children. "She has written to beg she may come over with Lord D. and Bess for one month only," Harriet told Lady Melbourne in April, "and then return to me. He never writes to her and seldom to Bess, and the last letter was in so harsh a style that I have little hopes of good; but at least the pretence of returning to me will always save a formal separation as long as I am away."[21]

Only Lady Spencer still hoped for an eventual reconcilement. Firm in this belief, she forbade Georgiana to risk upsetting the Duke by going home now. Georgiana's mask of determined cheerfulness slipped when she broke the news of her prolonged exile to Little Georgiana: "Oh my dear child, I can only assure you that your Love and the hopes that you will not forget me is the comfort of my life now that I am absent from you—when I am to return is now very uncertain—I hope it will be soon as I do not feel that I have strength to bear so long an absence." "When shall I see you all," she wrote plaintively a month later. "It will not be long now I trust and I beg of you dst love to make your Papa come and fetch me soon."[22] Lord Duncannon went home in June and did not return for six months, but Bess stayed with Georgiana.

The children were deeply upset by Georgiana's banishment. "Mama gone, Mama gone," Hart wailed over and over. The Duke never saw them; they remained in Devonshire House under Selina's sole care. Lady Melbourne and George and Lavinia were good about visiting them and, surprisingly, Lady Jersey often brought her own children to play. Selina, for all her peculiarities, showed a hitherto unexpressed sensitivity towards Georgiana and did her utmost to help to maintain contact with the children. Her first letter on Georgiana's departure was kind and betrayed no hint of judgement: "It is impossible to say how much I long to hear you are all safe and well in France. . . . Lady Georgiana's letter is quite her own." Subsequently she wrote, "How happy I am to be of any use to you and how much I wish to comfort you by telling you how all your sweet children go on."[23]

Lady Spencer asked Selina to make a special effort to become friendly with the Duke, although the result was not quite what she intended:

She writes me word she found it very heavy work [Lady Spencer reported]. But as I thought it (which I do) of great consequence to those under her care, she persisted and thought she began to gain some ground. . . . Now I have begun to take fright, tho' I think there can be no occasion for it, his attachments are of such a nature that they are not likely to alter and as for her I never can have a fear about her—but as he is at present perfectly desoeuvré he may mistake her attentions for coquettry or partiality, and it is not impossible that he may behave in such a manner as to distress her.[24]

The exiles whiled away the time quite pleasantly, socializing with their French and English acquaintances. As Nice was part of the kingdom of Savoy the town was thronging with refugees from France. Georgiana had formed a plan to follow her children's lessons so that she would be able to share in whatever they were learning, and perhaps even help them a little. She began a course of self-improvement, learning Italian, practising her drawing and music, and studying natural science, which became very important to her in later life. She now filled her letter journals to the children with colourful maps and sketches of the places she visited, enlivened with individual accounts of their social and political histories.

Quite by chance Georgiana discovered that Mary Graham was also in Nice. The Grahams had been abroad for several years in the vain hope that a Mediterranean climate might improve Mary's health. She was now in the final stage of consumption and beyond help. The two women had a short but emotional reunion. She died on June 26, 1792; according to Mrs. Nugent, who sat with her as she struggled for breath, one of her last conversations concerned her friendship with Georgiana: no other woman had claimed such an important part in her life. Mary used curious words to describe Georgiana: clever, safe, and benevolent. "Tell her," she added, "to thank Lady Spencer for all her kindness to me. The poor Duchess had had affliction enough, without my adding to it, with poor Lady Duncannon. Tell her I hope she will continue to see as much of Charlotte [Mary's younger sister] as she can, and to love her, and tell her exactly anything that occurs to her."[25] The party had moved on to Switzerland when the news of Mary's death reached them. "I shall never forget her," Georgiana avowed. "Her goodness, her sense, her sweetness have left a strong impression on my mind; she thought too much of me I am sure; but I have a pride in feeling that she loved me. I wish I deserved her friendship, but the contemplation of what she was adds to one's discontent with oneself. . . . how proud I feel in the certainty of her love for me—how humbled in the consciousness of deserving it so little."[26]

Georgiana's self-criticism was not an affectation. "The result of *thought* in me is always remorse and condemnation of myself," she once said of herself.[27] It was not only Mary's death which made her reflect on the past with pain; several old friends had died within a few months of each other. Sheridan, stricken with remorse over his philandering, wrote to say that his wife, Elizabeth, had died of consumption. Georgiana and Harriet received several guilt-ridden letters, although he could not help adding to Harriet, "you are the only creature whom I find it a relief to think of."[28] Georgiana heard that Lady Derby and the Prince of Wales's first love, Perdita, were also terminally ill. Even though many friends rallied to her side, writing letters of support and promising to visit, she felt wretched and unworthy. Up to twenty or thirty letters arrived at each post, of which only a fraction survive. The Duke of Dorset was particularly kind to her: "*aimez moi un peu toujours*"*[29] was all he asked in return. Although he was ignorant of the true cause of Georgiana's exile, the Prince of Wales also exhibited a rare display of loyalty. Exactly a year after her banishment he wrote:

> Out of sight out of mind, I know, is an old proverb, and but too often the case with many people in this world, but yt. is not in the least, my dearest Dss., applicable to me . . . *my best beloved friend,* that no circumstance in life *can ever cause any change in ye the sentiments of yt heart with wh. you have long been acquainted.* . . . my ever dearest friend must be fully persuaded yt no *human event* can ever cause any alteration in my sentiments respecting her.[30]

People knew that a separation between the Duke and Georgiana must have taken place despite official denials, and everyone except the Cavendishes blamed the Duke for the split. A typical conversation was recorded by the young Whig Thomas Pelham after a dinner with friends; Dudley North had brought up the subject of the Devonshires: "He complained of [the Duke's] selfishness and want of attention, and said . . . that if the Dss had been married to — or to any man who had shown her proper attention and done justice to her merits she would have been one of the most perfect women in England."[31] Although Lady Spencer would never have said such a thing to Georgiana, she agreed with North. Writing from Switzerland to Mrs. Howe, she described how helpful and generous George had been to them: "What would not my Daughters have been had their husbands been like him."[32]

Even under the most trying circumstances Lady Spencer had the bitter-

* Always love me a little.

sweet satisfaction of watching Georgiana and Harriet attract friends and laughter about them. By the time the party had reached Lausanne it had grown into a bulging caravan of English and foreign travellers. "Chemistry and mineralogy in the morning and draw all the evening; in short nothing can be more instructive or pleasant than their society," was how one of the newcomers, Henry Pelham, described it.[33] "Not to adore her [Georgiana] seems an odd thing to any person who lives with her," wrote another.[34] They spent the summer on Lake Geneva, at Edward Gibbon's house, enjoying the view over the valley with its silver rivers and dark green forests. The author of *The Decline and Fall of the Roman Empire* had retired from politics to a contented bachelor existence in Lausanne, where he regularly received visits from scholars and admirers. This sedate lifestyle was completely overturned by Georgiana's arrival; within days he had thrown his house open to all her guests. The two Carolines, Caroline Ponsonby and Caroline St. Jules, found him fascinating and played with him as if he were a doll:

> Mr. Gibbon is very clever but remarkably ugly [Georgiana told Little Georgiana], and wears a green jockey cap to keep the light from his Eyes when he walks in his garden. Caroline was quite entertained with it and made him take it off and twist it about. . . . He comes to us almost every day and sometimes whilst we are dressing they undertake to amuse him. . . . One day Caroline Ponsonby out of kindness, wanted one of the footmen who had been jumping her to jump Mr. Gibbon, which was rather difficult as he is one of the biggest men you ever saw. . . . we take lessons in mineralogy and chemistry and Mr. Gibbon attends them with us and in the Evenings we have a great deal of music. . . . [35]

Ironically, Lady Spencer was very much taken with Caroline St. Jules, and preferred her to Harriet's Caroline. Even at seven years old Caroline Ponsonby was an alarming and unpredictable girl, given to hysterical fits and rages. "She is very naughty and says anything that comes into her head, which is very distressing," wrote Georgiana, who wanted to slap her when she was rude to Harriet. "She told poor Mr. Gibbon, who has the misfortune of being very ugly, that his big face frightened the little puppy with whom he was playing."[36] Since Lady Spencer was the only one who could control Caroline, she was obliged to spend more time with her than she liked. Despite her robust attitude to other people's failings, she was not good at self-analysis. When Georgiana failed to notice her efforts to overcome her cold she became difficult and petulant until she had everyone's attention. "The happiness of my children," Lady Spencer wrote in justification of this incident, "I think I do not deceive myself by saying, is that on which mine entirely depends. I have had much disappointment and I have felt it bitterly. I sometimes shew it more than I could wish, but it is difficult to keep it always concealed."[37]

Lord and Lady Palmerston stopped by with some friends for a few weeks, although Lady Palmerston was not able to appreciate the scenery quite as much as Georgiana. "I never felt anything equal to the heat of the Inn or the stink or the dirt."[38] They were greatly relieved to be invited to the cooler enclave down by the lake, where the party had rented two houses near Gibbon's. It was through the Palmerstons that Georgiana met the scientist Sir Charles Blagden, with whom she formed a life-long friendship. With his encouragement she became an amateur chemist and mineralogist of note, later endowing Chatsworth with a collection of stones and minerals of museum quality. Lady Palmerston made some astute observations on the company: "The Duchess is grown ten years younger, but Lady Spencer seems unhappy and as if she wished to get away from herself."[39] Even though she knew the Duke only slightly, she thought Georgiana was mistaken in her hope that he would come to fetch her: "I do not believe the Duke of Devonshire will come. The idea of some political arrangements may be a reason for detaining him, but he wants little more excuse than the trouble of setting off."[40]

The escalation of war along France's borders in October provided Lady Spencer with the opportunity to take a short break from Bess and her artificial laugh. Switzerland was no longer deemed safe, and the party decided that Harriet should go to Italy, where the warmth and relative quiet would continue to mend her health. Georgiana and Bess remained in Lausanne, still hoping the Duke would keep to his word and fetch them. The others began their tortuous journey, avoiding main roads in case they met soldiers, and fearful of going into the mountains, which would be too cold for Harriet. On several occasions Lady Spencer was very frightened: "Everything in these countries is in the greatest confusion—the whole road and every Inn full of Troops marching to the frontier and to Geneva which is supposed to be in great danger."[41] Georgiana had not seen her children for twelve months, and the separation was growing even harder for her to bear. On November 30, 1792, she wrote to Little G:

Your letter dated the 1st of Nov was delightful to me tho' it made me very melancholy my Dearest Child. This year has been the most painful of my life. . . . when I do return to you, never leave you I hope again—it will be too great a happyness for me Dear Dear Georgiana, & it will have been purchased by many days of regret—indeed ev'ry hour I pass away from you, I regret you; if I amuse myself or see anything I admire I long to share the happyness with you—if on the contrary I am out of spirits I wish for your presence which alone would do me good.[42]

The party travelled slowly in the new year until it reached Pisa, where Duncannon rejoined the group. George had found him much improved when he saw him in London—less awkward and calmer than the old Duncannon. Lady Spencer knew her son-in-law well enough to be sceptical of any lasting change: she had witnessed his true character often enough. However, she noticed that he was behaving better towards Harriet and hoped it was not all show.[43] Georgiana and Bess caught up with them there, having waited until the last possible moment for the Duke. They were forced to cross into Italy through the snow and ice. The French had taken control of the Savoy mountains, leaving open only the dangerous passage over St. Bernard. Fortunately, Pelham had stayed behind to escort them: on several occasions the servants had refused to continue until persuaded by a combination of threats and pleading.

The news of Louis XVI's execution had reached Georgiana before she set off for Italy. Most countries, including Britain, recalled their ambassadors at this point, much to the relief of Lady Sutherland; "you have no idea of the horror of being at Paris since the 10th," she had written to Georgiana. "The King and Queen confined in the Temple and not suffered to have servants. Mde de Lamballe *est à hotel de la Force.* They do nothing but arrest, interrogate, and guillotine, in short it is too bad."*[44]

---

* In June Lafayette attempted to halt the revolution by ousting the Jacobins from power. He failed, and two months later, on August 16, defected to the Austrians, who promptly imprisoned him as a spy. The Princesse de Lamballe was less fortunate; a mob burst into La Petite Force during the September massacres, breaking down every door until they found her. They dragged her screaming from her cell into the yard, where she was raped, tortured, and finally hacked to death. Afterwards, they stuck her head and breasts on pikes and paraded them through Paris until they stopped beneath Marie Antoinette's window and called out for her to see her friend.

Georgiana had known it was only a matter of time before they came for Marie-Antoinette, but she was still unprepared for the manner of her death, which took place on October 16, 1793. "I cannot express to you the horror I feel," she told Coutts.[45] The public trial, the corrupting of her son, the malicious abuse by her guards, and the stories about her mistreatment tormented Georgiana in her dreams and waking thoughts. "The impression of the Queen's death is constantly before my eyes," she wrote.[46] The Little Po, still in exile in Switzerland, died shortly after they brought her the news.

Georgiana had certainly kept in contact with her, as well as with Calonne and many other French émigrés, but such letters were dangerous to keep and they were always burnt. Occasional references to "letters of great consequence" only hint at her activities. One which has survived concerns the plight of the French émigrés residing in Italy, many of whom were destitute. Georgiana and Bess organized a network of friends to help to raise money for the poorest of them. Madame de Fitzjames, once a darling of the court, was a typical refugee: reduced to a miserable existence in a dirty pension, she lived off charity; when it was not forthcoming she starved.

London heard about Louis XVI's execution on January 23, 1793. The government immediately expelled the Marquis de Chauvlin, the French ambassador. In retaliation, the French declared war on Britain and urged all British patriots to rise up in favour of the ideals of the revolution. Georgiana's friends in London insisted she should come home. "I wish most sincerely that you were in England," wrote Lady Sutherland. "The Duke of Dorset often talks of you *con amore* as do many other people. . . . The best thing I can say of [London] is that the Dss of Gordon is *cut* almost generally."[47] Lady Jersey had reverted to her old self and was spreading tales about Georgiana, but she was the only one as far as Lady Sutherland was aware. Bess's brother Lord Hervey sweetly forwarded a letter from the Duke, saying in a postscript that he wished its contents contained the news that will "pour balm into your heart and soothe away anxious feel with the hopes of speedy return and the calm prospect of future comfort and tranquillity."[48] But the Duke could only bring himself to write short, curt notes to Georgiana about nothing in particular. Devonshire House was reported to be "dismal and dirty" without her, which at least showed that he was not cheerful at her absence. James Hare had been writing faithfully to Georgiana with social and political news from home but, disappointingly, he could no better determine the Duke's intentions than she could. "I have seen the Duke very frequently," he wrote, "and often dine with him tête-à-tête; he is not (as you know) very communicative . . . so that I learn nothing from him."[49]

Lord Bessborough died on March 11, 1793, aged eighty-nine. As soon as he heard, Lord Duncannon, now the third Earl of Bessborough, set off for London, leaving the exiles to make themselves at home in Naples. The city and its environs was a favourite tourist spot for English travellers. It was one of the highlights of the Grand Tour, and a place which invited extravagant descriptions. One traveller writing home in the second half of the eighteenth century praised its

> olive groves and well-tilled fields of corn, intermixed with ranks of elms, every one of which has its vine twining about it, and hanging in festoons between rows from one tree to another. The great old fig-trees, the oranges in full bloom, and myrtles in every hedge, make one of the delightfullest scenes you can conceive; besides that, the roads are wide, well-kept, and full of passengers. . . . the number of people outdoes both Paris and London. The streets are one continued market, and thronged with populace so much that a coach can hardly pass. . . . it is on the most lovely bay in the world, and one of the calmest seas. . . .[50]

The King and Queen of Naples and the ubiquitous Hamiltons—Sir William and Lady Hamilton—made the group extremely welcome and they were frequent guests at court. An eminent group of scientists, which included Sir Joseph Banks and Sir Charles Blagden, had gathered to study such phenomena as the volcanic Mount Vesuvius and they graciously made room for Georgiana at their meetings. These months were some of the happiest and most fulfilled of her life. She climbed up to the top of Mount Vesuvius to watch smoke billowing from the crater, took boat trips around the islands, and investigated the ancient ruins with her new companions.

However, she had no money or jewellery left and Coutts's patience was at an end. He had endured her pleadings and excesses for almost two years, and urged her to return some of the £20,000 she owed him. On several occasions he had even approached the Duke, who refused to talk to him. The new Lord Bessborough reached London just in time to prevent Georgiana's name from appearing on a list of defaulting debtors. He and

Harriet were enjoying one of their brief periods of *rapprochement;* he managed to control his irritation on discovering that she too was on the list: "for God's sake tell me all your debts, there is no use in concealing them. I don't say I can pay them, but we might make some arrangement of them to make them less ruinous. . . . I can think of nothing but you."[51]

Georgiana was beginning to give up hope when a letter from the Duke arrived on May 18.

> Oh my G [she wrote immediately], how can I express my happyness to you. We were dining today at the Arca Felice—or rather under it—it is the most picturesque situation in the world—when the post arrived and your dear dearest Papa's letter telling me to return to you in the middle of the summer. God of heaven bless him for his kindness to me—in three months at the latest I shall be with you my Dearest children and this cruel absence will be amply made up by the delight of seeing you. Oh my dearest love what joy it will be and how very good your dear Papa is to me.[52]

The party hastily decamped and began the long journey home. They got no farther than Rome when Harriet suffered a relapse. Lady Palmerston saw her:

> We dined at the Websters and went together to the Borghese Villa. We met there the Duchess of D. and in the evening went to see Lady Bessborough who makes my heart ache. She looks and is so ill. She coughs and spits blood again. She was quite free from either complaint at Naples, but the travelling has brought it on. She is so excessively interesting that one cannot bear to see her in so precarious a state. They will, I fancy pass the winter at Naples. The Duchess is as enchanting as ever. We looked over drawings of the doings, Lady Elizabeth draws in a most capital style. The Duchess certainly returns to England this summer. The Duke has written a most affectionate letter to desire her to return.[53]

Harriet was not fit to travel, and Lady Spencer elected to stay behind with her in Italy. Harriet was distraught at the idea of being separated from Georgiana: "This dreaded and horrible day has passed my Dearest Georgiana far better than I expected," Lady Spencer reported after Georgiana and Bess had set off alone. "Your sister cried violently when she first got into the chaise," but after several hours her tears subsided and, exhausted, she fell into a deep sleep.[54]

Georgiana was equally affected, but she had Bess to comfort her. However, as they neared Ostend both became oppressed by fears of what the future held for them in England. Georgiana in particular felt burdened by worries and regrets. Forgetting her science lessons and how much she had taught herself, she confessed to Lady Spencer:

> I condemn myself as much almost for the misuse of time in my *bannishment,* as anything else. I think I ought to have done so much better and the worst is that I have often given you cause of uneasiness and complaint, tho' I would have sacrificed my life for your care and to do a little away the cruel blows I have given you. My mind and my heart always wish'd to do well, but despair at myself and my situation often depriv'd me of all energy, and drew me into errors. Sometimes it was better, when I had hope I then could rouse myself, but at times I have sunk to a situation of despair that made me fly to anything for resource.[55]

What sort of things Georgiana had resorted to she did not say, but she swore that her life would be different. She would never disobey the Duke in anything ever again: "I return impressed with [a] very deep humility, and the wish of atonement, by doing more for another, and by perfect acquiescence in all *his* intentions and wishes. I hope likewise to make use of the very great good fortune that has attended me by increas'd prudence and care. I fear and tremble, but my only dependence is on my penitence and gratitude to God and on my adoration to my children."[56]

They arrived at Ostend just as the French were forcing the Duke of York's army to retreat. Having escaped from besieged Maastricht, risking the bombardment as they crept through its streets, Georgiana and Bess ignored warnings to turn back. "We came on against all advice and heard of the English disasters. . . . between Bruges and Ostend some soldiers stopped to ask us if we had seen any French etc.,—At Ostend everybody advised us to get off as fast as possible."[57] There was not a single space on any of the boats leaving the port. Fortunately, in the midst of the general panic Georgiana came across a friend, Lord Wicklow, just as he was heading for his pleasure boat. Eyeing their baggage and servants rather doubtfully he nevertheless squeezed them on to his little yacht. As the men cut the moorings some English refugees rushed up and begged to be allowed on. Georgiana was distraught at being forced to leave them behind but there was nothing they could do. The boat pulled away from the stragglers, and she watched them standing forlornly on the quayside as the city burned behind them.[58]

CHAPTER 17

RETURN

1794—1796

Lord Egremont's superb mansion in Piccadilly . . . is sold to Mr. Mills, of Yorkshire for the sum as is said, of £16,000. The tenanting of this mansion and of Devonshire House, with the completion of Mr. Drummond's and Mr. Crauford's [sic], will restore, in the ensuing spring, some of the former splendour of Piccadilly.

London Chronicle, *January 2–4, 1794*

The Duke was waiting at Dartford with the children to greet Georgiana and Bess. "I have seen them, I have seen them," Georgiana wrote to Lady Spencer after the reunion. "Georgiana is very handsome. . . . Harryo is still fat, but with the whitest complexion. . . . Hartington is very pretty, but very cruel to me. He will not look at me or speak to me, tho' he kiss'd me a little at night. . . . The Duke has the gout but looks pretty well. There was never anything equal to the attention I have met with from him—to the generosity and kindness."[1] He had surprised her with a welcome-home present: a smart new carriage with light blue panels and silver springs. They travelled back in it to London, reaching Devonshire House on September 18, 1793. The entire household was waiting in the courtyard as the carriage drove through the gates. "I never knew anything so touching as the reception of the servants," Georgiana recorded. As for herself, she admitted she was "so happy and so anxious."

The certainty that she would find many unpleasant changes made Georgiana unwilling to venture from Devonshire House. "I have been in town 4 days and have been too agitated to look about me or do anything," she wrote on September 23; "too happy, too agitated and perhaps after so long a journey, too idle. I get up early to see the children sooner, I sit by the fire, and the litter in my room wd make you bless yrself."[2] Even within the safe confines of Devonshire House she could not avoid some upsetting discoveries. The only good piece of news seemed to be that Charlotte Williams was at last off their hands, having married Heaton's nephew.[3] For the rest, there was only regret and disappointment.

Georgiana's two-year separation from the children had affected them badly. She was heartbroken to find that ten-year-old Little G had no self-confidence. She had become "the most interesting dr child I ever saw and very pretty," Georgiana wrote. However, "she never would let me out of her sight could she help it and today she told me I did not know all her faults."[4] Little G had developed a morbid religious sensibility which made her dwell relentlessly on her sins, real and imagined.[5] Fortunately, eight-year-old Harryo did not share Little G's religious terrors. On the other hand she had become reserved and prickly towards other people. She was also less pretty than her sister, being rather short and plump.

Yet Harryo seemed to have suffered the least, while Hart, now three and a half, had suffered the most. He did not recognize his mother—indeed he screamed whenever Georgiana tried to hold him. He had been so deprived of maternal affection that he associated physical contact with nasty sensations such as smacks and cold baths. For months he resisted all Georgiana's entreaties to let her touch him. The full reason for his behaviour did not emerge until later: he was almost deaf—an infection had destroyed most of his hearing. The sweet-natured infant of Georgiana's memory had turned into a furious toddler who kicked and bit anyone who came near. Georgiana always blamed herself for his condition and she spoilt him by way of compensation, which further deformed Hart's character. The fact that he had caught the infection while under Selina's care added to the tensions between the two women. Georgiana's relationship with the governess on her return was fraught. Selina had grown used to caring for the children on her own and she resented Georgiana's interference. They argued constantly over how the children should be disciplined. It was three years before they ceased to be suspicious of each other.* In the meantime Georgiana had to fight to regain control of the nursery.

---

* It didn't help that Selina remained Lady Spencer's spy. In April 1796 Selina reminded Lady Spencer not to reveal their correspondence to Georgiana "as we are now going on so well I would not wish her Grace to think I tell you everything that passes between us." Chatsworth 1333, Selina Trimmer to LS, April 11, 1796.

The Duke was also marked by the past two years; the pain from his gout, added to a natural tendency to hypochondria, had reduced him to an invalid. "As soon as he can move we shall go to Hardwick, certainly till after Xmas and probably for all the years," Georgiana wrote on September 30 to Lady Spencer. She had made a conscious decision regarding the Duke, and he was pleased to see that he was now her first priority. "As it is I never go out," she continued in her letter, "but receive 3 or 4 men of the Duke's acquaintance who sit with him and when he is tired come into my room; these are generally Craufurd, Hare, Mr James and Mr Grenville. . . . I am impatient to be with the children whom I scarcely leave all day."[6]

Georgiana kept to her resolution even though neither time nor distance had diminished her love for Grey. "Don't imagine by this that the Duchess of Devon is supposed to have changed her Ideas; they still appear to remain *Grey*," Lady Stafford wrote after seeing her at a dinner in February 1794.[7] Initially at least, Grey was keen for them to resume their relationship. Lady Webster, who later eloped with Fox's nephew Lord Holland, watched them together and recorded her observations in her diary. In December 1793 she wrote: "Mr Grey is le bien aimé of the Dss, he is a fractious, exigeant lover," and added, he is a "man of violent temper and unbounded ambition."[8] But Georgiana not only made strenuous efforts to hide her feelings, she also refused to bend to Grey's demands. Her sacrifice helped to smooth away any lingering bitterness in the Duke, who, for his part, remained angry with Bess for leaving him and taking Caroline St. Jules. She continued to be his mistress, but he no longer loved her with the same ardour, nor did he trust her. There was, however, no question of Bess moving out of Devonshire House: Georgiana would never have allowed it. Bess was more important to her than any other human being. When confronted by the choice of celebrating Little Georgiana's birthday or nursing Bess, who had a high fever, Georgiana chose the latter, "for I dare not leave my poor friend," she explained.[9] Still, Bess left nothing to chance, and she sought out the Duke of Richmond, just in case.

When Georgiana finally ventured into society her re-entry was quiet and subdued. The *Morning Post* reported that Lady Melbourne had held a dinner in her honour; after that there was little about Georgiana in the press.[10] Her first presentation at court confirmed the change. This time, she deliberately wore something sober and unremarkable. She knew it would be foolish to pretend she was still the leader of the *ton*, although Lady Spencer couldn't help writing to remind her "Let [the dress] be sim-

ple and noble, but pray do not let it be singular. . . . The credit such a conduct would be to your character would far outweigh the trivial and really
false idea of your looking more shewy. There must be some period for taking up a different character of dress, and when can you find a better than
now at your return after so considerable an Absence. . . ."[11]

Lady Spencer was right to point out that Georgiana's two-year absence
made it easier for her to retire gracefully. She also had little choice—in addition to the rumours about her exile, she was known to be bankrupt, and
her banishment had only added to her debts. The Duke was helping to
clear some of them, but as usual he could never be brought to sign anything and Georgiana was too frightened to remind him. A return to her old
way of life would also expose her to the temptation of gambling. Paradoxically, Georgiana had been free of the urge to gamble during her exile; she
had been so preoccupied by other interests, especially her scientific studies,
that the problem had never arisen. Even at Naples, where the opportunity
to gamble was everywhere, Georgiana preferred to spend her time at Father
Patrini's house, the gathering place for visiting scientists, talking to Sir
Charles Blagden about his work.[12] On her return to London she continued
to pursue her new interests and filled her days with lectures at the Royal
Academy, conducting chemistry experiments in a back room at Devonshire
House, and studying mineralogy. The fossils and minerals she had acquired while abroad formed the core of a collection to which she was continually adding.[13] On October 23 Lady Sutherland described Georgiana's
routine to Lady Stafford as being quite reformed and sensible: "the Duke
has got the gout, & the Dss is 'at home' every night at 12 o'clock, afterwards
she sits with him till 3. She is busy studying *Chemistry,* and goes out little,
she is going this morning to a chemical lecture."[14]

Politics was now a source of much grief to her; the Whigs were hated
by the King, despised by the government, and mistrusted by the whole
country. The press labelled them "the French Faction," James Hare complained to her, because of their supposed sympathies with the revolution,
when ironically they were "completely divided and disagreeing amongst
themselves."[15] Grey, Sheridan, and some of the younger Foxites had set up
a radical political reform group called "The Association of the Friends of
the People," which called for annual elections and greater democracy. The
Association's anti-aristocratic stance sharply divided the party.

Pitt naturally capitalized on the party's troubles. He began a successful
campaign to poach the most talented of the disaffected Whigs. Georgiana
spent her first few months trying to heal the rifts in the party by bringing

members together at small dinners at Devonshire House. "I have continued receiving all the world without any attention to what has passed in my
absence," she told her brother.[16] But two obstacles handicapped her efforts
to reunite the party: her own guilt at her disgrace, which made her unwilling to be seen too much in public, and the promise extracted by her
mother while they were abroad never to meddle in politics again. In Lady
Spencer's opinion Georgiana's political power had given her too much
freedom. Writing from Florence where Harriet was convalescing, she
warned Georgiana of the "serious consequences of your interesting yourself in this subject."[17] Georgiana's reply reveals the confusion she felt after
her return: "I never talk politics, not only from hating them but from
every person one speaks to having 7 different opinions."

For the first time in her life Georgiana disagreed with Fox. He saw no
threat in the revolution; she did. He thought England should make peace
with France; she didn't. "I by no means am an advocate for peace for I
don't see how it could be made," she told Lady Spencer on October 22.[18]
"I am said to see people of all partys but to be a great Royalist," she wrote
a few weeks later. "Another report is that I am making a coalition and this
is founded, I suppose, on my having seen a good deal of Lady Chatham."
The bickering within the party so disillusioned her that she toyed with the
idea of retiring from politics altogether. In early November she made a
dramatic announcement to her mother: "I promise you from this day, November 2, 1793, I never will say one word of politics in any way whatsoever."[19] Georgiana did not, of course, keep her promise, and embarked on
a campaign to reconcile Grey and Sheridan with Fox.

Fox continued to dither throughout the winter and the whole of the
spring. By the summer, however, he was leaning more towards the Association than the conservative faction. The Portlands fell out with Georgiana and the Duke over their continued support for Fox. "You can have
no conception how despised and abused both the D and Dss are by every
creature," Lavinia told George with relish in February. "Indeed their conduct well deserves it—Montagu tells me that the Dss of Portland is quite
outrageous—so much as to speak to him of them both in the bitterest
terms which she never did before."[20] The Duchess of Portland died a short
time later of cancer on June 3; her death seemed to be the catalyst for Portland, enabling him to cut his ties with the Cavendishes. The following
month he went over to Pitt, taking more than half the party with him.
Among the defectors was George, whom Pitt appointed as First Lord of
the Admiralty. Georgiana was devastated by her brother's decision. How-

ever, realizing that she would not change his mind, she wrote him a generous letter in which she absolved him of treachery to the party. "I have often told you, that I (as well as you) would have prefer'd seeing you out of place," she wrote in July. "But I think your reasons for coming in are the noblest and most upright."[21]

Devonshire House became a refuge for the eighty or so Foxites who remained—so much so that they were sometimes referred to as the "Devonshire House party." Many of Georgiana's closest friends, including Thomas Grenville and the Prince of Wales, stopped coming at all.*[22] The Duke of Devonshire was not a supporter of the Association, nor did he agree with Fox's position that Britain should make peace with France; nevertheless his allegiance to the party remained firm. His adherence to Whiggery was based on a sense of *noblesse oblige,* history, and on the certain belief that the Cavendishes had a divinely ordained role in government. Robert Adair wrote a posthumous sketch of him which had this to say about his political courage:

> In his political principles, the Duke of Devonshire was a thorough Whig. With all due respect for the Crown, he felt that the foundation of the Whig Character is laid in a love for the liberties of the People. To support the Crown in its lawful authority he considered at all times to be proper and decorous, but he felt that his more immediate duty was to defend the People, and the popular part of the Constitution. . . . He saw, therefore, the necessity of keeping the [royal] prerogative strictly within its limitations.[23]

It was some comfort to Georgiana that the Duke shared her loyalty to the party, and to Fox. But the Whig split of 1794 was a personal disaster for her.

---

* The Prince had fallen out with the Devonshires politically and personally. Having abandoned the Whigs, he also renounced Mrs. Fitzherbert and agreed to marry his cousin Caroline of Brunswick. By this time he did not care whom he married since he was prepared to do anything so long as the King agreed to pay off his debts. But he had also fallen under the baleful influence of Lady Jersey. At forty-one she was still a beautiful and captivating woman, even after bearing nine children. The Prince had always looked on her with a keen eye, and she, seeing that a vacancy was about to open up, manoeuvred herself into position. She was insufferable, making it a point to be as vicious as possible to any woman who had once been connected with the Prince. She was vile to Mrs. Fitzherbert and sneering towards Georgiana and Lady Melbourne. There could be no real reconciliation between the Prince and Georgiana as long as Lady Jersey remained his mistress.

Georgiana's skill and experience in party organization and political strategy belonged to the golden era of opposition. There was little or nothing for her to do now that the party had almost ceased to exist. The swift change to her status and reputation dented her self-confidence; she found it almost impossible to do things which only a few years ago would never have given her a moment's thought. Prodded by Richard Fitzpatrick to help poor Lafayette, still imprisoned in Austria, Georgiana finally wrote a humble letter to George in August 1794, begging him to intercede on the Frenchman's behalf. Her justification for writing took up as many lines as her request for help. "You will think it odd I should interfere on a political subject," she wrote—rather absurdly considering her previous experiences—"but as I am actuated by motives of gratitude and as the Duke agrees with me in wishing it I am sure you will forgive me."[24]

Georgiana's embarrassment at putting herself forward was also a reaction to the conservative backlash of the 1790s against women who crossed over into "masculine" areas. Until the French Revolution aristocratic women with a taste and aptitude for politics could carve out a role for themselves, and many did.[25] However, the opportunity was not theirs by right and, as Georgiana discovered, access was conditional on having a compliant husband, sufficient wealth, and a regiment of male supporters. Having enjoyed a prominent and successful part in politics, Georgiana had difficulty in accepting its premature end when the Whig party dissolved. She was not the first woman, nor the last, to resent watching men with considerably less talent than herself enjoy far greater and challenging opportunities. Ten years earlier the widow of the Marquess of Rockingham had struggled in vain to maintain her position within the Whig hierarchy and was condemned for it because she seemed to be exhibiting the "male" attribute of personal ambition. Lady Mary Coke said nastily of her, "it seems as if politics was her first passion and that even her great misfortune in losing Lord Rockingham is insufficient to make her forget her favourite amusement."[26]

The 1780s had been a decade of extraordinary freedom for women, and not only in the political sphere. During the American War of Independence newspaper reports of British women who disguised themselves as men in order to fight were not uncommon, and their patriotism was applauded as much as their actions were derided. In contrast, during the present war with France women concentrated their sartorial efforts on making warm clothes for volunteers. The *Oracle* trumpeted that the "brightest ornament of exalted life," the Duchess of Devonshire, "is *liter-*

ally employed in making FLANNEL SHIRTS for the brave fellows in *Flan-ders.*"*[27] Social commentators urged the return to a traditional society in which women knew their place. The Whigs' unashamed use of their female supporters during the 1780s tainted the notion of publicly active women with the slur of radicalism. A later critic of Fox thought his habit of treating women such as Georgiana on the same terms as his male friends a gross character flaw.[28]

Georgiana could not reconcile her desire for a career with eighteenth-century notions of female propriety. It was not in her nature to act outside the established political boundaries of the time. There is no evidence that she ever read Mary Wollstonecraft's *Vindication of the Rights of Woman* or that she knew of the writings of such early feminists as Mary Hays and Catherine Macaulay.†[29] Georgiana was more interested in practical political issues than with philosophical debates about women's rights and social equality. This enabled her to hold seemingly contradictory views, supporting the Polignacs in France and the patriots in Belgium. It also made it difficult for her to decide what to do. Georgiana became increasingly defensive about her own contribution: once shut out of politics she decided that women did not belong there anyway. Their role in life was to act as facilitators in the works of great men—but only when requested. She stated unequivocally: "If women would only meddle as moderators they wd do good instead of mischief."[30] In effect she was denying that a woman had the right to personal ambition. A woman's mission was not to bring out the best in herself but to inspire others. Such opinions were a far cry from the confidence—even arrogance—that she had exuded before the Regency crisis. Lavinia had hated her then for the careless way in which she talked of "we" and "us" when discussing the party.

Georgiana's interest in mineralogy prevented her from sinking into inactivity. She exchanged political meetings for scientific lectures and, with the help of Sir Charles Blagden, continued to enlarge her mineral collection. On August 22, 1794, an excited Blagden informed the president of the Royal Society, Sir Joseph Banks, that Georgiana had managed to acquire a piece of "elastic marble" from Italy.[31] Her progress gave Lady Spencer the opportunity to boast about her: "[she has] a genius for it," she

---

* Georgiana was disappointed to learn that the garments were later sold for gin.

† But she was a patron of Charlotte Smith, a semi-successful poet and playwright whose prevailing theme throughout her work was the misery caused to good wives by their feckless husbands.

wrote in September; "Padre Patrini, one of the first men in that line in Italy, and Sir Ch. Blagden here have both assured me . . . that the degree of knowledge the Dss has acquired and her observations were very extraordinary. Mr Cavendish* too I find is delighted with her. He calls upon her frequently."[32] Georgiana became a patron of promising scientists just as in the old days she had been a patron of young actors. One of her notable successes was Dr. Thomas Beddoes, whose Pneumatic Institute she helped to establish in 1798, resulting in the discovery of "laughing gas." Beddoes almost ruined his chances of finding favour with the government through his vociferous support for French republicanism. Georgiana struggled to help him to achieve recognition:

> It is these three years since I have known him [she wrote to her brother in 1795], and followed his discoveries in pneumatical chemistry and his application of them to health, and in my own mind I have not the least doubt that in many cases they would cure disorders and in almost all give great relief. His proposals are very fair and candid, and he is full of genius and good sense in everything but the one subject of politics, in which he has neither judgement, taste or temper.[33]

Harriet, now the Countess of Bessborough, joined Georgiana in her scientific studies. She had returned in September 1794 with her health almost restored, except for a lingering weakness in her legs, which necessitated the use of walking sticks. When Georgiana last saw her sister she had been thin and wan; now her face glowed with a light Mediterranean tan and she radiated good spirits. Harriet had fallen in love while in Naples. The man in question was Lord Granville Leveson Gower, a twenty-year-old, who was travelling through Italy before embarking on a career in the diplomatic corps.[34] He was clever, self-centred, and extraordinarily attractive. His looks conformed to the late eighteenth-century romantic ideal of manhood: his soft curly brown hair flopped over large dark eyes ("those eyes where I have looked my life away," Harriet later wrote) above a full, sensitive mouth. He was politically ambitious, but also hedonistic: he gambled too much, drank too much, and was constantly falling in love. It

---

* Henry Cavendish (1731–1810), a second cousin of the Duke's. He was an eminent natural scientist, discovered the constitution of water and atmospheric air, and in 1776 conducted ground-breaking experiments in electricity. A shy man like his cousin, he nevertheless loathed the Duke but developed a kindness for Georgiana.

had never been Harriet's intention to fall in love with him; "I trust and hope I am grown old and wise enough to be certain of never again involving myself in the misery of feeling more than the common Interest of friendship for any one," she told him on June 1, 1794.*[35] He was unabashed by her rebuffs and they were lovers before she departed for home.

Harriet had returned just in time to comfort Georgiana. Grey had become engaged to Mary Ponsonby, a cousin of Lord Bessborough's. Too cowardly to inform Georgiana himself, Grey allowed her to hear of his engagement through the newspapers. The marriage followed quickly afterwards in November. For a while Georgiana was rendered almost speechless with grief. The news arrived while she was taking the sea air at Teignmouth with Harriet, Bess, and the children. Both women did their best to distract her, as did Lady Melbourne, who sent frequent letters from London.

> I read most of your letter to the Dss [Bess informed Lady Melbourne on January 8], I thought it a favourable moment, and that it would sink deep and do good; she has been very low upon the whole, nor can I wonder at it, and it is the knowledge of what she suffers and has suffer'd that made me give way on some things in London, perhaps foolishly, but it was not where *he* was concerned, only in what alone can never change for her. He is a brute, a beast and I have no patience with him—there is a want of feeling and consideration for her that makes me quite mad with him. I think she does all she can to arm herself against the present and the future, but it is a difficult task and requires time to succeed in. I wish I could blot four years out from my memory—we shall not probably return till April, and then I hope she will have acquired strength enough to mind him less—I promise you on my part to be as prudent for her and little weak as possible.[36]

Georgiana waited until she was calmer before replying to Lady Melbourne. "You are wrong in your fears," she insisted. "I had one kind letter from him

---

* Leveson Gower's mother, Lady Stafford, was horrified by the thought of her son's becoming Harriet's lover. She warned him to be wary of "that Sort of Woman. . . . once she gets possession of a Young Man's mind, he thinks what she feels and is what she wishes him to believe her to be. All the flattery which she administers with Art appears to him her genuine, undisguised Thoughts . . . on the Person, on whom she fixes her Claws . . ." Lady Granville, ed., *Correspondence of Lord Granville Leveson Gower* (London 1916), I, pp. 82–83, Lady Stafford to LGLG, February 16, 1794.

and that is all and I have wrote to him twice such letters as the universe might see, and I think our correspondence is likely to end there."[37] They were brave words, although Lady Melbourne did not believe them, and nor, probably, did Georgiana herself.

Grey's marriage increased Georgiana's sense of isolation. She had devoted the past seventeen years of her life to the Whig party; its ideology had become a religion for her, its leaders she had obeyed and venerated. The disintegration of the party, followed by Fox's retreat to St. Anne's Hill, and now Grey's rejection, robbed Georgiana of her all-important role of political confidante. Without these props she had no means of expressing her own suppressed political ambition. Yet she could not imagine a life where she was not in a position to influence a powerful man. In desperation she turned all her attention to George.

> My only comfort is my brother [she wrote to Lady Spencer in April 1795]. Thinking so ill of the war as I do and being disgusted with politics and lamenting the ruin and downfall of that glorious phalanx ... of probity and property which so long had stood between the people and the crown *The Rockinghams*; ... for I see him amidst the wreck sacrificing everything to the prosperity of our only stay and Hope, our Navy—and I see his evident endeavours crown'd with merited success.[38]

Georgiana began to send him unsolicited advice and information. She could not help herself; her need to be involved—to do something important—was sometimes overwhelming, especially when she was unhappy. Writing from Teignmouth in February 1795, she described to him the condition of the fleet in nearby Torbay.

> I went to Torbay to see the fleet yesterday, and on board the Queen Charlotte—it was the finest sight and finest fleet I ever saw;—but they seem to think it very difficult for the W[est] I[ndian] fleet to get out of Portsmouth—as there are such numbers and it is so difficult in [the] harbour.—I had just got a letter from Pelham with the plan for the increase of men; and I told it to Ld Howe; he made an observation which I will mention to you—he said the only objection to the men raised in Parishes, is what happened [in] the last war: their send[ing] to the service of the navy, their poachers and troublesome people whom they want to get rid of—and that these men were both

useless and dangerous on board. . . . Bless you Dr Br., how provoking that the winds were against us; I think we should have caught
their fleet; Don't teaze yourself to write to me.

Georgiana justified the breaching of her promise never to take part in anything political by saying that she was only passing on information, which
did not count. "Sometimes, people may say to me what they would not
venture to you and a hint may be of use."[39]

She stayed in the country as much as she could for the rest of 1795, oc-
cupying herself with her mineral collection and writing to George whenever she had information she thought might be useful. The Duchess of
Gordon had taken Georgiana's place as the leading political hostess in society, although the press still made fun of her attempts to set the fashion.[40]
Georgiana lived much more quietly than in previous years, which lost her
none of her old friends and earned her many more. "She dined with me
yesterday and we sat talking all the evening," wrote Lady Stafford; "had a
most [illeg.] and interesting conversation, & talked ourselves almost out
of our senses before we concluded."[41] She was pleased to see Georgiana
"living in a pleasanter way this year than usual, with a good society, & less
of the nonsense that was formerly."[42]

Lady Spencer thought it would be no bad thing if Georgiana withdrew
a little while social and political disputes continued to divide the *ton*. The
behaviour of the Prince of Wales had once more drawn society into op-
posing camps. He was flagrantly unfaithful to his new wife, Princess Caroline of Brunswick, whom he married on April 8, 1795, and humiliated
her by parading Lady Jersey in public as his consort. He also bullied Caroline in a manner which did him no credit and elevated her in the eyes of
the public. Nor did Lady Jersey help her own cause by seizing every opportunity to insult the young princess deliberately. Harriet commented
dryly that she was the sort of woman who could not be happy "without a
rival to trouble and torment." Lady Jersey had even contrived to have herself appointed one of Caroline's Ladies of the Bedchamber. "Lady J. is in
everything, and by everybody most thoroughly disapproved. What a
prospect of wretchedness seems gathering round for every individual of
that sad group," wrote Lady Spencer. "I feel happy that you and your sister are unconnected with them all."[43]

Lady Jersey's malice towards Caroline became the chief topic of conversation, as did her greedy insistence that the Prince place all the patronage at
his disposal in her hands. "It is very odd," mused Georgiana, "that clever as

she is she should not have guessed that the extent of patronage she took would be unpopular."[44] People were amazed by her effrontery when she drove about in a carriage accompanied by servants wearing the Prince's livery. However, by January 1796 there were whispers of a revolt. "She has reigned with too much despotism to last long," was Lady Spencer's opinion. "I would wish you both to remember that she has fairly dropt you, and that there is no necessity when others drop her that you should take her up. In a good cause such a conduct is highly laudable, but surely not in a bad one."[45]

Within less than six months of her prediction Lady Jersey was the most reviled woman in England, while Caroline was loudly applauded whenever she appeared in public. The Prince's attempt to obtain a formal separation from his wife had brought universal condemnation of Lady Jersey. This was most eloquently expressed at a ball given by the Duchess of Gordon. Lady Jersey arrived, proud as usual, but was checked by the cold reception she received on entering the ballroom. No one went up to her, and whenever she approached a group of people the conversation ceased and they immediately dispersed. The lower classes showed their disapproval in a more trenchant style: a mob stoned her house, and when she visited Brighton in the summer the locals performed a skimmington* which drove her away in shame.

Lady Jersey's downfall coincided with Georgiana's brief reappearance in public. In June 1796 Fox was re-elected for Westminster and his supporters carried him to Devonshire House. It was the last time the Whigs enjoyed anything that resembled a celebration. The Duke was not present to congratulate Fox on his victory, fearing that it would imply that he supported Fox's advocacy of peace. Instead, at the last minute he asked Georgiana to organize the reception herself. She did as requested but felt wretched throughout, haunted by the memory of happier occasions, and embarrassed lest the Lady Mary Cokes of the world should accuse her of putting herself forward without the Duke's consent. She managed the event with considerable style in spite of her reservations. Later she felt ashamed at having enjoyed herself so much and wrote a somewhat incoherent letter to George, insisting that she had not broken her promise to remain out of politics.

---

* Two figures dressed as the Prince and Lady Jersey were paraded through the town on a donkey.

I certainly should not have refused myself to an act of friendship to Mr Fox, [but] I certainly feel that I ought to avoid taking any part that was separate and not under the particular guidance of the Duke of Devonshire. . . . for tho' you forgive me I know if some of my opinions are not the same as yours (well knowing how ardently my wishes tend to your success and wishes), yet I could not bear that you should think I had been coming forward in a manner very unbecoming any woman—I therefore repeat it Dr Br. this was arrang'd without my knowledge. The little alone that took place was very disagreeable but had not any bad consequence.[46]

The victory celebration was the last time anyone saw Georgiana for over a year.

CHAPTER 18

INTERLUDE

1796

"Dear Georgiana," Lady Spencer had written on January 2, 1796, "your headaches so often proceed from Vexation, and your saying you are low about yourself dwells sadly upon my mind."[1] For the past few years Georgiana had often complained about an ache in her eyes during and immediately after one of her migraines. In July she went to bed with a headache, but the pain did not abate, and after a few days her right eyeball had swelled to the size of an apricot.[2] Dr. Warren examined her and summoned three of the best eye surgeons in the country, including John Gunning, who was Senior Surgeon-Extraordinary to the King. The children were dispatched to Chiswick so that they would not hear their mother's screams. Harriet and Lady Spencer joined Bess's vigil by Georgiana's bedside, her troubles once again uniting them.

Georgiana's illness and the experiments performed on her in the name of medicine were appalling even by eighteenth-century standards. There was no anaesthetic except laudanum, no appreciation of cleanliness or even a basic understanding of the origins of infections. One of the doctors almost strangled her when he tried to force the blood up to her head in the belief that the eye needed to be "flushed" through. Harriet told her lover, "After hearing what I did tonight I can bear anything."[3] On August 4 Lady Spencer forced herself to describe Georgiana's appearance to Selina Trimmer.

The inflammation has been so great that the eye, the eyelids and the adjacent parts were swelled to the size of your hand doubled, and projecting forward from the face. Every attempt was made to lower this inflammation so as to prevent any ulceration, but this has been in vain. A small ulcer has formed on the top of the cornea and has burst, and as far as that reaches the injury is not to be recovered. If the inflammation should increase, the ulcer form again, and again burst, it would destroy the whole substance of the eye, which would then sink. . . . The eyelids are still much swelled and scarred with the leeches, and the little opening between them is always filled with a thick white matter. The eye itself, to those who see it (for I cannot) is still more horrible.[4]

They darkened her room after the operations so that she would not know how badly her sight had been damaged. The Cavendishes came to see her and tried not to pull faces at the ugly lump protruding from her eye. Georgiana's sister-in-law Lady George enraged Harriet by her customary insensitivity: she "is jabbering to my Sister, and putting me in a fever by saying things to her which I see make her nervous, and by peeping under her green shade to try to see her eye, which is of all things what my Sister dreads the most. She is talking to her now of the breaking of her eye, which she has never yet been told of, and now is wondering that the other eye is not affected, and fears it will. I must stop her."[5] Bess tried to explain Georgiana's illness to the children in a way that would not frighten but would prepare them; their mother was "in a very low and nervous state from the long pain and the quantity of opium which she has taken," she wrote. "The complaint I believe was entirely owing to sudden cold, caught by her opening her windows as she got up late one day in a perspiration from her last headache, the eye was bad the next day, and has certainly been in some danger but is now nearly its proper size again and the inflam'd look very much diminished indeed."[6]

News of the calamity at Devonshire House spread very quickly. Most newspapers reported her illness but with little of the speculation which would have accompanied such news in previous years. Now that Georgiana was no longer the object of envy, people could sympathize sincerely. The Spencer sisters were viewed as tragic and even, in some circles, as noble examples of sibling devotion; pundits remembered how Georgiana had cared for Harriet during her long illness. Such behaviour in an ordinary family would hardly have been commented on, but the members of the *ton* seemed so inhuman at times, so devoid of normal feelings, that the sisters appeared all the more remarkable. Their friends worried what effect Georgiana's illness would have on Harriet's fragile health. She was known to be badly affected. "Her care of herself is so little, and her attachment to her sister is so great," wrote Lord Morpeth to Granville Leveson Gower, who was fretting that she would have another relapse.

Fortunately, Georgiana's health, although not her sight, began to recover quickly. Four weeks after the attack any light or motion still brought on spasms of pain. The right eye could only detect shapes, and the left had also suffered some damage during the treatment and as a consequence her sight was slightly blurred. Yet she remained so hopeful of a full recovery that when Dr. Warren announced that the shades around the lights at Devonshire House could be removed since there was nothing more he could do, they remained in place so that Georgiana would think that she was still under treatment. "There is little hope of her eye recovering properly, she however is always in hopes and tis best it should be so," wrote a friend sadly.[7] The other unmentionable subject was her looks. Georgiana could not see herself properly for the first two months, and that too was a blessing. The children were brought to her in September and warned specifically not to stare or show any fear at her face. She was pathetically glad when they came, and their unrestrained tears enabled her to cry with them without shame.

Lady Spencer was proud of Georgiana's courage. Not once had she indulged in hysterics or acted the part of a spoilt invalid. Her harsh experiences during Eliza's birth had taught her a greater fortitude than either she or anyone else had imagined. It supported her now during the worst moments of her life and afterwards, for the infection did not disappear for several months and each time the doctors returned they subjected her to hours of torture.

When Georgiana finally emerged from her sickroom, everyone immediately noticed the changes to her personality: there was no laughter or lightness in her, she had also lost too much weight and looked much older than her thirty-nine years. The bottom half of her face was unscarred but her right eye now drooped. She tried to show interest in those around her, but the illness had made her introverted. She would pick up on innocuous comments and dwell on them for hours afterwards in a way which alarmed her mother. There was no reason why Georgiana could not leave the house, make little visits and receive callers, but she was too shy. Her friends gently tried to help her retrieve some semblance of her old routine, but without success. Lady Melbourne invited Georgiana to spend a few weeks at Brocket Hall in comfort and seclusion. At the last minute she decided not to go. She explained to Little Georgiana that it was partly due to her eye aching but also "I had another reason, I saw Mr Beauclerk who returned from thence today and told me that Ly E. Bentinck and many ladys were expected so that my courage was not sufficient for the enterprise."[8] This was exactly, Lady Spencer told Selina, what she feared would happen:

> All my consolation, from the very moment I had got over the shock of seeing her poor eye, has been the benefit I have hoped she may derive from it, and for some weeks her sentiments seemed so exactly what I wished that my confidence was very great that this would be one of the happiest epochs of her life, but before I left Chiswick I feared that the fatal enemy to her peace—the world—was gaining ground imperceptibly and that a barren mortification was all she would reap. . . . [9]

While Georgiana retreated into darkness, Bess was enjoying an excess of good fortune. Mr. Foster died unexpectedly in November, so her sons Augustus and Frederick could at last come over from Ireland; her widow's jointure would make her financially independent and, most important of all, she was now free to marry again. As if on cue, the Duchess of Richmond died. Although she had never reproached her husband for resuming his affair with Bess two years ago, she had nevertheless remained an obstacle. "The Dss of Richmond has at last slipt off merely out of attention to Ly E.F.," Lady Sutherland commented sarcastically. "It is odd that Mr Foster and she should have calculated so nearly."[10]

Georgiana generously invited the Foster boys to stay, adding that although she was "half-blind" she was still anxious to meet them. "I do not know if you remember me, but I assure you that I never have forgot you since Bath," she wrote in a shaky hand.[11] They arrived on December 17, the four resident children safely out of the way so that the reunited family could have its first moments in privacy. "Bess is ill with happiness," Georgiana told her mother. "I never saw a more touching sight. They clung to poor Bess, who cried terribly. Mr Foster [Frederick] is plain but a very interesting and sensible young man. Augustus a very fine boy of 16."[12] Little Georgiana and Harryo, thirteen and eleven respectively, did not share their mother's satisfaction and rather resented the intrusion of two shy and gauche Irishmen in their midst. No one would explain why the Fosters did not have their *own* home.

No doubt Georgiana's motives in offering to provide the Fosters with a home were prompted by genuine feeling. But the action also contained a message to Bess, a plea that she should not reject her surrogate, Cavendish, family. The possibility that Bess and the Duke of Richmond would be conveniently widowed at the same time had never occurred to Georgiana. Until this untoward event Bess's relationship with the Duke of Richmond had posed no threat to the stability of the *ménage à trois*. It is impossible to know whether the Duke of Devonshire minded about the Duke of Richmond. His thoughts do not survive and one can only surmise that his dislike of change would make him hostile to the idea of Bess marrying. Georgiana could not accept such a possibility: she wrote Bess a letter, in the form of a poem, which asked her to stay:

> I regret not the freedom of will,
> Or sigh, as uncertain I tread;
> I am freer and happier still,
> When by thee I am carefully led.
>
> Ere my Sight I was doomed to resign,
> My heart I surrendered to thee;
> Not a thought or an Action was mine,
> But I saw as thou badst me to see.
>
> Thy watchful affection I wait,
> And hang with Delight on Thy voice;
> And Dependance is softened by fate,
> Since Dependance on Thee is my choice.[13]

Bess promised to do nothing in the short term. She was not sacrificing anything by agreeing to Georgiana's request; the lovers fully intended to observe twelve months' mourning for their respective spouses to avoid accusations of over-haste. Georgiana was reassured, although if she had seen Bess's behaviour at Bath in April 1797 it would have been all too clear that her friend was determined to make a new life for herself. As one of the ladies at Bath observed, "Lady Eliz. Foster is here all in a *tender wee waw high ho!* sort of mood with coquettish weeds and demi caractère grief, agreeable and pleasant enough I think when she forgets to Devonsherise her mouth."[14] Bess was happy in the certainty that when she became the Duchess of Richmond she would at last have the life she craved. Her jealousy of Georgiana's wealth and influence need never trouble her again; indeed she would atone for it by being generous towards her friend: inviting Georgiana to political soirées, bringing Georgiana to the opera as her companion—in short, in the nicest possible way achieving her secret wish to outrival her dearest and best friend.

CHAPTER 19

ISOLATION

1796—1799

The daughter of the Duchess of Devonshire, a sweet bud of loveliness, is to be intro-
duced to the circle of fashion in the course of next winter. Devonshire House has of late
undergone considerable improvements, and will, ere long, be ready for the reception of
its noble owners.

Morning Herald, *June 28, 1799*

My sister continues mending," Harriet wrote in December 1796 to
her lover, Leveson Gower. "But it was thought necessary to perform a most painful operation on her, applying causticks behind her ears
and a blister to the back of her neck for four hours. I never saw anything
like the agony she suffer'd, & the exertion I made to hold & soothe her
brought my old complaint of spasms with great violence."[1] Georgiana's
recovery was hindered by the exceptional cold of the winter. The whole
country was suffering: animals froze to death on the hills, people went
hungry (although they weren't starving like the peasants in France), and
the mortality rate among the young and the old rose sharply. The Duke's
uncle, Lord John Cavendish, succumbed at the age of sixty-four, dying
just two weeks after Georgiana's operation. "Your papa was very much affected," she told Little G.[2] Lord John had been a surrogate father and mentor to him. He was also the last Cavendish to have held office during the
Duke's lifetime.

The thought that he had failed his uncle by not becoming a statesman in the Cavendish mould may have been uppermost in the Duke's mind when he returned from Lord John's funeral. He arrived at Chatsworth in an emotional state and went immediately to Georgiana, who comforted him while he cried. She had seen him cry only three times before: once when his brother Richard died in 1781, and twice thirteen years later, in 1794, over the successive deaths of his sister Dorothy and uncle Lord George. Georgiana could sense that on this occasion the Duke was upset by more than just the loss of Lord John. The past few months had been deeply unsettling for him. At one point he had feared that he would lose his wife to illness and his mistress to a rival. He was shaken by the experience and yearned for a more stable life. Now that Georgiana was thought to be out of danger he wanted them to live as husband and wife. On February 3, 1797, less than six weeks after Lord John's death, Georgiana informed her mother that she had received a visit from Dr. Croft. "It has been Croft's opinion lately that I miscarry'd," she wrote. "I was not much past therefore tis not possible to judge but it appear'd so."[3]

Bess was in Bath when Georgiana suffered her miscarriage. She was there ostensibly to visit her younger sister Louisa, although people looked out for the Duke of Richmond's carriage outside their door. Bess's stay was somewhat marred by the rumour that the city was about to be invaded by French troops. "Louisa and I feel as if we were going to be carried off," she told Georgiana.[4] She was referring to the invasion force which had landed in February at Fishguard in Wales. In fact it consisted of only 2,000 men who were easily captured, but it was the French government's second attempt. A few months earlier 15,000 troops had sailed to Bantry Bay in south-west Ireland, where poor weather had prevented them from landing.

The thought that luck was all that stood between Paris and London was no comfort to the British. William Pitt and his inner war cabinet tried to maintain the appearance of calm although in private they were frantic. Spain had switched sides in 1796 and joined France, leaving Britain without a single ally. Napoleon Bonaparte was now Commander-in-Chief and had led the French army to victory against Austria. Georgiana's brother dreaded to think how they would defend the country if Napoleon led his armies to England. His fear was considerably heightened when in May two of the navy's largest fleets at Spithead and Nore briefly mutinied within weeks of each other over poor pay and conditions. Understandably, George was described by those who saw him during this time as "very nervous."

Georgiana explained to Little G that "your dear Uncle Spencer's honour and happyness is at stake—any bad success would fall (tho' undeserving) on him."*[5]

The invasion scare started a run on the banks, which Pitt was only able to contain by allowing the Bank of England to suspend cash payments until the situation was restored. The people who suffered most were ordinary debtors who found themselves inundated with calls they could not oblige. Georgiana and Harriet were both caught out by the panic, and Harriet frightened Georgiana by exhibiting the same kind of hysteria that had preceded her collapse in 1791. Since then Georgiana had assumed responsibility for both their debts. "At that time," she explained to a cousin, "I put myself at the head of her affaires, as indeed I ought its having been my example and folly that had drawn her in."[6]

When Coutts brought up the subject with Harriet instead of with Georgiana, she "was thrown into violent hystericks and past the day very ill indeed."[7] Georgiana penned him a letter in frail and shaky writing, begging him never to do it again: "tho' she feels and knows she has vast unpaid debts, I have from the time of her illness kept off all agitation, all talk of money by desiring everybody to address themselves to me. . . . All I entreat, Dr. Sir, in the future, is that you wd apply to me, but oh, for God's sake never, never to her. . . . the calamity of my nearly losing my eye, and, if I recover sight, being in part disfigur'd, has not render'd her state of health more prosperous or her affairs in better plight." She added simply: "Were I to abandon her because I have not my former health, I should betray that adoration I have ever felt for her."[8]

The burden of carrying Harriet's debts as well as her own forced Georgiana to go to the Duke. "The expectation of having these discussions made me such a coward about applying to D. of D. but it was necessary and will do good," she told Lady Spencer.[9] In May she wrote over-optimistically that he seemed inclined to help and "my difficulties [are] settled."[10] She was not telling the truth since the Duke did not know the full extent of the difficulties. He also put off paying the debts which she had disclosed. Georgiana was loath to press him when he was disturbed by other worries: Ireland appeared to be on the brink of civil war and, like many of the Whig

* Naval chiefs pulled themselves together after this, and the following year was full of notable victories. By Christmas 1797 the enemy fleets were locked in their ports in Cherbourg, Brest, Cádiz, and Toulon.

grandees, the Duke still derived considerable income from his Irish estates. His land holdings and family connections within the Protestant ascendancy gave the Cavendishes almost as much influence in Irish politics as they had in English. Georgiana told Little G, "the accounts from Ireland are so various that your Papa does not like my leaving him in this anxious moment. . . . if any misfortune should happen in Ireland we should be very much reduc'd in our circumstances."[11]

Georgiana had become reclusive since her illness, but the events taking place in Ireland revived some of her former energy. She was convinced that a policy of cross-party co-operation over Ireland would be in the island's best interests. The Duke agreed to her request to vote in support of George in the Lords. But her brother took a different view and berated Georgiana for interfering.

She lapsed into silence for a while until rumours that there was an anti-Spencer cabal forming in government prompted her to resume writing to him. She sent a letter with their names attached: "I do give you my word of honour that what I said is true for I have heard it from ministerial people," she wrote, "that there is amongst the supporters of Govt a strong party crying up Ld Hood and abusing you when they dare."[12]

It was ironic that Fox should choose to resign from active politics just as Georgiana was beginning to emerge from her own retirement. He kept his seat in Parliament, but he decided that attending was a depressing and futile effort. He retreated to his house at St. Anne's Hill. Some party members—mostly his close friends—applauded his action; however, the majority resented him for leaving them in the lurch. Even Georgiana's small dinners for three or four of her friends often ended in acrimonious arguments. Sheridan still went to Devonshire House, accompanied by his new wife, Hecca, a pert, talkative girl half his age, but he invariably provoked violent quarrels with the other guests. He was torn between wishing to show himself a good Foxite and taking advantage of Fox's absence in Parliament. Yet he was outraged when he learned that Fox was grooming Grey (who briefly seceded with Fox and then changed his mind) to be his eventual successor.

Georgiana judged Fox's decision less harshly than the others. She believed that the majority of the House secretly sympathized with Fox's assertion that Pitt was a dangerous Prime Minister who held no respect for civil liberty. The House supported Pitt, Georgiana theorized, because "they respect him, as often a wife does her husband; think him a very disagreeable fellow, but a good manager of their views and happiness; and now, though they think he has been going and going on too far, yet they still cling to their spouse, lest the separation or divorce should bring on immediate ruin."[13] However, Georgiana's loyalty to Fox clouded her judgement. The House had no sympathy for Fox and regarded him as a demagogue with suspect views. His secession from Parliament was a tactical error in a career stunted by poor judgement and self-indulgence. With most of the Foxites out of the way, the debating talent in Parliament was now all on Pitt's side.

Georgiana tried not to let Fox's retirement distract her from her own project of reentering the political realm. She continued to write to George about Irish affairs. Her commitment, as well as the quality of her comments, finally earned her a grudging respect from him. As pockets of unrest spread to other parts of Ireland she often sent George the private reports of their local agent in the hope that the relatively impartial information might be useful for cabinet discussions. The government's policy of repression struck her as counter-productive, and she argued that legal and civil discrimination against Irish Catholics would only make rebellion inevitable.[14] However, Georgiana was always careful to couch her disagreements with George in a respectful tone: "Alas connected as I am with all sides it must be my hope that things yet may not come to the horrors of civil war. I hate some of your colleagues, but I am really quite come over to Mr Pitt, because I believe he is sincerely attach'd to you," she wrote, "and knows and values you as you deserve. But I think both you and him too often cede your opinion to that of others. God bless you. I never knew till now how much I love you."[15]

"I believe the Government is coming over to the opinion of Duke of D. and indeed all reasonable people, about granting emancipation to the Catholics," Georgiana triumphantly told her mother, meaning that George had proved receptive to her arguments. Government policy, however, did not change. The King and his ministers would never espouse what was in any case a Whig position.

The Duke was moved by her interest in Ireland even though he disliked anything which distracted her attention away from him. He was in continual pain from his gout and he expected Georgiana to act as his nurse. She was kind towards him and they were more receptive to each other now than at any time past. His habitual reserve with her gradually faded and, after two decades of marriage, they managed to forgive and accept one another. Bess rarely accompanied them to Chatsworth any more. She preferred to remain at Devonshire House, holding soirées of her own which she would describe in chatty letters to Georgiana. In December 1797 Lady Spencer went to stay with Georgiana and the Duke at Hardwick. The scenes she had witnessed made her hope that Bess's marriage would take place soon. She attributed the happy family atmosphere to Bess's absence:

> The Dss said a few nights ago that Lady E's time at Goodwood [with the Duke of Richmond] was nearly over and she did not know whether she would come here or go to Chiswick—it will not be a matter of indifference to me, for our present party is so pleasant and one that I shall be sorry to have any change—I have not for many years seen the D and Dss seem so happy in each other—she looks extremely well and he seems delighted with her civility to the neighbouring families who occasionally come, he listens often with attention to her conversation with other people, and I often see a cheerful whisper between them which is very pleasant and in her last headache he was in and out of his room perpetually to know how she did—all this and the acquaintance he is making with his children induced me to wish to prolong our stay as long as we can go on as we now are.[16]

Georgiana's life had indeed changed. It proceeded at a slower and more gentle rhythm. Before, she had lived in a "perpetual hurry," always surrounded by people. When the remnants of the Devonshire House Circle visited her now they often found her engaged in writing a poem, or designing a new flower bed. She had the opportunity to indulge her considerable creative talents, and with the Duke's acquiescence she amused herself by refurbishing their houses. Chiswick House received the most attention with an ambitious plan to repair it using Lord Burlington's original drawings. Built in 1729 to resemble Palladio's Villa Rotonda, it was much smaller than Devonshire House, yet infinitely more elegant in design. Lord Burlington had always intended the villa to be his country retreat and had overseen every detail. Georgiana spent some of her happiest moments at Chiswick, calling it "My earthly paradise." She planted lilac, honeysuckle, and climbing roses along the walls by her window so that her bedroom would be filled with scent through the spring and summer.

When Harriet was in London or Roehampton, it was not unusual for Georgiana to spend many hours on her own at this time. The experience, though sometimes painful, helped her to gain insight and strength. She became less afraid to be direct with people; no longer was she frightened of disagreeing or of saying the word "no." With Selina, for example, she was able to talk frankly about the tensions between them:

> Surely you must know the infirmity of my nature, that with a heart not bad (I humbly trust) I have an instability of nature that is some-times madness. The only alleviation of this to my friends is that it is only to those I love I have ever shown these odious destructive paroxysms. A thousand little fancys, little suspicions and jealousys had long, perhaps, been brooding in my mind. A spark, I know not what, brought it out. Dearest Selina, if I hurt you or offended you I ask your pardon from the bottom of my heart. . . . Never, never in the future shall you have the least cause of complaint . . . and do not refuse me an entire oblivion for the past. . . . indeed, Dr. Selina, I never knew before how much I lov'd you. . . . I am sure you cannot misunderstand the sincere and grateful affection that dictates this, and the tears that run down my cheeks whilst I write would prove it to you.[17]

Georgiana also invited Charles Grey and his wife to Devonshire House. Incredibly, Mary had no knowledge of the love affair or Eliza. She had no notion why Georgiana should make such an effort to know her, but the friendship which developed was genuine on Mary's part. Georgiana's motives were obviously mixed in the beginning, and were almost cer-tainly driven by a desire to be close to Grey. Nevertheless her letters to Mary breathe unfeigned warmth: "Dear Mary, my heart is still young in enthusiastick love of my friends and my children," she wrote in 1798. "And amongst them I do indeed love and value you and feel interested in your happiness beyond expression." In some way, Mary's affection com-pensated Georgiana for the loss of Grey's. Their first child, Louisa, also became the recipient of Georgiana's particular regard: "Your little Loo, too, I consider as *mes petites entrailles** and feel like her grandmother," she wrote with a far deeper, and poignant, meaning than the words con-

---

* My own flesh and blood.

veyed.[18] It was not lost on Grey. In time the relationship between the two women enabled Georgiana and Grey to achieve their own private rapprochement.

In the same year, some twenty months after her illness, Georgiana acknowledged that the partial loss of her eyesight had brought her a kind of peace. It had forced her to learn to be honest with herself. There was, therefore, something symbolic in Georgiana's choice of Mary Grey as the person to whom she described her new life. Mary represented the future for Grey, while Georgiana knew that she represented his past.

> My eye goes on well [she wrote] tho' I know I shall be blind: but I have learnt a degree of philosophy and think you would all take care of me. It really is so much my idea at times that I see all the pretty places I can and examine all the flowers and prospects to store my mind with images if I lose my sight. Music would be my greatest resource and I play more than I us'd, but dependence I fear would be my chief evil. But alas Dr. Mary, I was 40 years old last June and at that age one must use oneself to personal disasters. I have learnt however to love my age, and not be ashamed of it and my illness perhaps was a benefit in making me relinquish at once the ridiculous trade of an *old beauty*.[19]

Georgiana's period of reflection was cut short in May 1798 by the long-anticipated uprising in Ireland. She blamed the government for "not consulting enough with the great Irish Lords," meaning the Whigs.[20] Two immediate issues concerned her: first, the fate of the Cavendish estates, and second, the prospect of the rebellion becoming a religious war. She was fervently opposed to the use of executions and terror to cow the Catholic population. "I think the mode of torturing to extract confession so disgraceful and horrid that were it sure of saving Ireland I should deprecate it," she wrote.[21] It was her opinion, which ran contrary to the majority, that the absentee Whig landlords should show that they

> feel for the people of Ireland whilst they disapprove of the Rebels. In the indiscriminate manner in which our troops have burnt villages, etc., how many innocent must perish—and tho' it is very well for those who have no lands in Ireland to talk big and say that extermination is the only means. We who receive the produce of the labour

of the Irish and whose tenants still call the D. of D. their father must feel that this mode of conquest is but a bad [decision] . . . the rebels are a bloody, cruel set, but that is no example for us and if it is possible to keep some right by mercy and coaxing how far better."[*22]

Lord Camden, the Lord Lieutenant of Ireland, resigned in June, and Lord Cornwallis, who was both a diplomat and an experienced general, was dispatched with the greatest urgency to take his place. Georgiana decided that this was the moment for the Duke to make a statement in the House of Lords. The absentee landlords, Georgiana reasoned, were the people most affected by the uprising; it was up to them to reassure their tenants in Ireland and to make it clear to the government that repression was neither desirable nor practical. The Duke was reluctant to speak but after much prodding by Georgiana and the other Whig magnates he agreed to speak in support of the Duke of Leinster's motion for an inquiry into the state of Ireland. His speech was short, lasting for less than half an hour, perhaps on account of his being "sadly nervous and frightened," and simply reiterated the Whig view that the government should be conciliatory but firm. Georgiana, however, regarded the occasion as one of the greatest triumphs of her life. "It was a proud evening for me," she told her mother. "I heard from a supporter of [the] ministry that [the speech] was manly, calm, elegant and impartial. My brother answered the motion but there was no warmth, it was truly the great Council of the Nation debating on the best ways of doing good."[23]

Cornwallis stopped the rebellion without resorting to the destruction and bloodshed that Georgiana and the Duke had feared. A small French contingent landed in County Mayo in support of the rebels on August 22, but they were too late to offer any useful assistance to the rebels. The danger was over. For Georgiana, the crisis in Ireland had been a lesson in political independence; instead of taking her cue from Fox, who refused to get involved, she had acted on her own initiative.[24] She had argued

---

* There were indeed unspeakable cruelties inflicted by both sides. The Protestant yeomanry, recruited by the Lord Lieutenant of Ireland Lord Camden to assist the overstretched British troops, used the opportunity to terrorize Catholic neighbours. Innocent people were arrested and tortured on the slightest suspicion. A school teacher, for example, was interrogated and flogged because he knew French. However, the rebels were not far behind in vindictiveness, and in one infamous incident massacred their Protestant captives after being repulsed from New Ross.

with George, sent him information and advice, and diligently pursued her own line. It was ironic that the demise of the Whig party had, in part, solved her dilemma about showing a masculine interest in politics. Georgiana called the Irish debate in the Lords "the great Council of the Nation" to show that she considered the Irish question to be above politics. Party politics, she could rationalize to herself, was the consequence of private ambition, but *national* politics was an expression of individual patriotism. She was not guilty of female impropriety, in her view, so long as the beneficiary was the country. Not even George could take issue with such pious sentiments.[25]

Ireland still occupied Georgiana's thoughts in September. "I am sorry to say that the people in this neighbourhood are determined to join the French when they arrive," confided General Frederick St. John, who was stationed near their estates. "If they come *in force* the country is gone."[26] The only comfort in his report was that the Cavendish name was still popular because of the charity distributed by their agent at Lismore. A month later, however, the threat of an imminent French invasion was removed by news of Nelson's dramatic victory at the Battle of the Nile. This was the first major British success in six years. Britain now controlled the Mediterranean while Bonaparte's army remained stranded in Egypt. "We intend all of us to wear laurels on our heads at the public day," Georgiana wrote on October 8. "I wish to God Buonaparte would do the only thing I think he can do now, surrender himself and his troops to so great and generous a foe [Nelson]."[27]

Further trouble concerning Ireland prevented Georgiana from withdrawing into herself as she had done the previous winter. She still had bouts of depression, however, and so disliked the idea of people looking at her that she contemplated wearing a mask. "I am sorry to say that I grow more shy ev'ry day and hate going anywhere except to my own boxes at the play and opera," she told Lady Spencer. "I have not seen Ly Sutherland these 3 months, and ev'ry day makes me worse, I think. I shall be oblig'd to take *le saut perileux* for Georgiana when she comes out but till then it is not worth teazing myself with visits and going to assemblys . . ."[28]

Georgiana was perhaps overly sensitive about her appearance. A visitor to Chatsworth in November 1798 thought that reports had been exaggerated: "the dss looks amazingly handsome when she is dressed, notwithstanding her eye which is I fear quite gone—it disfigures her less than one could have conceived possible but there it is, a sad thing."*[29] Horace Walpole gave his opinion that she looked "much altered." But Georgiana was by no means ugly: indeed she was not so unattractive as to prevent Sir Philip Francis from falling in love with her.

The sixty-year-old Whig politician paid a visit to Chatsworth in the autumn. Francis was almost certainly the author of the notorious "Junius" letters, a series of anonymous letters published in the early 1770s by the *Public Advertiser* which had ferociously attacked George III's ministers. Afterwards, he moved to India and returned with a fortune in 1780. He had sudden and strong passions, such as the one which seized him for Georgiana now. He told his wife that he was bored with his stay: "As for Silence, the Abbaye de la Trappe is a mere Babel to this house. . . . the Dutchess tried to bring conversation into fashion, but to no purpose; and even poor Lady Elizabeth is not allowed to talk."[30] The letters Francis wrote to Georgiana after he left suggest a different story. "You talk of the shortness of our acquaintance, why, then," he urged, "if all this be not mere moonshine, and if we are really and seriously to be friends, we have no time to lose."[31]

He had not expected to fall in love again at his age, and the experience awoke unaccustomed feelings in him. His letters alternated between elation and jealousy. Francis was not ashamed to confess that he had always admired Georgiana from afar: "The fact, however, is that *I* have known *you* many years, and long before the date of our acquaintance. It is true I saw you at a great distance, and as a bird of passage. The planet passed by, and knew nothing of, the poor astronomer who watched her motions and waited for transit. Hereafter, I hope, you will not insist on my seeing you through a telescope." Georgiana's admiration for Charles Fox tormented him. "Not at all, however, in the sense of being in love with him," he hastily added. But the fear that "while you were writing to *me,* you thought of nobody but C.F." kept him distracted: "I feel liked gummed velvet, and wish I could hate you for half an hour, that I might cut you into a thousand little stars, and live under the canopy."[32]

---

* The ambitious Lady Holland wrote a startlingly opposite description of Georgiana. She resented her, and the power of Devonshire House, as the chief obstacles to the establishment of Holland House as the primary residence of the Whig party. Her view of Georgiana perhaps ought to be understood in the spirit in which it was uttered. "Her figure is corpulent," she wrote spitefully in April 1799, "her complexion coarse, one eye gone, and her neck immense. How frail is the tenure of beauty." Earl of Ilchester, *Journal of Elizabeth, Lady Holland* (London 1908), p. 244.

Georgiana was at first more frightened by her own feelings than by the strength of his. "I am ashamed of sending this letter, so incorrect, and so mad as I fear it is," she wrote. "But I am really extremely ill indeed. I will write again when I am better; but pray write to the one who knows so well the pleasure of receiving your letters. . . . Tell me that you are not angry, and that I may write on as I think."[33] Gradually she felt more secure in expressing whatever thoughts came into her head. Francis was delighted and flattered that she was prepared to take him into her confidence. An obsessive politician himself, he enjoyed nothing more than a dispute with Georgiana over the future of Whig politics. He resented Fox's secession from Parliament and felt that he had sacrificed the careers of his followers to feed his own vanity. "Why, what, in the name of your own idol, would you have him do?" Francis demanded to know regarding a mutual acquaintance. "Would you have him hang himself because C.F. chooses to live at St. Ann's [*sic*] Hill?"[34]

There is no record of how or when the correspondence ended; someone destroyed the rest of their letters. Evidence suggests that their relationship cooled after a while, although its effects were beneficial and long-lasting. Her confidence had returned and she began to venture out again in public. Little G was now seventeen, only a few months away from her presentation at court, and society mothers were extremely anxious to invite the Duchess of Devonshire and her daughter to their parties. Georgiana cautiously accepted a few invitations and was touched by the kindness she encountered. "I am overpower'd by the court all these great ladies pay me," she wrote, half pleased and half in jest. "Lady Chatham, Ly Hardwick, Ly Leicester, Mrs Bowles, Ly Auckland, all trying to engage me to take the children to them." But, she added, "I never dare engage anything without being sure of my company."[35]

Georgiana's relationship with all three children had improved considerably during the past two years. Hart had started at Harrow (Clifford went with him), and the experience of living with other boys was making him less temperamental and more outgoing. Harryo was, in Georgiana's opinion, turning into "a very clever nice girl, but I do not guess what she will be as to person, however I should not despair—I remember how many people us'd to run down my poor G—and now the same people are puffing her too much. She is a very pleasing sweet girl but no regular beauty, but she is natural and interesting and is uncommonly clever."[36] Georgiana was closest to Little G. "[You are] my dear and chosen little friend," she told her, "for such you would have been to me had I not had the happyness of being your mother."[37] Despite their contrasting temperaments—Little Georgiana was still quiet and shy—they understood each other and shared many interests, particularly a love of books. Georgiana treasured Little G's company so greatly that she could never bear to say a harsh word towards her. Only once was there a serious disagreement between them, when Little G was rude to Selina. Georgiana remonstrated with her, but in the gentlest of tones:

> I write to you from the bottom of my heart and with the conviction that you look upon me as your best and most affectionate friend— my life, both you and I have obligations of the most serious nature to Selina. When I was banish'd from you her watchful care preserv'd you to me. Her judgement I value beyond my own—and I feel how right she is in fearing the effect of dissipation for you—I have been desirous to indulge you—indeed doing so is the greatest pleasure my heart knows, but let me entreat you my dst G to prove to Selina by redoubled care and affection to all your dutys and employments that such indulgements are rather incitements to exertion in you than the cause of negligence or idleness. Besides she has given up so much of family contact to us that it is but fair to seem cheerful—pleased with being at Chiswick (which is likewise so good for you and given me such opportunities of coming to you).[38]

But there was one subject which divided Georgiana from her children, and that was Bess. None of the Cavendish children liked her even though they accepted Caroline St. Jules and Clifford. Their view of Bess was coloured by Lady Spencer's and Selina's antipathy, but their dislike needed no extra encouragement. They thought her silly and affected and, in the way of children, they could sense Bess's ambivalence towards their mother. "My mind was early opened to Lady Elizabeth's character," Harryo wrote many years later, "unparalleled I do believe for want of principle and delicacy, and more perverted than deceitful, for I really believe she hardly herself knows the difference between right and wrong now. Circumstances have altered her conduct and situation at different times but she has invariably been what even [as] a child I understood and despised."[39] Both Harriet's and Georgiana's children enjoyed tormenting Bess, although Caroline St. Jules never joined them. Harriet's daughter Caroline Ponsonby once satirized Bess's artificial manner.

I have been studying to make myself Mad and uncommon and everything thats dear and delightful but Have not been able to attain to the perfection of giving all the House a Headache. My dearest Love, believe me that all my professions of *amitié* I made you at Chiswick are sincere as Lasting. Ah, what pleasure I enjoyed whilst the children (pronounced with a contemptuous mean) amused themselves at the Bench; what pleasure I say, we enjoyed pacing up and down the Lawn and expressing by words and actions our sincere Friendship.[40]

Georgiana could not properly explain Bess's place in the household without going into embarrassing details. But she tried to show her children that she loved Bess and trusted her implicitly. "Think of Dearest Bess," she told Little G on one occasion. "She thought I wanted some money and sent me, Dear Love, £100. I did not want it but feel equally her dear kindness."[41] The fact that the Duke of Richmond had still not proposed to Bess made Georgiana sad for her, knowing that she had staked her future on the marriage. Georgiana, Harriet, and Bess had been waiting since 1797 for him to formalize the relationship, and at various times, when an announcement seemed imminent, said their goodbyes and exchanged their fond reminiscences. During one of these false alarms Harriet wrote to Leveson Gower: "What adds I believe to my stupidity is great anxiety at this moment concerning Bess if she marries the D. of Richmond (mind there is nothing settled). It seems quite a separation from us all, and changing the habits of fifteen years standing is always a serious thing, especially at our age."[42]

The Duke of Richmond's hesitation became an embarrassment to Bess. Not only did it highlight the objections of his family, it reminded people of Bess's history. There was much conjecture at the delay: Lady Holland, whose elopement with Lord Holland gave her no right to comment on Bess's morals, thought it a wonderful joke. "His conduct by Ly E. Foster is very unaccountable," she wrote in her diary on March 26, 1799. "He is always talking and writing as if he intended to marry her, and yet the marriage is not more advanced than it was two years ago. . . . Lady E. is very hopeful for it."[43] When Bess brought up the subject of their marriage the Duke's answers were reassuring and yet equivocal, leaving her with little alternative but to wait until he made up his mind. "Burn this when you have read it," Georgiana wrote to Little G after Bess had confronted Richmond over the delay:

I found dr Bess tollerably well tho' a good deal push'd. I find from her that she is perfectly satisfied with the D of R's conduct to her. That she has had conversations with him in which he has entrusted her with circumstances that acct for everything that may appear odd to others and that she has every reason to be satisfyed with his conduct towards [her] and to feel secure of his friendship and esteem and attachment—time alone therefore can decide as to the event. . . . Upon the whole I think Bess [illeg.] and right in wishing to avoid the questions and remarks of people by keeping out of the way—it is an embarrassing situation—but it must be a satisfaction to her to have no cause of complaint against a person she has known so long.[44]

Bess's frustration with her own life was increased by her jealousy of Georgiana. There was as yet, however, no real cause for her to worry. The Duke of Richmond still showed every sign of proposing, and Georgiana still suffered from many handicaps, not least her debts. Periodically she would have a crisis—a call for repayment or trouble from an angry creditor—and she would beg her weary friends and family for further assistance. In April 1799, after another of her dramatic appeals for money, George complained to Lady Spencer that there was "always a great degree of mystery and concealment about the whole subject."[45] "She assures me there is no more owing (but alas I know not how to rely upon her)," wrote Lady Spencer.[46] Georgiana had sworn she had confessed all her debts to the Duke after her return from exile; although everyone wanted to believe her they suspected she was concealing the truth. "She is and always will be imprudent in the highest degree," Lady Spencer was forced to admit, "but I trust in God she is not intentionally dishonest."[47]

The only fragment that remains from Georgiana's personal diary illustrates the extent to which her secret debts made her suffer. Although undated, it refers to the shipwreck of her friend Thomas Grenville, who was on a diplomatic mission to Berlin. His ship, the *Proserpine,* sank in February 1799 after hitting ice. Grenville was one of the few passengers who survived. His death was presumed for over a week and the news affected Georgiana quite badly for "tho' I seldom saw him now, but a friendship of 20 years in above circumstances. I heard so kindly from him during the little interval of his voyages."[48] In the diary her grief at his supposed drowning is interposed with despair about her financial situation—someone was harassing her for money.

It begins on a Monday: "I heard of Grenville." For Tuesday she wrote, "the climax of everything disagreeable. Teazings of all kinds and my own mind almost worn out—I did what I could, but by an omission I miss'd the only favourable opportunity of improving my situation." On Wednesday she slipped off to church unaccompanied and "humbled myself in the most lowly manner and prayed devoutly for poor Grenville." Thursday: "I rode with G and just before heard the confirmation of millions of unpleasantnesses and humiliations. The horses started and I was very nervous." A few days later: "the joy of Mr Grenville's safety—great happiness all day." Then, the following week, on Monday, "a vexatious letter"; however: "happy terminations of some things and relief; but my poor child ill." Tuesday: "My child ill, but some good circumstances to other things." Wednesday: "In some things very much teazed and unhappy. But my child better." Thursday: "extremely good day." Friday: "remarkably good day. Saturday also." But on Monday, disaster: "One of the wretched days of my life. I have too much perhaps presumed on my relief, and am again plunged deep and whole series of black and ungrateful perfidy has come to my knowledge." Tuesday: "What this day will bring I know not. It begins ill enough and looks like a day of trouble but I trust and hope. New wounds of perfidy. I have not made a proper use of the short liv'd prosperity. I have not done ill but I have suffered some evil to creep over me. *Ah misera, quanto sera da me.*"[49]

As terrible as the fragment sounds, Georgiana did not live like this every day. There were often long periods of calm. She grew less reluctant to receive visitors and resumed the practice of holding select dinners for the Whigs who still attended Parliament. Charles Grey once again stopped by every evening to discuss the day's events in the Commons.[50] When Sheridan began work on a tragedy called *Pizarro,* adapted from the highly successful play by Kotzebue, *Die Spanier in Peru,* he invited Georgiana to contribute a song. The play's patriotic theme of an embattled people fighting against a barbaric opponent struck a chord with audiences. It opened on May 24, ran for an unprecedented thirty-one nights, and sold more than 30,000 copies.[51] According to Sheridan's biographer, Georgiana's song became a success in its own right.[52]

She followed up her collaboration with Sheridan by preparing one of her poems for publication. She had started *The Passage of the Mountain of St. Gothard,* which describes her homeward crossing from Italy into Switzerland, when she was still in exile. Although she wrote *The Passage* in the form of a travel poem ("I wander where Tesino madly flows,/from cliff to

cliff in foaming eddies tossed") it contained a veiled apology to her children for leaving them. "Italy, farewell!" Georgiana wrote in the first
stanza. "To thee a parent, sister I consign . . . Whilst every step conducts
me nearer home." She climbed the winding pass, "My weary footsteps
hoped for rest in vain, / Steep on steep in rude confusion rose," seeking
shelter where she could, "where some bright hours are found / Amidst the
darkest, dreariest years of care." The path took her behind waterfalls and
around hanging rocks until she reached Lucerne. Pausing only long
enough to say, "Farewell, Helvetia! from whose lofty breast Proud Alps
arise, and copious rivers flow," Georgiana continued on her journey
home. In the last stanza she spoke directly to her children:

> Hope of my life! dear children of my heart!
> That anxious heart, to each fond feeling true,
> To you still pants each pleasure to impart,
> And more—O transport!—reach its home to you.

Once Georgiana was satisfied with *The Passage* she distributed a number
of copies to her friends and family, telling them she would add her own illustrations later. Somehow a printer got hold of one of the copies and a pi-
rate edition appeared in the *Morning Chronicle,* full of mistakes and misprints
which horrified and embarrassed Georgiana. However, the poem was an
immediate success, far outselling a prose work of hers entitled *Memorandums
of the Face of the Country in Switzerland.*[*53] There is no record of the children's
reaction to the poem; only Little G, possibly, would have been old enough
to understand Georgiana's feelings when she wrote it.

* On December 24, 1799, the *Morning Post* printed a parody of *The Passage* by Samuel
Taylor Coleridge, which gently poked fun at its popularity:

> Thenceforth your soul rejoiced to see
> The shrine of social Liberty
> O beautiful! O Nature's child!
> Twas thence you hailed the platform wild,
> Where once the Austrian fell
> Beneath the Shaft of Tell!
> O! Lady nursed in pomp and pleasure
> Where learnt you this heroic measure. . . .

In 1802 the Abbé Delille translated *The Passage* into French, which proved very popular.
Italian and German translations followed, all of which earned Georgiana considerable
plaudits, but no money.

Mother and daughter had become inseparable. Georgiana wanted Little G's coming out to be a success, and she forced herself to chaperone her daughter to every party. The Devonshires held a magnificent ball and supper at Devonshire House to mark her first season. The household clattered with activity in the days before the ball: chairs were pushed back against the walls of the drawing room, the chandeliers polished, and extra glasses brought out from the store. No one turned down Georgiana's invitation. Some came out of curiosity, others out of loyalty, and a few out of nostalgia; all were surprised by the ease with which she had recaptured the atmosphere of Devonshire House parties. According to the *Morning Herald* the ball was a triumph: "On Friday evening the Duchess of Devonshire gave a brilliant Ball and supper at Devonshire House, at which all the first fashion of both sexes were present."[54]

Georgiana's re-entry into society coincided with the Prince of Wales's return to respectability after his notorious affair with Lady Jersey. Freed from Lady Jersey's influence, the Prince was anxious to be re-admitted into the Devonshire House Circle. His friendship with Georgiana resumed at the level of its former intimacy, as if there had never been a breach. The *Morning Herald* announced their reconciliation in September 1799, with a report of their joint trip to the theatre: "The Prince of Wales, Lord Moira, the Duchess of Devonshire, and her accomplished daughters, were at the Haymarket Theatre on Saturday night. On the entrance of his Royal Highness, *God Save the King,* was loudly called for and sang, amidst the reiterated plaudits of the whole audience, who seemed to feel an ecstatic pride in the presence of their Prince."[55]

Those who knew Georgiana well noticed how she had gained in self-assurance since her illness: she was more confident not only about her appearance but also about her intellectual capabilities. She stopped apologizing for her enthusiasm for politics and made no attempt to disguise her interest in Napoleon's progress. In her opinion Pitt had badly misjudged the French in fighting them on land rather than on the seas. "These are my own ideas," she wrote in a letter dated October 13, 1799:

> I think myself a very deep politician for I really have always been judg'd right. . . . I have told my dr Brother and every body always the same thing—that the French owe their success and even existence to the attacks made on them—We draw out the only Virtues they have, energy as soldiers, and enthusiasm from Vanity. Could a cordon have been drawn and no fighting [but] by sea, they would soon tire of

their miseries and the frivolity of their character would tell against them. But as it is Pride of La République is food and drink to them and heals their sores. Meanwhile, they wear out the internal peace of every other country, and the best blood is spilt without effect. I hope therefore that we shall withdraw our troops (unless aided by the Dutch people) and depend on our Tarr [navy].[56]

In a revealing aside, she added, "tis my single opinion for all here are great warriors"; she had at last found her own voice. The fact that Georgiana's view of the war was based on a fundamentally flawed Whig reading of the character of Napoleon—who, she thought, had no interest in further conquest—does not detract from the sophistication of her comments. The troubles in Ireland, and the war against France in general, had persuaded her that she could explore the possibilities of a political life outside the party.[57]

For the first time in her adult life Georgiana questioned the assumptions which caused men and women to be segregated into different spheres. She felt that she had the same qualities as a man; it was simply her sex, not her capability, which barred her from taking part in politics. "Would I were a man," she told Sir Philip Francis. "To unite my talents, my hopes, my fortune, with Charles's, to make common cause, and fall or rule, with him."[58] Georgiana's great ambition was to work with Fox on an equal footing. Such an achievement would bring fulfilment that went far beyond the satisfaction she had enjoyed as the leader of the *ton*. Yet, under the present circumstances there was no prospect of Fox ever leaving retirement. The fortunes of the party depended upon Pitt. Only if he were to resign could the two halves of the party reunite. As it was, the Whigs were weak and Georgiana had no role to play.

PART FOUR

Georgiana Redux

CHAPTER 20

GEORGIANA REDUX

1800—1801

Busy preparations are on foot for a course of splendid galas, next month, in the higher circles of fashion: the Duchesses of Devon, Rutland, and Gordon are to take the lead.

Morning Herald, *April 23, 1800*

Both [the Prince of Wales and Mrs. Fitzherbert] dined at the Duchess of Devonshire's on Thursday. Mrs. Fitzherbert had not been at Devonshire House for many years.

Morning Herald, *September 1, 1801*

Georgiana's first few days of the new century were troubled. She was again hunted by creditors and all she had managed to raise was £50 from George. The Duke of Bedford rescued her by offering a loan of £6,000: "I think it is not more than you may, in the opinion of the most scrupulous, accept from a friend," he wrote compassionately. Knowing her well, however, he insisted on a strict timetable for repayment and even drew up a "memorandum of the transaction between us that there may be no possible mistake."[1] The memorandum was, of course, useless as a legal document, and if he believed that its existence would guarantee the safety of his money, then he did not know Georgiana well at all. Lady Spencer bitterly acknowledged the failure of her hopes in this regard: "Your motives in everything are generous and benevolent, but you have never accustomed yourself to any degree of order or regularity, on the contrary you rather hold it in contempt, nor will you bear the least control when your too liberal heart has conceived any idea of expence. In all this the last 27 years has repeatedly give me reason to fear you are incorrigible."[2]

Georgiana was not alone in her difficulties. George was worried about money, and several of her cousins were severely pressed. However, for Harriet and Lord Bessborough the situation was already hopeless. They had never managed to curtail their expenses (he was an avid collector of prints), and the combination of his and Harriet's previous gambling debts had bankrupted them. They had turned to the Duke in November 1799, and at first it seemed as if their problems would be solved. The family, principally the Duke, Lord Frederick Cavendish, and Lord Fitzwilliam, were to contribute £10,000 each into a trust which would be administered on the Bessboroughs' behalf. However, this plan foundered when Harriet's husband objected at being given no say in the trust. "I am quite in despair about the Bessboroughs," wrote Lady Spencer to George on February 11, 1800. "Heaton [the Duke's financial agent] I believe, was harsh and insolent, but if his plan or any of that kind had been adopted I should have been delighted, both your sisters, I am assured, have done their utmost to bring this to bear but if Lord B. will give up no gratification— nothing can be done."[3]

The Duke became so exasperated with his cousin that he threatened to give him nothing. This forced Bessborough to change his obdurate attitude and eventually he agreed to an arrangement with Thomas Coutts whereby the banker would lend him the money to keep Roehampton during his lifetime, after which the estate would belong to the bank. The ever-generous Duke of Bedford submitted to being appointed one of the trustees. The new arrangement freed Georgiana from the additional burden of Harriet's debts; "my heart is full of gratitude for the ameliorated prospect before me. Years might not have done on the score of circumstances what the last two months have done," she told Lady Spencer on January 22, adding an unnecessary falsehood: "By May I shall be clear of any debt."[4]

In the short term, the Duke of Bedford's £6,000 enabled Georgiana to forget about her debts. What she might have been able to achieve if she had not burdened herself in this way was a favourite theme with Lady Spencer.

> She is so overwhelmed with difficulties of one sort or another [she had lamented to Selina in 1797]. I only wonder her constitution has not long ago sunk under the keen sensibilities she feels. If she would

be open upon the single subject of money matters I would live upon bread and water to relieve her, if I saw a possibility of doing it, but extreme difficulties have long inured her to deceive herself and others that I am persuaded she knows not how she stands with regard to debts or engagements.[5]

"How lamentable," she continued in another letter, "to think that a heart and head like hers should have been so little profitable and that the invaluable talents of money, time, example and abilities she had in her power should have been lavished away so very uselessly."[6]

As if to bear out Lady Spencer's observation Georgiana began writing seriously again after the Duke of Bedford's timely intervention. In April she ruefully confessed to George "that I am guilty of having wrote the epilogue to 'de Montfort' to be spoken by Mrs Siddons tomorrow. I did not mean it should be spoken but Mrs Siddons has taken a liking for it."[7] She started work on a religious drama and a few months later collaborated with Harriet on a tragedy. "My sister work'd very hard at it at Hardwick, and now we are going on again, and it is almost done," Harriet told Leveson Gower in 1802. "But hers is much the most considerable part. I suppose you will think it vanité d'auteur or sisterly partiality if I tell you I really do not think it very bad. . . . It is the story of Siegendorf in the Canterbury Tales."[8]

However, Georgiana was mainly preoccupied with Little G's preparation for her presentation at court on May 22. Georgiana wanted it to be perfect. Lady Spencer had provided her daughter with the best masters in London and her training had been impeccable. Georgiana was determined to do the same for Little G. The rituals of a court presentation were extremely demanding: grace and a dignified ease were paramount—the poor execution of a curtsy could ruin a girl's first season. Unfortunately Little G had not inherited her mother's poise or co-ordination. Georgiana was worried by her tendency to keep her head down, and she seemed unable to effect the same curtsy twice. A débutante was required to walk slowly up to the Queen, make a deep curtsy to her knees and, if she was the daughter of a peeress, wait while Her Majesty kissed her forehead, and then rise and make another curtsy to the Queen and a smaller one to each of the royal members present, and then walk backwards out of the room, keeping her eyes on the throne.

Women's fashion and court dresses had parted company many years previously. While simple white robes with puckered sleeves were all the rage in London, at St. James's Palace, hoops, three-yard trains, and bare shoulders were still *de rigueur.* The latest hair fashion, called *à la Titus,* called for cropped hair which made the regulation court feathers difficult to wear and awkward in appearance. The style was affected by few women over the age of forty—except Bess, who took advantage of the fact that she was thin and youthful-looking to dress younger than her years. Georgiana had the compensation of being able to dress her daughters. By every account Little G's court dress was a dramatic success: white crêpe trimmed with blonde (a form of silk lace), cords, and tassels. She wore the Cavendish diamonds and, importantly in Georgiana's opinion, no rouge.

Devonshire House was in a twitter of excitement on the morning of the twenty-second. The footmen were dressed in special liveries, and Harryo and Caroline, who tried not to be jealous, watched from the stairs as bouquets arrived hourly from well-wishers. All the family were there, except Lady Spencer. Bess's presence, and the fear that the weight of memories would make her cry, caused her to stay away. Lady Clermont went in her place and was herself tormented by the scene. "I never thought I should have seen the poor Dutchess look so well," she scribbled at three o'clock after the party had left for St. James's. "The Duke figited in and out while the Dss was dressing, wanting to know when Georgiana was to come down that he might dress to follow them. I wish you had been there and yet I believe it was better you should not. You would have been effected as I was very much. It put me so in mind of old times."[9]

The Poyntzes, Cavendishes, and Spencers, including the Duchess of Marlborough and the Marchioness of Blandford, accompanied the Devonshires to court in a grand statement of family pride and loyalty. The *London Chronicle* reported that it was the most crowded Drawing Room since the Regency crisis. Someone counted over 1,000 carriages passing through the gates. However, it must be said that the crush was partly due to the excitement of the previous week when a madman had tried to shoot the King at the theatre. One of the women who paid a visit to court, Lady Jerningham, described the scene to her daughter: "we went to the Drawing Room at three o'clock, and remained standing till six, in the most violent crowd I ever yet saw: the three Rooms filled with hoops, swords, and each step thro' the Crowd bringing danger of suffocation. Everybody had made it a point to go there."[10]

Her description of Little G was kind but, considering Georgiana's former reputation as a beauty, hardly enthusiastic. "Lady Georgiana is a tall fair girl," she wrote, "not ugly, but not handsome either." This was better than the reports of Harryo, "who is said to be very stout," although Lady Jerningham had heard that "little *Caroline* is very pretty."[11] Georgiana reported the day as a success "beyond my warmest hopes." Little G remembered to keep her head up, and the Queen was extremely civil, which was remarkable considering that only three years earlier she had banned all opposition ladies from appearing at court.

A few days later Georgiana gave the first of a series of balls following Little G's presentation and was pleased to note how many compliments her daughter received for her unpretentious manner and elegant dancing. Georgiana unobtrusively assessed her dancing partners for signs of interest. Two stood out by the end of the first evening: the Duke of Bedford and Lord Morpeth. At thirty-five Bedford was certainly not too old for Little G, although he had several illegitimate children and currently enjoyed two mistresses—Lady Melbourne and a Mrs. Palmer. The Duke's liaisons aside, his wealth, Whig credentials, and generosity recommended him to Georgiana. She may even have hoped that having Bedford for a son-in-law would ease the £6,000 debt she owed him. Morpeth Georgiana was not so sure about even though he too was a personal friend. His father, the fifth Earl of Carlisle, had offended the Devonshire House Circle by defecting to William Pitt, and Morpeth belonged to the younger set of Pittites which included Leveson Gower and George Canning. On the other hand, he was only twenty-seven, which was in his favour, but this was offset by his manner, which Georgiana sometimes found a little pompous. "I believe he has many great qualities and would make a woman happy," she decided; "he is rather too *cold* for [Little G]."[12] He had been linked with several women, including Lady Jersey and Lady Anne Hatton, Harriet's best friend. The previous year Morpeth had almost proposed to Lady Georgiana Gordon, the Duchess of Gordon's youngest daughter, and Georgiana liked to think that she might succeed where the Duchess of Gordon had failed.

Georgiana observed the two men closely at each of their encounters with Little G, but neither revealed his intentions. In the meantime she was energetically taking Little G around London. "I am very busy in my new life and it does pretty well with me," she wrote contentedly to Lady Spencer. "She is so much admired—it is said they are glad that at last a civil Duchess's daughter is come out."[13] The *ton* hailed each of her parties as triumphs and they received fulsome plaudits in the newspapers. Georgiana was determined not to allow politics to interfere with Little G's coming out and no one was excluded from the guest list. "It was a tow-row indeed but succeeded amazingly well and is reckon'd the finest given for many years," Georgiana recorded in June after a supper ball for 1,000 people. "The decoration part was all my own invention for no one person knew what I intended to do till the very day when all met."[14] She had garlanded all the rooms with a mixture of real and paper roses to create a fantasy spring bower.

The season was over by July, and Georgiana gave her final, and most lavish entertainment—a breakfast at Chiswick. Lady Jerningham attended and recorded her impressions, although after six weeks of continuous socializing it is clear from her tone that the indefatigable party-goer was tired and jaded.

> I am returned living from *the Breakfast* [she wrote], I found it extremely pleasant and was very much amused. We got there a little after Three, and were told the Duchess was in the Pleasure Ground. We accordingly found her sitting with Mrs. Fitzherbert by an urn. Several Bands of Musick were very well placed in the garden, so that as soon as you were out of the hearing of one Band, you began to catch the notes of another; thus Harmony always met your ears. This sort of continued concert has always a pleasant effect upon my nerves. There is a Temple which was destin'd to be the Prince's Entertainment and was very prettily decorated with flowers.
>
> There were about 20 covers, and when we understood that the Duchess and these fine People were in their Temple, we Goths took possession of the House, where we found in every room a table spread, with cold meat, fruit, ice, and all sorts of Wine. It is a fine House, and there are the most delightful pictures in it. After the eating and quaffing was over, the young ladies danced on the Green. Lady Georgiana Cavendish (a tall, Gawkey, fair Girl, with her head poked out and her mouth open) dances however very well. . . .[15]

On July 30 the *Morning Herald* reported that Georgiana "and her two lovely daughters," along with the rest of the family, had removed to the southern coastal resort of Bognor Regis for the summer. Georgiana was exhausted but extremely satisfied with her work. There were only a few irritants to mar her enjoyment. Mrs. Fitzherbert's reappearance was one of them. The Prince had humbly asked her forgiveness, and on June 16 she gave a public breakfast to mark her return to society as his "wife." The *ton* had no choice but to include her whenever the Prince was invited. Georgiana was forced to treat her with exaggerated honour for the sake of her friendship with Prinny, although neither woman was misled by the other's friendliness. Lady Jerningham could not hear the conversation between Mrs. Fitzherbert and Georgiana at the breakfast; if she had she would no doubt have noticed the strain between them. Georgiana hoped that the rapprochement was only temporary. "I wanted to tell you how gracious Cadet [the Prince of Wales] was," she told Lady Melbourne. "But I cannot quite believe his *entire* reconciliation with Mrs F—I think it certainly is in a way—but not complete, at least she certainly takes great pains to persuade the contrary. He certainly never appeared more calm and contented."[16]

Lady Jersey was the other irritant. She had convinced herself that Devonshire House had colluded in her disgrace by poisoning the Prince's mind against her. There was no truth in the accusation, but Georgiana was fearful, knowing that she was capable of petty acts of revenge.

> I hear [she] is furious with me [she told Lady Melbourne], and thinks we were all in league against her. It would be easy enough to undeceive her—but perhaps it is better to let time do that. . . . My mother and her friends are all in a fever now, least my thinking her unhappy should give her an opening to regain her sway over me—I believe she is too proud to attempt it, and indeed it is long since she had any power over me except of tormenting; however, on G's account I meant to be very cautious for once in my life—for should Peste [Lady Jersey] reproach me and accuse me, I should be distrest not to shew her some kindness and she would be a bad person for my girls in every way. . . . but I will do nothing without telling you.[17]

It was a relief to Georgiana to be by the sea, out of reach of both women. Throughout August she strolled along the sand and, when the sun was hot enough, daintily stepped out of her changing cabin into the water. Her letters for these weeks have disappeared, probably because Harriet was nine months pregnant with Leveson Gower's child and waiting to come to term. It is extraordinary that they managed to keep the pregnancy a secret. Harriet had told no one for several months and, when her condition became obvious, she had absented herself from London. This time there was no anonymous letter to Lord Bessborough, no exposure or disgrace. Harriet simply remained out of the way for a time. There were, however, unnamed complications during the birth—Harriet gave out the story that she had fallen down the stairs—and she was extremely ill for a couple of months. The baby was a girl, and Harriette Stewart, as she was named, the surname coming from Leveson Gower's maternal side, was farmed out to foster parents. The certainty that she couldn't keep Harriette did not make the separation any easier. Like Georgiana with Eliza, Harriet tried to keep in contact with her by acting as the girl's godmother. Only one letter mentioning Harriette escaped the censors who later went through Harriet's correspondence. When Harriette was two years old Harriet obtained a little locket. "Pray," she begged Leveson Gower, "give me a scrap of your Hair to put into it for her."[18]

The family went to Chatsworth in the autumn so that Little G would be able to mix with her possible suitors in a more relaxed setting. Georgiana was perplexed by the Duke of Bedford's behaviour: he seemed interested and yet disinclined to act, as if he knew what was expected of him but was half minded to rebel. James Hare agreed with Georgiana that "a certain person's behaviour is unaccountable."[19] Little G gave no indication that she had a preference for anyone, and Georgiana, remembering how her own parents had influenced Harriet and herself without meaning to, did not want to press her. By November Bedford was still dilly-dallying when Morpeth started a determined campaign to woo Little G. The courtship proved to be awkward since Little G was so shy. "It is impossible to explain exactly the state of things here," wrote Georgiana. "It is no fancy of mine, but Hare and D of D who have no doubt of his intentions, and she certainly *retards* the declaration, but yet she seems to like his society . . ."[20]

By mid-December everyone at Chatsworth was watching the couple with undisguised interest. There was a collective sigh of relief just before Christmas when Morpeth finally had the courage to propose and was accepted. Georgiana still had reservations, however; she feared that his total disregard for religion would upset Little G, and his penchant for gambling reminded her too much of herself. But Little G seemed genuinely happy, and although Georgiana had hoped her daughter would become the Duchess of Bedford, Morpeth was not a bad match. Lady Spencer also approved: "Indeed," she told George, "I see much to hope and think well of this marriage—especially if one thinks of what might have happened surrounded as she is by Fosters, Lambs, and a D of Bedford."[21] The Duke of Devonshire showed his pleasure with a generous settlement of £30,000 on Little G, and arranged for her to have £1,500-a-year pin money. It was unfortunate that Morpeth had only a small allowance, which his father was not prepared to increase. Georgiana, who had learned a good deal about the psychology of money over the years, advised the Duke not to be too generous in the beginning because it would circumscribe his actions later when, for example, Morpeth entered Parliament and required more help.

Charles and Mary Grey were among the first people to be informed by Georgiana, who knew how much it would mean to Mary that she had taken the trouble to inform her personally. Mary was genuinely attached to her: some years after Georgiana's death she gave Hart a portrait of his mother which she had held in safekeeping: "I value it more than anything I possess," she explained.[22] The Prince of Wales was particularly effusive when he heard the news, calling Georgiana "my dear sister," and referring to the widespread joy in "the numerous circle in which you are so beloved."[23] It was as if he had banished the past ten years with a stroke of the pen. Lady Jersey was not quite so generous in her letter of congratulation. Georgiana was indignant when she saw that the letter contained no mention of Little G, referring only to Morpeth's peerless qualities. This was a great cheek, she complained, "especially as where she founds her affection for him upon [their short-lived affair], long acquaintance cannot be full of very favourable recollections."[24]

Everyone else was sincere or, as in Bess's case, sincerely trying to be sincere. "I have ever lov'd you so much as if you were mine," she declared. "Believe me, no mother ever pray'd more fervently for her dear child's happiness than I do for yours."[25] What she said was no doubt true but it was not the whole truth. Her own Caroline, handicapped by her illegitimacy, could never hope to make such an illustrious marriage. She would never be presented at court, never have her "year" like Georgiana's daughters. Little G's engagement also reminded Bess of how poorly her own marriage prospects had progressed. She was miserable waiting for the Duke of Richmond to propose; the years were slipping away and she was beginning to wonder if she had fallen into a trap, wasting her looks and the residue of her youth on a worthless venture.

While Bess was endeavouring to be happy for Little G she received news that Lady Bristol had died. She and her mother had been growing apart for some time and Bess had not even known she was ill, but it provided the perfect outlet for her feelings. She took to her bed and produced such alarming physical symptoms that the household interrupted its rejoicing to wonder whether Bess was about to die of grief. Some of the less sympathetically inclined dismissed it as an act. Even James Hare found her performance mildly funny and upset Georgiana by pointing out that Bess was so affected she did not know what it meant to be natural. Georgiana guessed that Bess's unhappiness was complicated by the Duke of

Richmond's prevarication. She informed him of her illness and added, "I am afraid previous to this she was, with reason, extremely uneasy."[26] Two weeks later Bess tried to force Richmond into action by announcing that she had decided to quit England on account of her mother's death: "But a little time and I shall probably leave this dear country forever." It would be all right, she wrote disingenuously, because Caroline will have "abler protection from the Dss and Georgiana than I could give her."[27] Richmond gave no sign that he even recognized the hint.

Bess was, therefore, in some desperation when she offered to stay behind and nurse the Duke of Devonshire while Georgiana took Little G down to London to buy her trousseau.* The marriage was set for March 21. Bess's "altruism" set people talking at once although Georgiana defended her to Hare and anyone else who referred to the situation. Meanwhile, Bess wrote to the Duke of Richmond assuring him there was nothing to worry about: "I am aware how much it may renew old stories, and he has been uneasy about it, but I have told him how little I mind if it does so, and have made him consent to my staying. For myself I feel a gratification in having an opportunity of shewing how deep I feel the excessive kindness of all his conduct to me."[28] It was a clear threat to Richmond that if he did not propose soon he would find himself replaced by the Duke.

⊙⊙

"Seriously," James Hare wrote to Georgiana on January 27, 1801, "I am very much delighted at having got so well acquainted with you, for before I went to Chatsworth this year I never fancied, and never even gave myself the air of knowing you."[29] This was from the man who knew about her debts, Charles Grey, and Eliza. He was remarking on something that other people had also noticed: Georgiana had become more open, more approachable. Devonshire House was filled with callers again, as in former times, although Georgiana could not always receive them: her health had never properly recovered since the infection in 1796. The sight in her remaining eye was poor and she was becoming frail, continually subject to coughs, colds, migraines, and intestinal troubles. Dr. Erasmus Darwin, the grandfather of Charles, recommended the dubious practice of sub-

---

* It was one of those rare occasions when Georgiana could relive the happier times when she had unlimited money to spend. The bill from Nunn and Barber, lacemen and haberdashers to the aristocracy, alone amounted to £3,368 9s 6d.

mitting Georgiana to powerful electric shocks, using primitive electrodes placed above the temples as a way of "galvanizing" her eye. As a form of ocular therapy the contraption was useless, but bizarrely it may have worked as an early form of shock treatment. It certainly did her no obvious harm despite the fact that it could deliver a hundred shocks a minute.

Reading and writing were difficult for Georgiana now, and sometimes the pain in her eye forced her to dictate letters. But she did not allow her disability to interfere with her voluminous correspondence. There had been important developments since the crushing of the Irish rebellion and Napoleon's defeat in Egypt. Napoleon had set sail for France in August 1799 and on November 9 seized power from the Directory in a *coup d'état*. Since its members were distrusted as a collection of "thieves in white linen" by the French, and despised as fanatics and amateurs in Europe, Napoleon's audacity in proclaiming himself First Consul caused little ripple. He was a successful soldier and seemed to be above politics. Most people, both inside and outside France, hoped his arrival signalled the end of the revolution and the return of calmer times.

Napoleon certainly encouraged the thought: in December he made a personal offer of peace to each of France's enemies. However, the British government did not take his overtures very seriously since he had broken every treaty he had ever made: Prussia, Naples, and Venice had all suffered for their misplaced trust. William Pitt went down to the House of Commons on February 3, 1800, and announced to the assembled MPs that the government was determined to pursue the war. The House voted on the issue and Pitt won decisively by 265 to 64. The numbers were misleading, however: 64 was a respectable showing for the opposition. More importantly, the debate brought Fox out of his retirement. He made one of his most impassioned speeches, pointing to the intransigence of a government that was not even prepared to consider peace. Fox's allegation that Pitt was blinkered by his hostility to the revolution met with approval outside Parliament. People were tired of the war, and expressing a desire for peace was no longer considered treacherous talk. The Whigs sensed this shift in national opinion and attendance at the Whig Club meetings reached double figures again. In July 1800 Sheridan went to Woburn Abbey, the Duke of Bedford's seat, and found the core of the party present, including Fox, the Duke of Devonshire, Richard Fitzpatrick, and Charles Grey. Even if they weren't sure why—there was no chance of defeating Pitt—the Whigs were coming together.

The threat that a rebellious Ireland posed to British security convinced

Pitt that the two countries had to become united under a single government. If Ireland became part of Britain like Scotland and Wales, he reasoned, it would have equal status and enjoy equal prosperity with the rest
of the country. Pitt also wanted emancipation for Irish Catholics, seeing it
as the only guarantee against civil war. The Devonshires supported
Catholic emancipation but could not see the point of a Union. Georgiana
dismissed the idea as "madness" because of the destabilizing effect it
would have on the existing hierarchy. Sheridan was also opposed, arguing
that it represented nothing less than the annexation of a separate country.
Fox had refused to become involved: "I therefore consider my political life
as over," he explained to Robert Adair.[30] Pitt used every means available to
persuade both the English and Irish parliaments to vote for his measure,
offering bribes, jobs, and peerages where needed. The Union officially
took place on January 1, 1801, and 100 Irish MPs were added to the House
of Commons, bringing the total number to 658.

Five weeks later, on February 5, 1801, to the astonishment of the nation, Pitt stepped down from office, ostensibly over the King's refusal to
grant Catholic emancipation. He felt it would be national suicide to leave
in Ireland a permanent underclass of disenfranchised and disaffected
Catholics. The King, on the other hand, believed that giving Catholics the
same political rights as Protestants, including admitting them as MPs to
Parliament, would be a betrayal of his Coronation Oath to uphold the
Constitution. George III was taking an extremely narrow view, although
widespread at the time, about the constitutional position of minority
faiths. Pitt disagreed with him and he therefore resigned as a matter of
principle. No one believed this at the time: Fox thought there had been a
"juggle" of some kind. After seventeen years of uninterrupted and unchallenged rule no one dreamt that Pitt could just walk away.

There were, of course, several contributing factors to Pitt's resignation.
He was exhausted from months of unremitting strain—indeed, he had
suffered a minor nervous breakdown in October 1800. He was ill, crip-
pled with gout, demoralized by the lack of progress in the war, fed up with
the infighting of his cabinet, tired of having to placate George III over
Britain's military setbacks, and genuinely appalled by the King's refusal to
allow Catholic emancipation alongside Irish Union. All these played a
part. But Pitt's decision was ultimately prompted by the loss of George
III's support. When the King heard that Pitt definitely planned to introduce legislation regarding the Catholics, he publicly stated his opposition
at a crowded levée. He approached Henry Dundas, the minister for war,

and said in a raised voice: "What is the Question which you are all about to force upon me? . . . I will tell you, that I shall look at every Man as my personal Enemy, who proposes that Question to me," and added, "I hope *All* my Friends will not desert me."[31] This was exactly the same language, even the same words, that the King had used seventeen years earlier when he turned Charles Fox out of office. Pitt had ridden into power on the back of the King's message to the Lords that "whoever voted for [Fox's] India Bill was not only not his friend but would be considered by him as an enemy."[32] When Pitt heard about the King's attack on Dundas he knew he was finished and rather than wait to be dismissed, as Fox had done, he resigned.

PEACE

1801—1802

The Duchess of Devonshire was last week much indisposed, but her friends were yes-
terday gratified by her re-appearance in public. In the evening her Grace attended a
musical party, under her patronage, at the King's Head, for the Benefit of Mademoi-
selle Morelle, a celebrated performer on the harp. The company consisted upwards of
300 distinguished characters. She is a charming performer, and a graceful figure. A
small stage was erected for her, at the upper end of the room which is lofty. Her per-
formance consisted of a military slow movement, Rondo, Sonata, with Cramer's
Grand March, followed by Mazzinghi's favourite sonata in G. with several airs, by
the Duchess's particular desire. The evening went off with great éclat and was suc-
ceeded by a Ball, which continued to a late hour.

London Chronicle, *October 5–7, 1802*

The Prince of Wales was pacing up and down the courtyard when
Georgiana's carriage arrived at Devonshire House. She had been
travelling for several days and had not heard the news of Pitt's resignation.
The Prince told "me as he came up the stairs," she wrote, "that Mr. Pitt
and Dundas, my Brother and Ld Camden and all the Grenvilles were out.
When he left me Lord Morpeth and Ld Carlisle confirmed the news."[1]
Their visits left her exhausted but also exhilarated.

Pitt was out but he had urged his colleagues to remain at the pleasure of
the new Prime Minister, Henry Addington, the former Speaker of the
House of Commons. Half the cabinet, including George, had ignored his

request, but the rest remained in their places—among whom, "I am sorry to say," wrote Georgiana, was the Duke of Portland. People could hardly believe the choice of Addington. He was a quiet, respectable nobody; perfect as the Speaker, incredible as Prime Minister. Georgiana had met him a few times at Bognor Regis and found him pleasant enough. "I like both him and Mrs Addington very much," she had written a little condescendingly. "He is simple and good-natured, and interesting from their attachment to their children and their being so little us'd to live in the World."[2] His father was one of the King's physicians, and in the rarefied world of aristocratic politics no one could really accept a *doctor's* son as the King's First Minister. It seemed almost indecent.

From her first day back in London Georgiana began keeping a political diary; news was coming in by the hour. She was the recipient of confidences from all sides. Either through friendship, family, or mutual interest, she was connected with the leaders of all the main parties. Lord Morpeth kept her informed about Pitt's circle of friends, George about the ex-members of the cabinet, Fox and Grey about the Whigs, and the Prince of Wales about his own plans. During the first heady days after Pitt's resignation she listened, speculated, and occasionally offered her advice. She thought it was too soon to have "any clear insight into public affairs—I think these new men will never do and that it is a pity Pitt pressed them to stay."[3] What hope could there be for Addington's administration, she wondered, "with all the talents of opposition on one side against it and the talents of this administration at least neutral?"[4]

Her first concern was that the opposition should not further damage its tattered reputation by behaving rashly. Consultation with Grey and the others reassured her slightly and she recorded, "I think they will keep quiet, and I hope not take any violent measures." Her second was for her brother's reputation, but his subsequent actions made both his sisters extremely proud. "He crowns the most brilliant administration by the most honourable retreat," was Georgiana's characterization of his prompt resignation.

Everyone was waiting for Pitt's next move when the King suffered a return of his old malady on February 21. Dr. Willis was recalled to Windsor, and the Prince once more faced the possibility of a Regency. However, the Whigs were saved from a repetition of the 1789 Regency crisis. The King recovered after only three weeks, too soon for the party to become embroiled in vicious leadership struggles. As it was, the Prince avoided seeing most people, including Georgiana, while he deliberated over whom he would choose as Prime Minister if he became Regent. He had reservations about all the main contenders and was probably relieved when the restoration of the King's sanity closed the matter. Pitt handed in his Seals of Office on March 14 and Addington officially became Prime Minister.

George III's recovery heralded a return to normality, of a sort, in Parliament. Fox resumed his seat in the Commons, but it was not his return which received the most attention. The House held its breath the first time Pitt took his seat on the back benches. He betrayed no emotion except to "hear, hear" Addington and MPs became bored of watching him. A familiar routine returned to Devonshire House as more Whigs followed Fox's example and began to attend debates. Lady Holland still wanted Holland House to be the centre of the Whig universe, but despite having married Fox's nephew she had neither Georgiana's popularity nor her experience. Georgiana was once more hosting political dinners for the party, and the Prince resumed his practice of consulting her on every issue, much to Mrs. Fitzherbert's annoyance.[5]

There is also circumstantial evidence that Georgiana and Grey were, if not lovers again, closer than ordinary friends. Their letters to each other do not survive, but he came to Devonshire House most days while Mary Grey remained tucked away in the country with the children. He also gave her a locket containing their hair and a lock of Eliza's with the words IL M'EST FIDEL (he is true to me) inscribed on it, and other people noticed some sort of unspoken understanding between them.[6] Georgiana was gratified by the return of Grey's affections, but it was far from being the passionate, reckless affair it once had been. He couldn't quite tear himself away from Georgiana, but nor was he truly in love with her. "Black [Grey] is now very good-natured to me," Georgiana told Lady Melbourne, to whom she always had to play down the affair.[7] "But I do not see him often [alone] and I do not believe anybody knows I do see him."[8] One reason she saw less of him was because he had also taken up with Hecca, Sheridan's unpopular second wife. Grey played them off against each other—to the distress of both women. "His manner to the Dss in the last 5 years [of her life] was much alter'd," Hecca claimed in self-justification after her affair with Grey was exposed.[9] But Harriet, who had witnessed everything, knew that Hecca was lying, although the truth hardly brought her more comfort. Mary Grey also became aware of Grey's relationship with Mrs. Sheridan; in the manner of Lady Jersey, Hecca had made sure of that.[10]

Yet the resemblance between the present situation and the politics of twenty years earlier was only superficial. There was a new generation of clever women and ambitious young men, and even though the old guard was still in command it would not be long before youth pushed aside old age and infirmity. Some of the younger Foxites, such as George Tierney, complained with some truth that Fox was out of touch with political realities. They were encouraged by Sheridan, who wanted to capitalize on Addington's pro-peace stance to make a pact in exchange for seats in the cabinet. Fox, on the other hand, was at best neutral towards Addington— or the "Doctor," as he was nicknamed. There were endless discussions at Devonshire House over which strategy the Whigs should adopt. Every month the Doctor remained in office consolidated his position.

Georgiana's own views were definite on the matter: the brief talk of a general coalition the previous spring had planted an idea which had grown into a conviction for her—that the old party rivalries were an irrelevance. She was willing to erase eighteen years of hostility towards Pitt in order to achieve an ideal: a coalition government which combined the best talent of all sides. She confided to Little G, who was anxious to learn about politics:

> My being here is rather fortunate as I keep the Prince a little from Sheridan's power and as my Brother means to attend for a few days, I should perhaps have made Fox and him meet. But it cannot be helped and there are such difficulties in the only thing that could do good, the junction of the old and new opposition (tho' I believe neither Fox or Pitt would be averse to it) that perhaps in being away I only spare myself mortification. Besides a woman has no business in these things unless very sure of serving La Patrie. . . .[11]

This short paragraph demonstrates the development of Georgiana's political beliefs. She had abandoned Fox's "influence of the crown" ideology as irrelevant to the politics of the day. She did not rate Addington's skills as a politician and saw it as the duty of the Whigs to end the war; this, she believed, could only be achieved in coalition with Pitt. Regarding her own place in politics, patriotism, she repeated, gave her the right to interfere.

By October 1801 Addington had worked out a peace proposal for the French. Although the Whigs laughed at his inability to string a logical sentence together ("to doubt is to decide" was one of his more baffling pronouncements from the dispatch box), his government remained on course. Perhaps his very dullness lay behind his success. Hare told Harriet that "he heard but one sentence in Mr. Addington's Speech the other night. He woke from his sleep, and heard 'For as this is that which was said to!' " He was "quite satisfied, and turn'd to sleep out the rest. . . ."[12] Nevertheless Addington achieved in less than a year what had eluded Pitt for almost a decade—peace. On March 25, 1802, France and Britain concluded the Treaty of Amiens and war was officially over.

CHAPTER 22

POWER STRUGGLES

1802—1803

A decent regard to female dress, is we trust, about to be restored. In consequence of a notification on the cards of invitation, the Marchioness of Townshend's late rout was composed of persons in full dress. The Duchess of Devonshire has given the same precautionary hint, and the decorous example, will, it is hoped, run the whole line of female fashion!

Morning Herald, *April 4, 1803*

Not everyone shared Georgiana's enthusiastic response to the treaty ("Peace! Peace!" she wrote to her mother). Lord Grenville's party sulked because it disliked the terms, and the Whigs were gloomy because it appeared to confirm Addington's position. Bess also had little reason to celebrate; five months earlier, in October 1801, the Duke of Richmond had finally admitted that he had no intention of marrying her. After the initial shock Bess felt rage and disappointment. He had "exposed me to much censure without in fact increasing his comfort," she wrote bitterly to Lady Melbourne.[1] She knew that his decision had been partly influenced by the objections of his family, particularly his niece Lady Charlotte Lennox. "He must be conscious of how wrong his conduct has been to me," Bess continued the theme in another letter. "Tho' had he not luckily for me, broke thro' my romance by showing me he had to a certain degree not only resisted but subdued his attachment to me, I might have long gone on as I did these four years."[2] When the treaty was announced Bess was still dwelling on her disappointment: "As to the D of R," she wrote, "I am quite certain that he now both feels and laments the line of conduct he adopted. I answered some of his questions fairly and told him where I thought he had acted ill by me, and what alter'd my conduct to him. He said he should answer me (which he never has) and that he was a helpless wretched Man. Lady C[harlotte] L[ennox] is an odious being and I should like to be certain of never seeing her again."[3]

Georgiana understood her friend well enough to know how her pride suffered, and tried to include Bess in as many of her activities as possible. When Lord Carlisle invited the Devonshires to visit Little G and Morpeth at Castle Howard Georgiana made sure that Bess was one of the party. It was not Georgiana's fault that she was content in her life, not least in her happy relations with Little G and Morpeth; "they do seem to prefer coming to me to anything," she told her mother proudly. She also derived considerable satisfaction from her writing. In April 1802 the *Morning Herald* reported that Georgiana was working on an opera which, it optimistically predicted, would be "brought forward at Covent Garden Theatre in the course of the next season."[4] This was something Georgiana would never do. There were aristocratic women who had their plays performed: Lady Craven, who had since married the Margrave of Ansbach, had been a serious playwright in the 1780s. But Georgiana no longer sought to be in the public eye. Now, especially, she was loath to do anything that might embarrass her children. She discussed with her mother the possibility of publishing anonymously a sacred drama and a children's story she had written: "Mr. Fox and others encouraged me of letting them pass without my name but without any adopted name and trusting Johnson—he will give me more and there is no reason why they should not be guess'd."[5] The printer in question, Joseph Johnson, accepted Georgiana's submission from "her friend" and encouraged her to send him more writing so that he might publish the work in a single volume, but Georgiana changed her mind.[6]

She missed Little G's company when the couple left London to live with the Carlisles, as custom demanded they should until Morpeth's father died. However, another young girl came into her life as a consolation—the Little Po's granddaughter Corisande de Grammont. Her mother had tuberculosis and the Duc de Grammont was relieved when Georgiana offered to look after Corise, who reminded her strongly of her late friend in both looks and manner: "I am sure you will be delighted with Corise and allow me to bring her," she wrote to Lady Spencer. "I long for her to see you and you to know her. I am sure you will be delighted with her and she is prepared to revere and admire you."[7] She was even more enthusiastic to Lady Melbourne: "Corisande will make me very gay. She is a delightful girl and D of D is so good natured about her, he thinks I cannot be too gay for her."[8]

Georgiana entertained regularly now, and her parties always received favourable attention in the press. After one supper the *Morning Herald* congratulated her on gathering together so many English and French royal dukes under one roof.[9] She also continued to be on good terms with the Duke even though their respective ailments often made them crotchety with each other. Lady Spencer felt that the Duke's tendency to morbid hypochondria placed an extra strain on Georgiana and agreed with Hare that "by his conversation one should suppose health was the principal object of his life—but by his conduct one must imagine he had come to some decided plan of destroying it."[10]

It was inevitable that something would interfere with Georgiana's happiness. By the end of 1801 the Duke of Bedford's money had run out and she had no means of paying him the interest on the loan. When she first hinted to him that she might default on her payments he was shocked. Georgiana had assured him that the £6,000 would clear all her debts. "I am truly sorry for all your plagues, both since and before you left London, but it is a source of vexation and the cause of it seems inexhaustible," he replied, not unreasonably.[11] When he realized that no payments would be forthcoming his sympathy turned to anger. He was furious, thinking she had used him, and, unlike so many of Georgiana's friends who shrugged their shoulders and knew better the next time she asked for money, he resolved never to speak to her again. "Alas when he only sees me as he does now, by starts," Georgiana lamented, "he can make no allowances, all my faults are in full force and I have not the power to do them away."[12] Bedford's disavowal of their friendship, after his unwavering loyalty during her years in exile, was the first time Georgiana had ever suffered a direct rebuff for her deceitfulness. The experience finally made her realize that she could no longer live by lying and prevaricating.

Georgiana turned to religion for strength. She had always maintained her faith in God, although for most of her life religion had been a source of guilt rather than comfort to her. She went to hear her friend Dr. Randolph, the Duke of York's chaplain and a regular preacher at Bath, and felt inspired by his sermons. On Christmas Day 1801 she wrote to him about her resolution. She had just come from church, where she had prayed for courage:

I am determined to give up all vain hope, to meet my situation and to form some plan thro' my relations and to gain their confidence, by sacrifices in expence, etc., and then to write to all those with whom I have form'd engagements, state my case to them and see if they will be satisfied with gradual payment—If not, as I cannot now speak to the Duke (who is not well) I must get them to give me a few months before I do speak to him and during that space endeavour to form some plan that may satisfy the Duke and put him in a way of assisting me by savings I could find out elsewhere—all this my sanguine mind sees with the return of hope. But on the other hand I shrink from the task before me—the task of viewing myself with the Eye of severe Truth—of viewing the disgrace and shame of having ever made engagements upon slight grounds of hope in the fear of hurting others—the knowledge of the harm I have done myself and all belonging to me—the certainty that my friends will doubt my steadyness, etc., are the objects I must dwell on. I have pray'd sincerely to be guided right.

. . . I feel could I ever be relieved from these [chains] of distresses I should be a different person and the happiness of many would be benefited. But I fear it is impossible. I fear being again driven to escape from pain by neglecting investigation—in short it has been to strengthen myself in every way and to meet the worst, that I have made the chief objects of my meditations today.[13]

She had already started to work with Coutts on the daunting process of listing and classifying her debts. It was a sad task; each one had a little story or an excuse attached. Georgiana entrusted a letter to Coutts's care, which in the event of her death he was to present to the Duke, exculpating the banker from any wrong doing and urging her husband to take "my character and my children's welfare into consideration."

Georgiana wanted to tell the Duke of Bedford about her repentance and show him the steps she was taking as a result, but he wouldn't see her. Shortly after writing to Dr. Randolph she heard news that could not have been more unwelcome—Bedford was courting the Duchess of Gordon's youngest daughter Lady Georgiana. The thought that her mean-spirited rival might steal the greatest prize in the Whig matrimonial field made Georgiana weep with frustration. Nor did she like to think of the slight to Little G, even though her daughter was happy with Morpeth. Bedford's

sin was compounded by his failure to inform Lady Melbourne of his intentions. "Indeed we are all undone," Georgiana commiserated with her;
"no possible event could have so thoroughly overturned the habit of our
society as this."[14] She feared the Duchess of Gordon would turn him
against the party. Reconciliation between Bedford and herself, she was
certain now, would be impossible. Three weeks later the Duke of Bedford
was dead, having collapsed while playing tennis.

Georgiana was distraught. "The family mourn and D of D allows me
to mourn as deeply as I chuse," she told her mother on March 8. "I go in
a few days with the Morpeths to Chiswick as I cannot bear the sight and
commiseration of people who think they have a right to see me."[15] She
did not attend his funeral in case she betrayed her feelings. Her absence
was noticed: the London Chronicle reported on March 16, "The Duchess
of Devonshire was so much affected on receiving the account of the
Duke of Bedford's death that her Grace has ever since been indisposed."[16] But her secret was safe; Bedford had ordered the destruction of
all his papers and no one knew about the loan. Georgiana had some satisfaction in watching the Duchess of Gordon make a fool of herself by insisting that the two had been officially engaged, in flat contradiction of
Bedford's brother, now the sixth Duke, who claimed that his brother had
never expressed any intention of marrying Lady Georgiana.

In answer to Lady Melbourne's anxious enquiries about Georgiana,
Bess wrote: "The Dss really scarcely coughs—she eats well (generally) and
is in good spirits and tho' very nervous at times, yet on the whole she is
well. . . . her cold was not of that kind, and her vessels in general appear'd
full—for you know when she is well she is apt to forget all caution and eats
and drinks a good deal and yet don't take exercise enough, but I really
think her well or nearly so."[17] Georgiana was determined not to fail in her
resolution to change. She curbed her personal expenditure and dedicated
herself to organizing charity galas and fund-raisers. Among the artists who
had cause to be grateful to her was Mrs. Jordan. "Was not this very handsome?" she asked the Duke of Clarence after Georgiana offered to be the
patron of her benefit night.[18] In June the London Chronicle carried a typical
report: "On Saturday evening the Duchess of Devonshire gave a very superb entertainment to about 200 persons of distinction. . . . Previous to
the supper there was music. The Prince of Wales was of the party, and the
company did not depart till near four o'clock in the morning."[19] Something of Georgiana's former celebrity had returned and she was mobbed

whenever she appeared in public. Lady Spencer was not very sympathetic, "as to the crowds that follow you," she wrote, "it is a small inconvenience to anybody used to crowds as you have been."[20]

However, Georgiana was plagued by more than crowds. Everyone in the family began to receive spiteful anonymous letters, even her daughters. Harriet wrote, "I found my Sister in a great fuss at one she had also receiv'd, very abusive of us all—Bess, K [the Duke of Devonshire], our whole Society, not omitting your Brother's wife and Lord Carlisle, but chiefly again attacking me, saying my Sister had forbearance enough to stop short of danger and only took money from her lovers but that I . . ."[21] Harriet suspected that the author was the same person behind the nasty paragraphs which appeared about them in the *Morning Post:* Sheridan. He had altered since his marriage to Hecca. Instead of being a drinker he was now a drunk, his love of melodrama had turned into a propensity for hysteria, and his humour had slipped into sarcasm and cynicism. Harriet was revolted by Sheridan now, but she had become an obsession for him. He stalked her movements and terrified her with his violent monologues. In August 1802 she was at home on her own, writing to Leveson Gower who was away ("alas! no chance of hearing your Step upon the stair"), when Sheridan barged his way into her hall. "I do not know why," she related to Granville, "but I took a horror of seeing him, and hurried Sally down to say I was out. I heard him answer: 'Tell her I call'd twice this morning and want particularly to see her, for I know she is at home.' Sally protested I was out, and S answer'd: 'Then I shall walk up and down before the door till she comes in,' and there he is walking sure enough."[22]

It was no wonder that Georgiana and the Duke discouraged Sheridan from visiting Devonshire House. However, he was not their only worry. In the spring of 1803, a satiric novel about aristocratic society called *A Winter in London* became a cause célèbre. Its author, a previously unsuccessful writer named T. S. Surr, cruelly caricatured Georgiana in it as the Duchess of Belgrave, a well-meaning but hopelessly muddled woman who is continually involved in scrapes with fraudsters. In one incident she is tricked into paying a bribe to stop the publication of a libellous memoir about herself. In another, she tries to pawn some borrowed jewels, but is robbed by the maid she sends to the jeweller's. "The Duchess was dreadfully hurt at the novel," remembered Samuel Rogers, a Devonshire House acquaintance. "It contained various anecdotes concerning her which had been picked up from her confidential attendantes, and she thought, of course, that the little great world in which she lived was intimately acquainted with all her proceedings."[23] The portrayal was a hideous distortion and yet also accurate in some respects. The Duchess of Belgrave lends money she doesn't have to people whom she has helped to get into debt, thereby compounding the evil to herself and others. "I will own to you I have been deeply hurt," Georgiana told Coutts. It did not help that the Duchess of Gordon was also caricatured: in fact she received far worse treatment as the scheming Duchess of Drinkwater, who is ugly, badtempered, and only interested in securing rich dukes for her daughters.

It hurt Georgiana to be reminded of her past just when she longed to make a fresh start. In a letter to Coutts she wrote, "I must make my future life (if I can snatch it from blame) an eminent example of good. And how is this to be done?" No one seemed to be prepared to forget. A few months before, she had been mortified when, during the general election in July 1802, the *Morning Herald* had mischievously claimed, "The Duchess of Devonshire, reports say, has commenced an active canvass in favour of Sir Frances Burdett."[24] Georgiana hastily denied the report:

> pray, Dst M., remember that tho' Sir Francis is as a Derbyshire man supported by the D. and the Cavendishes, I never canvas, and have never done so since the great election [of 1784]. It was our stupid lawyer gave the toast meaning to allude to former times. The Duke says as he supports Sr. Francis I ought not to contradict the paragraphs because, if I ever did canvas, I must, of course, for the person he supports. But I wish you could convey this to my brother and Lavinia, that since the year 84 I never have ask'd a vote for Westminster or Middlesex, and the toast would not have been given but in the zeal of Mr Lowton our lawyer, who, I suppose, having the Duke's orders for Byng and Burdett thought it right to pay a compliment to my former patriotism.[25]

She was relieved when the Prince personally contradicted the story to the Queen, who, naturally, had been ready to believe the worst.

Bess was not much help to Georgiana. All she could think about was her humiliation at the hands of the Duke of Richmond. She could not bear to live as Georgiana's dependent friend again, so she chose instead to go to France. After the peace thousands of British tourists were flocking to Paris. Bess left in October 1802 with Caroline St. Jules and Frederick Foster to join the sightseers. She had an excuse for being there, and for her wretchedness, since they travelled with her niece Eliza Ellice, who was dying of tuberculosis. Georgiana had wanted the whole family to accompany her, but the Duke would not travel because of his gout. Her distress at being separated from her friend may have cheered Bess up a little. Georgiana wrote to her almost immediately after her departure:

> but I must not allow myself to tell you what I have felt and do still feel. I have been battling with my sad self all day not to make my head ache or make Ca uncomfortable, for he is very sorry too for our dr Racky [Bess]. And indeed I only feel now what I shall feel all the time you are gone. We had so pleasant a drive that Ca did not but regret the not having gone with you to Calais. . . . December may perhaps take us to you, and December will then become July. . . . Write me all the gossip dearest, and all the news. . . . Do you perfectly understand what it is to be separated by the sea? Since 87 we have breath'd the same atmosphere, and our separations have always been within the power of our own will to be reunited in a very few hours, but I will only hope as I most sincerely pray that ev'ry good and happiness may attend you. . . .[26]

Bess was not alone for long: Harriet and Lord Bessborough followed with their son Duncannon, who had recently alarmed them all by falling in love with Harryo, only to jilt her for Lady Jersey's daughter Elizabeth. Harriet declared it would kill her to have Lady Jersey as her son's mother-in-law, and the family hurriedly decamped to Paris. Morpeth and Little G, who was pregnant, also went to visit. Half of Whig society, including Fox and Mrs. Armistead, the Hollands, James Hare, and Robert Adair, followed. Just before his departure Charles Fox had informed his friends that he and Mrs. Armistead had been secretly married for seven years. The inhabitants of Devonshire House accepted the news calmly, and Georgiana wrote congratulating him; but "all his friends are very angry with him," Harriet recorded. For herself, she saw nothing wrong in his formalizing a liaison of sixteen years. "The odd thing is that people who were shock'd at the immorality of his having a mistress are still more so at that mistress having been his wife for so long."[27] The new Mrs. Fox's appearance created a squall among the English society ladies in Paris; no one wanted to recognize her, but no one wanted to be the first to issue the snub lest a duchess or some great lady broke ranks. Her visit proved to be a mixed success.

Georgiana was miserable at being left behind to nurse the Duke. She promised her French friends that she would come over as soon as possible, knowing the Duke would find an excuse not to go. The English visitors found Paris much changed; no money had been spent on maintaining the fabric of the city for the past ten years because of the political instability there, and the centre was run-down and dirty. Bess complained that deference among the lower orders was non-existent, although she encountered little actual hostility. She made a half-hearted attempt to socialize with the new and *ancien* nobility. She was also aware of how much Georgiana's children disliked her, and dreaded the Morpeths' arrival. Georgiana argued with Little G about Bess and succeeded in making her promise to be kind. "I know how painful it is to force oneself, but in cases like this one must and for your sake as well as Bess's," she wrote. For them to ignore her "all the time you remained in Paris would have been extraordinary and would have been as bad for poor Bess as for you."[28]

The letters exchanged between Georgiana and Bess show the deep bond that existed between the two women. When they wrote to each other it was in the language of parted lovers: *"My dear Bess,"* Georgiana wrote plaintively in December. *"Do you hear the voice of my heart crying to you? Do you feel what it is for me to be separated from you,* or do new scenes and occupations obliterate the image of a poor, dull, useless, insignificant being such as myself?"[29] In turn, when Bess was low she imagined Georgiana no longer needing her: "don't forget," she pleaded. "I don't mean that, but don't accustom yourself to do without poor little me."[30] The reports of Georgiana's activities as the doyenne of the Whig party made her feel unwanted and insignificant. Devonshire House was regaining its former stature, and with the peace looking unsteady there was speculation that Addington's government would have to go.

Georgiana was better informed of Napoleon's intentions than most government ministers. In the manner of his predecessor, Count d' Adhémar, the French ambassador Andreossi treated Devonshire House as if it were his club, coming to dine most days in order to glean information which was casually exchanged there.[31] After the French annexed Piedmont in September, and invaded Switzerland in October, it was clear to almost everyone that they had no intention of honouring the Treaty of Amiens. But Georgiana hoped—mistakenly, since Napoleon had no wish for peace with Britain—that if Fox were Prime Minister his reputation as a Francophile might make it easier for him to negotiate with the First Consul. She wrote to Fox at the end of October 1802, asking him to return quickly to resume his old place in politics.

Only three issues, Fox claimed, interested him now: parliamentary reform "in some shape or other—Abolition of all Religious Tests as to Civil Matters, and Abolition of the Slave Trade."[32] He replied to Georgiana's letter, saying, "I am more and more for complete retirement." She did not believe him and as soon as he arrived in London arranged for him to meet her brother for an informal talk. George and the Grenvilles were debating whether to make a stand against Addington, and a coalition with Fox was not out of the question. Georgiana was certain that if they did not make the mistakes of the nineties, the old opposition and new opposition might coalesce. "Do you not therefore think we may at least see Mr Fox in office? It is not only my ardent wish from my opinion of him independent of my love for him, but I have 1,000 reasons for wishing it."[33] Georgiana spent the next few months consolidating her contacts in each of the factions by holding political dinners almost every night. There were sympathizers from the old Whig party who had joined Pitt, such as Lord Fitzwilliam and Thomas Grenville, who were more than happy to sit down with their former colleagues.

Fox, however, was still absurdly insisting that Napoleon wished for peace with England right up until the French invasion of Malta. He refused to attack Addington as long as the Prime Minister maintained his pacific stance. Since Fox was not interested in participating, Georgiana could do little with the links she was forging between the main political factions.

Bess returned to England just before Britain declared war on France on May 18, 1803. Eliza Ellice, her niece, had died. Bess had wanted to stay longer to look after her sister-in-law Lady Hervey, but it was not prudent for English visitors to remain abroad. Several thousand of them, including James Hare, were trapped and declared prisoners of war when war broke out. Bess's depression lifted when she saw how the domestic situation at Devonshire House had changed during her absence. The Duke and Georgiana had entered a bad patch and were both desperate for her company. Georgiana's re-emergence as a popular political figure may have been the cause, since she no longer had the time nor the inclination to devote herself to his needs. The Duke missed having her constant attention, and remembered with nostalgia how well Bess had played the part of nurse. He wrote to her several times emphasizing how anxious he was for her to come and assuring her of his "fixed and unalterable" friendship. Bess accepted his offer of her old position without hesitation. She resumed her role as intermediary between the Duke and Georgiana even before she reached home: "Ca tells me that he has not been quite well for these ten days," she counselled Georgiana. "I think perhaps you have mistaken his not being well for being in a moo."[34]

Bess's arrival in London coincided with Harryo's and Caroline Ponsonby's presentation. She made no attempt to have Caroline St. Jules presented as a French émigrée, although some people thought she might, but watched enviously as Georgiana's daughter rode off in a train of carriages. Whatever had been given to her in life, she felt, had been offset by what lay out of her reach. She also noticed that Georgiana's welcome was a little distracted; politics was consuming all her time. As usual, there was fierce debate in the party over strategy. The resumption of war was an important development, but Fox was not sure what benefits it would bring the Whigs: "But tho' the present state of things has certainly given a kind of importance to our Party which it has not had of late years," he mused, "it is by no means clear how we ought to use what little power we have."[35]

Georgiana disagreed. The way forward was clear to her: the Whigs should join forces with the other opposition parties.

CHAPTER 23

THE DOYENNE
OF THE WHIG PARTY
1803—1804

The Duchess of Gordon pretends to have traced to a rival Duchess, the expressions attributed to Lord Cun[ningha]m. Their Graces met at the Drawing Room on Saturday last and exchanged looks.

Morning Herald, *June 8, 1803*

His Grace the Duke of Bedford has erected in the Garden at Woburn, a Temple consecrated to Friendship, and decorated with busts and poetical tributes to his most valued intimates. The bust of Mr. Fox is honoured with some beautiful lines, from the elegant pen of the Duchess of Devonshire.

Morning Herald, *July 2, 1804*

Among the tourists returning from France was the new Duchess of Bedford, the former Lady Georgiana Gordon. The sixth Duke had naturally gone out of his way during his visit to Paris to be courteous to his late brother's putative fiancée and, almost in spite of himself—certainly in spite of his Whig friends—found himself proposing before he departed. Georgiana attributed the engagement to the Duke's generosity of heart, which had prompted him to rescue the girl from her ambitious mother. The woman in question strode into the Opera House on her return to London with an air of triumph such as befits a mother who has married off her daughters to three dukes and a marquess. The audience turned as one to hail the Duchess of Gordon's entrance and applauded her as she took her seat.

Georgiana tried very hard not to be bitter about the marriage and in-stead concentrated on preparing Harryo for her season. She did not feel as comfortable with Harryo as she had with Little G: Harryo was too quick to judge and not afraid to speak her mind, which disconcerted her mother. Harryo's obvious contempt for Bess also strained relations be-tween them. The terms under which Bess had returned to Devonshire House had not escaped Harryo's notice, and it made her resent the woman more than ever. As for her father—she despised him for prefer-ring the ridiculous Bess to her mother. While the family was staying in Bath she complained to Little G: "Our mode of life is not diversified. We are still in this Hotel, Papa thinking it, I believe, Paradise regained. Lady Eliz. and Sidney [the dog] both unwell, both whining and both finally as agreeable as you know I always think them. Mama, in an hotel, as every-where else, kinder more indulgent and more unlike the Lady or the Dog, than I can express."[1]

Harryo was not looking forward to her coming out. She was aware that she had not inherited her mother's looks or figure, and her lack of inter-est in fashion was partly a defence against unfavourable comparisons. But she was not shy like Little G and her witty conversation made a strong im-pression on visitors to Devonshire House.* Georgiana sensed her daugh-ter's dread of being teased because she was plump, and went to considerable lengths to ensure that she was never allowed to feel left out. The *Morning Post* reported a typical incident at a ball given by a Mr. M. P. Andrew on April 21. The heat combined with poor management of the ball had emptied the dance floor.

> The music ceased. The gay scene then degenerated into a mere dull *tête-à-tête* party, from which however it was soon rescued by the Duchess of Devonshire. Her Grace introduced *French Cotillions*, which were led off by Lady Harriet Cavendish, Lord Viscount Os-sulston, and Mr and Mrs Johnstone. In these dances, all those who comprehended them joined the set. . . . The grace and activity dis-played by Lady Harriet Cavendish was unusually admired. . . . The

---

* In his memoirs Colonel Greville described her as having "a great deal of genius, hu-mour, strong feelings, enthusiasm, delicacy, refinement, good taste, *naïveté* which just misses being affectation, and a *bonhomie* which extends to all around her." Lytton Strachey and Roger Fulford, eds., *The Greville Memoirs* (London 1938), I, p. 63.

Goddesses of Youth and Beauty seemed united in this lovely off-spring of gentle Devon.[2]

The "lovely offspring," however, did not attract any suitors.

As soon as the season was over Georgiana turned her attention to politics again. The outbreak of war had reshuffled political alliances to some extent, but not enough to make a difference to Addington's hold on power. Georgiana would devote the next two and half years of her life to one cause—that of seeing Fox in office, in a government made up of all the most talented men in Parliament, which would bring peace to Europe.

When Georgiana wrote in 1782 that behind the accepted version of any political history lies a secret tale of the "intrigues and combination of Society" that are known only to a few, she was highlighting a problem encountered by all political historians who search in vain for missing links. "I have been in the midst of action," she continued. "I have seen parties rise and fall, friends be united and disunited." Georgiana's privileged position had given her both knowledge and power, and she had often contemplated writing a "secret history of the times."[3] It was to her later reputation's disadvantage that she did not. As a general rule, the Victorian descendants who took it upon themselves to preserve their grandparents' papers employed a rigorous policy of sexual segregation: women's letters were destroyed, men's letters were preserved. In many archives Georgiana's letters are mentioned but have not themselves survived. The meetings, the confidential conversations, the whispered advice and secret messages have been blanked out. In most printed accounts of the Addington and Pitt ministries Georgiana receives only the briefest mention, sometimes only a line to indicate her shadowy presence. The following account, pieced together from fragments, restores her to the tableau of political history, uncovering the face that was painted out.

The Whigs had no interest in supporting the government once the war was in process. Georgiana canvassed the Prince of Wales for his opinion on the war and found him hysterical about the dangers facing the country if France invaded. The Prince wanted to do something, to fight like his brothers, but his father would not allow him to hold a military position. The only outlet for his thwarted energy was politics. He began to toy with the idea of saving the country by organizing a coalition against Addington. He discussed his plans with Georgiana, who promptly offered her services as a go-between for his meetings with the different factions.

Meanwhile she sounded out Fox on the Prince's behalf and was delighted by his encouraging reply. However, he was cautious about becoming involved with the Prince.* Robert Adair had also forwarded the Prince's request and Fox's letter to him survives:

> I have just received your letter and the Duchess's and can only say that if the P of W wants to see me, it will of course be my duty to wait upon him either in London or wherever else he chuses to appoint, but that as to attending Parliament at present, it appears to me impossible that any good can come of it. . . . At the same time you may tell his R. H. that I am very happy to find that my general opinions are nearly the same as his. . . . I think the best chance is to wait for the effect which these violent measures and untoward events will produce, and then if much Discontent should arise, a junction such as the P seems to wish may be produced and the exertion of his R. H.'s influence may very much contribute to give strength.[4]

Fox was prepared to contemplate co-operation with his former opponents but only if their aim was to bring peace to Europe rather than seek to defeat France. If they could agree on this, and on Catholic emancipation, there would be grounds for discussing some sort of provisional arrangement for the next parliamentary session. But Fox was frankly pessimistic, and wary of risking the ire of his supporters by entering into talks that would be futile and divisive.

Georgiana was not deterred by Fox's lack of enthusiasm. She and the Prince agreed that their next move should be to collar individual members of Grenville's party, notably the former Foxites, and convert them to the idea of a coalition before approaching Lord Grenville. The obvious candidate for Georgiana's initial approach was George, and she wrote to him on July 8, 1803. The letter is worth quoting in full:

> You will think there is no end of my annoying you but this is not about a ball or a dinner, but by desire of the Prince, who has just left me—I would give anything to see you for ten minutes in your way thro' town tomorrow if you will let me know the time—if you cannot come I will write what I have to say and convey it to you by a safe

---

* Pitt was also blunt about the Prince; "I fear no very certain dependence is to be placed on any language he holds." Philip Ziegler, *Addington* (London 1965), p. 209.

hand. Do not be alarm'd for it is nothing immediate, but the Prince wishes to state to you thro' me (unless he could see you which he would prefer) what has pass'd between him and several people and I want to tell you the substance of a letter of Fox's.

The only use of this now is a future consideration. That so far some concert may be established that nothing should arise before the next session to create new difficulties to a union of Talent and respectability.

Fox's expression of you and Ld Grenville are that you are persons of whose abilities he has an high opinion as perfectly unexceptional men whom he has, and would still live on terms of friendship with, and whom he likes.

I quote from the letter because from circumstances it was one he had no idea would be seen.

The Prince I believe dines with Wyndham [*sic*] at Francis's tomorrow. Dr. Brother write me word if you can see me tomorrow—remember it leads to nothing that conditions you . . . I do believe that the opinions of the wisest men are so near meeting in everything essential.[5]

As a result of Georgiana's efforts the idea of some sort of co-operation gained currency. Fox considered the Prince to be malleable, Sheridan "treacherous," and Carlton House—as people referred to the Prince of Wales's political cronies because that was where they could be found—unreliable at best. Sheridan did not improve his position with the Prince by ranting in public that Georgiana had polluted his mind with the "Grenville infection" and tricked him into abandoning faithful friends like himself.[6] As he continued to pursue Harriet, he had seen several of Pitt's associates surreptitiously enter Devonshire House for short visits, and he surmised from this that Georgiana was attempting to forge an understanding between the Prince of Wales, Fox, and Pitt. Harriet told Leveson Gower that Sheridan had confronted Fox with the words, " 'Can you say upon your honour that *all those meetings between* Mr Canning and the Dss at D. H. were not purposely to carry messages backwards or forwards between you and Pitt?' Mr Fox laugh'd, assur'd S. he had not heard of the meetings, but was glad to hear there was so good a prospect of a strong opposition, and came away leaving Sheridan in a fury."[7] Sheridan's fears were premature; neither man had any intention of working with the other—it was Canning's idea and his visits to Devonshire House were made on his own initiative. On the other hand Georgiana was convinced by Canning's arguments that if the two men could meet they might reach an understanding. She wrote Fox a confidential letter pointing out that it could only be to his advantage if Pitt joined them:

> After saying all this to you, pray dear Mr Fox do not think that I am advising you to a junction with Pitt unless you yourself see the necessity of something being done. I have not altered my opinion of him. . . . Even if he only plans to make you the means of his return to power I should not think that ought to deter you, granting that his sentiments and opinions coincide with yours and that he is sincere in working for Peace and for that Peace to be made by you.
>
> All I wish therefore, is to put yourself in the way of opportunities of intercourse without seeming particularly to seek them—If neither part will make a step how can they ever meet.
>
> [Do not] betray what I have now written. I should never care for Politicks if it was not for you and Mr Grey, but when I think the country may be sav'd by a little exertion from the two men I think most highly of I should be a mauvaise amie et mauvaise citoyenne if I did not tell you my opinions.[8]

Georgiana fell ill shortly after writing the letter. Her health had become a serious handicap. The problem this time was a stone in her kidneys. "She had a very bad night," wrote Lady Spencer to George on September 15. "Sir Walter and the Duke sat up with her almost the whole night."[9] Harriet was also at her side and cried as she watched her sister's sufferings: "No Medicine, not the strongest, nothing that can be given her, has as yet taken effect. Six and thirty hours have already elapsed in the dreadful pain. I sat up with her last night. She was put into a warm bath and bled, which reliev'd her at the time so much that she slept from four till near seven leaning on my Arm and quite still."[10] It was almost a month before the *Morning Herald* reported that Georgiana was receiving "daily visits of the Nobility, who warmly congratulate her Grace on her perfect recovery."[11] Although the attack had left her weak it also increased her determination to promote her plan. Fox groaned when he received a summons from her to come to a meeting at Devonshire House.

> I suppose I must obey [he replied on October 20, 1803]. I suppose you can give me some dinner. I dislike the thing more because I can

expect no good from the P[rince], considering certain circumstances. I have not yet seen your speech, but the speeches of ladies
can make no great figure now, because they can hardly . . . be allowed to make use of the words Scoundrel, Bloodhound, Atheist
etc., which are the great ornaments of speeches on these occasions.[12]

However, the meeting was successful in galvanizing the Whigs; the general consensus afterwards was in favour of limited co-operation if the occasion was appropriate.

For most of the session Georgiana remained at Bath with the Duke,
Bess, and Harryo, drinking the waters and trying to wean herself off laudanum. The heavy doses prescribed by Dr. Farquhar had left her with an
addiction to the drug. Having fallen into the trap of "false tranquillity," as
Lady Spencer termed it, several times before, Georgiana was determined
not to succumb again. Fox helped to sustain her interest in events taking
place in London with a continuous stream of reports of political developments. However, she was not idle: the Prince's "unsteadyness" required
continual vigilance. He was far too susceptible to flattery from any quarter.

London filled up after the Christmas recess, but Georgiana and the
Duke did not stir from Bath, both lying like invalids on chaise-longues
in the overheated drawing room, nursing themselves with delicate self-
absorption. Georgiana was now forty-six and the damp weather had
brought on an attack of rheumatism. She was bored, even though there
was plenty to occupy her time: despite her remorse and her genuine attempts to re-structure her debts the unpaid bills continued to pile up in
her closet in Devonshire House; their sheer number made it impossible
for her to clear them without help. She was once more begging her
friends for money, the Prince in particular. Writing from Bath she asked
him, "if you should happen to be at all rich, a very small *cadeau* would
make me comfortable, and if you do, send it by a half note in two letters,* but if you are not rich, I entreat you not, for owing to *you* I have
been less tormented than I could have supposed when you found me in
that anxiety last spring."[13]

She cheered up considerably when the new Duke of Bedford invited
her to write a poem about Charles Fox. The Duke was having busts made
of all his friends, which he intended to arrange in a pantheon to Whiggery

---

* So as to avoid detection.

at Woburn and he thought it appropriate for Georgiana to provide the inscription for Fox. She took it as one of the highest honours ever bestowed on her to be singled out from among the plethora of talent in Whig society. "There is nothing I would not do to make [the poem] succeed at last," she humbly told the poet and playwright Richard Fitzpatrick, who had offered to help.[14] She wanted his opinion because "I can assure you I shall very willingly yield my place" if her efforts proved to be a failure. There was no need for her to worry: after reading the poem he wrote back, "I can however with perfect truth assure you that the very first reading of inscription entirely relieved me from all apprehension of this sort. I admire it extremely and think that, (like everything I have seen of your writing) it bears the marks of true poetical genius. . . ."[15] True genius or not ("And whilst extending dedication for/Ambition spread, the baneful flames of war/fearless of blame, and eloquent to save, Twas he, twas Fox," etc.), the inscription bears witness to Georgiana's and Fox's remarkable friendship, as well as to the adoration he inspired among the Whigs.

❀

Now that Harryo was out of the nursery, Selina would have to find another family, yet no one except Bess wanted her to go. Princess Charlotte was in need of a governess, and Georgiana felt that releasing Selina to the Prince of Wales, who liked the proposal, would be almost like keeping her in the family. But the objections of the Queen, who thought the job should go to a person of rank, and Princess Caroline, who disliked the appointment going to someone in the Prince's "camp," stopped the plan. In the end, Selina remained loosely attached to Devonshire House, somewhat removed from the day-to-day running of the house but close enough for Bess to feel her presence.

Georgiana remained at Bath for the rest of January and February until the Prince wrote to her with the news that his father had once again become deranged. This was the second time in three years. The Devonshires dismissed their doctors and hurried to London to prevent Sheridan or anyone else from monopolizing the Prince at this crucial moment. "Everything is absorbed in politics," Georgiana informed her mother a few days after her return. She had reached the Prince in time, and Devonshire House "is the only place he goes to and he only sees the D. and me, for he very wisely has resolved to see nobody till this is over."[16]

Two weeks later the doctors were reporting an improvement in the

King's condition and the Prince put away his plans for a Regency government. Georgiana had been so caught up with affairs in London that she failed to take note of the bad reports coming from Bath about Hare, who died on March 10, 1804. He had never recovered from his ordeal as a prisoner-of-war in France, and a long walk with Lady Spencer on a chilly and damp afternoon had turned a head-cold into pneumonia. Georgiana was shocked: "Having deceiv'd ourselves about the progress of poor Hare's disorder we had the Prince to supper here on Saturday."[17] She was aghast by the false reports in some newspapers that they had continued to entertain as normal even after receiving the news. "No one has been admitted," Georgiana asserted to her mother. His death had torn a hole through the middle of the Devonshire House Circle and both she and the Duke wished to be alone. Bess shared their grief; Hare had known all their secrets, helped them in many of their scrapes, and had never betrayed his knowledge.

When Georgiana re-emerged from her mourning she found that Sheridan and his friends were still trying to secure the Prince's support for Addington. Sheridan's liking for the Prime Minister was a case of *faute de mieux:* he was not Pitt, nor Grenville, whom Sheridan hated with such intensity that he would leave the room rather than tolerate his proximity, and nor was he Fox.* Apart from Sheridan there seemed to be two further major obstacles to all the opposition parties working together. The first was the antipathy between Fox and Pitt, and the second was the Prince's aversion to having any dealings with Pitt. Although many people played a part in bringing these antagonistic men together, Georgiana's contribution was particularly effective—perhaps even decisive—in each case.

George Canning watched the Fox–Grenville–Carlton House alliance work well together and decided that Pitt was making a mistake in staying aloof from the opposition coalition when its chances of success seemed higher than ever. Once again he turned, via Granville Leveson Gower, to Georgiana, and asked her to persuade Fox to see Pitt. Even though Fox still thought Pitt was a "mean," "low-minded dog," he now accepted that

---

* Thomas Moore recalled in his journal: "Sheridan was so jealous of Mr Fox and showed it in so many ways that it produced at last a great coolness between them—he envied him particularly his being a Member of Westminster, & in 1802 had nearly persuaded him to retire from Parliament, in order that he might himself succeed to that honour." Wilfred S. Darden, *Journal of Thomas Moore* (London 1983), I, p. 61.

the coalition could not succeed without him. But the Prince was less practical and still objected to his inclusion.

The next time the Prince visited Devonshire House Georgiana asked

> if he had vow'd eternal enmity to Mr P., which his wish to oppose
> him on the admiralty question, and the language of his people, had
> led her to imagine. He answer'd: "Certainly not; the enmity is on Mr
> Pitt's side, not mine." [and] . . . that no one party alone was strong
> enough to do any good, but that a union of all the great talents in the
> country was what he look'd to as the only measure that could be of
> any use. . . . "I am ready to meet him half way, but surely some little
> advance on his part is due to me."[18]

Leveson Gower was duly given the message to take to Pitt. The outcome
of these delicate manoeuvres was that a broad understanding between the
parties (Sheridan excluded) was reached and Addington's government
was doomed. By the middle of April Pitt, Fox, and Grenville were co-
ordinating strategy and by the sixteenth the government saw its majority
slip to 21 on the third reading of the Augmentation of the Irish Militia
Bill. On April 19 the government was defeated by one vote in a debate
about India. It staggered on for several more days until Addington finally
gave up and resigned on April 30, 1804.

Georgiana had already begun to feel sceptical about Pitt's intention to
include Fox in the new government. She had heard rumours that he was
holding private meetings with his own friends. Fox wrote to Grey as soon
as the rumours were confirmed: "I understood pretty distinctly from Lord
G[renville] today that if P[itt] found His Majesty impracticable upon the
idea of an extended administration, he (P.) should feel himself bound to try
one himself. These were not the words; but nearly the substance and exactly the same idea that we heard thro' the Duchess. . . ."[19] Their fears soon
proved to be justified: the King had no intention of allowing Fox into the
cabinet and told Pitt it was a "personal insult" to suggest his name. Fox was
magnanimous when he heard the news; at a crowded meeting at Carlton
House he urged his side to work without him. Considering the extent to
which the coalition owed its success to his efforts this was a ludicrous suggestion. The meeting closed with a unanimous decision to remain aloof
from the new government. A meeting of the Grenvillites at Camelford
House produced the same result; without Fox there could be no alliance

with Pitt. This was splendid news for the Whigs. It meant that Pitt would be as isolated as Addington had been, and that his government would be vulnerable to attack. A Pittite strategist estimated that he would face 79 Foxites, 68 Addingtonians, 23 Grenvillites, 41 supporting the Prince of Wales, and 29 whose leadership was doubtful: 240 in all.[20] The opposition was in no doubt that the struggle would continue.

Georgiana performed her usual trick of arranging delightful entertainments at Chiswick to boost party morale. The sense of collective strength remained high when the season ended and London emptied for the summer. In June Gillray commented on the Whigs' new-found solidarity in a cartoon of the coalition entitled "L'Assemblée Nationale:—or—Grand Co-operation Meeting at St. Anne's Hill," which showed Mr. and Mrs. Fox hosting a party. Pictured in the middle was Georgiana, holding a fan with the words THE DEVONSHIRE DELIGHT OR THE NEW COALITION REEL written across it. Although the cartoon was inimical towards the party in general, it affirmed, if there was ever a doubt, Georgiana's pre-eminence among the Whigs.

CHAPTER 24

"THE MINISTRY
OF ALL THE TALENTS"
1804—1806

A woman more exalted in every accomplishment of rapturous beauty, of elevated genius, and of angelic temper, has not adorned the present age. . . .

Morning Chronicle, *March 31, 1806*

As was his right, Pitt did not call Parliament into session for six months. It gave him ample time to look for means to shore up his weak government. Almost all the debating talent was on the other side, and he did not expect much from some of his new cabinet members. The opposition could do little except wait for the battle to begin.

The Devonshires went to the seaside for their health and busied themselves with family matters. Georgiana was worried about Harryo, who was argumentative and miserable because of Duncannon. He still could not make up his mind between Harryo and Lady Elizabeth Villiers, Lady Jersey's daughter, and was pursuing both girls. Even more galling to Georgiana and Harriet was the fact that Lady Jersey had succeeded in making the impressionable Duncannon infatuated with her; if she ordered him to marry Lady Elizabeth there was no doubt that he would. Only when Duncannon was away from her long enough for her spell to be broken did he remember his cousin. "I feel anxious about Harriet and Duncannon," Georgiana wrote to Little G. "It must not go on—something must be decided and that is one reason why I wish her to go to you as I think you will judge better than I can." She perfectly understood and forgave her nephew's enthralment: "I think when Lady J pleases there is quite a fascination about her, at least I have often and often gone to her resolving to arm myself against her flattery and have found myself quite forgetting all I resolv'd and believing her as sincere as myself. Yet she is not a person one should trust—it would be the height of folly to suppose she was not as [false] to oneself as she is to all the world."[1]

Georgiana was frightened when she saw Harryo's common sense overruled by her passions. If she suspected she was being manipulated, Harryo would do something perverse simply to prove that no one had control over her.[2] Her behaviour made it difficult for Georgiana to be candid with her or talk to her as a friend when her intentions were so often misunderstood. Harryo's adolescence was a complete contrast to that of Little G's who had never subjected her mother to sullen silences or nurtured slow-burning resentment. Little G was pregnant with her third child in September 1804, when she wrote to Georgiana: "One cannot know till one has separated from you how different you are from everybody else, how superior to all mothers, even good ones."[3]

However, Georgiana's persistence succeeded in wearing down some of her daughter's defences. At the age of eighteen Harryo finally discovered the element of friendship which had been missing in her relationship with Georgiana. While she stayed with Little G at Castle Howard she wrote to thank her mother for her advice about Duncannon: "You have made my situation with regard to Duncannon just what I wished it to be."[4] She added, with a touching earnestness, that her feelings towards her had changed: "I never knew thoroughly what I felt for you till I left you." As if to make up for the years of quiet estrangement, Harryo felt a rush of emotion for her mother: "I am sure you alone could inspire what I feel for you, it is enthusiasm and adoration, that for anybody else would be ridiculous, but that to deny it [to] you would be unnatural."[5] Georgiana's reply has not survived but there is no doubt of her happiness at having at last connected with her second daughter.

It seemed to her that nothing would ever atone for the years her children had spent as orphans, with only Selina for company. She had come to accept Harryo's reserve as part of her punishment for abandoning them, but Hart's partial deafness and isolation hurt her most. When he was eleven Georgiana had expressed her worry to the Duke, admitting that she may have been responsible for spoiling him, but also pointing out that he usually rejected her advances and seemed to prefer the company of servants.[6] Harrow had helped to draw him out, but he still disliked physical contact, and sisterly teasing provoked hysterics. Bess was the only one whom he seemed to trust, which might have made Georgiana jealous had she not been relieved to see Hart talking to someone. She arranged for him to stay with Bess at the seaside while Harryo was at Castle Howard. "I am full of anxiety on this subject and the fortnight he is away shall be very anxious," she confided to her mother. But "I have great dependence on Ly E's care and she has influence with him about hours."[7]

With her children away, Georgiana was able to devote her energies to the crisis developing around the Prince. Since the King's illness the power of Carlton House had increased: it was no longer merely the allegiance of a few men but a recognizable party in Parliament. After Pitt's return to government the Prince gave a series of political banquets for the opposition which unnerved the present ministry. No one connected with Pitt doubted that as soon as the King died or lapsed into insanity the Prince would have his revenge on his father's men. Almost immediately after taking office Pitt began negotiating with the Prince's friends to see what would gain his support for the government. Lord Moira and George Tierney thought he should arrange a reconciliation between father and son and even suggested a basis for the talks: the Prince's desire to hold a military rank, and the education of Princess Charlotte. The first was a hopeless pursuit—the King would never permit his son to join the army (the Prince had never even been allowed to go abroad). The second, the Princess Charlotte matter, looked promising. The King wanted the Princess to be brought up with her unmarried aunts at Windsor, while the Prince was anxious to remove her from the care of his wife, Princess Caroline. Pitt's idea was to reconcile father and son (they had not spoken for almost a year), using Princess Charlotte as the bait; then, in the aftermath of warm feelings, to invite the Prince's friends to join his government. Fortunately for the Whigs, Carlton House followers were divided over the wisdom of co-operating with Pitt. Sheridan, of course, was vehemently against the idea, but Lord Moira, who had already been softened by an offer of a cabinet post, was eager for the Prince to agree.

The interview was set for November 12, 1804, and as the day approached the Prince showed all the signs of a man set to betray his friends. There were crowded discussions at Brooks's and Devonshire House about how best to prevent the wayward Prince from deserting the coalition. The Whigs feared that if they pressed him too hard he would run into Pitt's arms, but they agreed to allow Georgiana to talk to him in private. In a frank letter she pointed out that "they court him in proportion as he approaches power, and that he therefore ought to be beware [of] shackling himself or being too much oblig'd to them for giving him power when they cannot perhaps much longer deprive him of it."[8] She also managed to persuade the Prince to see her and after several intensive counter-propaganda sessions at Devonshire House had persuaded him to free the reconciliation of its political implications.

On the eleventh, however, the Prince sent a message to Georgiana begging her to see him before he went to Kew. She found him "hurried and agitated" and sensed that he was torn between his desire for power and his wish to be loyal to his friends. Someone from their side had to counteract Pitt's promises, and she knew it would sound unconvincing coming from her. Thinking quickly, she sent for Fox, who was at Woburn. London buzzed with the news that something significant was about to happen. The *Morning Herald* reported: "yesterday Mr Fox arrived in town at five o'clock from Woburn. He is come alone, and said to have been *sent* for."[9] Thomas Grenville was at Devonshire House keeping his colleagues informed of developments. "I have in fact seen F[ox], just getting out of his chaise," he scribbled to Georgiana's brother. "But as the P[rince] immediately came up I retired, the P just seeing me enough to stop me and to tell me that F. should repeat to me all that passed."[10] Together, Georgiana and Fox primed the Prince on what he should say to the King and then waited anxiously for his return.

The interview was a disaster for Pitt. Father and son attempted to be polite, but as the King spoke almost non-stop and barely listened to the Prince's replies it was hardly a reconciliation. The Prince returned to London in a much steadier frame of mind, and Georgiana was able to inform George that "he has put a stop *in fact* to all proceedings, tho' he will still have a written proposal about Princess Charlotte. He conveyed to Mr Pitt thro' Ld Moira that he could not enter into any negotiation that did not include all his friends. Tho' he was ready at any turn to listen to any that did."[11] Pitt was astonished and dismayed when he discovered that his plan had failed at the last moment. To make matters worse a misunderstanding had arisen over Princess Charlotte. The King wrongly assumed that the Prince had given his assent to having her brought up at Windsor. The Prince was furious when he learned of this and blamed Pitt for meddling.

Fox was jubilant; as a result of Georgiana's and his intervention the Prince had remained firm. He told Grey: "Opposition *seems* now restored (at least) to what it was before the Duke of Portland's desertion, and the other adverse circumstances of those times."[12] He ended his letter by saying, "you will be glad to hear that the Duke of Devonshire is doing something handsome and kind about the Duchess's debts." The combination of her creditors' harassment and her friends' pleading had forced Georgiana to own up to her husband. "Be freed, dearest, I conjure you," Bess wrote while Georgiana dithered over her decision; "it is better things should be as [bad] as they are, than you go on temporising as you have done, promising I am afraid and not able to perform and therefore exasperating people—whereas make but one effort and tell dear Ca . . . and [shed] these shackles that really render useless the finest heart and mind any being was blessed with and withholds happiness from you."[13] In another letter she tried to play on Georgiana's guilt: "If you knew how terrible it is to me to have dear Ca say sometimes that I do not check you enough, that I know everything and ought to control you and this when I know how little I do know and how impossible to prevent things, and how much happier you would be if I could."[14] Bess's pleas were echoed by Fox, who feared that even if she did confess to the Duke she would lie about the sum, "and then new debts, new borrowing and a new series of distress and misery."[15] Robert Adair tried to frighten her into being honest: "Count up, I repeat it. . . . you are now drawing out your last stake. . . . it is not I alone who speak to you now, it is your fame, your quiet, and your happiness, it is every friend you have living, it is our common and ever lamented friend who is no more [James Hare], who invokes you from the grave to put an end once and forever to that system which has caused you such endless anxiety and alarm."[16]

Georgiana knew her friends were right. She was exhausted and no longer had the energy to fight off her creditors. She would be mortified, she confided to the Prince, if her children ever learned the truth about her, and described the "constant anxiety and humiliation of knowing one has been to blame for want of caution and getting into bad hands, and yet feeling the impossibility of escaping, and besides the constant and incessant dread of some great alarm and fuss, and shrinking from the idea of being expos'd to the most painful conversations."[17] However, Georgiana was fortunate that Bess and Harriet were there to give support just as they had after the great confrontation thirteen years earlier. Harriet waited nervously for the moment:

Ca knows everything except the amount. He look'd grave and agitated, but answer'd nothing. I am extremely anxious as I think it far more than mere relief, but literally a concern of life and death. She has been all this while taking courage and he in some degree suspecting and avoiding it. . . . I am sure he really will let it be put in the hands of F[arrar] and A[ltman], and not let Heaton have anything to do with it, that all may be settled, and she restor'd to health and peace and *honour,* which now really is sadly injured.[18]

The Duke had been expecting a sum of £5,000 or £6,000, not the £50,000 Georgiana eventually presented to him. Bess stepped in immediately to act as a buffer between the two of them, but her fears proved exaggerated. The Duke did not shout or threaten a separation from Georgiana; at the moment of truth he saw not a liar or a cheat but a tragic figure in need of assistance. "There never was anything so angelic as the Duke of Devonshire's conduct," wrote Bess in her syrupy way to her son Augustus Foster. "The many conversations I had with him on the subject, though it made me so nervous at the time, have made me happier now, and if possible, increased my admiration and attachment to him. I feel secure now that she will avoid things of this kind for the future and though the sum is great, yet it will end well I am convinced."[19] Georgiana was not quite so sanguine as Bess because she feared that Heaton might interfere, "which I know will stop everything. However, I hope [the Duke] will be persuaded, it will require time and unfortunately the state of the debts will not allow of time."[20]

The Duke took so long to make up his mind that she had to borrow £800 from the Prince in the meantime. The decision, when it came, was more than generous. It took into account Georgiana's requirements as well as her foolishness with money. Her income was doubled to £2,000 a year, but the extra thousand was consigned to Mssrs. Farrar and Altman, who were to be in charge of the liquidation of her debts. Her creditors would be paid by degrees, and by the time Hart came of age the restrictions in the fourth Duke's will against raising a mortgage on the Cavendish estates would have expired, thereby allowing for the residue of Georgiana's debts to be paid off in one lump sum. The Duke even saw to it that her extra expenses such as her opera box and charitable subscriptions would be taken care of by Mssrs. F and A. "I shall never have a plague of money," Georgiana wrote joyfully to Little G. "I have kept from you the agitation which this has occaision'd. And am very happy and grateful to the blessed author of my happyness.[21]

Matters were never simple where Georgiana's finances were concerned, however, and even though she had made as full a confession as was possible for her, there were many debts which she had forgotten or

hoped had gone away. Once the news leaked out that the Duke of Devonshire was going to settle the Duchess's debts, literally hundreds of creditors came forward with further claims. Some of them were genuine but
others were frauds, and Georgiana herself had trouble distinguishing between the two. Six months after her confession, in July 1805, Harriet was
disheartened by the lack of progress: "I [am] drove mad with every day
hearing of some fresh Claim on my Sis., whose affairs are to be put into
my hands as the only person she will entirely trust, and K. [the Duke] *says*
he has so high an opinion of my *integrity* that if I give him my word that no
new debt shall be enter'd into, that he will trust implicitly to me and not
enquire the names or circumstances; but you cannot think how worrying
this is."[22] For the rest of the year, more claims continued to trickle in, depriving Georgiana of the relief she had earned through her courage. A
friend commented sadly, "The poor Duchess of D has had a severe attack
in her *bad* eye and continues very unwell. I am fearful that the total de-
rangement of her affairs, owing chiefly to her own imprudence is a material cause of her present illness and confinement."[23]

Shortly after her confession Georgiana suffered excruciating pain from
another kidney stone. The entire household remained awake for several
nights until it passed. Following the unpleasant experience, in the midst of
her difficulties with her creditors, Georgiana felt a ghoulish sense of humour about her predicament, which she expressed in a short poem.

ENQUIRIES AT DEVONSHIRE HOUSE

Is she sick; or at Chiswick; in or gone out
is she shamming a headache; or giving a rout
    She's been ill—
twas a stone—but she's now in good trim
a stone! you amaze me—more likely a whim,
But what is its substance? a feather or lead!
is it soft as her heart, or as light as her head,
is it gall cries a foe—is it gold cries a Dun
—alas the poor Duchess of either has none
But smile on the errors she tries to disown
and perhaps it will prove the philosopher's stone.

However, Georgiana tried not to dwell on her debts and returned to
politics as soon as she had recovered. Her understanding, not to mention

her enjoyment, of the intricacies of party politics made her indispensable. Fox asked her to work alongside him and she became one of his chief whips. The Whigs were weak in the Lords; Georgiana organized a recruitment drive just before the opening of Parliament urging supporters to register (no peer may vote in the Lords unless he declares his intention at the start of each year). It was precisely this sort of activity which distinguished factions from parties, and amateurs from professionals. Georgiana and Fox were determined to let nothing fall to chance.[24] "Pray give everybody you see notion of an active commencement of the session," he had ordered her in January.[25] When it came to hunting down wayward votes Georgiana was tireless, ill or not, and was prepared, in the case of the slave trade debate in March, to pick up some of the lazier members and convey them to the House in her own carriage.[26]

Although Pitt had managed to persuade Addington (who accepted a peerage as Viscount Sidmouth) and his followers to join the government, his support could not counterbalance the coalition. The government was tottering. On February 10, 1805, the Commission of Naval Enquiry had published its Tenth Report, which contained allegations of malfeasance against the current First Lord of the Admiralty Henry Dundas (recently ennobled to Viscount Melville). The report claimed that Melville had, as Treasurer to the Navy, knowingly allowed public funds to be misappropriated by a member of his staff. Melville was Pitt's oldest and best friend, his chief support in the cabinet, the man who controlled all Scottish patronage and delivered the Scottish MPs at every election: he was the heart and lungs of Pitt's ministry. The opposition scented victory. On April 9 MPs packed into a crowded Commons to debate whether or not to impeach Melville. Pitt gave one of the worst speeches in his life while MP after MP, led by Fox and Thomas Grenville, stood up to denounce the First Lord. The debate continued until 5 a.m., when the exhausted members agreed to divide. The result, however, defied expectation: the numbers were exactly even—216 to 216. It was now up to the Speaker, Charles Abbot, to decide. According to eye-witnesses he sat in his chair for ten minutes, staring straight ahead as the blood drained from his face. The House remained silent in anticipation. Then he roused himself and cast his vote in favour of impeachment. Members of the opposition leapt to their feet in jubilation as Pitt collapsed in tears and had to be helped from the chamber by his friends. Two months later Sidmouth resigned, bringing the government to its knees; experience had taught him to recognize a dying ministry.

The opposition continued to harry the government. The Prince wrote

Lady Harriet Spencer (1761–1821), by Reynolds, after she became Lady Bessborough. When the Duke ordered Georgiana into exile, Harriet declared, "Wherever she goes I will go with her."

Attributed as Frederick, Lord Bessborough (1758–1844), after Reynolds. His treatment of Harriet appalled those who witnessed it.

"The Devonshire, or Most Approved Method of Securing Votes," April 12, 1784. Caricature of Harriet and Georgiana canvassing during the 1784 Westminster election, by Rowlandson. BM Cat. 6520.

R. B. Sheridan (1715–1816), by John Hoppner. "He cannot resist playing a sly game,"
Georgiana complained.

James Hare (1749–1804), after Reynolds.
Hare helped Georgiana through some of
her worst troubles.

Whig statesmen and their friends, c. 1810, by William Lane. *From left to right*: William, fifth
Duke of Devonshire; Henry, third Lord Holland; William, second Earl Fitzwilliam; bust of
Charles James Fox; John, first Lord Crewe; Frederick, third Earl Bessborough; John, sec-
ond Earl of Upper Ossory; Dudley Long North; General Richard Fitzpatrick; George, first
Marquess Cholmondeley; George, second Marquess Townshend; Lord Robert Spencer;
St. Andrew, thirteenth Baron St. John.

Above left: Francis, fifth
Duke of Bedford (1765–
1802), by John Hoppner.
Although one of the many
friends who lent Georgiana
money for her gambling
debts, he was one of the
few who would not be pla-
cated when she failed to
repay him.

Above right: Elizabeth, Viscountess Melbourne
(1752–1818), by Thomas
Phillips. She was a successful Whig hostess before
Georgiana entered society
but took great pains not to
be seen in competition
with her.

Right: Georgiana, Lady
Melbourne, and Mrs.
Dawson Damer depicted
as the "Witches Round the
Cauldron," by Daniel
Gardner.

Left: George, second Earl Spencer, by John Singleton Copley. Georgiana's brother is wearing robes of the Order of the Garter, an honour awarded to him in 1799 in recognition of his services as First Lord of the Admiralty.

Below: House of Commons in 1793, by K. A. Hickel. Pitt is shown addressing the House. Addington, later Prime Minister, is in the Speaker's Chair. Fox is seated on the right, wearing a hat.

Lord Morpeth (1773–1848), by Henry Birch. After his marriage to "Little G," he joined the Whig party.

George Canning (1770–1827), after Lawrence. Canning convinced Georgiana in 1803 that Pitt and Fox might reach an understanding.

South view of Castle Howard, by William Marlow.

The ballroom of Devonshire House, c. 1920, shortly before the house was sold.

The demolition of Devonshire House. In 1925 developers tore it down to make way for a block of luxury flats.

Duchess of Devonshire.

A Certain Dutchess kissing Old SWELTER-IN-GREASE the Butcher for his Vote
O' Times! O' Manners!
The Women Wear Breeches & the Men Petticoats

RAYFORD SCULP

"A Certain Duchess Kissing Old Swelter-in-Grease the Butcher for his Vote," April 1784.
This caricature of Georgiana during the Westminster election was one of the many cartoons
that accused her of kissing butchers in exchange for votes. BM Cat. 6533.

"L'Assemblée Nationale: — or — Grand Co-operation Meeting at St. Ann's [*sic*] Hill," by Gilray, published in 1804, shows a reception given by Mr. and Mrs. Fox for various factions of the Opposition. The three Grenville brothers — Lord Buckingham, Lord Grenville, and Thomas Grenville — are in the foreground bowing to Fox. Georgiana, Harriet, and George, second Earl Spencer, are pictured together, standing behind the seated Mrs. Fox. Georgiana carries a fan inscribed *The Devonshire Delight or the new Coalition Reel*. Among the many guests who have come to pay court is the Duchess of Gordon (far left), wearing tartan drapery. Mrs. Fitzherbert is sitting on the sofa in semi-state, while she receives the fawning attention of Lord Carlisle. BM Cat. 10253

confidently to Georgiana on May 1: "The most perfect good understanding and harmony, as well as firmness, exists between *all* our political
friends." A few weeks later Georgiana held a joint ball with Lavinia in honour of the coalition. Despite their long rivalry Lavinia behaved graciously
for the first and only time in their acquaintance, and invited Georgiana to
"do the honours." After the remains of "the old famous champagne" were
drunk Georgiana "took the Prince and his party, consisting of my Br., all
our family, Ly Stafford, etc., 26 in all, down the private back stairs from the
Musick room where we assembled and we got in without the rush. In
short it was the most solidly magnificent ball I ever saw at least of late
years." It was also Georgiana's final and most public triumph: 340 guests
watched her usher the Prince to his place and then glide to her own at the
head of the table. All those present understood the symbolism of her actions. Georgiana herself related to her mother: "I do not know I was ever
more flattered than being told by everybody when I undertook the honours, that I looked as if I belong'd to the fate."[27]

There were many who had their reasons for wanting to see the link between Devonshire House and the Prince broken. Mrs. Fitzherbert was
one of the most virulent enemies of the coalition, partly because of her hatred of Fox but mainly because of her jealousy of Georgiana. She had
watched Georgiana's influence increase while her own diminished as the
Prince found greater attractions in the company of Lady Hertford. By November 1805 she was an embittered woman ready to air her grievances to
anyone who would listen. Taking tea with Mrs. Creevey one day, she surprised and delighted her hostess by bursting into a tirade against Georgiana, declaring that the Prince now knew "everything" about her,

> above all, how money is made by promises, unauthorised by him, in
> the event of his having power; that he knows how his character is in-
> volved in various transactions of that house, and that he only goes
> into it from motives of compassion and old friendship, when perse-
> cuted to do so. In short he tells Mrs F all he sees and hears, shows
> her all the Duchess's letters and notes, and she says she knows the
> Dss hates her. . . .[28]

Only the last part was certainly true.

Georgiana paid no attention to Mrs. Fitzherbert; she was surrounded by
her family and friends and happily engaged in the light-hearted pursuit of
amateur theatricals with Lady Melbourne and the Lambs. To her relief Har-

ryo was no longer fretting over her cousin Duncannon, although this was because he had since dropped both her and Lady Elizabeth Villiers. Harryo was philosophical when she learned of his engagement to Lady Maria Fane, telling Little G: "One hears more of their furniture than of their love, of their home than of themselves and it is all so comfortable, proper and uninteresting that until you reminded me of them, they had nearly escaped my memory."[29] Georgiana was also pleased to notice a marked improvement in sixteen-year-old Hart's behaviour towards her. He had started to respond to her overtures of friendship with small movements of his own. The change had come about following Caroline Ponsonby's sudden engagement to William Lamb, the future Viscount Melbourne.* Hart was so distraught by the news that Georgiana summoned Dr. Farquhar to give him a sedative. It transpired that he secretly loved Caroline and had planned to marry her when he came of age. As she had done with Harryo, Georgiana managed to break through Hart's reserve and comfort him. When he went away to stay with his tutor in the country they embarked upon a correspondence which later held some of his most precious memories of her. They chatted and gossiped, exchanged thoughts and news as if they had always been friends. Georgiana was finally able to share her political activities with him and began to instil in him that reverence for Whiggery which had already taken hold in Little G. As the new parliamentary session neared Georgiana wrote her letters in the style of a journal, detailing for Hart "the secret history of the times." "Tho' you do not yet care about politics, I must tell you what has pass'd. . . ." the first letter opened.[30]

The combatants were in their places by mid-January. Pitt had been buoyed by the success of the Battle of Trafalgar on October 21 which, though it had resulted in the death of Nelson, had also destroyed Napoleon's fleet and with it his ambition to launch an invasion of England. But Pitt's elation had turned to despair six weeks later. Napoleon regained and increased his advantage by defeating the Austrian army at the Battle of Austerlitz on December 2. His victory destroyed the Third Coalition agreed between Russia, Prussia, Austria, Sweden, and Britain earlier that

---

* Georgiana was resigned to the news: "It has long been evident to me how much she was in love with William Lamb, but till lately she had suppressed it," she told Lady Spencer. "I really believe—so does the Duke, that any check would be productive of madness or death." Harriet did not hide her disappointment to Leveson Gower: "My poor Caroline's fate is probably deciding for ever," she wrote. Relations had cooled between Harriet and Lady Melbourne and she doubted whether William would be able to control Caroline.

year. Pitt's diplomacy was in ruins; the political future of the government looked bleak.

Nevertheless, the Duchess of Gordon launched the home offensive by arranging her ministerial parties to coincide with Georgiana's opposition parties. "The Duchess of Gordon has a great supper to which she has not asked me," Georgiana wrote to Hart; "it will make my supper very thin."[31] But a few days later the struggle abruptly halted. Pitt collapsed at his home. He had been ill for some time and people had commented on his shrunken body and grey face: the port, for so long a prop, was poisoning him. He died on January 23, 1806, at the age of forty-six, having sat in the Commons for twenty-five years to the day.[32] According to reports, he cried just before lapsing into unconsciousness, "Oh my country! how I leave my country!"

The Pittite hegemony was over. Fox expressed his disbelief at the news "as if there was something missing in the world—a chasm, a blank that cannot be supplied."[33] Georgiana echoed his sentiments to Hart. She had devoted over twenty years of her life to fighting one man who had "fill'd an immense space in the universe."[34] Scarcely a day had passed without Pitt's name being mentioned. He had shaped their lives to such an extent that for a brief period the Whigs were at a loss. Georgiana summed up the orthodox Whig view of his career to Hart:

> Mr Pitt's fault as an Englishman and statesman was that he came into place against the constitution and supported himself in place by exercising the power of the throne. As a statesman he was chiefly brilliant as a financier. In war he was a bad leader, not from his own want of powers but from his trusting too much to incapable individuals. But his eloquence was so great he could explain even ev'ry disaster into almost the contrary. His choice of words was perfect, his voice beautiful, and his way of putting aside the question when he chose, and fascinating the minds of men, extraordinary.[35]

The King searched for alternatives to the Fox-Grenville Coalition but no one was willing to take the job. Bracing himself for the worst, he sent for Lord Grenville and invited him to form his own ministry. The government was quickly dubbed "The Ministry of all the Talents" since Fox and Grenville invited Addington (now Sidmouth) to join them. The new government was the broadest and most inclusive of the entire reign of George III. However, after the initial euphoria there was a vicious scramble for places. Georgiana was dismayed: "I am weary and tired to death," she told Hart. "Mr Fox had no difficulty with the great offices of State, but now that he comes to the lesser it is inconceivable. I have plagued him amongst the others without knowing his situation, but never will again . . ."[36] "I cannot bear it, I cannot," Fox complained to Thomas Grenville; he felt that the Grenvilles were being greedy with the places.[37] It was an unfortunate and unseemly beginning. However, it was eventually settled that Lord Grenville was to be Prime Minister, Fox Foreign Secretary, George Spencer Home Secretary, Charles Grey First Lord of the Admiralty, and Sheridan Treasurer to the Navy, a generous position considering his past antipathy to the coalition.

Georgiana wisely remained in the background until the government was formed, but once the ministers had kissed hands she re-emerged to head the celebrations. "Last night we had a splendid assembly of the new ministry," she informed Hart. "We met in my room and then crossed the hall and the middle room to sup in the dining room. The Prince sat up late with us till Mr Fox (who looks quite smart in powder) went to sleep by me or nearly so."[38] In the spirit of reconciliation and co-operation she held a supper for the outgoing ministers and their wives, telling Hart: "The Dss of Gordon came and was very gracious, it was very forgiving of me to ask her." Nothing was more amusing than the sight of the Duchess "paying great court to Mr Fox. She asked him and Mrs Fox to a party tomorrow." She even extended an invitation to Georgiana, but she was too busy with party matters to accept. Night after night London society passed through the doors of Devonshire House to pay their respects to the newly anointed leaders. Some were respectful, others sullen, and a few made such obvious attempts to curry favour (such as the Duchess of Gordon), that they made themselves ludicrous.* "The Dss of Gordon has made it up with me I perceive," Georgiana joked to Hart, "for she has asked us to a ball on the 6th. I hear she calls me, 'the head of the administration.' "[39] Twenty years earlier Georgiana had been called the "head of the opposition public" by Fanny Burney; this new title filled her with far greater satisfaction: "we the administration," she crowed. She joked with Little G, "We are all statesmen and stateswomen and grown very dull and important."[40]

---

* The Whigs were amused to hear that the Duchess of Gordon was literally running after them. Catching sight of the Duke of Bedford at a party, she ran towards him and in her haste tripped over her shoes and fell flat on her face. Chatsworth 1863, GD to Mq. Hartington, Feb. 26, 1806.

On March 9, in the middle of all the dinners, balls, meetings, and attendances at court, Georgiana stole a few hours to write a long and serious letter to Hart. Perhaps she had some presentiment of what was about to happen, or perhaps, having reached the summit of her ambitions, she had stopped to assess her life.

> I feel and fear that I give too much latitude to my pleasure in writing to you, but indeed no mother ever lov'd a son as I do you. I live in you again. I adore your sisters, but I see in you still more perhaps than even in them what my youth was. God grant that you may have all its fervours and cheerfulness without partaking of many of the follies which mark'd the giddyness of my introduction into the world. . . . You will have great temptations in the same way, but you have judgement and sense to protect you. . . .
>
> *I hope to live* to see you not only happy but the cause of happyness to others, expending your princely fortune in doing good, and employing the talents and *powers of pleasing,* with which nature has gifted you, in exalting the name of Cavendish even beyond the honour it has yet ever attain'd. God bless you Dst Dst Hart. If it will not bore you I have sometimes the idea of sending you a history of your House, from the time of Elisabeth [Queen Elizabeth I] to the present day, to show you what you have belong'd to. But believe me, Dst Hart, when I tell you I *do* expect you to surpass them all, all except your Dr father. He has a mind of most uncommon endowments, a rectitude few others could boast. Mr Fox and the finest of men of the time look up to his judgment and sence. Dear Hart, banish but indolence, and add but a little activity to this character of your dr father, and you will bring him back with the only thing he wanted—*power to conquer idle habits, and to make the virtues that endear'd him to his friends of use to his country.*[41]

A few days later Georgiana fell ill with what appeared to be jaundice. When Lady Spencer received a request from her for £100 she suspected that "her illness is owing to the old and hopeless story of money difficulties." Her daughter was indeed being harassed by a new creditor, but the illness was real. At first the doctors thought it was another kidney stone and she seemed to rally for a few days. She was well enough to write to her mother that the jaundice was "going off." But on March 22 she rapidly deteriorated. Harriet moved into Devonshire House and sat up all night with her while she suffered a prolonged shivering fit. On March 25 Bess wrote in her diary: "a better day—the attack of fever was slighter this morning though the interval was dreadful to see, but the rest of the day the Dss has been more collected."[42] She complained that "crowds come to enquire." People sensed that Georgiana's illness was serious this time. Fox visited Devonshire House and thought Georgiana's four doctors far too sanguine, telling Leveson Gower, "The Physicians think there is now no danger, but those who love her cannot be easy till the fever has entirely quitted her."[43] Lady Spencer was torn between staying at St. Albans and coming into town. She decided that Georgiana had enough people nursing her, with Bess and Harriet, as well as her three children at hand (by chance Little G was in town with Morpeth since she was eight months pregnant), but Harriet's letters persuaded her to come. On the twenty-sixth Georgiana suffered a fit which lasted eight and a half hours. The doctors shaved her head and put blister-plasters on her skin which did nothing to alleviate her illness and only increased the pain. The doctors did not know it but she had an abscess on her liver; there was nothing they could have done for her except make her comfortable, and in this they miserably failed.

By the twenty-seventh everyone in Devonshire House knew that Georgiana was dying. The family, friends, and servants waited for the end to come. The crowd outside the gates grew in size. The Duke wrote to Selina on March 29: "If the worst should happen I hope you will be so good as to stay at Devonshire House for the present, for I shall not be in a state of mind to attend to anybody, or to receive or give any comfort whatever."[44] Georgiana was struggling to talk and Harriet later wrote of the "agony of seeing eager efforts to speak, of listening with agonising attention to inarticulate sounds which it was impossible to understand and seeing the pain this gave."[45] Her seizures became worse throughout the day and the memory of her pain imprinted itself on all those who witnessed her final hours. "I saw it all," wrote Harriet, "held her thro' all her struggles, saw her expire, and since have again and again kiss'd her cold lips and press'd her lifeless body to my heart—and yet I am alive."[46]

Georgiana died at 3:30 a.m. on March 30, 1806. The Duke, Bess, Harriet, Lady Spencer, and Little G were with her until "nearly the end" and were reported to be "quite delirious." "The Duke has been most deeply affected," wrote a friend to Leveson Gower, who was on a diplomatic mission to St. Petersburg. "And has shown more feeling than anyone thought possible— indeed every individual in the family are in a dreadful state of affliction—

Oh God what a loss they all have to lament—all who knew her lament her. . . ."[47] Thousands of Londoners, many of whom remembered Georgiana's street campaign for Fox in 1784, streamed into Piccadilly to pay their respects. Friends came to Devonshire House to share their grief with the family. Fox sat on a sofa, tears rolling down his cheeks. Harriet later told Leveson Gower that she could do nothing to comfort the Whig leader: "I was so stupefied I could not even speak to him."[48] The Prince was stunned: "the best natured and best bred woman in England is gone," he said. Both Harriet and Bess wrote eloquently and at length of their grief, but nothing remains of Lady Spencer's or the children's thoughts. Nothing, except for a tiny scrap of paper. It contained a message from Little G:

Oh my beloved, my adored departed mother, are you indeed forever parted from me—Shall I see no more that angelic countenance or that blessed voice—You whom I loved with such tenderness, you who were the . . . best of mothers, Adieu—I wanted to strew violets over her dying bed as she strewed sweets over my life but they would not let me.[49]

EPILOGUE

For no less than 33 years have we seen [the Duchess of Devonshire] regarded as the glass and model of fashion, and amidst the homage which was paid to her, she moved with a simplicity that proved her to be unconscious of the charm which bound the world to her attraction.

Morning Chronicle, *March 31, 1806*

Wednesday morning, the remains of the Duchess of Devonshire were interred with great funeral pomp in the Family Vault, at St. Stephen's Church, Derby. The hearse was met 3 miles from Derby by the whole of the County Nobility and the Duke's tenantry residing there, who conducted the remains to the place of interment.

The Times, *April 10, 1806*

The recollection alone remains, and regrets, never ceasing regrets," Bess wrote to her son Augustus six weeks after Georgiana's death. "Regrets only to be equalled by the angelic, the unequalled qualities of the friend of my heart, my dear, my loved, my adored friend. . . . I am and ought to be grateful for the friend that is preserved to me, and for such affectionate sons, but she was the only female friend I ever had. . . ."[1]

Bess was alone and unprotected without Georgiana. The day after her death, she wrote in her diary, "we are a family of sufferers."[2] But she was not part of the family and even though she referred to "we" and "our loss," she was frightened that Georgiana's children and Lady Spencer would insist on her leaving Devonshire House. Georgiana's body lay in state for five days beneath the gaze of an unending file of mourners. On April 5 the lid was hammered into place and the coffin removed from the Great Hall. "I am no longer calm," Bess wrote in her diary, "no longer soothed. I cannot describe my own feelings." A few hours later, she scribbled:

> We have seen the coffin pass—we have heard the deep sound of the hearse—we saw the long procession leave the Court and pass through the gates of Devonshire House. . . . It is done. It is over. And we have scarcely wept. Involuntarily we kneeled as it passed.
>
> Never shall I forget Hartington's look and figure as I saw him in the Great Hall as if to attend on his poor Mother there and then on the steps—fixed without his hat—his innocent, interesting countenance and looks bent to the last on the coffin as it was carried slowly down the steps, and on the Hearse as it was placed within. He did not appear to weep but his whole soul seemed absorbed by what was passing.
>
> The morning just began to dawn—all was reviving to light and life but her—her who was our light and life.
>
> Lady Bessborough and I hurried back to my room—our maids brought us something and we parted for the night, but scarcely to sleep, but to think and wonder how we had borne what we have witnessed.[3]

The Duke remained in his room, except for one night when, Bess claims, "he was hysterical. I stayed late, very late with him. I then went feebly to my room—when I got there I saw in his anxiety he had followed me."[4] The family abandoned Devonshire House after the departure of Georgiana's coffin; the children and the Duke went to Chiswick House, Bess to Roehampton with Harriet. In her diary Bess wrote that she had had an "interesting conversation" with Little G and Harryo. Georgiana's children were undecided as to how to treat her. Hart wrote to Little G after an inconclusive discussion: "Perhaps you understood more than I meant today about the person we talked of. I only think that as she has been calumniated, some little care ought to be taken and difference made at a time when her enemies would talk more. If she does that I shall be the first to pay her every respect and attention."[5]

Georgiana had anticipated that her death would jeopardize Bess's situation at Devonshire House, not to mention that of Clifford and Caroline St. Jules. To safeguard her friend, she had made Bess the sole guardian of her papers, ensuring that Bess would remain indispensable to the family—at least for a while. "Lady Elizabeth has you know the care of all papers and letters entrusted to her—it was *her* particular wish," Little G wrote in bewilderment to her mother-in-law, Lady Carlisle. Georgiana had left behind thousands of letters: it would take weeks, if not months, to sort through them, and Bess had absolute discretion to do as she pleased with every one. The importance of Georgiana's gift did not escape her, nor did it leave the family in any doubt as to Georgiana's wishes concerning Bess. For perhaps the only time in their acquaintance, Bess made a special attempt to be sensitive to Lady Spencer and refrained from making the most of this last victory. On May 8 she sent Lady Spencer a lock of Georgiana's hair curled inside a piece of paper which read: "Dear Madam, The enclosed paper is the only thing that I *can* take the liberty of asking you to accept." Lady Spencer's reply has not survived.

There is no doubt that Bess arranged Georgiana's papers to suit herself, selectively destroying or preserving letters to leave a record that was detrimental to Georgiana's reputation and beneficial to hers. She was not being deliberately unfaithful to Georgiana; she was simply incapable of behaving in any other manner. Her grief was real. In July she wrote to Augustus, who was in America: she felt numb, she said, although Dr. Farquhar had told her "it was always so" after terrible shock. "She is so present to me," she continued, "and I am so constantly occupied by her that I feel as if she was absent on a journey and I catch myself saying, 'I'll tell her this.'"[6] Georgiana was "the constant charm of my life. She doubled every joy, lessened every grief. Her society had an attraction I never met with in any other being. Her love for me was really 'passing the love of woman.'"[7] But now that Georgiana was gone there were no further impediments to Bess taking her place.

Events overtook the children's desire for Bess to leave Devonshire House. First Clifford came home on leave from the navy, then Hart fell ill and Bess offered to nurse him. The Duke naturally found that he could not do without Bess to look after him. Then Charles Fox developed dropsy in August and his condition became so serious that the Duke offered him Chiswick House as a quiet refuge from London. Bess made all the arrangements concerning the servants, and took it upon herself to issue bulletins to the public about his health. "She is a disgusting beast," raged Lavinia, who was furious at the way Bess had succeeded in taking centre stage.[8] Bess was also among those present when Fox died on September 13, 1806, just six months after Georgiana's death: ("It don't signify, my dearest, dearest Liz," were his last words, addressed to his wife.) She also attended Fox's funeral and sat with Georgiana's children while the Duke performed his duty as one of the eight pall-bearers. The cabinet and over a hundred MPs followed the coffin from St. James's to Westminster Abbey. Thousands lined the streets and, unlike that at Pitt's state funeral, the crowd was silent and well behaved.[9] Four months later the King dismissed the coalition after it attempted to grant Irish Catholics the right to hold officer rank in the army. The Whigs did not form another government until Grey became Prime Minister in 1830.

Bess remained at Devonshire House after Fox's death; her manner subtly changed, as if Georgiana had bequeathed to her not only all her papers but her position too. In November Harryo informed Little G that Bess was shameless in her "laying down the law when Lord M. and you are away."[10] It also annoyed her to watch Bess exact her petty revenge on Selina, "forcing her to say things that she may dispute them." Worst of all, she had to watch Bess usurping her mother's place: by rights Harryo should have sat at the head of the table. "Lady E. F. is very disagreeable in doing the honours instead of me," she told Little G; "which for every reason in the world is painful to me."[11] Harryo feared a confrontation with Bess; Caroline, Harriet's daughter, however, had no compunction in goading her when the opportunity arose. According to Harryo's letter of November 19,

> Caroline began last night, before the Bessboroughs and all of us assembled, reading *out loud* a letter of Madame de Maintenon, in which she excuses her conduct towards Louis and says, "*si je ne vais dans sa chambre, à qui pourrait il confier ses secrets.*"* or words to that effect, and describing in short scenes too like what we are so often witnessing. This was to lead to every sort of question to Lady E., whether Madame de Maintenon was right in her conduct, whether she was ambitious or only making generous sacrifices, etc. I fancied Lady E. was embarrassed.[12]

Bess was not so embarrassed by Caroline that she altered her behaviour. Sheridan, who had always been able to see through her, told people that "Bess had *cried* to him because she 'felt it her severe duty to be the Duchess of Devonshire.' "[13] She indignantly denied the story; however, his com-

---

* If I did not go to his room, to whom would he be able to confide his secrets?

ments made her more careful. A year later Little G felt obliged to write to Hart, asking him not to avoid his father because of Bess's presence. "She behaves better than I expected and does not assume so much as I feared, tho' too much a great deal, but that must be in the situation in which she has chosen to place herself. . . . I feel all her conduct and hate it as you do, but I wish you to behave towards and concerning her as Harryo does, never giving her a handle against you or a just cause of complaint to my father."[14]

The only person who took Bess's side was Harriet. But even she hoped that Bess would not try to marry the Duke and usurp Georgiana's place as the Duchess of Devonshire. "Tho' we have no right to expect it," she admitted. Georgiana's death had destroyed something vital in Harriet: "no one knows, G," she told Leveson Gower, "not even you—how I suffer." One night she stayed up late reading Georgiana's letters; the painful recollection of her voice made Harriet realize "it will be long, long before that wound would heal. . . . I take this bitter misfortune as a punishment to me and a release to [Georgiana]. The latter miserable years of her life and her agonising death were, I hope and trust, the retribution and full atonement of *her* errors . . . but while I acknowledge the justice of the blow that kills me, I sink under its severity."[15] The worst part was having her memory of her sister's last years sullied by Hecca Sheridan's revelation that Grey had been her lover.[16]

Grey shamefacedly visited Harriet on August 19, 1807. "I could not resist reproaching him bitterly for what I think from first to last abominable conduct," Harriet wrote after the interview. "I never saw such violence; he beat his head, call'd himself by a thousand harsh names, cried and threw himself at my feet. It was impossible not to be agitated by such a scene. . . ." She blamed herself for having been deceived by Grey's manner. "I admired too much one, who, whatever he is among Men, is anything but honourable among women, or classes them low indeed in society." Harriet was almost prepared to forgive him, but he ruined his tearful apology by grasping her knees, "and then when I least dreamt of it clasp'd me in his Arms," and tried to kiss her. "I am asham'd of it for him, and for myself. I cannot account for it: was it resentment at my just indignation for his conduct to her, and did he take this strange way of marking? It is impossible a man of common decency should not know . . ."[17]

Two years after Harriet learned how Grey had betrayed Georgiana, she heard more distressing news. In Autumn 1809 Bess and the Duke announced their engagement. Harriet tried hard to forgive her, telling Leveson Gower:

I really love Bess, and think she has many more good and generous qualities than are allowed her, but I think she has the worst judgement of any body I ever met with; and I begin to think she has more *Calcul,* and more power of concentrating her wishes and intentions, than I ever before believ'd. In the midst of all this I have a distressing letter from my Mother, who from something W. Spencer said has taken alarm, and is coming up to Town with the intention of consulting my Brother upon laying down some plan for our whole family to follow in case of such an event having taken place and having to be declar'd. If my Mother trusted to herself alone she would do as I do, grieve over what renews so painfully former recollections, but no more; but I know my Brother's opinion, sway'd by Ly Spencer, and Ly Morpeth too, and seems to intimate that on such an event all connection should cease between Devonshire House and us, and Harriet quit her Father. This I highly disapprove of. Yes, Dear G., I shall stand alone against my whole family and *her* [Georgiana's] children as favouring an event which God knows pains me more than any I believe, and taking part against them and against the Memory of what I lov'd best on earth. . . .[18]

The Duke informed the children and Lady Spencer of the marriage a few days after the event. "I wish you, my Dear Lady Spencer, not to answer this letter," he wrote on October 17, 1809, "as it must be disagreeable to you to do it, and I shall know by other means whether you approve or disapprove of my conduct."[19] Hart wrote a cold acknowledgement to his father which made no mention of Bess, and a heated letter of complaint to his cousin Lady Caroline Lamb: "Hardly till I see it can I believe that the woman could have the assurance to take that name always so sacred to us, and hence forward to be so polluted."[20] Harryo did not know how she would bear living at Devonshire House with Bess as her stepmother. Fortunately, a suitor stepped forward to ask for her hand. Harryo had been in love with him for some time, but the connection was nevertheless surprising—the suitor was Granville Leveson Gower, Harriet's lover and father of her two illegitimate children. He was thirty-six and anxious to have a legitimate family of his own. Harriet had accepted that she could not hold him and had given him her blessing to woo Harryo. Her love for him, however, had not diminished and his marriage to her niece caused her intense anguish. "I must put down what I dare tell nobody," she wrote in 1812. "I have heard or spoke that language [of love] and for

17 years of it lov'd almost to idolatry the only man from whom I could have wish'd to hear it, the man who has probably lov'd me least of all those who have profess'd to do so—tho' once I thought otherwise."[21]

The Duke made it clear which daughter he preferred—the illegitimate Caroline or the legitimate Harryo—when he decided their marriage portions. In 1809, when Caroline St. Jules married George Lamb, the younger brother of the future Lord Melbourne, the Duke gave them £30,000. A few months later, when Harryo married Leveson Gower, he gave them only £10,000. Bess made no effort to rectify the Duke's unfairness.

Although Bess had finally taken Georgiana's title, she never possessed her popularity or her influence, and the Cavendishes and Spencers were never more than civil to her. Shortly after her marriage she wrote a polite note to Lady Spencer requesting leave to visit, but was refused. "It is needless to say that many very bitter reflections will occur when we meet, which has made me rather wish it might not be just yet," Lady Spencer replied on December 9, 1809. "But believe me when I assure you that I sincerely hope the latter part of your life may be happier—much happier than the former part of it has been."[22] Eight months later she expressed her feelings more honestly to Harriet: "Pray that this wretched woman may feel and repent, before it is too late, of all the mischief she has done, and among other things that you, my dear Harriet, may no longer be deceived by her."

Bess may have indeed repented some of her "mischief" since the Duke gave her a taste of what Georgiana had experienced for so many years. Shortly before their marriage, he and Bess made friends with a Mrs. Spencer, a young woman who had lived in Germany for most of her life before marrying William Spencer, an impecunious rake on the Churchill side of the Spencer family. Extraordinarily, considering that there had already been two Spencers in the Duke's life, the couple adopted her as a new companion. As she had no money to speak of, and few relatives living in England, the widow was excessively grateful for any show of friendship. She soon became so attached to the Devonshires that she was one of the few witnesses at their wedding. But afterwards Harryo remarked that her father's phaeton was seen outside Mrs. Spencer's door every day, "sometimes till past 8." "Can the Duchess like this?" she asked. "Especially after having made Mrs. S. her Cat's Paw and therefore put herself under obligations to her."[23]

The Duke did not live long enough for Mrs. Spencer to become a serious threat to Bess. He died on July 29, 1811. Bess, however, was not ready to relinquish the fruits of her campaign. She demanded money and jewels from Hart, and even insisted that the Duke had written a secret codicil which gave her Chiswick for life. To support her claims, Bess announced the true paternity of Caroline and Clifford—a shocking act in eighteenth-century society—and tried to insist that Clifford had the right to use the Cavendish arms. There were ugly rows between herself and the Cavendishes which, to her embarrassment, somehow found their way to the public. Finally, at the end of the year Hart bribed Bess to leave in "a single week" with a generous ex gratia settlement on herself and his two half-siblings. Bess moved out of Chiswick and built a small house in Richmond. She divided her time between there and a house in London, 13 Piccadilly Terrace, where she entertained with great formality as Elizabeth, Duchess of Devonshire. But she was restless and dissatisfied with her new life. After five years of respectable widowhood she packed up her belongings and moved to Rome. An old acquaintance of Georgiana's, Sir William Gell, visited her there:

> There is an instance for example, where charm of countenance and of manner fascinate, and make one like her, despite all that has been reported of her character. Her room is filled with books, and literature is now the pursuit in which she takes, or pretends to take, an interest. I suspect, she is come to that time when nothing of this world's amusements can charm; she has tasted pleasure in all its varieties; she has drunk it to the very dregs; and the lees are bitter. If there be a source of interest to her, it is the Cardinal.[24]

The Cardinal Consalvi was Bess's last great love. "No girl of fifteen ever betrayed a more romantic passion for her lover than did this distinguished, but then antiquated lady for the Cardinal," wrote Sir William. The Cardinal had the thankless job of the Pope's Secretary of State. He shared Bess's interest in classical architecture and antiquities and helped her to plan her own excavation site in the Forum. "That Witch of Endor the Duchess of Devon," Lady Spencer wrote just before she died on March 18, 1814, "has been doing mischief of another to what she has been doing all her life by pretending to dig for the public good in the Forum."[25] Bess made Italy her permanent home, although she sometimes visited England and eventually regained her former influence with Hart, much to Little G's and Harryo's annoyance. She died in Rome on March 30, 1824, eighteen years to the day after Georgiana's death. A locket carrying one of her friend's reddish-gold curls, and also a hair bracelet of Georgiana's, were next to her bed. Hart was at Bess's side during her last moments, and so, surprisingly, was Georgiana's daughter Eliza Courtney, now Mrs. Ellice.[26] Afterwards Hart arranged for Bess's remains to be brought to England and interred alongside those of Harriet, who had died three years previously in 1821, and Georgiana and the Duke.

Georgiana's daughters had mixed feelings when they heard the news of Bess's death. "It has shocked us very much, she had so much enjoyment of life and I feel so unhappy and anxious about poor Mrs. Lamb [Caroline St. Jules]," wrote Harryo. "It also brings past times to one's mind, and many nervous and indefinable feelings. This is a bitter cup, dearest sister."[27] The eight children belonging to Georgiana and Bess: Hart, Little G, Harryo, Eliza Courtney, Caroline St. Jules, [Augustus] Clifford, and Frederick and Augustus Foster remained on good terms with each other all their lives. Bess's Caroline was fortunate in enjoying a close relationship with Georgiana's children that circumstances denied to Eliza Courtney. On the other hand, Caroline's marriage to George Lamb was a tragic mistake—it was never consummated—while Eliza was extremely happy with Robert Ellice. Harryo was forbearing about her half-brother and step-brothers.

> Clifford and the *two* Fosters are here, but it does very well [she wrote on October 30, 1812] Clifford is improved in looks but in conversation he really is nothing and his constant little nervous laugh makes even his silence appear less negative than that of another person. I am very kind but with the "Spirits low that bore bestows." He has no conversation at all and having quite left off the familiarity and childishness of manner he once had, he has nothing at all in its place. F. Foster is in tearing spirits and most excessively amusing. A. Foster rather better than he used to be.[28]

Hart took his duties as head of the family very seriously.* He looked after all the interests of his siblings; his first act on becoming the sixth Duke was to raise Harryo's marriage portion from £10,000 to £30,000. He also paid Thomas Coutts some of the money that was still outstanding from

---

* The old rumour that Bess was his real mother resurfaced in 1818 and caused a brief stir while Lord George Cavendish, Hart's uncle, interrogated Georgiana's former maid Ann Scafe on the circumstances surrounding Hart's birth.

Georgiana's debts. Clifford particularly benefited from Hart's help: through his influence he received the royal appointment of Gentleman Usher of the Black Rod and was eventually made a baronet. Frederick Foster, who settled down to become a country gentleman, and Augustus, who was knighted in 1835 for his services to diplomacy, were frequent visitors to Chatsworth. Georgiana's two legitimate daughters never achieved, nor sought, the celebrity of their mother, although Harryo and Leveson Gower presided over the British embassy in Paris with great éclat for almost seventeen years.

Hart did not fulfil Georgiana's expectations; his deafness prevented him from entering politics or playing a significant role in the Whig party. He never married and died childless at the age of sixty-eight in 1858, which meant that the title moved sideways to his second cousin William Cavendish. During his lifetime Hart displayed many of Georgiana's traits. He was a serious collector of minerals, an enthusiastic modernizer who spent hundreds of thousands of pounds altering and improving Chatsworth and Devonshire House, and a famously generous host. As well as enjoying the sisterly adoration of Harryo and Little G, Hart was a popular society figure. However, when Georgiana told him, "I see in you still more perhaps than even in them [the girls] what my youth was," she may have been hinting at something in Hart which only became clear in adulthood. He imitated the pattern of her life by maintaining close, passionate friendships with members of his own sex. He formed a lifelong attachment to the gardener and architect Joseph Paxton, who lived with his wife in a house on the Chatsworth estate. Their relationship provoked comment but not scandal and Hart led a contented if unremarkable life.

⟨⟩

Georgiana's obituary in the *Gentleman's Magazine* was typical of the notices which appeared following her death. It praised her compassion, spirit, and intelligence, calling them "qualities . . . of a rare and superior kind." But it was Louis Dutens in his memoirs who best described Georgiana's effect on her generation. "Without any intention, she became the directress of the *ton*. She changed the hours, and set the fashions. Everybody endeavoured to imitate her, not only in England, but even at Paris. Everyone enquired what [Georgiana] did, and how she dressed, anxious to act and dress in the same style. She had an uncommon gracefulness in her air rather than her figure; and appeared always to act entirely from the impression of the moment."[29]

However, just as no painter ever captured a true likeness of Georgiana during her life, no obituary conveyed the true complexity of her character after her death. Georgiana was pre-eminently a woman of paradoxes. She once confided to Alexandre Calonne, just before the Regency crisis in 1788, "I have opened my heart to you and you have seen that despite all my gaiety, it is often quite tormented."*[30] She wrote in a similar vein to Mary Graham in 1778, and to Sir Philip Francis twenty-one years later in 1799. Throughout her adult life Georgiana struggled to reconcile the contradictions that enveloped her. She was an acknowledged beauty yet unappreciated by her husband, a popular leader of the *ton* who saw through its hypocrisy, and a woman whom people loved who was yet so insecure in her ability to command love that she became dependent upon the suspect devotion of Lady Elizabeth Foster. She was a generous contributor to charitable causes who nevertheless stole from her friends, a writer who never published under her own name, a devoted mother who sacrificed one child to save the other three, a celebrity and patron of the arts in an era when married women had no legal status, a politician without a vote, and a skilled tactician a generation before the development of professional party politics.

Georgiana should be credited with being one of the first to refine political messages for mass communication. She was an image-maker who understood the necessity of public relations, and she became adept at the manipulation of political symbols and the dissemination of party propaganda. The two-party system was still developing in the late eighteenth century and factions, with their problems of discipline and dependence upon personality, predominated. Despite this, Georgiana was successful in helping to foster a sense of collective membership among the Foxite Whigs; and she made Devonshire House the focal point for meetings during critical times, such as the Westminster election and the Regency crisis. She was simultaneously a public figurehead for the Whigs and an effective politician within the party. The faction leaders obeyed her summonses, sought her advice, employed her to negotiate, and relied on her to maintain the morale of supporters.

Dedicating herself to the Whig cause and to Fox's success (the two being inextricable in her mind), Georgiana achieved a number of political

---

* *Je vous ai bien ouvert mon coeur et vous avez vue que malgré toute ma gaieté ile [sic] est souvent bien tormenté.*

victories during what can legitimately be called her thirty-year career. First, she used her considerable powers of persuasion to prevent the Prince from splitting the Fox-North Coalition in 1783. The following year she rescued Fox from electoral defeat with her courageous campaign in the Westminster election. During the subsequent wilderness years before and after the 1789 Regency crisis, Georgiana succeeded in recruiting new blood to the party and in helping to stem the flow of desertions. Later, she was one of the leading instigators of the Fox-Grenville Coalition of 1804. More important, she held the Coalition together in 1805, when she once again persuaded the Prince not to desert the Whigs. It was her persistence which helped to sustain the momentum for the 1806 "Ministry of all the Talents." No other woman—indeed, very few men— achieved as much influence as Georgiana wielded during her lifetime.

Georgiana was not alone, however, in the duties she performed as a political wife. Her career exemplifies the political access granted to aristocratic women when politics was still a family enterprise. Lady Melbourne, Mrs. Crewe, and Lady Salisbury, for example, were expected to "work" by being prominent in the local community. They helped their male kin to fight elections, and used family and social ties to promote the careers of relatives. During the parliamentary season they presided over salons, organized political suppers, and provided opportunities for factions to mingle. They were the conduits for messages and the facilitators of meetings and informal alliances. They were no less partisan than the men and were sometimes more so: during the Regency crisis Foxite and Pittite hostesses struck off the opposition from their invitation lists.

By contrast, aristocratic women in the nineteenth century were granted considerably less access to politics. As the national mood swung against the "lassitudes" of the eighteenth century women were perceived as having been far too active in male preserves such as politics and business, and were encouraged to be content with domestic occupations. Femininity became equated with the home, the family, and religion, while masculinity became more strongly identified with the work place, politics, and power.[31] The accession of Queen Victoria in 1837 had a further dampening effect on women's participation in public life, as did the professionalization of party politics. Middle-class participation, the growth of centralized party control over constituencies, and the transformation of politics from public service into a vocational career, all contributed to the exclusion of women. They were never entirely removed, as the lives of Lady Palmerston, Princess

Lieven, the wife of the Russian ambassador to London from 1812, and Lady Waldegrave make clear, but nineteenth-century women were denied the same degree of political co-operation as their predecessors.

Ironically, Georgiana's political achievements, not to mention the activities of her female contemporaries, have been obscured by the rigidity of modern academic fashion. Most political historians generally follow a conservative approach and ignore the role of women *tout court*. Most feminist historians concentrate on "women's occupations" and therefore ignore the world of high politics. Marxist history, which is strongly allied to feminist history, concentrates on the lives of the many—the middle and working classes—at the expense of the few—the aristocracy. As a result, the theoretical model that has dominated women's history for the past three decades, the so-called "separate spheres" model, is a hybrid of class and gender theory. It argues that women lived in sealed communities, without autonomy or direction, being little more than passive victims of the whims of men who dominated social and institutional life.[32] The model also stresses the "sisterhood" of women, their separate consciousness from men, and their shared suffering from the effects of capitalism and patriarchy.[33]

Such an approach denies the experiences of a Duchess of Devonshire or a Duchess of Gordon as relevant or significant. Yet Georgiana's life is representative of a vital part of eighteenth-century society. Male and female relations were robust, multi-layered, and contradictory. Neither the public and private nor the social and political realms existed as separate entities. They blurred into each other, making divisions often subtle and nuanced. Rather than being an anomaly, Georgiana's political career demonstrates the fluidity which characterized relations between the sexes. The propensity of women's historians to ignore high politics, and of political historians to ignore women, has resulted in a profound misunderstanding of one of the most sexually integrated periods of British history.

A more appropriate model for the eighteenth century would be one of interlocking spheres, recognizing the flexibility of social conventions of the era: women's lives reflected the shifting patterns of society and were equally susceptible to the pressures caused by class, locality, economy, and age.[34] The perceived "proper role" of women was a much-debated question which led to disagreements between family members, both within the aristocracy and in society as a whole. Georgiana herself agonized about whether she was pushing the limits of her role too far. On the other hand, she continued to explore those limits until the time of her death. Nor was she alone. Linda Colley's study of women's political and social participation at the end of the century led her to conclude that they were much more active than the literature of the time would have us believe. The vociferous critics who called for women to remain in the domestic sphere were fighting a rearguard action against the great number who were already outside it.[35]

At various times Georgiana had access to real power and encountered men who were willing for her to use it. At others, she was barred from participation at the joint instigation of her male and female contemporaries.[36] The pattern of her friendships was similarly complex. Georgiana had close and confiding relationships with members of both sexes. Though it would not be appropriate to apply twentieth-century preconceptions about heterosexual and homosexual behaviour to Georgiana's relationships with Mary Graham and Lady Elizabeth Foster—the evidence remains inconclusive—if, indeed, Georgiana and Bess were lovers it would merely confirm that eighteenth-century sexuality was no less inclusive than its modern counterpart.

Historians have begun to question the idea that in the eighteenth century women and men lived in distinctly separate spheres.[37] Georgiana's political career is a compelling example of how such a view contradicts the reality of eighteenth-century life, stripping it of its richness and diversity. Her history is as much a part of the history of men and the wider world as it is of the women's community. She is remarkable for being a successful politician whose actions brought about national events; for attaining great prominence in spite of the fact she was a woman in a society which favoured men; and for achieving these successes while enduring great personal suffering in her search for self-fulfilment.

Long after the scattering of the Whig party and the destruction of Devonshire House Georgiana continues to fascinate because of her single-minded determination to be the heroine of her own story. "I was but one year older than you when I launched into the vortex of dissipation—a Duchess and a beauty," Georgiana wrote to Hart three weeks before she died, "however . . . all that I have seen never weaken'd my principles to devotion to almighty God or took from my love of virtue and my humble wishes to do what is right."[38]

NOTES

1: DÉBUTANTE

1 Carlisle MSS J18/20/95: GD to Lady Georgiana Morpeth, August 1799.
2 L. Dutens, *Memoirs of a Traveller in Retirement* (London 1806), IV, p. 209.
3 Spencer MSS at Althorp: Mrs. Spencer to Thea Cowper, Sept. 30, 1758.
4 Chatsworth MSS [henceforth Chatsworth] 22: Georgiana, Duchess of Devonshire [GD] to Lady Spencer [LS], Sept. 23, 1774.
5 E. S. de Beer, ed., *The Diary of John Evelyn* (Oxford 1959), p. 886.
6 Joseph Friedman, *Spencer House: The Chronicle of a Great London Mansion* (London 1993), p. 194.
7 D. Douglas, ed., *The Letters and Journals of Lady Mary Coke* (Edinburgh 1889–96), I, p. 96.
8 Brian Connell, *Portrait of a Whig Peer* (London 1957), pp. 46–7.
9 BL Althorp MSS [henceforth BL Althorp] F122: Miss Georgiana Poyntz to Miss Thea Cowper, [1754].
10 Lady Llanover, ed., *The Autobiography and Correspondence of Mary Granville, Mrs Delany* (London 1861–2), IV, p. 186.
11 Friedman, *Spencer House*, p. 55.
12 Brian Masters, *Georgiana, Duchess of Devonshire* (London 1981), p. 4.
13 A. Aspinall and Lord Bessborough, eds., *Lady Bessborough and Her Family Circle* (London 1940), p. 23.
14 Ibid., p. 27.
15 BL Althorp F40: LS to first Earl Spencer, [Oct. 26, 1769].
16 BL Althorp F37: LS to GD, July 17 [1768].
17 Lawrence Stone, *The Family, Sex and Marriage in England 1500–1800* (London 1979), p. 276.
18 BL Althorp F183: Althorp household accounts.
19 Chatsworth 7: Lord Althorp to GD, April 14, 1773.
20 BL Althorp F40: GD to first Earl and Countess Spencer, March 16, 1764.
21 W. T. Whiteley, *Artists and Their Friends in England 1700–1799* (London 1928), II, p. 397.
22 Connell, *Portrait of a Whig Peer*, p. 51.
23 Spencer MSS at Althorp House: diary of Mrs. Poyntz, August 27, 1763.
24 Ibid., June 30, 1764.
25 Ibid., July 10, 1764.
26 BL Althorp F122: LS to Thea Cowper, July 1764.
27 BL Althorp F122: LS to Thea Cowper, Dec. 7, 1765.
28 BL Althorp F40: GD to LS, Feb. 29 [1766]. Note the juxtaposition in the following sentence: "Betty's child is dead But she is very well my grandmamma went to Wimbleton [*sic*] this

morning and found my sisters Hariot and Charlote very well." It is very common for children surprised by a new arrival to fantasize about its removal. The fact that Georgiana linked the death of Betty's child with Harriet and Charlotte being well suggests the turn of her thoughts.

29 Chatsworth C.2014: diary of Lady Spencer.

30 BL Althorp F122: LS to Thea Cowper, Nov. 21, 1766.

31 SNRA Douglas-Home MSS TD95/54: diary of Lady Mary Coke, August 8, 1787.

32 Aspinall and Lord Bessborough, *Lady Bessborough*, p. 23.

33 Ibid., p. 20.

34 Althorp F37: LS to GD, July 30, 1769.

35 Ibid.

36 BL Althorp F42: LS to Mrs. Howe, Nov. 29 [1769].

37 BL Althorp F122: LS to Thea Cowper, Nov. 29, 1771.

38 Chatsworth 9: E. Carter to Hon. Mrs. Howe, Oct. 14, 1773.

39 Evelyn Farr, *Before the Deluge, Parisian Society in the Reign of Louis XVI* (London 1994), p. 73.

40 Henry Wheatley, *The Historical and Posthumous Memoirs of Sir Nathaniel Wraxall* (London 1884), II, p. 344.

41 Sir George Leveson Gower and Iris Palmer, eds., *Harry-O: The Letters of Lady Harriet Cavendish* (London 1940), p. 249.

42 Wheatley, *Historical and Posthumous Memoirs*, I, pp. 113–14.

43 Lady Llanover, *Mary Granville, Mrs Delany*, III, p. 584.

44 *Morning Herald and Daily Advertiser*, Saturday March 30, 1782.

45 Chatsworth 36: first Earl Spencer to GD, Oct. 26, 1774.

46 Chatsworth 13: Miss Georgiana Shipley to GD, Feb. 22, 1773.

47 Chatsworth 12: LS to Mrs. Henry, Jan. 31, 1774.

48 Randolph E. Trumbach, *The Rise of the Egalitarian Family* (New York 1978), p. 97.

49 Chatsworth 12: LS to Mrs. Henry, May 15, 1774.

50 Chatsworth 11: LS to GD, Nov. 26, 1773.

51 Chatsworth 10: LS to GD, Nov. 21, 1773.

52 Elizabeth and Florence Anson, eds., *Mary Hamilton at Court and at Home* (London 1925), p. 27.

53 Lady Llanover, *Mary Granville, Mrs Delany*, IV, p. 587.

54 BL Althorp F183: bills and accounts for 1774.

55 Lady Llanover, *Mary Granville, Mrs Delany*, IV, pp. 593–4.

56 Charlotte Spencer's papers have not survived and there is only scant information about her.

2:FASHION'S FAVOURITE

1 Georgiana's jewellery was a present from the Duke. The earrings alone, consisting of a large single-drop diamond each, cost £3,994 and newspapers speculated that the entire ensemble was worth over £10,000.

2 SNRA Douglas-Home MSS TD95/54: diary of Lady Mary Coke, June 23, 1774.

3 André Parreaux, trans. Carola Congreve, *Daily Life in England in the Reign of George III* (London 1969), p. 45.

4 Andrew C. Bruyn, *The Torrington Diaries* (London 1935), I, p. 37.

5 Mark Girouard, *Life in the English Country House* (London 1978), p. 194.

6 Althorp House MSS: diary of Mrs. Poyntz, July 26, 1764.

7 Chatsworth 20: LS to GD, Sept. 22, 1774.

8 Chatsworth 21: GD to LS, Sept. 23, 1774.

9 Chatsworth 23: LS to GD, Sept. 25, 1774.

10 Chatsworth 28: GD to LS, Oct. 9–15, 1774.

11 Chatsworth 43: GD to LS, Nov. 6–11, 1774.
12 Chatsworth 648: GD to LS, Sept. 22, 1784.
13 F. O'Gorman, *The Rise of Party in England. The Rockingham Whigs 1760–1782* (London 1975), p. 429.
14 Chatsworth 28: GD to LS, Oct. 9, 1774.
15 Chatsworth 32: GD to LS, Oct. 16, 1774.
16 Chatsworth, Curr's Lists, 86/Compartment I: Ben Granger to Unknown, Nov. 3, 1774. Also, F. O'Gorman, *Voters, Patrons and Parties: The Unreformed Electorate of Hanoverian England, 1734–1832* (Oxford 1989), p. 61.
17 Chatsworth 29: LS to GD, Oct. 11–14, 1774.
18 Chatsworth 27: LS to GD, Oct. 9, 1774.
19 Chatsworth 49: GD to LS, Nov. 24, 1774.
20 Chatsworth 37: LS to GD, Oct. 27, 1774.
21 Ibid.
22 Chatsworth 58: GD to LS, Dec. 11, 1774.
23 Johann von Archenholtz, *A View of the British Constitution and of the Manners and Customs of the People of England* (London 1794), I, p. 119.
24 Parreaux, *Daily Life,* p. 83.
25 James Ralph, *A Critical Review of the Public Buildings, Statues, and Ornaments in and about London and Westminster* (rep. London 1971), p. 184.
26 Hugh Stokes, *The Devonshire House Circle* (London 1917), p. 22.
27 *Covent Garden Magazine,* 4, 14, 1752.
28 J. Timbs, *Clubs and Club Life in London* (London 1872), p. 88.
29 Lady Llanover, ed., *The Autobiography and Correspondence of Mary Granville, Mrs Delany* (London 1861–2), II, p. 98.
30 W. S. Lewis, *Horace Walpole's Correspondence* (New Haven, Conn. 1937–80), XXXII, p. 232: Horace Walpole to Lady Ossory, Feb. 1, 1775.
31 William LeFanu, ed., *Betsy Sheridan's Journal* (Oxford 1986), p. 143, n. 49: Jan. 3–6, 1789.
32 SNRA Douglas-Home MSS TD95/54: diary of Lady Mary Coke, July 15, 1774.
33 BL Add. MSS 48218, ff. 40–40d: Anne Robinson to Frederick Robinson, April 4, 1775.
34 SNRA Douglas-Home MSS TD95/54: diary of Lady Mary Coke, June 9, 1776.
35 Chatsworth 65: LS to GD, April 22, 1775.
36 Lady Llanover, *Mary Granville, Mrs Delany* II, p. 114.
37 Chatsworth 65: LS to GD, April 22, 1775.
38 Chatsworth 66: LS to GD, May 8, 1775.
39 BL Althorp F123: Lady Clermont to LS, March 12, 1775.
40 Chatsworth 63: LS to GD, April 14, 1775.
41 *Morning Post,* Friday April 7, 1775.
42 Ibid.
43 Lord Malmesbury, *The Diaries and Correspondence of Lord Malmesbury* (London 1844), I, p. 299. Mrs. Harris wrote to her son in Berlin that one of her friends tried to buy her plumes from the local undertaker, who "sent word back his horses were all out but they were expected home in a few days and then he hoped to accommodate her Ladyship."
44 A. Ribeiro, *Dress and Morality* (London 1986), p. 106.
45 *London Chronicle,* 41, April 29–May 1, 1777.
46 *Morning Post,* Wednesday May 24, 1775.
47 *Morning Post,* Tuesday April 25, 1775.
48 Olivier Bernier, *Imperial Mother, Royal Daughter: The Correspondence of Marie Antoinette and Maria Theresa* (London 1986), p. 171.

49 Chatsworth 80: LS to GD, August 9–15, 1775.

50 Ian Dunlop, *Marie Antoinette* (London 1993), p. 149.

51 Chatsworth 93: GD to LS, Sept. 10, 1775.

52 BL Althorp F125: Miss Lloyd to LS, Oct. 30, 1775.

53 Iris Palmer, *The Face Without a Frown* (London 1944), p. 28.

54 *Morning Post,* Monday March 11, 1776.

55 *Morning Post,* Friday April 12, 1776.

56 John Ashton, *The History of Gambling in England* (London 1871), p. 54.

57 BL Althorp F123: Lady Clermont to LS, July 1776.

58 Chatsworth 163: LS to GD, Nov. 1, 1776.

3:THE VORTEX OF DISSIPATION

1 Chatsworth 156: GD to LS, Oct. 2–11, 1776. The letter is written in French.

2 Chatsworth 219: LS to GD, August 5, 1778.

3 Leslie Mitchell, *Charles James Fox* (Oxford 1992), p. 96.

4 Chatsworth 582: GD to LS, Jan. 12, 1784.

4 Brian Masters, *Georgiana, Duchess of Devonshire* (London 1981), p. 65.

5 BL Add. MSS 51705, f. 54, Lord Pelham to Lady Webster, Dec. 4, 1791.

6 W. Sichel, *Sheridan* (London 1909), I, p. 167.

7 Nat. Lib. Scot. Lynedoch MSS 3624, f. 276: GD to Mary Graham, circa 1778.

8 Chatsworth 184: GD to LS, August 27–Sept. 2, 1777.

9 Christopher Hibbert, *George IV, Prince of Wales* (London 1972), I, p. 131.

10 Francis Bickley, ed., *The Diaries of Sylvester Douglas, Lord Glenbervie* (London 1928), II, p. 23.

11 BL Add. MSS 45911, f. 10: GD to Lady Melbourne, circa 1780–87.

12 BL Add. MSS 45548, f. 1: GD to Lady Melbourne, [after 1785].

13 Chatsworth 310: GD to LS, August 6, 1780.

14 *Morning Post,* Monday Dec. 30, 1776.

15 The gravest charge against her was the bad example her excessive frivolity set for the rest of society. It is unlikely the pamphlets could have escaped her notice, with titles such as *A Letter to Her Grace the Duchess of Devonshire* and *The Duchess of Devonshire's Cow; A Poem.* In the latter, the author praised her generosity, citing the occasion when she spotted a lean and hungry cow in a field. Guessing its owner must be suffering hardship, she had the man located and made him a present of some money. A mocking reply soon came, entitled, *An heroic epistle to the Noble Author of the Duchess of Devonshire's Cow,* which begged for information on further examples of Georgiana's goodness other than a soft spot for cows. A new title appeared almost every month. But in fact the entire controversy was a fabrication, a commercial venture by William Combe, a debt-ridden profligate, who hoped to capitalize on Georgiana's fame. The thirty-five-year-old author, nicknamed "Count Combe" because of his extravagance, had been reduced to translating travels and histories for booksellers before he hit upon the idea of creating paper wars about celebrities. He had enjoyed a considerable success with his satire on Lord Irnham, "The Diaboliad," the year before. Georgiana was only one of his many victims in a series of fake *Letters* he composed to leading figures in society. Eventually the public grew tired of his contrived polemics and Combe became a propaganda writer for the government.

16 Hugh Stokes, *The Devonshire House Circle* (London 1917), p. 140.

17 Chatsworth 178: GD to LS, August 6, 1777.

18 Chatsworth 146: GD to LS, Sept. 21–30, 1776.

19 Chatsworth 641: LS to GD, August 26, 1784.

20 Lady Ilchester and Lord Stavordale, *The Life and Letters of Lady Sarah Lennox* (London 1901), II, p. 261.

21 BL Althorp F125: Lady Clermont to LS, Oct. 16, 1777.

22 Chatsworth 199: GD to LS, Oct. 21, 1777.

23 Nat. Lib. Scot. Lynedoch MSS 3624, f. 277: GD to Mary Graham, circa Dec. 1777. Partly written in French.

24 Chatsworth 202: LS to GD, April 12, 1778.

25 Nat. Lib. Scot. Lynedoch MSS 3590, f. 227R: GD to Mary Graham, circa 1778. Partly written in French.

26 BL Add. MSS 45548, f. 14: GD to Lady Melbourne, nd.

27 Nat. Lib. Scot. Lynedoch MSS 3624, f. 275: GD to Mary Graham, circa 1778. Partly written in French.

28 Ibid.

29 Nat. Lib. Scot. Lynedoch MSS 3590, f. 227R, GD to Mary Graham, circa 1778. Partly written in French.

30 Richard Brinsley Sheridan, *The School for Scandal,* in Eric S. Rump, ed., *The School for Scandal and Other Plays* (London 1988), p. 217, act II, scene ii.

31 Lord Bessborough, ed., *Georgiana, Duchess of Devonshire* (London 1955), p. 35.

32 Lord Herbert, *Henry, Elizabeth and George* (*The Pembroke Papers*) (London 1939), p. 298: Lady Pembroke to Lord Herbert, Oct. 20, 1779.

33 Claude Manceron, trans. Nancy Amphoux, *The Age of the French Revolution: Toward the Brink* (New York 1983), IV, p. 94.

34 Masters, *Georgiana,* p. 68. Lady Louisa Stuart wrote to Lady Caroline Dawson: "We both read the same book, and it furnished us with a great deal of conversation; it was La Nouvelle Héloïse, with which I am charmed, perhaps more than I should be, yet, I do not think I feel the worse for it. . . . indeed I believe it might be very dangerous to people whose passions resembled those he describes. But I have nothing to do with love, so it is safe with me, and I do think it, notwithstanding several absurdities, the most interesting book I ever read in my life."

35 Chatsworth 126: Lady Jersey to GD, August 1, 1776.

36 Almost £8.5 million in today's money. Lord Holland was deeply wounded by his son's behaviour but couldn't bear to remonstrate with him: "never let Charles know how excessively he afflicts me," he begged.

37 John Ashton, *The History of Gambling in England* (London 1871), p. 75.

38 *Oxford Magazine,* June 1770.

39 Chatsworth 180: GD to LS, August 12–19, 1777.

40 Chatsworth 179: GD to LS, August 9, 1777.

41 J. W. Derry, *Charles James Fox* (New York 1972), pp. 46–7.

42 Leslie Mitchell, *Charles James Fox* (Oxford 1992), p. 32

43 BL Add. MSS 40763, f. 250: GD to Sir Philip Francis, Nov. 29, 1798.

44 Chatsworth 206: GD to LS, April 18, 1778.

45 The following notice appeared in the *London Chronicle* on November 26, 1778: "On Tuesday next will be published, in Two Volumes, 12 mo. price 5s sewed, or 6s bound. 'The Sylph: A Novel.' Printed for T. Lowndes in Fleet Street, where may also be had, just published, in 5 vols. 'Evelina, a Novel,' price 7s, 6d. sewed." *Evelina, or A Young Lady's Entrance into the World* had first appeared anonymously in January, and was an immediate success. The clamour to know the author was so great that the first-time novelist was forced to step out from obscurity and reveal herself to be

Fanny Burney. She was still unmarried at twenty-six and somewhat shy,
but within a few months Mrs. Thrale,
who knew her father, Charles Burney,
had introduced her to all the notable
figures on the literary scene. Thomas
Lowndes, Fanny's publisher, was so
pleased with her sales that he deliberately advertised *The Sylph* to make it
appear to be one of hers. This little
commercial ploy outraged the Bur-
neys, and Charles Burney ordered
Lowndes to stop. Their anger was not
merely pique at his selling techniques
but also genuine fear over the harm
The Sylph might do to Fanny's reputation. Unlike *Evelina, The Sylph* was
less a novel than an exposé of the corrupting mores of the *ton.*
46 Chatsworth 32: GD to LS, Oct.
16–22, 1774.
47 K. Balderston, ed., *Thraliana, The
Diary of Mrs Hester Lynch Thrale (Later
Mrs Piozzi), 1776–1809* (Oxford
1951), I, p. 363, Jan. 20, 1779.

4:A POPULAR PATRIOT

1 *London Chronicle,* 43, June 4–6, 1778.
2 Ibid., June 13–16, 1778.
3 BL Althorp G287: GD to Lord Althorp, May 4, 1778.
4 Chatsworth 212: GD to LS, May
6–12, 1778.
5 *Morning Post,* Saturday July 18, 1788.
6 Ibid., Wednesday Sept. 23, 1778.
7 BL Althorp F123: Lady Clermont to
LS, circa August 1778.
8 Chatsworth 182: GD to LS, August
21, 1777.
9 BL Althorp F123: Lady Clermont to
LS, circa August 1778.
10 Chatsworth 218: LS to GD, July 30,
1778.
11 Chatsworth 223: LS to GD, August
20, 1778.
12 Reginald Blunt, *Mrs Montagu* (Edinburgh 1923), II, p. 58.
13 BL Althorp F8: Lord Althorp to LS,
Oct. 20, 1778.

14 Chatsworth 235: GD to LS, Nov. 4,
1778.
15 Chatsworth 248: GD to LS, Oct.
12–14, 1779.
16 Chatsworth 233: GD to LS, Oct. 26,
1778.
17 SNRA Douglas-Home MSS
TD95/54: diary of Lady Mary Coke,
June 28, 1778.
18 Ibid., Dec. 17, 1778.
19 Duke of Argyll, ed., *Intimate Society
Letters of the Eighteenth Century* (London 1910), I, p. 267: Lady Sarah
Lennox to Lady Sarah O'Brien, Feb.
1779.
20 SNRA Douglas-Home MSS
TD95/54: diary of Lady Mary Coke,
Dec. 3, 1778.
21 Chatsworth 236: GD to LS, Dec. 4,
1778.
22 Chatsworth 237: LS to GD, Dec. 5,
1778.
23 SNRA Douglas-Home MSS
TD95/54: diary of Lady Mary Coke,
Dec. 11, 1780.
24 Chatsworth 237: LS to GD, Dec. 5,
1778.
25 *Morning Herald and Daily Advertiser,*
Sept. 15, 1779.
26 Ibid., Sept. 30, 1779: "The gallant conduct of Capt. Garner of the Fly sloop
in the late engagement with the two
French Cutters, cannot be sufficiently
extolled. Having exhausted all his am-
munition, he ordered a boat out, in
which he rowed on board the packet
to procure more and appeared before
the noble passengers on the deck with
one side of him almost covered with
the blood of that brave officer, his
master Mr Armourer, who was killed
close by him. Lord Spencer here addressing him said he had given the
strongest testimony of his courage,
and therefore begged he 'would no
longer contend with a force so superior at the hazard of his ship and crew,
for it was of very little consequence
whether the Duchess of Devonshire,

Lady Spencer, and himself, were carried into France or not.'—'It may be of no consequence to your Lordship,' replied the brave Garner, 'but it is of the utmost consequence to *me,* and therefore you shall not be taken while I have life, by G—!' "

27 Chatsworth 244: GD to LS, Oct. 1–3, 1779.

28 Chatsworth 246: GD to LS, Oct. 6–10, 1779.

29 Chatsworth 253: GD to LS, Oct. 21, 1779.

30 BL Althorp F121: Lord Frederick Cavendish to LS, Nov. 11, 1779.

31 Chatsworth 248: GD to LS, Oct. 12–14, 1779.

32 Chatsworth 252: LS to GD, Oct. 1779.

33 PRO 30/29/4/7, f. 74: Miss R. Lloyd to Lady Stafford, July 8, 1780.

34 *Morning Herald and Daily Advertiser,* April 16, 1781.

35 Chatsworth 287: GD to LS, May 9, 1780.

36 Chatsworth 284: LS to GD, May 1, 1780.

37 Chatsworth 281: LS to GD, April 26, 1780.

38 Chatsworth 287: GD to LS, May 9, 1780.

39 BL Althorp F9: Lord Althorp to LS, April 10, 1780.

40 BL Althorp G287: GD to Lord Althorp, May 9, 1780.

41 *Morning Herald and Daily Advertiser,* March 21, 1781.

42 PRO 30/29/4/7, f. 77: Miss R. Lloyd to Lady Stafford, Sept. 7, 1780.

43 Chatsworth 321: Lady Harriet Spencer to Miss Shipley, circa Oct. 1780.

44 Ibid.

45 PRO 30/29/4/7, f. 76: Miss R. Lloyd to Lady Stafford, August 24, 1780.

46 Chatsworth 306: GD to LS, July 28, 1780.

47 BL Althorp F125: Miss Lloyd to LS, Oct. 30, 1775.

48 Chatsworth 269: Edmund Burke to GD, March 17, 1780. The excitement surrounding the Duke's speech offended those who were unimpressed by the Cavenish wealth. Mrs. Thrale wrote in her diary, "what a Bustle they make about the Duke of Devonshire's speaking, one would think it was Balaam's Ass." K. Balderston, ed., *Thraliana, The Diary of Mrs Hester Lynch Thrale (Later Mrs Piozzi), 1776–1809* (Oxford 1951), VI, p. 434: March 26, 1780.

49 Chatsworth 279: GD to LS, April 24, 1780.

50 Chatsworth 280: GD to LS, April 25, 1780.

51 Chatsworth 287: GD to LS, May 9, 1780.

52 F. O'Gorman, *The Rise of Party in England* (London 1975), p. 420.

53 Ibid.

54 Henry Wheatley, *The Historical and Posthumous Memoirs of Sir Nathaniel Wraxall* (London 1884), V, p. 371.

55 The relationship fits easily within the patterns of the Prince's love life. The first time he fell in love was over one of his sister's attendants, Mary Hamilton, granddaughter of the Duke of Hamilton. Like all the women he ever fancied, she was several years older than he. She had no idea of his passion until he bombarded her with daily letters. The rather shy and upright twenty-three-year-old was shocked by her unwanted suitor's intemperate ravings—he loved her "beyond the idea of everything that is human." He sent a lock of his hair and requested she return one of hers in the engraved locket he had provided. After a few weeks of enduring the brunt of his extreme passion, she managed to convince him that his suit was futile and he agreed to address her as "friend and sister." Calling himself her dearest brother, he sought her advice on everything, but especially on

clothes and even went so far as to send her patterns from his tailor. His attentions abruptly ceased when he met Perdita, and they rarely spoke again. As a model, this early relationship makes the Prince's later infatuation with Georgiana plausible.

56 Chatsworth 401.1: Lady Melbourne to GD, circa June 1782. Lady Melbourne managed to keep the affair going for almost two years, and in 1784 gave birth to his son, George. The newspapers only really began to pass comment when she and Georgiana helped the Prince to refurbish Carlton House in 1783. That gave the *Morning Herald* the opportunity to write slyly, "the alterations now making at Carlton House . . . by Lady Melbourne, has the guidance of most of the *erections* on this spot." Lady Melbourne profited from the liaison in many ways, not least in having her husband made a Gentleman of the Bedchamber.

57 Chatsworth 297: GD to LS, June 5, 1780.

58 Chatsworth 289: GD to LS, June 7, 1780.

59 Chatsworth 303: GD to LS, June 9, 1780.

60 Chatsworth 296: GD to LS, May 30, 1780.

61 C. Price ed., *The Letters of Richard Brinsley Sheridan* (Oxford 1966), I, p. 135: R. B. Sheridan to GD, Sept. 19, 1780.

5: INTRODUCTION TO POLITICS

1 *Morning Herald and Daily Advertiser,* Jan. 19, 1781.

2 Carlisle MSS J14/1/558: W. Fawkener to Lord Carlisle, March 2, 1781.

3 BL Althorp F123: Lady Clermont to LS, June 8, 1780.

4 Chatsworth 329: LS to GD, Feb. 14, 1781.

5 Chatsworth 323: GD to LS, Dec. 21, 1780.

6 Chatsworth 371: LS to GD, Oct. 4, 1781.

7 Chatsworth 325: GD to LS, Feb. 12, 1781.

8 *Morning Herald and Daily Advertiser,* March 21, 1781.

9 Ibid., March 24, 1781.

10 Chichester R. O. Lord Bessborough MSS 231: Dorothy, Duchess of Portland to Lord Duncannon, April 1, 1781.

11 Ibid., April 3, 1781.

12 Chatsworth 261: LS to GD, Nov. 17, 1779.

13 Chatsworth 369: LS to GD, Sept. 29, 1781.

14 Carlisle MSS J/14/1/267: George Selwyn to Lord Carlisle, May 28, 1781.

15 Colonel George Hanger, *The Life, Adventures, and Opinions of Colonel George Hanger* (London 1801), II, p. 126.

16 S. Rogers, *Recollections of the Table Talk of Samuel Rogers* (London 1856), p. 190.

17 SNRA Douglas-Home MSS TD95/54: diary of Lady Mary Coke, June 17–22, 1781.

18 *Morning Herald and Daily Advertiser,* June 11, 1781.

19 Chatsworth 362: GD to LS, Sept. 3–12, 1781.

20 N. Mckendrick, J. Brewer, and J. H. Plumb, eds., *The Birth of a Consumer Society* (London 1982), p. 112.

21 Ibid. Georgiana's popularity served many purposes. Authors frequently dedicated their books to her with an eye to associating their work with fashion. She did not have the heart to refuse such dedications although sometimes the work was abominable. "A thousand thanks for Mr Garrick's very pretty verses," wrote Mrs. Montagu, disgusted by the dross sometimes associated with Georgiana. "I was glad to see something address'd to the Duchess of Devonshire of which wit and good nature would make her amends for the austerity

and dullness of some things in prose which had been addressed to her Grace." Reginald Blunt, *Mrs Montagu* (Edinburgh 1923), II, p. 18; Mrs. Montagu to Mrs. Vesey, June 1, 1777.

22 *Morning Herald and Daily Advertiser,* Dec. 3, 1781.

23 P. G. Thomas, *Lord North* (London 1976), p. 111.

24 Carlisle MSS J14/1/337: George Selwyn to Lord Carlisle, March 1782.

25 Ibid., March 22, 1782.

26 *Morning Herald and Daily Advertiser,* March 30, 1782.

27 Carlisle MSS J14/1/345: George Selwyn to Lord Carlisle, March 21, 1782.

28 Nathaniel Wraxall, *Posthumous and Historical Memoirs of My Own Time* (London 1904), II, p. 196.

29 Basil Cozens-Hardy, ed., *The Diary of Silas Neville, 1767–1788* (Oxford 1950), p. 29.

30 *London Chronicle,* April 2–4, 1782.

31 *Morning Herald and Daily Advertiser,* May 21, 1782.

32 Chatsworth 387: LS to GD, May 22, 1782.

33 Carlisle MSS J/14/1/570: James Hare to Lord Carlisle, Feb. 11, 1782.

34 Chatsworth 433: Annecdotes Concerning HRH the Prince of Wales, Sept. 1782.

6: THE NEWCOMER

1 The *Morning Herald and Daily Advertiser* erroneously reported that month that Georgiana was pregnant, but there is no mention in Georgiana's letters of a pregnancy. Lady Mary Coke had heard she was pregnant in November and the papers hinted at it in January. It is likely that Georgiana miscarried before the spring: she would not have been allowed on to the hustings with Charles Fox if she had been pregnant.

2 Chatsworth 390: GD to LS, May 22–24, 1782.

3 Chatsworth 393: GD to LS, June 1, 1782.

4 Chatsworth 397: GD to LS, June 8, 1782.

5 Dorothy Stuart, *Dearest Bess* (London 1955), p. 2.

6 It was only when Frederick Hervey was offered the Bishopric of Derry that the family had their first permanent home. Once safely installed, the new Bishop indulged his heterodox interests. He was good about employing Irish rather than English clergy and, as one would expect from a friend of Voltaire, he despised religious bigots. But he spent as little time as possible at his duties. One of his greatest pleasures was to play humiliating tricks on unsuspecting victims. Once he entertained the fattest clergymen of his acquaintance, and after feeding them a sumptuous dinner announced a competition: a race across his park and the winner would receive a newly vacant, and plum, living. He lined them up outside while they groaned and shivered and sent them running off into a bog, where they almost drowned in the thick oozing mud. After much crying and floundering about in the darkness they managed to climb back on to the bank, and returned wet and filthy to the house. They found their horses waiting for them and the door locked. It was this sort of behaviour which confirmed that the Bishop was a true Hervey.

7 Chatsworth 532.4: Lady Elizabeth Foster [henceforth Bess] to GD, circa Sept. 1782.

8 Brian Fothergill, *The Mitred Earl* (London 1988), p. 47.

9 Ibid., p. 84.

10 Caroline Grosvenor, *The First Lady Wharncliffe and Her Family* (London 1927), I, pp. 9–10.

11 Ibid.

12 The paid companion was the only bona fide job for an upper-class indi-

gent. Often she was a poor, distant relation of the family who received no regular salary but bed and board, and the occasional cast-offs. She dined with the family, was expected to amuse or keep quiet when the occasion demanded, fetched, carried, listened and generally undertook anything that was tedious. An outsider was hired on the basis of her personality and her willingness to please, hence the paid companion's reputation for sycophancy.

13 Vere Foster, *The Two Duchesses* (Bath 1974), pp. 199–200: Bess to Augustus Foster, circa 1804.

14 Chatsworth 397: GD to LS, June 8, 1782.

15 Chatsworth 1565: James Hare to GD, Jan. 27, 1801.

16 Chatsworth 396: LS to GD, June 7, 1782.

17 Chatsworth 398: GD to LS, June 10, 1782.

18 Chatsworth 413: GD to LS, June 15–19, 1782.

19 Chatsworth 435: GD to LS, Sept. 30, 1782.

20 Ibid.

21 Chatsworth 440: GD to LS, Oct. 11–18, 1782.

22 Chatsworth 446: GD to LS, Oct. 22, 1782.

23 Chatsworth 443: LS to GD, Oct. 19, 1782.

24 Chatsworth 440: GD to LS, Oct. 11–18, 1782.

25 Chatsworth 454: GD to LS, Oct. 29, 1782.

26 Chatsworth 457: GD to LS, Nov. 5, 1782.

27 Chatsworth 1332: LS to Selina Trimmer, Nov. 9, 1796.

28 Chatsworth 403: LS to GD, June 28, 1782.

29 Chatsworth 459: LS to GD, Nov. 9, 1782.

30 Chatsworth 460: GD to LS, Nov. 12, 1782.

31 BL Althorp F37: LS to Lady Harriet Duncannon, Nov. 16, 1782.

32 Chatsworth 426: GD to LS, Dec. 1, 1782.

33 Chatsworth 472: LS to GD, Dec. 8, 1782.

34 BL Althorp F37: LS to Lady Harriet Duncannon, Jan. 9, 1783.

35 Chatsworth 472: LS to GD, Dec. 8, 1782.

36 Chatsworth 466: LS to GD, Dec. 3, 1782.

37 BL Althorp F37: LS to Lady Harriet Duncannon, Jan. 16, 1783.

38 Chatsworth 476: GD to LS, Dec. 24, 1782.

39 Chatsworth 482: GD to Bess, Jan. 25, 1783.

40 Foster, *The Two Duchesses,* pp. 94–8: Lady Bristol to Bess, March 13, 1783.

7: AN UNSTABLE COALITION

1 Chatsworth 475: GD to LS, Dec. 23, 1782.

2 J. Ehrman, *The Younger Pitt* (London 1969–96), I, p. 100.

3 Chatsworth 492: GD to Bess, circa Feb. 1783.

4 Ibid.

5 Chatsworth 492.1: GD to Bess, circa Feb. 1783.

6 Chatsworth 490: GD to Bess, April 5, 1783.

7 Ibid.

8 BL Althorp G287: GD to Lord Althorp, April 1783.

9 Ibid.

10 SNRA Douglas-Home MSS TD95/54: diary of Lady Mary Coke, May 28, 1783.

11 Ian Dunlop, *Marie-Antoinette* (London 1993), p. 155.

12 Chatsworth 495: GD to LS, May 8, 1783.

13 *London Chronicle,* May 27, 1783.

14 SNRA Douglas-Home MSS TD95/54: diary of Lady Mary Coke, May 28, 1783.

15 Chatsworth 507.1: Bess to GD, circa June 1783.
16 Chatsworth 508: GD to Bess, June 20, 1783.
17 Leslie Mitchell, *Charles James Fox* (Oxford 1992), p. 62.
18 A. Aspinall, *The Correspondence of George, Prince of Wales, 1770–1812* (London 1964), I, no. 91: GD to Prince of Wales, circa June 17, 1783.

8: A BIRTH AND A DEATH

1 Brian Masters, *Georgiana, Duchess of Devonshire* (London 1981), p. 103.
2 Dr. Amanda Vickery's study of Elizabeth Shackleton, a member of the provincial gentry living in a small Lancashire valley, reveals that, among other things, she was fascinated (and sometimes appalled) by Georgiana's fashions. But while she had no intention of wearing a "wax kitchen garden in her hair," something not quite so conspicuous, like the "picture hat" was a more attainable style. "Women and the World of Goods: a Lancashire consumer and her possessions, 1751–1781" in John Brewer and Roy Porter, eds., *Consumption and the World of Goods* (London 1993), pp. 274–304.
3 SNRA Douglas-Home MSS TD95/54: diary of Lady Mary Coke, July 12, 1783.
4 Chatsworth 508.1: GD to Bess, July 1783.
5 Chatsworth 512: GD to Bess, July 1783.
6 *Morning Post,* July 16, 1783.
7 Women had used wet-nurses for over 700 years, and it was only recently that social commentators had begun to challenge the practice. The fashion of décolletage played a large part in discouraging breast-feeding. It was as important to have an attractive cleavage as it was to have clear skin and good hair. As soon as a pregnancy was over, women resorted to elaborate procedures to drive back the milk and reduce the size of the breasts. One remedy was to apply lint around the nipple, another was the use of hareskin treated with ointments. The various methods frequently caused infections and inflammations, and many women developed tumours as a result. Medical opinion held that a woman's milk was converted blood, through which her characteristics, and her diseases, could be passed on to the child. In consequence, the criteria for a wet-nurse were extremely precise. A whole list of features barred women from wet-nursing: redheads or those with freckles or blemishes were automatically disqualified, for example. Height and intelligence were important factors too. The most highly sought-after wet-nurse was a woman in her early twenties, with clear skin, blue eyes, brown hair, and a good disposition.
8 Chatsworth 516: GD to LS, August 6, 1783.
9 Chatsworth 529: GD to LS, Sept. 1–16, 1783.
10 Chatsworth 507.1: Bess to GD, circa June 1783.
11 Chatsworth 511: Bess to GD, July 20, 1783.
12 Ibid.
13 Chatsworth 513: fifth Duke of Devonshire to Bess, July 29, 1783.
14 Chatsworth 507.1: Bess to GD, circa June 1783.
15 Chatsworth 532.2: GD to Bess, circa Sept. 1783.
16 Vere Foster, *The Two Duchesses* (Bath 1974), p. 88: Lady Bristol to Bess, Feb. 7, 1783.
17 Chatsworth 519: GD to Bess, August 19, 1783.
18 Ibid.
19 Chatsworth 530: Bess to GD, Sept. 8, 1783.
20 An early promissory note of Georgiana's to a money lender appears in the published diary of Lady Charlotte

Bury, edited by A. Francis Steuart, *The
Diary of a Lady-in-Waiting by Lady
Charlotte Bury* (London 1908): "December 18, 1779. Mr D——ll, having
lent me two thousand six hundred
and fifty pounds, I do hereby promise
to pay him two hundred and fifty
pounds every three months, at the
usual quarter days . . . allowing five
per cent and five percent for insurance
of my life per annum, until principal,
interest, and insurance, shall be fully
paid." The lender in question added:
"My agreement is that in case the
Duchess does not pay me two hundred and fifty pounds quarterly that I
shall acquaint the Duke of D with this
transaction . . . as I have lent her the
money to relieve her from play debts,
under a solemn promise that she will
not play in future."

21 SNRA Douglas-Home MSS
TD95/54: diary of Lady Mary Coke,
May 30, 1783.

22 *Morning Herald and Daily Advertiser,*
Sept. 30, 1783.

23 Chatsworth 542: GD to LS, Oct. 7,
1783.

24 W. S. Lewis, *Horace Walpole's Correspondence* (New Haven, Conn.
1937–80), XXXIII, p. 408: Horace
Walpole to Lady Ossory, July 23,
1783.

25 Chatsworth 533: GD to LS, Sept. 15,
1783.

26 M. D. George, *Catalogue of Political and
Personal Satires Preserved in the Depart-
ment of Prints and Drawings in the
British Museum* (London 1947), VIII,
C. 6263: "The Ladies Church Yard,"
Sept. 23, 1783.

27 Chatsworth 533: GD to LS, Sept. 15,
1783.

28 Chatsworth 538: LS to GD, Sept. 28,
1783.

29 Chatsworth 534: GD to LS, Sept. 17,
1783.

30 Chatsworth 549: GD to LS, Oct. 21,
1783.

31 Chatsworth 547: GD to Bess, Oct.
18, 1783.

32 Chatsworth 508: GD to Bess, June
20, 1783.

33 Henry Wheatley, *The Historical and
Posthumous Memoirs of Sir Nathaniel
Wraxall* (London 1884), I, p. 10.

34 BL Althorp F40: diary of Lady
Spencer, Nov. 1 and 2, 1783.

35 BL Althorp G287: GD to Lord
Spencer, Nov. 6, 1783.

36 Chatsworth 573: GD to Bess, Jan. 3,
1784.

37 Ibid.

38 Chatsworth 576: GD to Bess, Jan. 6,
1784.

39 Chatsworth 569.1: fifth Duke of
Devonshire to Bess, circa Dec.
1783.

40 Chatsworth 603: Bess to GD, Feb.
1784.

41 Evelyn Farr, *Marie Antoinette and Count
Fersen* (London 1995), p. 41.

42 Chatsworth 604: Bess to GD, Feb.
1784.

43 Chatsworth 749: GD to Bess, July 3,
1786.

44 Chatsworth 603: Bess to GD, Feb.
1784.

45 BL Althorp F123: Lady Clermont to
LS, Feb. 26, 1784.

46 Chatsworth 595: GD to LS, Feb. 5,
1784.

47 Chatsworth 607: GD to Bess, March
8, 1784.

48 Chatsworth 591: GD to LS, Jan. 21,
1784.

49 Chatsworth 610: GD to LS, circa
April 1784.

50 Chatsworth 598: GD to LS, Feb. 8,
1784.

51 Chatsworth 582: GD to LS, Jan. 12,
1784.

9: THE WESTMINSTER ELECTION

1 BL Althorp F121: Lord Frederick
Cavendish to LS and GD, Dec. 1783.

2 Chatsworth 575: GD to Bess, Jan. 3,
1784.

3 Chatsworth 598: GD to LS, Feb. 7, 1784.

4 Chatsworth 573: GD to Bess, Jan. 3, 1784.

5 Chatsworth 608: GD to LS, March 17, 1784.

6 Chatsworth 609: GD to LS, March 20, 1784.

7 M. D. George, *Catalogue of Personal and Political Satires* (London 1935–54), VIII, C. 6484: "The Coalition Party Beating Up for Recruits," circa March 1784.

8 J. Ehrman, *The Younger Pitt* (London 1969–96), I, p. 141.

9 PRO 30/8/103, f. 93: George III to William Pitt, April 13, 1784.

10 F. O'Gorman, *Voters, Patrons and Parties* (Oxford, 1989), p. 129.

11 Hugh Stokes, *The Devonshire House Circle* (London 1917), p. 205.

12 *London Chronicle,* March 30–April 1, 1784.

13 Henry Wheately, *The Historical and Posthumous Memoirs of Sir Nathaniel Wraxall* (London 1884), III, p. 346.

14 Stokes, *Devonshire House Circle,* p. 203.

15 PRO 30/8/21, ff. 183–4: Mrs. Boscawen to Lady Chatham, April 12, 1784.

16 Chatsworth 610.3: GD to LS, circa early April 1784.

17 HMC XIV Report, Part I, Rutland MSS, Appendix, pp. 87–88: Earl Temple Nugent to Duke of Rutland, April 12, 1784.

18 Chatsworth 610.1: GD to LS, circa early April 1784.

19 Brian Connell, *Portrait of a Whig Peer* (London 1957), p. 155.

20 Chatsworth 36: first Earl Spencer to GD, Oct. 26, 1774.

21 A. Aspinall, *Politics and the Press, c. 1780–1850* (London 1949), p. 67.

22 BL Althorp G276: LS to second Earl Spencer, April 11, 1784.

23 BL Althorp F38: LS to Lady Duncannon, April 13, 1784.

24 Reginald Blunt, *Mrs Montagu* (Edinburgh 1923), II, p. 169: circa April 1784.

25 Florence and Elizabeth Anson, *Mary Hamilton, Afterwards Mrs John Dickenson, at Court and at Home* (London 1925), April 27, 1784.

26 Chatsworth 611: Duchess of Portland to GD, April 13, 1784.

27 Chatsworth 612: Duke of Portland to GD, April 14, 1784.

28 BL Althorp F121: Lord John Cavendish to LS, April 14, 1784.

29 BL Althorp G287: GD to second Earl Spencer, April 23, 1784.

30 Chatsworth 638: LS to GD, August 14, 1784.

31 *Morning Herald and Daily Advertiser,* April 15, 1784.

32 George, *Catalogue,* VIII, C. 6597: "The Apotheosis of the Duchess," May 25, 1784.

33 *Morning Post,* April 19, 1784.

34 *Morning Herald and Daily Advertiser,* April 21, 1784.

35 J. Hartley, ed., *History of the Westminster Election* (London 1784), p. 494.

36 Ibid., p. 254.

37 *Morning Herald and Daily Advertiser,* April 28, 1784.

38 Ibid., May 1, 1784.

39 BL Althorp G289: Lavinia, Lady Spencer, to second Earl Spencer, April 24, 1784.

40 Chatsworth 615: LS to GD, May 15, 1784.

41 Leslie Mitchell, *Charles James Fox and the Disintegration of the Whig Party* (Oxford 1971), p. 95.

42 HMC XIV Report, Part I, Rutland MSS, Appendix, p. 88: Daniel Pultney to Duke of Rutland, May 6, 1784.

43 *London Chronicle,* May 15–18, 1784.

44 Joyce Hemlow and Althea Douglas, eds., *The Journals and Letters of Fanny Burney (Madame d'Arblay)* (Oxford 1972–84), I, p. 61.

45 See Linda Colley, *Britons, Forging the Nation 1707–1837* (London 1992), p. 244.

46 Lady Granville, ed., *The Private Correspondence of Lord Granville Leveson Gower* (London 1916), I, p. 243: Lady Bessborough to Lord Granville Leveson Gower [henceforth LGLG], March 5, 1799.

10: OPPOSITION

1 Chatsworth 620: GD to LS, June 16, 1784.
2 Ibid.
3 Chatsworth 614: GD to Bess, June 27, 1784.
4 BL Althorp F123: Lady Clermont to LS, August 4, 1784.
5 PRO 30/8/21, f. 189: Mrs. Boscawen to Lady Chatham, May 29, 1784.
6 "His Highness is making fierce love to ye Widow Fitzherbert, & I think will succeed," wrote Lady Milbanke to Wentworth Noel, March 10, 1784. Malcolm Elwin, *The Noels and the Milbanks* (London 1967), p. 233.
7 Lord Bessborough, *Georgiana, Duchess of Devonshire* (London 1955), p. 87.
8 BL Althorp F123: Lady Clermont to LS, August 4, 1784.
9 Chatsworth 641: LS to GD, August 26, 1784.
10 BL Althorp F38: LS to Lady Duncannon, Sept. 27, 1784.
11 Chatsworth 645: GD to LS, Sept. 4–10, 1784.
12 Chatsworth 643: GD to LS, August 28–Sept. 4, 1784.
13 BL Althorp F12: second Earl Spencer to LS, Sept. 27, 1784.
14 BL Althorp F125: Miss Lloyd to LS, Sept. 29, 1784.
15 Chatsworth 651: GD to LS, Sept. 26, 1784.
16 Chatsworth 653: GD to LS, Oct. 12, 1784.
17 BL Althorp G276: LS to second Earl Spencer, Nov. 22, 1784. Even Lady Spencer noticed her thinness: "If she is grown leaner since, she must be a shadow."
18 BL Althorp G289: Lavinia, Lady Spencer to second Earl Spencer, Dec. 2, 1784.
19 Chatsworth 584: Bess to GD, Jan. 17, 1784.
20 Ibid.
21 Chatsworth 667.1: Bess to GD, Feb. 1785.
22 Chatsworth 679: GD to Bess, June 1785.
23 Ibid.
24 SNRA Douglas-Home MSS TD95/54: diary of Lady Mary Coke, May 21, 1785.
25 Bath Public Library ALB. 2289: Elizabeth Sheridan to Mehitabel Patrick Canning, July 11, 1785.
26 Chatsworth 673: LS to GD, May 6, 1785.
27 Chatsworth 677: GD to LS, June 7, 1785.
28 SNRA Douglas-Home MSS TD95/54: diary of Lady Mary Coke, Sept. 8, 1785.
29 Ibid., Nov. 18, 1785.
30 Dorothy Stuart, *Dearest Bess* (London 1955), p. 28: July 10, 1785.
31 Chatsworth 678: Bess to GD, June 21, 1785.
32 Chatsworth 681: fifth Duke of Devonshire to Bess, August 11, 1785.
33 Chatsworth 682: fifth Duke of Devonshire to Bess, August 29, 1785.
34 Stuart, *Dearest Bess,* p. 33.
35 Ibid., p. 35.
36 Chatsworth 744: fifth Duke of Devonshire to Bess, May 16, 1786.
37 Lord Bessborough, *Georgiana,* p. 103.
38 BL Add. MSS 37843, f. 5: Edmund Burke to William Windham, Oct. 14, 1784.
39 *Morning Herald and Daily Advertiser,* Dec. 1, 1784.
40 Thomas Campbell, *The Life of Mrs Siddons* (London 1832), I, p. 89.
41 Almost all Georgiana's patronage had a social, and hence political, dimension. On June 14, 1784, the *Morning*

Herald and Daily Advertiser announced that the Prince of Wales and Georgiana "are at the head of a subscription for building the new theatre near Grosvernor Place. . . . It will be called the 'The Prince of Wales' Theatre,' built by Mr Harris for fashionable people, and will have a suite of ballrooms and apartments like that at Ranelagh and Vauxhall."

42 SNRA Douglas-Home MSS D95/54: diary of Lady Mary Coke, Sept. 12, 1787.

43 Ibid., Oct. 28, 1785.

44 A. Ribeiro, *The Dress Worn at Masquerades in England, 1730–1790, and its Relation to Fancy Dress in Portraiture* (London 1984), p. 131.

45 Chatsworth 639: GD to LS, August 14–18, 1784.

46 A. Ribeiro, *Dress in Eighteenth-Century Europe, 1715–1789* (London 1984), p. 155.

47 *Morning Herald and Daily Advertiser,* Jan. 19, 1785.

48 Ibid., April 22, 1785.

49 If it were only her cleverness with designs, Georgiana might have been important in the fashion world without being a popular figure, like Lady Jersey or Lady Melbourne. But what endeared her to the public was her diligence in carrying out public commitments. Her name appeared on every subscription list, whether for orphans, new theatres, or public assembly rooms. However, people often took advantage of her generosity. That year Miss George received a similar boost to her career, despite the *Morning Post*'s dismissive remark: "The Duchess of Devonshire, with that liberality of sentiment, for which she is distinguished, was particularly conspicuous in her plaudits to modest merit." *Morning Post,* August 5, 1786. Its criticism was less an attack on Miss George than on the commercialization of Georgiana's reputation. Her inability to rebuff requests for patronage made a farce of the system of dedication. On April 10, 1788, the *Morning Herald* complained: "We are sorry to observe the name of the Duchess of Devonshire is frequently prefixed to execrable writing, boasting her Grace's 'permission' for the dedication. Mrs Hill's despicable effusions may be adverted to in proof." The newspaper was unaware that Georgiana had fought a tiresome battle with the printer, Mr. Thompson, to prevent him from livening up Mrs. Hill's book with an engraved portrait and a long letter of dedication.

50 Lord Bessborough, *Georgiana,* p. 88: GD to Prince of Wales, circa Dec. 1785.

51 Lord John Russell, *Memorials and Correspondence of Charles James Fox* (London 1853–7), II, pp. 283–4: Prince of Wales to Fox, Dec. 11, 1785.

52 Chatsworth 717: GD to LS, Feb. 7, 1786.

53 Christopher Hibbert, *George IV, Prince of Wales* (London 1972), p. 59.

54 SNRA Douglas-Home MSS TD95/54: diary of Lady Mary Coke, Jan. 19, 1785.

55 Chatsworth 753: Lady Melbourne to GD, July 24, 1786.

56 Borthwick Institute Hickleton MSS A1.2.7, f. 9: Duchess of Portland to Lady Louisa Ponsonby, Feb. 1782.

57 Lewis Melville, ed., *The Berry Papers* (London 1914), p. 39: Hon. Mrs. Damer to Mary Berry, June 20, 1791.

58 BL Althorp G287: GD to second Earl Spencer, circa July 1786.

59 BL Althorp F14: second Earl Spencer to LS, July 6, 1786.

60 BL Althorp G290: Lavinia, Lady Spencer to second Earl Spencer, August 11, 1786.

61 BL Althorp F13: second Earl Spencer to LS, Dec. 14, 1785.

62 Chatsworth 692: Bess to GD, Dec. 10, 1785.

63 Stuart, *Dearest Bess*, p. 24.

64 Chatsworth 744: Bess to GD, June 7, 1786.

65 Stuart, *Dearest Bess*, p. 37.

66 *Morning Post*, August 4, 1786.

67 Borthwick Institute Hickleton MSS A1.2.6, f. 9: Lord John Cavendish to Louisa Ponsonby, circa Dec. 12, 1784.

68 *Morning Post*, Sept. 1, 1786.

69 BL Althorp G278: LS to second Earl Spencer, Sept. 23, 1786.

70 BL Althorp G278: LS to second Earl Spencer, Oct. 12, 1786.

71 Chatsworth 759: GD to LS, Oct. 15, 1786.

72 Stuart, *Dearest Bess*, p. 38.

73 Ibid.

74 Chichester RO Bessborough MSS 268: LS to Lady Duncannon, Oct. 31, 1786.

75 BL Althorp F14: second Earl Spencer to LS, Oct. 29, 1786.

76 BL Althorp G278: LS to second Earl Spencer, Nov. 2, 1786.

77 BL Althorp G278: LS to second Earl Spencer, Oct. 31, 1786.

78 Ibid.

79 Chatsworth 762: GD to LS, Oct. 19–25, 1786.

80 BL Althorp G278: LS to second Earl Spencer, Dec. 29, 1786.

81 BL Althorp F14: second Earl Spencer to LS, Dec. 31, 1786.

11: QUEEN BESS

1 Chatsworth 766: GD to LS, Nov. 5, 1786.

2 Chatsworth 772: GD to LS, Nov. 15, 1786.

3 Chatsworth 792: GD to LS, Jan. 11, 1787.

4 Chatsworth 791: GD to LS, Jan. 7, 1787.

5 Chatsworth 796: GD to LS, Jan. 25, 1787.

6 Chatsworth 853: Sir Richard Arkwright to GD, Jan. 21, 1788.

7 Chatsworth 802.1: GD to Thomas Coutts, March 12, 1787.

8 Chatsworth 782.1: GD to Thomas Coutts, circa 1787.

9 Chatsworth 819: GD to LS, July 3, 1787.

10 Chatsworth 814: Thomas Coutts to GD, May 23, 1787.

11 Chatsworth 816: GD to Thomas Coutts, May 24, 1787.

12 Chatsworth 814: Thomas Coutts to GD, May 23, 1787.

13 Chatsworth 800: LS to fifth Duke of Devonshire, Feb. 28, 1787.

14 Chatsworth 816: GD to Thomas Coutts, May 24, 1787.

15 BL Althorp F15: second Earl Spencer to LS, Feb. 5, 1787.

16 BL Althorp G278: LS to second Earl Spencer, Feb. 7, 1787.

17 HMC Rutland MSS, p. 388: Daniel Pultney to Duke of Rutland, May 7, 1787.

18 Ibid., p. 395: Daniel Pultney to Duke of Rutland, July 3, 1787.

19 Chatsworth, Georgiana, Duchess of Devonshire Misc.: GD to Bess, circa Feb. 1787.

20 Dorothy Stuart, *Dearest Bess* (London 1955), p. 40.

21 Chatsworth 811: GD to LS, May 10, 1787.

22 Rowlandson drew a caricature in November of the Whigs attending church with Fox standing in the corner, wearing a sinner's cape for playing cards on a Sunday and Georgiana vainly trying to wake the sleeping politicians in the gallery. M. D. George, *Catalogue of Political and Personal Satires* (London 1935–54), IX, C.7182: "Reformation—Or the Wonderful Effects of a Proclamation," Nov. 5, 1787.

23 HMC Rutland MSS, p. 386: Daniel Pultney to Duke of Rutland, Feb. 6, 1787.

24 Ibid.
25 W. S. Lewis, *Horace Walpole's Corre-*
    spondence (New Haven, Conn. 1944),
    XXV, p. 486.
26 Chatsworth 796: GD to LS, Jan. 25,
    1787.
27 BL Add. MSS 45911, f. 10: GD to
    Lady Melbourne, circa 1787–8.

12: MÉNAGE À TROIS

1 BL Althorp G278: LS to second Earl
   Spencer, Oct. 3, 1787.
2 PRO 30/29/4/7, f. 65: Lady Augusta
   Murray to Lady Stafford, circa Sept.
   6, 1787. Written partly in French.
3 Dorothy Stuart, *Dearest Bess* (London
   1955), p. 25.
4 Ibid., p. 40.
5 BL Althorp G279: LS to second Earl
   Spencer, May 27, 1788.
6 Chatsworth 854: GD to LS, Feb. 2,
   1788.
7 BL Althorp G278: LS to second Earl
   Spencer, August 9, 1787.
8 Chatsworth 828: GD to LS, August
   20, 1787.
9 Stuart, *Dearest Bess,* p. 41: circa Feb.
   1788.
10 Ibid., p. 44.
11 Ibid.
12 Chatsworth 856: fifth Duke of Dev-
    onshire to LS, Feb. 7, 1788.
13 BL Althorp G279: LS to second Earl
    Spencer, May 27, 1788.
14 Chatsworth 861A: GD to Bess, Feb.
    25, 1788.
15 Lewis Melville, ed., *The Berry Papers*
    (London 1914), p. 63: Mrs. Damer to
    Mary Berry, August 15, 1791.
16 Chatsworth 871: Duke of Dorset to
    GD, June 12, 1788.
17 BL Add. MSS 45548, f. 2: GD to Lady
    Melbourne, fragment, circa summer
    1788. Dorset left Paris in 1789 so the
    letter could not have been written
    earlier and the comment "I send the
    Children to C. tomorrow" makes the
    suggestion of 1788 credible.
18 Lady Minto, *Life and Letters of Sir*

Gilbert Elliot, First Earl of Minto,
    1751–1806 (London 1874), I, p. 180:
    Sir Gilbert Elliot to Lady Elliot, Feb.
    22, 1787.
19 E. A. Smith, *Lord Grey, 1764–1845*
    (Oxford 1990), p. 135.
20 Chatsworth 861A: GD to Bess, Feb.
    25, 1788.
21 Chatsworth 920.1: Bess to GD, circa
    Feb. 1788.
22 Chatsworth 890: GD to LS, July 29,
    1788.
23 BL Althorp G290: Lavinia, Lady
    Spencer to second Earl Spencer, July
    28, 1788.
24 PRO 30/29/4/7, f. 94: Miss Lloyd to
    Lady Stafford, August 3, 1788.
25 Stuart, *Dearest Bess,* p. 43.
26 BL Althorp G278: LS to second Earl
    Spencer, Feb. 12, 1787.
27 Chatsworth 891, LS to GD, August 8,
    1788.
28 Chatsworth 953, GD to LS, May 12,
    1789.
29 Duke of Argyll, *Intimate Society Letters*
    of the Eighteenth Century (London
    1910), pp. 314–17.
30 Chatsworth 902: GD to LS, Sept. 15,
    1788.

13: THE REGENCY CRISIS

1 T. More, *Memoirs of R. B. Sheridan*
   (London 1817), II, p. 26. The King's
   illness is generally accepted by historians to have been a form of a rare
   hereditary disorder known as porphyria, which afflicted the Stuarts and
   was transmitted to the Hanoverians by
   George III's great-great-grandmother,
   the Electress Sophia. Porphyria sufferers experience discoloured urine,
   stomach pains, hallucinations, hysteria,
   paranoia, and rambling speech. To
   doctors in the eighteenth century all
   these medical indicators would have
   pointed to simple madness.
2 *Morning Post,* Oct. 31, 1788.
3 Leslie Mitchell, *Charles James Fox*
   (London 1992), p. 80.

4 See John Derry, *The Regency Crisis and the Whigs, 1788–9* (Cambridge 1963), for a comprehensive account of the event. Also Leslie Mitchell, *Charles James Fox and the Disintegration of the Whig Party,* J. Ehrman, *The Younger Pitt,* I, and Christopher Hibbert, *George IV, Prince of Wales,* I.

5 Chatsworth 921: J. Craufurd to GD, circa Nov. 7, 1788.

6 Lady Minto, *The Life and Letters of Sir Gilbert Elliot, First Earl of Minto, 1751–1806* (London 1874), I, p. 312: Sir Gilbert Elliot to Lady Elliot, May 21, 1789.

7 Chatsworth 936: diary 1788–9.

8 W. Sichel, *Sheridan* (London 1909), ii, p. 249: Sheridan to Harriet, circa 1788.

9 Chatsworth 937: LS to GD, Dec. 10, 1788.

10 Duke of Buckingham and Chandos, eds., *Memoirs of the Court and Cabinets of George III* (London 1853–5), II, p. 56.

11 Ibid., II, p. 64: Grenville to Buckingham, Dec. 17, 1788.

12 SNRA Douglas-Home MSS TD95/54: diary of Lady Mary Coke, June 29 and July 18, 1787.

13 J. Ehrman, *The Younger Pitt* (London 1969–96), I, p. 583.

14 *Morning Herald,* July 6, 1787.

15 Henry Wheatley, *The Historical and Posthumous Memoirs of Nathaniel Wraxall* (London 1884), III, p. 267.

16 Chatsworth 936: diary.

17 BL Althorp F29: Lavinia, Lady Spencer to second Earl Spencer, Dec. 13, 1788.

18 Lady Granville, ed., *The Private Correspondence of Lord Granville Leveson Gower* (London 1916), I, p. 14: Lady Stafford to LGLG, Feb. 12, 1789.

19 PRO Hampshire Malmesbury MSS 9M73/150: GD to Lord Malmesbury, [1789?].

20 Lady Granville, *Lord Granville Leveson Gower,* I, p. 15: Lady Stafford to LGLG, Feb. 20, 1789.

21 William LeFanu, ed., *Betsy Sheridan's Journal* (Oxford 1986), p. 153, n. 54: March 2–3, 1789.

22 Lady Minto, *Sir Gilbert Elliot,* I, pp. 323–4.

23 BL Althorp F16: second Earl Spencer to LS, March 26, 1789.

24 A. Aspinall and Lord Bessborough, eds., *Lady Bessborough and Her Family Circle* (London 1949), p. 48: Lady Duncannon to LS, March 26, 1789.

25 Ibid.

26 Ibid., p. 49: March 30, 1789.

27 R. Brimley Johnson, *The Letters of Lady Louisa Stuart* (London 1926), p. 98.

28 Lady Minto, *Sir Gilbert Elliot,* I, p. 300.

29 *The Times,* April 24, 1789.

30 Lady Granville, *Lord Granville Leveson Gower,* I, pp. 13–14: Lady Stafford to LGLG, Feb. 12, 1789.

31 C. Ross, ed., *Correspondence of Charles, First Marquis Cornwallis* (London 1859), I, pp. 406–7: Lord Sydney to Cornwallis, Feb. 21, 1789.

32 Quoted in Leslie Mitchell, *Charles James Fox and the Disintegration of the Whig Party* (Oxford 1971), p. 140: Lord Palmerston to Lady Palmerston, Dec. 26, 1788.

33 Durham Univ. Lib. Grey MSS, box 70: Lord George Cavendish to Mrs. Ponsonby, Dec. 25, 1788.

34 For example, Leslie Mitchell, *Charles James Fox* (Oxford 1992), p. 85.

35 Chatsworth 936: diary.

14: THE APPROACHING STORM

1 In March Georgiana may have been so desperate that she briefly contemplated suicide. There is a note preserved in Castle Howard, dated March 18, 1789, which reads: "Dear Georgiana, I leave you, and give you the only valuable gift in my power; wrote in my blood; my Blessing. May God Bless you my Dear Child, Your affectionate Mother, G. Devonshire.

Wear the inclos'd chain as a memorandum of my Affection." Carlisle MSS J18/20: GD to Lady Georgiana Cavendish, March 18, 1789.

2 Lord Bessborough, *Georgiana, Duchess of Devonshire* (London 1955), p. 143: Thomas Coutts to GD, April 2, 1789.

3 William Galley, who owned a betting office and lottery shop, was one of those making a fortune out of Georgiana as she tried everything to raise ready cash. "I am resolved never again to be a burthen to the Duke and never to borrow," she had written to him in 1789. She offered him an annuity instead: "that it may fall on me alone should I infringe it . . . my debt to you: £1000, the surplus unpaid, £500 the interest—make it up to £3000 by lending me £1500 more, and I will give you a note promising to pay you £500 a year during my life, annuity. You need fear no deceit as I would not for the universe have it come to the Duke. Do this for me, Dear Sir, I entreat you and the payments shall be regular and quarterly." Walpole Library Devonshire MSS: GD to William Galley, circa winter 1789.

4 O. Browning, ed., *Despatches from Paris, 1784–90* (Camden Third Series 1909–10), II, p. 217.

5 Chatsworth 961: GD to LS, Tuesday June [25], 1789.

6 Peter Burley, ed., *Witness to the Revolution: British and American Despatches from France 1788–94* (London 1989), pp. 52–3.

7 Chatsworth 961: GD to LS, Friday June [26], 1789.

8 PRO 30/29/5/3, f. 41: Lady Sutherland to Lady Stafford, July 14, 1789.

9 Burley, *Witness* p. 53.

10 Chatsworth 961: GD to LS, June 22–8, 1789.

11 Ibid.

12 Chatsworth 963: GD to LS, June 29–July 1, 1789.

13 Chatsworth 962: GD to LS, June 27, 1789.

14 Chatsworth 963: GD to LS, June 29–July 1, 1789.

15 BL Althorp G287: GD to second Earl Spencer, July 5, 1789.

16 Chatsworth 964: GD to LS, July 5, 1789.

17 A. Aspinall and Lord Bessborough, eds., *Lady Bessborough and Her Family Circle* (London 1949), p. 55: GD to Harriet, circa June–July 1789 [misdated October].

18 PRO 30/29/5/3, f. 39: Lady Sutherland to Lady Stafford, July 12, 1789.

19 Chatsworth 972: GD to LS, July 18, 1789.

20 Chatsworth 966: GD to LS, July 14, 1789.

21 Chatsworth 993: James Hare to Bess, Sept. 15, 1789.

22 Chatsworth 993: James Hare to Bess, Sept. 15, 1789.

23 Chatsworth 991: James Hare to GD, Sept. 8, 1789.

24 Lord Bessborough, *Georgiana,* p. 158: Coutts to GD, Sept. 9, 1789.

25 Chatsworth 998: James Hare to GD, Oct. 9, 1789.

26 Chatsworth 995: GD to LS, Sept. 25, 1789.

27 Chatsworth 994.2: GD to Coutts, Sept. 23, 1789.

28 Chatsworth 1010: GD to LS, Nov. 8, 1789.

29 Chatsworth 1018: GD to Calonne, Nov. 19, 1789. In French.

30 BL Add. MSS 45548, f. 4: GD and Bess to Lady Melbourne, Dec. 24, 1789.

31 Chichester RO Bessborough MSS: Harriet's diary, March 19, 1789.

32 William LeFanu, ed., *Betsy Sheridan's Journal* (Oxford 1986), no. 60: p. 167: June 14 and 15, 1789.

33 Bath Reference Library Sheridan MSS ALB. 2304: Elizabeth Sheridan to Mrs. Mehitabel Canning, Feb. 5, 1790.

34 Chatsworth 1051: Duke of Dorset to GD, March 17, 1790.

35 Chatsworth 1022: Memorandum, Nov. 25, 1789. The draft from Denne on the other hand haunted her, since it contravened an "oath in which I pledged my wishes for the Salvation of my Children, and of the Duke and Ly Eliz; not to sign any paper, to raise money *upon interest.*" She wrote a memorandum to herself to explain why she had broken her promise. But her excuses were rendered almost un-intelligible by her circumnavigations round the truth. It was a secret con-fession and yet she still lied about the actual sum borrowed, reducing it by half.

36 Walpole Library Devonshire MSS: GD to William Galley, March 9, [1790].

37 A. Aspinall, ed., *The Correspondence of George, Prince of Wales 1770–1812* (London 1964), II, no. 465: GD to Prince of Wales, July 22, 1789.

38 Chatsworth 1029: GD to LS, Dec. 21, 1789.

39 Chatsworth 1036: fifth Duke of Dev-onshire to Bess, Jan. 22, 1790.

40 Chatsworth 1052.1: GD to fifth Duke of Devonshire, circa March 1790.

41 Aspinall, *George, Prince of Wales,* II, no. 508: GD to Prince of Wales, circa May 1790.

42 Chatsworth 991, James Hare to GD, Sept. 8, 1789. It was the sort of over-anxious care which infuriated James Hare. He often warned Georgiana against overloading them with ser-vants. "I think it is a great disadvan-tage to children to have five nurses and footmen to attend them, to see their parents but seldom, and under a sort of constraint, which prevents their behaving naturally and being as entertaining as they would be other-wise. It also gives them an early habit of dissimulation, which they would have soon enough without help."

43 Chatsworth 1041: GD to LS, Feb. 18, 1790.

44 Chatsworth 1044: GD to LS, Feb. 23, 1790.

45 Croft was a successful doctor until he attended Princess Charlotte during her labour in November 1817. She died in agony after two days of labour and people blamed him for her death. Croft was so griefstricken by the event that he committed suicide.

46 Chatsworth 1030: GD to LS, Dec. 21, 1790.

47 Reginald Blunt, ed., *Mrs Montagu* (Edinburgh 1923), II, p. 245: Lord Erskine to Mrs. Montagu, June 6, 1790.

48 BL Althorp F17: second Earl Spencer to LS, May 7, 1790.

49 BL Althorp G280: LS to second Earl Spencer, May 20, 1790.

50 Chatsworth 1054.1: journal of Ann Scafe, May 1790.

51 Chatsworth 1056.1: Lord George Cavendish to GD, June 9, 1790. Many years later the rumours about Hartington's birth resurfaced. Lord George believed an absurd story which maintained that both women had been pregnant but Bess had given birth to the boy while Geor-giana's was either stillborn or a girl. They swapped the babies and Hart-ington was illegitimately brought up as the true heir. Lord George con-templated suing for the dukedom after his brother's death until he read Ann Scafe's diary and accepted her account as incontrovertible evi-dence.

52 BL Althorp G281: LS to second Earl Spencer, June 19, 1790.

53 Chatsworth 1056: GD to LS, August 11, 1790.

54 Dorothy Stuart, *Dearest Bess* (London 1955), p. 53.

55 PRO 30/29/5/3, f. 56: Lady Suther-land to Lady Stafford, circa August 1790. In French.

56 Ibid., f. 55: Lady Sutherland to Lady Stafford, circa July 1790.

57 Ibid., f. 56: Lady Sutherland to Lady Stafford, circa August 1790.

15: EXPOSURE

1 Chatsworth: diary of Lady Elizabeth Foster, November 25, 1790.

2 W. S. Lewis, ed., *Horace Walpole's Correspondence* (New Haven, Conn. 1937–80), XI, p. 263: Walpole to Mary Berry, May 12, 1791.

3 Chatsworth 936: GD Regency crisis diary, introduction.

4 Chatsworth 971: anonymous, undated letter to GD, "1789" erroneously added by another hand; almost certainly written by Lafayette in July 1791.

5 Chatsworth 1072: Duke of Dorset to GD, Nov. 1, 1790.

6 Chatsworth 1086: Duke of Dorset to GD, June 30, 1791.

7 BRBL Yale University: Duke of Dorset to GD, August 1791.

8 Chatsworth 1062: GD to LS, Sept. 9, 1790.

9 Ibid.

10 Chatsworth 1064: GD to LS, Sept. 10, 1790.

11 Chatsworth 1063: LS to GD, Sept. 10, 1790.

12 Chatsworth 1075: GD to LS, Nov. 12, 1790.

13 SNRA Douglas-Home MSS TD95/54: diary of Lady Mary Coke, Feb. 27, 1791.

14 Ibid.

15 Vere Birdwood, ed., *So Dearly Beloved, So Much Admired: The Letters of Lady Chatham* (London 1994), p. 217: Mrs. Trevor to Lady Hester, March 7, 1791.

16 BL Althorp G291: Lavinia, Lady Spencer to second Earl Spencer, May 1789.

17 Chatsworth 1078.1: GD to Coutts, circa March 1791.

18 Lewis Melville, ed., *The Berry Papers* (London 1914), p. 39: Hon. Mrs. Damer to Mary Berry, June 20, 1791.

19 Henry Wheatley, *The Historical and Posthumous Memoirs of Nathaniel Wraxall* (London 1884), I, p. 50.

20 Chatsworth 1099.1: GD to Coutts, circa March 1791.

21 *Morning Post,* July 11, 1791.

22 Chatsworth 1095: GD to Coutts, July 17, 1791.

23 Joyce Hemlow and Althea Douglas, eds., *The Journals and Letters of Fanny Burney (Madame d'Arblay)* (Oxford 1972–84), I, p. 38: August 31, 1791.

24 Ibid.

25 Ibid., I, p. 41: August 31, 1791.

26 Ibid., I, pp. 61 and 49.

27 Ibid., I, p. 49: August 31, 1791.

28 Lady Granville, *The Private Correspondence of Lord Granville Leveson Gower* (London 1916), I, p. 117: Lady Bessborough to LGLG, Oct. 6, 1795.

29 BL Add. MSS 45548, f. 79: Bess to Lady Melbourne, circa May 1791.

30 C. Price, ed., *The Letters of Richard Brinsley Sheridan* (Oxford 1966), I, pp. 225–6: Sheridan to GD, circa July 20, 1791.

31 BL Add. MSS 45548, f. 79: Bess to Lady Melbourne, circa May 1791.

32 BL Althorp F17: second Earl Spencer to LS, June 10, 1791.

33 Chatsworth 1098: GD to Coutts, July 17, 1791.

34 BL Add. MSS 45911, f. 15: Lady Duncannon to Lady Melbourne, circa Oct. 1791.

35 BL Add. MSS 45548, f. 36: Lady Duncannon to Lady Melbourne, circa Oct. 1791.

36 BL Add. MSS 45911, f. 18: GD to Lady Melbourne, Oct. 15, 1791.

37 Ibid.

38 BL Add. MSS 45548, f. 44: Lady Duncannon to Lady Melbourne, circa Oct. 1791.

39 BL Add. MSS 45911, f. 15: Lady Duncannon to Lady Melbourne, circa Oct. 1791.

40 Ibid., f. 22: Bess to Lady Melbourne, Oct. 23, 1791.
41 BL Add. MSS 45548, f. 42: Lady Duncannon to Lady Melbourne, circa Oct. 1791.
42 Ibid., f. 44: Lady Duncannon to Lady Melbourne, circa Oct. 1791.
43 Ibid.
44 BL Add. MSS 45911, f. 20: GD to Lady Melbourne, Oct. 24, 1791.
45 BL Add. MSS 45548, f. 40: Lady Duncannon to Lady Melbourne, circa Oct. 1791.
46 BL Add. MSS 45911, f. 25: GD to Lady Melbourne, Nov. 20, 1791.

16: EXILE

1   Chatsworth 1115: GD to Marquess of Hartington, circa Jan. 27, 1792.
2   Carlisle MSS J18/20: GD to Lady Georgiana Cavendish, circa Feb. 1792.
3   Papers of Hugh Seymour, Esq.: "Verses copied by Lady Charlotte Cholomondeley in her common place book, circa 1816," attributed to GD.
4   Francis Bickley, *The Diaries of Sylvester Douglas, Lord Glenbervie* (London 1928), I, p. 70: Sept. 5, 1796.
5   NRO 324/L.8/42: Mrs. Creevey to Mr. Creevey, circa 1805.
6   Papers of Hugh Seymour, Esq.: GD to Eliza Courtney, circa 1803.
7   Ibid: GD to Eliza Courtney, circa 1804.
8   Ibid., circa 1803–4.
9   Ibid.
10 Carlisle MSS, J18/20/95: fragment, GD to Lady Georgiana Cavendish, circa 1798.
11 Chatsworth 1464: Lady Georgiana Cavendish to Selina Trimmer, April 1, 1799.
12 Lady Granville, ed., *The Private Correspondence of Lord Granville Leveson Gower* (London 1916), II, p. 320: Lady Bessborough to LGLG, August 22, 1808.
13 Henry Broughton, *Recollections of a Long Life* (London 1865), I, p. 92.
14 Papers of Hugh Seymour, Esq.: diary of Eliza Ellice, February 28, 1828.
15 BL Add. MSS 45548, f. 48: Lady Duncannon to Lady Melbourne, Dec. 11, 1791.
16 Ibid., f. 35: GD to Lady Melbourne, Feb. 16, 1792.
17 BL Add. MSS 45911, f. 28: Lady Duncannon to Lady Melbourne, Feb. 28, 1792.
18 PRO 30/29/5/4, f. 13: Lady Sutherland to Lady Stafford, March 29, 1792.
19 BL Add. MSS 45548, f. 50: Lady Duncannon to Lady Melbourne, Dec. 29, 1791.
20 BL Add. MSS 45911, f. 32: Lady Duncannon to Lady Melbourne, March 24, 1792.
21 Ibid., f. 34: Lady Duncannon to Lady Melbourne, April 15, 1792.
22 Carlisle MSS J18/20: GD to Lady Georgiana Cavendish, May 20, 1792.
23 Carlisle MSS J18/21/97: Selina Trimmer to GD, Nov. 4, 1791, and circa Nov./Dec. 1791.
24 BL Althorp F71: LS to Mrs. Howe, Dec. 7, 1791.
25 E. M. Graham, *The Beautiful Mrs Graham* (London 1927), p. 282.
26 Lynedoch MSS, 3594, ff. 261–4: GD to Thomas Graham, July 17, [1792].
27 Chatsworth 1176: GD to LS, Sept. 9, 1793.
28 C. Price, ed., *The Letters of Richard Brinsley Sheridan* (Oxford 1966), I, p. 241: Sheridan to Lady Duncannon, May 3, 1792.
29 Chatsworth 1130: Duke of Dorset to GD, August 10, 1792.
30 A. Aspinall, ed., *The Correspondence of George, Prince of Wales 1770–1812* (London 1964), II, n. 696: Prince of Wales to GD, Sept. 26, 1992.
31 BL Add. MSS 51705, f. 115: Henry Pelham to Lady Webster, [April] 16, 1792.

32 BL Althorp F72: LS to Mrs. Howe, May 4, 1792.

33 BL Add. MSS 33,129, f 88: Henry Pelham to Earl Chichester, Sept. 19, 1792.

34 Brian Connell, *Portrait of a Whig Peer* (London 1957), p. 285: Lady Palmerston to Benjamin Mee, May 26, 1793.

35 Carlisle MSS J18/20: GD to Lady Georgiana Cavendish, August 7, 1792.

36 Carlisle MSS J18/20: GD to Lady Georgiana Cavendish, Sept. 30, 1792.

37 A. Aspinall and Lord Bessborough, eds., *Lady Bessborough and Her Family Circle,* p. 74: LS to Lady Duncannon, circa Dec. 1792.

38 Broadlands MSS, BR11/18/7: Mary Mee to Benjamin Mee, Sept. 6, 1792.

39 Connell, *Portrait,* p. 268: Lady Palmerston to Benjamin Mee, Sept. 7, 1792.

40 Ibid., p. 269: Sept. 10, 1792.

41 BL Althorp F72: LS to Mrs. Howe, Oct. 6, 1792.

42 Carlisle MSS J18/20: GD to Lady Georgiana Cavendish, Nov. 30, 1792.

43 BL Althorp F72: LS to Mrs. Howe, June 1, 1792.

44 Chatsworth 1131: Lady Sutherland to GD, August 31, 1792.

45 Chatsworth 1191: GD to Coutts, Oct. 31, 1793.

46 Chatsworth 1192: GD to LS, Nov. 1, 1793.

47 Chatsworth 1152: Lady Sutherland to GD, March 24, 1792.

48 Suffolk RO, Hervey, MSS, Acc. 941/56/93: Lord Hervey to GD, March 7, 1793.

49 Chatsworth 1147.1: James Hare to GD, circa late 1792.

50 Roger Hudson, ed., *The Grand Tour 1572–1796* (London 1993), pp. 187–8.

51 Aspinall and Lord Bessborough, *Lady Bessborough,* p. 85: Lord Bessborough to Lady Bessborough, May 10, 1793 and May 14, 1793.

52 Carlisle MSS J18/20: GD to Lady Georgiana Cavendish, May 18, 1793.

53 Connell, *Portrait,* p. 385: Lady Palmerston to Benjamin Mee, May 26, 1793.

54 Chatsworth 1155: LS to GD, July 30, 1793.

55 Chatsworth 1174: GD to LS, Sept. 9, 1793.

56 Ibid.

57 Chatsworth 1179: GD to LS, Sept. 16–18, 1793.

58 Ibid.

17: RETURN

1 Chatsworth 1180: GD to LS, Sept. 18, 1793.

2 Chatsworth 1183: GD to LS, Sept. 23, 1793.

3 Charlotte may have been slightly mentally impaired.

4 Chatsworth 1183: GD to LS, Sept. 23, 1793.

5 BL Althorp F40: Lady Georgiana Cavendish to LS, April 26, 1795. She wrote that she was too young and unworthy to talk about her faith. But "by endeavouring to strengthen my faith in God may I not hope by these reflections to become better—may I acquire a settled composed devotion—may it dictate my actions and may it help me to correct my faults."

6 Chatsworth 1185: GD to LS, Sept. 30, 1793.

7 Lady Granville, ed., *The Private Correspondence of Lord Granville Leveson Gower* (London 1916), I, p. 82: Lady Stafford to LGLG, Feb. 16, 1794.

8 BL Add. MSS 51927, ff. 108–9: diary of Lady Holland, Dec. 1793.

9 Chatsworth 1297: GD to LS, July 11, 1795.

10 *Morning Post,* Oct. 1, 1793.

11 Chatsworth 1188: LS to GD, Oct. 19, 1793.

12 Royal Society: diary of Sir Charles Blagden, March–April 1793 *passim.*

13 Among the specimens were "por-
    phyry. This specimen was broken off
    from the very top of the highest point
    of the Mount St. Gothard August 2,
    1793, by Lieutenant Genl. Count
    Rumford, and by him presented to
    her Grace the Duchess of Devonshire
    at Bern, August 21, 1793." Quoted in
    Michael P. Cooper for the Russell So-
    ciety, "Notes on the Mineral Collec-
    tions of Georgiana Cavendish,
    Duchess of Devonshire and the Sixth
    Duke of Devonshire at Chatsworth
    House, Derbyshire;" Chatsworth
    Cataloguing Project 1992. Cooper
    notes the systematic nature of the col-
    lection, as well as its considerable
    breadth.

14 PRO 30/29/5/5, f. 49: Lady Suther-
    land to Lady Stafford, Oct. 23, 1793.

15 Chatsworth 1147.1: James Hare to
    GD, circa 1793.

16 BL Althorp G287: GD to second Earl
    Spencer, Nov. 14, 1793.

17 Chatsworth 1186: LS to GD, Oct. 11,
    1793.

18 Chatsworth 1189: GD to LS, Oct. 22,
    1793.

19 Chatsworth 1192: GD to LS, Nov. 1,
    1793.

20 BL Althorp G291: Lavinia, Lady
    Spencer to second Earl Spencer, rec.
    Feb. 28, 1794.

21 BL Althorp G287: GD to second Earl
    Spencer, rec. July 16, 1794.

22 Lady Granville, *Lord Granville Leveson
    Gower,* I, p. 359: Lady Bessborough to
    LGLG, Sept. 21, 1802/BL Add. MSS
    45911, f. 44: GD to Lady Melbourne,
    circa Jan–March 1795/ Chatsworth
    1386: LS to GD, Jan. 8, 1796/ James
    Greig, *The Farington Diary* (London
    1922–8), I, pp. 199–200.

23 R. Adair, *A Sketch of the Character of the
    Late Duke of Devonshire* (London
    1811), p. 13.

24 BL Althorp G287: GD to second Earl
    Spencer, August 28, 1794. George
    replied that he would do everything

in his power but "it is not very easy to
interfere personally on a subject of
this sort, as everything that is said and
done by anyone in the situation in
which I am here is the subject of
much speculation and jealousy, and as
it would be impossible for me to do
or say anything which would at all in-
volve the government at home without being expressly authorised by
them." BL Althorp G287: second Earl
Spencer to GD, August 28, 1794.
Lady Holland's diary reveals that
Georgiana pressed on, undaunted by
George's pessimistic response: "Ld
M[Malmesbury?] thinks he shall not
succeed in his attempts to attain La
Fayette's release; *he has no instructions
whatever from Ministry* and all must be
done through his own influence. The
Dss of Devon suggested the measure
to him, she did intend writing herself
to the Empress of Russia to beg her
interference on behalf of the poor
Captive—but all [illeg.] be fruitless."
BL Add. MSS 51927, f. 114: diary of
Lady Holland, marked Dec. 1793
[1794].

25 However, there was considerable
    hypocrisy regarding the role of
    women. Female participation in any
    activity outside the domestic sphere
    was haphazard and unpredictable;
    character and circumstances were
    often more important in determining
    a woman's life than social conven-
    tion. Widowhood could force a
    woman to take up her husband's oc-
    cupation, for example in running a
    printing press or owning a shop,
    while spinsterhood brought its own
    hardships but also its own opportuni-
    ties. The arts and education offered
    the most opportunity for women, as
    the careers of Mary Wollstonecraft,
    the playwright Elizabeth Inchbald,
    and the moralist Hannah More illus-
    trate. Although the majority of tracts
    and pamphlets on the role of women

argued for passivity and delicacy, constantly reminding women of their subordinate status, these were, in the main, prescriptive works on how women *ought* to be. See H. Barker and E. Chalus, eds., *Gender in Eighteenth Century England: roles, representations and responsibilities* (London 1996), in which the eight contributors argue against the case for separate spheres and therefore, by implication, against the notion that women's history is a separate discipline within the field of history. In the past, historians have argued that men and women lived in increasingly rigid separate spheres, controlled and demarcated by the functions of gender. More recently, the argument has turned in favour of idiosyncrasy, of integration and pluralism, with a greater dependence on individual case histories rather than theoretical models.

26 SNRA Douglas-Home MSS TD95/54: diary of Lady Mary Coke, August 17, 1782.

27 L. Werkmeister, *A Newspaper History of England, 1792–1793* (Lincoln, Nebraska 1967), pp. 426–7: Nov. 22, 1793.

28 J. Parkes and H. Merivale, eds., *The Memoirs of Sir Philip Francis* (London 1867), II, p. 400.

29 Mary Hays, *Appeal to the Men of Great Britain in Behalf of Women* (London 1798); Catherine Macaulay, *Letters on Education* (London 1790).

30 Chatsworth 1210: GD to LS, Feb. 1, 1794. Harriet shared Georgiana's view that there were unbreachable boundaries between men and women. Defending her right to disagree politically, Harriet nevertheless conceded that "nothing can be more ridiculous than a female politician." Lady Granville, *Lord Granville Leveson Gower,* I, p. 102.

31 BL Add. MSS 33272, ff. 133–4: Sir Charles Blagden to Sir Joseph Banks,

August 22, 1794. On September 8, 1794, Sir Charles Blagden wrote that Georgiana had recommended three men: B. Watson, Barker, and French. Barker was almost certainly the scientist Thomas Barker (1722–1809). B. Watson was White Watson (1760–1835), a mineral dealer and pioneer of Derbyshire geology who catalogued Georgiana's collection in 1799 and again in 1804.

32 BL Althorp G282: LS to second Earl Spencer, Sept. 25, 1794.

33 BL Althorp G287: GD to second Earl Spencer, June 1, 1795.

34 Granville Leveson Gower came from a complicated family background. His mother, Lady Stafford, was the third wife of Lord Gower (later Marquess of Stafford). His half-brother, Lord Gower's elder son, as well as being the future Marquess became Earl of Sutherland when he married Elizabeth, Countess of Sutherland, *suo jure.* He later became the first Duke of Sutherland.

35 Lady Granville, *Lord Granville Leveson Gower,* I, p. 91: Lady Duncannon to LGLG, June 1, 1794.

36 BL Add. MSS 45911, f. 40: Bess to Lady Melbourne, Jan. 8, 1795.

37 Ibid., f. 44: GD to Lady Melbourne [Jan./Feb. 1795].

38 Chatsworth 1286: GD to LS, April 14, 1795.

39 BL Althorp G287: GD to second Earl Spencer, Feb. 5, 1795.

40 *Bon Ton Magazine,* no. 56, Oct. 1795.

41 PRO 313/744: Lady Stafford to Lady Harriet Douglas, Oct. 30, 1795.

42 Ibid., Thursday, circa Nov. 1795.

43 Chatsworth 1334: LS to GD, April 12, 1795.

44 BL Add. MSS 45911, f. 44: GD to Lady Melbourne, [Jan./Feb. 1795].

45 Chatsworth 1386: LS to GD, Jan. 8, 1796.

46 BL Althorp G287: GD to second Earl Spencer, June 17, 1796.

18: INTERLUDE

1 Chatsworth 1211: LS to GD, Jan. 2, 1796.
2 Modern medical opinion differs as to the cause of the illness. Arthur Calder-Marshall suggests "unilateral exophthalmos of endocrine origine" or perhaps "orbital cellulitis." Arthur Calder-Marshall, *The Two Duchesses* (London 1978), p. 179.
3 Lady Granville, ed., *The Private Correspondence of Lord Granville Leveson Gower* (London 1916), I, p. 126: Lady Bessborough to LGLG, [August 1796].
4 Chatsworth 1358: LS to Selina Trimmer, August 4, 1796.
5 Lady Granville, *Lord Granville Leveson Gower,* I, p. 127: Lady Bessborough to LGLG, [August–Sept. 1796].
6 Carlisle MSS J18/37: Bess to Lady Georgiana Cavendish, Wednesday [August 1796].
7 PRO 30/29/6/2, f. 17: Lady Elizabeth Monck to LGLG, Dec. 10, 1796.
8 Carlisle MSS J18/20/96: GD to Lady Georgiana Cavendish, circa early 1797.
9 Chatsworth 1387: LS to Selina Trimmer, Jan. 8, 1797.
10 PRO 30/29/5/5, f. 65: Lady Sutherland to Lady Stafford, circa Nov. 1796.
11 Vere Foster, *The Two Duchesses* (Bath 1974), p. 130: GD to Frederick Foster, Nov. 18, 1796.
12 Chatsworth 1379: GD to LS, Dec. 17, 1796.
13 Foster, *Two Duchesses,* p. 131: "To Lady Elizabeth Foster, from Georgiana, Duchess of Devonshire, when she was apprehensive of losing her eyesight—1796."
14 BL Add. MSS 51960: Lady Crewe to Caroline Fox, April 1797.

19: ISOLATION

1 Lady Granville, ed., *The Private Correspondence of Lord Granville Leveson Gower* (London 1916), I, pp. 141–2:

Lady Bessborough to LGLG [Dec. 1796].
2 Carlisle MSS J18/20: GD to Lady Georgiana Cavendish, Dec. [20], 1796.
3 Chatsworth 1391: GD to LS, Feb. 3, 1797.
4 Chatsworth 1396: Bess to GD, March 2, 1797.
5 Carlisle MSS J18/20: GD to Lady Georgiana Cavendish, Dec. 1796.
6 Chatsworth 1392: GD to Lady Jones, Feb. 11, 1797.
7 Chatsworth 1375: GD to Coutts, Oct. 19, 1796.
8 Ibid.
9 Chatsworth 1383: GD to LS, Dec. 22, 1796.
10 Chatsworth 1401: GD to LS, May 12, 1797. Georgiana's habit of ignoring certain debts was incorrigible. For example, she still owed £1,160 to Calonne, who was languishing in Italy, almost bankrupt, forced to sell his jewellery and watches while he waited with diminishing hope for repayment.
11 Carlisle MSS J18/20: GD to Lady Georgiana Cavendish, Dec. 1796.
12 BL Althorp G287: GD to second Earl Spencer, May 17, 1797. George was not free of doubts about his abilities until Nelson's famous victory over Napoleon in the Battle of the Nile in August 1798.
13 J. Parkes and H. Merivale, eds., *The Memoirs of Sir Philip Francis* (London 1867), II, p. 309: GD to Sir Philip Francis, Nov. 29, 1798.
14 BL Althorp G287: GD to second Earl Spencer, March 24, 1797. She wrote: "As to the subject of Ireland, I wish to God, as I always do *when we differ* yt you may be right—and my whole soul goes with you in good wishes. But the times give an awful lesson and for God's sake Dr. Brother do not take very violent measures without much reflection. I am far from disapproving of Energy and strong

measures, I think them necessary but why may not they be enforc'd with kindness at the same time to the Catholicks? Who certainly deserve it and would greatly strengthen the hands of Government."

15 BL Althorp G287: GD to second Earl Spencer, May 13, 1797.

16 Chatsworth 1421: LS to Selina Trimmer, Dec. 30, 1797.

17 Chatsworth 1400: GD to Selina Trimmer, April 2, 1797.

18 Borthwick Institute Hickleton MSS, A1, 4, 11, 9, f. 2: GD to Mary Grey, circa 1798.

19 Ibid.

20 Chatsworth 1439: GD to LS, June 16, 1798.

21 Chatsworth 1438.1: GD to LS, June 12, 1798.

22 Ibid.

23 Chatsworth 1439: GD to LS, June 16, 1798.

24 Bess's jealousy over Georgiana's success with the Duke is reflected in the way she described the event in her diary. In her account it was *she* who used her influence with him; Georgiana has a mere walk-on part as an anxious observer during the tense deliberations. The truth of Bess's description must be judged against the context of her relationship with the Duke of Richmond and the fact that it was assumed they were about to be married.

25 Lady Granville, *Lord Granville Leveson Gower*, I, p. 218: Harriet to LGLG, [August] 1798. Harriet finally answered in response to Leveson Gower that politics was in their blood: "for notwithstanding all my violence in politicks & talking so much on that subject, I perfectly agree with you that no woman has any business to meddle with that or any other serious business, farther than giving her opinion. . . . You will tell me I do not practise the doctrine I preach, and I

allow it as far as talking goes, because from my childhood I have accustom'd to hear politicks the constant and eager subject of conversation." George had to accept the same argument from Georgiana.

26 Chatsworth 1445: General Frederick St. John to GD, Sept. 3, 1798.

27 Lord Bessborough, *Georgiana Duchess of Devonshire* (London 1955), p. 229: GD to LS, Oct. 8, 1798.

28 Chatsworth 1435: GD to LS, June 5, 1798.

29 Chatsworth 1453.1: Mrs. Louisa Ponsonby to Louisa O'Calaghan, Nov. 23, 1798.

30 Chatsworth 1448: Sir Philip Francis to Lady Francis, Sept. 18, 1798.

31 Parkes and Merivale, *Sir Philip Francis*, II, p. 311: Sir Philip Francis to GD, Dec. 3, 1798.

32 Ibid.

33 Ibid., II, p. 310: GD to Sir Philip Francis, Nov. 29, 1798. Partly written in French.

34 Ibid., II, p. 312: Sir Philip Francis to GD, Dec. 3, 1798.

35 Chatsworth 1466: GD to LS, April 13, 1799.

36 Borthwick Institute Hickleton MSS, A1, 4, 11, 9, f. 2: GD to Mary Grey, circa 1798.

37 Carlisle MSS J18/20/95: GD to Lady Georgiana Cavendish, circa 1798–9.

38 Ibid.

39 Sir George Leveson Gower and Iris Palmer, eds., *Harry-O: The Letters of Lady Harriet Cavendish* (London 1940), pp. 329–30: Lady Harriet Cavendish to Marquess of Hartington, Oct. 14, 1809.

40 Leveson Gower and Palmer, *Harry-O*, p. 4: Lady Caroline Ponsonby to Lady Georgiana Cavendish, Oct. 31, 1796.

41 Carlisle MSS J18/20/95: GD to Lady Georgiana Cavendish, circa 1799.

42 Lady Granville, *Lord Granville Leveson Gower*, I, pp. 194–5: Lady Bessborough to LGLG, [Feb. 16–18, 1798].

43 BL Add. MSS 51928, f. 74: diary of Lady Holland, March 26, 1799.

44 Carlisle MSS J18/20/95: GD to Lady Georgiana Cavendish, circa 1799.

45 BL Althorp F21: second Earl Spencer to LS, April 4, 1799.

46 BL Althorp G287: LS to second Earl Spencer, March 30, 1799.

47 BL Althorp G287: LS to second Earl Spencer, April 4, 1799.

48 Chatsworth 1460: GD to LS, Feb. 21, 1799.

49 Chatsworth Misc.: Blue Notebook, diary fragment.

50 Lady Granville, *Lord Granville Leveson Gower,* I, p. 245: Lady Bessborough to LGLG, Saturday [1799].

51 Linda Kelly, *Richard Brinsley Sheridan: A Life* (London 1997), p. 229.

52 W. Sichel, *Sheridan* (London 1909), II, pp. 276–7.

53 Chatsworth Misc. *Memorandums of the Face of the Country in Switzerland,* attributed to Georgiana, Duchess of Devonshire, 1799, printed by Cooper and Graham. There is a copy of the book in the John Rylands Library in Manchester. The core of the library is owed to the acquisition of the book collection belonging to Georgiana's brother, which by the time of his death was one of the greatest private collections in Europe.

54 *Morning Herald,* May 27, 1799.

55 Ibid., Sept. 17, 1799.

56 Chatsworth 1492: GD to LS, Oct. 13, 1799.

57 She once revealed in a letter to George the stratagems she sometimes had to employ to help him: "I shall send you a letter from our agent in Ireland, if I can steal it, for the Duke thinks it absurd in me to trouble you." BL Althorp G287: GD to second Earl Spencer, rec. Sept. 27, 1797.

58 BL Add. MSS 40763, f. 250: GD to Sir Philip Francis, Nov. 29, 1798.

20: GEORGIANA REDUX

1 Chatsworth 1501: fifth Duke of Bedford to GD, Jan. 8, 1800.

2 Chatsworth 1601: LS to GD, August 21, 1801.

3 BL Althorp G282: LS to second Earl Spencer, Feb. 11, 1800.

4 Chatsworth 1505: GD to LS, Jan. 22, 1800.

5 Chatsworth 1421: LS to Selina Trimmer, Dec. 30, 1797.

6 Chatsworth 1600: LS to Selina Trimmer, Aug. 20, 1801.

7 BL Althorp G287: GD to second Earl Spencer, rec. April 28, 1800.

8 Lady Granville, ed., *The Private Correspondence of Lord Granville Leveson Gower* (London 1916), I, p. 332: Lady Bessborough to LGLG, [February 1802]. The "Canterbury Tales" is not Chaucer's but Harriet Lee's, novelist and dramatist (1757–1851). Count Siegendorf was a character in "Kruitzner," one of the "Tales." The play is now lost and there is no way of clearing up the mystery which surrounds it. It was still extant in 1822 when Little G, now Lady Morpeth, sent a copy to a friend, but by 1899 all the MSS had been lost or destroyed. Thus there was no way to prove or deny the extraordinary assertion by Georgiana's grandson Frederick Leveson Gower that Byron had plagiarized *Werner,* from Georgiana's *Siegendorf.* He claimed, "My Sister, Lady Georgiana Fullerton, told me many years ago that this was the case. Her statement was that the Duchess wrote the poem and gave the manuscript of it to her niece, Lady Caroline Ponsonby, and that she, some years later, handed it over to Lord Byron, who subsequently published it in his own name." Quoted in Hugh Stokes, *The Devonshire House Circle* (London 1917), p. 277. If there is any truth to the story, the likelihood is that Byron saw Georgiana's play and was inspired to write *Werner.*

9 BL Althorp F124: Lady Clermont to LS, May 22, 1800.

10 Egerton Castle, *The Jerningham Letters, 1780–1843* (London 1896), I, pp. 178–9: Lady Jerningham to Charlotte Bedingfeld, May 24, 1800.

11 Ibid., I, p. 187: Lady Jerningham to Charlotte Bedingfeld, June 12, 1800.

12 Chatsworth 1533: GD to LS, Nov. 6, 1800.

13 Chatsworth 1519: GD to LS, June 2, 1800.

14 Chatsworth 1521: GD to LS, June 14, 1800.

15 Castle, *Jerningham Letters,* I, pp. 192–3: Lady Jerningham to Charlotte Bedingfeld, July 1800.

16 BL Add. MSS 45548, f. 33: GD to Lady Melbourne, circa 1800–1801.

17 Ibid.

18 Lady Granville, *Lord Granville Leveson Gower,* I, p. 318: Lady Bessborough to LGLG, Jan. 6, 1802.

19 Chatsworth 1525: James Hare to GD, Sept. 11, 1800.

20 Chatsworth 1539: GD to LS, Dec. 19, 1800.

21 BL Althorp G282: LS to second Earl Spencer, Dec. 23, 1800.

22 Chatsworth: Sixth Duke's Series, 2512.

23 Chatsworth 1550: Prince of Wales to GD, Dec. 25, 1800.

24 Chatsworth 1564: GD to LS, Jan. 14, 1801.

25 Carlisle MSS J18/37: Bess to Lady Morpeth, March 21, 1801.

26 Chatsworth 1554: GD to Duke of Richmond, circa Dec. 30, 1800.

27 Chatsworth 1562: Bess to Duke of Richmond, Jan. 12, 1801.

28 Chatsworth 1567: Bess to Duke of Richmond, Jan. 29, 1801.

29 Chatsworth 1569: James Hare to GD, Jan. 27, 1801.

30 BL Add. MSS 47569, f. 111: Charles Fox to William Smith, circa 1801.

31 J. Ehrman, *The Younger Pitt* (London 1969–96), III, p. 503: John Ehrman's

last volume of his magisterial biography of Pitt offers, in my opinion, the most thorough and convincing explanation for his resignation.

32 Ibid., I, p. 127.

21: PEACE

1 Chatsworth V1611C: GD's diary, Feb. 7, 1801.

2 Chatsworth 1305: GD to LS, Sept. 2, 1795.

3 Chatsworth 1581: GD to LS, Feb. 19, 1801. Georgiana's first concern was to encourage all her friends not to stay in government because they would be regarded as traitors by those going out and, as members of the old guard, by those coming in. In this vein she wrote to Lord Hervey and Henry Pelham urging them not to accept any offers from Addington. "My private reason," she told Pelham, "is that no one but myself would perhaps dare tell you the kind of contempt and scorn in which those who stay in are held not only by opposition but by all the friends of the Govt. You know how much I see of all sides. . . ." BL Add. MSS 33, 107, f. 12: GD to Thomas Pelham, circa Feb. 1801. Pelham did not accept her advice and Georgiana's prediction proved true. He was never accepted by the new administration and was eventually dropped in ignominious circumstances.

4 BL Add. MSS 33, 107, f. 12: GD to Thomas Pelham, circa Feb. 1801.

5 For example, Georgiana canvassed the Whigs on the Prince's behalf when he asked Parliament to grant him the arrears on his income from the Duchy of Cornwall. Lady Granville, ed., *The Private Correspondence of Lord Granville Leveson Gower* (London 1916), I, p. 332: Lady Bessborough to LGLG, Feb. [1802].

6 It is, of course, impossible to be accurate when all the evidence has been

destroyed. But a letter of Mrs. Sheridan's to Granville Leveson Gower reveals that "to the last moment she thought herself belov'd," and that Georgiana and Grey allegedly met at third places, although how often and when remains in dispute. PRO 30/29/6/2, f. 63: Mrs. Sheridan to LGLG, circa August 1807.

7 The friendship between the two women had not changed with time: Lady Melbourne still behaved like a bossy older sister towards Georgiana, and Georgiana was always slightly afraid of her and anxious to retain her approval. The *London Chronicle* noted on October 5, 1802 that Lady Melbourne "is, of course, in all the Devonshire Parties." In contrast, Harriet now resented Lady Melbourne as a tiresome know-it-all and nicknamed her "The Thorn."

8 BL Add. MSS 45548, f. 24: GD to Lady Melbourne, circa 1801–2.

9 PRO 30/29/6/2, f. 63: Mrs. Sheridan to LGLG, circa August 1807.

10 Harriet visited Howick in 1808 and complained, "It is hardly possible to have a moment's conversation with Ld Grey, for either [Mary] (from thinking, I suppose, that I am a friend of Hecca's)—or Mr Bennet, who is here, and whose head always intervenes between any two people who are talking—makes all conversation so general one dares say nothing that may not be discuss'd by the whole room." Lady Granville, *Lord Granville Leveson Gower,* II, p. 320: Lady Bessborough to LGLG, August 22, [1808].

11 Carlisle MSS J18/20/96: GD to Lady Georgiana Morpeth, circa 1801.

12 Lady Granville, *Lord Granville Leveson Gower,* I, p. 306: Lady Bessborough to LGLG, circa late 1801.

22: POWER STRUGGLES

1 BL Add. MSS 45548, f. 81: Bess to Lady Melbourne, Oct. 26, 1801.

2 Ibid., f. 83: Bess to Lady Melbourne, Oct. 31, 1801.

3 Ibid., f. 85: Bess to Lady Melbourne, Feb. 20, 1802.

4 *Morning Herald,* April 15, 1802.

5 Chatsworth 1645: GD to LS, Sept. 1, 1802.

6 Claire Tomalin in *The Times Literary Supplement,* Dec. 2, 1994.

7 Chatsworth 1602: GD to LS, August 31, 1801.

8 BL Add. MSS 45548, f. 24: GD to Lady Melbourne, circa 1801/2.

9 *Morning Herald,* July 14, 1801.

10 BL Althorp G283: LS to second Earl Spencer, Feb. 3, 1802.

11 Chatsworth 1606: fifth Duke of Bedford to GD, Oct. 22, 1801.

12 BL Add. MSS 45548, f. 24: GD to Lady Melbourne, circa 1801/2.

13 Chatsworth 1609: GD to Dr. Francis Randolph, [Dec. 25, 1801].

14 BL Add. MSS 45548, f. 28: GD to Lady Melbourne, circa Feb./March 1802.

15 Chatsworth 1622: GD to LS, March 8, 1802.

16 *London Chronicle,* March 16–18, 1802.

17 BL Add. MSS 45548: f. 85: Bess to Lady Melbourne, Feb. 20, 1802.

18 A. Aspinall, *Mrs Jordan and Her Family: Unpublished Correspondence of Mrs Jordan and the Duke of Clarence* (London 1951), p. 50: [Sept. 3], 1802. Mrs. Jordan wrote, "I thought it proper as the Duchess of Devonshire sent to know how long I stayed to let her know that my night was fixed for Friday, on which she sent me the most civil letter, highly pleased with the attention, desiring me to keep both stage boxes, & if her name would be of any use, to say by her desire. The Duke is very unwell, but if it is possible he will come that night; if not, she will quit him on that occasion, tho' she goes nowhere. Was not this handsome?"

19 *London Chronicle,* June 5–8, 1802.

20 Chatsworth 1750: LS to GD, Dec. 13, 1803.
21 Lady Granville, ed., *The Private Correspondence of Lord Granville Leveson Gower* (London 1916), II, p. 17: Lady Bessborough to LGLG, Feb. 14, [1805].
22 Ibid., p. 351: Lady Bessborough to LGLG, Aug. 23, [1802].
23 S. Rogers, *Recollections of the Table Talk of Samuel Rogers* (London 1856), p. 191.
24 *Morning Herald,* July 21, 1802.
25 Chatsworth 1637: GD to LS, July 21, 1802. Sir Francis Burdett and George Byng won the contest but Burdett was later unseated on appeal in 1804.
26 Chatsworth 1655: GD to Bess, Oct. 1802.
27 Lady Granville, *Lord Granville Leveson Gower,* I, p. 344: Lady Bessborough to LGLG, [July 1802].
28 Carlisle MSS J18/20/95: GD to Lady Georgiana Morpeth, Feb. 7, 1803.
29 Chatsworth 1690: GD to Bess, [Dec. 26], 1802.
30 Chatsworth 1668: Bess to GD, Nov. 15, 1802.
31 Mrs. Damer told Mary Berry that all the information she was passing on about France came from Georgiana, who appeared to be in contact with "everyone." Lewis Melville, *The Berry Papers* (London 1914), p. 283: Mrs. Damer to Mary Berry, June 12, 1803.
32 BL Add. MSS 47569, f. 111: Charles Fox to William Smith, circa 1801.
33 Mabel, Countess of Airlie, *In Whig Society* (London 1921), p. 59: GD to Lady Melbourne, Nov. 24, 1802.
34 Chatsworth 1707: Bess to GD, Jan. 16, 1803.
35 A. D. Harvey, *Britain in the Early Nineteenth Century* (London 1978), p. 135.

23: THE DOYENNE OF THE WHIG PARTY

1 Sir George Leveson Gower and Iris Palmer, eds., *Harry-O: The Letters of Lady Harriet Cavendish* (London 1940), p. 79: Lady Harriet Cavendish to Lady Georgiana Morpeth, Nov. 19, 1803.
2 A. Aspinall and Lord Bessborough, eds., *Lady Bessborough and Her Family Circle* (London 1949), pp. 125–6.
3 Chatsworth 433: Anecdotes concerning HRH the Prince of Wales, Sept. 1782.
4 BL Add. MSS 47565, f. 224: Fox to Robert Adair, circa June 1803.
5 BL Althorp G287: GD to second Earl Spencer, July 8, 1803.
6 Lady Granville, ed., *The Private Correspondence of Lord Granville Leveson Gower* (London 1916), I, p. 427: Lady Bessborough to LGLG, Aug. 17, 1803.
7 Ibid., I, p. 437: Lady Bessborough to LGLG, [circa Oct. 1803].
8 PRO 30/29/6/7, f. 5: GD to Fox [1803].
9 BL Althorp G283: LS to second Earl Spencer, Sept. 15, 1803.
10 Lady Granville, *Lord Granville Leveson Gower,* I, p. 433: Lady Bessborough to LGLG, Sept. 15, 1803.
11 *Morning Herald,* Oct. 11, 1803.
12 Chatsworth 1741: Fox to GD, Oct. 20, 1803.
13 Aspinall, *George, Prince of Wales,* IV, n. 1862: GD to Prince of Wales, [Nov. 1803].
14 BL Add. MSS 51454, f. 115: GD to Richard Fitzpatrick, [Jan. 1804].
15 Chatsworth 1755: Richard Fitzpatrick to GD, Jan. 25, 1804.
16 Chatsworth 1758: GD to LS, Feb. 27, 1804.
17 Chatsworth 1761: GD to LS, March [13], 1804.
18 Lady Granville, *Lord Granville Leveson Gower,* I, pp. 451–2: Lady Bessborough to LGLG, [March 1804].
19 BL Add. MSS 47565, f. 125: Fox to Grey, April 18, 1804.
20 J. J. Sack, *The Grenvillites 1801–1829* (Chicago 1979), p. 79.

24: "THE MINISTRY OF ALL THE TALENTS"

1 Carlisle MSS J18/20/96: GD to Lady Georgiana Morpeth, [Sept. 1804].

2 Many years later Harryo wrote about "My wish of doing right and really acting up to my own ideas of what is so," and then continued with a rare reference to her mother about her desire "to become worthy of her." Sir George Leveson Gower and Iris Palmer, eds., *Harry-O: The Letters of Lady Harriet Cavendish* (London 1940), p. 282: Lady Harriet Cavendish to Lady Georgiana Morpeth, [1808].

3 Carlisle MSS J18/21/99: Lady Georgiana Morpeth to GD, [Sept. 1804].

4 Leveson Gower and Palmer, *Harry-O,* p. 108: Lady Harriet Cavendish to GD, Oct. 1804.

5 Ibid., pp. 107–8: Lady Harriet Cavendish to GD, Oct. 1804.

6 Chatsworth 1332: GD to fifth Duke of Devonshire, [1801].

7 Chatsworth 1782: GD to LS, Oct. 9, 1804.

8 Durham Univ. Lib., Grey MSS, Box 11: GD to Grey, Nov. 10, 1804.

9 *Morning Herald,* Nov. 13, 1804.

10 BL Althorp G55: Thomas Grenville to second Earl Spencer, Nov. 13, 1804.

11 BL Althorp G287: GD to second Earl Spencer, Nov. 21, 1804.

12 BL Add. MSS 47565, f. 134: Fox to Grey, Dec. 17, 1804.

13 Chatsworth 1787: Bess to GD, Nov. 1, 1804.

14 Chatsworth 1834: Bess to GD, [1805].

15 Chatsworth 1789: Fox to GD, Dec. 11, 1804.

16 Lord Bessborough, *Georgiana, Duchess of Devonshire* (London 1955), p. 270: Sir Robert Adair to GD, [1804].

17 A. Aspinall, *The Correspondence of George, Prince of Wales 1770–1812* (London 1964), V, n. 2287: GD to Prince of Wales, [1804].

18 Lady Granville, ed., *The Private Correspondence of Lord Granville Leveson Gower* (London 1916), I, p. 472: Lady Bessborough to LGLG, Nov. 1804.

19 Vere Foster, *The Two Duchesses* (Bath 1974), p. 191: Lady Elizabeth Foster to Augustus Foster, Dec. 5, 1804.

20 Chatsworth, Letters between the Prince of Wales and GD, no. 54, [1804].

21 Carlisle MSS J18/20/96: GD to Lady Georgiana Morpeth, [Jan. 1805].

22 Lady Granville, *Lord Granville Leveson Gower,* II, p. 92: Lady Bessborough to LGLG, 12 [July 1805].

23 PRO 30/29/9/1, f. 70: Lord Boringdon to LGLG, July 10, 1805.

24 Durham Univ. Lib., Grey MSS, Box 11: GD to Grey, Nov. 10, 1804.

25 Chatsworth 1792: Fox to GD, Jan. 7, 1805.

26 "Pray speak to everybody you can to come down or we shall be lost on the Slave Trade. Morpeth, Ossulston, Ld A. H., Ld H. Petty all away, Pray, pray send anybody you see," Fox begged. Foster, *The Two Duchesses,* p. 263: Fox to GD, [April 31], 1805. Georgiana joked that in obeying his orders she "lost, by patriotism, the best scene of Young Roscius in Frederick." Lady Granville, *Lord Granville Leveson Gower,* II, p. 34, GD to LGLG, March 1, [1805]. Young Roscius was a boy actor called William Henry West Betty, whose performances in *Hamlet* and *Richard III* at the age of thirteen enraptured London for several seasons. Pitt actually adjourned the House of Commons earlier so that members could watch the phenomenon play Hamlet. Georgiana was one of those who took up the cry on his behalf and even invited him to dinner at Devonshire House.

27 Chatsworth 1811: GD to LS, May 30, 1805.

28 Northumberland R. O. Creevey

MSS, 324/L8/42: Mrs. Creevey to Mr. Creevey, Nov. 1805.

29 Leveson Gower and Palmer, *Harry-O: Lady Harriet Cavendish to Lady Georgiana Morpeth*, Oct. 11, 1805.

30 Chatsworth 1843: GD to Marquess of Hartington, Jan. 18–20, 1806.

31 Chatsworth 1841: GD to Marquess of Hartington, Jan. 19, 1806.

32 J. Ehrman, *The Younger Pitt* (London 1969–96), III, p. 829.

33 Lady Granville, *Lord Granville Leveson Gower*, II, pp. 162–3: Lady Bessborough to LGLG, Jan. 23, 1806.

34 Chatsworth 1845: GD to Marquess Hartington, Jan. 23, 1806.

35 Ibid.

36 Chatsworth 1853: GD to Marquess of Hartington, Feb. 7, 1806.

37 BL Add. MSS 41856, ff. 196–205: Fox to Thomas Grenville, Jan. 1806.

38 Chatsworth 1854: GD to Marquess of Hartington, Feb. 12, 1806.

39 Chatsworth 1863: GD to Marquess of Hartington, Feb. 26, 1806.

40 Carlisle MSS J18/20/95: GD to Lady Georgiana Morpeth, circa Feb. 1806.

41 Chatsworth 1873: GD to Marquess of Hartington, March 9, 1806.

42 Dorothy Stuart, *Dearest Bess* (London 1955), p. 141: March 25, 1806.

43 Lady Granville, *Lord Granville Leveson Gower*, II, p. 185: Fox to LGLG, March 25, 1806.

44 Chatsworth 1887: fifth Duke of Devonshire to Selina Trimmer, March 29, 1806.

45 Lady Granville, *Lord Granville Leveson Gower*, II, p. 210: Lady Bessborough to LGLG, Sept. 14, 1806.

46 Ibid., II, p. 185: Lady Bessborough to LGLG, [March? 31, 1806].

47 PRO 30/29/6/2, f. 22: Lady E. Monck to LGLG, March 31, 1806.

48 Lady Granville, *Lord Granville Leveson Gower*, II, p. 187: Lady Bessborough to LGLG, April 15, [1806].

49 Carlisle MSS J18/20/96: Lady Geor-
giana Morpeth, circa 1806. "Strew" and "strewed" could also be read as "shew" and "shewed;" the writing is not clear.

EPILOGUE

1 Vere Foster, *The Two Duchesses* (Bath 1974), pp. 280–81: Lady Elizabeth Foster to Augustus Foster, May 18, 1806.

2 Dorothy Stuart, *Dearest Bess* (London 1955), p. 142.

3 Ibid., p. 143.

4 Ibid., p. 144.

5 Lord Bessborough, *Georgiana, Duchess of Devonshire* (London 1955), p. 283.

6 Foster, *Two Duchesses*, pp. 287–91: Lady Elizabeth Foster to Augustus Foster, July 9, 1806.

7 Ibid., p. 286: Lady Elizabeth Foster to Augustus Foster, July 3, 1806.

8 BL Althorp G294: Lavinia, Lady Spencer to second Earl Spencer, rec. Sept. 12, 1806.

9 Leslie Mitchell, *Charles James Fox* (Oxford 1992), p. 239.

10 Sir George Leveson Gower and Iris Palmer, eds., *Harry-O: The Letters of Lady Harriet Cavendish* (London 1940), p. 166; Lady Harriet Cavendish to Lady Georgiana Morpeth, Nov. 19, 1806.

11 Ibid., p. 170: Lady Harriet Cavendish to Lady Georgiana Morpeth, Nov. 22, 1806.

12 Ibid., p. 166: Lady Harriet Cavendish to Lady Georgiana Morpeth, Nov. 19, 1806.

13 Stuart, *Dearest Bess*, p. 149.

14 Lord Bessborough, *Georgiana*, p. 283: Lady Georgiana Morpeth to Marquess of Hartington, Nov. 26, 1807.

15 Lady Granville, ed., *The Private Correspondence of Lord Granville Leveson Gower*, II, p. 230: Lady Bessborough to LGLG, Dec. 4, 1806.

16 Hecca Sheridan claimed that she was faithful to Sheridan for seven years,

but that he tortured her over his love for Harriet. She, in turn, began an affair with Grey in 1802. Mrs. Sheridan wrote Leveson Gower a long letter of self-justification in which she admitted she had been jealous of Georgiana, but that she had not meant to reveal the truth to Harriet. It was Harriet's remark, "that to the last moment [Georgiana] thought herself belov'd [by Grey]," that provoked Hecca. "It was said in a moment of abandon & when I was wounded too by the confession that *anything* had passed. The immense confidence [Grey] had in me was one of my greatest consolations. . . . Lady B in her first indignation asserted as strongly as she does anything now that he was in the habit of meeting her at 3rd places, that she could prove it—She now gives up that assertion excepting in *one* instance since his marriage many years ago, which he owns—she says 'we all thought he lov'd her to the last, & never did I feel so much affection for him as after her death.' In her next breath she says 'both Lady E and myself were *convinced* of his intercourse with you— Lord G, are not these contradictions. She also admits that his manner to the Dss in the last 5 years was much alter'd and that together with the above mention'd the conviction hastened her death." PRO 30/29/6/2, f. 63: Mrs. Sheridan to LGLG, [August 1807?].

17 Lady Granville, *Lord Granville Leveson Gower,* II, pp. 274–5: Lady Bessborough to LGLG, August 19, [1807].

18 Ibid., II, p. 345: Lady Bessborough to LGLG, Monday [August 1809].

19 Stuart, *Dearest Bess,* p. 169: fifth Duke of Devonshire to LS, Oct. 17, 1809. Letter drafted in Lady Elizabeth Foster's hand.

20 A. Aspinall and Lord Bessborough,

eds., *Lady Bessborough and Her Family Circle* (London 1940), p. 194: Marquess of Hartington to Lady Caroline Lamb, Oct. 11, 1809.

21 Lady Granville, *Lord Granville Leveson Gower,* II, p. 434: note by Lady Bessborough, April 1812. Harryo became jealous and suspicious of Harriet—as her husband's former mistress—and would not see her aunt unless forced to do so. Yet she adopted Harriet's two children by him, Harriette Stewart and George Stewart. She doted on them, which must have been hard for Harriet, who rarely saw either child.

22 BL Althorp f. 40: LS to Lady Elizabeth Foster, Dec. 9, 1809.

23 Betty Askwith, *Piety and Wit: A Biography of Harriet, Countess Granville* (London 1982), p. 74.

24 A. Francis Steuart, *Diary of a Lady-in-Waiting* (London 1908), II, p. 18: Sir William Gell to Lady Charlotte Bury, July 1815.

25 Stuart, *Dearest Bess,* p. 214.

26 Brian Masters, *Georgiana, Duchess of Devonshire,* (London 1981), p. 293.

27 Virginia Surtees, *A Second Self: The Letters of Harriet Granville 1810–1845* (London 1990), p. 182: Lady Harriet Leveson Gower to Lady Georgiana Morpeth, Sunday [April 11, 1824].

28 Ibid., p. 53: Lady Harriet Leveson Gower to Lady Georgiana Morpeth, Friday [Oct. 30, 1812].

29 L. Dutens, *Memoirs of a Traveller in Retirement* (London 1806), IV, p. 209.

30 Lord Bessborough, *Georgiana, Duchess of Devonshire,* p. 134: GD to M. de Calonne, Lundi [Sept. 1788].

31 E. Chalus and H. Barker, eds., *Gender in Eighteenth-Century England* (London 1997), p. 19.

32 For example, Richard Leppert, *Music and Image: Domesticity, Ideology and Socio-Cultural Formation in Eighteenth-Century England* (Cambridge 1988). Leppert states, "Females, young and

old alike, lived out their lives within the metaphorical or literal confines of domestic walls" (p. 29).

33 For example, Sally Alexander, "Feminist History," *History Workshop Journal,* 1 (1976).

34 See the introduction in H. Barker and E. Chalus, eds., *Gender in Eighteenth-Century England.*

35 Linda Colley, *Britons: Forging a Nation* (Yale 1992), pp. 241ff.

36 Women were self-conscious about appearing too interested in politics lest they encountered ridicule. Lady Stafford wrote to a friend in January 1805, "you see I write to you whatever comes uppermost just as I should talk to you, but to others I am more reserved and quiet, thinking it unbecoming for a female to meddle with Politics." Sutherland MSS DB13/744: Lady Stafford to Lady Harriet Douglas, Jan. 16, 1805.

37 They argue that it is outmoded and riddled with inconsistencies. For example, Amanda Vickery, "Golden age to separate spheres? A review of the categories and chronology of English women's history," *Historical Journal* 36, 2 (1993). See also Ann-Louise Shapiro, ed., *Feminists Revision History* (New Brunswick, NJ, 1994).

38 Chatsworth 1873.9: GD to Marquess of Hartington, March 9, 1806.

SELECT BIBLIOGRAPHY

I. MANUSCRIPT SOURCES

BATH PUBLIC LIBRARY
Canning MSS. Correspondence of Elizabeth Ann Sheridan

BIRMINGHAM UNIVERSITY LIBRARY
Stafford MSS. Papers and Correspondence of Susanna Leveson Gower

BORTHWICK INSTITUTE
Hickleton MSS. Papers and Correspondence of Ponsonby family

BODLEIAN LIBRARY, OXFORD
C. A. Clayton, "The Political Career of Richard Brinsley Sheridan" (Oxford D.Phil 1992)
V. E. Chancellor, "The Ministry of All the Talents" (Oxford D.Phil 1978)
A. I. M. Duncan, "A Study of the Life and Public Career of Frederick Howard, Fifth Earl of Carlisle" (Oxford D.Phil 1981)
Burdett-Coutts MSS. Papers and Correspondence of Thomas Coutts
Lovelace Byron MSS. Papers and Correspondence of Noel family
Misc. English Letters MSS. Correspondence of Richard Brinsley Sheridan
Montagu MSS. Correspondence of Georgiana, Duchess of Devonshire
North MSS. Papers and Correspondence of Sylvester Douglas, Lord Glenbervie

BRITISH LIBRARY
Adair MSS, Add. MSS 47565, 51609–10. Papers and Correspondence of Robert Adair
Althorp MSS, unfol. Papers and Correspondence of Spencer family
Auckland MSS, Add. MSS 34412–57. Papers and Correspondence of William Eden, first Baron Auckland
Georgiana Duchess of Devonshire MSS, ST 755, Eg. 32137, 33107, 37282, 37308, 37916, 40763, 10763, 48252, 48412–13, 46916, 60484
Gibbon MSS, Add. MSS 34886. Correspondence of Edward Gibbon
Foster MSS, Add. MSS 41579. Journal of Lady Elizabeth Foster
Holland House and Fox MSS, Add. MSS 41851–9, 47559–601, 51454–960
Francis MSS, Add. MSS 40763. Correspondence of Sir Philip Francis

Grenville MSS, Add. MSS 58880–85, 60487, Correspondence of Thomas Grenville and William Grenville, first Baron Grenville

Melbourne MSS, Add. MSS 45550, 45546–9, 45911. Papers and Correspondence of Elizabeth, Lady Melbourne

Pelham MSS, Add. MSS 33100–112, 33629–31, 53269–31, 33126–30, 33100–105, 33108, 33112, 33117, 64813. Correspondence of the second Earl of Chichester

Sheridan MSS, Add. MSS 35118, 58274–7, 6341

Windham MSS, Add. MSS 37843–5, 37847–8, 37873, 37909

CASTLE HOWARD, YORKSHIRE

Carlisle MSS. Papers and Correspondence of the fifth Earl of Carlisle and Georgiana, Lady Carlisle

CHATSWORTH, DERBYSHIRE

Chatsworth MSS. Correspondence of fifth Duke of Devonshire, Georgiana, Duchess of Devonshire, and Lady Elizabeth Foster

W. L. CLEMENTS LIBRARY, ANN ARBOR, MICH.

Correspondence of Comte Perregeaux

Correspondence of Lord John Russell

DURHAM UNIVERSITY LIBRARY

Grey MSS. Papers and Correspondence of Charles, second Earl Grey

EDINBURGH, NATIONAL LIBRARY OF SCOTLAND

Edinburgh, Nat. Lib. of Scotland, Elliot Murray Kynynmound MSS. Papers of Sir Gilbert Elliot

Edinburgh, Nat. Lib. of Scotland, Leveson Gower MSS. Papers of Elizabeth, Duchess of Sutherland

Edinburgh, Nat. Lib. of Scotland, Minto MSS. Papers of Sir Hugh Elliot

EDINBURGH, NATIONAL REGISTRY OF ARCHIVES

Edinburgh, SNRA, Douglas-Home MSS, diary of Lady Mary Coke

CENTRE FOR KENTISH STUDIES

North MSS. Papers and Correspondence of Sylvester Douglas, Lord Glenbervie

Sackville MSS. Papers and Correspondence of third Duke of Dorset

NOTTINGHAM UNIVERSITY LIBRARY

Nottingham Univ. Lib., Portland MSS. Papers and Correspondence of the third Duke of Portland

NORTHUMBERLAND RECORD OFFICE

Creevey MSS. Papers and Correspondence of Thomas Creevey

NORTHERN IRELAND RECORD OFFICE

Blackwood MSS. Papers and Correspondence of Richard Brinsley Sheridan and Elizabeth Sheridan

Foster MSS. Papers and Correspondence of Lady Elizabeth Foster

PUBLIC RECORD OFFICE, LONDON
Calonne MSS. Papers and Correspondence of Charles Alexandre de Calonne
Chatham MSS. Papers and Correspondence of William Pitt
Granville MSS. Papers and Correspondence of Leveson Gower family

ROYAL SOCIETY
Blagden MSS. Papers of Sir Charles Blagden

SOUTHAMPTON UNIVERSITY LIBRARY
Broadlands MSS. Papers and Correspondence of Palmerston family

SUFFOLK RECORD OFFICE
Hervey MSS. Papers and Correspondence of Hervey family

EAST SUSSEX RECORD OFFICE
Holroyd MSS. Correspondence of Earl of Sheffield

WEST SUSSEX RECORD OFFICE
Bessborough MSS. Papers and Correspondence of Bessborough family

YALE UNIVERSITY, BEINECKE RARE BOOK LIBRARY
Osborn MSS. Correspondence of Earl of Bessborough

II. PRINTED SOURCES

A. Primary Sources

1. HISTORICAL MANUSCRIPTS COMMISSION
V   Report *Manuscripts of the Duke of Sutherland*
X   Report *Manuscripts of the Marquess of Abergavenny*
XIII   Report *Manuscripts of J. B. Fortescue, Esq.*
XIV   Report *Manuscripts of the Duke of Rutland*
XV   Report *Manuscripts of the Earl of Carlisle*
XVI   Report *Manuscripts of the Marquess of Lothian*
XX   Report *Manuscripts of Reginald Rawdon Hastings, Esq.*

2. NEWSPAPERS AND PERIODICALS
Bon Ton Magazine
Covent Garden Magazine
Gentleman's Magazine
London Chronicle
Morning Chronicle
Morning Herald and Daily Advertiser
Morning Post
The Times

3. BOOKS
Adair, R., *A Sketch of the Character of the Late Duke of Devonshire* (London 1811)
Mabell, Countess of Airlie, *In Whig Society, 1775–1818* (London 1921)

Earl of Albemarle, *Memoirs of the Marquis Rockingham and His Contemporaries* (London 1852)

———*Fifty Years of my Life* (London 1876)

[Almon, John,] *Biographical, Literary, and Political Anecdotes of several of the most eminent Persons of the Present Age* (London 1797)

Angelo's Pic Nic or, Table Talk, including numerous recollections of Public Characters (London 1834)

Anson, Florence and Elizabeth, *Mary Hamilton, Afterwards Mrs John Dickenson, at Court and at Home, from Letters and Diaries, 1756–1816* (London 1925)

Archenholtz, Johann von, *A View of the British Constitution and of the Manners and Customs of the People of England* (London 1797)

Duke of Argyll, *Intimate Society Letters of the Eighteenth Century* (London 1910)

Aspinall, A., *The Later Correspondence of George III* (Cambridge 1971)

———*The Correspondence of George, Prince of Wales 1770–1812* (London 1964)

———*Mrs Jordan and Her Family: Unpublished Correspondence of Mrs Jordan and the Duke of Clarence* (London 1951)

Aspinall, A., and Lord Bessborough, *Lady Bessborough and Her Family Circle* (London 1940)

Aspinall, A., and Smith, E. A., *English Historical Documents 1783–1832* (London 1959), XI

Balderston, K., *Thraliana, The Diary of Mrs Hester Lynch Thrale (Later Mrs Piozzi), 1776–1809* (Oxford 1951)

Baring, Mrs. Henry, *The Diary of the Right Hon. William Windham, 1784–1819* (London 1866)

Barrington, Jonah, *Personal Sketches of His Own Times* (London 1827)

Bernier, Olivier, *Imperial Mother, Royal Daughter: The Correspondence of Marie Antoinette and Maria Theresa* (London 1986)

Lord Bessborough, *Georgiana, Duchess of Devonshire* (London 1955)

Bickley, Francis, *The Diaries of Sylvester Douglas, Lord Glenbervie* (London 1928)

Birdwood, Vere, *So Dearly Beloved, So Much Admired: The Letters of Lady Chatham* (London 1994)

Bishop of Bath and Wells, *Journals and Correspondence of Lord Auckland* (London 1861–2)

Bladon, F. M. *The Diaries of Colonel the Honourable Robert Fulke Greville* (London 1930)

Blunt, Reginald, *Mrs Montagu* (Edinburgh 1923)

Brimley Johnson, R., *The Letters of Lady Louisa Stuart* (London 1926)

Broadley, A. M., and Melville, L., *The Beautiful Lady Craven* (London 1914)

Brougham, Henry, *Historical Sketches of Statesmen who Flourished in the time of George III* (London 1839–43)

Broughton, Henry, *Recollections of a Long Life* (London 1865)

Broughton, Mrs. Vernon, *Court and Private Life in the Time of Queen Charlotte: being the Journals of Mrs Papendiek, Assistant Keeper of the Wardrobe and Reader to Her Majesty* (London 1887)

Browning, O., *Despatches from Paris, 1784–90* (Camden Third Series, 1909–10)

Bruyn, Andrew C., *The Torrington Diaries* (London 1935)

Duke of Buckingham and Chandos, *Memoirs of the Court and Cabinets of George III, from Original Family Documents* (London 1853–5)

Burley, Peter, *Witness to the Revolution: British and American Despatches from France 1788–94* (London 1989)

Campbell, Thomas, *The Life of Mrs Siddons* (London 1832)

Castle, Egerton, *The Jerningham Letters, 1780–1843* (London 1896)

Cave, K., *The Diary of Joseph Farington* (London 1982–4)

Colburn, Henry, *The Private Correspondence of David Garrick* (London 1835)

Lord Colchester, *The Diary and Correspondence of Charles Abbot, Lord Colchester* (London 1861)

Coleridge, E. H., *The Life of Thomas Coutts, Banker* (London 1920)

Connell, Brian, *Portrait of a Whig Peer, Compiled from the Papers of the Second Viscount Palmerston, 1739–1832* (London 1957)

Copeland, T., *The Correspondence of Edmund Burke* (Cambridge 1961–3)

Cozens-Hardy, Basil, *The Diary of Silas Neville, 1762–1788* (Oxford 1950)

de Beer, E. S., *The Diary of John Evelyn* (Oxford 1959)

Defoe, Daniel, *A Tour Through England and Wales* (London 1928)

Douglas, D., *The Letters and Journals of Lady Mary Coke* (Edinburgh 1889–96)

Dowden, Wilfred, *The Journal of Thomas Moore* (London 1983)

Dutens, L., *Memoirs of a Traveller in Retirement* (London 1806)

Edgecombe, Richard, *The Diary of Frances, Lady Shelley, 1787–1813* (London 1913)

Fitzgerald, B., *Correspondence of Emily, Duchess of Leinster* (Dublin 1957)

Fortescue, J., *The Correspondence of King George the Third from 1760 to December 1783* (London 1973)

Foster, Vere, *The Two Duchesses* (Bath 1974)

George, M. D., *Catalogue of Political and Personal Satires Preserved in the Department of Prints and Drawings in the British Museum* (London 1935–54)

Ginter, Donald, E., *Whig Organization in the General Election of 1790: Selections from the Blair Adam Papers* (Los Angeles 1967)

Gore, John, *The Creevey Papers* (London 1963)

Graham, E. M., *The Beautiful Mrs Graham* (London 1927)

Lady Granville, *The Private Correspondence of Lord Granville Leveson Gower* (London 1916)

Grieg, James, *The Farington Diary, by Joseph Farington* (London 1922–8)

Hanger, Colonel George, *The Life, Adventures and Opinions of Colonel George Hanger* (London 1801)

Harcourt, L. V., *The Diaries and Correspondence of George Rose* (London 1860)

Hartley, J., *History of the Westminster Election* (London 1784)

Hemlow, Joyce, and Douglas, Althea, *The Journals and Letters of Fanny Burney (Madame d'Arblay)* (Oxford 1972–84)

Lord Herbert, *Henry, Elizabeth and George (The Pembroke Papers)* (London 1939)

Lord Holland, *Memoirs of the Whig Party* (London 1852–4)

———*Further Memoris of the Whig Party* (London 1905)

Home, J. A., *The Letters of Lady Louisa Stuart* (Edinburgh 1899)

Lady Ilchester and Lord Stavordale, *The Life and Letters of Lady Sarah Lennox* (London 1901)

Earl of Ilchester, *The Journal of Elizabeth, Lady Holland* (London 1908)

Jennings, Louis J., *The Croker Papers* (London 1885)

Jesse, J. H., *George Selwyn and his Contemporaries* (London 1843–4)

Jupp, P., *The Letter Journal of George Canning, 1793–95* (London 1991)

Langdale, Charles, *Memoirs of Mrs Fitzherbert* (London 1920)

LeFanu, William, *Betsy Sheridan's Journal* (Oxford 1986)

Leighton, Rachel, *Correspondence of Charlotte Grenville* (London 1920)

Leslie, Shane, *The Letters of Mrs Fitzherbert and Connected Papers* (London 1940)

Leveson Gower, Sir George, and Palmer, Iris, *Harry-O: The Letters of Lady Harriet Cavendish* (London 1940)

Lewis, Theresa, *Extracts from the Journal of Miss Berry From the Year 1783–1852* (London 1865)

Lewis, W., *Notes by Lady Louisa Stuart on George Selwyn and his Contemporaries by John Heaneage Jesse* (New York 1928)

Lewis, W. S., *Horace Walpole's Correspondence* (New Haven, Conn. 1937–80)

Lincoln, Anthony and McEwen, Robert, *Lord Eldon's Anecdote Book* (London 1960)

Lady Llanover, *The Autobiography and Correspondence of Mary Granville, Mrs Delany* (London 1861–2)

Malcolm, J. P., *Anecdotes of the Manners and Customs of London* (London 1808)

Lord Malmesbury, *The Diaries and Correspondence of Lord Malmesbury* (London 1844)

Maxwell, the Rt Hon. Sir Herbert, *The Creevey Papers* (London 1912)

Melville, Lewis, *The Berry Papers* (London 1914)

Lady Minto, *The Life and Letters of Sir Gilbert Elliot, First Earl of Minto, 1751–1806* (London 1874)

More, T., *Memoirs of R. B. Sheridan* (London 1817)

Norton, J. E., *The Letters of Edward Gibbon* (London 1956)

Parkes, J., and Merivale, H., *The Memoirs of Sir Philip Francis* (London 1867)

Price, C., *The Letters of Richard Brinsley Sheridan* (Oxford 1966)

Ralph, James, *A Critical Review of the Public Buildings, Statues, and Ornaments in and about London and Westminster* (rep. London 1971)

Rogers, S., *Recollections of the Table-Talk of Samuel Rogers* (London 1856)

Roscoe, E. S., and Clergue, H., *Letters and Life of George Selwyn* (London 1899)

Ross, C., *Correspondence of Charles, First Marquis Cornwallis* (London 1859)

Lord John Russell, *Memorials and Correspondence of Charles James Fox* (London 1853–7)

———*The Memoirs, Journal, and Correspondence of Thomas Moore* (London 1853–6)

Steuart, A. Francis, *The Diary of a Lady-in-Waiting by Lady Charlotte Bury* (London 1908)

———*The Last Journals of Horace Walpole* (London 1910)

Surr, T. S., *A Winter in London* (London 1806)

Surtees, Virginia, *A Second Self: The Letters of Harriet Granville, 1810–1845* (London 1990)

Walpole, Horace, *Memoirs of the Reign of George III* (London 1894)

Wheatley, Henry, *The Historical and Posthumous Memoirs of Sir Nathaniel Wraxall* (London 1884)

Wraxall, Nathaniel, *Posthumous and Historical Memoirs of My Own Time* (London 1904)

Wright, J., *The Speeches of the Right Honourable Charles James Fox in the House of Commons* (London 1815)

4. PAMPHLETS

Anon., *History of the Westminster Election* (London 1784)

Anon., [Combe, William,] *A Letter to Her Grace the Duchess of Devonshire* (London 1777)

———*A Second Letter to Her Grace the Duchess of Devonshire* (London 1777)

———*The Duchess of Devonshire's Cow; a Poem* (London 1777)

———*An Heroic Epistle to the Noble Author of the Duchess of Devonshire's Cow, a Poem* (London 1777)

———*The Duke of Devonshire's Bull to the Duchess of Devonshire's Cow: a Poetical Epistle* (London 1777)

———*A Letter to Her Grace the Duchess of D. Answered cursorily, by Democritus* (London 1777)

Piggott, Charles, *The Female Jockey Club* (London 1794)
——*The Whig Club* (London 1792)

B. Secondary Sources

1. BOOKS

Arnold, Walter, *The Life and Death of the Sublime Society of Beefsteaks* (London 1871)
Ashton, John, *The History of Gambling in England* (London 1871)
Askwith, Betty, *Piety and Wit: Biography of Harriet, Countess Granville, 1785–1862* (London 1982)
Aspinall, A., *Politics and the Press, c. 1780–1850* (London 1949)
Ayling, S., *A Portrait of Sheridan* (London 1985)
Barker, H., and Chalus, E., *Gender in Eighteenth Century England: roles, representations and responsibilities* (London 1997)
Barnes, D., *George III and William Pitt* (London 1939)
Battiscombe, Georgina, *The Spencers of Althorp* (London 1984)
Bayne Powell, R., *The English Child in the Eighteenth Century* (London 1939)
Biddulph, Violet, *The Three Ladies Waldegrave* (London 1938)
Black, J., *The English Press in the Eighteenth Century* (Beckenham 1987)
Bleackely, Horace, *Ladies Fair and Frail, Sketches of the Demi-monde during the Eighteenth Century* (London 1926)
——*The Beautiful Duchess* (London 1927)
Bolt, Christine, *The Women's Movements in the United States and Britain from the 1790s to the 1920s* (Amherst, Mass. 1993)
Borer, Mary Cathcart, *An Illustrated Guide to London in 1800* (London 1988)
Boucé, P., *Sexuality in Eighteenth Century Britain* (Manchester 1982)
Boucé, P., and Porter, Roy, *Sexual Underworlds of the Enlightenment* (Manchester 1987)
Bovill, E. W., *English Country Life, 1780–1830* (London 1962)
Brewer, John, and Porter, Roy, *Consumption and the World of Goods* (London 1993)
Brooke, J., *King George III* (London 1972)
Browne, Alice, *The Eighteenth Century Feminist Mind* (London 1987)
Buck, A., *Dress in Eighteenth Century England* (London 1979)
Cannon, J. A., *Aristocratic Century: The Peerage of Eighteenth Century England* (Cambridge 1984)
——*The Fox–North Coalition: Crisis of the Constitution* (Cambridge 1969)
——*The Whig Ascendancy: Colloquies on Hanoverian England* (London 1981)
Cecil, Lord David, *The Young Melbourne* (London 1939)
Chaloner, W. H., and Richardson, R. C., *Bibliography of British Economic and Social History* (Manchester 1984)
Christie, I. R., *Myth and Reality in Late-Eighteenth Century British Politics and other Papers* (London 1970)
——*The End of North's Ministry, 1780–1782* (London 1958)
——*Wilkes, Wyvill and Reform* (London 1962)
Colley, Linda, *Britons, Forging the Nation 1707–1837* (London 1992)
Cunnington, C. W. and P., *Handbook of English Costume in the Eighteenth Century* (London 1972)
Davidoff, L., *The Best Circles* (London 1986)
Davidoff, L., and Hall, C., *Family Fortunes: Men and Women of the English Middle Class, 1780–1850* (London 1992)

Davis, I. M., *The Harlot and the Statesman* (London 1986)

Derry, J. W., *The Regency Crisis and the Whigs, 1788–9* (Cambridge 1963)

——*Charles James Fox* (New York 1972)

——*Charles, Earl Grey* (Oxford 1992)

Deborah, Duchess of Devonshire, *The House: A Portrait of Chatsworth* (London 1982)

Dickinson, H. T., *Liberty and Property: Political Ideology in Eighteenth Century Britain* (London 1977)

Duffy, M., *The English Satirical Print, 1600–1832* (Cambridge 1986)

Dunlop, Ian, *Marie-Antoinette* (London 1993)

Ehrman, J., *The Younger Pitt* (London 1969–96)

Elwin, Malcolm, *The Noels and the Milbanks* (London 1967)

Farr, Evelyn, *Before the Deluge, Parisian Society in the Reign of Louis XVI* (London 1994)

Foster, Elizabeth, *Children of the Mist* (London 1960)

Fothergil, Brian, *The Mitred Earl* (London 1988)

Fraser, Flora, *Beloved Emma* (London 1986)

Friedman, Joseph, *Spencer House: The Chronicle of a Great London Mansion* (London 1993)

Fritz, Paul, and Morton, Richard, *Women in the Eighteenth Century and Other Essays* (Toronto 1976)

George, M. D., *English Political Caricature to 1702: A Study of Opinion and Propaganda* (Oxford 1959)

——*Hogarth to Cruickshank: Social Change in Graphic Satire* (London 1967)

——*Johnson's England* (Oxford 1933)

——*London Life in the Eighteenth Century* (London 1992)

Girouard, Mark, *Life in the English Country House* (London 1978)

Griffiths, Arthur, *Clubs and Clubmen* (London 1907)

Grosvenor, Caroline, *The First Lady Wharncliffe and Her Family* (London 1927)

Harvey, A. D., *Britain in the Early Nineteenth Century* (London 1978)

Hibbert, Christopher, *George IV, Prince of Wales* (London 1972)

——*The French Revolution* (London 1982)

Hill, Bridget, *Women, Work, and Sexual Politics in Eighteenth Century England* (London 1989)

——*Eighteenth Century Women, An Anthology* (London 1978)

Hinde, W., *George Canning* (London 1973)

Hudson, Roger, *The Grand Tour 1592–1796* (London 1993)

Hufton, Olwen, *The Prospect Before Her* (London 1995)

Jarret, Derek, *The Begetters of Revolution* (London 1973)

Jesse, J. H., *Selwyn and His Contemporaries* (London 1843–4)

Jones, L. C., *The Clubs of the Georgian Rakes* (New York 1942)

Jones, Vivien, *Women in the Eighteenth Century: Constructions of Femininity* (London 1990)

Jupp, P., *Lord Grenville* (Oxford 1985)

Kanner, Barbara, *The Women of England* (Hamden, Conn. 1979)

Kelly, Linda, *Richard Brinsley Sheridan, A Life* (London 1997)

Langford, Paul, *A Polite and Commercial People: England 1727–1783* (Oxford 1989)

Lees-Milne, James, *The Bachelor Duke* (London 1991)

Leppert, Richard, *Music and Image: Domesticity, Ideology and Socio-Cultural Formation in Eighteenth-century England* (Cambridge 1988)

Lewis, J. S., *In the Family Way. Childbirth in the British Aristocracy, 1760–1860* (London 1988)

Lonsdale, Roger, *Eighteenth Century Women Poets* (Oxford 1989)

Lumis, Trevor, and Marsh, Jan, *The Woman's Domain. Women and the English Country House* (London 1990)

Macfarlane, A., *Marriage and Love in England* (Oxford 1986)

Manceron, Claude, trans. Amphoux, Nancy, *The Age of the French Revolution: Toward the Brink* (New York 1983)

Marshall, Arthur Calder, *The Two Duchesses* (London 1978)

Masters, Brian, *Georgiana, Duchess of Devonshire* (London 1981)

Mavor, E., *The Ladies of Llangollen* (New York 1981)

Mckendrick, N., Brewer, J., and Plumb, J. H., *The Birth of a Consumer Society: The Commercialisation of 18th Century England* (London 1982)

Mingay, G., *English Landed Society in Eighteenth Century Society* (London 1963)

Mitchell, Leslie, *Charles James Fox and the Disintegration of the Whig Party* (Oxford 1971)

———*Holland House* (London 1980)

———*Charles James Fox* (Oxford 1992)

Mullan, John, *Sentiment and Sociability. The Language of Feeling in the Eighteenth Century* (London 1988)

Myers, Sylvia, *The Blue Stocking Circle: Women, Friendship and the Life of the Mind in Eighteenth Century England* (London 1990)

Norris, J., *Shelburne and Reform* (London 1963)

O'Dowd, Mary, and Wichert, Sabine, *Chattel, Servant or Citizen* (Belfast 1995)

O'Gorman, F., *The Whig Party and the French Revolution* (London 1967)

———*The Rise of Party in England. The Rockingham Whigs 1760–1782* (London 1975)

———*Voters, Patrons and Parties: The Unreformed Electorate of Hanoverian England, 1734–1832* (Oxford 1989)

Olphin, H. K., *George Tierney* (London 1934)

Olson, A., *The Radical Duke* (Oxford 1961)

Outhwaite, R. B., *Marriage and Society: Studies in the Social History of Marriage* (London 1981)

Palmer, Iris, *The Face Without a Frown* (London 1944)

Pares, Richard, *George III and the Politicians* (London 1953)

Parreaux, André, *Daily Life in England in the Reign of George III* (London 1969)

Pearson, John, *Stags and Serpents. The Story of the House of Cavendish and the Duke of Devonshire* (London 1983)

Powis, J., *Aristocracy* (Oxford 1984)

Raymond. J., *A Passion for Friends: Toward a Philosophy of Female Affection* (Boston 1986)

Ribeiro, A., *A Visual History of Costume: The Eighteenth Century* (London 1983)

———*Dress in Eighteenth-Century Europe, 1715–1789* (London 1984)

———*The Dress Worn at Masquerades in England, 1730–1790, and its Relation to Fancy Dress in Portraiture* (London 1984)

———*Dress and Morality* (London 1986)

Rodgers, Katharine, *Feminism in the Eighteenth Century* (London 1990)

Roth, W., *The London Pleasure Gardens of the Eighteenth Century* (London 1986)

Rudé, G., *Hanoverian London 1714–1808* (London 1971)

Sack, J. J., *The Grenvillites 1801–1829, Party Politics and Factionalism in the Age of Pitt and Liverpool* (Chicago 1979)

Shapiro, Ann-Louise, ed., *Feminists Revision History* (New Brunswick, NJ, 1994)

Sichel, W., *Sheridan* (London 1909)

Smith, E. A., *Whig Principles and Party Politics* (Manchester 1975)

———*Lord Grey, 1764–1845* (Oxford 1990)

Steinmetz, Andrew, *The Gaming Table: Its Votaries and Victims* (London 1870)

Stokes, Hugh, *The Devonshire House Circle* (London 1917)

Stone, Lawrence, *Broken Lives: Separation and Divorce in England 1660–1857* (Oxford 1993)

———*The Family, Sex and Marriage in England 1500–1800* (London 1979)

———*Road to Divorce: England 1530–1987* (Oxford 1990)

Stone, Lawrence and Fawtier, Jeanne C., *An Open Elite?* (Oxford 1984)

Stuart, Dorothy, *Dearest Bess* (London 1955)

Sykes, Christopher Simon, *Private Palaces: Life in the Great London Houses* (London 1985)

Thomas, P. G., *Lord North* (London 1976)

Thorne, R. G., *The House of Commons* (London 1986)

Tillyard, Stella, *Aristocrats* (London 1994)

Timbs, J., *Clubs and Club Life in London* (London 1872)

Tomalin, Claire, *Mrs Jordan's Profession* (London 1995)

Trumbach, Randolph E., *The Rise of the Egalitarian Family* (New York 1978)

Wardroper, John, *Kings, Lords and Wicked Libellers* (London 1973)

Werkmeister, L., *The London Daily Press, 1772–1792* (Lincoln, Nebraska 1963)

Whiteley, W. T., *Artists and Their Friends in England 1700–1799* (London 1928)

Wilkins, W. H., *Mrs Fitzherbert and George IV* (London 1905)

Ziegler, Philip, *Addington* (London 1965)

2. ARTICLES

Alexander, Sally, "Feminist History," *History Workshop Journal,* 1 (1976)

Berkeley, Eliza, "Singular Tale of Love in High Life," *Gentleman's Magazine,* 66 (August 1796)

Boucé, Paul Gabriel, "Aspects of Sexual Tolerance and Intolerance in Eighteenth Century England," *British Journal for Eighteenth Century Studies,* 3 (Autumn 1980)

Butterfield, H., "Charles James Fox and the Whig Opposition in 1792," *Cambridge Historical Journal,* 9 (1949)

Clay, Christopher, "Marriage, Inheritance, and the Rise of Large Estates in England, 1660–1835," *Economic History Review,* 2nd ser., 38 (1968)

Deutsch, Phyllis, "Moral Trespass in Georgian London: Gaming, Gender, and Electoral Politics in the Age of George III," *Historical Journal,* 39, 3 (1996)

Dinwiddy, J. R., "Charles James Fox and the People," *History,* 55 (1970)

George, E., "Fox's Martyrs: The General Election of 1784," *Transactions of the Royal Historical Society,* 21 (1937)

Laprade, W. T., "William Pitt and the Westminster Election," *American Historical Review,* 23 (1912)

Plumb, J. H., "The new world of children in eighteenth century England," *Past and Present,* 67 (May 1975)

Vickery, Amanda, "Golden age to separate spheres? A review of the categories and chronology of English women's history," *Historical Journal,* 36, 2 (1993)

INDEX

Abbot, Charles, 364
Aberdeen, Mr., 235
Act of Settlement, 157
Adair, Robert, 281, 328, 342, 349, 361
Addington, Henry, 330–34, 335, 344, 348,
    354–56, 364, 367
Addington, Mrs., 331
Addington (Ziegler), 349*n*
Adelphi, 70
Adhémar, Comte d', 113–14, 117–18,
    136, 190, 343
Ahrenberg, Duc d', 237
Ahrenberg, Duchesse d', 237–38
Ailesbury, Lady, 123–24
Almack's, 32, 44*n*, 55
Althorp, George, Viscount, *see* Spencer,
    George Spencer, 2nd Earl
Althorp, Lavinia, Viscountess, *see* Spencer,
    Lavinia Bingham, Countess
Althorp Park, 4, 5, 12, 23, 25, 29, 51, 127,
    179
Altman, Mr., 362
American War of Independence, 137, 282
    Battle of Yorktown in, 89
    French and Spanish support in, 62, 89
    Whig support for, xix, 44, 61–62, 64,
        75, 89
Amiens, Treaty of, 334, 343
Andreossi, Antoine, Comte, 343
Andrew, M. P., 347–48
Annenberg, Duchess of, 91
Ansbach, Margrave of, 336
Anson, 88
Archenholtz, Baron, 32, 143

Arkwright, Sir Richard, 184
Armistead, Elizabeth, 78
    Fox and, 127, 206, 213, 342
Artois, Comte d', 227, 229
Association Movement, 79, 81
Association of the Friends of the People,
    279, 280, 281
Auckland, Eleanor, Lady, 307
Augmentation of the Irish Militia Bill, 355
Austerlitz, Battle of, 366–67
Austin, Mr., 171
Austria:
    French victory against, 297
    Lafayette imprisoned in, 270*n,* 282

Baker, George, 188, 204–5, 234, 235
Bank of England, 81, 298
Banks, Sir Joseph, 272, 283
Bath, 95–96, 127–28, 132, 160, 169, 188,
    213, 243, 248–54, 293–94, 297, 347,
    352–53
Batoni, Pompeo, 8
Beauchamp, Catherine, Lady, 173*n,* 189–90
Beauclerk, Topham, 47, 293
Beaufort, Elizabeth, Duchess of, 131
Beddoes, Thomas, 284
Bedford, Duchess of, 21
Bedford, Francis Russell, 5th Duke of, 324
    death of, 339
    Lady Melbourne and, 206, 339
    loans to Georgiana by, 317–19, 321,
        337–39
    mistresses of, 206, 321, 339
    political interests of, 198–99, 327

Bedford, Georgiana Gordon, Duchess of,
    338, 339, 341, 346–47
Bedford, John Russell, 6th Duke of, 339,
    346–47, 352–53, 368*n*
Bentinck, Lady E., 293
Bernis, Cardinal, 129
Berthe, Lady Charlotte, 157
Bertin, Mlle., 238
Bésenval, Baron de, 114
Bessborough, Frederick Ponsonby, 3rd
    Earl of (brother–in–law), 120, 238,
    265, 342
  character and personality of, 73, 85–86,
    118, 175, 187, 196, 270
  divorce proceedings initiated by,
    232–33, 249
  engagement and marriage of Harriet
    Spencer to, 72–73, 84
  gambling and debts of, 118, 175, 187,
    256, 318
  Lady Bessborough's relationship with,
    84–86, 118, 165, 175, 187, 196, 207,
    232–33, 245, 247, 249–50, 254–55,
    264, 270, 273
Bessborough, Harriet Spencer Ponsonby,
    Countess of (sister), 40, 68, 105, 106,
    120, 126, 143, 342
  Bessborough's relationship with,
    84–86, 118, 165, 175, 187, 196, 207,
    232–33, 245, 247, 249–50, 254–55,
    264, 270, 273
  Cavendish family and, 73, 84, 85–86
  character and personality of, 10, 72,
    249–50
  childhood of, 9, 10–11, 13–14, 20,
    23–24
  death of, 380
  diary of, 232
  dowry and income of, 73, 86, 187, 245
  Duke of Devonshire and, 247–48, 255
  engagement and marriage of, 72–74,
    84
  gambling and debts of, 186–88, 203,
    246, 256, 273, 298, 318
  Georgiana's relationship with, 10,
    72–74, 86, 118, 158, 169, 186–88,
    189, 201–2, 203, 228, 232, 235, 238,
    246–48, 253–56, 263–65, 273–74,
    284–85, 290–92, 298, 318, 369–70
  illness and fragile health of, 246–48,
    249–50, 253–54, 264, 269, 273–74,
    280, 284, 291–92, 298
  Lady Spencer and, 179, 187, 194,
    248–49, 269, 273–74
  love affairs of, 174–76, 207, 232–33,
    249, 284–85, 290, 292, 296, 309, 319,
    323–24
  physical appearance of, 4, 72, 249
  political activism of, 138, 140, 142,
    144–45, 152–53, 198–99, 215–16
  pregnancies and childbirths of, 84,
    85–86, 118, 164–65, 323–24
Bessborough, William Ponsonby, 2nd Earl
    of, 73, 233, 249, 264, 272
Bezier, M., 238
Bingham, Lady Lavinia, *see* Spencer,
    Lavinia Bingham, Countess
Blagden, Sir Charles, 269, 272, 279,
    283–84
Blanchard, Jean-Pierre, 168
Blandford, Susan, Marchioness of, 320
Blenheim Palace, 7*n*
Blue Stocking Circle, 59, 143
Blunt, Reginald, 163*n*
Bolingbroke, Frederick Saint-John, 2nd
    Viscount, 47
Bolton Abbey, 17
Bon Ton Magazine, 71, 258
Boodles, 32
Boscawen, Mrs., 139, 157
Boston Massacre, xix
Boswell, James, 9
Bouverie, Harriet, 47, 139
Bowles, Mrs., 307
Boyle, Lady Charlotte, 17
Bristol, Augustus Hervey, 3rd Earl of, 97*n*
Bristol, Elizabeth Hervey, Countess of,
    98–99, 100, 107, 122, 177, 180, 212,
    325–26
Bristol, Frederick Augustus Hervey, 4th
    Earl of, 96, 97–100
Britain, *see* Great Britain
British Library, xv
British Navy, 69, 280, 286–87, 297–98
British Parliament, xvii–xviii, 4, 6–7, 15,
    31–32, 74–76, 209
  coalition governments and, 108–10,
    116, 133–36, 152, 348–57

mob attack on, 79–80
reform movement in, 75–76, 79–81, 82, 109, 344
see also House of Commons; House of Lords
Brocket Hall, 292
Brooks's club, 16, 32, 34, 55, 56, 58, 78, 109, 116, 163*n,* 206, 209, 223, 359
Broughton, Henry, Lord, 262
Brown, Lancelot "Capability," 23
Buckinghamshire, Albinia Hobart, Countess of, 87*n*
Buckinghamshire, Caroline Hobart, Countess of, 214
Burdett, Sir Francis, 341
Burke, Edmund, 47, 75
   Fox and, 57, 136, 240–41
   on French Revolution, 240–41
   political ideology and career of, 44, 80, 167–68, 213, 240–41
   Sheridan and, 45*n,* 240–41
Burlington, Richard Boyle, 3rd Earl of, 17, 301
Burlington House, 17
Burney, Fanny:
   Georgiana and, 248–52
   on Lady Bessborough, 249–50
   on Lady Foster, 251–52
   as Second Keeper of the Queen's Robes, 248
   works of, 33–34, 60, 99
Burr, Aaron, xx
Bury, Lady Charlotte, 123*n*
Bute, John Stuart, 3rd Earl of, 16
Byron, George Gordon, 6th Lord, 164*n,* 197

Cadogan, William Cadogan, 1st Earl of, 18*n*
Calonne, Charles Alexandre de, 190
   Georgiana and, 203, 231, 241–42, 243, 382
   Georgiana's loans from, 203, 223–24, 235
Camden, Charles Pratt, 1st Earl, 78, 110
Camden, John Jeffreys Pratt, 2nd Earl, 304, 330
Campbell, Lord Frederick, 212
Canada, xix, 11

Canning, George, 321, 350–51, 354
Carbery, Mr., 148
Carlisle, Frederick Howard, 5th Earl of, 55*n,* 87, 89, 114, 321, 330, 340
Carlisle, Lady Margaret Howard, Countess of, 67, 68, 139, 336, 374
Carlton House, 137, 149, 151, 158, 174, 190, 350, 354
Caroline of Brunswick, Princess of Wales, 281, 287–88, 353, 359
Castle Howard, xv, 336, 358, 359
Cater, Mr., 188
Cathcart, Charles Cathcart, 9th Baron, 50
Cathcart, Charlotte, 50
Cathcart, Jean, Lady, 50
Cavendish, Georgiana Dorothy "Little G" (daughter):
   birth of, xix, 118–20
   character and personality of, 277, 307, 308, 324
   childhood and adolescence of, 118–21, 124, 126, 127–28, 163, 195, 224, 236, 239, 258–59, 261–62, 265, 268–70, 276, 277, 278, 292–93, 298, 299, 307–8, 312–13, 319–22
   court and society presentation of, 296, 305, 313, 319–22
   courtship and marriage of, 324–25, 326
   dowry and income of, 324–25
   Georgiana's correspondence with, 258–59, 265, 268, 269–70, 273, 307–8, 309–10, 333, 343, 357–58
   Georgiana's relationship with, 124, 163, 258–59, 265, 270, 277, 307–8, 312–13, 336, 371
   Lord Morpeth and, 321, 324–25, 336, 338, 339, 342, 370
   physical appearance of, 276, 307, 320, 322
   pregnancies and childbirths of, 342, 358, 370
   prospective suitors of, 321, 324–25
Cavendish, Harriet "Harryo" (daughter):
   birth of, 164
   childhood and adolescence of, 171, 195, 224, 236, 261–62, 276, 277, 293, 307, 308, 320–21, 342, 347, 357–59, 365–66, 375

Cavendish, Harriet "Harryo" (daughter)
  (*cont.*):
  court and society presentation of, 345,
    347–48
  marriage of, 377–78
  physical appearance of, 276, 277, 307,
    321
Cavendish, Henry, 284
Cavendish, Lady Dorothy, *see* Portland,
    Dorothy Cavendish, Duchess of
Cavendish, Lady George, 106*n,* 125
  Georgiana and, 102, 126, 291
  political activism of, 199
Cavendish, Lord Frederick, 28, 70, 134,
    318
Cavendish, Lord George, 17, 24, 125,
    218
  Georgiana and, 174*n,* 238, 380*n*
  mistresses of, 78
Cavendish, Lord John, 170
  death of, 296–97
  political career of, 80, 109, 110, 116,
    144–45, 149, 208, 296
Cavendish, Lord Richard, 17, 20, 24, 81,
    297
Cavendish, Sir William, 15
Cavendish, William, 381
Cavendish family, 14–18, 23–25, 56, 73,
    84, 120, 173, 223, 232, 320
  disapproval of Georgiana by, 23–25, 27,
    29, 50, 52–53, 65*n,* 70, 81, 119–20,
    144–45, 148, 203, 238, 240, 245,
    246–48, 255, 267, 291
  drawl affected by, 29, 44–45
  Lady Bessborough and, 73, 84, 85–86
  political influence of, 14–16, 28, 29, 81,
    281, 296–97, 299
  wealth and power of, 15–16, 112, 136
Cecilia (Burney), 33–34
Charles James Fox (Mitchell), 55*n,* 185*n*
Charlotte, Princess, 353, 359, 360
Charlotte, Queen of George III, 21, 36,
    65–66, 75, 76, 77, 90, 115, 248, 252,
    341
  Georgiana's presentation to, 21–22,
    215–16
  Little G's presentation to, 319–21
  Regency Crisis and, 204, 205, 211,
    215–16, 217

Chartres, Duc de, 113–14, 226
Chatham, John Pitt, 2nd Earl of, 137
Chatham, Mary Elizabeth Pitt, Countess
    of, 139, 157, 280, 307
Chatham, William Pitt, 1st Earl of, xvii,
    62, 109
Chatsworth, xv, 17, 22–31, 54, 56, 68,
    111, 132, 134, 159, 180, 182–83, 194,
    297
  architecture and furnishings of, 23,
    124, 130
  archives of, xv, 259
  daily routine at, 202–3
  dining and entertainment at, 24–25, 26,
    27–28, 126, 160, 169, 177, 202–3
  Georgiana as chatelaine of, 23–31,
    64–65, 202–3
  grounds and garden of, 23
  parishioners and tenants of, 24, 27–28,
    372
  Public Days at, 23, 27–28, 126
  rugged and isolated situation of, 22–23
  staff of, 24–25, 31, 381
Chauvlin, Marquis de, 271
Chesterfield, Philip Stanhope, 4th Earl of,
    17, 30
Chiswick House, 17, 301, 308, 322, 339,
    356, 373, 379
Cholmondeley, George James Chol-
    mondeley, 4th Earl of, 44, 69, 78
Church of England, 97
  Thirty-nine Articles of, 55
Clarence, William, Duke of, 339
Clarissa (Richardson), 31
Clermont, Frances Fortescue, Countess
    of, 35–36, 47, 49, 50, 66, 159
  on Georgiana, 64–65, 84, 156
  Georgiana and, 41, 49, 65, 320
Clermont, William Henry Fortescue, Earl
    of, 46
Clifford, William James, 195, 373, 374,
    379, 380
  childhood and adolescence of, 224, 229,
    239, 255, 307, 308
  education of, 307
Clubs and Club Life in London (Timbs),
    56*n*
Coke, Lady Mary, 7, 163, 282, 288
  on Duchess of Gordon, 211–12

on Duke of Devonshire, 22, 118, 246
on Georgiana, 22, 34–35, 88, 113, 115, 123–24, 156, 164, 169, 245, 246
on Lady Derby, 66–68
Coleraine, George Hanger, 4th Baron, 47
Coleridge, Samuel Taylor, 312n
Colley, Linda, 385
Condé, Prince de, 229
Condorcet, Marie Jean de Caritat, Marquis de, 225
Consalvi, Cardinal, 379
Conway, Henry Seymour, 110, 124
Cornwallis, Charles Cornwallis, 1st Marquis, 89, 211, 304
Correspondence of Lord Granville Leveson Gower (Granville, ed.), 285n
Courier de l'Europe, 190
Courtney, Eliza, see Ellice, Eliza Courtney
Coutts, Thomas, 228–29, 246, 247, 380–81
Duke of Devonshire and, 185, 272
Georgiana's correspondence with, 246, 247, 253, 271, 298, 341
Georgiana's financial arrangements with, 185–86, 223–24, 230, 231, 235, 253, 272, 338
Covent Garden, 32, 46, 61, 90, 133, 144, 199, 336
Cowper, Thea, 12
Coxheath, 61, 62–66, 74, 75, 197
Craufurd, James, 46, 159, 206, 213, 276, 278
Craufurd, Quentin, 46
Craven, Elizabeth, Countess of, 336
Creevey, Eleanor, 260, 365
Crewe, Frances Anne, Lady, xiv, 47, 49, 135, 151, 207, 383
Georgiana and, 63, 65, 69–70, 138
Croft, Richard, 236, 237, 239, 297
Cromwell, Oliver, 135
Cumberland, Anne, Duchess of, 83
Cumberland, Henry Frederick, Duke of, 90
Cunningham, Lord, 346

Daily Life (Parreaux), 25n
Dalrymple, Grace, 78
Damer, Anne Seymour, 46, 138, 175, 196, 247

Damer, John, 46, 59n
Darwin, Erasmus, 326–27
Declaration of Independence, 61
Decline and Fall of the Roman Empire, The (Gibbon), 268
Defoe, Daniel, 22
Delany, Mary, 8, 17, 19, 20, 34, 35
Delille, Abbé, 312n
Denman, Thomas, 119, 236
Denne, Cornelius, 234, 235
Derby, Edward Stanley, 12th Earl of, 44, 46, 66, 68, 170
Derby, Elizabeth Stanley, Countess of, 46, 47, 66–68, 191, 253, 267
Derbyshire Militia, 61, 62–66, 68–70, 88
Devonshire, Elizabeth, Duchess of, see Foster, Lady Elizabeth
Devonshire, Georgiana Spencer, Duchess of:
accusations of swindling and bribery against, 124–25, 153
as amateur chemist and mineralogist, xvi, 269, 272, 279, 283–84
attention-seeking behavior of, 10, 34, 36–38, 48–49, 153, 201
autobiographical novel of, xvi, 58–60, 68, 187
banking arrangements of, 185–86, 223–24, 245
Belgian revolutionary sympathies of, 231, 236–37, 239, 283
birth of, xix, 4
blackmail of, 178, 183n, 224n
breastfeeding by, 119–20, 130, 164, 243, 258
celebrity and fame of, xvi, 37–38, 48–49, 67, 88–91, 140, 152, 153–54, 168–71, 339–40, 382
charm and sophistication of, xv, 3, 10, 14, 24, 34, 184, 228, 251–52
childhood and adolescence of, 3–6, 9–14, 17–20, 24, 131
courage of, xv, 292, 363
court presentations of, 21–22, 215–16
criticism and caricature of, 34–36, 38, 49, 65, 66, 124–25, 136, 139–42, 143–44, 145–46, 147, 148, 150–51, 152, 153, 156, 157, 170, 171, 200
death of, xx, 233n, 325, 370–71

Devonshire, Georgiana Spencer,
  Duchess of (*cont.*):
  debts of, 41–42, 58, 88, 102, 123–24,
    130–31, 136, 155–56, 163–64, 178,
    179, 182–86, 187, 223–24, 230–31,
    233–35, 239, 243, 245–46, 255, 259,
    272–73, 279, 298, 310–11, 317–19,
    321, 326, 337–38, 352, 360–63
  dependency and malleability of, xv, 11,
    12, 30, 35, 36, 49, 50, 66, 68, 103,
    105, 188–89, 382
  depressions of, 105–6, 160, 252, 305
  Derbyshire Militia and, 61, 63–66,
    68–70, 88
  diminished eyesight of, 291–93, 298,
    303, 305–6, 326–27, 363
  dissipation and drinking by, 19, 21,
    35–36, 40–42, 48, 49–50, 53, 86–88,
    153, 163–64
  dowry and trousseau of, 18, 19–20
  early failure to produce an heir as con-
    cern of, 70, 84, 102, 120, 127, 160,
    164, 180, 203, 224, 231, 234
  eating disorder of, xvi, 50, 105
  education and reading of, 9, 11, 14, 30,
    54, 57, 246, 266, 268, 274, 319
  egalitarian instincts of, 44*n,* 153–54,
    300
  exile of, xx, 255–75, 311–12
  family background of, 3–9
  farewell letters to children by, 258–59
  fashionable life rejected by, 43, 53, 58,
    69–70, 132
  fashion innovations of, 95, 117, 118,
    155, 168, 169–71, 211
  female auxiliary corps organized by, 64,
    75
  fictional parodies of, 49, 53, 340–41
  French aristocracy and, 39–40, 53,
    68–69, 88, 161, 169–71, 190, 223,
    224–28, 238, 241–42, 271
  French royalist sympathies of, 231, 236,
    239, 240, 241–43, 283
  funeral and burial of, 372–73
  gambling addiction of, xvi, 35, 41–42,
    43, 49, 58, 71, 86–88, 123–24,
    130–31, 136, 156, 163, 178, 186–89,
    191, 234, 246, 279
  gardening of, 301

generosity and charity of, 24, 121, 123*n,*
    186, 240, 271, 283, 284, 317, 339,
    382
giddy and hysterical tendencies of, xv,
    19, 34–35, 49, 51, 65, 124
hair and hair styles of, 7, 36
hot-air balloon publicity event spon-
    sored by, 168, 215
illnesses of, xx, 40–41, 49–50, 127–28,
    178–79, 237, 238, 290–92, 296, 303,
    307, 326, 330, 350–51, 363–64,
    369–70
insight and wisdom gained by, 301–3,
    313–14
involvement in French court politics
    of, 190
legal will of, 258
lesbianism suspected of, 161–62
loans and gifts solicited from friends
    by, 184, 203, 234, 235, 245, 246, 310,
    317–19, 337, 352
loneliness of, xv, 11, 26, 60, 66, 84, 100,
    132
medical treatments of, 70, 290–91, 292,
    296, 326–27, 352, 370
miscarriages of, 38, 40–41, 50, 86, 95,
    131–32, 297
musical compositions of, xvi, 136, 311
obituary of, 381
passionate nature of, 13, 22, 39, 40,
    51–54, 246
as patron of arts, xvi, 25, 26, 45–46,
    84–85, 153, 168–69, 177, 284, 382
personal ambition of, xvi, 91–92, 314
personal diary of, 310–11
physical appearance and stylishness of,
    3, 7, 10, 18, 21, 28, 34, 36, 37–38, 83,
    88, 95, 117, 118, 155, 168, 169–71,
    251, 305–6
plays written by, 102, 319, 336
poetry and verse letters of, xiii, 10, 30,
    51, 167, 259–60, 294, 301, 311–12,
    352–53, 363
political awakening and career of, 54,
    58, 61, 74–76, 81–83, 90–91, 108,
    110, 113–16, 133–54, 167–68,
    198–99, 208–16, 382–85
political campaigning of, xiv, xv–xvi,
    xviii, 58, 61, 74–76, 81–82, 90–91,

133, 137–54, 208–9, 211–13, 217–18, 239, 279–83, 286

political cartoons on, 141, 142, 150, 151, 156, 170, 171, 200, 356

as political hostess, xiv, xv, 74, 89–90, 113–15, 117, 149, 152, 198, 199, 213–14, 223, 279–80, 288–89, 311, 332, 356

popular public events organized by, 168–69, 190, 217

portraits of, ii, 3, 88, 91, 118, 192, 325

press accounts of, xvi, 21, 24, 36, 37–38, 40–41, 43, 48, 61, 64, 72–73, 75, 83, 85, 88–91, 95, 108, 114, 117, 119, 124, 132, 133, 140–43, 145–46, 153, 155, 156, 171, 177, 240, 258, 278, 282–83, 291, 296, 317, 322, 330, 335, 336, 337, 339, 341, 346, 347–48, 351, 357, 372

promise to avoid politics exacted from, 280, 287

reckless behavior of, xvi, 35–36, 40–42, 86–88, 155–58, 163–64, 186–91, 246

Regency Crisis diary of, 205–6, 218–19

religious faith of, 337–38

self-assurance gained by, 313–14

self-criticism of, 266–67, 274, 277, 298, 302

self-doubt and insecurity of, xv, 10, 11, 12, 22, 24–25, 26–27, 29, 65, 66, 101–2, 106, 234–35

social obligations of, 21–22, 24–29, 30, 52–53, 152

social skills and talent of, 9–10, 14, 22, 24–25, 27, 34–38, 65, 74, 177

and status of women, xviii, 58, 282–83, 314

successful pregnancies and deliveries of, xix, 105–6, 108, 113, 117–20, 162–64, 166, 171, 231–38, 252–60

on women in politics, 283, 314

writing style of, xiv, xvi, 58–60, 91–92, 259–60, 311–12

Devonshire, William Cavendish, 1st Duke of, 15, 23

Devonshire, William Cavendish, 3rd Duke of, 33, 112

Devonshire, William Cavendish, 4th Duke of, 14, 15–16, 17

Devonshire, William Cavendish, 5th Duke of (husband):

adultery of, 64–66, 70–72, 126, 127, 244–45

apathy and reserve of, 16, 17, 19, 29–30, 40, 52, 90, 300

childhood and adolescence of, 16–17

courtship and marriage of Georgiana and, xvii, xix, 17–20, 50, 91, 120

death of, 378–79

education and intelligence of, 16, 30, 369

family deaths as source of grief to, 296–97

Fox and, 55, 90, 115–16, 280, 288–89

Georgiana's political influence of, 299, 304

Georgiana's relationship with, xv, 17–18, 19–22, 25, 26, 29–31, 34, 39, 40–42, 43, 49, 50, 52, 63–64, 70, 71, 84, 95–96, 113, 118–19, 124–26, 127, 130–31, 156, 160, 163, 164, 174*n*, 179–84, 186, 188–89, 195–96, 223–24, 230–31, 234–35, 243, 245–48, 254–57, 264–65, 267, 269, 271–72, 273, 274, 276, 278, 296–97, 298–99, 300–301, 337, 342–44, 360–63

heir born to, 237–38

illnesses and hypochondria of, 127–28, 177, 276, 278, 279, 300, 337, 342–43

inherited income and property of, 17, 33–34, 163, 299

Irish post offered to, 112–13

Lady Foster's relationship with, xvi, 100, 101, 103, 104–5, 112, 121, 128–29, 156, 159, 162, 165–67, 176–80, 182–83, 189–90, 192–95, 229–30, 232, 244, 245, 248, 271, 274–75, 278, 326, 347, 376–78

Lady Spencer and, 21, 22, 65, 195, 201, 244

lifestyle of, 16, 21, 26, 31, 34, 84, 163*n*, 186

maiden speech in House of Lords by, 75

militia organized by, 61, 62–66, 68–70, 88, 101

political posts declined by, 122–13, 208

Devonshire, William Cavendish, 5th
    Duke of (husband) (*cont.*):
  separation and divorce threatened by,
    179–84, 200, 240, 243, 251, 254–57
  Whig party loyalty of, 16, 20, 28, 46*n*,
    74, 79, 90, 109*n*, 110, 281
Devonshire, William Cavendish, 7th
    Duke of, *see* Cavendish, William
Devonshire, William George Cavendish,
    6th Duke of, *see* Hartington, William
    George Cavendish, Marquis of
Devonshire House, 17, 20, 31, 34, 66, 68,
    70, 81, 84–88, 108, 111, 117–18, 129,
    132, 183, 271
  architecture and decoration of, 33, 89,
    124
  dining and entertainment at, 33, 74, 78,
    83, 86–88, 89–90, 113–14, 117, 149,
    152, 158, 168–69, 175, 195, 206–7,
    216, 223, 280, 313, 317
  domestic staff at, 196, 276, 370
  Georgiana's return from exile to,
    276–78
Devonshire House Circle, 44–49, 59*n*,
    73–74, 77–79, 86–90, 157, 173, 253,
    301, 313, 321, 354
  gambling and indebtedness in, 185
  patois and drawl affected by, 44–45,
    207*n*
  sexual license in, 44, 47, 48, 53, 64–68,
    78, 126, 162, 174*n*, 207
Diary of a Lady-in-Waiting, The (Steuart,
    ed.), 123*n*
Dillon, Mrs., 99–100
Dorset, John Frederick Sackville, 3rd
    Duke of, 56, 192
  cricket developed as national game by,
    46
  as French ambassador, 162–63, 190,
    224, 225, 230, 243
  Georgiana's relationship with, 178,
    190–91, 193–94, 196–97, 198, 224,
    227, 233, 242–43, 267, 271
  Lady Foster and, 106*n*, 112, 162–63,
    178, 193
  marriage of, 242
Douglas, Lady, 47
Drummond, Mr., 276
Drury Lane Theatre, 32, 49, 77, 155

Dublin Castle, 113
Dumouriez, M., 121
Duncannon, Frederick Ponsonby, Lord,
    see Bessborough, Frederick Pon-
    sonby, 3rd Earl of
Duncannon, Harriet, Lady, *see* Bessbor-
    ough, Harriet Spencer Ponsonby,
    Countess of
Duncannon, John William Ponsonby,
    Lord, 86, 342, 357, 358, 366
Dundas, Henry:
  Lady Gordon and, 212
  political career of, 212, 218, 328–29,
    330, 364
Dunning, John, 76
Dutens, Louis, 3, 381

East India Bill, 134, 135, 329
East India Company, 33, 134, 135
Egremont, Sir George O'Brien, 3rd Earl
    of, 47, 66, 88, 276
elections:
  of 1780, 81–82, 83, 90, 212
  of 1782, 90–91
  of 1784, 137–54, 206, 218
  of 1788, 198–99
  of 1796, 288
Elizabeth I, Queen of England, 15, 369
Ellice, Edward, 262
Ellice, Eliza (Lady Foster's niece),
    341–42, 344
Ellice, Eliza Courtney (daughter), 380
  birth of, 259–60, 262, 264, 292, 380
  character and personality of, 262
  Charles Grey's paternity of, 252–60,
    262, 302, 326, 332
  childhood of, 260–62, 324
  Georgiana's relationship with, 259–62
  Grey family's rearing of, 259, 260–62
  marriage of, 262
Ellice, Hannah Alethea Grey, 262
Ellice, Robert, 262, 380
Elliot, Sir Gilbert, 197–98, 207
Elliot, William, 215, 216
Elphinstone, Captain, 212
Erne, Lady Mary, 96, 98, 100, 111–12
Erskine, Thomas Erskine, 1st Baron,
    236–37
Et in Arcadia Ego (Poussin), 33

Eton, 55, 58, 197
Evelina (Burney), 60
Evelyn, John, 5

Fane, Lady Maria, 366
Farington, Joseph, 210*n*
Farington Diary, The (Greig, ed.), 210*n*
Farquhar, Dr., 352, 374
Farrar, Mr., 362
Farren, Elizabeth, 170*n*
Fawkener, Georgiana "Jockey," 174
Fawkener, William, 174*n*
Fersen, Count, 129, 242
Fielding, Henry, 33
Fielding, Miss, 131
Fitzgerald, Lord Robert, 237
Fitzherbert, Maria:
    Georgiana resented by, 172, 260, 332,
        365
    Prince of Wales and, 157–58, 171–74,
        206, 232, 260, 281*n*, 317, 322–23,
        365
Fitzjames, Duc de, 114
Fitzjames, Madame de, 271
Fitzpatrick, Richard, 46, 87, 114, 185, 207,
    213, 282, 327, 353
Fitzwilliam, William Wentworth
    Fitzwilliam, 2nd Earl, 318, 344
Fly, The, 69
Foley, Lady Harriet, 34–35
*Footsteps: Adventures of a Romantic Biogra-
    pher* (Holmes), xiii
Forbes, John, xix
Foster, Augustus, 165*n*, 362, 372, 374,
    380, 381
    childhood and adolescence of, 98, 100,
        111, 112, 129, 195, 224, 293–94
    Devonshires and, 111, 112, 293–94
    education of, 111
Foster, Frederick, 96, 98, 123, 129,
    293–94, 341, 380, 381
Foster, John Thomas, 98–99, 106*n*,
    110–12, 224
    death of, 293
    as Irish member of parliament, 194
Foster, Lady Elizabeth "Bess":
    Cavendish children's antipathy for,
        308–9, 343, 347, 374–76
    death of, 379–80

Devonshires' financial arrangements
    with, 121–22, 161, 263
diary of, 165, 166, 177, 179, 189, 193,
    194, 195, 199, 210, 372–73
Duke of Devonshire's marriage to,
    376–78
Duke of Devonshire's relationship
    with, xvi, 100, 101, 103, 104–5, 112,
    121, 128–29, 156, 159, 162, 165–67,
    176–80, 182–83, 189–90, 192, 193,
    194–95, 229–30, 232, 244, 245, 248,
    271, 274–75, 278, 326, 347, 376–78
Duke of Richmond and, 192–93, 195,
    211, 278, 293–94, 297, 301, 309–10,
    325–26
European sojourns of, 108, 110–12,
    115, 120–23, 128–31, 156, 161,
    176–77, 193–96, 224–36, 255–75,
    341–43
failed first marriage of, 96, 98–99, 100,
    106*n*
family background of, 96–98
financial independence gained by, 293
frail health of, 101–2, 103, 106, 120,
    160–61, 278, 325–26
Georgiana's correspondence with,
    110–12, 115–16, 118–19, 120–23,
    126, 128–31, 156, 161–63, 176–77,
    188–89, 196, 301, 342, 343
Georgiana's relationship with, xvi, xix,
    xx, 95, 96, 100–107, 110–13, 115,
    120–23, 128, 159–65, 176–78, 179,
    180, 182–84, 188–90, 193–95,
    199–201, 232, 239, 243–45, 250–52,
    254–55, 258, 262–65, 274–76, 278,
    294–95, 309, 342–43, 373–74, 385
Georgiana's role usurped by, 178, 180,
    189, 199–201, 375–78
Georgiana's wealth and influence as
    cause of jealousy to, 120–21, 294–95,
    310
as governess of Charlotte Williams,
    106–7, 115, 122, 129–30, 161, 243
impoverishment of, 97, 98, 99–100,
    121–22, 161, 194
ingratiating, seductive manner of, 96,
    100–101, 105, 127, 159, 160, 308
insincerity and affectation of, 160, 162,
    308, 325

Foster, Lady Elizabeth "Bess" (*cont.*):
  Lady Melbourne and, 177, 231, 236,
    252, 253, 254, 335
  Lady Spencer's hostility toward, 101,
    104–5, 107, 156, 159–60, 177–79,
    180–81, 192, 193–94, 199–200, 201,
    237, 238, 243–45, 250–51, 255, 256,
    264, 269, 301, 308
  motherhood of, 96, 98–100, 111, 112,
    123, 129, 165, 224, 229–30, 236,
    293–94, 325, 341–42
  physical appearance of, 96, 160, 320
  romantic attachments and lovers of,
    106–7, 112, 122–23, 129–30, 159,
    162–63, 166–67, 192–93, 195, 211,
    278, 293–94, 297, 301, 309–10,
    325–26, 335–36, 379
Fox, Charles James, 50, 171
  adultery of, xiv, 127, 206, 213
  birth and childhood of, 54–55
  death of, xx, 374–75
  dissolute lifestyle of, xiv, 54, 55–56, 57,
    78, 87, 109, 135
  Duke of Devonshire and, 55, 90,
    115–16, 280, 288–89
  East India Bill of, 134, 135, 329
  Edmund Burke and, 57, 136, 240–41
  as Foreign Secretary, 90–91, 109, 110,
    115–16, 117–18
  Georgiana's campaigning for, xiv, 61,
    90–91, 133, 137–54
  Georgiana's political disagreements
    with, 280, 304, 333
  as Georgiana's political mentor, 54,
    57–58, 75, 81–82, 90–91, 108, 110, 304
  Georgiana's relationship with, xiv, 54,
    56–58, 74, 75, 126–27, 163, 189, 241,
    280, 283, 288–89, 299–300, 306–7,
    314, 342, 343–44, 348–53
  illness of, 208–9
  Mrs. Armistead and, 127, 206, 213, 342
  open and generous nature of, 55, 58, 109
  political cartoons on, 135, 141, 142
  political opposition to, 14*n,* 109–10,
    133–38, 143–46, 148, 152, 207–8,
    209–10, 211, 217, 280–81, 283, 300,
    328–29
  political retirement of, 299–300, 307,
    314

  Prince of Wales and, 78, 115–16,
    172–73, 208–10, 211, 213
  unconventional personal appearance of,
    56, 78
  Whig party career of, xiv, 54, 55, 57–58,
    62, 74, 75, 81–82, 90–91, 108–10,
    115–18, 133–53, 167, 205, 206–13,
    219, 223, 240–41, 279–80, 288–89,
    299–300, 331, 333, 348–53
  William Pitt's rivalry with, 14*n,* 109–10,
    134–37, 143–44, 148, 152, 209–10,
    327, 354–56
Fox, Henry, *see* Holland, Henry Fox, 1st
  Baron
Fox, Stephen, 97*n*
France:
  American War of Independence and,
    62, 89
  aristocracy and royal court of, 7, 14,
    38–40, 53–54, 68–69, 113–15, 136,
    161, 162, 224–28, 238, 239
  British hostilities with, 10–11, 55,
    68–69, 88, 271, 274–75, 280, 281,
    286–87, 297–98, 305, 313–14,
    327–28, 344
  constitutional reform demanded in,
    225–26
  Directory government in, 327
  drought and food shortages in, 224–25,
    296
  National Assembly of, 225, 238
  peace negotiations of Britain and, 11,
    114, 117, 333–34, 335, 343
  peasantry of, 22
  Royal Council of, 225
  storming of the Bastille in, 229
  Third Estate in, 225–26, 228
  see also French Revolution; Paris; Ver-
    sailles
Francis, Sir Philip, 306–7, 314, 382
Frederick William II, King of Prussia,
  243
Freemason's Tavern, 147–48
French and Indian War, xix
French Fleet, 69, 88
French Revolution, xix, 153, 190, 280,
  282, 327
  Georgiana's royalist sympathies in, 231,
    236, 239, 240, 241–43, 283

Jacobins in, 270*n*
plight of the royal family in, 225, 227–29, 238, 241–43, 270–71
political unrest leading to, 223–30, 232, 238, 241, 263–64, 269, 270–71
refugees of, 266, 271
republican constitution adopted in, 241
September massacres in, 270*n*
Whig party debate on, 239–42, 279
Fulford, Roger, 347*n*

Gainsborough, Thomas, 3, 51, 52, 88, 118
Galley, William, 234, 245
Galway, Robert Monckton-Arundell, 4th Viscount, 199
Gardner, Mrs., 71, 106
Garner, Captain, 69
Garrick, David, 6, 8–9, 32, 45–46
Gaussé, Mlle., 238
Gell, William, 379
Gentleman's Magazine, 59, 381
George I, King of England, 76
George II, King of England, xix, 8, 14*n*
George III, King of England, xix, 16, 62, 65–66
American War of Independence and, 62
anti-constitutional activities of, 134–35
assassination attempt against, 320
Fox and, 133–37
ill health of, 185, 204
Irish question and, 328–29
madness and recovery of, 204–6, 208–9, 213, 214, 217, 331–32, 353–54
Pitt and, 134–37, 152, 328–29
Prince of Wales and, 76–78, 83, 115–16, 151, 173, 204–6, 215, 216, 348, 359–60
proclamation on suppression of vice from, 190
Whig opposition to, 57, 74–76, 79, 89–90, 108–9, 110, 115, 134–36, 152, 248, 279, 300, 306
George IV (as Prince of Wales), 91, 148, 232
character and personality of, 76–78, 157–58, 205, 209, 211, 216
debts of, 173–74, 185, 281*n*

education of, 77
Fox and, 78, 115–16, 172–73, 208–10, 211, 213
George III's relationship with, 76–78, 83, 115–16, 151, 173, 204–6, 215, 216, 348, 359–60
Georgiana on, 76–77, 80, 115–16
Georgiana's loans from, 234, 235, 245, 352
Georgiana's relationship with, 77–78, 84, 89–90, 114, 115–16, 119, 124–25, 149, 152, 157–58, 171–74, 208–9, 234, 235, 245, 260, 267, 281*n*, 313, 322–23, 325, 330, 331–32, 348–49, 353–54, 359–61
marriage of, *see* Caroline of Brunswick, Princess of Wales
mistresses of, 47, 77, 78–79, 153, 157–58, 171–74, 206, 267, 281*n*, 287–88, 313
Mrs. Fitzherbert and, 157–58, 171–74, 206, 232, 260, 281*n*, 317, 322–23
profligate lifestyle of, 78, 151, 209, 214, 281*n*, 287–88
Regency Crisis and, 204–19
Sheridan and, 206–8, 216, 353–54
Whig alliance of, 76, 78, 83–84, 89–90, 115–16, 137, 149, 151, 168, 172, 173, 185, 216–17
Giardini, Felix, 25, 56
Gibbon, Edward, 96, 268, 269
Gilbert (hairdresser), 233*n*
Gillray, James, 135, 356
Glenbervie, Sylvester Douglas, Baron, 47, 260
Goodwood, 301
Gordon, Jane, Duchess of:
daughters of, 212, 321, 338–39, 346–47
Georgiana's rivalry with, 218, 338–39, 346
political activism of, 211–13, 218, 367, 368, 384
social position of, 155, 212, 213, 216, 218, 271, 287, 288, 346
Gordon, Lady Georgiana, *see* Bedford, Georgiana Gordon, Duchess of
Gordon, Lord George, 79, 81, 82
Gower, George Granville Leveson-Gower, Earl, 226

Grafton, Augustus Henry Fitzroy, 3rd
    Duke of, 110
Graham, James, 70
Graham, Mary, 96, 382
    beauty and gentle nature of, 51, 266
    Gainsborough portraits of, 51, 52
    Georgiana's relationship with, 50–54,
        58, 101, 184, 266, 385
    illness and death of, 50, 54, 266–67
Graham, Thomas, 50, 54, 266
Grammont, Corisande de, 336–37
Grammont, Duc de, 336
Granby, Lady Mary Isabella, Marchioness
    of, 64
Granville, 1st Earl, *see* Leveson Gower,
    Lord Granville
Granville, Lady, 285*n*
Great Britain:
    aristocratic oligarchy of, xvii–xviii, 6–7,
        23–25, 31–32, 43–49, 74
    French hostilities with, 10–11, 55,
        68–69, 88, 271, 274–75, 280, 281,
        286–87, 297–98, 305, 313–14,
        327–28, 348
    French invasions of, 297–98
    French peace negotiations with, 11,
        114, 117, 333–34, 335
    Glorious Revolution of 1688 in, 31,
        241
    imperial interests of, xvii, 11, 134, 306
    industrial power of, xvii
    mass circulation of newspapers in, 37,
        140–43
    monarchy and rules of succession in,
        15, 157, 172
    political system of, xvii–xviii, 6–7, 28,
        74
    population of, xvii, 37
    Regency Crisis in, 204–19, 331
    rural villages of, 22
    sport and gaming in, 35, 46, 87–88,
        186–88, 234
    status of women in, xvi, xviii, 58, 86,
        98–99, 152–54, 282–83, 383–85
Greig, J., 210*n*
Grenville, Fox, 136
Grenville, Thomas, 126, 278, 364
    Georgiana and, 46, 88, 310–11

shipwreck survival of, 310–11
    Whig party career of, 46, 281, 310, 344,
        349, 360, 368
Grenville, William, 211
Grenville, William Wyndham Grenville,
    Baron, 335, 349, 350, 354–56, 367
Gresse, John, 9
Greville, Charles Cavendish Fulke, 347*n*
Greville Memoirs, The (Strachey and Ful-
    ford, eds.), 347*n*
Grey, Charles, xiv
    Association of the Friends of the People
        formed by, 279, 280
    family background of, 197
    Georgiana's daughter by, *see* Ellice,
        Eliza Courtney
    Georgiana's relationship with, xiv, xvi,
        198, 211, 244–45, 252–54, 256–57,
        278, 285–86, 302–3, 311, 325, 326,
        331, 332, 376
    impulsive, moody nature of, 198, 207
    maiden speech in Commons by,
        197–98
    marriage of, 285–86
    physical appearance of, 197
    political career of, 197–98, 206–7, 208,
        213, 214, 215, 279, 280, 299, 327,
        368, 375
    as Prime Minister, 375
Grey, Louisa, 302
Grey, Mary Ponsonby, 285, 332
    Georgiana and, 302–3, 325
Grey family, 197, 259, 260–61
Grove, Lord, 74
Guardian (London), 41
Guémène, Madame de, 39
Guérin, M., 238
Gunning, John, 290

Hamilton, Douglas Hamilton, 8th Duke
    of, 67
Hamilton, Emma, Lady, 272
Hamilton, Lady Betty, 18
Hamilton, Mary, 19, 143–44
Hamilton, Sir William, 123, 272
Hampton Court, 35
Hanger, George, 59*n*
Hanoverians, 76

Harcourt, George Simon Harcourt, 2nd
   Earl, 192
Harcourt, Lady, 87
Hardwick, Bess of, 15
Hardwick, Elizabeth Yorke, Countess of,
   307
Hardwick House, 17, 59, 84, 85, 278, 301,
   319
Hare, James, 108, 178, 278, 337
   death of, 354
   as French prisoner of war, 344, 354
   gambling and debts of, 46*n,* 87, 185
   on Georgiana, 91, 202–3
   Georgiana and, 46, 229, 230–31, 235,
      245, 271–72, 279, 324, 326, 354
   on Lady Foster, 100–101, 202–3,
      229–30, 325
   on life at Chatsworth, 202–3
   political career of, 126, 137, 240, 334
Harrington, Jane Stanhope, Countess of,
   21, 83
Harrow, 9, 10, 307, 358
Hartington, William George Cavendish
   "Hart," Marquis of (son), 3, 325,
   380–81
   birth of, 237–38
   character and personality of, 277, 307,
      358–59, 381
   childhood and adolescence of, 239, 243,
      248, 253, 258, 265, 276, 277, 307,
      358–59, 362, 366
   deafness of, 277, 358, 381
   education of, 307, 358
   Georgiana's correspondence with, 258,
      367, 368–69
   Georgiana's relationship with, 239, 265,
      276, 277, 358–59, 366, 369, 385
   Lady Foster and, 358–59, 373, 374, 377,
      379, 380
   physical appearance of, 276
Hartshorn and Dyde's, 91
Hatham, Miss, 27
Hatton, Lady Anne, 321
Haymarket Theatre, 38, 313
Hays, Mary, 283
Heaton, John, 24, 179, 184, 318, 362
   Georgiana accused by, 124–25, 136
Henry VI, King of England, 209

Henry VIII, King of England, 5*n,* 15
Herbert, George Augustus Herbert, Lord,
   53, 114
Hertford, Isabella Seymour, Countess of,
   88, 365
Hervé, François, 124
Hervey, Carr Hervey, Lord, 97*n*
Hervey, John Augustus Hervey, Lord,
   111–12, 162, 165, 166, 192, 193, 271,
   344
Hervey, Lady, 344
Hervey family, 96–97, 123, 251
Hicks, Mr., 102
Hobart, Mrs., 140, 147, 152, 163
Holland, Elizabeth, Lady, 278, 306*n,* 309,
   332
Holland, Henry Fox, 1st Baron, 54–55, 57
   Lord Chatham's rivalry with, 14*n,* 109*n*
Holland, Henry Richard Vassall Fox, 3rd
   Baron Holland, 286, 309
Holland, Lady Caroline, 109
Holland House, 306*n,* 332
Holmes, Richard, xiii
Holroyd, Captain, 81
Hood, Samuel Hood, Baron, 137, 139,
   148, 199, 299
Hope, Miss, 169
Hopetoun, Elizabeth Hope, Countess of,
   190
Horton, Sir Watts, 188
Hotwells, 104–5
House of Commons, 6, 74–76, 110
   democratic reform urged in, 75–76,
      79–81
   elections to, 28, 74, 76, 81–82, 90–91
   Irish MPs added to, 328
   membership in, xvii–xviii, 28, 74, 328
   mob attack on, 79–80
   political influence of peers in,
      xvii–xviii, 6, 28, 135
   speeches, debate and votes in, 55, 76,
      79, 80, 134, 135–36, 213, 214, 216,
      223, 241, 327–28
   Whig minority in, 74–76, 151–52,
      167–68
House of Lords, 6, 134
   Duke of Devonshire's Irish speech in,
      304

House of Lords (*cont.*):
  Irish debate in, 304–5
  mob attack on, 79–80
  peers' membership by right of birth in, xvii, 74
  speeches and debate in, 62, 74, 304
House of Representatives, U.S., 75
Howe, Lord, 286
Howe, Mrs., 267

Ickworth Park, 97, 98, 99
Ilchester, Earl of, 306n
Immortal Seven, 15
India, 11, 134, 306
Inns of Court, 76
Ireland, 129, 159, 194, 232, 293, 297
  British unification of, 328
  Cavendish family interests in, 112–13, 299, 303–5
  discrimination against Catholics in, 300, 303–4, 328
  French support of rebels in, 304, 305
  political unrest and rebellion in, 75, 113, 298–99, 300, 303–5, 314, 327–28
  Protestant ascendancy in, 299, 300, 304n, 328
Italian Opera, 32, 177

Jacobins, 270n
James, Mr., 278
James I, King of England, 5n, 15
James II, King of England, 15, 31
Jefferson, Thomas, 226
Jerningham, Lady, 320–21, 322–23
Jersey, Frances Villiers, Countess of, 47, 67, 68, 132, 139, 232, 265, 332, 342
  Duke of Devonshire and, 64–66, 126
  Georgiana's relationship with, 48, 49, 54, 58, 64–65, 66, 132, 271, 325, 357–58
  Princess of Wales and, 287–88
  sexual liaisons of, 47, 64–66, 78, 126, 192, 281n, 287–88, 313, 321, 323, 325
  social downfall of, 288, 323
Jersey, George Villiers, 4th Earl of, 64, 114, 192
Jersey, Lady Elizabeth, *see* Villiers, Lady Elizabeth

Jocelyn, Lord, 68
Jockey Club, The, 240
Johnson, Joseph, 336
Johnson, Samuel, 15n, 27n, 64
Johnstone, Mr. and Mrs., 347
Jones, Sir William, 9, 81
Jordan, Dorothy, 339
Joseph II, Emperor of Belgium, 231
Journal of Thomas Moore (Dowden, ed.), 45n, 354n
Julie ou La nouvelle Héloïse (Rousseau), 53–54
"Junius letters," 306

Kent, William, 33
King's Theatre, 84–85
Kingston, Duke of, 97
Kingston, Elizabeth, Duchess of, 97n
Kotzebue, August von, 311

Lady's Magazine, 171
Lafayette, Marie Joseph, Marquis de, 228
  American War of Independence joined by, 89
  Austrian imprisonment of, 270n, 282
  French Revolution and, 225, 237, 242, 270n
La Marck, Comte de, 114
Lamb, George, 378, 380
Lamb, Lady Caroline Ponsonby, 375, 377
  birth of, 164–65
  character and personality of, 268
  childhood of, 256, 268
  court presentation of, 345
  engagement and marriage of, 366
  on Lady Foster, 308–9
  Lord Byron's affair with, 164n
  madness of, 164n
Lamb, William, 164n, 366
Lamballe, Princesse de, 190, 227, 270
Lamb family, 365–66
Langham, Sir James, 28–29
Lansdowne, George Granville, Baron, 8
Leeds, Catherine, Duchess of, 260
Lefanu, Betsy Sheridan, 207, 214, 232
Leicester, Charlotte Townshend, Countess of, 307
Leinster, William Robert Fitzgerald, 2nd Duke of, 304

Lennox, Lady Caroline, 54
Lennox, Lady Charlotte, 335–36
Lennox, Lady Sarah, 49, 50, 67, 68
Lepel, Molly, 97n
Letters to His Son (Chesterfield), 30
Leveson Gower, Lady, *see* Cavendish, Harriet
Leveson Gower, Lord Granville:
  character and personality of, 284
  Harriet Cavendish's marriage to, 377–78
  Lady Bessborough's affair with, 284–85, 290, 292, 296, 309, 319, 323–24, 340, 350, 371, 377
  political career of, 153, 284, 321, 354–55, 370, 377–80
Lévis, Duc de, 129
Lincoln, Anna Maria Pelham-Clinton, Countess of, 120
Linley, Elizabeth, *see* Sheridan, Elizabeth Linley
Linley, Thomas, 9
Lismore Castle, 17, 305
Lloyd, Miss, 40, 70, 79–80, 160, 199
Locke, John, 9
Londesborough, 180
London:
  aristocratic society in, 31–36, 43–49, 58–60, 115, 152, 185, 218
  Cavendish family homes in, 31, 33–34
  City of, 32
  coal dust fog in, 33
  commerce and clubs of, 31–33, 143
  1780 mob riots and fires in, 79–81, 82
  Spencer family homes in, 4–6
  West End vs. East End of, 31–33
London Chronicle, 62–63, 90, 139, 149–51, 320
  on Georgiana, 37–38, 61, 83, 114, 330, 339
London Opera, 25
Loughborough, Alexander Wedderburn, 1st Baron, 213
Louis XIV, King of France, 15, 30
Louis XVI, King of France, 38, 39, 113, 196
  deposition of, 241–42
  execution of, 270, 271
  imprisonment of, 241, 270
  revolt of Third Estate against, 225–28
Louis (servant), 166, 195
Lovattini, Signor, 38
Lowton, Mr., 34
Lucan, Charles Bingham, Earl of, 72
Lucan, Lady, 190
Lucille (maidservant), 195
Lunardi, Vincenzo, 168
Luttrell, Lady Elizabeth, 87n

Macaroni Club, 56
Macaulay, Catherine, 283
Macbeth (Shakespeare), 46
Maintenon, Madame de, 375
Malden, George Capel-Coningsby, Viscount, 136
Malmesbury, James Harris, 1st Earl, 213–14
Manchester, Duchess of, 44n
Manners, Lord Robert, 81
Mansfield, William Murray, 1st Earl, 79, 80
Marie-Antoinette, Queen of France, 119, 196, 225, 227–29
  character and personality of, 39–40, 190, 230
  execution of, 38, 271
  Georgiana and, 38–40, 88, 169–71, 190, 227, 228, 238, 241–42
  imprisonment of, 241–43, 270
  Madame de Polignac and, 39–40, 53–54, 69, 161, 190, 238, 271
  portrait of, 169–71
Marie-Thérèse, Empress, 38–39
Marlborough, Caroline, Duchess of, 21, 157, 320
Marlborough, Charles, 2nd Duke of, 7n
Marlborough, John Churchill, 1st Duke of, 7n
Marlborough, Sarah, Duchess of, 7n
Marshall family, 255
Martindale, Mr., 87–88, 178, 179, 183, 184, 224n
Masham, Lady Frances, 70
Mazzinghi, Count Joseph, 177, 330
Melbourne, Elizabeth Lamb, Viscountess, 49, 59, 114, 125n, 177, 265, 281n
  character and personality of, 47–48

Melbourne, Elizabeth Lamb, Viscountess (*cont.*):
  children of, 47, 66, 164
  Georgiana and, 47–48, 52, 63, 78–79, 80, 88, 132, 174–75, 191, 197, 256, 278, 292–93
  Georgiana's correspondence with, 52, 78–79, 80, 197, 232, 255–56, 257, 263, 285–86, 323, 332, 337, 339
  Lady Bessborough's correspondence with, 254, 255, 263, 265
  Lady Foster and, 177, 231, 236, 252, 253, 254, 335
  love affairs of, 47, 78–79, 206, 321
  social position of, 47–48, 383
Melbourne, Peniston Lamb, 1st Viscount, 47, 114
Melbourne, 2nd Viscount, *see* Lamb, William
Melville, Viscount, *see* Dundas, Henry
Memoirs of George II (Hervey), 97n
Memorandums of the Face of the Country in Switzerland (Duchess of Devonshire), 312
Mills, Mr., 276
Mitchell, Leslie, 55n, 185n
Moira, Francis Rawdon Hastings, 2nd Earl of, 313, 359, 360
Montagu, Elizabeth, 65, 143, 163n, 236–37
Montagu, Lady Mary Wortley, 97
Montgolfier brothers, 168
Moore, Thomas, 45n, 354n
Morelle, Mlle., 330
Morning Chronicle, 312, 357, 372
Morning Herald and Daily Advertiser, 70n, 148, 168, 182, 212, 296
  on Georgiana, 69, 72–73, 84, 85, 88, 89–90, 95, 108, 117, 119n, 124, 133, 143, 146–47, 148, 155, 169n, 313, 317, 322, 335, 336, 337, 341, 346, 351
Morning Post (London), 204, 205, 312n, 340
  on Georgiana, 21, 37, 38, 40–41, 48, 61, 64, 83, 117, 119, 133, 140, 145–46, 148, 153, 155, 171, 177, 192, 233, 248, 278, 347–48
Morpeth, George Howard, Lord, 292, 321
  Little G and, 321, 324–25, 336, 338, 339, 342, 370
  political alliances of, 321, 325, 330, 331
Morpeth, Georgiana, Lady, *see* Cavendish, Georgiana Dorothy
Mortimer, Fanny, 233n
Mrs. Montagu (Blunt), 163n
Murray, Lady Augusta, 192
Mutiny Bill, 136

Naples, 122–23, 129, 166, 176, 272–73, 279, 284, 327
Naples, King and Queen of, 123, 272
Napoleon I, Emperor of France, 313–14
  Austria captured by, 297
  French *coup d'état* by, 327
  military defeats of, 305, 327, 366
  military victories of, 343, 344, 366
Necker, Jacques, 190
Nelson, Horatio, Viscount, 305, 366
Neville, Silas, 90
Newcastle, Thomas Pelham-Holles, Duke of, 7
Newgate Prison, 80
Newton, Mrs., 131
Nile, Battle of the, 305, 327
Noailles, Vicomte de, 228
North, Dudley, 267
North, Frederick, 8th Lord, 91, 109–10, 134, 136, 152
  political opposition to, 74–76, 82, 89, 110
  as Prime Minister, xix, 57, 62, 74–76, 81, 82, 83, 89, 110, 116, 133
  resignation of, xix, 89
Northington, Robert Henley, 2nd Earl of, 116
Northumberland, Duchess of, 153
Nugent, Mrs., 266
Nunn and Barber, 326n
Nunns, Mrs., 169n

O'Gorman, Frank, 137–38
Old Man in Turkish Dress (Rembrandt), 33
Onslow, George, 158
Opera House (London), 89, 217, 346
Oracle, 282–83
Ord, Mrs., 248–49

Orléans, Duc d', 226, 227
Ossulston, Viscount, 347
Oxford Magazine, 56
Oxford University, xv, 81

Paine, Thomas, xx
Palais-Royal, 226
Palladio, Andrea, 301
Palmer, Iris, xiv
Palmer, Mrs., 321
Palmerston, Henry Temple, 2nd Viscount, 7, 140, 218, 269
Palmerston, Mary Temple, Viscountess, 269, 273
Paris, 13, 14, 36, 38–40, 114, 161, 194
  post-Revolution, 342–43
  unrest and rioting in, 223–30, 232, 238, 241, 270–71
Paris Opéra, 227–28, 237
Parker, Mr., 81
Parliament, British, *see* British Parliament
Parreaux, André, 25*n*
Passage of the Mountain of St. Gothard, The (Duchess of Devonshire), 311–12
Patrini, Father, 279, 284
Paxton, Joseph, 381
Payne, Jack, 234
Pelham, Henry, 268, 270
Pelham, Thomas Pelham, Baron, 45, 267, 286
Pembroke, Elizabeth Herbert, Countess of, 53, 127
Perdita, *see* Robinson, Mary
Pérregeaux, Comte, 186
Peterborough, Bishop of, 74
Peterson, Mrs., 233*n*
Pigott, C., 240
Pitt, Mrs., 169
Pitt, Thomas, 110
Pitt, William (the Elder), *see* Chatham, William Pitt, 1st Earl of
Pitt, William (the Younger):
  childhood of, 109
  death of, xx, 367
  Duchess of Gordon and, 211–13, 218
  George III's alliance with, 134–37, 152, 328–29
  illness and demoralization of, 328
  physical appearance of, 109

  political rise of, 109–10, 134–40, 152, 167, 329
  as Prime Minister, 134–37, 139–40, 193, 205, 208–18, 279–81, 297, 298, 299–300, 313, 314, 327–29, 348, 356–57, 364–67
  public support for, 213, 215, 217–18, 299–300
  Regency Crisis and, 205, 208–18
  resignation of, 328–29, 330–31, 332
  rivalry of Fox and, 14*n,* 109–10, 134–37, 143–44, 148, 152, 209–10, 327, 354–56
  Whig members' alliance with, 279, 280–81, 321, 344
Pizarro (Sheridan), 311
Plympton House, 101, 188
Pneumatic Institute, 284
Polignac, Duc de, 39–40, 108, 190, 203, 227, 229
Polignac, Duchesse de "Little Po," 108, 113–14, 161–62, 203, 229
  death of, 271
  Georgiana's relationship with, 39–40, 53, 68–69, 161, 223, 224, 227, 228, 271
  Marie-Antoinette and, 39–40, 53–54, 69, 161, 190, 238, 271
  political intrigue against, 190
Ponsonby, Caroline, *see* Lamb, Lady Caroline Ponsonby
Ponsonby, Frederick, 118, 120
Ponsonby, John William, *see* Duncannon, John William Ponsonby, Lord
Ponsonby, Lady Emily, 233*n*
Ponsonby, Mary, *see* Grey, Mary Ponsonby
Ponsonby family, 56
Pope, Alexander, 97*n*
Portarlington, Caroline Dawson, Countess of, 216
Portland, Dorothy Cavendish, Duchess of (sister-in-law), 17, 85–86, 112, 139, 141, 142, 175
  death of, 280, 297
  Georgiana and, 118–19, 120, 144, 148, 246, 280
  marriage of, 20
  political activism of, 144, 148, 152, 199, 280

Portland, William Henry Cavendish-
    Bentinck, 3rd Duke of, 20, 110,
    130–31
    political career of, 28, 112–13, 134,
    144, 149, 167, 206, 210, 213, 223,
    280, 331
*Posthumous and Historical Memoirs of My
    Own Time* (Wraxall), 27n
Poussin, Nicolas, 33
Poyntz, Anna Maria (grandmother),
    11–12, 24
Poyntz, Stephen (grandfather), 8
Poyntz family, 8, 174, 259, 320
Proserpine, 310
Protestant Association, 79
Public Advertiser, 306
Pultney, Daniel, 187–88, 190, 214

Quebec, 241
Queen Charlotte, 286
Queensberry, Charles Douglas, 3rd Duke
    of, 8

Ralph, James, 33
Randolph, Francis, 337–38
Ranelagh pleasure gardens, 21, 32, 35,
    37–38, 190, 214
"Rational Day in the Country, A" (Hare),
    202–3
Reflections on the Revolution in France
    (Burke), 240
Regency Bill, 214, 216
Reine de Golconde, La, 136
Rembrandt, 33
Reveillon, 225
Revolutionary War, *see* American War of
    Independence
Revolution Settlement, 15
Revolutions in Sweden (Vertot), 57
Reynolds, Joshua, 47
Richardson, Samuel, 31
Richmond, Charles Lennox, 1st Duke of,
    18n
Richmond, Charles Lennox, 2nd Duke
    of, 18n, 54, 62
Richmond, Charles Lennox, 3rd Duke of,
    78–79, 90, 206
    constitutional reform urged by, 79

Lady Foster and, 192–93, 195, 211, 278,
    293–95, 297, 301, 309–10, 325–26,
    335–36, 341
Richmond, Mary, Duchess of, 193, 216,
    293–94
Richmond, Sarah, Duchess of, 18n
Rights of Man, The (Paine), xx
Rivals, The (Sheridan), 45
Road to Divorce (Stone), 86n
Robinson, Mary "Perdita," 77, 78,
    168–69, 267
Robinson, Mr., 29
Rockingham, Charles Watson-Went-
    worth, 2nd Marquess of, 80, 108–9
    Burke and, 44
    death of, 109, 282
    political influence of, 28, 54, 286
Rockingham, Mary, Marchioness of, 282,
    286
Roehampton, 302, 318
Rogers, Samuel, 340–41
Rolliad (Fitzpatrick), 46
Roman Catholic Church, 79, 300, 303–4,
    328
Rothes, Mary Leslie, Countess of, 9
Rousseau, Jean-Jacques, 9, 53–54
Royal Academy, 279
Royal Marriages Act of 1774, 157
Royal Society, 283
Rutland, Charles Manners, 4th Duke of,
    69, 81, 88, 139–40, 187–88, 190
Rutland, Mary Isabella, Duchess of, 88,
    120, 136, 159, 232

Saint-Fond, Faujas de, 25n
St. Helen, Alleyne Fitzherbert, Baron,
    237
St. James's Palace, 21–22, 31, 62, 84, 110,
    137, 320–21
St. John, Frederick, 305
St. Jules, Caroline Rosalie:
    birth of, 165, 166
    childhood of, 166–67, 177, 179, 189,
    195, 224, 228, 229–30, 236, 239, 248,
    250, 251, 256, 258, 259, 263, 268,
    278, 308, 320, 321, 325, 341, 345, 373
    marriage of, 378
    physical appearance of, 321

St. Jules, Comte, 177, 263
St. Leger, Colonel, 114, 136
St. Paul's Cathedral, 217
Salisbury, Mary Amelia Cecil, Countess
    of, 137n, 140, 147, 152, 153, 155,
    383
Sandwich, John Montagu, 4th Earl of,
    210
Savile, Sir George, 80
Scafe, Ann, 380n
School for Scandal, The (Sheridan), 49, 53
Scotland, 212, 328
Scott, Mrs., 163n
Sefton, Isabella Molyneux, Countess of,
    51, 120
Selwyn, George, 86–87, 89
Senate, U.S., 75
Seven Years' War, 10–11, 55
Shakespeare, William, 16, 57, 96, 101
Sharp of Fleet Street, 171
Shelburne, William Petty, 2nd Earl of, 89,
    90, 108–10, 113, 133, 143
Sheridan, Betsy, see Lefanu, Betsy Sheri-
    dan
Sheridan, Elizabeth Linley, 45, 207,
    232–33, 267
Sheridan, Hecca, 299, 332, 340, 378
Sheridan, Richard Brinsley, 9, 178, 193,
    234
    Burke and, 45n, 240–41
    character and personality of, 45, 81,
        205, 206–7, 210, 232, 267, 299, 340
    debts of, 185, 247
    on Georgiana, 87–88, 213
    Georgiana and, 81, 183, 190, 207, 208,
        245, 247, 253, 267, 311
    Lady Bessborough's love affair with,
        207, 232–33, 249, 267, 340, 350
    plays of, 45, 49, 53, 311
    political ambition and career of, 45, 81,
        136, 206–8, 210, 211, 213, 223,
        239–41, 279, 280, 299, 327, 328, 333,
        350–51, 354, 468
    Prince of Wales and, 206–8, 216,
        353–54
Siddons, Sarah, 96, 169, 217, 319
Sidmouth, Viscount, see Addington, Henry
Sloper, Mrs., 137n

Smith, Charlotte, 283n
Smith, E. A., xiv
Smith, Mrs., 120
Southampton, Charles Fitzroy, 1st Baron,
    158
Southill, 262
Spain, 69, 297
Spanier in Peru, Die (Kotzebue), 311
Spencer, Charlotte (Devonshire's mis-
    tress), 20, 40, 70–71, 100
Spencer, Charlotte (sister), 12, 13
Spencer, George Spencer, 2nd Earl
    (brother), 114, 127, 137n, 148, 192
    birth of, 4
    character and personality of, 10, 250, 267
    childhood and adolescence of, 9–11,
        13–14, 20
    education of, 9, 10, 81
    financial concerns of, 318
    as First Lord of the Admiralty, 280,
        286–87, 297–98, 330–31
    Georgiana's loans from, 224, 310, 317
    Georgiana's relationship with, 10, 63,
        72, 113, 132, 143, 178–81, 224, 228,
        280–81, 282, 286–87, 288–89, 300,
        305, 310, 313, 349–50
    inheritance of, 131, 246
    on Lady Foster, 159–60, 176
    Lady Spencer's correspondence with,
        178–80, 187, 194, 199–200, 237, 238,
        253, 310, 318, 324
    political career of, 143, 280–81, 286–87,
        297–98, 330–31, 349–50, 368
    resignation of, 331
    Spencer family concerns of, 175–76,
        178–81, 187, 194, 200, 203, 237, 246,
        256, 265
Spencer, Harriet, see Bessborough, Har-
    riet Spencer Ponsonby, Countess of
Spencer, Hon. John (grandfather), 4, 7n
Spencer, John, 5n
Spencer, John Spencer, 1st Earl (father),
    23–24, 179
    classical antiquities collection of, 5, 6,
        131
    diffidence and moodiness of, 7, 10, 11,
        17
    estate of, 131, 246

Spencer, John Spencer, 1st Earl (father)
(*cont.*):
  Georgiana's relationship with, 4, 17,
    41–42, 51, 67–68
  ill health and death of, 4, 10, 86, 91,
    103, 127–28
  inherited wealth and property of, 4–7,
    17, 131
  Lady Spencer's relationship with, 7,
    8–9, 10–11, 12, 127, 140
  lifestyle of, 6, 7
  physical appearance of, 7, 16, 72
  political influence of, 7, 28–29, 81
Spencer, Lady Diana, 47
Spencer, Lady Georgiana, *see* Devonshire,
  Georgiana Spencer, Duchess of
Spencer, Lavinia Bingham, Countess
  (sister-in-law), 213, 341, 365
  George Spencer and, 72, 159, 161,
    173*n,* 176, 179, 246, 265
  Georgiana disparaged by, 72, 148, 161,
    179, 199, 246, 280, 283
Spencer, Louise (sister), 12, 13
Spencer, Margaret Georgiana Poyntz,
  Countess (mother), 47, 137
  correspondence of Georgiana and,
    26–30, 35, 36, 39, 40, 42, 44, 48–52,
    57–59, 63, 65–74, 76, 81, 84, 85, 86,
    96, 100–105, 114, 119–20, 125, 131,
    139, 159, 160, 163–64, 183–84, 191,
    194, 206, 208–9, 226, 229, 234,
    244–45, 274, 278–79, 280, 287–88,
    290, 301, 305, 310, 317–19, 336–37,
    340, 353–54
  daily regimen of, 51
  death of, 379
  Duke of Devonshire and, 21, 22, 65,
    195, 201, 244
  gambling of, 12, 13, 86, 87, 131, 186
  George Spencer's correspondence
    with, 178–80, 187, 194, 199–200,
    237, 238, 253, 310, 318, 324
  Georgiana's relationship with, 4, 9–14,
    18–19, 23–26, 28–30, 34, 35–36,
    38–39, 42, 48, 51, 67–68, 91, 100–106,
    118–19, 131, 140, 143–45, 148–49,
    156, 159, 164, 174*n,* 193–94, 243–45,
    253, 262–63, 265, 267–69, 274,
    369–70

  as grandmother, 224, 236–39, 243–44,
    256
  intelligence and erudition of, 8
  interference in daughters' lives by, 175,
    191, 194, 195, 243–45, 253, 264,
    265–66
  Lady Foster distrusted by, 101, 104–5,
    107, 156, 159–60, 177–79, 180–81,
    192, 193–94, 199–200, 201, 237, 238,
    243–45, 250–51, 255, 256, 264, 269,
    301, 308, 378
  Lord Spencer's relationship with, 7,
    8–9, 10–11, 12, 127, 140
  motherhood and family life of, 3–4,
    9–14, 269
  physical appearance of, 7–8
  political campaigning of, 28–29, 140
  religious fanaticism of, 12–13
  widowhood of, 127–28, 131, 179,
    194
Spencer, Mrs. William, 378
Spencer, Robert, 1st Baron Spencer, 5
Spencer, William, 378
Spencer family, 4–6, 18, 29, 72–74, 81, 86,
  91, 120, 173, 175–76, 320, 378
Spencer House, 5–6, 131
Stafford, Susannah, Marchioness of, 70,
  279
  on Georgiana, 278, 287
  on Lady Bessborough, 285*n*
  on Regency Bill, 214
Stanhope, Lady Hestor, 246
Stanhope, Mrs., 199
Sterne, Laurence, 6
Steuart, A. Francis, 123*n*
Stewart, Harriette, 324
Stockholm Syndrome, xiii, xv
Stock Exchange, 246, 247
Stone, Lawrence, 86*n*
Storer, Anthony, 35
Stormont, David Murray, 7th Viscount,
  36
Strachey, Lytton, 347*n*
Stuart, Lady Louisa, 36, 169, 216
Surr, T. S., 340–41
Sutherland, Elizabeth, Countess of, 226,
  270, 305
  on Georgiana, 228, 239, 271, 279
  on Lady Foster, 239, 293

Sydney, Thomas Townshend, 1st Viscount, 211
Sylph, The (Duchess of Devonshire), xvi, 58–60, 68, 187

Talman, William, 23
Temple, George Grenville, 3rd Earl, 113, 134, 149
Tessier, M., 44*n*
Thanet, Sackville Tufton, 9th Earl of, 178
Thompson, Lady D., 27
Thompson, Lord Charles, 27
Thrale, Hester, 59–60
Thynn, Miss, 73
Tierney, George, 215, 333, 359
Timbs, J., 56*n*
Times (London), 217, 372
Tollemache, Lady Bridget, 155
Tollemache, Mr., 28–29
Tollemache, Mrs., 29, 140
Tory party, 15, 212, 218, 223
Town and Country Magazine, 71
Townsend, Caroline, 233
Townsend, Mr., 57, 233*n*, 256
Townshend, Anne, Marchioness of, 335
Townshend, Charles, 2nd Viscount Townshend, 8
Townshend, Lord John, 174, 207
Trafalgar, Battle of, 366
Treaty of Amiens, 334, 343
Trevelyan, George, xiv
Trevor, Mrs., 246
Trimmer, Sarah, 243*n*
Trimmer, Selina, 370, 375
    Georgiana and, 265, 277, 302, 353
    as governess, 243–44, 250, 256, 262, 265, 277, 308, 353, 358
    Lady Spencer's alliance with, 243–44, 250, 265–66, 277*n*, 290–91, 293
Tristram Shandy (Sterne), 6
Tunbridge Wells, 65, 87, 189

United States, 75
    see also American War of Independence

Van Dyck, Anthony, 89
Vasa, Gustavas, 57

Vaudreuil, Comte de, 114
Vauxhall Gardens, 33, 88
Versailles, 38–39, 47, 129, 161, 162, 168, 226–28
Vertot, Abbé de, 57
Vestris, Auguste, 84–85
Victoria, Queen of England, 383
Vigée-Lebrun, Élisabeth, 171
Villa Rotonda, 301
Villiers, Lady Elizabeth, 342, 357, 366
Vindication of the Rights of Woman (Wollstonecraft), 283

Waldegrave, Elizabeth, Countess, 83, 139, 145, 152
Waldegrave, Frances, Countess, 139, 145, 152, 384
Waldegrave, Lady Maria, 136, 139, 145, 152
Walpole, Horace, 22–23, 35, 39, 97*n*, 191, 241
    on Georgiana, 34, 124, 306
Wanderer, The (Burney), 99
Warren, Richard, 248, 253–54, 255–56, 290, 292
Washington, George, xix, xx, 89
Webster, Elizabeth, Lady, *see* Holland, Elizabeth, Lady
Wedgwood, Josiah, 88–89
Weltje, Mr., 234
Westminster Association, 79
Westminster Hall, 137
Westmorland, John Fane, 10th Earl of, 76
Whig Club, 327
Whig party:
    American cause supported by, xix, 44, 61–62, 64, 75, 89
    ascendancy of, xx, 82, 89–91, 110, 115, 135
    divisiveness and decline of, 214–19, 223–24, 239–42, 279–82, 286, 305, 314
    Duke of Devonshire's loyalty to, 16, 20, 28, 46*n*, 74, 79, 90, 109*n*, 110, 281
    Fox and, xiv, 54, 55, 57–58, 62, 74, 75, 81–82, 90–91, 108–10, 115–18, 133–53, 167, 205, 206–13, 219, 223, 240–41, 279–80, 288–89, 299–300

Whig party (*cont.*):
   French Revolution debated in, 239–42,
     279
   Georgiana's campaigning and support
     for, xv–xvi, xviii, 58, 61, 74–76,
     81–82, 90–91, 133, 137–54, 208–9,
     211, 212–13, 217–18, 239, 279–83,
     286, 348–51, 353–56, 382–85
   Irish interests of, 303–5
   as minority in House of Commons,
     74–76, 151–52, 167–68
   political ideology of, 44, 57, 61–62, 64,
     74–76, 80, 279, 281, 286, 304
   Prince of Wales and, 76, 78, 83–84,
     89–90, 115–16, 137, 149, 151, 168,
     172, 173, 185, 216–17
   social and political dominance of, xx,
     15–16, 31, 43–44, 89–91, 190
Whitbread family, 262
White's, 32, 55, 137, 216, 218
Wicklow, Lord, 274–75
William III, King of England, 15, 31, 182
Williams, Charlotte, 131
   birth of, 20
   childhood of, 70–72, 84, 106–7, 115,
     122, 129–30, 160, 161, 195, 224, 229,
     239

   Lady Foster as governess to, 106–7,
     115, 122, 129–30, 161, 243
   marriage of, 277
Willis, Francis, 218, 331
Wimbledon Park, 5, 8, 20, 88, 91
Windsor Castle, 13, 204, 216, 331, 359,
   360
Winter in London, A (Surr), 340–41
Winter's Tale, The (Shakespeare), 77
Woburn Abbey, 327, 346, 353, 360
Wollstonecraft, Mary, 283
Wraxall, Nathaniel, 16, 27*n*, 90, 139, 212,
   247
   on Georgiana, 27*n*, 78, 127, 247
Wray, Sir Cecil, 137, 139, 144, 147, 148
Württemberg, Frederick, Duke of, 5*n*
Wyndham, Charles, 174–76, 191, 207,
   350
Wyvill, Christopher, 79

York, Frederick Augustus, Duke of, 172,
   215, 216, 217, 274, 337
Yorktown, Battle of, 89
Young, Arthur, 5–6, 226

Ziegler, Philip, 349*n*
Zyllia (Duchess of Devonshire), 102

ABOUT THE AUTHOR

AMANDA FOREMAN was born in London in 1968. She attended Sarah Lawrence College and Columbia University in New York. Since 1991 she has been a researcher at Lady Margaret Hall, Oxford. In 1993 she was awarded the Henrietta Jex Blake Senior Scholarship. She has written for many newspapers, including the *Independent, The Times,* the *Sunday Telegraph,* and the *Express,* and is a contributor to the Longman "Gender in History" series (1997) and the Oxford *New Dictionary of National Biography.*

ABOUT THE TYPE

This book was set in Bembo, a typeface based on an old-style Roman face that was used for Cardinal Bembo's tract *De Aetna* in 1495. Bembo was cut by Francisco Griffo in the early sixteenth century. The Lanston Monotype Company of Philadelphia brought the well-proportioned letterforms of Bembo to the United States in the 1930s.

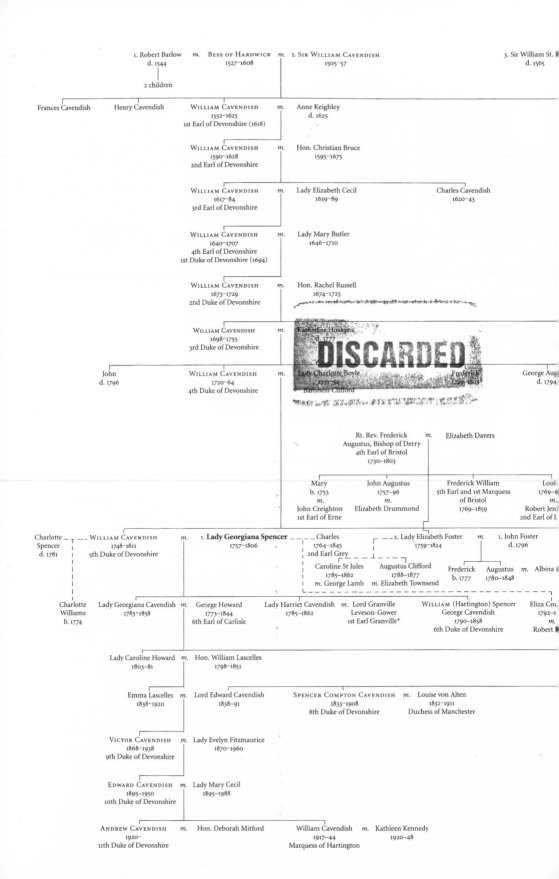

1. Robert Barlow   *m.*   **Bess of Hardwick**   *m.*   2. **Sir William Cavendish**   3. Sir William St.
d. 1544   1527–1608   1505–57   d. 1565

2 children

Frances Cavendish   Henry Cavendish   **William Cavendish**   *m.*   Anne Keighley
1552–1625   d. 1625
1st Earl of Devonshire (1618)

William Cavendish   *m.*   Hon. Christian Bruce
1590–1628   1595–1675
2nd Earl of Devonshire

William Cavendish   *m.*   Lady Elizabeth Cecil   Charles Cavendish
1617–84   1619–89   1620–43
3rd Earl of Devonshire

William Cavendish   *m.*   Lady Mary Butler
1640–1707   1646–1710
4th Earl of Devonshire
1st Duke of Devonshire (1694)

William Cavendish   *m.*   Hon. Rachel Russell
1673–1729   1674–1725
2nd Duke of Devonshire

William Cavendish   *m.*   Katherine Hoskyns
1698–1755   d. 1777
3rd Duke of Devonshire

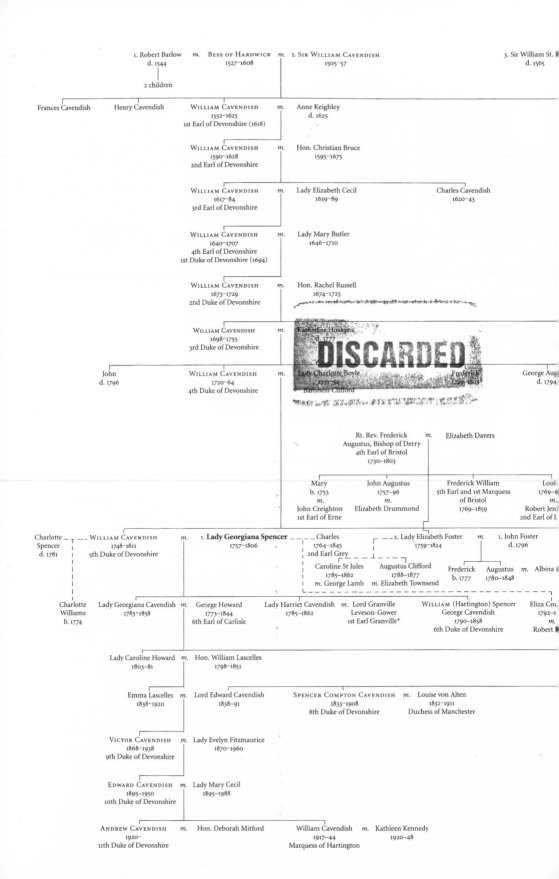

DISCARDED

John   **William Cavendish**   *m.*   Lady Charlotte Boyle   Frederick   George Aug
d. 1796   1720–64   1731–54   1729–1803   d. 1794
4th Duke of Devonshire   Baroness Clifford

Rt. Rev. Frederick   *m.*   Elizabeth Davers
Augustus, Bishop of Derry
4th Earl of Bristol
1730–1803

Mary   John Augustus   Frederick William   Loui
b. 1753   1757–96   5th Earl and 1st Marquess   1769–1
m.   *m.*   of Bristol   *m.*
John Creighton   Elizabeth Drummond   1769–1859   Robert Jen
1st Earl of Erne   2nd Earl of I

Charlotte   **William Cavendish**   *m.*   1. **Lady Georgiana Spencer**   Charles   2. Lady Elizabeth Foster   *m.*   1. John Foster
Spencer   1748–1811   1757–1806   1764–1845   1759–1824   d. 1796
d. 1781   5th Duke of Devonshire   2nd Earl Grey

Caroline St Jules   Augustus Clifford   Frederick   Augustus   *m.*   Albina
1785–1862   1788–1877   b. 1777   1780–1848
m. George Lamb   *m.* Elizabeth Townsend

Charlotte   Lady Georgiana Cavendish   *m.*   George Howard   Lady Harriet Cavendish   *m.*   Lord Granville   **William** (Hartington) Spencer   Eliza Cou
Williams   1783–1858   1773–1844   1785–1862   Leveson-Gower   George Cavendish   1792–1
b. 1774   6th Earl of Carlisle   1st Earl Granville*   1790–1858   *m.*
     6th Duke of Devonshire   Robert

Lady Caroline Howard   *m.*   Hon. William Lascelles
1803–81   1798–1851

Emma Lascelles   *m.*   Lord Edward Cavendish   **Spencer Compton Cavendish**   *m.*   Louise von Alten
1838–1920   1838–91   1833–1908   1832–1911
     8th Duke of Devonshire   Duchess of Manchester

Victor Cavendish   *m.*   Lady Evelyn Fitzmaurice
1868–1938   1870–1960
9th Duke of Devonshire

Edward Cavendish   *m.*   Lady Mary Cecil
1895–1950   1895–1988
10th Duke of Devonshire

Andrew Cavendish   *m.*   Hon. Deborah Mitford   William Cavendish   *m.*   Kathleen Kennedy
1920–   1917–44   1920–48
11th Duke of Devonshire   Marquess of Hartington